SAINTS & PILGRIMS
IN THE DIOCESE OF ST ALBANS

ALAN SMITH
BISHOP OF ST ALBANS

WITH A FOREWORD BY
THE ARCHBISHOP OF CANTERBURY

+ Alan St Albans

AP
THE AMPHIBALUS PRESS

The Amphibalus Press
Abbey Gate House
Abbey Mill Lane
St Albans
AL3 4HD

First published in 2013

ISBN 978-0-9575982-0-1

Design, layout and typesetting: Richard Ponsford Graphic Design
Printed and bound in India by Replika Press Pvt. Ltd.

The Amphibalus Press, St Albans

This book has been written to celebrate the centenary of the
incorporation of Bedfordshire into the Diocese of St Albans.
It is dedicated to the Christian women and men who have
served God in this area, and to those who draw inspiration
from them in their life of faith today.

Let us now sing the praises of famous men,

our ancestors in their generations.

The Lord apportioned to them great glory,

his majesty from the beginning.

There were those who ruled in their kingdoms,

and made a name for themselves by their valour;

those who gave counsel because they were intelligent;

those who spoke in prophetic oracles;

those who led the people by their counsels

and by their knowledge of the people's lore;

they were wise in their words of instruction;

those who composed musical tunes,

or put verses in writing;

rich men endowed with resources,

living peacefully in their homes—

all these were honoured in their generations,

and were the pride of their times.

Some of them have left behind a name,

so that others declare their praise.

But of others there is no memory;

they have perished as though they had never existed;

they have become as though they had never been born,

they and their children after them.

But these also were godly men,

whose righteous deeds have not been forgotten;

their wealth will remain with their descendants,

and their inheritance with their children's children.

Their descendants stand by the covenants;

their children also, for their sake.

Their offspring will continue for ever,

and their glory will never be blotted out.

Their bodies are buried in peace,

but their name lives on generation after generation.

The assembly declares their wisdom,

and the congregation proclaims their praise.

Ecclesiasticus 44. 1–15 from the Authorised Version of the Bible

Contents

Foreword by
The Archbishop of Canterbury

———

Centenaries provide an opportunity to look back and to reflect on the journeys that have brought us to the present day. The novelist E. M. Forster is reputed to have said that 'Unless we remember, we cannot understand.' His words remind us that we are all products of our history. We inherit a complex of ideas, traditions and customs which shape our self-understanding as well as the life of the Church today. Unless we reflect on our roots, we may fail to understand fully the issues that are confronting us, or the opportunities for service that present themselves.

The centenary of the incorporation of the County of Bedfordshire into the Diocese of St Albans presents a good opportunity to pause and thank God for his faithfulness. The stories of 'saints and pilgrims' assembled here invite us to think about how we can witness to God's love and truth in our day, and how best we can pass on the baton of the faith to the next generation.

I hope that this book, recounting the lives of some of the ordinary and extraordinary Christians of the past, will encourage the people of the Diocese of St Albans to deepen their faith, and renew their witness to Jesus Christ who 'is the same yesterday, today, and for ever.'

+ Justin Cantuar:

The Most Reverend and Right Honourable Justin Welby
Archbishop of Canterbury
Lambeth Palace
June 2013

How to use this book

———

Saints & Pilgrims in the Diocese of St Albans celebrates the centenary of the incorporation of Bedfordshire into the diocese in 1914. It is hoped that those who say the Daily Office will use it to enhance their prayers; others may wish to start or end the day by reading the entry set for the day to reflect on the life and example of one of our forebears and find inspiration for their own Christian discipleship.

The book is also designed to be put on display in every church, school and chaplaincy in the diocese, opened to that day's page, so that visitors can read about our common history and, by God's grace, be encouraged to become pilgrims too.

Acknowledgements

Many people have helped in the production of this book. I am grateful to those who work in my office who have contributed to its production, and particularly Rosamund Adlard who spent many days chasing up information, marshalling material, typing and checking the text, proof reading as well as making many helpful suggestions. Mary Handford and Claire Wood typed a great deal of the material. Andy Crooks worked with me on finding and selecting photographs and illustrations, sorting out copyright and checking information. Several people have read the text and made helpful suggestions including Andy Piggott, Paul Bayes, Richard Atkinson, Jonathan Smith, Paul Hughes, Trevor Jones and Susan Pope.

Thanks also to many people who provided suggestions and biographical material, in particular Chris Beales, Lyn Bridger, Jan Brookshaw, James Burgess, Sister Catherine, Lindsay Dew, Don Dowling, Michael Eggleton, Bob Franklin, Will Gibbs, John Griffiths, Sue Groom, Suzannah Hart, Sister Hazel, Ailsa Herbert, Pauline Higham, Stephen Holroyd, Elizabeth Inall, Philip Jewell, David and Jane Kelsall, Doreen Lawrence, Mary Leonard, Philip McDonough, Janet McKenzie, Jim May, Stephen Nuth, Jackie Osborne, Barry Pate, James Runcie, Gill Smith, Rebecca Tabor, Derwyn Williams, Tanya Willington, Pam Wise, Evelyn Wright, Dennis Yates and Patricia Yates.

I am grateful for permission to reproduce a number of photographs:

The icon of St Alban and the picture of Alfred Smith were photographed by David Kelsall and used by permission of the Dean and Chapter of St Albans Cathedral.

The Annunciation from the Alban Psalter, the bust of Lord Grimthorpe and the statue of Nicholas Breakspear were taken by Arun Kataria and are used by permission of the Dean and Chapter of St Albans Cathedral.

Jennifer Worth: used by permission of the Worth family.

Lord and Lady Runcie: used by permission of the Runcie family.

Gay Perry: used by permission of the Perry family.

Anna Constantia (née Beresford) Thynne. Artist: Richard James Lane © National Portrait Gallery, London. Used with permission.

(Geoffrey) Leonard Cheshire, Baron Cheshire: Sue Ryder. Artist: Rosalind Cuthbert. © National Portrait Gallery, London. Used with permission.

Trevor Huddleston. Artist: Nancy Culliford Sharp © Estate of Nancy Sharp/National Portrait Gallery, London. Used with permission.

John Bunyan. Stained Glass Window at the Bunyan Meeting, Bedford. By kind permission of the trustees of Bunyan Meeting, Bedford, England.

The photographs of the portraits of Bishop Thomas Claughton and Bishop Michael Furse, which belong to the See of St Albans, were taken by Arun Kataria.

The readings and prayers come from different periods and sources. In order to give the book coherence spelling and punctuation have, in most cases, been standardised though I have not attempted to change ancient texts to make them gender-neutral; for example when 'man' or 'men' is used. The writing of this book has been fitted into odd moments. As a consequence and despite much checking of facts, there may be mistakes for which I take responsibility. I would be grateful to know any errors so that, if a second edition is printed, they can be corrected.

Introduction

────

When in 2008 I learnt that I was to be the tenth Bishop of St Albans, I had little knowledge of the diocese, its towns and villages, its communities and history. Since then I have come to know and to treasure its rich heritage, and feel honoured to be part of its worshipping life.

The incorporation of Bedfordshire into the diocese in 1914 was hugely significant. During discussions about how best to mark the centenary, I came across two books: a slim volume from the Diocese of Gloucester called *Companions in the Faith: A Diocesan Calendar*, and the beautifully-produced *Saints and Sinners of the Marches*, by Michael Tavinor, Dean of Hereford. These two books gave me the idea that we should produce a similar book about the people who have shaped our diocese. What better way to celebrate our heritage than by reflecting on the faith and discipleship of our forebears?

Sadly, there are not as many women featured as I would have liked. Much of our history has been written by men and, despite strenuous efforts, it has not proved easy to unearth the stories of the women who contributed so much to the Christian story in our two counties. The other difficulty is that with a limit of 366 short chapters (one for each day of the year) it has been impossible to mention every church in the diocese of which there are over four hundred.

Inevitably there is a subjective element in this compilation. Beyond fulfilling three criteria: namely, that the persons commemorated are dead, were practising Christians, and had a connection with Bedfordshire and Hertfordshire, the choice of individuals is my own. With some people I feel an instinctive affinity. Others strike me as rather odd, at least judged from a modern perspective. For this reason I have sometimes chosen a reading which critiques the person featured or which is by someone with a contrasting theological view. Each entry ends with a prayer, most of which I have written myself. Taken together, I hope the entries will inform our thinking and deepen our desire to follow Christ.

A long and rich history

St Albans claims with good reason to be the site of longest continuous Christian worship in Britain. The first martyr of our islands needs no introduction. When Alban was executed by the Romans around the year 209 the English were a wave of immigrants who had yet to arrive on these shores. Sadly neither Bedfordshire nor Hertfordshire boasts any Christian Romano-British remains or artefacts, at least not to my knowledge, though Roman bricks were re-used in constructing some of our churches, including St Albans Abbey, Sandridge and Great Gaddesden.

By contrast, Saxon remains abound. There is a Saxon figure of Christ carved in Totternhoe stone in St Mary, Walkern, near Stevenage; and outside Elstow Abbey is the base of an ancient Saxon cross. Later preaching crosses are to be found at Stevington, Oakley and Biddenham, symbols of our calling 'to proclaim Christ, and him crucified'. Saxon remains are also to be found in a number of Bedfordshire churches, such as St John, Bedford; St Peter de Merton, Bedford; Caddington, Turvey, Kempston, Biddenham, Clapham, Stevington, Carlton, Harrold, Riseley and Shelton. In Hertfordshire, Saxon masonry and remains are to be found in churches at Northchurch, Walkern, St Michael St Albans, Reed and Westmill.

The Norman Conquest left its mark on the ecclesiastical landscape, not least in several churches which date from this period; notably, St Mary the Virgin, Great Wymondley; Holy Trinity, Weston; St Mary, Kensworth; St Peter, Milton Bryan; and St Mary Magdalen, Meesden, which is also notable for its unusual early fourteenth-century tiled floor. A handsome Norman door survives at St Mary, Stapleford. But there are later medieval churches which are equally beautiful such as those of Felmersham, Sundon and Billington.

As well as fine architecture, many of our churches represent notable repositories of sculpture and funerary art. The memorials in the Lytton Chapel in St Mary and St Thomas, Knebworth, and the de Grey Mausoleum in Flitton, are both of national importance. Other churches tantalise us with the untold and now long-forgotten lives of our forebears. Who was John Thompson whose fine alabaster memorial graces the walls of Husborne Crawley church? A tour around the diocese uncovers other funerary monuments such as the memorial to Sir Robert Whittingham and his wife in the Pendley Chapel in St John the Baptist, Aldbury; or the memorial to Margaret Sparhauke in St Mary's, Graveley. Then there is the distinguished black floor slab to Robert Elwes carved by the Flemish sculptor Johannes Rysbrack in Holy Trinity, Throcking.

But it is the glimpses into an earlier age that fascinate me most, such as the plaque under the tower at All Saints, Clifton, commemorating the ministries of the Reverend D. S. Olivier and his son, the Reverend D. J. Olivier, who were rectors of the parish for 36 and 31 years respectively. A parish's communion plate can also tell a story. The restoration of the cup to the laity at the Reformation meant that chalices had to be large enough to communicate an entire congregation, not merely the priest. Many of our ancient parish churches are the proud custodians of these wonderful treasures, such as St Mary Magdalen, Dunton, which has a paten and chalice dated 1569 from the reign of Queen Elizabeth I.

As a child I loved to go brass rubbing and it has been a particular delight for me to discover so many memorial brasses in our churches. Fine collections of early brasses are to be found in St Mary, Albury; St John, Digswell; and All Saints, Cople. The wanton destruction of buildings and images during the Reformation era is well documented. Many brasses were grubbed up with the result that some of our churches have just one or two left, such as the small memorial to Thomas Hundon in St Andrew, Langford, dated 1520; or the memorial to John Fysher in All Saints, Clifton, dated 1528.

The Elizabethan injunctions of 1559 attempted to bulldoze away all memory of a Catholic past, and that included the destruction of all stained glass that portrayed 'feigned miracles, pilgrimages, idolatry and superstition'. The proximity of so many of our churches to London meant that much was destroyed, but some outstanding medieval glass did manage to survive the zeal of the iconoclasts. As well as complete windows, many churches contain fragments, such as that found from the fourteenth century in St Mary's, Stocking Pelham. Ecclesiastical fashions change and today some of our churches boast more modern windows, such as those in St Michael and All Angels, Waterford, with its extraordinary collection of art by Burne-Jones, William Morris and Ford Madox Brown.

The sixteenth century also saw the dismantling of rood screens, the defacing of images of the saints, and the whitewashing of church walls. Ironically the whitewash often resulted in the preservation of imagery, the medieval painting leaching through the whitewash with the passing of the years as at St Albans Abbey. Less well known, but equally important, are the medieval wall paintings that survive in the churches in Flamstead, Kimpton and Langford. Sadly few parishes retained their painted screens. But one that did survive, at least in its lower sections, complete with its depiction of saints, stands in St Mary's, Roxton.

Countless generations of people have been baptised in the fonts of our churches down the centuries. To the casual observer all fonts are much the same. But the informed eye will admire the different features of ancient fonts such as that in St Peter's, Tempsford; All Saints, Tilsworth; and St Peter, Arlesey; not to mention the handsome octagonal font of St Mary the Virgin, Harlington. You will find a simple Norman font tucked away in St Peter and All Saints, Battlesden; an early English font in St Michael's, Eggington; and somewhat bizarrely, a font in the shape of a cauldron in St Mary Magdalene, Westoning.

T. S. Eliot in his poem 'Little Gidding' talks of places 'where prayer has been valid'. However beautiful the building and however significant the architecture, it is the people who worship and pray in our churches that enliven them, and it is this spiritual currency that impresses me most as I have travelled around the diocese. As the New Testament reminds us, the Church is not a building, but the people of God.

Why saints and pilgrims?

In the early centuries Christians instinctively gave honour to the *martyrs*, to those like Alban who died for their faith in the persecutions. They were the great heroes of the Church. With the cessation of the persecutions in the fourth century, we find Christians publicly remembering not only the martyrs, but also men and women whose holiness was evident in their devotion and service to others. The Letter to the Hebrews says that we are surrounded by a 'great cloud of witnesses', an unseen army who enfold us with prayer in our journey through life.

It is good to honour the witness of outstanding Christians, but we need to remember that in the Bible the word 'saint' refers not to a spiritual elite, but to ordinary women and men like you and me. As the entries in this book reveal, none of us is perfect. We are all a strange mixture of goodness and godliness, muddled up with self-centredness and sinfulness. Holiness comes from the Holy Spirit working in and through us. We call certain people saints because we glimpse something of God in what they say or do.

The word 'saint' occurs several times in the New Testament. By contrast, the word 'pilgrim' occurs only three times. It refers to those who are strangers and foreigners, those who have yet to arrive at their heavenly destination (Hebrew 11.13). The word 'pilgrim' reminds us that the Christian life is a journey, and it is of particular relevance to us, given that St Albans is probably the oldest site of pilgrimage in the British Isles. For around eighteen hundred years women and men have come to honour the memory of Alban and to pray for grace to emulate his faith.

The choice of title for this centenary volume consequently seeks to honour both some of the ordinary and the extraordinary people who have shaped our diocese. Those commemorated are not exclusively Anglican. They are drawn from a range of Christian traditions. Indeed I have deliberately included both Protestants and Catholics, as well as Dissenters who were ejected from the Church of England during the seventeenth century. In an age which often scorns the gospel, there is no place to distance ourselves from our fellow Christians. We need to learn from the mistakes and failings of our forebears, as well as their triumphs, and pray more earnestly for the unity which is Christ's will for his Church.

Only one local person featured in this volume is recognised by the wider Church as a 'saint' and that is Alban. Christina of Markyate is honoured locally (see the entry for 31 July), but she is little known outside Bedfordshire and Hertfordshire. Some churches in the diocese are dedicated to medieval saints from other parts of the country. For example, there are two churches dedicated to St Dunstan, the great Saxon Archbishop of Canterbury, at Bolnhurst and Hunsdon. St Etheldreda of Ely is honoured at Bishop's Hatfield. Rye Park is dedicated to St Cuthbert, the great hero of the north, buried at Durham. Chells and Lewsey are dedicated to St Hugh of Lincoln (see the entry for 17 November); Croxley Green to St Oswald of Northumbria; and Sandy to St Swithun, on whose day we hope it doesn't rain.

Every diocese has churches dedicated to biblical saints and our diocese is no exception. The most popular dedication by far is to Mary, the mother of Jesus, but the diocese has no less than twenty-five churches dedicated to the apostle Peter. There are other popular dedications such as to St Lawrence and St Giles, both of whom are featured in the book. St Leonard has no less than seven churches dedicated to him: Sandridge (11th century), Old Warden (12th century), Bengeo (12th century), Flamstead (12th century), Stagsden (13th century), Heath and Reach (1829) and Bedford (1913). Given that Leonard is the patron saint of prisoners, it has been suggested that the medieval churches dedicated to him may have had a parish gaol, but this is pure speculation.

The founding of the Diocese of St Albans in 1877

Nearly half of the churches in our diocese were built in the fifteenth century or earlier. The seventeenth and eighteenth centuries saw a lull in church building, with only eight new churches being built in the two counties. St Peter, Buntingford, was built in the seventeenth century. The rest, St Catherine and St Paul, Hoddesdon; St John the Baptist, Markyate; Ayot St Lawrence; St Mary Magdalene, Melchbourne; and St Andrew, Totteridge, were built in the eighteenth century. With the dawn of the nineteenth century, however, everything changed.

The industrialisation of England and consequent migration of people from the countryside to the towns, in combination with the fervour generated by the Evangelical Revival on the one hand and the Oxford Movement on the other, fuelled a wave of church building. As a result, half of the churches in the diocese have been erected over the last two hundred years.

The diocese was founded in 1877. It was still in its infancy when in 1914 Essex was formed into the Diocese of Chelmsford, and the county of Bedfordshire transferred from the Diocese of Ely to the Diocese of St Albans. It was not a propitious year for such pastoral reorganisation, with the nation on the verge of the First World War. Even so, under the leadership of Bishops Thomas Claughton, Michael Festing and Edgar Jacob, over forty new churches were built. And in the hundred years since Bedfordshire became part of the diocese, a further sixty-five new churches have been built, mostly to cater for the rapidly growing urban population.

Bedford

Until the Reformation, the town of Bedford was served by the ancient parish churches of St Paul, St John and St Peter de Merton, together with a number of monastic foundations, but with the explosion in the population during the Victorian era more parish churches were needed. St Martin was built in 1888, and this was followed by All Saints in 1914, St Andrew in 1920, The Transfiguration, Kempston, in 1939, Christ Church in 1956, St Michael and All Angels in 1965, and St Mark in 1984. St Leonard's Church Centre replaced the Victorian church which had been destroyed in a fire. Currently there is a new church being planted in the Wixams, to the south of the town.

Further afield, new places of worship were built to serve the rural population. All Saints, Upper Stondon, was almost completely rebuilt in 1857. In 1897 Stevington Church Room was opened, followed two years later by the mission room in Haynes. Down the A421 we find the model village of Stewartby with its ecumenical congregation which meets in Stewartby United Church, built in the 1950s. To the south St Andrew's, Flitwick, was opened to serve new areas of housing in the town.

Luton and Dunstable

With the coming of the railway, the small town of Luton grew faster than Dunstable, its older sister community, and today is much larger. New housing was built in neighbouring villages. The old village of Stopsley had a new church built, dedicated to St Thomas, in 1862. Biscot was another ancient settlement, but with its expansion it was formed into a new parish and in 1867 Holy Trinity Church was built. This was followed by two more churches in the area: St Andrew, Woodside (1889) and St Saviour (1897). Meanwhile the nearby village of Cockernhoe put up a 'tin tabernacle' in 1903.

Building continued across Luton with the opening of All Saints (1922), St Andrew (1931), St Christopher (1936), St Anne (1937), St Luke's, Leagrave (1956), St Francis (1959), St Augustine of Canterbury, Limbury (1964), St Hugh, Lewsey (1967), St John the Baptist, Farley Hill (1969) and Holy Cross, March Farm (1970). Church building has continued in recent decades with the opening of St Peter, Harefield Road, St Paul, New Town Street (1991, replacing an older church) and, most recently, Christ Church, Bushmead (2003).

Dunstable, known to the Romans as *Durocobrivis*, grew more slowly than Luton, but even so needed new churches as the community spread north and south along the A5. St Augustine's was built in 1959 and replaced with a new building in 1992. In 1968 St Fremund the Martyr and St Katherine of Genoa (a United Reformed Church which is home to an ecumenical congregation) were built. To the north of the town St Thomas's Mission Room was opened in 1988 in the parish of All Saints, Houghton Regis.

West Hertfordshire travelling south along the a41

The last century saw new housing developments along the A41. In 1868 Holy Trinity, Potten End was built, followed by All Saints, Berkhamsted (1906) and in 1909 by the consecration of St Michael and All Angels, Sunnyside. St Francis of Assisi, Hammerfield in Boxmoor was opened in 1914. After the Second World War it was decided to develop Hemel Hempstead into a new town. Large estates were built served by six new churches: St Stephen, Chaulden; St Barnabas, Adeyfield; The Resurrection at Grovehill and Woodhall Farm; St Benedict, Bennett's End; St Paul, Highfield, and finally St Albans, Warner's End and Gadebridge.

To the east of Hemel is Leverstock Green. There is evidence that there were settlements here in prehistoric and Roman times. Holy Trinity Church was opened in 1846 and a new ecclesiastical parish carved out of the older parishes of St Michael St Albans, Abbots Langley, and Hemel Hempstead.

Watford

Nearer London, but still on the A41, the Anglo-Saxon settlement of Watford clustered around the thirteenth-century church of St Mary, but with the massive rise in population this ancient parish church could no longer cater for the town. As a result in 1857 St Andrew's was built, followed by St John the Evangelist (1891), Christ Church (1905), St Michael and All Angels (1911), St Mark (1931), St Luke (1938) which was replaced by another building in 2006, and St Peter (1967).

The expansion of the railway network made outlying areas within easier reach of London and as a result the communities surrounding Watford began to expand as well. All Saints, Leavesden, designed by George Gilbert Scott, opened in 1853. Bushey was home to a Roman settlement and for centuries was served by the parish church of St James. But again the rise in population prompted the erection first of St Paul in 1904, and in 1958 of Holy Trinity Church.

The village of Chipperfield, six miles to the west of Watford, was originally part of the parish of Kings Langley. It did not have its own church until 1837 when St Paul's was opened. It became a separate parish in 1848. To the north of Watford, the Church of the Ascension in Bedmond, known in the village as 'The Tin Church', was opened in 1880. Still further to the east St Luke, Bricket Wood, was erected in 1936.

To complement the ministry of All Saints, Croxley Green (1872), St Oswald, Croxley Green, was opened in 1937 to the west of the town. The south of Watford was served by St Matthew, Oxhey (1880) and an additional building was required when Oxhey Chapel was deemed too small for the size of the population. The All Saints' Centre of Worship was erected in 2000.

In the south-west corner of the diocese, the church of St Thomas of Canterbury, West Hyde, was opened in 1844. St Peter, Mill End, opened thirty-one years later and then in 1886 the brick-built St John, Heronsgate, was built to serve the Chartist settlement founded by Feargus O'Connor. To the north-west a new church was built in 1966 in Chorleywood, dedicated to St Andrew.

The twentieth century saw massive housing developments in the area now bounded by the M1, M25 and A1. All Saints, Borehamwood, was built in 1906, followed by Holy Cross (1951) and St Michael and All Angels, Borehamwood (1954). St John, Radlett (1953), was built to complement the ministry at Christ Church, Radlett (1864). These churches are now linked with the red brick church of St Martin, Shenley (1841), which replaced the medieval church of St Botolph, the burial place of the architect Nicholas Hawksmoor (see the entry for 25 March).

St Albans

The town had grown up around the monastery. In the mid-tenth century Abbot Ulsinus built the three churches of St Michael, St Peter and St Stephen to cater for the vast numbers of pilgrims coming to pray at Alban's shrine. During the Victorian era the town saw significant growth and since then six new churches have been built: the elegant church of St Saviour, designed by William Woodward (1902), St Paul (1910), St Mary, Marshalswick (1955), St Julian (1956), Christ Church (1968) and St Luke (1968).

Nearby in Harpenden St Mary's was built in 1860 and, to serve the south of the town, a fine church dedicated to St John the Baptist was designed by F. C. Eden and consecrated in 1908. More recently, All Saints, not far from the River Lea, was opened in 1965.

Wheathampstead is thought to have been an important settlement of the Catuvellauni tribe and some think that Julius Caesar fought against them here in AD 54. The chancel of the stunning church of St Helen dates from 1280, and as the population of the village increased St Peter's was built to the north in 1910 to serve Gustard Wood.

The Great North Road and its hinterland

Barnet is reputedly the place where the 'Grand old Duke of York' marched his soldiers up and down the hill. For centuries the people of Chipping Barnet worshipped in the church of St John the Baptist. In 1840 this was supplemented by the building of St Peter, Arkley. Further churches were erected to serve the mushrooming population: Holy Trinity Lyonsdown (1866), St Stephen (1896), St Mark (1898) and St James, New Barnet (1911).

The old A1, the 'Great North Road', was the artery connecting London with the north for centuries, and along its path villages and communities have gradually expanded and merged. Potters Bar, for example, was originally in the parish of South Mymms, but in the nineteenth century it was formed into a separate parish. St Mary the Virgin and All Saints Church were built in 1915, and during the Second World War the church of King Charles the Martyr was opened in 1941. St Mark, Colney Heath, had been built in 1845. Today it has an impressive modern extension on the south side of the building.

Travelling north we arrive in Hatfield, or to give it its proper name Bishop's Hatfield; so called because the bishops of Ely used to live there. The Bishop's Palace was built in 1497 but seized by the Crown at the Reformation. Close by the Old Palace is the thirteenth-century parish church dedicated (of course) to St Etheldreda, the patron saint of Ely. As the communities around Hatfield grew, additional churches were needed. St Luke, Bishop's Hatfield, was built first in 1877, followed by St Mary Magdalen, Hatfield Hyde, in 1882. Two other churches have since been built, both put up after the Second World War: St John, and St Michael and All Angels.

Although an ancient settlement, the new village of Knebworth needed a church and Sir Edwin Landseer Lutyens (1869–1944) was commissioned to design it. The result is the beautiful church of St Martin, opened in 1915.

St Michael, Woolmer Green, had been built in 1899, long before Ebenezer Howard had begun work on his plans for the new Garden City developments at Letchworth and Welwyn. As part of this ambitious project a wide range of public buildings were erected in Welwyn Garden City, including the church of St Francis of Assisi (1934), and later on Christ the King, Digswell (1965), and Panshanger Church (1977).

Further north still is Stevenage, originally another Roman settlement. The new town we see today was built around the ancient village with its twelfth-century church of St Nicholas. During the Victorian period the community had already expanded, and first Holy Trinity was built in 1861, and in 1865 St Mary, Shephall, adjacent to the beautiful village church of St Mary, Aston. With the construction of the new town, however, additional churches were opened: St Peter, Broadwater (1955), St Michael and St George (1956), St Hugh and St John, Chells (1965), All Saints, Pin Green (1974), and the ecumenical church of Christ the King.

To the west of Stevenage and south of Hitchin is the village of Preston. The church of St Martin was opened in 1900. St Peter, Holwell, to the north of Hitchin was almost completely rebuilt in 1877. In the town itself St Faith was opened in 1894 and St Mark in 1936.

Letchworth Garden City was planned around three ancient villages, each with a medieval church: St Mary the Virgin, Letchworth, St Nicholas, Norton, and All Saints, Willian. The new Garden City required new churches to serve its vastly increased population and St Paul was built in 1924, followed by St Thomas of Canterbury, Wilbury (1935), St George, Norton (1962), and finally in 1966 St Michael the Archangel.

East Hertfordshire

We turn finally to East Hertfordshire. Whilst no new towns were built in this part of the county, overspill from London has generated significant increases in the populations of the communities that straddle the A10.

Christ Church, Waltham Cross, was consecrated in 1834, and St Clement, Turnford, in 1898. The parish of St Laurence, Wormley, opened a new Church Room after the Second World War. Up the road in Rye Park, the Church of St Cuthbert was built in 1908. St James, Goffs Oak was built in 1861, St Thomas à Becket, Northaw (replacing an older church) was consecrated in 1882, and in 1965 the Church of St Andrew at Cuffley was opened. The little chapel at Brickendon of Holy Cross and St Alban in the parish of Bayford was opened in 1932 (see the entry for 29 August).

Christ Church, Ware, was opened in 1858 and All Saints, Hertford, in 1895, replacing a medieval church which had burnt down. Other new churches in the area include St Andrew, Stanstead Abbotts (1880), Holy Trinity, Little Amwell (1863), Holy Trinity, Wareside (1841), and more recently St Francis, Hunsdon. To the north of Hertford, the old parish church of Thundridge was abandoned and a new church dedicated to St Mary opened in 1853. To strengthen the parish work at St John, High Cross (1846), St Mary, Colliers End was built in 1911. In the north-east of the county the old church of St Mary the Virgin, Therfield, was almost totally rebuilt in 1878.

Bishop's Stortford was served for centuries by St Michael's Church. In the Victorian period Holy Trinity was opened (1859) and, more recently, the beautifully-proportioned church of All Saints, Hockerill, designed by Dykes Bower, was consecrated in 1937.

New forms of mission and ministry

If the population of the diocese has generated the building of huge numbers of churches, recent years have seen significant developments in the mission and ministry of the Church.

Readers and Self-Supporting Ministers

Since the first Lay Readers were commissioned in the Church of England in 1866, their numbers have continued to increase steadily. Currently in the Diocese of St Albans there are just over two hundred licensed Readers supported by the Diocesan Readers' Association. There are also around eighty Self-Supporting Ministers (SSMs, formerly known as Non-Stipendiary Ministers or NSMs, and before that as Auxiliary Pastoral Ministers, APMs). Without the work and commitment of the Readers and SSMs the diocese could not possibly function today.

Different models of staffing

Changes have also taken place in staffing parishes and today a number of different models have emerged across the diocese. In rural areas there are many multi-parish benefices, the largest of which is the Stodden Churches in Sharnbrook Deanery which brings together the six parishes of Dean, Melchbourne, Pertenhall, Shelton, Swineshead and Yelden.

Currently there are also five *Group Ministries*, which mainly serve rural areas. A good example of how well this works can be seen in the Ivel Group Ministry which draws together three united benefices: Caldecote, Northill, Old Warden; Cople, Moggerhanger and Willington; and Great Barford, Blunham, Roxton and Tempsford with Little Barford.

Much more common are *Team Ministries* of which there are currently seventeen in the diocese. These often serve a town and its surrounding villages. A typical example is the Tring Team Ministry which centres around St Peter and St Paul's Church and four village churches: St John the Baptist, Aldbury; St Mary, Puttenham; All Saints, Long Marston; and St Cross, Wilstone.

Ecumenism

In recent years relations with other Christian denominations have developed considerably. There are over thirty Local Ecumenical Partnerships (LEPs) in the diocese, mainly involving congregations, although the chaplaincy of Hertfordshire University is an LEP, as is the Methodist Queenwood School in Hatfield. There are many excellent and varied models of ecumenical cooperation. There are single congregation LEPs such as at Lidlington, where the congregation unites Anglicans and Baptists. Elsewhere a church building is shared by two or more denominations, which retain their separate church services. In other places the LEP is between two churches in the same area. They have retained their separate buildings and services, but are working together in mission and ministry. A good example is St Mary the Virgin, East Barnet, and Brookside Methodist Church.

Ministry among young people

In partnership with the parishes are our 135 church schools. The two most recent are both in Dunstable. All Saints Academy opened in 2009, and St Augustine's Academy opened in 2012. Church schools are supported by the Diocesan Board of Education. There are also around fifteen chaplains employed by independent schools in the diocese.

A significant development in recent years has been the increase in the number of full-time and part-time youth and children's workers in the diocese. There are currently around twenty-six full-time workers. These work in partnership with a phalanx of volunteers and a large number of unpaid youth and children's leaders. They are supported by a full-time Children's Work Adviser and a full-time Youth Officer. The University of Bedfordshire and the University of Hertfordshire both have chaplains, as does Cranfield University and the Royal Veterinary College (Hawkshead Campus) at Potters Bar.

Healthcare Chaplaincy

In recent decades there has been a huge increase in the number of chaplains in healthcare. There are approximately ten full-time or part-time Anglican hospital chaplains, six hospice chaplains and two mental health chaplains serving in the diocese. Most of these have groups of lay volunteers who work with them. Together they offer a network of spiritual and pastoral care to both patients and their local communities.

Other Specialist Chaplaincies

There are a number of specialist chaplaincies, most of which are linked together by *Workplace Matters*. These include chaplains to London Luton Airport and Vauxhall UK. There are chaplains to the police, fire and rescue, and ambulance and paramedic services. There are also several Retail and Leisure Chaplains along with Town Centre Chaplains in most of our large urban areas. There are chaplains working in prisons, crematoria, agriculture, inland waterways, and with the deaf, Roma, travellers and gypsies. Many volunteer chaplains support the uniformed organisations including the Army Cadet Force and Sea Cadet Corps.

The future

The Diocese of St Albans continues to serve the growing populations of Bedfordshire, Hertfordshire, Luton and Barnet, and to witness to the good news of Jesus Christ. My hope and prayer is that this book will help us not only to celebrate the past but to look with confidence to the future and to *Live God's Love:*

> *Living God,*
> *draw us deeper into your love;*
> *Jesus our Lord, send us to care and serve;*
> *Holy Spirit, make us heralds of good news.*
> *Stir us, strengthen us, teach and inspire us to live your love*
> *with generosity and joy, imagination and courage;*
> *for the sake of your world and in the name of Jesus. Amen.*

+ Alan St Albans

The Feast of St Albans
21 June 2013

Florence Louisa Barclay 1862–1921

Rector's wife and novelist

———

FLORENCE LOUISA CHARLESWORTH was the daughter of an Anglican priest who ministered in Limpsfield. During her childhood the family moved to Limehouse, in east London, where she lived until she married. One of her sisters, Maud, was to become a leader of the Salvation Army in America. Florence married the Reverend Charles Barclay in 1881 and they moved to Hertford Heath, where they had eight children.

During a time of prolonged ill health she began to write novels and her first book, *The Wheels of Time*, was published in 1908. However, it was her second novel, *The Rosary*, which became a best seller. It was translated into no less than eight languages, made into a film and also performed as a stage play in Paris. Florence went on to write another nine books. She died at the age of fifty-five and shortly afterwards her biography was published, written by one of her daughters.

An insight into beauty from one of Florence Barclay's novels

'At present I have only painted her from memory; but she is to sit for me in October.' 'From memory?' questioned Jane. 'Yes, I paint a great deal from memory. Give me one look of a certain kind at a face, let me see it at a moment which lets one penetrate beneath the surface, and I can paint that face from memory weeks after. Lots of my best studies have been done that way. Ah, the delight of it! Beauty – the worship of beauty – is to me a religion.' 'Rather a godless form of religion,' suggested Jane. 'Ah no,' said Garth reverently. 'All true beauty comes from God, and leads back to God. "Every good gift and every perfect gift is from above, and cometh down from the Father of lights." I once met an old freak who said all sickness came from the devil. I never could believe that, for my mother was an invalid during the last years of her life, and I can testify that her sickness was a blessing to many, and borne to the glory of God. But I am convinced all true beauty is God-given, and that is why the worship of beauty is to me a religion. Nothing bad was ever truly beautiful; nothing good is ever really ugly.' 'Then are plain people to be denied their share of goodness, Dal?' she asked. 'Plainness is not ugliness,' replied Garth Dalmain simply. 'I learned that when quite a small boy. My mother took me to hear a famous preacher. As he sat on the platform during the preliminaries he seemed to me quite the ugliest man I had ever seen. He reminded me of a grotesque gorilla, and I dreaded the moment when he should rise up and face us and give out a text. It seemed to me there ought to be bars between, and that we should want to throw nuts and oranges. But when he rose to speak, his face was transfigured. Goodness and inspiration shone from it, making it as the face of an angel. I never again thought him ugly. The beauty of his soul shone through, transfiguring his body. Child though I was, I could differentiate even then between ugliness and plainness. When he sat down at the close of his magnificent sermon, I no longer thought him a complicated form of chimpanzee. I remembered the divine halo of his smile.'

From *The Rosary*

Heavenly Father, we thank you for the gift of imagination:
bless all authors and writers, that through their creativity
our horizons may be widened, our sympathies broadened,
and our compassion deepened;
through Jesus Christ our Lord. Amen.

Samuel Ryder 1858–1936

Businessman and golfer

———

S AM RYDER IS best remembered as the person behind the Ryder Cup, the golf competition which has been held biannually between America and Britain since 1927. He took up the sport when he was forty-nine for health reasons. What is less well known is that throughout his life Ryder was also a committed Christian. He was brought up in the north-west of England and as a young man taught in the Sunday School in Sale. However, he moved to St Albans and by 1911 he had become president of the Mid-Hertfordshire Sunday School Union, whilst he worshipped at the Congregational Chapel in Spicer Street. Ryder later joined what is now Trinity United Reformed Church where he was a deacon. Ryder was also a successful businessman, having set up a seed business in his garden shed at his home in Folly Lane, St Albans, selling packets of seeds for a penny by post. As the business expanded, he moved several times, eventually ending up on Holywell Hill, where he built an Exhibition Hall next to the head office. For many years he was a town councillor and in 1905 he was the Mayor of St Albans. He died on this day in 1936.

Josef Pieper reflects on the importance of leisure

Leisure is a form of that stillness that is the necessary preparation for accepting reality; only the person who is still can hear, and whoever is not still, cannot hear. Such stillness as this is not mere soundlessness or a dead muteness; it means, rather, that the soul's power, as real, of responding to the real – a *co*-respondence, eternally established in nature – has not yet descended into words. Leisure is the disposition of receptive understanding, of contemplative beholding, and immersion – in the real. Leisure is not the attitude of the one who intervenes but of the one who opens himself; not of someone who seizes but of one who lets go, who lets *himself* go, and 'go under,' almost as someone who falls asleep must let himself go (you cannot sleep, unless you do so). And in fact, just as sleeplessness and restlessness are in a special way mutually related, just so the man at leisure is related to someone sleeping; as Heraclitus said of those who sleep, that they 'are active and co-operative in the business of the world.'

From *The Basis of Culture*

———

O God, the creator of all things,
who made us in your own image
so that we should seek joy in creative work,
we give thanks for your creation
and for those whose work brings joy to others.
We pray for those who find their work hard and dull,
and for those who are unemployed.
Help us to order our public life,
so that everyone may have the opportunity to work,
and may find satisfaction in doing it;
through Christ our Lord. Amen.

From *New Parish Prayers*

Richard Shepherd c.1732–1809

Priest and poet

———

RICHARD SHEPHERD STANDS in a long line of clerics who were scholars and poets. The son of a priest, he had originally wanted to be a soldier, but after studying at Oxford was ordained into the Church of England. He spent much of his life in Oxford until he was appointed chaplain to Thomas Thurlow, the Bishop of Lincoln, who in 1783 made him Archdeacon of Bedford. Shepherd had a distinguished academic career, being elected as a Fellow of the Royal Society in 1783 and five years later giving the Bampton Lectures in Oxford which were published under the title *Ground and Credibility of the Christian Religion.* As well as composing a considerable body of poetry, he translated works from Latin, wrote a commentary on the Gospel and the Epistles of John. He also wrote a book on warfare, entitled *Polyænus's Stratagems of War.*

And daily in the temple, and in every house, they ceased not to teach and preach Jesus Christ (Acts 5.42)

In my last discourse I considered the nature of miracles, as proper and satisfactory vouchers for a divine commission. Let us next examine the character, and note the zeal of those, to whom such commission was entrusted. When they were convened before the Jewish council, to be questioned concerning their faith, and warned with an authoritative interdict against the propagation of it, they were enjoined in silence, but refused to obey men counteracting in contradiction to God. They were beaten, but they persisted; they were threatened, but not deterred. They even *rejoiced, that they were counted worthy to suffer for the name* of their maker. What could actuate, what could sustain, this inflexibility of resolution? Not surely the spirit of deception. Mankind usually balances the chances of gain with those of loss; and, before they embark in an undertaking, satisfy themselves that it is feasible. If therefore the Apostles were deceivers, they must presumably have projected some advantage superior to the pains; otherwise they would have acted without common sense: and without that it would surpass every degree of credulity, to suppose them capable of deluding many of the wisest men in the world. But as the state of things were at that time, considering the treatment they received, what advantage could they propose; what had they to anticipate? Disappointment, alienation of friends, and all the evils which malevolence, armed with power, could inflict. If therefore deceivers, they were deceivers of a strange cast; contrivers of a project with temptation, which exposed them to inconveniences without an equivalent. And as this is not credible, it remains to account for their behaviour, from the zeal of conscious honesty in the cause of truth.

From a sermon by Richard Shepherd

———

Everlasting God
we thank you for the apologists of the faith:
give them an eloquence that they may speak of your glory
with conviction and integrity.
Through their endeavours may the hearts and minds of our generation
be expanded and inspired to wonder and to worship
through your Son, Jesus Christ our Lord. Amen.

Offa d.796

King of Mercia

―――――

KING OFFA IS best known for the dyke that bears his name – the extensive earthworks which were constructed to separate the Anglo-Saxons from the Welsh. As King of Mercia his kingdom covered much of what we call 'the Midlands'. He was a powerful ruler and is remembered locally for an important military success at Pirton close to Hitchin when he defeated Beornred in around the year 657. It is thought that the village of Offley is named after him. Offa was a Christian and towards the end of his life he founded the monastic community at St Albans. He was not afraid to disagree with bishops, and is known to have fallen out with the Bishop of Worcester and with Jaenberht, Archbishop of Canterbury. So determined was Offa to have his way that he appealed directly to Pope Adrian I over the Archbishop's head and persuaded him to divide the Archdiocese of Canterbury into two, creating a new Archdiocese of Lichfield. King Offa was buried in Bedford.

Alcuin's letter to Bishop Speratus

Your reverence should often consider the various happenings in the world and enquire with an alert mind what fortune awaits us. The whole human race provides examples to teach us how dangerous a day and how fearful a judgement awaits us at a time we know not. Let us prepare to meet the great king, whom none can escape, that we may find him gracious. We must think each day what gift we bring – as Scripture says: 'Appear not empty-handed in the sight of the Lord your God' (Ecclus. 35.4). No precious metals, no sparkling gems, no vain dress, no worldly luxury will be acceptable before that most just of judges; only generous alms and an increase of good deserts will avail. Whatever is done here will be judged there. All goodness will be crowned with eternal reward, and all wickedness damned to eternal torment. Let our hearts hold to this with wise foresight, that on that day the soul may not mourn its lack of good deserts, but we must take great care to think how it may rejoice in the simple fruit of goodness…You know well how the illustrious king [Alcuin here is referring to Offa] prepared for his son to inherit his kingdom, as he thought, but as events showed, he took it from him. Hence you can judge worldly wisdom, and how truly the psalmist said: 'Unless the Lord build the house, they labour in vain who guard it' (Psalm 127.1). Man plans but God decides.

From Letter 160 in Stephen Allott's *Alcuin of York*

―――

Generous God
who delights to give wisdom to those who ask:
give us enquiring minds, questioning spirits,
and an insatiable curiosity that may always be open to you.
In your mercy, grant that we may not only seek your will,
but finding it, may be obedient to it;
for we ask this for the sake of your Son, Jesus Christ. Amen.

Richard Hartwell d.1739

Quaker philanthropist

ALTHOUGH QUAKERS HAVE always been few in number they have often made a disproportionate impact on the communities in which they have lived. One such person was Richard Hartwell. We do not know a great deal about his life. However, we do know from his wills dated 1734 and 1739 he wanted to build some almshouses in Cranfield, Bedfordshire. Three houses were built which were designed to provide accommodation for up to six residents. Three places were to be retained for Quakers and three for people who lived in Cranfield. Hartwell endowed the almshouses by providing the income from Hartwell Farm. Richard Hartwell died on 16 June 1739 and he is buried in the grounds of Hartwell Farm.

The American scholar Rodney Stark writes about the impact of practical acts of service in sharing the good news of Jesus Christ

The power of Christianity lay not in its promise of other-worldly compensations for suffering in this life, as has so often been proposed. No, the crucial change that took place in the third century was the rapidly spreading awareness of a faith that delivered potent antidotes to life's miseries here and now! The truly revolutionary aspect of Christianity lay in moral imperatives such as 'Love one's neighbour as oneself,' 'Do unto others as you would have them do unto you,' 'It is more blessed to give than to receive,' and 'When you did it to the least of my brethren, you did it unto me.' These were not just slogans. Members did nurse the sick, even during epidemics; they did support orphans, widows, the elderly, and the poor; they did concern themselves with the lot of slaves. In short, Christians created 'a miniature welfare state in an empire which for the most part lacked social services.' It was these responses to the long-standing misery of life in antiquity, not the onset of worse conditions, that were the 'material' changes that inspired Christian growth. But these material benefits were entirely spiritual in origin. Support for this view comes from the continuing inability of pagan groups to meet this challenge.

From *Cities of God*

Lord, make me an instrument of your peace.
Where there is hatred, let me sow love.
Where there is injury, pardon.
Where there is doubt, faith.
Where there is despair, hope.
Where there is darkness, light.
Where there is sadness, joy.
O Divine Master,
grant that I may not so much seek to be consoled, as to console;
to be understood, as to understand;
to be loved, as to love.
For it is in giving that we receive.
It is in pardoning that we are pardoned,
and it is in dying that we are born to Eternal Life. Amen.

Francis of Assisi

William Harpur c.1496–1574

Merchant and founder of the Harpur Trust

———

MOST PEOPLE WHO live in and around Bedford will know of the Harpur Trust which provides financial support to five independent schools in the town. The Trust has three charitable objects: the promotion of education; the relief of those who are sick or in need, hardship or distress; and the provision of recreational facilities with a social welfare purpose. It is thought that William Harpur went to school in Bedford before moving to London, where in 1533 he joined the Merchant Taylors' Guild. Some twenty years later the records show that he was an Alderman for the Bridge-Without Ward, and later still that he was elected Alderman of Dowgate Ward. He was deeply involved in public service, serving as Treasurer of St Bartholomew's Hospital, Sheriff of the City of London in 1556–7, and in 1561 as Lord Mayor of London, the year after which he was knighted. Harpur had been instrumental in founding Bedford Grammar School some years earlier. In 1562 he purchased some land in Holborn, London, for the sum of £180. He and his wife, Dame Alice, gave the land to the Bedford Corporation in 1566 to endow the Trust. As well as supporting the school, Harpur specified that dowries should be given to 'poor maids' and that poor children should be 'nourished and informed'. The Harpur Almshouses were also funded from the endowment. He died in 1574 and is buried in the churchyard of St Paul's, Bedford. His memorial brass reads 'Hereunder lieth buried the body of Sir William Harpur, knight, alderman and late Lord Mayor of the city of London, with Dame Margaret, his last wife.'

The German theologian Hans Küng writes about education

The Christian message gives no detailed information as to how the scholastic and vocational training system is to be better and more effectively organized, how curricula are to be worked out, training and educational programmes implemented, educational problems solved, institutions governed and children educated. But the Christian message has something essential to say about the attitude and approach of the teacher to the child and the child to the teacher, and also about the reason for commitment even in the face of disappointments and failures: that in the light of the person of Jesus education can never be for the sake of my own prestige, repute, interest, but for the sake of the one who is entrusted to me. Education is understood therefore as non-repressive, as mutual service regardless of precedence. This means that the children never exist simply for the sake of the teachers, nor indeed the teachers simply for the sake of the children; that the teachers may never exploit their children, nor indeed the children their teachers; that the teachers may never impose their will in an authoritarian spirit on their children, nor however may the children impose their will in an anti-authoritarian spirit on their teachers. Mutual service regardless of precedence in a Christian spirit means for the teacher unconditional trust, goodness, loving good will, in advance and without any compelling reasons. And in all this he will refuse to let anything deter him.

From *On being a Christian*

———

Almighty God, you are the source of truth and your Spirit leads us into the truth:
may all who teach and all who learn in our schools, colleges and universities
be set free from everything that might hinder their search for the truth;
and finding truth, may they learn to use it for the good of mankind
and for your greater glory. Amen.

James M. Todd

Kenneth Harold Pillar 1924–2011

Bishop of Hertford

———

BORN IN PLYMOUTH and educated at Devonport High School for Boys, Ken Pillar served in the Royal Navy in 1943–6. He graduated from Queens' College, Cambridge, in theology and trained for the ministry at Ridley Hall. He was ordained deacon in 1950 by Clifford Martin, Bishop of Liverpool, and served as curate of All Saints, Childwall. From there he moved to Devon where he was Chaplain of the Lee Abbey Community. He served incumbencies in Beckenham and Bredin before returning to Lee Abbey as Warden. In 1970 Pillar was appointed as Vicar of Waltham Abbey. During the twelve years of his incumbency the population of the parish grew rapidly and he was involved in building a new church school and worship centre. In 1982 he was consecrated Bishop of Hertford. Throughout his ministry he regularly led parish missions and was actively involved in the Church Missionary Society. For many years he chaired the council of Scargill House at Kettlewell in Yorkshire, and he was a pastoral adviser to the Archbishops of Canterbury and York in 1990–2000. In his retirement Ken served as an Assistant Bishop in the Diocese of Sheffield. He married Margaret Elizabeth Davies in 1955, and they had one son and three daughters.

Dietrich Bonhoeffer writes about the Ministry of Meekness

He who would learn to serve must first learn to think little of himself. Let no man 'think of himself more highly than he ought to think' (Rom. 12.3). 'This is the highest and most profitable lesson, truly to know and to despise ourselves. To have no opinion of ourselves, and to think always well and highly of others, is great wisdom and perfection' (Thomas à Kempis). 'Be not wise in your own conceits' (Rom. 12.16). Only he who lives by the forgiveness of his sin in Jesus Christ will rightly think little of himself. He will know that his own wisdom reached the end of its tether when Jesus forgave him. He remembers the ambition of the first man who wanted to know what is good and evil and perished in his wisdom. That first man who was born on this earth was Cain, the fratricide. His crime is the fruit of man's wisdom. Because the Christian can no longer fancy that he is wise he will also have no high opinion of his own schemes and plans. He will know that it is good for his own will to be broken in the encounter with his neighbour. He will be ready to consider his neighbour's will more important and urgent than his own. What does it matter if our own plans are frustrated? Is it not better to serve our neighbour than to have our own way?

From *Life Together*

———

Lord Jesus Christ,
you humbled yourself in taking the form of a servant,
and in obedience died on the cross for our salvation:
give us the mind to follow you and to proclaim you as Lord and King,
to the glory of God the Father, Amen.

From *Common Worship*

Henry Tattam 1788–1868

Priest and scholar

———

EXPERTISE IN THE Coptic language may not have been the most essential ability for a Rector of St Cuthbert's, Bedford, but Henry Tattam was no ordinary priest. He had travelled to the Holy Land and Egypt, where he had obtained a number of Coptic and Syriac manuscripts which are now housed in the British Library. He wrote a grammar of the Coptic language (with the racy title *A Compendious Grammar of the Egyptian Language as contained in the Coptic and Sahidic dialects, with observations on the Bashmuric: together with alphabets and numerals in the hieroglyphic and enchorial characters; and a few explanatory observations*) and translated a number of the Coptic texts into English. Tattam was also the author of a number of theological books. His scholarship was so widely recognised that he was not only elected as a Fellow of the Royal Society, but he was also awarded honorary degrees from the universities of Dublin, Göttingen and Leiden. Towards the end of his life he was appointed Archdeacon of Bedford and Chaplain-in-Ordinary to Queen Victoria. He died on this day in 1868.

Egypt was the birthplace of monasticism. Here are three of the sayings of the Desert Fathers

A brother asked Abba Poemen, 'Some brothers live with me; do you want me to be in charge of them?' The old man replied, 'No, just work first and foremost, and if they want to live like you, they will see to it themselves.' But the brother said to him, 'But it is they themselves, Father, who want me to be in charge of them.' The old man said to him, 'No, be their example, not their legislator.'

A teacher ought to be a stranger to the desire for domination, vain-glory, and pride; one should not be able to fool him by flattery, nor blind him by gifts, nor conquer him by the stomach, nor dominate him by anger; but he should be patient, gentle, and humble as far as possible; he must be tested and without partisanship, full of concern for people, and a lover of souls.

An old man was asked, 'How can I find God?' He replied, 'In fasting, in watching, in labours, in devotion, and above all in discernment. I tell you, many people have injured their bodies without discernment and have gone away from us having achieved nothing. Our mouths smell bad through fasting, we know the scriptures by heart, we can recite all the Psalms of David, but we do not have that which God seeks: charity and humility.'

From *The Sayings of the Desert Fathers* translated by Benedicta Ward

---

Lord Jesus Christ,
who chose to walk the path of self-sacrifice:
bless those who follow your example
by leaving homes and families
to embrace the way of obedience, conversion of life and stability;
grant that their willingness to offer their lives
may inspire your whole Church in the way of holiness;
for your name's sake. Amen.

Gilbert Bourne d.1569

Archdeacon of Bedford and Bishop of Bath and Wells

———

GILBERT BOURNE LIVED in volatile and violent times when Catholics and Protestants were busy persecuting one another. Ordained a priest, he became first a Fellow of All Souls College, Oxford, before becoming first a Prebendary of St Paul's Cathedral, and then Archdeacon of Bedford. In 1554 during the reign of Queen Mary, he was consecrated Bishop of Bath and Wells and appointed Lord President of the Council of Wales. Bourne was known for his humanity and kindness. He was not involved in persecutions and there are no records of any executions in his diocese. When Elizabeth I came to the throne, however, he refused to take the Oath of Supremacy and in 1559 was deprived of his bishopric. He died after nearly ten years' imprisonment, part of which was spent in the Tower of London. A memorial in the English College in Rome numbers him among those who 'died for their confession of the Roman See and Catholic faith, worn out by the miseries of their long imprisonment'.

A reading about finding peace in the face of conflict

There liveth no man on earth who may always have rest and peace without troubles and crosses, with whom things always go according to his will; there is always something to be suffered here, turn which way you will. And as soon as you are quit of one assault, perhaps two will come in its place. Wherefore yield thyself willingly to them, and seek only that true peace of the heart, which none can take away from thee, that thou mayest overcome all assaults. Thus then, Christ meant that inward peace which can break through all assaults and crosses of oppression, suffering, misery, humiliation and what more there may be of the like, so that a man may be joyful and patient therein, like the beloved disciples and followers of Christ. Now he who will in love give his whole diligence and might thereto, will verily come to know true eternal peace which is God Himself, as far as it is possible to a creature; insomuch that what was bitter to him before, shall become sweet, and his heart shall remain unmoved among all changes …

From the fourteenth-century work *Theologia Germanica*

———

Forgive us, Gracious Lord,
when Christians have taken up arms against one another,
and pursued the way of violence.
Take from us all hatred, bitterness and enmity.
Banish from our hearts anger, envy and greed
and teach us the way of love and forgiveness;
through Jesus Christ our Lord. Amen.

Elizabeth Fuller 1644–1709

Philanthropist

———

ELIZABETH FULLER PAID for a new Free School in Watford in 1704. It was built next to St Mary's Church in the centre of the town and was planned for forty boys and twenty girls. A few years later she endowed it with £52 per annum. It was this school which was later to become Watford Grammar School for Boys and Watford Grammar School for Girls. She is still remembered each year in the Founder's Day Service. Elizabeth also provided funds for the distribution of bread each year to the poor of Watford, and specified that the Vicar of Watford should be paid £1 each year for preaching a sermon.

Ernest Burgmann explores the relationship between playing and learning

Education begins in play. It continues in play, and remains possible while ever the spirit of play survives. Play is spontaneous living, and in it we enter into relations with our world and with our fellows. Play is the activity by which we explore not only our world, but our own capacities. In play we try things out. We are not really old till we can no longer play. While we can play we can retain our interest in life and our education can still go on. We were born to play. The purpose of education is to take hold of our spontaneous play activities and to bring into them a social discipline and a sense of responsibility. The art of education is to do this without reducing the energy of play, in fact, we should aim at enhancing and increasing it. We also equip the play activity with knowledge and understanding. For instance, the child's capacity to pretend is the scientist's ability to fashion a hypothesis, the philosopher's vision of a universal system of thought, and the saint's ground for faith. The child pretends he is the butcher or baker, the father or doctor, and by degrees he settles down to become one or more of the things he pretended to be. He eventually makes his play dream come true by dealing faithfully with the facts of life. He begins that faithful dealing in play. The form of the play can be transformed into work. The play spirit can keep the work fresh and resilient and creative to the end of his days. The scientist says in effect, 'Let us pretend that this hypothesis is true' and then he proceeds to test it out on facts. The play spirit will keep his imagination alert and sensitive. He will be able to see all the more quickly and modify his hypotheses all the more readily if he keeps that spirit fresh.

From *The Education of an Australian*

———

Bless, Lord, our schools, colleges and universities,
that those who teach may do so with inspiration and flair,
and those who learn may do so with commitment and diligence.
We pray that minds may be deepened,
imaginations kindled, and sympathies broadened,
in the name of Jesus Christ our Lord. Amen.

Philip Henry Loyd 1884–1952

Fifth Bishop of St Albans

———

PHILIP LOYD WAS educated at Eton and King's College, Cambridge. He was ordained in 1911 and served his title at St Mary-of-Eton, Hackney Wick, in East London. He then spent three years as Vice-Principal of Cuddesdon College before going to India with the Society for the Propagation of the Gospel Mission in 1915. After periods at Miri and Ahmednagar, he was made Assistant Bishop of Bombay in 1925, and then Bishop of Nasik in 1929. In 1944 he was appointed Bishop of St Albans where he served until his resignation in 1950. He died on this day in 1952 and is buried at St Albans Abbey. He wrote a number of books on the Gospels, including *The Way according to St Mark*, *By Faith with Thanksgiving*, *The Life according to St John*, *The Treasures of the Heart of Jesus*, *Doers of the Word* and *Teach Me Thy Statutes*.

Philip Loyd preaches about vocation

'And Barnabas and Saul returned from Jerusalem, when they had fulfilled their ministration, taking with them John whose surname was Mark'. Picture him [John Mark] then, a young man, taking the first step on the path of service. Was it the imprisonment and deliverance of St Peter that stirred him to offer himself for this work? We do not know. But we do know that wherever there are servants of Christ who are filled with the spirit of consecration and are giving their witness fearlessly, there the supply of recruits to the ministry is always more abundant. So let us pray for more vocations to the ministry of the Church; and let us pray that we may have such a spirit of service and consecration in the Church, that young men may be attracted to the ministry, not as to a respectable or advantageous career, but as to the appointed path along which they are to follow in service and self-denial the Lord Jesus who, when He gave His charge to St Peter by the Sea of Galilee, ended by saying *Follow Me* (John 21. 19).

From *The Holy Spirit in the Acts*

Lord God, the harvest is plentiful
but the labourers are few,
And so we pray that you,
the Lord of the harvest,
will send forth labourers into your harvest,
to preach the good news to the nations,
to build up your Church in every land,
and to serve the needs of mankind everywhere;
for the sake of Jesus our Saviour. Amen.

Frank Colquhoun

Mary Abney 1676–1750

Benefactress who lived near Waltham Cross

———

FOR MANY YEARS the Manor at Stoke Newington had belonged to St Paul's Cathedral, but it came into the possession of Mary's brother, Thomas Gunston, and following his death in 1701 she inherited the property. Mary was living at Theobalds, a large estate in Cheshunt, with her husband Sir Thomas Abney. Thomas, a former Lord Mayor of London, was nearly forty years older than Mary and was an influential figure in the city. Thomas and Mary retained both properties, keeping the manor at Stoke Newington, now known as Abney House, as their second home. In 1736 Thomas died and Mary became one of the few lady Lords of the Manor in England, something which was uncommon in eighteenth-century England. Mary was a Nonconformist and worshipped in what was to become the Congregational Church. She was friends with a number of leading Nonconformist figures such as Philip Doddridge and Selina Hastings, the Countess of Huntingdon, who built a number of churches which are now known as the Countess of Huntingdon's Connexion. Mary also entertained Isaac Watts at Abney House and Theobalds. He became her chaplain and a life-long friend, and collaborated with her in landscaping the park around Abney House. It was there that he wrote many of his most famous hymns, inspired by the surroundings. When Watts died, Mary contributed to the building of a memorial to him in Bunhill Fields. Mary died in 1750 and is buried at Old Stoke Newington Church.

When I survey the wondrous cross
on which the Prince of Glory died;
my richest gain I count but loss,
and pour contempt on all my pride.

Forbid it, Lord, that I should boast,
save in the death of Christ, my God;
all the vain things that charm me most,
I sacrifice them to his blood.

See, from his head, his hands, his feet,
sorrow and love flow mingled down.
Did e'er such love and sorrow meet,
or thorns compose so rich a crown.

Were the whole realm of nature mine,
that were an offering far too small;
love so amazing, so divine,
demands my soul, my life, my all.

Isaac Watts

Almighty God
whose Son, though he was rich, yet for our sakes become poor,
that we through his poverty might become rich:
grant us the spirit of generous self-giving
that we may further the work of your church
and relieve those who are in need.
Help us who have received so freely from you to give as freely in our turn,
and so share the blessedness of giving as well as the happiness of receiving.
We ask this in the name of him who gave himself for the life of the world,
your Son, Jesus Christ, our Lord. Amen.

Adapted from a prayer by George Appleton

Henry Edward Manning 1808–92

Cardinal Archbishop of Westminster

——

HENRY MANNING WAS born in Totteridge, Hertfordshire, in 1808. Educated at Harrow School and Balliol College, Oxford, he had wanted a career in politics and took a position in the Colonial Office. In 1833, however, he was ordained in the Church of England and served his title at Lavinton-with-Graffham in Sussex where he later became Rector. He married Caroline Sargent, but she died only four years later. A devout high churchman, he was appointed Archdeacon of Chichester and in 1842 wrote *The Unity of the Church*. This was followed by four volumes of his sermons. In 1850, however, following the Gorham Judgment, Manning converted to Roman Catholicism and a year later was re-ordained a Catholic priest. In 1865 he was appointed Archbishop of Westminster, and made cardinal. Manning was responsible for building Westminster Cathedral. He was a close ally of Pope Leo XIII and a passionate supporter of the doctrine of papal infallibility. He had a strong social conscience and one of his stranger contributions was to help settle the London Dock Strike in 1889. Several volumes of his sermons were published along with *Rule of Faith, Unity of the Church* and *The Eternal Priesthood*.

In this sermon Manning speaks of the power of praise

'Ye shall have a song, as in the night when a holy solemnity is kept; and gladness of heart as when one goeth with a pipe to come into the mountain of the Lord, to the mighty One of Israel' (Isaiah 30.29). This sets vividly before us a state of heart, a temper of love and thanksgiving, a filial and almost childlike simplicity of grateful joy; and in this way it brings out, more clearly than any words, what is the full meaning of praise; from what source it springs, and in what ways it is expressed. If we are to define it in words, we may say that praise is thankful, lowly, loving worship of the goodness and majesty of God. And therefore we often find the word 'praise' joined with 'blessing' and 'thanksgiving': but though all three are akin to each other, they are not all alike. They are steps in a gradual scale – a song of degrees. Thanksgiving runs up into blessing, and blessing ascends into praise: for praise comprehends both, and is the highest and most perfect work of all living spirits.

From *Sermons IV*

————————————

O Holy Spirit of God, take me as Thy Disciple.
Guide me, illuminate me, sanctify me.
Bind my hands that they may do no evil.
Cover my eyes that they may see it no more.
Sanctify my heart that evil may not dwell within me.
Be Thou my God. Be Thou my Guide
Whithersoever Thou leadest me I will go.
Whatsoever Thou forbiddest me I will renounce.
And whatsoever Thou commandest me,
in Thy strength I will do.
Lead me then unto the fullness of Thy truth. Amen.

Henry Manning

Gay Perry 1939–2009

Mother and clergy wife

———

GAY PERRY REPRESENTS all those wives, husbands and children who have selflessly supported clergy in their ministry, usually behind the scenes and at great personal cost. Born in Ruislip, Gay Brown was the elder of two sisters and was educated at Preston Manor County Grammar School. She was profoundly influenced by the Covenanters, a youth movement, and the Billy Graham Crusades, and made a Christian commitment in her teenage years. She worshipped at Emmanuel Northwood, where she was involved in running the youth work and taking services in the local hospitals. After leaving school she worked for Scripture Union for a year. In 1959 Gay married John Perry, who had just been ordained to serve a curacy at Christ Church, Woking, and in the years that followed they had five children. Throughout her life, Gay was deeply involved in Christian ministry, not only supporting her husband but offering hospitality, running young wives' groups and leading Bible studies. In 1962 Gay and John came to St Andrew's, Chorleywood, where they spent the next fifteen years. In 1977 they moved to the Lee Abbey Community near Lynton, in North Devon. Here Gay's creative gifts of homemaking and gardening came to the fore as she took a leading role in running the large house and extensive grounds. She was greatly valued as a listener and counsellor. In 1989 Gay found herself as a bishop's wife, first in Southampton and then in 1996 in Chelmsford, which gave ever wider scope for her hospitality.

John Main writes about the importance of learning to listen to one another

Marriage and prayer are intimately related in Paul's vision of the Christian life.

In both prayer and marriage the call is to full selfhood by loss of self in the other. The giving of self must become total. Both prayer and marriage are creative of life because of the generosity and faith that enable us to lay down our lives in love. I suppose it wouldn't be an exaggeration to say that one of the principal causes of the breakdown of so many marriages is a lack of the spirit of obedience. No word in the religious vocabulary is so much misunderstood by our contemporaries as 'obedience'. Obedience is nothing else than the capacity to listen to the other. We stray from God when we lose this attentiveness and no amount of talking or thinking about God can truly substitute for this openness to him. The Latin root of 'obedience' is *ob-audiere*, to hear, to listen. We are to be listeners. Obedience here is in essence sensitivity, deep sensitivity to the other, to the others. The readiness to think, in the first place, of the other and not of oneself. As you know it is impossible for us to love one another unless we serve one another.

From *The Joy of Being*

God our Father, who made men and women to live together in families;
we pray that marriage may be held in honour;
that husbands and wives may live faithfully together according to their vows;
and that the members of every family may grow in mutual love and kindness,
so that they may bear one another's burdens and so fulfil the law of Christ;
for His name's sake. Amen.

The Mothers' Union

Paul of Caen 11th century

Abbot of St Albans

———

PAUL WAS A Benedictine monk of the Abbey of Saint-Étienne in Caen in Normandy. In 1077 his uncle, Lanfranc, who had become Archbishop of Canterbury, appointed Paul as Abbot of St Albans, a post he held for sixteen years. His Anglo-Saxon predecessors Ealdred and Easmer had amassed building material from Verulamium, the ruined Roman city situated just below the present Abbey building, and he used these materials to erect the present building which we know today as our Cathedral. As well as recycling old Roman bricks, archaeological work has shown that Paul also used some of the stonework from the Anglo-Saxon abbey, such as tombs, which have survived in the foundations. Today we can see Paul's legacy in the massive central tower of the Abbey which stands forty-eight metres high and is estimated to weigh around five thousand tons.

St Benedict gives instructions about worship

As soon as the signal for the divine office is heard, let everyone abandon whatever he is doing and hasten to the oratory with all speed, yet with gravity, so that there is no cause for levity. Let nothing be preferred to the Work of God. If at Matins any brother arrives after the Gloria of the 95th psalm, which on that account we wish to be much recited slowly, let him not stand in his place in the choir. Rather let him stand last of all, or in a place which the Abbot has designated for such careless persons, so that he may be seen by all. When the Work of God is ended, he should make satisfaction by public penance. The reason why we think such brothers should stand in the last place, or apart from the rest, is so that being seen by all they may amend their ways for very shame. For if such brothers are permitted to stay outside the oratory, there might be one who would go back to sleep, or else sit down outside and indulge in idle gossip, and give a 'chance to the devil'. Let the brother come inside the oratory, therefore, so that he may not lose the whole of the office and may amend for the future. At the times of prayer during the day, if someone fails to arrive for the Work of God by the verse and the Gloria of the first psalm, then let him stand in the last place, according to the rule which we stated above; and let him not attempt to join the choir of the chanters until he has made satisfaction, unless the Abbot has given him leave to do so, with the understanding that he atone for his fault later.

From Chapter XLIII of *The Rule of St Benedict*

Almighty God,
you have so linked our lives one with another that all we do affects,
for good or ill, all other lives:
so guide us in the work we do,
that we may do it not for self alone,
but for the common good;
and, as we seek a proper return for our own labour,
make us mindful of the rightful aspirations of other workers,
and arouse our concern for those who are out of work;
through Jesus Christ our Lord, who lives and reigns with you
and the Holy Spirit, one God, for ever and ever. Amen.

Anonymous

Edward George Earle Lytton Bulwer-Lytton 1803–73

Man of letters and politician

————

Revenge is a common passion; it is the sin of the uninstructed. The savage deems it noble;
but Christ's religion, which is the sublime civiliser, emphatically condemns it. Why?
Because religion ever seeks to ennoble man; and nothing so debases him as revenge (Bulwer-Lytton)

BULWER-LYTTON'S LITERARY OUTPUT included many phrases which are now part of the English language, including 'It was a dark and stormy night', 'The great unwashed' and 'The pen is mightier than the sword'. He became a best-selling author and made a fortune from his writing. His father, General William Bulwer, came from Norfolk and his mother, Elizabeth Barbara Lytton, from Knebworth in Hertfordshire. After his father died when he was just four years old, Bulwer-Lytton was taken to live in London. He was sent to boarding school and at the age of fifteen published his first collection of poetry, *Ismael and Other Poems*. In 1822 he went up to Trinity College, Cambridge, where in 1925 he won the Chancellor's Gold Medal for English Verse. Soon afterwards he published his second collection of poetry, *Weeds and Wild Flowers*. He was first elected to Parliament as the Member for the seat of St Ives. He then represented Lincoln for nine years and, after a break, returned as Member of Parliament for Hertfordshire. In 1866 he was made Baron Lytton of Knebworth. Bulwer-Lytton wrote twenty-nine novels (several of which have been translated into other languages), three plays and published three volumes of poetry. At least two of his works were turned into operas, one by Richard Wagner. He died on this day in 1873 and is buried in Westminster Abbey.

> What a mistake to suppose that the passions are strongest in youth! The passions are not stronger, but the control over them is weaker! They are more easily excited, they are more violent and apparent; but they have less energy, less durability, less intense and concentrated power than in the maturer life.
>
> There is no such thing as luck. It's a fancy name for being always at our duty, and so sure to be ready when good time comes.
>
> The best teacher is the one who suggests rather than dogmatises, and inspires his listener with the wish to teach himself.
>
> From the works of Edward George Earle Lytton Bulwer-Lytton

Heavenly Father, we pray for the leaders of our nation,
for our politicians and civil servants:
give them a vision of a society which protects the weak and the vulnerable,
which gives opportunity for the less fortunate,
and which encourages responsibility for the privileged;
that all may have the opportunity to thrive and flourish;
for we ask this in the name of Jesus Christ our Lord. Amen.

Claud Thomas Thellusson Wood 1885–1961

Bishop of Bedford

———

EDUCATED AT ETON and Trinity College, Cambridge, Wood was ordained in the Diocese of St Albans and served his title at Hatfield. He spent ten years as Chaplain to the Territorial Army and served with the British Expeditionary Force in 1914–18. He was mentioned in dispatches, and in 1916 awarded the Military Cross. After a curacy in Croydon, Wood became Vicar of St Saviour's in St Albans. In 1930 he was appointed Vicar of St Peter and St Paul, Tring, and four years later he took on the additional responsibility of Rural Dean of Berkhamsted. In 1942 he became Archdeacon of St Albans and then in 1948 Bishop of Bedford. He retired in 1953 and died on this day in 1961. Bishop Wood Junior School at Tring is named after him.

Gregory the Great explores the responsibility of leadership

It is vital that Christian leaders when occupied with exterior matters should not lessen their solicitude for the inner life, and by the same token, when occupied with their inner life should not relax their watch on exterior concerns. Otherwise, by being engrossed in the pressing duties that assail a leader, they will experience an interior collapse; or by being preoccupied with the things that concern the inner life, they will end up neglecting their external duties to their neighbours. It often happens in the Church that some leaders, forgetting that they have been given oversight of their brothers and sisters for the sake of their souls, end up devoting the energies of their heart to secular causes. These they gladly attend to as often as occasion demands; and when occasion is not present, find themselves bereft, hankering after engagements day and night, their minds disoriented and awry. If they discover they have some free time because they have no commitments, they suddenly feel exhausted – not through stress, but by the emotional vacuum. The reality of their situation is that they have found significance in being weighed down by external duties, and find it impossible to stop working. They rejoice in being weighed down by the many heavy demands of the world, but neglect their inner life which ought to be the well from which they teach others. As a direct consequence of this, it is inevitable that the life of their people will languish. Although their people want to make spiritual progress, in the example of their leaders they are confronted by a stumbling-block. As long as the head languishes, the members will degenerate. It is a waste of time for an army, seeking to engage the enemy in battle, to hurry behind the general if he has lost his way. No exhortation will succeed in raising the minds of people, no rebuke will succeed in amending their faults, if it issues from a spiritual guardian who prefers to be immersed in secular duties: the shepherd's care of the flock will be missing. People cannot see the light of truth, for when secular affairs take over a pastor's mind, dust, driven by the winds of temptation, blinds the eyes of the Church.

From the treatise *Pastoral Care*

———

Almighty God, the light of the faithful and shepherd of souls,
who set your servant Claud to be a bishop in the Church
to feed your sheep by the word of Christ
and to guide them by good example:
give us grace to keep the faith of the Church
and to follow in the footsteps of Jesus Christ your Son our Lord. Amen.

From *Common Worship*

John Whethamstede d.1465

Abbot of St Albans

———

JOHN'S SURNAME DERIVES from being born in Wheathampstead in Hertfordshire. He was educated at St Albans School and at the age of sixteen entered the monastery. In 1420 he was elected Abbot. Records indicate that in 1423 he was present at the Council of Siena. He paid great attention to restoring the monastic buildings which had fallen into disrepair following the first Battle of St Albans. He resigned as abbot but, following the unexpected death of his successor, he was appointed for a second term. He is buried in the Abbey in St Albans.

St Benedict speaks of the importance of perseverance in the Christian life

The fourth step of humility is when, in the act of obeying, you encounter trials, opposition, and even abuse, and do not complain, but rather keep a firm grip on patience and endure it. You should neither grow faint nor run away. As scripture says, 'Those who stand firm to the end will be saved,' and again, 'Let your heart take courage and hope in the Lord.' Furthermore, to demonstrate how a faithful person will suffer even painful things for the Lord's sake, scripture gives voice to those who suffer in the words, 'For your sake are we afflicted by death all the day long, and are reckoned as sheep for the slaughter.' Unperturbed because of their hope of a divine reward they persevere with joy, saying, 'These are trials through which we triumph on account of him who loved us.' And elsewhere scripture says, 'You have tested us, O God; you have refined us in the fire as silver is refined; you led us into the net; you laid tribulations on our backs.' And to show that we ought to be under a superior, scripture continues, 'You have set men over our heads.' These are people who patiently fulfill the command of the Lord in trials and setbacks. When struck on one cheek, they offer the other. When someone robs them of their tunic, they give him their cloak too. When forced to go one mile, they go two. Like the Apostle Paul, they put up with false brethren, and bless those who curse them.

From *The Rule of St Benedict*

———

Grant, O God, that the same mind that was in Christ Jesus
may be in all the ministers of your Church:
his self-forgetting humility; his interest in common things;
his love for common people; his compassion for the fallen;
his tolerance with the mistaken; his patience with the slow;
and in all their work and converse make them continually sensitive to your guidance
and ready for your will, through Jesus Christ our Lord. Amen.

Adapted from the *Book of Offices* of the Methodist Church

William Jenkyn 1613–85

Dissenter who ministered in Kings Langley

———

THE LIFE OF William Jenkyn raises sharp questions during the Week of Prayer for Christian Unity. He was an Anglican priest and a strong supporter of the monarchy. After studying at Cambridge, he became Rector of St Leonard's, Colchester, and then Vicar of Christ Church, Newgate. However, in 1650 he was suspended from the ministry because of his support of Charles I. He was part of the plot for the restoration of the monarchy, for which he was imprisoned in the Tower of London. He only narrowly avoided being executed by submitting a grovelling petition to Parliament. Jenkyn welcomed the restoration of the monarchy in 1660, but two years later was ejected under the Act of Uniformity. In 1664 he moved to Kings Langley, Hertfordshire, from where he continued to exercise a ministry. In 1684 he was arrested, having attended a prayer meeting, and was sent to Newgate Prison. He was allowed visitors but not permitted to pray with them. Jenkyn published a number of his sermons and also wrote a number of books including *The Busie Bishop, or the Visitor Visited* and *An Exposition of the Epistle of Jude*. He died on this day in Newgate Prison in 1685. Eight months later his son, William Jenkyn, was executed for his part in the Monmouth Rebellion.

> There can be no ecumenism worthy of the name without interior conversion. For it is from newness of attitudes of mind, from self-denial and unstinted love, that desires of unity take their rise and develop in a mature way. We should therefore pray to the Holy Spirit for the grace to be genuinely self-denying, humble, gently in the service of others and to have an attitude of brotherly generosity toward them. The Apostle to the Gentiles says: 'I, therefore, a prisoner for the Lord, beg you to lead a life worthy of the calling to which you have been called, with all humility and meekness, with patience, forbearing one another in love, eager to maintain the unity of the spirit in the bond of peace' (Eph. 4:1-3).
>
> Decree on Ecumenism, *Unitatis Redintegratio*, from the Second Vatican Council

---

> *O God, the Father of our Lord Jesus Christ, our only Saviour, the Prince of Peace:*
> *give us grace to lay to heart the great dangers we are in by our unhappy divisions.*
> *Take away all hatred and prejudice, and whatever else may hinder us*
> *from godly union and concord;*
> *that, as there is but one body and one Spirit, one hope of our calling,*
> *one Lord, one faith, one baptism, one God and Father of us all,*
> *so we may henceforth be all of one heart and of one soul,*
> *united in one holy bond of peace, of faith and charity,*
> *and may with one mind and one mouth glorify you;*
> *through Jesus Christ our Lord. Amen.*
>
> From *The Book of Common Prayer*

John Howard 1726–90

Philanthropist and prison reformer

————

JOHN HOWARD SPENT much of his childhood in Cardington and went to school in Hertford and London. As a young man he was captured by privateers and imprisoned in France, an experience which awakened his interest in prisons. He returned to live on the family estate in Cardington where he became known for his care of the tenants and for his generosity in paying for the education of twenty-three children. When he was appointed as High Sheriff of Bedfordshire, Howard decided to undertake an inspection of the county gaol. He was so shocked by what he saw that he began to visit other prisons and, as a result, wrote *The State of the Prisons.* Howard's concern for prisoners took him to many parts of the world. It was during such a visit to the Crimea that he caught typhoid and died on this day in 1790. He is buried at Dophinovka. His work inspired the founders of the Howard Association which today is known as the Howard League for Penal Reform. Other groups in New Zealand, Canada and the United States of America are also named after him.

John Howard describes his growing horror at the plight of prisoners

The distress of prisoners, of which there are few who have not some imperfect idea, came more immediately under my notice when I was Sheriff of the Country of Bedford; and the circumstance which excited me to activity on their behalf was, foreseeing some, who by the verdict of juries were declared not guilty; some, on whom the ground jury did not find such an appearance of guilt and subjected them to trial; and some, whose persecutors did not appear against them; after having been confined for months, dragged back to gaol, and locked up again till they should pay sundry fees to the gaoler, the clerk of assize. In order to address this hardship, I applied to the justices of the county for a salary to the gaoler in lieu of his fees. The bench were properly affected with the grievance, and willing to grant the relief desired: but they wanted a precedent for charging the county with the expense. I therefore rode into several neighbouring counties in search of a precedence; but I soon learned that the same injustice was practised in them; and looking to the prisons, I beheld scenes of calamity, which I grew daily more and more anxious to alleviate. In order therefore to gain a more perfect knowledge of the particulars and extent of it, by various and accurate observation, I visited most of the county gaols in England.

From *The State of the Prisons in England and Wales*

Heavenly Father,
we pray for those who make our laws,
those who interpret them,
and those who enforce them.
May our systems of justice be free from corruption,
that those convicted of crime may face up to what they have done,
find ways to make restitution,
and contribute to the good of society;
for the sake of Jesus Christ. Amen.

Seth Ward 1617–89

Bishop, mathematician and astronomer

———

SETH WARD WAS born in Aspenden, Hertfordshire. He studied at Sidney Sussex College, Cambridge, where in 1643 he was appointed a lecturer in mathematics. However, the following year he was deprived of his fellowship because he refused to support the Solemn League and Covenant. In 1649 Ward moved to Oxford where he took up the post of Savilian Professor of Astronomy. He wrote *In Ismaelis Bullialdi astro-nomiae philolaicae fundamenta inquisitio brevis* (1653) and *Astronomia geometrica* (1656). He was involved in founding the Royal Society and was appointed President of Trinity College, Oxford, a post he held for only a short time. Ward held a number of ecclesiastical appointments, including St Lawrence Jewry in London, Uplowman in Devon, St Breock in Cornwall and the Deanery of Exeter Cathedral. In 1662 he was consecrated Bishop of Exeter and five years later was translated to Salisbury. In 1671 he was appointed Chancellor of the Order of the Garter. Ward was passionately opposed to Nonconformity and enforced the Conventicle Acts of 1664 and 1670 which prevented meetings of more than five people for religious purposes, unless they were part of the Church of England. In his will Ward left £12 to provide apprenticeships for boys. He paid for and endowed some almshouses in Buntingford. He also had a memorial stone to his parents erected outside the church at Aspenden.

Bill Bryson describes the enormity of the solar system

Such are the distances, in fact, that it isn't possible, in any practical terms, to draw the whole solar system to scale. Even if you added lots of fold-out pages to your textbooks or used a really long sheet of poster paper, you wouldn't come close. On a diagram of the solar system to scale, with the Earth reduced to about the diameter of a pea, Jupiter would be over 300 metres away and Pluto would be two and a half kilometres distant (and about the size of a bacterium, so you wouldn't be able to see it anyway). On the same scale, Proxima Centauri, our nearest star, would be 16,000 kilometres away. Even if you shrank down everything so that Jupiter was as small as the full stop at the end of this sentence, and Pluto was no bigger than a molecule, Pluto would still be over 10 metres away. So the solar system is really quite enormous. By the time we reach Pluto, we have come so far that the Sun – our dear, warm, skin-tanning, life-giving Sun – has shrunk to the size of a pinhead. It is little more than a bright star.

From *A Short History of Nearly Everything*

———

O Lord, whose name is majestic in all the earth,
who has set your glory above the heavens:
when I consider the moon and the stars
who am I that you should care for me?
Yet you have adopted me as your child,
crowned me with glory and honour,
and allow me to share in your work of creation! Amen.

Based on Psalm 8

Noel Martin Kennaby 1905–94

Dean of St Albans

———

NOEL KENNABY WAS born in 1905 and educated at Queens' College and Westcott House, Cambridge, before being ordained in 1930. Following a curacy in Epsom, he became Priest-in-Charge of Christ Church, Scarborough; then Vicar of St Andrew's, Handsworth, before being appointed to the living of Tynemouth. In 1947 he became the Provost and Vicar of Newcastle Cathedral. After fifteen years he moved to be senior chaplain to the Archbishop of Canterbury. From 1964 until 1973 he served as Dean of St Albans. He died on this day in 1994.

Noel Kennaby writes about prayer

A Christian at his prayer is never alone; he is in the company of other praying Christians. It does not matter whether he is on a mountain-top thanking God for the beauty of the scene, or whether he is on the shore quietly remembering the presence of God while no other human being is in sight, or whether he is in a noisy, clattering factory offering an arrow-prayer for help in difficulty or temptation, or whether he is a stranger feeling utterly lonely in a busy, crowded street; when he prays, either in muttered word or unspoken thought, he is no more alone that when he is one of a vast congregation in the biggest cathedral in Christendom; for Christian fellowship in prayer and worship is a spiritual reality and does not depend on physical proximity. It is true, of course, that the supreme act of Christian prayer and worship, the Holy Eucharist, can be offered only in the fellowship of a congregation, and it is also true that men most easily realise their spiritual fellowship with one another when they are close to one another physically; that is why we are commanded 'not to forsake the assembling of ourselves together as the manner of some is.' But Christian fellowship is the treasured possession which each member of Christ's Body, the Church, shares with each other member, wherever each may be.

From *To Start You Praying*

Lord Jesus Christ,
pierce my soul with your love so that I may always long for you alone,
who are the bread of angels and the fulfilment of the soul's deepest desires.
May my heart always hunger and feed upon you,
so that my soul may be filled with the sweetness of your presence.
May my soul thirst for you, who are the source of life, wisdom,
knowledge, light and all the riches of God our Father.
May I always seek and find you, think on you, speak to you,
and do all things for the honour and glory of your holy name.
Be always my only hope, my peace, my refuge and my help
in whom my heart is rooted so that I may never be separated from you. Amen.

St Bonaventure

John Berridge 1716–93

Hymn writer and vicar

——

FOR NEARLY FORTY years John Berridge was Vicar of St Mary's, Everton. Although Everton is in Bedfordshire the parish is in the Diocese of Ely. Berridge was a friend of John and Charles Wesley and knew George Whitfield personally. In 1756 he had a spiritual awakening which resulted in a revival among the parishioners. It was said that during his sermons there were sometimes outbreaks of hysteria, not something which was very common in Anglican churches, then or now. Berridge is buried just outside the church at Everton. The words on this tomb are a sermon in their own right, posing the question 'Art thou born again?':

> *Here lay the earthly Remains of JOHN BERRIDGE*
> *late Vicar of Everton and an itinerant Servant*
> *of JESUS CHRIST who loved his Master and his Work*
> *and after running on his Errands many Years was called*
> *up to wait on him above. Reader art thou born again*
> *No salvation without a new Birth*
> *I was born in Sin Feb 1716*
> *Remained ignorant of my fallen State till 1730*
> *Lived proudly on Faith & Works for Salvation till 1754*
> *Admitted to Everton Vicarage 1755*
> *Fled to Jesus alone for Refuge 1756*
> *Fell asleep in Jesus Christ Jan 22nd 1793*

An earthly heart I have,
And earthly made by sin!
No good, but sensual, it will crave,
And sweetly drinks it in.

Who can the spirit turn,
And unto God unite,
And make the heart with fevour burn,
And in its God delight?

Thou, Holy Spirit, must
The mighty work perform,
Awake the sleeper from his dust,
And wing the grovelling worm.

Oh, let thy breath inspire
All needful power and will
And make my soul to God aspire,
And with his presence fill.

John Berridge

Heavenly Father,
by the power of your Holy Spirit
you give your faithful people new life in the water of baptism.
Guide and strengthen us by the same Spirit,
that we who are born again may serve you in faith and love,
and grow into the full stature of your Son, Jesus Christ,
who is alive and reigns with you in the unity of the Holy Spirit
now and for ever. Amen.

From the service of confirmation in *Common Worship*

Clarissa Robinson 1925–2009

Musician, embroiderer and hospice founder

———

AS A YOUNG woman Clarissa studied at the Royal College of Music. In 1955 she moved to Bedfordshire, was appointed as the Manager of the Carlton Approved School for Boys, and married James Robinson. She took on his two sons, and she and James went on to have three children of their own. Clarissa had a lifelong interest in healthcare and served on the committee of the Friends of Bedford Hospital for many years. She became chair of the North Bedfordshire Community Health Council in 1970 and was one of the group who founded St John's Hospice at Moggerhanger, built in memory of Bishop John Hare. Her interest in the hospice movement had come largely from nursing her husband through his terminal cancer. James died in 1980. In the same year St John's Hospice opened and Clarissa became its first almoner. Drawing on her work with the North Bedfordshire Cruse Group and her diploma in counselling, she set up one of the first hospice bereavement support services in the country. Niece of Michael Furse, Bishop of St Albans, Clarissa was a deeply committed Christian. During her life she served variously as churchwarden, Reader and as a member of Bishop's Council. For twenty years she was the choir mistress and organist of All Saints Church, Great Barford. As well as being a talented musician, she acquired a national reputation as an ecclesiastical embroiderer. More than forty-five pieces of her work are in use today, including copes, stoles, altar frontals, and the vestments she made for both Bishop Robert Runcie and Bishop John Taylor during their time as Bishops of St Albans.

A poem for embroiderers

Man's life is laid in the loom of time
To a pattern he does not see,
While the weavers work and the shuttles fly
Till the dawn of eternity.

Some shuttles are filled with silver threads
And some with threads of gold,
While often but the darker hues
Are all that they may hold.

But the weaver watches with skillful eye
Each shuttle fly to and fro,
And sees the pattern so deftly wrought
As the loom moves sure and slow.

God surely planned the pattern:
Each thread, the dark and fair,
Is chosen by His master skill
And placed in the web with care.

He only knows its beauty,
And guides the shuttles which hold
The threads so unattractive,
As well as the threads of gold.

Not till each loom is silent,
And the shuttles cease to fly,
Shall God reveal the pattern
And explain the reason why

The dark threads were as needful
In the weaver's skillful hand
As the threads of gold and silver
For the pattern which He planned.

Anonymous

God grant that I may see to stitch until my dying day
when the last thread is cut and the scissors tucked away.
May the work that I have done live on
that other folk may see
the pleasure I have known, Lord,
from the gift you gave to me. Amen.

A Prayer for Embroiderers by Anonymous

Mary Spencer 17th century

Diarist and social historian

———

LADY MARY SPENCER was married to Sir Richard Spencer, the grandson of the builder of Offley Place in Great Offley. From 1683 until 1686 she kept a diary which contains a vivid account of daily life. We read of her frequent journeys to visit relatives in Hornsey and Highgate, and from there to London and Westminster. Her journal contains many references to diseases and their cures, including how she took her son to receive 'the King's touch' to cure him of scrofula. She was an excellent housekeeper and kept both an account book and a meticulous inventory of every household and personal item. She corresponded regularly with family and friends, receiving from them national news, including from her brother Charles in London the news that the Thames had frozen over in January 1684. It is clear from her diary that she went to church regularly, although holy communion was celebrated only at the main Christian festivals. However, in 1687 she was widowed and then her only child, Jack, died when he was just twenty-one. She made provision for an annual sermon to be preached on Jack's birthday.

E. M. Forster reflects on the power of words

Just as words have two functions – information and creation – so each human mind has two personalities, one on the surface, one deeper down. The upper personality has a name. It is called S. T. Coleridge, or William Shakespeare, or Mrs Humphry Ward. It is conscious and alert, it does things like dining out, answering letters, etc., and it differs vividly and amusingly from other personalities. The lower personality is a very queer affair. In many ways it is a perfect fool, but without it there is no literate, because, unless a man dips a bucket down into it occasionally he cannot produce first-class work. There is something general about it. Although it is inside S.T. Coleridge, it cannot be labelled with his name. It has something in common with all other deeper personalities, and the mystic will assert that the common quality is God, and that here, in the obscure recesses of our being, we near the gates of the Divine. It is in any case the force that makes for anonymity. As it came from the depths, so it soars to the heights, out of local questionings; as it is general to all men, so the works it inspires have something general about them, namely beauty. The poet wrote the poem no doubt, but he forgot himself while he wrote it, and we forget him while we read. What is so wonderful about great literature is that it transforms the man who reads it towards the condition of the man who wrote, and brings to birth in us also the creative impulse. Lost in the beauty where he was lost, we find more than we ever threw away, we reach what seems to be our spiritual home, and remember that it was not the speaker who was in the beginning but the Word.

From *Anonymity, An Enquiry*

———

Almighty God,
we thank you for our inner world
of reflection, thought and imagination:
give us grace to enter into the hidden depths of our being
to find you, the source of all life and truth,
for we ask it in the name of Jesus Christ our Lord. Amen.

Halley Stewart 1838–1937

Politician and philanthropist

———

THE SON OF a Congregational minister, Halley Stewart was born into a large family in Barnet. He had a varied career in banking, coal, brewing and in the oil seed processing business. Although never ordained, he was pastor of two Congregational churches for several years. Halley became editor of a newspaper that he himself founded and went on to be elected as Liberal Member of Parliament, firstly in Spalding, and then in Greenock. Later in life he turned his attention to the manufacture of bricks and his company eventually became the London Brick Company. Halley was renowned for his philanthropy, supporting the poor and funding medical research. His generosity enabled Harpenden District Council to buy the common on the edge of the town and he bequeathed his house to become a hospital. He was knighted when he was ninety-three and died in Harpenden on this day in 1937.

Kenneth Leech writes about prayer and political action

Christian prayer is rooted in a revolutionary vision, it is Kingdom-directed prayer. It is therefore marked by a sense of fulfillment, of yearning, of stretching out into the future and tasting the powers of the age to come. It is never the prayer of security, ease, and smug certainty. It is a crying out for the Kingdom that is coming. Prayer and politics meet at the point at which this vision of the new age comes into collision, as it must, with political structures based upon a different view of man and of human life. At the heart of our Gospel and our prayer there lies an inescapable core of conflict. This core of conflict is central to the Kingdom which must be the motive force and the visionary cumulus for Christian action.

From *The Meaning of Prayer and Politics*

O Righteous Lord, who loves righteousness,
may your Holy Spirit be with our rulers,
with our Sovereign and all in authority under her,
that they may govern in thy faith and fear,
striving to put down all that is evil and to encourage all that is good.
Give your spirit of wisdom to those who make our laws,
grant that they may understand how great a work thou has given them to do;
that they may not do it lightly, but gravely and soberly,
to the putting away of all wrong and oppression
and to the advancement of the true welfare of the people. Amen.

Thomas Arnold

Mother Mary Clare 1906–88

Nun

———

MARY CLARE BEGAN her religious life as a sister of the Community of St Margaret in East Grinstead at the age of twenty-four. However, sensing a call to the contemplative life she transferred to the Convent of the Incarnation, at Fairacres in Oxford. The community, known as the Sisters of the Love of God, is an enclosed order, which for many years had a daughter house at Boxmoor. Mary Clare was elected as Mother General, and acquired a reputation as a wise counsellor and spiritual director to many. She maintained a correspondence with Thomas Merton, the American Trappist monk, and wrote a number of books on spirituality including *Encountering the Depths: Prayer, Solitude, and Contemplation, Aloneness not Loneliness, Intercession, Learning to Pray, Carmelite Ascent* and *The Simplicity of Prayer*. Known affectionately by her sisters as MMC, she was clear-sighted, formidable and vivacious, with an irrepressible sense of humour. She died in 1988.

Mother Mary Clare teaches about prayer

Prayer is the gateway to the vision of God for which we were created. It is the means for free and conscious intercourse between the creature and his creator, and it expresses the union between the two. It is the art of spiritual living, and it will be incomplete if it includes only the presence of God without the presence of man. The first lesson we have to learn about prayer is that it is God's activity in us, and not a self-activated process of our own. The Desert Fathers, those great masters of the spiritual life, knew all about the essential condition of learning to pray. They called it 'purity of heart', without which there could be no true *metanoia* or conversion. We can pray only if our hearts are truly pure in the sense of Jesus' teaching in the Sermon on the Mount, where the pure in heart shall see God. Prayer and daily life are individable. We must learn to pray as we are, and accept ourselves as we are, and not as the ideal people we would like to imagine ourselves to be. We must grow to understand ourselves and accept that it is at the time when our natural passions are most active, and our minds most distracted, that we can grow to a knowledge of ourselves as real persons. That is the point of tension at which we must offer ourselves to God in prayer. At the beginning of our learning to pray, therefore, we must relate prayer to conversion of life. Prayer, which is the fruit of true conversion, is an activity, an adventure, and sometimes a dangerous one, since there are occasions when it brings neither peace nor comfort, but challenge, conflict and new responsibility.

From *Encountering the Depths*

Gracious Father,
still our wandering minds,
settle our restless bodies,
and open our hearts and minds to your presence.
In the power of your Holy Spirit
pray in us and through us
to the glory of your holy name,
through Jesus Christ our Lord. Amen.

Amelia Long 1772–1837

Watercolour artist

———

AMELIA LONG WAS the daughter of Sir Abraham Hume, Member of Parliament and High Sheriff of Hertfordshire in 1774. Her mother, also called Amelia, was the daughter of the Bishop of Durham. In 1793 Amelia married the politician Charles Long, and in 1801 the couple moved to Bromley Hill Place where Amelia used her horticultural skills to design extensive gardens. She was a keen plantswoman, collecting and growing new species that were being introduced from abroad during the period. She even has a plant named after her: *Lady Long's Camellia.* In 1826 Charles was raised to the peerage by King George IV, taking the title Baron Farnborough. Both Amelia and her husband were interested in the arts and amassed an extensive collection of paintings and sculptures. She took painting lessons from Thomas Girtin and was influenced by her artist friends Henry Edridge and Thomas Monroe. Although she used various mediums, she is remembered today as one of the most influential watercolourists of her generation. Some of her paintings are in the collections at the National Gallery, Tate Britain, and the Victoria and Albert Museum. She is buried in St Laurence's Church, Wormley, Hertfordshire.

John Miller describes how an artist sees the world in new ways

For a long time I could find no way to speak of these things. I spent days drawing and making watercolour studies of everything from the boats: the single fishermen who perch along the water's edge; children playing and bathing or flying kites to the ever changing atmosphere of sea and sky in sunshine and shadow from dawn until dusk. I nearly always started soon after dawn and sometimes worked through twelve hours…but when it came to painting, the day frequently ended in frustration. One lunchtime when I was walking Michael's dog, Boss, along the cliff top I looked down over the vast area of water occupying the Bay of St Ives with Godrevy lighthouse away in the distance and a tiny fishing boat floating in an endless ocean, everything appeared to be beyond the conventional space that I had been painting – a space with a single viewpoint. I instantly realised that the only way to speak about all this was to defy conventional space. I returned to the studio and, at once, everything fell into place and after months of frustration the work flowed as though the flood gates had been opened.

From *New Paintings: Annual Exhibition*

God of all grace,
we thank you for the skills you have given to men and women,
so that through the arts our lives may be inspired and uplifted.
Grant that those who create such works, and we who appreciate them
may be concerned only with what is true, noble, pure, lovely and gracious,
so that all artistic expression may direct us to the fullness of truth and beauty
as revealed in Jesus Christ your Son our Lord. Amen.

Michael Botting

Matthew Paris c.1200–59

Chronicler, artist and monk

———

MATTHEW PARIS WAS a medieval chronicler, cartographer, biographer and artist. Although his name suggests he was French, it is thought that he was born in England. He entered the Benedictine Community at St Albans in 1217 and nineteen years later was made the official chronicler of the Abbey. He wrote in both Latin and French. Of his many works, the most famous are his three-volume *Chronica Majora*, which is partly a re-working of two of his predecessor's chronicles, along with material which he himself wrote, and his *Life of St Alban*. Paris's sources were letters and the reminiscences of the many guests who stayed at the monastery, including King Henry III and the Earl of Cornwall. Despite being a lowly monk, he was not slow to criticise people in authority including the King and the Pope. Paris used tinted drawings to illuminate his manuscripts, drawing on a wide range of images. His illumination of an elephant is often reproduced. He also drew many maps including those of the British Isles and the Holy Land.

St Benedict instructs the monks on restraint in speech

Let us do what the prophet says, 'I have resolved to keep watch how I behave and not to let my tongue lead me into sin. I will set a muzzle on my mouth. I stayed dumb, I was humbled, I refrained from speaking even good words.' Here the prophet teaches us that if we should sometimes for the sake of the virtue of silence refrain from even good conversation, we should do so all the more refrain from speaking evil words for fear of committing sin. Therefore, because of the great importance of keeping silence, permission to speak should rarely be given even to exemplary disciples, even for conversation that is good, holy and edifying. For it is written, 'If you talk, you cannot avoid falling into sin.' And elsewhere it says, 'Death and life are in the power of the tongue.' Indeed, it is fitting for the master to talk and to teach; the disciple's part is to be still and to listen. If it is necessary to ask a superior for something, then the request should be made humbly and respectfully. But as for loose talk, idle chatter and gossip that leads to laughter, we condemn this with a permanent ban in all places. We do not permit a disciple to open his mouth for that kind of speech.

From *The Rule of St Benedict*

And give me, good Lord,
an humble, lowly, quiet, peaceable, patient,
charitable, kind and filial and tender mind,
every shade, in fact, of charity,
with all my words and all my works, and all my thoughts,
to have a taste of thy holy blessed Spirit. Amen.

Sir Thomas More

Charles I 1600–49

King and martyr

———

T HE ONLY CHURCH dedicated to Charles, King and Martyr, in the Diocese of St Albans is in Potters Bar. Charles was the second son of James I and not expected to come to the throne, but his elder brother, Arthur, Prince of Wales, died. Charles succeeded his father at the age of twenty-five. Like him, Charles believed himself to be divinely ordained to be king and consequently found himself in almost constant conflict with Parliament and with the Puritanism that was gaining power in the land. He was often thwarted by Parliament in his attempts to raise revenue through taxes. The Puritan party was already suspicious of Charles following his marriage to the Catholic Henrietta Maria in 1625, with whom he had seven children. The conflict intensified when in 1633 he appointed William Laud as Archbishop of Canterbury who was opposed to Calvanistic theology and tried to impose religious uniformity on the Church, using the courts where necessary. The English Civil War broke out in 1642. In January 1649 Charles was tried, convicted and executed. Just before he was beheaded in Whitehall he said 'I shall go from a corruptible to an incorruptible Crown, where no disturbance can be.'

Just before his execution, King Charles writes to his son

With God, I would have you begin and end, who is King of Kings, the sovereign disposer of the kingdoms of the world, who pulleth down one and setteth up another. The best government and highest sovereignty you can attain to is to be subject to him, that the sceptre of his word and spirit may rule in your heart. The true glory of princes consists in advancing God's glory, in the maintenance of true religion and the Church's good; also in the dispensation of civil power, with justice and honour to the public peace. Above all, I would have you, as I hope you are already, well grounded and settled in your religion, the best profession of which I have ever esteemed that of the Church of England, in which you have been educated; yet I would have your own judgement and reason now sealed to that sacred bond which education hath written, that it may be judiciously your own religion, and not other men's custom or tradition which you profess. Let nothing seem little or despicable to you in matters which concern religion and the Church's peace, so as to neglect a speedy reforming and effectually suppressing errors and schisms. What may seem at first but as a hand-breadth, by seditious spirits, as by strong winds, are soon made a cover and darken the whole heaven.

From a letter delivered to the King's chaplain, the Bishop of London, 30 January 1649

———

Almighty and most merciful Father, look down upon us thy unworthy servants through the mediation and merits of Jesus Christ, in whom only thou art well pleased. Purify our hearts by thy Holy Spirit, and as thou dost add days to our lives, so good Lord, we beseech thee to add repentance to our days; that when we have passed this mortal life we may be partakers of thine everlasting kingdom; through the merits of Jesus Christ our Lord. Amen.

King Charles I

Henry John Rose 1800–73

Linguist and Archdeacon of Bedford

———

FORTUNATELY, A MASTERY of Greek, Latin, German, Hebrew and Syriac is not an essential qualification for an archdeacon today. Henry Rose, however, was an accomplished linguist who had studied at Peterhouse and St John's College, Cambridge. The College was patron of the parish of Houghton Conquest in Bedfordshire and Rose was appointed to the living in 1837. The following year he married Sarah Caroline and before long they had five children. Both of their sons were ordained. In 1866 Rose became the Archdeacon of Bedford, a post he held in plurality with the living of Houghton Conquest until his death. Although he was an academic (he gave the Hulsean Lectures at Cambridge University) he did not neglect the parish and oversaw a major restoration of the church and school. Henry Rose wrote extensively about the Bible and church history and he translated a number of books into English. He died on this day in 1873 and is buried in Houghton Conquest. Among his published works are *The Law of Moses in connection with the History and Character of the Jews* and *Answer to the Case of the Dissenters.*

Henry Rose gives a lecture on death and Christian hope

The Gospel never attempts to persuade man that pain is no evil, but it teaches him to look beyond the present hour, and gives him that which the wounded spirit craves beyond all the other balm – the balm of hope. With death, indeed, it deals after another manner. Whatever of evil death has in a Christian's view, that evil arises from sin alone – 'the sting of death is sin'; and the Gospel disarms death of its power to wound man, by breaking the power of sin, and by bringing the spirit to look on death, for the sincere believer and faithful Christian, only as a passage from a life of trial and of difficulty and darkness, to a state where the pure in heart shall see God, and be satisfied with his goodness! It therefore requires him to prepare himself for death, by daily renouncing all the sinfulness that still clings to his nature, and daily asking of the Holy Spirit more of the power to change his heart into the likeness of the model which his Saviour left for man, and thus to take away the sting from death, because it professes no power to chase away the shadows of darkness from the dying bed of the sinner, and because only in proportion to the faith and the holiness of the Christian are its promises of power or its hopes available.

From the *Hulsean Lectures*, 1833

Heavenly Father,
whose Son suffered and died on the cross,
and on the third day was raised to new life:
give us grace to place our lives into your hands,
that in times of both joy and suffering we may have confidence
in your promise of resurrection;
through the merits of Jesus Christ our Lord. Amen.

Francis Egerton 1736–1803

The Father of Inland Navigation

———

THOSE WHO ENJOY walking in the countryside will be familiar with the paths on the Ashridge Estate in West Hertfordshire. The area is dominated by the Bridgewater Monument, dedicated to Francis Egerton, the third Duke of Bridgewater, on which he is described as 'The Father of Inland Navigation'. Egerton was the younger son of the second Duke of Bridgewater, a title he inherited at the age of twelve. He was not a robust child and had many periods of illness, which caused much worry to his family. However, as an adult he became a brilliant entrepreneur. Needing to find a better way to transport coal from the mines on his land in Lancashire, he commissioned James Brindley to build what is now known as the Bridgewater Canal. This was so successful that Egerton then made significant improvements to the waterway between Manchester and Liverpool. These projects made Egerton one of the richest men in England. He amassed a large art collection and also used his wealth to build and repair churches including St Mary Magdalene Winton, St Mark Worsley, and St Peter and St Paul Little Gaddesden. Towards the end of his life he decided to demolish Ashridge Priory and to build a new house at Ashridge but it was not completed until 1814, some years after his death. He is buried in the family vault in Little Gaddesden Church.

A reading about the dignity of work and the rights of workers

The economy must serve people, not the other way around. Work is more than a way to make a living; it is a form of continuing participation in God's creation. Employers contribute to the common good through the services or products they provide and by creating jobs that uphold the dignity and rights of workers – to productive work, to decent and just wages, to adequate benefits and security in their old age, to the choice of whether to organise and join unions, to the opportunity for legal status for immigrant workers, to private property, and to economic initiative. Workers also have responsibilities – to provide a fair day's work for a fair day's pay, to treat employers and co-workers with respect, and to carry out their work in ways that contribute to the common good. Workers, employers, and unions should not only advance their own interests, but also work together to advance economic justice and the well-being of all.

From *Faith Citizenship: A Call to Political Responsibility from the Catholic Bishops of the United States*

———

Creator God,
we thank you for those involved in industry and manufacture:
for the energy and drive of entrepreneurs,
for the administrative gifts of managers,
and for the expertise and skills of workers.
May they work together in harmony,
that each may receive a just and fair reward for their labours:
for we ask this in the name of Jesus Christ our Lord. Amen.

Peter Newcome 1656–1738

Vicar of Aldenham

—

NOT ONLY IS it unusual for families to have twelve children today, but it is even more unusual to have six of them die before their parents. Yet this was the experience of Peter and Ann Newcome. Newcome was the son of a well-known Nonconformist preacher, Henry Newcome. He studied at Magdalen College, Cambridge, and then at St Edmund Hall and finally Brasenose College, Oxford. He was curate at Crookham for three years before taking the living of Aldenham. His final post was as Vicar of Hackney in Middlesex where he wrote *A Catechetical Course of Sermons* (1702), *Being, an explanation of the church-catechism. In fifty two distinct discourses*, and published other single sermons between 1705 and 1737.

Ben Jonson's poem on the death of his son

Epigrams: On my first son
Farewell, thou child of my right hand, and joy;
My sin was too much hope of thee, lov'd boy.
Seven years tho' wert lent to me, and I thee pay,
Exacted by thy fate, on the just day.
O, could I lose all father now! For why
Will man lament the state he should envy?
To have so soon 'scap'd world's and flesh's rage,
And if no other misery, yet age?
Rest in soft peace, and, ask'd, say, 'Here doth lie
Ben Jonson his best piece of poetry.'
For whose sake henceforth all his vows be such,
As what he loves may never like too much.

O God, you have dealt very mysteriously with us. We have been passing through deep waters. You have reclaimed the lent jewels. Yet, O Lord, shall I not thank you now? I will thank you not only for the children you have left to us, but for those you have reclaimed. I thank you for the blessing of the last ten years, and for all the sweet memories of these lives. I thank you for the full assurance that each has gone to the arms of the Good Shepherd, whom each loved according to the capacity of her years. I thank you for the bright hopes of a happy reunion, when we shall meet to part no more. O Lord, for Jesus Christ's name, comfort our desolate hearts, may we be a united family in heart through the communion of saints; through Jesus Christ our Lord. Amen.

A prayer by Archbishop Tate, five of whose
daughters died in less than a month

William Butterfield 1814–1900

Architect

———

WILLIAM BUTTERFIELD IS one of the most famous English Gothic Revival architects of the nineteenth century. Born in London, the son of a chemist, he was apprenticed to a builder, decorator and furnisher in Middlesex. He then studied architecture before setting up his own practice in Lincoln's Inn Fields. Although he had been brought up in Nonconformity, he was deeply influenced by the Oxford Movement. Butterfield was awarded a Gold Medal by the Royal Institute of British Architects in 1884 'for his revival of Gothic Architecture' but, unusually, he declined the invitation to attend the ceremony. In the same year, he became a member of the Ecclesiological Society, and from then on most of his work was building and restoring churches. Butterfield was the architect of two churches in the Diocese of St Albans: Holy Saviour, Hitchin, and St Margaret of Antioch, Barley. He was responsible for the restoration of St Peter's, Great Berkhamsted, St Peter and St Paul, Flitwick, St George, Anstey, and for some of the furnishings in St Mark's, Barnet Vale.

St Augustine preaches on 'The building and dedication of God's house within us'

We are gathered together to celebrate the dedication of a house of prayer. This is our house of prayer, but we too are a house of God. If we are a house of God, its construction goes on in time so that it may be dedicated at the end of time. The house, in its construction, involves hard work, while its dedication is an occasion for rejoicing. What was done when this church was being built is similar to what is done when believers are built up into Christ. When they first come to believe they are like timber and stone taken from woods and mountains. In their instruction, baptism and formation they are, so to speak, shaped, levelled and smoothed by the hands of carpenters and craftsmen. But Christians do not make a house of God until they are one in charity. The timber and stone must fit together in an orderly plan, must be joined in perfect harmony, must give each other the support as it were of love, or no one would enter the building. When you see the stones and beams of a building holding together securely, you enter the building with an easy mind; you are not afraid of its falling down in ruins.

Most gracious Father,
we pray to you for your holy catholic Church.
Fill it with all truth; in all truth with all peace.
Where it is corrupt, purge it.
Where it is in error, direct it.
Where anything is amiss, reform it.
Where it is right, strengthen and defend it.
Where it is in want, provide for it.
Where it is divided, heal it and reunite it in your love;
for the sake of your Son, our Saviour Jesus Christ. Amen.

Archbishop William Laud

James Howard 1821–89

Agriculturalist and industrialist

——

H OWARD WAS A man of many interests. He and his brother started an iron foundry which manufactured agricultural machinery at the Britannia Works in Bedford. He bought an estate at Clapham, where he developed a model farm, using the latest methods of agriculture. Here Howard developed his passion for pig breeding which led to his appointment as vice-president of the National Pig Breeders' Association. He was Mayor of Bedford and served as the Liberal Member of Parliament in the county on two occasions. Like many Victorian entrepreneurs, Howard was a Methodist who sought to apply his faith to his everyday life. He was involved in a campaign in Bedford to provide a clean water supply and to eliminate typhoid. In 1865 he and his brother were the main donors towards the building of the new St Mary's Wesleyan Methodist Church (now closed) and a school in Cauldwell Street in Bedford. We still have a record of what he said: 'Mr. Howard, of Caldwell, in a truly characteristic speech, which delighted all present, gave an account of the Rise and Progress of Wesleyan Methodism in Bedford. He especially referred to the visit of the Rev. John Wesley, in 1758, when on Friday, March 10, of that year, he preached the memorable assize sermon before Sir Edward Clive in St. Paul's Church, the text being "We shall all stand before the judgement seat of Christ".'

Pope John Paul II on work

Through work man must earn his daily bread and contribute to the continual advance of science and technology and, above all, to elevating unceasingly the cultural and moral level of the society within which he lives in community with those who belong to the same family. And work means any activity by man, whether manual or intellectual, whatever its nature or circumstances; it means any human activity that can and must be recognized as work, in the midst of all the many activities of which man is capable and to which he is predisposed by his very nature, by virtue of humanity itself. Man is made to be in the visible universe an image and likeness of God himself, and he is placed in it in order to subdue the earth. From the beginning therefore he is called to work. Work is one of the characteristics that distinguish man from the rest of creatures, whose activity for sustaining their lives cannot be called work. Only man is capable of work, and only man works, at the same time by work occupying his existence on earth. Thus work bears a particular mark of man and of humanity, the mark of a person operating within a community of persons. And this mark decides its interior characteristics; in a sense it constitutes its very nature.

From *Laborem exercens*

O God our Father,
whose Son Jesus Christ worked in the carpenter's shop in Nazareth.
We pray for all those who work in industry, commerce and agriculture.
Strengthen in them the spirit of service, mutual respect and common purpose;
and may they receive a just reward for their labours,
through Jesus Christ our Lord. Amen.

William Garland Barrett d.1865

Missionary, apologist and geologist

───────

WILLIAM BARRETT WAS a Baptist minister who joined the London Missionary Society and was posted to Jamaica where he became involved with the campaign for the emancipation of slaves. He wrote several books including *Immigration to the British West Indies: Is it the Slave-Trade Revived or Not?* and *Geological facts*. He married Martha Fletcher. Their second son, William Fletcher Barrett (1844–1925), became a famous physicist and was knighted. Their daughter, Rosa Mary Bennett, became a well-known social reformer. In 1848 the family returned to England and settled in Royston, before they moved to Manchester in 1855.

William Barrett sets out the grounds for the basis of faith

Doubting and scorning are very opposite phases of mind: we here address the *doubter*; with the *scorner* we have nothing to do; if *ridicule* is his substitute for argument, by all means let him enjoy it; and if *calling names* is his substitute for patient investigation, let him enjoy that pastime also – hard words break no bones; but for the *doubter*, for the man who has his honest difficulties, and finds large stumbling-blocks in the path of unresisting acquiescence in household faiths, for such an one I have much to say in this chapter, if he will read it, – to him I stretch forth my hand in cordial greeting, and invite him to examine evidence, and consider facts; and then, whatever may be the result, whether I shake *his doubts* or he shake *my faith*, we shall at least have acted a manly and a straightforward part. At any rate, we ought ever to meet as friends, and to be candid and forbearing, as men liable to err through manifold besetments and biasses.

From *Geological facts; or, The crust of the earth, what it is, and what are its uses*

───────

Blessed be you, harsh matter, barren soil, stubborn rock: you who yield only to violence, you who force us to work if we would eat. Blessed be you, perilous matter, violent sea, untameable passions: you who unless we fetter you will devour us. Blessed be you, mighty matter, irresistible march of evolution, reality ever new-born; you who, by constantly shattering our mental categories, force us to go ever further and further in our pursuit of the truth. Blessed be you, universal matter, immeasurable time, boundless ether, triple abyss of stars and atoms and generations: you who by overflowing and dissolving our narrow standards or measurement reveal to us the dimensions of God. Blessed be you, impenetrable matter: you who, interposed between our minds and the world of essences, cause us to languish with the desire to pierce through the seamless veil of phenomena. Blessed be you, mortal matter: you who one day will undergo the process of dissolution within us and will thereby take us forcible into the very heart of that which exists. Without you, without your onslaughts, without your uprootings of us, we should remain all our lives inert, stagnant, puerile, ignorant both of ourselves and of God. You who batter us and then dress our wounds, you who resist us and yield to us, you who wreck and build, you who shackle and liberate, the sap of our souls, the hand of God, the flesh of Christ: it is you, matter, that I bless. Amen.

From *Hymn of the Universe* by Teilhard de Chardin

Catherine Parr 1512–48

Wife of Henry VIII who lived at Rye House, Hoddesdon

—

IT IS HARD to imagine a present-day member of the Royal Family writing a religious best seller, yet that is exactly what Catherine Parr did. Not only that, but her *Prayers or Meditations* was the first book published by a woman in England and in English. Catherine's book *The Lamentations of a Sinner* was also received with acclaim. Catherine Parr was an educated woman who was fluent in Latin, French, Italian and Spanish. Following the death of her father in 1531, she lived with her brother at Rye House, Hoddesdon. She had been widowed twice before coming to the attention of the King, who married her at Hampton Court in 1543. During the time he was fighting in France Henry appointed her Regent, so she controlled the country's finances and authorised Royal Proclamations. Although she was raised as a Catholic, Catherine was sympathetic to the new faith and her books reflect her Protestant views. After the King's death she married Thomas Seymour but died the following year after giving birth to her only child, Mary.

Catherine Parr writes about God's grace

But now, what maketh me so bold and hardy, to presume to come to the Lord with such audacity and boldness, being so great a sinner? Truly, nothing, but his own word. For he saith, 'Come to me, all ye that labour, and are burdened, and I shall refresh you'. What gentle, merciful, and comfortable words are these to all sinners! Were he not a frantic, mad, beastlike, and foolish man, that would run for aid, help, or refuge to any other creature? What a most gracious, comfortable, and gentle saying was this, with such pleasant and sweet words to allure his very enemies to come unto him! Is there any worldly prince, or magistrate, that would show such clemency and mercy to their disobedient and rebellious subjects, having offended them? I suppose they would not with such words allure them, except it were to call those whom they cannot take, and punish them being taken. But even as Christ is Prince of princes, and Lord of lords, so his charity and mercy exceedeth and surmounteth all others. Christ saith, If carnal fathers do give good gifts to their children when they ask them, how much more shall your heavenly Father, being in substance all holy, and most highly good, give good gifts to all them that ask him.

From *The Lamentations of a Sinner*

Most benign Lord Jesus, grant me thy grace,
that it may always work in me, and persevere with me unto the end.
Grant me that I may ever desire and will that which is
most pleasant and most acceptable to thee.
Thy will be my will, and my will be to follow always thy will.
Let there be always in me one will, and one desire with thee;
and that I have no desire to will or not to will, but as thou wilt.
Lord, thou knowest what thing is most profitable and most expedient for me.
Give, therefore, what thou wilt, as much as thou wilt, and when thou wilt.
Do with me what thou wilt, as it shall please thee, and shall be most to thine honour.
Put me where thou wilt, and freely do with me in all things after thy will. Amen.

From *Prayers or Meditations* by Catherine Parr

Richard Sampson d.1554

Composer

———

FOR A MAN who lived during the sixteenth century, Richard Sampson had a surprisingly broad education, which may account for his interest in both theology and music. After he left Trinity Hall, Cambridge, he studied at the Sorbonne in Paris and at Sens in Burgundy. He was awarded the degree of Doctor of Canon Law and Cardinal Wolsey appointed him Diocesan Chancellor and Vicar-General of the Diocese of Tournai. Among the many posts that Sampson held was the living of Wheathampstead in Hertfordshire. Sampson spent three years as the English ambassador to Charles V. This experience stood him in good stead when he assisted Henry VIII's attempts to obtain a divorce. As a result of his efforts Henry made him Dean of Lichfield. He also added the benefice of Hackney and the post of Treasurer of Salisbury Cathedral to his portfolio of responsibilities. His loyalty to the crown was called upon again when in 1536 he was made Bishop of Chichester. Eight years later he was translated to the See of Coventry and Lichfield. Sampson was also a composer, which was unusual, as the principal composers during the reign of Henry VIII were Gentlemen of the Chapel Royal, who with a very few exceptions were all clerics. Among his writings are commentaries on the Psalms and on the Epistle to the Romans. He died at Eccleshall in Staffordshire.

Thoughts on the power of music

Now, what is music? This question occupied me for hours before I fell asleep last night. Music is a strange thing. I would almost say it is a miracle. For it stands halfway between thought and phenomenon, between spirit and matter, a sort of nebulous mediator, like and unlike each of the things it mediates – spirit that requires manifestation in time, and matter that can do without space.

Heinrich Heine

Music is God's greatest gift. It has often so stimulated and stirred me that I felt the desire to preach.

Martin Luther

Music is a principal means of glorifying our merciful Creator, it heightens our devotion, it gives delight and ease to our travails, it expelleth sadness and heaviness of spirit, preserveth people in concord and amity, allayeth fierceness and anger; and lastly, is the best physic for many melancholy diseases.

Henry Peacham

God of music, the song of your love echoes down through the ages:
in the power of your Holy Spirit enable us your people
to play our part in the orchestra of your church;
may we live together in harmony, sensitive to the rhythm of your creation,
that at the last we may be part of your perfect cadence
when all things find their fulfilment in you; through Jesus Christ our Lord. Amen.

Walter Espec d.1153

Soldier and founder of Warden Abbey

———

WARDEN ABBEY WAS a foundation of the famous Rievaulx Abbey in Yorkshire. The Cistercians followed a strict interpretation of the Rule of St Benedict, with a strong emphasis on manual labour such as farming and brewing. Walter Espec was a soldier, remembered for his part in the fight against King David of Scotland at the Battle of the Standard at Northallerton in 1138. A senior figure in the Royal administration in Yorkshire under Henry I, Espec had acquired estates in both Yorkshire and Northumberland, as well as inheriting the Warden estate in Bedfordshire (the home of the famous 'Warden Pear'). Around the year 1135 he asked the community at Rievaulx to make a foundation on the estate. Espec was described as 'An old man and full of days, quick-witted, prudent in council, moderate in peace, circumspect in war, a true friend and a loyal subject. His stature was passing tall, his limbs all of a size as not to exceed their just proportions, and yet to be well matched with his great height. His hair was still black, his beard long and flowing, his forehead wide and noble, his eyes large and bright, his face broad but well featured, his voice like the sound of a trumpet, setting off his natural eloquence of speech with a certain majesty of sound.' Espec himself entered the community at Rievaulx just before his death around the year 1153 and was buried there. Warden Abbey, along with other monastic houses in England, was dissolved in 1537.

St Benedict instructs the monks on work

Idleness is the enemy of the soul. The brothers, therefore, should be employed in manual labour at stated times, and again at others, in sacred reading. Hence, we believe that the time for each of these duties can best be arranged as follows. From Easter till 14 September, they go out in the morning from the first hour till about the fourth hour to do the necessary work. From the fourth till about the sixth hour they should devote themselves to reading. After the sixth hour, however, when they have had their meal, let them rest in their beds in complete silence; or if anyone is minded to read, he may do so, provided he does not disturb anyone. Let None be said somewhat earlier, about the middle of the eighth hour, Then let them work again at what is necessary until Vespers. If, however, the needs of the place or their poverty means that they have to gather the harvest themselves, let them not be downcast. For then are they truly monks, if they live by the work of their hands, as did our fathers and the apostles. However, on account of the faint-hearted let everything be done with moderation. On Sundays let all devote themselves to reading, except those who are appointed to the various jobs.

From *Of the Daily Work* from *The Rule of St Benedict*

Loving Father, you promise to supply all our needs out of your abundant store:
prosper the labours of those who enable us to enjoy the resources of nature,
whether by farming, fishing or industrial work,
that we may render thanks and praise to you;
through Jesus Christ our Lord. Amen.

From *Collects with the New Lectionary*

Kate Smith 1862–1919

Parish nurse who worked in Rye Park

———

KATE SMITH WAS a parish nurse, who was employed by St Cuthbert's Church, Rye Park, between 1908 and 1913. At the beginning of the twentieth century, Rye Park was little more than a group of cottages inhabited by workers, tinkers and travellers, very few of whom would have been able to afford medical assistance. The PCC yearbook commented, 'Those who have had illness in their homes know how to appreciate the help given at all times so readily by Nurse Smith. There are many who have felt that they would not have known what to do without this help. It is of course impossible to give any record of work done but there are very few in Rye Park who have not either directly or indirectly felt the benefit of having such help at their service at all hours of the day and night.' The system of parish nurses had its origins in the seventeenth century when only the wealthy could afford medical help. The nurses were responsible for delivering a large proportion of parish relief. Their role lay somewhere between the workhouse and poor relief. From the churches' perspective they were responding to the gospel imperative to 'preach the Kingdom of God and to heal the sick' (Luke 9.2). Kate Smith died on this day in 1919, aged fifty-seven. She had only been in post five years, but suffered a breakdown and was buried in the family plot at Great Amwell. There is a plaque dedicated to her in St Cuthbert's Church.

The Christian vocation of nursing

The influences of an ever changing society have promoted the radical developments in nursing throughout time. First seen as a role suitable only for uneducated women or slaves in ancient times, Christianity along with other religious orders soon helped the nurse gain respect as the role of caregiver to the sick became an increasingly prominent practice. The Christian Church brought the formation of the Order of the Deaconesses in the first century, a group similar to public health or visiting nurses. This happened at a time when caring for the sick was a Christian duty, 'a sacred vocation based upon Christ's actual command.' The love and brotherhood of Christianity also led to the establishment of the first nursing order by the Augustinian Sisters during the Middle Ages. With the approach of the Protestant Reformation in England, monastic medicine (care given by monasteries and the monks and nuns who live there) and the nursing orders of the sixteenth century were destroyed, leaving hospitals overcrowded with the only care for the sick provided by illiterate, indigent women. Chaos ruled until the early eighteenth century when voluntary hospitals offered some relief for England, and the continued presence of nursing orders in Europe aided those in need. Reformation of societal factors, including prisons and social welfare during this dark period, led to the organization of new nursing orders to supply improved, humane services where none existed before.

From *Reflections on Nursing* by Anonymous

———

Gracious Father
we praise you for those who dedicate their lives
to heal the sick and to bring comfort to the suffering:
bless those who have responded to your call to be nurses,
and grant them skill, patience and tenderness in their work;
through Jesus Christ our Lord. Amen.

Daniel Dyke 1617–88

Minister

———

BORN IN EPPING in Essex, Daniel Dyke studied at Sidney Sussex College, Cambridge, before being ordained. He was appointed to two livings in Hertfordshire, first as Rector of Eastwick around 1636 and then Rector of Great Hadham (which is known as Much Hadham today). In 1651 Dyke became a chaplain-in-ordinary to Oliver Cromwell. He resigned his living after the Restoration. Despite several writs being served against him, which led to short periods of imprisonment, Dyke continued to exercise a public ministry. He became one of the pastors of the Particular Baptist Church in Devonshire Square, London, and remained there until his death in 1688. He was buried in the Dissenters' cemetery at Bunhill Fields in London. He published a number of books including a collection of his father's sermons, *The Quakers' Appeal Answered, and a full Relation of the Occasion, Progress, and Issue of a Meeting at the Barbican between the Baptists and the Quakers* and *The Baptists' Answer to Mr. Wills' Appeal*.

William Inge, former Dean of St Paul's Cathedral, writes about Christian unity

The unity of Christendom which alone we can desire and rationally seek to promote is not the unity of a world-wide centralised government, but unity of spirit based on a common faith and a common desire to see the Kingdom of God, which is 'righteousness and peace and joy in the Holy Ghost,' established on earth. There will be diversities of gifts, but the same Spirit; differences of ecclesiastical organisation, but the same Lord. We must not expect that India, China, and Japan, if they ever adopt Christianity, will be European Christians. They have their ancient traditions, unlike the Graeco-Roman traditions which formed Catholicism; they must build their national churches upon these, in complete independence. The sole bond of a spiritually united Christendom is the Person and the Gospel of the Divine Founder.

From *Lay Thoughts of a Dean*

———

O God,
bless and preserve your Church
dispersed over the face of the earth.
Restore to it unity and concord,
in the acknowledgement of the truth
and the practice of righteousness.
Remove out of it all errors and dissensions,
that they who profess the same faith
may no longer persecute and destroy one another,
but be kind and tender-hearted one towards another,
as it becomes brethren and those that are
heirs of the same common salvation. Amen.

King William III

Adrian Fortescue 1874–1923

Scholar, artist, composer, linguist and Roman Catholic priest

———

BORN INTO A distinguished Catholic family, Adrian Fortescue studied in Rome and Innsbruck before being ordained priest in 1889. So extraordinary were his academic abilities that he was awarded three doctorates and was presented with a prize by the Emperor of Austria in acknowledgment of his scholarship. Fortescue was a gifted linguist and spoke Greek, Hebrew, Syrian, Persian and Turkish, which stood him in good stead during his travels in Greece, Asia Minor and the Middle East. In 1907 Fortescue was made Missionary Rector of Letchworth, where he built a new church. Fortescue's interests were wide ranging. He wrote *Ceremonies of the Roman Rite Described.* As well as being an accomplished organist, Fortescue was also an artist of considerable talent and an authority on heraldry. Knowing he had cancer, Fortescue preached his final sermon on the Incarnation of Christ and died on this day in 1923.

C. S. Lewis describes the human longing for heaven

In speaking of this desire for our own far off country, which we find in ourselves even now, I feel a certain shyness. I am almost committing an indecency. I am trying to rip open the inconsolable secret in each one of you – the secret which hurts so much that you take your revenge on it by calling it names like Nostalgia and Romanticism and Adolescence; the secret also which pierces with such sweetness that when, in very intimate conversation, the mention of it becomes imminent, we grow awkward and affect to laugh at ourselves; the secret we cannot hide and cannot tell, though we desire to do both. We cannot tell it because it is a desire for something that has never actually appeared in our experience. We cannot hide it because our experience is constantly suggesting it, and we betray ourselves like lovers at the mention of a name. Our commonest expedient is to call it beauty and behave as if that had settled the matter. Wordsworth's expedient was to identify it with certain moments in his own past. But all this is a cheat. If Wordsworth had gone back to those moments in the past, he would not have found the thing itself, but only the reminder of it; what he remembered would turn out to be itself a remembering. The books or the music in which we thought the beauty was located will betray us if we trust to them; it was not in them, it only came through them, and what came through them was longing. These things – the beauty, the memory of our own past – are good images of what we really desire; but if they are mistaken for the thing itself they turn into dumb idols, breaking the hearts of their worshippers. For they are not the thing itself; they are only the scent of a flower we have not found, the echo of a tune we have not heard, news from a country we have never yet visited.

From *The Weight of Glory*

———

Be thou a light unto my eyes, music to mine ears, sweetness to my taste, and full contentment to my heart. Be thou my sunshine in the day, my food at table, my repose in the night, my clothing in nakedness, and my succour in all necessities. Lord Jesu, I give thee my body, my soul, my substance, my fame, my friends, my liberty and my life. Dispose of me and all that is mine as it may seem best to thee and to the glory of thy blessed name. Amen.

John Cosin

Astley Paston Cooper 1768–1841

Anatomist, surgeon and philanthropist

———

NOT MANY PEOPLE are honoured by having two roads and a school named after them, as well as a statue of them erected in St Paul's Cathedral. Yet during his lifetime Astley Cooper was so eminent that he was appointed surgeon to three monarchs: George IV, William IV and Queen Victoria. Born in Norfolk, the son of an Anglican clergyman and a novelist mother, Cooper studied at St Thomas' Hospital in London before being appointed surgeon at Guy's Hospital. In 1802 he was elected a Fellow of the Royal Society and a few years later became Professor of Comparative Anatomy at the Royal College of Surgeons. As a result of successfully operating on King George, he was made a baronet. He made important advances in vascular surgery and the treatment of aneurisms, and wrote a two-volume work on the treatment of hernias. He lived in Gadebridge House in Hemel Hempstead where he was known as a benefactor and founder of a cottage hospital at Piccotts End in 1827. He also gave land in Queen's Street, Hemel Hempstead, so that a new church, St Paul's, could be built. His ashes were interred under the chapel of Guy's Hospital and there is a memorial to him in St Mary's Church, Hemel Hempstead.

The writer of the book of Ecclesiasticus reflects on healing

Honour a physician with the honour due unto him for the uses which ye may have of him: for the Lord hath created him. For of the most High cometh healing, and he shall receive honour of the king. The skill of the physician shall lift up his head: and in the sight of great men he shall be in admiration. The Lord hath created medicines out of the earth; and he that is wise will not abhor them. Was not the water made sweet with wood, that the virtue thereof might be known? And he hath given men skill, that he might be honoured in his marvellous works. With such doth he heal men, and taketh away their pains. Of such doth the apothecary make a confection; and of his works there is no end; and from him is peace over all the earth. My son, in thy sickness be not negligent: but pray unto the Lord, and he will make thee whole. Leave off from sin, and order thine hands aright, and cleanse thy heart from all wickedness. Give a sweet savour, and a memorial of fine flour; and make a fat offering, as not being. Then give place to the physician, for the Lord hath created him: let him not go from thee, for thou hast need of him. There is a time when in their hands there is good success. For they shall also pray unto the Lord, that he would prosper that, which they give for ease and remedy to prolong life. He that sinneth before his Maker, let him fall into the hand of the physician.

From Ecclesiasticus 38, the *King James Version of the Bible*

———

Heavenly Father, source of health and wholeness,
we pray for those who give their lives to bring healing
to the sick in body, mind or spirit:
bless all doctors and nurses,
give them skill, empathy and compassion
as they share in the work of healing;
through Jesus Christ our Lord. Amen.

Alexander Nowell c.1507–1602

Dean of St Paul's

———

Alexander Nowell's unusual claim to fame is that during his time as Rector of Much Hadham he discovered how to bottle ale. Nowell studied at a school in Middleton and then at Brasenose College, Oxford, where he became acquainted with John Foxe, famous for his *Book of Martyrs*. From Oxford he moved to be Master of Westminster School in 1543 and later became a prebendary of Westminster. In 1553 Nowell stood for Parliament and was elected to represent West Looe in Cornwall. However, within months it was ruled that he could not remain in Parliament because his prebendal stall in Westminster entitled him to a seat in Convocation. In 1554, following the accession of Mary Tudor, he was deprived of his prebend and left the country to find sanctuary first in Strasbourg and later in Frankfurt with other Protestant exiles. It is during his time overseas that Nowell's Puritan sympathies deepened. Nevertheless, under Elizabeth I, he was willing to submit to the Elizabethan Settlement of Religion and before long he was appointed Archdeacon of Middlesex and to a canonry at Canterbury Cathedral. He found favour with the new queen and in 1560 was appointed Dean of St Paul's Cathedral, a post he held for forty-two years. Nowell was known for his controversial sermons and on one occasion the queen interrupted him, crying out, 'To your text, Mr Dean! Leave, that! We have heard enough of that!' Nowell is thought to be the author of the catechism in the 1549 Prayer Book, and of a later catechism published in 1570. He founded a school in Middleton. He died on this day in 1602.

Stewart Headlam reflects on the use of the catechism

The Catechism begins by calling out the sense of individuality in the person to whom it is being taught: by making the child feel, in a very real, practical way, that he in some sense stands alone: that whatever his circumstances and antecedents may be, he is personally responsible: the child is asked, generally in the presence of many others, often under circumstances of some solemnity, What is your name? and he has to answer, not the name of the family into which he was born, but his own name: thus from the beginning in the English child there is encouraged a healthy, sturdy independence. The bonds of the family are rightly round him in all their strength, his surname has for him most sacred associations, but the owners of that name had, he is taught, recognized that there was another society vaster than their family, other relationships on which theirs were grounded: his father and mother had let him be taken from the home to the church, and there from other lips than theirs his own name was given him. At the same time he was baptised. Of the meaning of baptism…we notice that the child is taught that he was made, constituted or set apart as a member of Christ, the Child of God, and an inheritor of the Kingdom of Heaven.

From *Priestcraft and Progress*

———

Our heavenly Father, your Son delighted in the happiness of children.
Bless our children and the children of our affection.
All things protect and guide their lives;
and as they enjoy the world of your gifts,
grant them the grace of gratitude to you, the Giver;
through Jesus Christ our Lord. Amen.

Michael Perry

Richard II 1367–1400

King

———

ONE OF THE Plantagenet dynasty, Richard was born in Bordeaux. Following the death of his father (known as 'The Black Prince'), Richard came to the throne when he was just ten years old. As a young man Richard played an important part in crushing the Peasants' Revolt in 1381. However, his reliance on a small group of favourite courtiers led him into conflict with Parliament and as a result five nobles (known as the Lords Appellant) took control. Richard was forced to collaborate with them but he slowly regained power, so much so that in 1397 he arrested and tried three of the Lords Appellant and in the following year he banished the other two, Thomas Mowbray and the Lancastrian, Henry Bolingbroke. When Richard went to war in Ireland in 1399, Bolingbroke seized his opportunity, raised an army and invaded England. Richard surrendered and abdicated. Bolingbroke was crowned as Henry IV. Shortly afterwards he sent Richard to Pontefract Castle where he died, probably of starvation. He was buried at Kings Langley in Hertfordshire, before his body was moved to its final resting place in Westminster Abbey alongside his wife, Anne.

William Tyndale writes about the responsibility of kings

The kings ought to remember that they are in God's stead, and ordained of God, not for themselves, but for the wealth of their subjects. Let them remember that their subjects are their brethren, their flesh and blood, members of their own body, and even their own selves in Christ. Therefore ought they to pity them, and to rid them from such wily tyranny, which increaseth more and more daily. And though that the kings, by the falsehood of the bishops and abbots, be sworn to defend such liberties; yet ought they not to keep their oaths, but to break them; forasmuch as they are upright and clean against God's ordinance, and even but cruel oppression, contrary unto brotherly love and charity. And let the kings put down some of their tyranny, and turn some unto a common wealth. If the tenth part of such tyranny were given the king yearly, and laid up in the shire-towns, against the realm had need, what would it grow to in certain year? Moreover one king, one law, is God's ordinance in every realm. Therefore ought not the king to suffer them to have a several law by themselves, and to draw his subjects thither. It is not meet, will they say, that a spiritual man should be judged of a worldly or temporal man. O abomination! See how they divide and separate themselves: if the lay-man be of the world, so is he not of God! If he believe in Christ, then is he a member of Christ, Christ's brother, Christ's flesh, Christ's blood, Christ's spouse, co-heir with Christ, and hath his Spirit in earnest, and is also spiritual. Because thou art put in office to preach God's word, art thou therefore no more one of the brethren?

From *The Obedience of a Christian Man*

———

King of Heaven and Earth,
we thank you for the life and example of Elizabeth our Queen:
may she and her ministers work for the good of all people,
and for a world where peace prevails and justice prevails;
we ask this in the name of Jesus Christ our Lord. Amen.

Joseph Holden Pott 1759–1847

Poet and Archdeacon of St Albans

———

JOSEPH POTT HAD a privileged upbringing: the son of a surgeon, he was educated at Eton and St John's College, Cambridge. He was ordained in the Diocese of Lincoln and became Rector of St Olave, Old Jewry with St Martin, Ironmonger Lane in the city of London. In 1789 he was appointed Archdeacon of St Albans. Over succeeding years he held the archdeaconry in plurality with parishes in Little Burstead, Northolt and St Martin in the Fields, London. In 1813 he ceased being the Archdeacon of St Albans and instead became the Archdeacon of London, and nine years later a canon of St Paul's Cathedral. His final post was Chancellor of Exeter Cathedral. In 1842 he retired from his Archdeacon's post, although he remained as a Canon of St Paul's and Exeter Cathedrals until he died, unmarried, leaving a valuable library. Pott published poetry, a play and several books including *Essay on Landscape Painting with Remarks on the Different Schools* and a theological work, *Testimonies of St Paul concerning Justification*.

Joseph Pott addresses the clergy of the St Albans Archdeaconry

How often do we hear it objected against the doctrine of the Holy Trinity, that it is collected only by inference and deduction, from scattered proofs, and occasional assertions. The charge itself is groundless. We have the form of Baptism appointed by our Lord: in which it is impossible to think that three Persons of an equal dignity could be joined together. The being of baptized [sic], signifies a dedication to the exercise of faith and worship in that name. We have the form of benediction used by the Apostle: concerning which it is also impossible to think, that he would have blessed his converts in other names beside that of God: and yet the Grace of Christ, and the Communion of the Spirit, are expressly included in the blessing. We have that compendious draught of our religion where 'our access to the Father, through the Son, and by the Holy Ghost,' is set forth: in which the same enumeration and conjunction indicate an equality of nature, and joint glory. We have even a more explicit and exact description of the several offices proper to each Person, in another passage; where the Apostle ascribes the calling and election of a chosen people to the Father, their justification to the Son, and their sanctification to the Holy Ghost: comprising once more the whole Gospel in a single sentence: 1 Peter 1.2.

From *A Charge Delivered to the Clergy of the Archdeaconry of St Albans*

Almighty and everlasting God,
you have given us your servants grace,
by the confession of a true faith,
to acknowledge the glory of the eternal Trinity
and in the power of the divine majesty to worship the Unity:
keep us steadfast in this faith,
that we may evermore be defended from all adversities;
through Jesus Christ your Son our Lord, who is alive and reigns with you,
in the unity of the Holy Spirit, one God, now and for ever. Amen.

The Collect for Trinity Sunday

Sue Ryder 1924–2000

Sue Ryder Centre at Stagenhoe and hospice at Moggerhanger

———

SUE RYDER IS a household name, due to the extensive charitable work that she undertook during her long and interesting life. She was born in Leeds in 1924 and attended Benenden School. At the age of fifteen, at the outbreak of the Second World War, she joined the First Aid Nursing Yeomanry. She then worked with the Special Operations Executive and later on in the war was posted to Tunisia and Italy. At the end of the war Ryder immersed herself in charitable work in Poland. However, it was the establishment of the Sue Ryder Foundation in 1953 which brought her to public attention. Initially she supported survivors of concentration camps, but this soon developed into a large network of nursing homes for the disabled. Much of the financial support for the foundation comes from the Sue Ryder Charity Shops. In 1959 she married Leonard Cheshire. They were both practising Roman Catholics. In recognition of her work Ryder was made a life peer in 1979. She played a prominent role in the House of Lords and used it to continue her lifelong interest in Poland. In 2000 Ryder set up another foundation which is now known as the Lady Ryder of Warsaw Memorial Trust. There is also a Community of the Sue Ryder Prayer Fellowship.

Jean Vanier reflects on how we can receive from those who are weak

People who are weak and fragile obviously need the help of those who are stronger. In L'Arche, however, we are discovering that the opposite is equally true: people who are stronger need those who are more fragile. We need others. People who are powerless and vulnerable attract what is most beautiful and most luminous in those who are stronger: they call them to be compassionate, to love intelligently, and not only in a sentimental way. Those who are weak help those who are more capable to discover their humanity and to leave the world of competition in order to put their energies at the service of love, justice and peace. The weak teach the strong to accept and integrate the weakness and brokenness of their own lives which they often hide behind masks. People who are well-situated in society, who know success, who have a certain influence and who exercise authority, but who are not in touch with their inner weaknesses and poverty, have trouble understanding the loving but demanding message of Jesus. He disturbs them. In the parable of the wedding feast (Luke 14), the poor, the crippled, the lame and the blind respond to the invitation to come. The rich and powerful refuse. They do not have time because they have other things to do. They are often seeking the knowledge of God, but their hearts are not humble and open enough simply to welcome the presence of God.

From *The Scandal of Serving*

Almighty God,
by whose grace alone we have been
accepted and called to your service:
strengthen and guide us by your Holy Spirit
in all our work and make us worthy of our calling;
through Jesus Christ our Lord. Amen.

Based on the Collect for the Fifth Sunday
before Lent in *Common Worship*

John Hacket 1592–1670

Bishop

NOT MANY ARCHDEACONS of Bedford have written a play which was performed in front of a king, yet this is precisely one of the achievements of John Hacket. The play, called *Loyola*, was written for the Spanish Ambassador, but later King James I visited Cambridge to see a performance. Hacket had been educated at Westminster School and Trinity College, Cambridge. He was ordained in 1618 and was appointed to the parishes of Stoke Hammond, Trumpington and Kirkby Underwood. By 1623 he had become chaplain to James I who appointed him to parishes in Holborn and Cheam. He was admitted to Gray's Inn in 1628 and was elected President of Sion College in 1633. From 1631 until 1661 Hacket was the Archdeacon of Bedford before being appointed Bishop of Lichfield and Coventry. He is remembered for his biography of John Williams, who was his patron and Archbishop of York in 1641–50. Hacket left his library and other bequests to Cambridge University when he died in 1670.

Peter Brook reflects on drama and imagination

I am calling it the Holy Theatre for short, but it could be called The Theatre of the Invisible-Made-Visible: the notion that the stage is a place where the invisible can appear has a deep hold on our thoughts. We are all aware that most of life escapes our senses: a most powerful explanation of the various arts is that they talk of patterns which we can only begin to recognize when they manifest themselves as rhythms or shapes. We observe that the behaviour of people, of crowds, of history, obeys such recurrent patterns. We hear that trumpets destroyed the walls of Jericho, we recognize that a magical thing called music can come from men in white ties and tails, blowing, waving, thumping and scraping away. Despite the absurd means that produce it, through the concrete in music we recognize the abstract, we understand that ordinary men and their clumsy instruments are transformed by an art of possession. We may make a personality cult of the conductor, but we are aware that he is not really making the music, it is making him – if he is relaxed, open and attuned, then the invisible will take possession of him; through him, it will reach us. This is the notion, the true dream behind the debased ideals of the Deadly Theatre. This is what is meant and remembered by those who with feeling and seriousness use big hazy words like nobility, beauty, poetry, which I would like to re-examine for the particular quality they suggest. The theatre is the last forum where idealism is still an open question: many audiences all over the world will answer positively from their own experience that they have seen the face of the invisible through an experience on the stage that transcended their experience in life.

From *The Empty Space*

We thank you for playwrights and all
who jolt us out of our comfortable assumptions
and open up new avenues of thought and imagination:
send your Holy Spirit that we too might dream of worlds yet unseen
as we work for the coming of your kingdom;
through Jesus Christ our Lord. Amen.

Constance Georgina Bulwer-Lytton 1869–1923

Suffragette

———

CONSTANCE LYTTON WAS the daughter of Robert Bulwer-Lytton, 1st Earl of Lytton, and Edith Villiers, but rejected her privileged upbringing and enlisted as a member of the Women's Social and Political Union to campaign for the political rights of women. She was imprisoned on four occasions and was force fed when on hunger strike. Receiving special treatment due to her position, she adopted a false identity for a time and was imprisoned under the name of Jane Warton. She campaigned tirelessly by lecturing, writing letters and articles and publishing a book, *Prisons and Prisoners*. She died, aged fifty-four, at the family home, Knebworth House. Her epitaph reads 'Endowed with a celestial sense of humour, boundless sympathy, and rare musical talent, she devoted the later years of her life to the political enfranchisement of women and sacrificed her health and talents in helping to bring victory to this cause.'

Constance Lytton described one of her stays in prison

I lay facing the window, which was high up, and very little light seemed to come from it. As the sun went down I saw the shadow of the wooden mouldings fall across the glass, – three crosses, and they were the shape of the three familiar crosses at the scene of Calvary, one in the centre and one on either side. It looked different from any of the pictures I had seen. The cross of Christ, the cross of the repentant thief, and the cross of the sinner who had not repented – that cross looked blacker than the others, and behind it was an immense crowd. The light from the other two crosses seemed to shine on this one, and the Christ was crucified that He might undo all the harm that was done. I saw amongst the crowd the poor little doctor and the Governor, and all that helped to torture these women in prison, but they were nothing compared to the men in the Cabinet who wielded their force over them. There were the upholders of vice and the men who support the thousand injustices to women, some knowingly and some unconscious of the harm and cruelty entailed. Then the room grew dark and I fell asleep. When the doctor came again with his apparatus he had bovril and brandy, and the tube was left for only one second in my body. The next morning, Thursday, January 20, I told him that the brandy, which at first had the effect of warming me, left me freezing cold after about two hours, and I thought it was no use. As for the bovril, I had the strongest objection to it of a vegetarian kind, and I begged him not to give it to me again; he said he would not. It was only when I was sick that I knew what were the ingredients put down my body. That morning it was again milk and plasmon that was given me, and I was horribly sick.

From *Prisons and Prisoners*

———

Gracious God,
who taught us through the apostle Paul
that in Christ there is neither male nor female:
help us celebrate the gifts and skills of men and women,
that together we may work for the coming of your kingdom
and for the glory of your Son, Jesus Christ. Amen.

Thomas Fowell Buxton 1786–1845

Abolitionist and social reformer

———

IN ST GEORGE'S Cathedral, Freetown, in Sierra Leone, you will find a bust of Thomas Fowell Buxton. It was paid for by Africans who described him as 'the Friend of the Negro'. Buxton lived much of his adult life at Easneye, near Stanstead St Margarets in Hertfordshire, and never actually visited Sierra Leone. As a young man he worked in a brewery in London and eventually took over ownership of the business. Although a life-long Anglican, Buxton was deeply influenced by members of his family and friends who were Quakers. This led to his participation in Elizabeth Fry's campaigns for women prisoners. From 1818 until 1837 he served as Member of Parliament for Weymouth and Melcombe Regis, during which time he maintained his interest in reforming the penal system, ending capital punishment, and protecting indigenous people in overseas parts of the Empire. He was one of the founders of the Society for the Mitigation and Gradual Abolition of Slavery and, following the retirement of William Wilberforce, headed up the movement which finally achieved its goal in 1833. Buxton's book, *The African Slave Trade and Its Remedy,* and his campaign had a profound effect on David Livingstone which contributed to his decision to become a missionary and anti-slavery campaigner himself. Buxton died on this day in 1845.

Thomas Buxton campaigns against the slave trade

I have already confessed that I am not experienced or skilful in matters which touch the commercial part of the question. I treat this ground with diffidence. I say no more, than that it appears to me that the soil in Africa being rich, and the people being found upon it, it is not advisable to carry them to a distance. It is possible, however, that some fallacy, unsuspected by me, may lurk under my theory, if theory of mine it can be called; but when I come to humanity, justice, and the duties of Christian men, I stand upon a rock. It may be, or it may not, that while we act under the impulse of charity to the most afflicted of mankind, we are also obeying the dictates of the most far-sighted policy, and the most refined ambition. It may prove, or it may not, that while we are leading Africa to grow at home, cheaper sugar than Brazil, and cheaper cotton than the United States, we are renovating the very sinews of our national strength. Be this as it may, without doubt it is the duty of Great Britain to employ the influence and strength which God has given her, in raising Africa from the dust, and enabling her, out of her own resources, to beat down Slavery and Slave Trade.

From *The African Slave Trade*

———

Your kingdom, O God, is among us as a seed growing secretly.
Let it burst into flower in our generation.
Where the poor are raised up, there is your kingdom;
where justice flows down like the mountain streams, there is your kingdom;
where men and women yield their lives to Christ and to the doing of his will,
there is the hidden treasure of your kingdom.
Help us, O God, to read the signs of the times, to discern the kingdom's presence,
and to make it known in prophetic words and committed lives;
through Jesus Christ our Lord. Amen.

John Kingsnorth

Charles Chauncy 1592–1672

Clergyman and educationalist

———

WHEN CHAUNCY WAS born in Ardeley, Hertfordshire, his parents could not have imagined that he would become President of Harvard College in Cambridge, Massachusetts, for eighteen years. Chauncy was a bright child and was educated at Trinity College, Cambridge, where he was later to teach Greek. He became the Congregational pastor at St Lawrence, Marston in Northamptonshire. In 1638 he emigrated to America and settled first at Plymouth before moving to Scituate in Massachusetts. Among other things, Chauncy is remembered for his strong conviction that the only way to baptise validly was by immersion. He was strongly against the practice of sprinkling water, a custom which was normative in many parts of North America due to the cold climate. His views were opposed by many, including other church leaders. During his time in Scituate he decided to baptise his two sons in public by full immersion. One of the sons fainted, at which point the parent of another child who was due to be baptised at the same time attacked Chauncy. He wrote a number of books, including *The Doctrine of the Sacrament*, *The Plain Doctrine of the Justification of a Sinner* and *Antisynodalia Scripta Americana*.

Dietrich Bonhoeffer explores the significance of baptism

Baptism therefore betokens a *breach*. Christ invades the realm of Satan, lays hands on his own, and created for himself his Church. By this act past and present are rent asunder. The old order is passed away, and all things have become new. This breach is not effected by man's tearing off his own chains through some unquenchable longing for a new life of freedom. The breach has been effected by Christ long since, and in baptism it is effected in our own lives. We are now deprived of our direct relationship with all God-given realities of life. Christ the Mediator has stepped in between us and them. The baptized Christian has ceased to belong to the world and is no longer its slave. He belongs to Christ alone, and his relationship with the world is mediated through him. The breach with the world is complete. It demands and produces the death of the old man. In baptism a man dies together with his old world. This death, no less than baptism itself, is a passive event. It is not as though a man must achieve his own death through various kinds of renunciation and mortification. That would never be the death of the old man which Christ demands. The old man cannot will his own death or kill himself. He can only die in, through and with Christ. Christ is his death.

From *The Cost of Discipleship*

Make yourself manifest, O Lord, in this water
and grant to those who are baptised in it so to be transformed,
that they may put off the old self, which is corrupted by deceitful lusts,
and may put on the new self,
which is formed fresh according to the image of the Creator.
Grafted through baptism into the likeness of your death,
may they become partakers also in your resurrection.
May they guard the gift of your Holy Spirit,
may they increase the measure of grace which has been entrusted to them,
and so may they receive the prize which is God's calling to life above,
being numbered among the first born whose names are written in heaven, Amen.

Part of *An Easter Orthodox blessing of a baptismal font*

Catherine of Aragon 1485–1536

'The Queen of Earthly Queens' (Shakespeare)

DAUGHTER OF FERDINAND II and Isabella, Catherine was born in Madrid. She was an intelligent and gifted girl who studied French, Spanish, Greek and Latin and was also knowledgeable in the classics, law and history. In 1509 Catherine married Henry VIII. Catherine was a powerful figure in her own right. In 1507 her father, Ferdinand, made her the Spanish Ambassador, which was the first time that a woman had ever held the role. A few years later, in 1513, she was made Henry's regent while he was campaigning in France. When the Scots invaded, although she was pregnant, Catherine rode with the army to Scotland and addressed the soldiers before the Battle of Flodden Field. In 1533, still with no male heir, Henry wanted a divorce, and a court was convened under Archbishop Thomas Cranmer. Whilst it sat in Dunstable, Catherine was sent to stay in Ampthill Castle in Bedfordshire, the home of Sir John Cornwall. Cranmer decided that Henry and Catherine's marriage was null and void, a decision which allowed Henry to marry Anne Boleyn and which he did within days of the judgement. Catherine was a deeply-religious woman, known for her personal piety and concern for the poor. For the last year of her life she was imprisoned in Kimbolton Castle where she lived in one room and wore a hair shirt, which was the practice of the Observant Franciscans of which she was a member. Henry refused to allow her to see, or to communicate with, her daughter Mary. She died on this day in 1536.

In December 1535, Catherine wrote her final letter to Henry

My most dear lord, King and husband, the hour of my death now drawing on, the tender love I owe thou forceth me, my case being such, to commend myself to thou, and to put thou in remembrance with a few words of the healthe and safeguard of thine soul which thou ought to prefer before all worldley matters, and before the care and pampering of thy body, for the which thoust have cast me into many calamities and thineself into many troubles. For my part, I pardon thou everything, and I desire to devoutly pray God that He will pardon thou also. For the rest, I commend unto thou our dughtere Mary, beseeching thou to be a good father unto her, as I have heretofore desired. I entreat thou also, on behalf of my maids, to give them marriage portions, which is not much, they being but three. For all mine other servants I solicit the wages due them, and a year more, lest they be unprovided for. Lastly, I makest this vow, that mine eyes desire thou above all things.

Katharine the Quene.

From *The Autobiography of Henry VIII* by Margaret George

Gracious God, your Son Jesus Christ,
asked forgiveness for his enemies as he hung on the cross:
give us grace to forgive those who hurt us or harm us,
that we may be set free from the bonds of anger and resentment
and enter into the freedom which you promise your people;
through Jesus Christ our Lord. Amen.

Alice Owen 1547–1613
Benefactor

———

ALICE OWEN'S MOTIVATION for founding a school resulted from a near tragic accident when she was a girl. Walking in the countryside near some archers who were practising their skill, a stray arrow went straight through her hat but missed her head and did not kill her. In thanksgiving to God for her survival, she made a solemn vow that if she were ever to become rich she would use her wealth to help others. During the years that followed Alice was married and widowed no less than three times. In 1613 she bought land in Islington with her money and built a boys' school and some almshouses. In remembrance of her close escape, three metal arrows were attached to the school wall. In 1886 a girls' school was opened by the Dame Alice Owen Foundation. Today the Foundation is administered by the Worshipful Company of Brewers. In 1973 the two schools were merged and moved to Potters Bar. The aims of the school include 'promoting respect and understanding of religious and moral values within the framework of the Christian tradition'. The school still observes two unique traditions, dating back to the seventeenth century. When the Governors make their annual inspection of the school the younger pupils wear white carnations and the Sixth Formers and Governors wear red carnations. The pupils are also given a small amount of 'beer money'.

Dietrich Bonhoeffer reflects on gratitude

Only he who gives thanks for little things receives the big things. We prevent God from giving us the great spiritual gifts he has in store for us, because we do not give thanks for daily gifts. We think we dare not be satisfied with the small measure of spiritual knowledge, experience and love that has been given to us, and that we must constantly be looking forward eagerly for the highest good. Then we deplore the fact that we lack the deep certainty, the strong faith and the rich experience that God has given to others, and we consider this lament to be pious. We pray for the big things and forget to give thanks for the ordinary, small (and yet really not small) gifts. How can God entrust great things to one who will not thankfully receive from him the little things?

From *Life Together*

Almighty God, Father of all mercies, we thine unworthy servants
do give thee most humble and hearty thanks
for all thy goodness and loving-kindness to us and to all men.
We bless thee for our creation, preservation, and all the blessings of this life;
but above all for thine inestimable love
in the redemption of the world by our Lord Jesus Christ;
for the means of grace, and for the hope of glory.
And, we beseech thee, give us that due sense of all thy mercies,
that our hearts may be unfeignedly thankful;
and that we show forth thy praise, not only with our lips, but in our lives,
by giving up our selves to thy service, and by walking before thee
in holiness and righteousness all our days;
through Jesus Christ our Lord, to whom, with thee and the Holy Spirit,
be all honour and glory, world without end. Amen.

The General Thanksgiving from *The Book of Common Prayer*

Richard Gough 1735–1809

Antiquarian

———

THE SON OF the Member of Parliament for Bramber, Richard Gough was born in Winchester Street, London. He was a highly intelligent child who was such a good linguist that his translations of two works from French were published during his teenage years. Gough studied at Corpus Christi College, Cambridge, where he became fascinated by antiquities which subsequently became a lifelong interest. Throughout his life he travelled around the United Kingdom, making extensive notes and detailed sketches. He became a member of the Society of Antiquaries in 1767 and four years later he was made its director. From 1775 until 1795 he was also a fellow of the Royal Society. Gough wrote many books, including *Anecdotes of British Topography*, *Sepulchral Monuments of Great Britain*, *An Account of the Bedford Missal*, *A Catalogue of the Coins of Canute, King of Denmark*, *History of Pleshey in Essex* and *An Account of the Coins of the Seleucidae, Kings of Syria*. Gough married Anne Hall of Goldings, near Hertford. He was a generous man, who made many bequests in his will. He is buried in St Laurence's Church, Wormley, in Hertfordshire.

The Venerable Bede writes 'To the Most Glorious King Ceolwulf'

Some while ago, at Your Majesty's request, I gladly sent you the history of the English Church and People which I had recently completed, in order that you might read it and give it your approval. I now send it once again to be transcribed, so that Your Majesty may consider it at greater leisure. I warmly welcome the diligent zeal and sincerity with which you study the words of Holy Scripture and your eager desire to know something of the doings and sayings of men of the past, and of famous men of our own nation in particular. For if history records good things of good men, the thoughtful hearer is encouraged to imitate what is good: or if it records evil of wicked men, the devout, religious listener or reader is encouraged to avoid all that is sinful and perverse and to follow what he knows to be good and pleasing to God. Your Majesty is well aware of this; and since you feel so deeply responsible for the general good of those over whom divine Providence has set you, you wish that this history may be made better known both to yourself and to your people.

From *A History of the English Church and People*

———

Everlasting God,
we thank you for the rich heritage
of our buildings and monuments.
We thank you for the history, art and poetry
that shapes and enriches our culture.
Help us to learn from the past,
and to look to the future with confidence,
through Jesus Christ our Lord. Amen.

Aubrey George Spencer 1795–1872

Bishop and missionary

————

AUBREY SPENCER WAS a direct descendant of the Duke of Marlborough. Born in London, he attended St Albans School before joining the navy. Having been discharged due to ill health he offered himself for the priesthood and went up to study at Magdalen Hall, Oxford. After ordination and a curacy in Prittlewell, Spencer went to Newfoundland as a missionary with the Society for the Propagation of the Gospel. However, the cold weather affected his health; so he moved to Bermuda where he was appointed as Archdeacon. It was there that he met and married Eliza Musson with whom he had four children. In 1839 he was consecrated the first Bishop of Newfoundland in the chapel at Lambeth Palace. Spencer was an energetic bishop with good organisational skills who built a number of churches and schools in Newfoundland. He ordained a significant number of clergy and laid the foundation stone of a new cathedral. He also set out his strong Protestant views in *A Brief Account of the Church of England, its Faith and Worship: as shown by the Book of Common Prayer* and *Sermons on various subjects*. In Newfoundland his health again suffered and he moved to be Bishop of Jamaica. In 1855 he retired to Torquay where he assisted the ageing Bishop of Exeter, and died on this day in 1872.

Aubrey Spencer addresses the clergy about their duties

But it is only by the faithful and assiduous performance of your duties that you can acquire the cordial goodwill and co-operation of your parishioners, without which much of your ministerial endeavours will prove ineffectual. In the performance of these duties I need hardly tell you that much piety, learning, prudence, patience, and knowledge of the world, will be requisite, and that a great portion of your time must therefore be dedicated to the cultivation of these attributes of the clerical character. Yours is a situation of high dignity and commensurate responsibility: while the sense of the one inspires you with a becoming humility, let the consciousness of the other excite you with a generous ambition to every Christian, every philanthropic virtue…A good minister will be *holy* in its purest sense, rather than *popular*. He will respect his office too highly to please at the expense of principle. He will love the people too sincerely to gratify them at the hazard of their real welfare; and then the influence which he acquires, if it be slow in its acquisition, will be durable in its materials, and beneficial in its results. And here I must be allowed to express my hope that the people will cheerfully predispose themselves by prayer and charitable constructions to profit by your tuition.

From *A Charge to the Clergy of Bermuda* in *Sermons on Various Subjects*

Good Shepherd,
who laid down your life for the sheep:
give grace to those you have called into the sacred ministry
that they may be faithful in teaching and diligent in caring for your people
that all may grow in faith and holiness,
and into the full stature of your Son, Jesus Christ. Amen.

Christopher Wren 1632–1723

Architect, scientist and politician

———

CHRISTOPHER WREN IS remembered chiefly as the architect of St Paul's Cathedral and fifty-one other churches following the Great Fire of London in 1666. However, during his lifetime he was equally famous as a mathematician and astronomer. He was also one of the founders, and later president, of the Royal Society. Born in East Knoyle in Wiltshire, Wren was privately educated at home. In 1650 he went up to Wadham College, Oxford, where he studied Latin, mathematics and science. He was elected a fellow of All Souls College, and in 1657 Gresham College in London appointed him Professor of Astronomy. Four years later he returned to Oxford as the Savilian Professor of Astronomy, and shortly afterwards King Charles II appointed him Surveyor of Works. His academic interests were wide and he wrote on many subjects including meteorology, medicine, optics and surveying. He was also elected Member of Parliament for Old Windsor on three occasions. Wren's interest in architecture developed from his study of physics and engineering and was further kindled by the need to repair St Paul's Cathedral, which was in a parlous state. However, before he had had an opportunity to submit plans, the Great Fire destroyed it, allowing him to produce an entirely new design. His work on the new cathedral was to continue for the next thirty-six years. Within the Diocese of St Albans he was the architect of Tring Manor House. He also designed a family pew for the Ashburnhams at Ampthill and the Temple Bar which for many years stood at Theobald's Park, Cheshunt, but which now once again is in London. He married twice and had four children. Wren is buried in St Paul's Cathedral. The inscription on his tomb reads 'Reader, if you seek his memorial – look around you.'

Anthony Bloom reflects on the significance of consecrating a church

When we build a church or set apart a place of worship we do something which reaches far beyond the obvious significance of the fact. The whole world which God created has become a place where men have sinned; the devil has been at work, a fight is going on constantly; there is no place on this earth which has not been soiled by blood, suffering or sin. When we choose a minute part of it, calling upon the power of God himself, in rites which convey his grace, to bless it, when we cleanse it from the presence of the evil spirit and set it apart to be God's foothold on earth, we reconquer for God a small part of this desecrated world. We may say that this is a place where the kingdom of God reveals itself and manifests itself with power. When we come to church we should be aware that we are entering upon sacred ground, a place which belongs to God, and we should behave accordingly.

From *Living Prayer*

———

God, our heavenly Father, make, we pray,
the door of this church wide enough
to welcome all who need human love and fellowship and a Father's care;
but narrow enough to shut out all envy, pride, and lack of love.
Here may the tempted find help, the sorrowing receive comfort,
the careless be awakened to repentance, and the penitent be assured of your mercy;
and here may all your children renew their strength
and go on their way in hope and joy;
through Jesus Christ, our Lord. Amen.

Bishop Thomas Ken

Geoffrey de Gorham d.1146

Scholar and abbot

———

GEOFFREY DE GORHAM was a Norman scholar from Maine which was then part of the Dukedom of Normandy. The Abbot of St Albans, Richard d'Aubeney, invited him to become master of the Abbey School. However it was a long time before he arrived, by which time someone else had been appointed to the post. So Gorham opened a school in Dunstable which is the setting for the events which were to lead him to become a monk of St Albans. A chronicle tells how he had written a miracle play for the pupils and borrowed some copes from St Albans Abbey for the performance. That evening there was a fire in his house and everything was destroyed, including the sacred vestments. In penitence he decided to become a monk. In 1119 he was elected abbot, a post which he held until 1146. The Abbey prospered under his wise administration. He is remembered for building the Abbey infirmary, for erecting a new shrine for St Alban, and for founding a leper hospital near St Albans. He was a close associate of Christina of Markyate and offered generous support to the nunneries at Sopwell and Markyate. He is also credited with saving the Abbey from destruction during the civil unrest in the reign of King Stephen.

The Leprosy Relief Association describes the curse of leprosy

It would be easy, but probably wrong, to suggest that prevention of infection was the reason for the instruction that a leper should move downwind before conversing with anyone. Indeed, if containment of infection was the purpose of seclusion in leper hospitals and lazar houses, why let inmates out at all (they were allowed out for farmwork and begging), and how can the punishment or expulsion from hospital for misbehaviour be explained? The regulations of the hospital of St Julian, near St Albans, put the general position with brutal simplicity: 'Amongst all infirmities the disease of leprosy is held in contempt.' The regulations continue by quoting Leviticus, ending that: 'When he is leprous and unclean he is to dwell alone without the camp.' (Leviticus 13 v 45.) The very strict programme of isolation for those with leprosy, as was practised in Europe, does not appear to have been either continuously or completely enforced in Britain. The Bishop of Exeter, in 1163, confirmed the rights of lepers to visit the market twice a week and collect food and alms, although in 1244 this right was rescinded. On the outskirts of a town in medieval times, travellers would have noticed a well-known landmark – a group of cottages with an adjoining chapel, clustering round a green enclosure. At a glance they would recognise it as the 'lazar house', and would prepare to throw alms to the crippled and disfigured representatives of the community. Lazar houses also provided spiritual care.

From *Leprosy in Britain*

———

Almighty Father, giver of life and health,
look mercifully upon those who are stricken with leprosy,
and stretch forth thy hand to cleanse and heal them,
as did thy blessed Son of old.
Grant wisdom to those who are seeking the cure
and treatment of this disease;
give tenderness and sympathy to those who minister to the sufferers;
and restore to their families and friends those who have been separated from them;
for the sake of the same Jesus Christ our Lord. Amen.

B. F. Westcott

Gerald Edgcumbe Hadow 1911–78

Missionary and linguist

———

NOT MANY ENGLISH clergymen can boast that they are fluent speakers of Kipdanga, a language spoken in a region of Tanzania. Gerald Hadow, an accomplished linguist who also spoke Swahili, learnt the languages during the thirty-eight years that he was a missionary. The son of a clergyman, Hadow had been a pupil at Haileybury College, Hertfordshire, before studying at Oriel College, Oxford. He came from a musical family (his uncle was Sir William Hadow, a well-known musician) and was himself an accomplished singer. He was ordained priest in 1936 in Bristol Cathedral but soon felt called to work overseas. He was sent to Africa by the Society for the Propagation of the Gospel and worked in several different parts of the country. He was awarded an OBE in 1961. In 1972 the Diocese of South West Tanganyika honoured him by making him a canon of the cathedral. He died on this day in 1978 in Cambridge.

Archbishop Michael Ramsey describes the missionary task

Yet all the time there is, for us whose hearts God has touched, the supreme task to bring home to the people of God himself, in his majesty, his compassion, his claim upon mankind, his astounding gift of his very self in Jesus the Word-made-Flesh. We cannot fulfil the task for this country unless we are striving to fulfil it towards the whole of the world. It therefore demands the service of men and women who will go anywhere in the world in Christ's obedience, who will witness to Christ's love in the insistence that races, black and white, are brothers of equal worth. Here at home our mission means for the Church a constant involvement in the community; we shall strive to penetrate the world of industry, of science, of art and literature, of sight and sound, and in this penetration, we must approach as learners as well as teachers. We need to be learning not only many new techniques, but also what God is saying to us through the new and exciting circumstances of our time. Yet because it is God to whom we witness, we need no less a constant detachment, a will to go apart and wait upon God in quiet, in silence, lest by our busyness we should rob ourselves and rob others of the realisation of God's presence: 'Be still and know that I am God.' Would that everyone whose heart God has touched would guard times of quietness amid our noisy, bustling life, to let God touch the heart again.

From *Canterbury Essays and Addresses*

———

*O God, who to an expectant and united church
granted at Pentecost the gift of the Holy Spirit:
give us the help of the same Spirit in all our life and worship,
that we may expect great things from you and attempt great things for you,
and show to the world your Son our Saviour Jesus Christ;
to whom with you and the Holy Spirit be honour and glory,
now and for evermore. Amen.*

Church of South India

Richard Grey 1694–1771

Archdeacon and author

A LTHOUGH GREY WAS Archdeacon of Bedford for fourteen years, he is better known today for his book *Memoria Technica; or a new Method of Artificial Memory*. Published in 1730, the book was so popular that it was reprinted many times over the next 130 years and was the inspiration for a number of other memory systems. He also wrote many other books, including a Hebrew grammar and a book of ecclesiastical law, for which he was awarded the degree of Doctor of Divinity by Oxford University in 1733. He was author of a book with the catchy title *An Answer to Barbeyrac's Spirit of the Ecclesiastics of all Ages as to the Doctrines of Morality*. Grey studied at Lincoln College, Oxford, and was ordained in 1710. He became chaplain to the Bishop of Durham and during subsequent years held a number of posts: he was Rector of Hinton in Northamptonshire as well as occupying the livings of Steane Chapel and of Kimcote, whilst also being appointed to a Prebendal Stall at St Paul's Cathedral. He was married to Joyce Thicknesse by whom he had three daughters. He died on this day in 1771 and is buried at Hinton.

Robert Atwell writes about memory

An ability to remember the past and to envision the future distinguishes us from the rest of the animal kingdom. At school we cultivate our memory so that it provides the context and means by which we store and evaluate information. A sense of journey begins to emerge, of where we have come from and where we would like to be. The older we get, the more precious becomes the carpet-bag of experiences we carry within us. Memories infused with gratitude are the wonderful consolation of old age. We savour events that shaped us for good. But we can also find ourselves mourning opportunities we missed or mistakes we made. Augustine likens memory to a royal court full of people: some familiar, others strange; some delightful, others threatening and disturbing. 'Inside me,' he says, 'is the huge court of memory in which I meet myself: I recall myself, what I have done, and how I was affected when I did it.' In our memories we do indeed meet ourselves: who we were and who we have become…Without a memory society can lose its way. Wisdom is lost in a morass of information. Shameful episodes in a nation's or community's history are not confronted. Memories of embarrassment or humiliation are suppressed. Bereaved of the past, society becomes imprisoned in the present, vulnerable to the claims of expediency. In his novel *Nineteen Eighty-Four*, George Orwell imagines a society in which the Ministry of Truth continuously edits newspapers to ensure that there is no memory of a time when Big Brother was not always right. Orwell realised that when you control people's memories you control their capacity to imagine a different future.

From *The Contented Life*

Everlasting God,
whose memory never fails,
you promise through your prophet
that our names are engraved on the palm of your hand:
bring healing and forgiveness to those memories that disturb us;
and give us grace to celebrate the good memories we cherish
that we may look to the future in confidence;
through Jesus Christ our Lord. Amen.

John de Benstede d.1323

Chancellor of the Exchequer

———

NOT A LOT is known about John de Benstede, though the fact that he was knighted and had an elaborate tomb indicates that he was an important person. His memorial sits in the Benstede chapel in the north-east corner of St Peter's Church, Benington. It is a handsome tomb chest bearing a life-size effigy of Benstede and his wife, Petronilla, who died in 1342. His family had long connections with the church and made substantial alterations to it over the years. Benstede held the prebendary of Sandiacre in Derbyshire from 1297 until he married in 1308. During the course of his long and distinguished career he built up an impressive estate. He held various positions in the royal household, including King's Secretary, Keeper of the Great Seal and Keeper of the Wardrobe for Edward I. He was also a prominent judge and ended up as Chancellor of England.

Bishop Peter Selby reflects on money

For years I have received and given spiritual direction, and have to say by way of confession that money has hardly figured; and I have gently broken enough silences to know that I am not alone in that experience. In years of attending worship and of preaching at it, I again have to admit that money seems to figure only when it is time to raise the question of 'Christian giving'; whenever the issue is raised it therefore arouses the instant defences of those who suspect, usually rightly, that they are about to be confronted with the Church in self-serving rather than world-serving mode. At the centre of this breaking of silence must be the matter of that which is primarily constitutive of the Church's life, its 'secret motive force', and that is its worship. For that is the point at which we act out in our shared life the dynamic of the Kingdom of forgiveness which enables mutual trust. We gather, after all, to celebrate pure gift, the act of God the Father, out of love and only love, in creating the world in freedom; the act of God the Son, out of love and only love, in restoring the economy of freedom; the act of the Holy Spirit, love and only love, in animating the Body of Christ in its freedom of response. We do not come to wait upon our demanding creditor or to make our expected down payments by the due date. What we are invited into is a context where our response may simply reflect as much as, and no more than, that 'out of love and only love' which is the character of God's action and is hoped for from those who have received it.

From *Grace and Mortgage*

Generous God,
you delight to give good gifts to your people:
teach us to practise generosity
not only among our family and friends
but also to our neighbour and the stranger in our midst;
through Jesus Christ our Lord. Amen.

Percy Malcolm Stewart 1872–1951

Industrialist and philanthropist

———

THE FOUR CHIMNEYS near the model village of Stewartby in Bedfordshire stand as a visual reminder of the old London Brick Company. The village was formerly called Wootton Pillinge but was renamed Stewartby in 1937. Percy Malcolm Stewart needed accommodation to house the LBC workers and commissioned a new village and church to the designs of Sir Albert Richardson. The village was built in the second half of the 1920s and during its most productive period the Stewartby Brickworks was able to fire eighteen million bricks annually in the world's largest kiln. Stewart was born into a deeply religious family who lived for a period on the Bramingham Shott Estate in Luton. He was educated at schools in England and in Germany. He bought the London Brick Company in the 1920s. It grew to such a size that it had its own fire engines, ambulances and even a sports club with a swimming pool. Stewart set up a charitable trust to 'advance religion and education, to relieve poverty…' and 'to establish a chapel for the village of Stewartby.' In 1934 he purchased a property at Sandy and three years later was created a baronet. He was the last Lord of the Manor of Potton. Stewart's ashes are buried in Stewartby United Church.

Pope Paul VI reflects on work

Human labour which is expended in the production and exchange of goods or in the performance of economic services is superior to the other elements of economic life, for the latter have only the nature of tools. This labour, whether it is engaged in independently or hired by someone else, comes immediately from the person, who as it were stamps the things of nature with his seal and subdues them to his will. By his labour a man ordinarily supports himself and his family, is joined to his fellow men and serves them, and can exercise genuine charity and be a partner in the work of bringing divine creation to perfection. Indeed, we hold that through labour offered to God man is associated with the redemptive work of Jesus Christ, who conferred an eminent dignity on labour when at Nazareth He worked with His own hands. From this there follows for every man the duty of working faithfully and also the right to work. It is the duty of society, moreover, according to the circumstances prevailing in it, and in keeping with its role, to help the citizens to find sufficient employment. Finally, remuneration for labour is to be such that man may be furnished the means to cultivate worthily his own material, social, cultural, and spiritual life and that of his dependants, in view of the function and productiveness of each one, the conditions of the factory or workshop, and the common good.

From 'Pastoral Constitution on the Church in the Modern World', *Gaudium et Spes*

———

Lord Jesus Christ,
son of the carpenter from Galilee,
who learnt from your father a craftsman's skills:
we thank you for all who work with their hands
to sculpt and carve and build.
As we honour their gifts and their labour
we pray for those whose work is dull or unrewarding.
May each of us have work and find delight in it;
for we ask it for your name's sake. Amen.

Robert Cecil c.1553–1612

Secretary of State

———

ROBERT CECIL WAS the son of the first Baron Burghley. The family lived at Theobalds in Hertfordshire. Following his studies at St John's College, Cambridge, he entered the House of Commons and became a Justice of the Peace. He was Secretary of State both to Elizabeth I and James I – as well as spymaster. Throughout his life Cecil was a passionate patron of the arts, supporting among others the composers William Byrd and Orlando Gibbons. He was also a strong advocate of education and was Chancellor of both the University of Cambridge and Trinity College, Dublin. In 1589 Cecil married Elizabeth Brooke, the daughter of Baron Cobham. They had a son, named William. Cecil died in 1612 and is buried in St Etheldreda's Church in Hatfield. His magnificent tomb, designed by Maximilian Colt, is a life-size effigy of Cecil dressed in the robes of a Knight of the Garter, holding the staff of the Lord Treasurer. He is supported by the four cardinal virtues of Justice, Fortitude, Temperance, and Prudence.

Pauline Croft describes Cecil's religious views

The chapel and the paintings at Hatfield House prove that as he grew older Robert Cecil somehow acquired a vivid appreciation of those visual aspects of the Christian tradition largely omitted from the godly protestantism of his childhood. The same progression can be seen in his will, a remarkable statement of his final doctrinal position written in March 1612, when he was already in severe pain and only two months from death. Fervently repenting his sins, begging and beseeching pardon 'at the hands of almighty God for his son Jesus Christ his sake the only saviour and redeemer of all mankind', he was

> in no way trusting or believing that any works of mine can be meritorious or coadjutors to my salvation but on the contrary…inutile and contemptible in respect of those great and grievous offences which nothing but the precious blood of Jesus Christ shed upon the cross for me and all mankind can wash away…

He avowed his belief in the Trinity, the communion of saints, and all points in the Apostles' creed, 'which because it is *summum credendum* I have always observed as the best rule of necessary faith and points of salvation', then went on to state his belief in baptism, 'the ordinary way and means appointed for our admittance into the Church, without which church whosoever is, is also without salvation'. Above all he spelt out his belief in the Lord's Supper.

From 'The Religion of Robert Cecil' in *The Historical Journal*

Let your mercy and blessing, O Lord of Lords, rest upon our land and nation;
upon all the powers which you have ordained over us:
our Queen and those in authority under her,
the ministers of state, and the great councils of the nation;
that we may lead a quiet and peaceable life in all godliness and honesty.
Rule the hearts of our people in your faith and fear;
rebuke the power of unbelief and superstition;
and preserve to us your pure Word in its liberty and glory even to the end of days;
through Jesus Christ our Lord. Amen.

Handley C. G. Moule

George Ratcliffe Woodward 1848–1934

Priest, poet and musician

————

Although GEORGE WOODWARD was an expert in plainsong, he is best remembered for three carols: *This joyful Eastertide, Ding, dong, merrily on high* and *Past three o'clock*. He was a prolific writer of poetry and set much of his own verse to music. He published several collections of carols and collaborated with the composer Charles Wood who provided musical settings. Woodward published a number of books on other subjects, including *Legends of the Saints, The Seven Sleepers of Ephesus* and *Poemata*. He was a man of varied interests, playing the euphonium and the cello, beekeeping and bell-ringing. His connection with the Diocese of St Albans was forged during his years at school in Elstree before going on to Harrow School and then Gonville and Caius College, Cambridge. In 1874 the Bishop of London ordained him to St Barnabas, Pimlico, from where he went on to serve in parishes in Norfolk and Suffolk. In 1894 he and his wife Alice moved back to Pimlico, where he founded the St Barnabas Choral Society and continued to write and publish hymns and carols. He died on this day in 1934 in London and is buried in Little Walsingham in Norfolk.

This joyful Easter-tide,
Away with care and sorrow!
My Love, the Crucified,
Hath sprung to life this morrow.

Had Christ, that once was slain,
Ne'er burst His three day prison,
Our faith had been in vain;
But now hath Christ arisen,
Arisen, arisen, arisen!

My flesh in hope shall rest,
And for a season slumber;
Till trump from east to west,
Shall wake the dead in number.

Death's flood hath lost his chill,
Since Jesus crossed the river:
Lover of souls, from ill
My passing soul deliver.

George Woodward

———

Heavenly Father,
we thank you for anointing men and women with the Holy Spirit,
the source of life and fount of inspiration:
bless all writers, poets and musicians;
through their psalms, hymns and songs draw us into your presence,
expand our minds with wonder and awe,
and inspire us to offer our lives in your service:
through Jesus Christ our Lord. Amen.

O God,
whom saints and angels delight to worship in heaven:
Be ever present with your servants who seek through art and music
to perfect the praises offered by your people on earth;
and grant to them even now glimpses of your beauty,
and make them worthy at length to behold it unveiled for evermore;
through Jesus Christ our Lord. Amen.

From *The Book of Common Prayer* of the Episcopal Church

Wulsin 10th century

Abbot of St Albans

————

WULSIN, ALSO KNOWN as Ulsinus, was a monk and subsequently Abbot of St Albans, during the first half of the tenth century. According to Matthew Paris, writing a chronicle of the period some three hundred years later, Wulsin was responsible for founding St Albans School around the year 948. By then, St Albans was already a major centre of pilgrimage and, in addition to the school, Wulsin is credited with founding three churches, built by the city gates, to welcome pilgrims before the final stage of their journey to the shrine of St Alban in the Abbey church. The parish churches of St Michael's, St Stephen's and St Peter's stand in testimony to his considerable achievements.

A Hymn for Pilgrims

Guide me, O thou great redeemer,
Pilgrim through this barren land;
I am weak, but thou art mighty,
Hold me with thy powerful hand;
Bread of heaven, bread of heaven
Feed me till I want no more;
Feed me till I want no more.

Open now the crystal fountain
Whence the healing stream doth flow;
Let the fire and cloudy pillar
Lead me all my journey through:
Strong deliverer, strong deliverer;
Be thou still my strength and shield;
Be thou still my strength and shield.

When I tread the verge of Jordan,
Bid my anxious fears subside;
Death of death, and hell's destruction
Land me safe on Canaan's side:
Songs of praises, songs of praises,
I will ever give to thee;
I will ever give to thee.

William Williams

————

O God our Father, who hast taught us that our citizenship is in heaven,
and hast called us to tread a pilgrim's path here on earth:
Guide us, we pray thee, on our journey
through this world to the Celestial City;
defend us from the perils that await us on the way;
give us grace to endure faithfully to the end;
and at the last bring us to thy eternal joy;
through the mercy of thy Son, Jesus Christ. Amen.

Frank Colquhoun

Alison Margaret Bonnard 1916–2011

Samaritan

———

SAMARITANS WAS FOUNDED in 1953 by the Reverend Chad Varah after he conducted a funeral of a fourteen-year-old girl who had committed suicide. Inevitably much of the work of the charity is hidden from public view because it consists of listening to those who are deeply troubled. It was typical of Alison Bonnard that, amongst her many activities, she should have trained as a Samaritan volunteer. She frequently undertook acts of service which were only known to a few. She paid for a snooker table for the youth club, supplied Bible reading notes, cleaned the brasses in her parish church and paid for the crosses for Palm Sunday. Alison served as a member of the Parochial Church Council at St Michael's, Woburn Sands, and as secretary to the group that supported overseas mission. There was another side to her personality: she loved to perform in amateur pantomimes. Alison was a child of the vicarage. Her father had been vicar of Edenbridge in Kent, and her mother was for many years Diocesan President of the Mothers' Union; consequently Christian faith was from the first a fundamental part of her life. She was deeply embedded into the life of Woburn Sands where she lived for more than sixty years. During her working life she taught at a private preparatory school in Aspley Heath called The Knoll, and then at Bow Brickhill Church of England Primary School. It was at The Knoll that she met her husband Basil, with whom she had three children.

Sister Jeanne D'Arc writes about the power of listening

Every one of our fellow men is in search of a heart ready to listen to him in such a way that he will no longer be another human being. Let us then try to give this kind of welcome, to pay him that depth of attention which comes from the bottom of the heart so that he will be at ease with us as he is with himself. So often the eyes of those who surround him and even of those closest to him are like so many distorting mirrors; instead, let him find in us a heart so clear and transparent that the refraction index, so to speak, is nil. 'Bear one another's burdens' (Galatians 6.2). We are so very weak that we are often unable to bear anyone else's burden. However we can always at least relieve him of his load by letting him pour it out into us. All we have to do is to listen with our heart. It is not simply a question of an interior welcome at a deep level, of a heart so full of fellow-feeling as to be on the alert for all that is best, and frequently most hidden and unexpressed, in all those with whom we come into contact. A silence impregnated with love, which listens in charity to the groans of the sufferer, is often far more effective than words of comfort…

From *The Listening Heart*

———

God of peace,
still our hearts and minds,
and banish the self-importance
which crowds out others
with our craving for an audience.
In your mercy, teach us truly to listen to others
that we may enter into their hopes and fears,
their anguish and their desires,
and journey alongside them;
through Jesus Christ our Lord. Amen.

Francis Owen Salisbury 1874–1962

Artist

———

FRANCIS SALISBURY PAINTED the portraits of some of the most famous people of his day, among them Queen Elizabeth II, Winston Churchill, Pope Pius XII, Benito Mussolini and Franklin D. Roosevelt. He had an intense dislike of modern art and was critical of many of his contemporaries. As well as portraiture, he was well known for his historical scenes, his illustrations and for his stained glass. Born in Harpenden, as a young man Salisbury worked in his father's bicycle repair shop. He obtained a position as an apprentice in a stained glass factory in St Albans where it quickly became evident that he had considerable artistic talent. He was awarded a scholarship to the Royal Academy where he won a number of prizes. He was a regular visitor to the United States of America and was in great demand. Salisbury was a lifelong Methodist which perhaps accounts for his teetotalism, pacifism and his insistence of not working on Sundays. He painted several pictures for the Salvation Army and the Methodist Church, including a portrait of John Wesley. He bequeathed Sarum Chase, his home in West Hampstead, to the British Council of Churches.

C.G. Jung explores the roots of the artistic impulse

Art is a kind of innate drive that seizes a human being and makes him its instrument. The artist is not a person endowed with free will who seeks his own ends, but one who allows art to realise its purposes through him. As a human being he may have moods and a will and personal aims, but as an artist he is 'man' in a higher sense – he is 'collective man', a vehicle and moulder of the unconscious psychic life of mankind. That is his office, and it is sometimes so heavy a burden that he is fated to sacrifice happiness and everything that makes life worth living for the ordinary human being. As K.G. Carus says: 'Strange are the ways by which a genius is announced, for what distinguishes so supremely endowed a being is that, for all the freedom of his life and the clarity of his thought, he is everywhere hemmed round and prevailed upon by the Unconscious, the mysterious god within him so that ideas flow to him – he knows not whence; he is driven to work and to create – he knows not to what end; and is mastered by an impulse for constant growth and development – he knows not whither.'

From *Psychology and Literature*

O God, whose Spirit in our hearts teaches us to desire your perfection,
to seek for truth and to rejoice in beauty:
enlighten and inspire all artists and craftsmen
in whatever is true, pure and lovely,
that your name may be honoured and your will done on earth;
through Jesus Christ our Lord. Amen.

Society of St Luke the Painter

Edward Michael Gresford Jones 1901–82

Sixth Bishop of St Albans

————

BORN INTO A clerical dynasty, Michael Gresford Jones served as Bishop of St Albans for twenty years from 1950 to 1970. He was educated at Rugby School, Trinity College, Cambridge, and Westcott House. He was ordained in 1927 in the Diocese of Manchester, serving his title at St Chrysostom's, Victoria Park. He returned to Trinity College, Cambridge, as Chaplain before being appointed Vicar of Holy Trinity, Blackpool, and Rural Dean of Fylde. In 1939 he moved to be Vicar of Hunslet in Leeds. In 1942 Gresford Jones was consecrated Bishop of Willesden in St Paul's Cathedral and appointed Rector of St Botolph-without-Bishopsgate. After eight years he was translated to the See of St Albans. He was the Lord High Almoner from 1953 to 1970 and was made a Knight Commander of the Royal Victorian Order in 1968. Although he was a member of the House of Lords for many years he spoke only on one occasion, in which he called for legislation to protect pit ponies. He died on this day in 1982 and is buried in the churchyard of St Albans Abbey.

The duties of a bishop

Bishops are called to serve and care for the flock of Christ. Mindful of the Good Shepherd, who laid down his life for his sheep, they are to love and pray for those committed to their charge, knowing their people and being known by them. As principal ministers of word and sacrament, stewards of the mysteries of God, they are to preside at the Lord's table and to lead the offering of prayer and praise. They are to feed God's pilgrim people, and so build up the Body of Christ. They are to baptize and confirm, nurturing God's people in the life of the Spirit and leading them in the way of holiness. They are to discern and foster the gifts of the Spirit in all who follow Christ, commissioning them to minister in his name. They are to preside over the ordination of deacons and priests, and join together in the ordination of bishops. As chief pastors, it is their duty to share with their fellow presbyters the oversight of the Church, speaking in the name of God and expounding the gospel of salvation. With the Shepherd's love, they are to be merciful, but with firmness; to minister discipline, but with compassion. They are to have a special care for the poor, the outcast and those who are in need. They are to seek out those who are lost and lead them home with rejoicing, declaring the absolution and forgiveness of sins to those who turn to Christ. Following the example of the prophets and the teaching of the apostles, they are to proclaim the gospel boldly, confront injustice and work for righteousness and peace in all the world.

From the *Ordination and Consecration of a Bishop* in *Common Worship*

————

Almighty God, who by thy Son Jesus Christ didst give thy holy apostles many excellent gifts, and didst charge them to feed thy flock: Give thy grace, we beseech thee, to all bishops, the pastors of thy Church, that they may diligently preach thy Word, and duly administer the godly discipline thereof; and grant to the people that they may obediently follow the same; that all may receive the crown of everlasting glory; through Jesus Christ our Lord. Amen.

Adapted from *The Book of Common Prayer*

James Cantlie 1851–1926

Doctor and pioneer of First Aid

———

BORN IN BANFFSHIRE, James Cantlie studied medicine at the University of Aberdeen and at Charing Cross Hospital, London. He was appointed a Fellow of the Royal College of Surgeons in 1877 and worked at Charing Cross until 1888 when he moved to a post in Hong Kong. Cantlie was one of the founders of the Hong Kong College of Medicine for Chinese, an institution which eventually became the University of Hong Kong. Whilst there, he undertook pioneering work into tropical diseases, including leprosy. When Cantlie returned to England, he launched the *Journal of Tropical Medicine* and was instrumental in setting up the London School of Tropical Medicine. He was also one of the founders of the Royal Society of Tropical Medicine and Hygiene. Throughout his working life, Cantlie was convinced of the importance of First Aid, a discipline that was practically unknown and untaught. During the First World War his interest in the subject developed and he became a passionate advocate of the provision of ambulance services. On his death he was buried in St John's Church, Cottered, in Hertfordshire.

Francis de Sales on coping with suffering

Complain as little as possible when you are ill. Inevitably, those who complain end up sinning because their self-preoccupation distorts the pain they are suffering, exaggerating their condition. Above all, never complain to emotional or censorious people. If you have to complain, either to remedy an offence or to secure peace of mind for yourself, then choose someone who is humble, generous and who truly loves God. Otherwise, instead of easing your heart, they will provoke you to greater pain. Instead of extracting the thorn, they will sink it deeper in your flesh. On the other hand, there are some who on becoming ill, upset, or hurt by others, refrain from complaining or revealing that they have been hurt lest it should appear as weakness or refusal to be open to the will of God. They much prefer others to sympathise with their lot, and find ways of encouraging them to do so. They want to appear brave *and* afflicted. By contrast, a truly patient person will neither complain nor want others to complain for him. When he speaks of his sufferings, he will speak honestly and straight-forwardly, without moaning, complaining or exaggeration. If he is pitied, he receives it with patience, unless he feels the pity is misplaced, in which case he will say so. When you are sick, offer to Christ all your pains, your suffering and your listlessness. Beg him to unite them with those he suffered for you. Obey your doctor, take your medicine, your food and other remedies, and all for the love of God, remembering how Christ tasted gall for the love of you. Desire to recover in order to serve him, but always be prepared to suffer on in obedience to his will, and be prepared to die when he calls you, that you may be with him and praise him for ever.

From *Introduction to the Devout Life* by Francis de Sales

———

Of your goodness, gracious Lord,
comfort and support all those who in this life
are in trouble, sorrow, need or sickness;
give us patience and compassion as we reach out to them
that they may know healing of body
and peace of mind;
through Jesus Christ our Lord. Amen.

Based on *The Book of Common Prayer*

Arthur Capell 1608–49

Member of Parliament

———

CAPELL WAS BORN at Hadham Hall, Hertfordshire, and educated at Queens' College, Cambridge. He was twice elected as the Member of Parliament for Hertfordshire. Initially he was critical of King Charles I but eventually was won over to the King's cause and became a strong Royalist. When he was elevated to the peerage in 1641 he took the title of Baron Capell of Hadham. He married Elizabeth Morrison from Cassiobury, Hertfordshire, a union which brought him great wealth. Together they had nine children. During the Civil War, Capell served in the Royalist army at the Battle of Edgehill and was made Lieutenant-General of Worcestershire, Shropshire, Cheshire and North Wales. He was appointed as one of the councillors to the Prince of Wales and was a commissioner at the Treaty of Uxbridge. Capell's military experience propelled him into leadership of the Royalist cause. However, after the Siege of Colchester he surrendered to Sir Thomas Fairfax, being promised that his life would be spared. He was incarcerated first at Windsor Castle and later in the Tower of London. He escaped but was recaptured and condemned to death by Parliament. On the morning of his execution he wrote:

> 'My dearest Life; My eternal life is in Christ Jesus: My worldly considerations in the highest degree thou hast deserved. Let me live long here in thy dear memory to the comfort of my family, our dear children, whom God out of mercy in Christ hath bestowed upon us. I beseech thee to take care of thy health, sorrow not, afflict not thyself too much; God be unto thee better than an husband; and to my children better than a father. I am sure He is able to be so. God be with thee, my most virtuous wife: God multiply many comforts to thee and my children…'

He was beheaded on this day in March 1649 and is buried at Little Hadham.

A meditation by Arthur Capell

My dear Saviour, inspire me with the true apprehension of thy infinite love towards me, who descendedst from the top of Majestie to the lowest degree of Servility, didst debase thyself to exalt me, cloathedst thyself with mortality to invest me with immortality, were poor to enrich me, enduredst the reproach of thine enemies to reconcile me to thy most incensed Father. Could I but truly conceive any part of this immense love, I could not but return more to Thee; to thine: I should then forget injuries from my weak Brethren, love my most malicious enemies, have none but those that undervalue this great goodnesse, whereas now mine affections are guided by my personall interests.

From *Daily Observations or Meditations: Divine, Morall*

Lord Jesus Christ,
we thank you that in sharing our life on earth
you also entered into the experience of our death and what follows.
As we trust you with our life, so we may surely trust you also with our death.
When that time comes, give us in your mercy a peaceful end free from fear,
knowing that you are with us and that at the last we shall be with you
in our Father's house for evermore. Amen.

Frank Colquhoun

John Joscelyn 1529–1603

Scholar and linguist

———

THE JOSCELYN FAMILY were Hertfordshire gentry who lived at Hyde Hall, Sawbridgeworth, and High Roding, Essex. John Joscelyn studied at Queens' College, Cambridge, and later became the bursar of the college. He taught both Latin and Greek in the University. We know that in 1555 he subscribed to the Marian articles, but two years later resigned his fellowship and became a passionate Protestant. In 1559 the new Archbishop of Canterbury, Matthew Parker, made Joscelyn his secretary. In 1557 he was presented to the rectory of Hollingbourne in Kent and in 1560 he was given a prebend at Hereford. As well as Latin and Greek, Joscelyn was a scholar of Hebrew and Old English. This enabled him to assist Archbishop Parker to publish his collection of medieval manuscripts, many of which were in Old English. Joscelyn made a significant contribution to Parker's *A Testimonie of Antiquitie Shewing the Auncient Fayth in the Church of England* and his *De antiquitate Britannicæ ecclesiæ*. Joscelyn became an expert in early English law codes and also wrote a history of Corpus Christi College, Cambridge. In his will he left money to establish a Hebrew lectureship at Queens' College. Most of his manuscripts are at Corpus Christi College, the British Library and the Bodleian Library in Oxford. He is buried at All Saints, High Roding.

Richard Hooker comments on the authority of Scripture

The main drift of the whole New Testament is that which St John setteth down as the purpose of his own history; 'These things are written, that ye might believe that Jesus is Christ the Son of God, and that in believing ye might have life through his name.' The drift of the Old that which the Apostle mentioneth to Timothy, 'The Holy Scriptures are able to make thee wise unto Salvation.' So that the general end both of Old and New is one; the difference between them consisting in this, that the Old did make wise by teaching salvation through Christ that should come, the New by teaching that Christ the Saviour is come, and that Jesus whom the Jews did crucify, and whom God did raise again from the dead, is he. When the Apostle therefore affirmeth unto Timothy, that the Old was able to make him wise to salvation, it was not his meaning that the Old alone can do this unto us which live since the publication of the New. For he speaketh with presupposal of the doctrine of Christ known also unto Timothy, and therefore first it is said, 'Continue thou in those things which thou hast learned and art persuaded, knowing of whom thou hast been taught them.' Again, those Scriptures he granteth were able to make him wise to salvation; but he addeth, 'through the faith which is in Christ.'

From *Of the Lawes of Ecclesiasticall Politie*

———

Blessed Lord,
who has caused all holy Scriptures to be written for our learning:
grant that we may in such wise hear them,
read, mark, learn, and inwardly digest them;
that, by patience and comfort of thy holy Word,
we may embrace and ever hold fast the blessed hope of everlasting life,
which thou hast given us in our Saviour Jesus Christ;
who liveth and reigneth with thee and the Holy Spirit,
one God, for ever and ever. Amen.

From *The Book of Common Prayer*

Reginald Bray c.1440–1503

Chancellor of the Duchy of Lancaster

———

BORN IN WORCESTER and educated at its Royal Grammar School, Reginald Bray entered the service of Lady Margaret Beaufort and her second husband, Lord Stafford, as Master of the Household. In 1485 he was appointed Chancellor of the Duchy of Lancaster by King Henry VII. As one of the king's 'new men', he was responsible for the king's finances and was, in effect, his prime minister. The king made him a Knight of the Bath at his coronation in 1485, and later on in his life a Knight of the Garter. Bray was also made Steward of the University of Oxford in 1496. He was elected as Member of Parliament for Hampshire on three occasions in the final years of the fifteenth century. As well as the manor in Eaton Bray (the village is named after him) he also had property in Houghton Regis and Totternhoe. Bray was particularly interested in architecture and buildings and played a major role in designing Henry VII's Chapel at Westminster and St George's Chapel in Windsor Castle. Around 1475 he married Catherine Hussey. He is buried in St George's Chapel, Windsor.

Edward Bouverie Pusey preaches about holiness

Holiness is made for all. It is the end for which we were made; for which we were redeemed; for which God the Holy Ghost is sent down and 'shed abroad in the hearts' which will receive him. God willed not to create us as perfect. He willed that we, through grace, should become perfect. We know not why our free will is so precious in the eyes of God that he waits for us, pleads with us, draws us, allures us, wins us, overpowers us with his love; but he will not force us. He made us to be like him. And what is this but to be holy? 'Be ye holy, for I your God am holy.' The mistake of mistakes is to think that holiness consists in great or extraordinary things beyond the reach of ordinary people. It has been well said, 'Holiness does not consist in doing uncommon things, but in doing common things uncommonly well.' Even in those great saints of God, the things which dazzle us most are not perhaps those which are the most precious in the sight of God…It is not by great things, but by great diligence in little everyday things that thou canst show great love for God, and become greatly holy, and a saint of God. Few ever do great things, and the few who do them can each do but few. But every one can study the will of God and can give great diligence to know it and to do what he knows. Everyone can, by the grace of God, be faithful to what he knows. Your daily round of duty is your daily path to come nearer unto God.

From *Parochial and Cathedral Sermons*

Heavenly Father,
whose servant St Paul called us to present our bodies
as living sacrifices, holy and acceptable to you:
forgive our sins and our self-obsessions,
and fill us anew with your Holy Spirit
that we may live lives worthy of our calling;
through Jesus Christ our Lord. Amen.

Carola Mary Anima Oman 1897–1978

Novelist and biographer

———

CAROLA OMAN WAS the daughter of the military historian Sir Charles Oman and his wife Mary. Carola's final book, *An Oxford Childhood*, describes her home, friends and holidays as an idyllic childhood. Even at a young age she was interested in drama, writing and directing plays for her friends to perform during the holidays. Throughout her life Carola was also a keen photographer. During the First World War, she worked as a probationary nurse in England and France, and these experiences contributed to a book of verse published in 1919. In 1922 she married Gerald Lenanton and settled at Bride Hall, a Jacobean mansion in Ayot St Lawrence, where their neighbour was George Bernard Shaw. During her writing career, which spanned more than fifty years, she produced over thirty books of fiction, history and biography for both adults and children, with a particular emphasis on historical biography. In later life, she was made a Trustee of both the National Maritime Museum and the National Portrait Gallery, and appointed CBE in 1957. She died at Ayot St Lawrence where there is a memorial in the church to both her and her husband.

Carola Oman writes about the life of a clergyman's wife

Visitors often told the Rector's wife that Ayot St Lawrence Parsonage was heavenly, but since this world is not really heaven, she had to confess, looking back, that the first two years of her married life had been embittered by the ungodly character of her servants. She longed for a kitchen which would be a model to the parish, and attendants who would sanctify their daily work by prayer and Bible reading. In 1834 she got the Ellises who were to stay. James was gardener, and his brother Tom was gardener to the Derings. Both had married Elizas. John had officiated at Thomas's wedding to a St Paul's Walden girl. Emma sent her sister a bright-faced pious Somerset girl who sounded perfection. Her fellow-workers found Hester Singer ignorant of the ways of service, pettish when spoken to. But Ellen persevered, finding her teachable, and good in Sunday school. Hester's health failed, after about a year. Eventually she had to be sent back to her native county. She was told it was for a few spring months, but she said farewell sadly to a number of poor people in the village who had come to love her kindness. When she had looked for the last time at the ivied ruin and laurelled schoolhouse her tears had fallen fast. She had died, aged twenty-six, consumptive.

From *Ayot Rectory*

Creator God
inspire, we pray, all writers and poets
that through their art
we may not only understand ourselves better,
but also know you more deeply
and serve you more faithfully;
through your Son,
the Word-made-flesh,
Jesus Christ. Amen.

Peter Clement Moore 1924–94

Dean

———

BORN IN 1924, Peter Moore was educated at Cheltenham College and Christchurch, Oxford. He was ordained to a curacy as a minor canon at Canterbury Cathedral, where he served under the 'Red Dean', Hewlett Johnson. After a second curacy at Bladon he moved back to Oxford where he was chaplain of New College. In 1952 he was appointed Vicar of Alfrick with Lulsley, and shortly afterwards also became librarian of the Hurd Library in Hartlebury Castle, until recently the historic home of the Bishops of Worcester. After several years as Vicar of Pershore, he moved to Ely first as a Canon Residentiary, then Canon Treasurer, and finally as Vice-Dean, before being appointed Dean of St Albans in 1973. He was Dean for twenty years until 1993, during which time he oversaw the restoration of the shrine to St Alban in time for the 1200th anniversary of the foundation of the Benedictine Abbey. He was also responsible for the building of a new, and rather controversial, Chapter House in the late 1970s. Moore was a member of the governing bodies of the Royal School of Church Music and the publishing firm SPCK. He was a passionate gardener. Moore was appointed OBE in 1993. He wrote and edited a number of books, including *Tomorrow is Too Late*; *Man, Woman and Priesthood*; *Footholds in the Faith*; *The Synod of Westminster*; and *Sharing the Glory*. He died in 1994 and is buried in the grounds of St Albans Abbey.

Peter Moore reflects on the need for an historical perspective

This leads us onto the matter of 'roots'. We are living in a society which is desperately in need of them: and I often think that the Church itself forgets to remember its own roots. It is inclined to reflect only too accurately our present rootless society, rather than exercise its proper function of redeeming society. It cannot and must not be wholly identified with society as it is – *we need roots*. It is like the hyacinth bulb. Before we can see any bloom, it has to throw out good and invisible roots; and without that root-system, which is fed by the manure of the past, the bulb cannot appear above the earth, let alone flower. If we keep digging it up, we wreck the root-system. It is far too delicate a thing; a child will dig up a bulb in its enthusiasm to see 'the works' three days after it is planted, and be surprised that there is nothing to see. If the bulb is dug up six weeks later, the child will ruin what it does see, and absolutely prevent the possibility of a flower. Many Christians nowadays approach the Christian faith as if its root-system needed cutting away.

From *Footholds in the Faith*

God of time and eternity,
in whom the past, present and future find their fulfilment:
give us humility to learn from those who have gone before us,
that drawing on their insights,
we may gain wisdom and perspective;
through Jesus Christ our Lord. Amen.

William Hale White 1831–1913

Author and civil servant

———

WILLIAM WHITE WAS born and educated in Bedford where his family worshipped at Bunyan Meeting. When his father became the doorkeeper of the House of Commons the family moved to London. Initially William trained as a Congregational Minister at the Countess of Huntingdon's College in Cheshunt, and later at New College in St John's Wood, London. However, he decided not to be ordained and instead worked as a schoolmaster for a time before becoming a clerk in the Admiralty where he remained for the rest of his life. White began writing to supplement his meagre income. For most of his life he wrote newspaper articles and was well known for his reports on the proceedings in the House of Commons. Later he also wrote novels, but was eager to remain anonymous and adopted the pseudonym Mark Rutherford for each of his six novels. He wrote late at night in order to hide his writing, even keeping it a secret from his invalid wife. He had married Harriet Arthur in 1856, but she died in 1890. At the age of seventy-nine White married again, this time to the novelist Dorothy Smith. He translated Spinoza's book *Ethics* from Latin into English and also wrote books on John Bunyan and William Wordsworth. He died on this day in 1913.

William Hale White writes about self-forgetfulness

Going through a churchyard one afternoon I noticed that nearly all the people who were buried there, if the inscriptions on the tombstones might be taken to represent the thoughts of the departed when they were alive, had been intent solely on their own personal salvation. The question with them all seemed to have been, shall *I* go to heaven? Considering the tremendous difference between heaven and hell in the popular imagination, it was very natural that these poor creatures should be anxious above everything to know whether they would be in hell or heaven for ever. Surely, however, this is not the highest frame of mind, nor is it one to be encouraged. I would rather do all I can to get out of it, and to draw others out of it too. Our aim ought not so much to be the salvation of this poor petty self, but of that in me which alone makes it worth while to save me; of that alone which I hope will be saved, immortal truth. The very centre of the existence of the ordinary chapel-goer and church-goer needs to be shifted from self to what is outside self, and yet is truly self, and the sole truth of self. If the truth lives, we live, and if it dies, we are dead. Our theology stands in need of a reformation greater than that of Luther's. It may be said that the attempt to replace the care for self in us by a care for the universal is ridiculous. Man cannot rise to that height. I do not believe it. I believe we can rise to it. Every ordinary unselfish act is a proof of the capacity to rise to it; and the mother's denial of all care for her own happiness, if she can but make her child happy is a sublime anticipation. It may be called an instinct, but in the course of time it will be possible to develop a wider instinct in us, so that our love for the truth shall be even maternally passionate and self-forgetting.

From *Mark Rutherford's Deliverance*

———

Almighty God, who knows our needs before we ask, and our ignorance in asking:
set free your servants from all anxious thoughts for the morrow;
give us contentment with your good gifts;
and confirm our faith that as we seek your kingdom,
you will not suffer us to lack any good thing;
through Jesus Christ our Lord. Amen.

St Augustine

Nehemiah Grew 1607–88

'Father of plant physiology' and a pioneer of dactyloscopy

———

NEHEMIAH GREW'S FATHER, Obadiah, was Vicar of St Michael's, Coventry. Grew went up to Cambridge and was a student at Pembroke College before undertaking further studies at Leiden University. Initially he worked as a doctor in London, but became fascinated by the physiology of plants. His essay *The Anatomy of Vegetables begun* led to his election as a Fellow of the Royal Society. While continuing his medical practice, he undertook further research which led in 1682 to the publication of his major work *Anatomy of Plants*. This comprised four volumes: *Anatomy of Vegetables begun*, *Anatomy of Roots*, *Anatomy of Trunks* and *Anatomy of Leaves, Flowers, Fruits and Seeds*. Grew wrote many other books including the *Seawater made Fresh*, *Tractatus de Salis*, and *Cosmologia Sacra*. He published a seminal work on pollen and was interested in dactyloscopy, the study of the patterning on human hands and feet. Grew was renowned for his 'religious practices' and died whilst visiting a patient. He is buried at St Mary's Cheshunt in Hertfordshire.

Johan Tangelder marvels at the wonder of creation

Exploring the wonders of nature can be one of the greatest pleasures of a summer holiday. In the complexity of nature we receive hints of the beauty, glory and majesty of God. Throughout the world, there are more than 700,000 species of insects and 250,000 varieties of plants. As Calvin put it, 'wherever you cast your eyes, there is no spot in the universe wherein you cannot discern at least some sparks of [God's] glory.' In creation we see the handiwork of the Designer. God made the sky blue, the grass green, and flowers of various colours and shapes. We look at beautiful and intricate flowers and we say, 'To display beauty: that was the purpose of God creating flowers.' God made birds to sing and trees to bear fruit. By immersion in the realm of the mundane in nature we discover untold marvels. A well-known stanza from one of William Blake's poems captured this point perfectly:

> To see a world in a grain of sand
> And a heaven in a wild flower,
> Hold infinity in the palm of your hand
> And eternity in an hour.

But nature displays not only beauty but also cruelty. We can't refer to nature as 'Mother.' The lamb and the lion are not friends. A cobra still kills. We live in a fallen world which 'waits in eager expectation for the sons of God to be revealed' (Romans 8.19). In other words, meditation on nature alone cannot lead us to an intimate knowledge of God. 'The things which are seen are temporal; but the things which are unseen are eternal' (2 Corinthians 4.18). With Isaac Watts we ask:

> Is this vain world a friend to grace,
> To help me on to God?

From *Reformed Reflections*

———

Eternal Father, source of life and light,
whose love extends to all people, all creatures, and all things:
grant us that reverence of life which becomes those who believe in you;
lest we despise it, degrade it, or come callously to destroy it.
Rather let us save it, serve it, and sanctify it,
after the example of your Son, Jesus Christ our Lord. Amen.

Basil Hume

Alfred Victor Smith 1891–1915

Choirboy and soldier

———

THE VICTORIA CROSS is the highest military decoration awarded for courage in warfare. It is of such importance that it is normally personally awarded to the individual, or to their next of kin, by the monarch at Buckingham Palace. Smith's citation reads:

For most conspicuous bravery. He was in the act of throwing a grenade when it slipped from his hand and fell to the bottom of the trench close to several officers and men. He immediately shouted a warning and jumped clear to safety. He then saw that the officers and men were unable to find cover and knowing that the grenade was due to explode at any moment, he returned and flung himself upon it. He was instantly killed by the explosion. His magnificent act of self-sacrifice undoubtedly saved many lives.

Soon after his birth in Guildford, Smith's family moved to St Albans, where he sang in the Cathedral Choir. In 1905 his father was appointed Chief Constable of Burnley and so the family moved north. Alfred joined the police and at the start of the war enlisted as a second lieutenant in the 1/5th East Lancashire Regiment. He was sent to the front line at Helles in Gallipoli on the coast of north-west Turkey. Smith is buried in Twelve Tree Copse Cemetery. For his courage he was also awarded the French Croix de Guerre. His bravery is still commemorated in a framed tribute which hangs in the Song School in St Albans Abbey: 'He glorified God by his voice as a Chorister in this Cathedral and by his death in the trenches of Gallipoli, when he laid down his life for his friends.'

At a Calvary near the Ancre

One ever hangs where shelled roads part.
In this war He too lost a limb,
But His disciples hide apart;
And now the Soldiers bear with Him.

Near Golgotha strolls many a priest,
And in their faces there is pride
That they were flesh-marked by the Beast
By whom the gentle Christ's denied.

The scribes on all the people shove
And bawl allegiance to the state,
But they who love the greater love
Lay down their life; they do not hate.

Wilfred Owen

———

Almighty God,
we long for the time when your kingdom shall come on earth:
when all people shall acknowledge your sovereignty,
seek your glory, and serve your good and righteous will.
Help us not only to pray but also to work for that new day;
and enable us by your grace to promote the cause of
justice and peace, truth and freedom,
both in our society and in the life of the world;
for the honour of Christ, our Saviour and our Lord. Amen.

Adapted from a prayer by Frank Colquhoun

Arthur Hinsley 1865–1943

Cardinal and ecumenist

———

ARTHUR HINSLEY SPENT most of his early years in the north of England, having been born at Carlton, near Selby, the son of a local carpenter. From the age of eleven, he studied at Ushaw College, the seminary near Durham, and where in later life he was to teach for a period. He completed his formation at the English College in Rome and was ordained in 1893. In 1900 he founded St Bede's Grammar School and served as its first headmaster for four years, before spending the next eleven years back in Rome as Rector of the English College. Hinsley was consecrated as a bishop in 1926 and in the following year appointed the Apostolic Visitor to British Africa. However, after seven years there, ill-health forced him to retire. To the surprise of many, he was called out of retirement in 1934 to become the fifth Archbishop of Westminster and two years later was made a Cardinal. During the Second World War, Hinsley spoke out courageously against totalitarianism and fascism, and became famous in homes throughout the land for his wartime radio chats and stirring encouragement. He was a committed ecumenist. Archbishop William Temple said he was 'a most devoted citizen of his country…a most kindly and warmhearted friend.' He died on this day in Buntingford in Hertfordshire and is buried in St Joseph's Chapel in Westminster Cathedral.

Arthur Hinsley calls Christians to witness to their faith

The Sword of the Spirit is the title of our campaign. This phrase of St Paul imposes on us the duty to see that our activity is first and foremost and all the time a vigorous spiritual effort if we are to contribute our small share in restoring true peace in the world. We ourselves must 'take unto us the armour of God' that we may be able to stand against the deceits of the devil. 'For our wrestling is not against flesh and blood; but against principalities and powers, against the rulers of the world of this darkness, against the spirits of wickedness in the high places.' The fight is keen as never before for God and for all we hold dear. God wills it, God is with us. But we must be with Him. We must turn to Him 'by all prayer and supplication, praying at all times in the spirit, and in the same watching with all instance and supplication for all the saints…' The Cross is our standard. The Cross is the pledge of victory. You have all gathered here because you can all play a part in this fight for truth, justice, and freedom. You can all play your part in defence of the supreme values of Christian civilisation. The Spirit divides His gifts to each according to His will to use them. Some can give their gift of speech, or pen, to the great cause. But all can devote their lives to Christian faith and discipline. And prayer is a sword every one, hale or sick, learned or unlearned, can wield against evil.

From *Launching the Sword of the Spirit*

We thank you for those leaders who in times of conflict
speak out fearlessly against evil and injustice.
Give us the grace and courage to stand up for what is right,
to defend the weak and to protect the vulnerable;
and hasten in the day when your kingdom will come on earth as it is in heaven;
through Jesus Christ our Lord. Amen.

Elizabeth Wigg 18th century

Benefactor

———

THE ORIGINS OF the village of Heath and Reach lie in two tiny hamlets in the Royal Manor of Leighton. Records refer to Heath as early as 1220 and to Reach in 1216. We first come across the Wigg family in 1639 when William Wigg, described as a 'yeoman', bought Stewkley Grange which had formerly been in the possession of Woburn Abbey. Originally Heath Chapel was in private hands but towards the end of the seventeenth century it came into the ownership of Richard Wigg. There is still a bell in the tower which bears the inscription 'Richard Wigg, Gentman, Owner of Me, 1695'. The church also possesses two pewter alms dishes inscribed, 'I do belonge to the Chappelle of Heath and Reach, 1697'. When Richard died he left his property to his daughter, Elizabeth, who in 1703 married John Frank. Two years later she gave 'her little Chappell and cell' as a gift 'to the inhabitants of the hamlets of Heath and Reach, their heirs and successors, together with the land it stands upon, with access through her close', on condition that they 'kept it in good repair for ever and ever'. Until 1850 the church was in the ecclesiastical parish of Leighton Buzzard and it was there that the parishioners had to be baptised, married and buried. The main body of the church was rebuilt in 1829 although the sixteenth-century tower survives.

James Woodforde's diary describes rural church life in the eighteenth century

Feb 9 I buried one John Greaves of East Tuddenham this afternoon at Weston – received for burying him as he was a stranger the sum of 6s 8d and which I gave back to his widow as she is poor and has many children.

Feb 14 To 36 children being Valentine's Day and what is customary for them to go about in these parts this day gave 3s being one penny apiece to each of them.

Mar 23 I read prayers and preached this morning at Weston. I gave notice this morning at church that there would be prayers on Friday night being Good Friday – there used to be none that day, which I think was very wrong.

Mar 25 My great pond full of large toads, I never saw such a quantity in my life and so large, was most of the morning in killing them.

Mar 28 I read prayers this morning at Weston church at 11 o'clock. No sermon. I had a tolerably good congregation. I did not dine today being Good Friday till 5 in the afternoon, and then eat only a few apple fritters and some bread and cheese.

Apr 6 I read prayers and administered the Holy Sacrament this morning at Weston. No sermon. My clerk Js Smith dined here today being Sacrament Day. About 9 o'clock this evening I saw in the element a prodigious Light, exactly the form of a Rainbow and near the breadth but vast deal larger…I apprehended it to be the Northern Lights, but I never saw them in that form before.

Heavenly Father, we thank you for our rich heritage of buildings,
for our forebears and past benefactors
who gave so sacrificially for their construction:
grant that as we gather in our churches week by week
we may worship you in spirit and in truth,
and be built into a living temple to your glory;
through Jesus Christ our Lord. Amen.

Thomas Ken 1637–1711

Bishop, non-juror and hymn writer

———

BORN IN LITTLE Berkhamsted, Thomas Ken was a pupil at Winchester College before studying at Hart Hall (the present-day Hertford College) and New College, Oxford. He was ordained in 1662 and ministered first in Essex, then on the Isle of Wight, and then at East Woodhay in the Diocese of Winchester. It was while a Fellow of Winchester College that he began to compose prayers and hymns. He served as chaplain to Charles II for two years before in 1685 being consecrated Bishop of Bath and Wells. With the king's death and the accession of the Roman Catholic James II, the new king proposed to rescind the Restoration penal laws and Ken, along with six other bishops, refused to comply. Ken was imprisoned, tried and acquitted. Such was his integrity that, when the king abandoned the throne and fled to France, and the throne was offered to the king's Protestant daughter Mary and her husband William of Orange, Ken felt unable in good conscience to forswear his oath to James as his living, anointed monarch. Hence Ken's title: 'non-juror'. As a result he was deprived of his See and lived in retirement for twenty years at Longleat House. Ken wrote much poetry, several books and many familiar hymns such as *Awake, my soul, and with the sun* and *Glory to Thee, my God, this night*. He died on this day in 1711.

A description of Thomas Ken's funeral in Frome, Somerset

When he was buried as dawn was breaking, the village children he had loved to teach gathered round his grave. They sang his verses:

> Glory to Thee who safe has kept
> And has refreshed me while I slept.
> Grant, Lord, when I from death shall wake
> I may of endless light partake.

And as they sang, the gloom was suddenly dispersed and upon the coffin and upon their own fresh faces, shone the radiant light of the rising sun. It was an augury of the future, of the glory that was to shine around Ken's memory, who in the turmoil of events had lived a life of uncompromising goodness in the surety of 'I can do all things through Christ which strengtheneth me.' No creed is complete, no historical event free from imperfection, no school of thought but has its critics; only the creation of character is the perfect answer to the mystery of existence. For though temporal disaster may overwhelm the Pilgrims and the kingdoms of the earth be destroyed by the vanity of men, something greater than themselves inspires to fresh endeavour each rising generation. A faith in God's abiding love and the courage to endure until faith passes into sight are based not upon theories nor achievements, but upon God's own promise, his sign-manual set ever and again upon the sequence of events that make up history, his own seal, the life of a good man.

From *Faith of our Fathers* by Florence Higham

———

Wherever I am, whatever I do, thou, Lord, seest me:
O keep me in thy fear all day long.
Lord, give me grace to keep always a conscience
void of offence towards thee and towards men.
Lord, teach me so to number my days,
that I may apply my heart to wisdom.
O let my mouth be filled with thy praise,
that I may sing of thy glory and honour all the day long. Amen.

Thomas Ken

Hannah Buxton 1783–1872

A godly grandmother

———

NONE OF US know the full effect of our prayers. So it was for Hannah Buxton who in 1868 wrote to her grandson as they moved into Easneye Mansion near Ware that the house 'might ever inhabited by faithful servants of God…that Christ might be honoured and served there…and that this place be a fountain of blessing to the church and to the world.' Little did she know that the house was later to become the home of All Nations Christian College, which for many years has been one of the most important training colleges for Christian missionaries in the United Kingdom. Hannah was born in 1783. Her brother was the well-known Quaker, Joseph John Gurney, and her sister was the prison reformer Elizabeth Fry. Hannah married Thomas Fowell Buxton, the anti-slavery campaigner and they had twelve children whom they brought up in the Christian faith. We have accounts of the whole family gathering together in the main hall for Bible reading and prayer each day. Her grandson was the missionary Barclay Fowell Buxton – see the entry for 20 September.

Martin Luther preaches about the life and example of the elderly Anna

'And there was one Anna, a prophetess, the daughter of Phanuel of the tribe of Asher (she was of a great age, having lived with a husband seven years from her virginity, and she had been a widow even unto fourscore and four years), who departed not from the temple, worshipping with fastings and supplications night and day.' Here some might say: From the example of Anna you see that good works are exalted, as for instance fasting and praying and going to church, therefore they must not be condemned. But who has ever condemned good works? We only reject hypocritical and spurious good works. Fasting, praying, going to church are good works, if they are done in the right spirit. But the trouble is that these blockheads explain the Scriptures so awkwardly, noticing only the works and examples of the saints and thinking that now they are able to learn from them and imitate them. Thus they become nothing but apes and hypocrites, for they do not perceive that the Scriptures speak more of the heart than of the deeds of men. The sacrifice and works of Abel are praised in Scripture, but he himself a great deal more. They however disregard the person and observe only the example, take notice of the works and pay no heed to faith, eat the bran and throw away the flour, as we read in Hosea 3.1: 'They turn unto other gods, and love cakes of raisins.' If you desire to fast and pray like Anna, well and good. But take good care that first of all you imitate her character, and then her works.

From *Of Simeon and Anna*

———

Lord Jesus Christ,
who was nurtured in the loving care of Joseph and Mary:
strengthen family life,
that parents may love and cherish their children,
that children may honour and respect their mothers and fathers;
be especially close to those who have no earthly family,
and grant that they may come to know the tender love of our heavenly Father;
we ask this for your name's sake. Amen.

Edmund Cosin c.1510–c.1574

Vice-Chancellor of Cambridge University

———

EDMUND COSIN LIVED through turbulent times. We do not know where in Bedfordshire he was born, but we do know that he studied as a Bible clerk at King's Hall, Cambridge, soon to be amalgamated with Michaelhouse and form Trinity College. He graduated in 1535 and was ordained. In 1538 Cosin was inducted into the living of Grendon in Northamptonshire. Three years later he returned to Cambridge to take up a fellowship at King's Hall, followed by a fellowship at St Catharine's Hall, and then back at Henry VIII's new foundation of Trinity College. His gifts were recognised when in 1554 he was elected Master of St Catharine's, which he held in plurality with several ecclesiastical livings. He received further preferment when he was elected Vice-Chancellor of the University in 1558. However, in that year Elizabeth I came to the throne and Cosin was not prepared to conform to the new Anglican settlement, so he resigned. Rather than have to deny his Catholic faith he went to live in exile.

Thomas Cranmer writes about God's grace

All men desire to have God's favour, and when they know the contrary, that they be in his indignation, and cast out of his favour, what thing can comfort them? How be their minds vexed! What trouble is in their consciences! All God's creatures seem to be against them, and do make them afraid, as things being ministers of God's wrath and indignation towards them, and rest or comfort can they find none, neither within them, nor without them. And in this case they do hate as well God, as the devil; God as an unmerciful and extreme judge, and the devil as a most malicious and cruel tormentor. And in this sorrowful heaviness, holy scripture teacheth them that our heavenly Father can by no means be pleased with them again, but by the sacrifice and death of his only-begotten Son, whereby God hath made a perpetual amity and peace with us, doth pardon our sins of them that believe in him, maketh them his children, and giveth them to his first-begotten Son Christ, to be incorporate into him, to be saved by him, and to be made heirs of heaven with him. And in the receiving of the holy supper of our Lord, we be put in remembrance of this his death, and of the whole mystery of our redemption. In the which supper is made mention of his testament, and of the aforesaid communion of us with Christ, and of the remission of our sins by his sacrifice upon the cross. Wherefore in this sacrament (if it be rightly received with a true faith) we be assured that our sins be forgiven, and the league of peace and the testament of God is confirmed between him and us, so that whosoever by a true faith doth eat Christ's flesh and drink his blood, hath everlasting life by him.

From *Miscellaneous Writings and Letters of Thomas Cranmer* by J. E. Cox

———

Heavenly Father,
who has promised us forgiveness
through the death and resurrection of your Son:
grant that as we partake of the bread of the messianic banquet
and the wine of the new covenant
we may be drawn afresh to the wonder of your grace.
Set us free from all that divides us
and equip us for your service
that we might be worthy of our calling;
for the sake of Jesus Christ our Lord. Amen.

Edmund 1249–1300

Earl of Cornwall

———

EDMUND WAS BORN at Berkhamsted Castle, the son of Earl Richard of Cornwall. In 1257 he joined his parents on a visit to Germany to pursue his father's nominal title as king and claimant to the Holy Roman Empire. In 1271 Edmund sailed with his cousin Edmund Crouchback to join the Crusades, but his father ordered him to return to England following the death of Edmund's elder brother, Henry. Edmund married Margaret, sister of the Earl of Gloucester, in the chapel at Ruislip. In October 1272, following the death of his father, Edmund was knighted by Henry III at Westminster Abbey and invested as Earl of Cornwall. When Henry III died, Edmund took on a role in the governing council of England until Edward I returned from the Crusades, and later during the king's absences abroad Edmund acted as Regent. Edmund was deeply religious. He set up a college of secular priests at Ashridge, between Aldbury and Little Gaddesden, which was later to become an order of Augustinian Bonshommes. After his death, Edmund's heart and flesh were buried at the priory there. Both during his life and in his will Edmund endowed a large number of abbeys and churches, and also left money to several religious orders.

Dom Denys Prideaux OSB meditates on Christian prayer

The Cross is the only key to prayer. You will never pray well unless you take the hammer and nails, and the spear and the thorns, and the hyssop dipped in vinegar, and go to Golgotha stripped and bare, and in physical agony as well as agony of mind and soul, re-enact the crucifixion in your own members, making up what is behind of the sufferings of Christ. You can only plead through lips that were once parched and cracked and stained with blood – your prayer can only be heard if it is joined to that stream of intercession that pours forth unceasingly in heaven from One who once was 'slain'. Impassible though he be now, he is not unfeeling, and his very memories of Good Friday wing your prayers. Oh yes; the Transfiguration Light may dazzle, and the soul sigh for the sweet cool converse of God walking in the evening peace of Eden, but there is no road to Eden except through the bloodsweat of Gethsemane and Calvery's long-drawn cry in the dark night of the soul – 'My God, My God, why hast thou forsaken Me?'

From 'Prayer and Contemplation' in *Laudate*

———

Most merciful God,
who by the death and resurrection of your Son Jesus Christ
delivered and saved the world:
grant that by faith in him who suffered on the cross
we may triumph in the power of his victory;
through Jesus Christ your Son our Lord, who is alive and reigns with you,
in the unity of the Holy Spirit, one God, now and for ever. Amen.

The Collect for the Fifth Sunday in Lent, *Common Worship*

Thomas Herring 1693–1757

Rectory of Barley and Archbishop of Canterbury

———

ONE OF THE main claims to fame of the small village of Barley in Hertfordshire is that two of its rectors have become Archbishops of Canterbury: Thomas Herring and William Warham (see 17 October). Herring was taught at Wisbech Grammar School and then studied at Jesus College, Cambridge. After he graduated he became a Fellow of Corpus Christi College until 1723. His abilities were recognised early on as he was made a chaplain to King George II in 1728. He was consecrated Bishop of Bangor in 1737 and, six years later in 1743, translated to become Archbishop of York. Herring's reputation was strengthened considerably during the Jacobite uprisings in September 1743 when he spoke powerfully in support of the king and helped raise an army to crush the rebels. He was strongly in favour of the Protestant Succession. Herring was appointed Archbishop of Canterbury in 1747. Some scholars believe that he was the author of *A New Form of Common Prayer* which was published anonymously in 1753. He died on this day in 1757.

Matthew 5.7. Blessed are the merciful: for they shall obtain mercy

The virtue of mercy, to the practice of which we are exhorted in the text, is one of the great duties of natural religion; I call it a *great* duty, because, whether we judge of its importance from its suitableness to the nature of the Deity, and his rules of acting in the creation, or from its friendliness to human society, or its usefulness to every individual, we shall find it equal to, if not exceeding in its influence and perfection, every other virtue. Our Saviour therefore, upon this great and solemn occasion, when he is delivering the substance of his doctrine for the instruction and observance of the world, takes care to distinguish this virtue, to give it a principal place in his system of religion, and to recommend it to the practice of men, as the best and happiest thing they can do for themselves or others – *Blessed are the merciful: for they shall obtain mercy.*

From a sermon by Thomas Herring preached on the Monday of Easter Week, 1739

———

Blessed are you, the Father of mercies and the God of all comfort,
who strengthens us in our suffering
that we might bring consolation to others:
grant us gifts of love and mercy,
that we may draw near to those in need
to offer them your healing and your hope;
through Jesus Christ our Lord. Amen.

Based on 2 Corinthians 1.2–4

Mary Augusta Ward 1851–1920

Novelist and philanthropist

———

THE GRANDDAUGHTER OF Thomas Arnold, headmaster of Rugby School, Mary Augusta Arnold was born in Tasmania. The family returned to England when she was five and she was sent to boarding school. Mary married Humphrey Ward, an editor and writer who was also a fellow and tutor of Brasenose College, Oxford. She was an accomplished linguist, both in modern European languages as well as in Greek and Latin, and began her literary career by contributing articles to the *Dictionary of Christian Biography*. She also wrote children's books, magazine articles and novels. Most of her books had a strong religious element and they were particularly popular in the United States. In 1908, Ward was one of the founders of the Women's National Anti-Suffrage League and became its first President, creating and editing the *Anti-Suffrage Review*. She used two of her novels to criticise the suffragettes. Mary Ward was involved in philanthropy, not least in the East End of London where she was one of the founders of what is now known as the Mary Ward Settlement, which provided sports facilities for children and a school for the physically handicapped. She was one of a group of people who helped set up Somerville College in Oxford to educate young ladies. She was also well known in the village of Aldbury, where she worshipped in the village church and where she visited the sick and organised entertainments. She died on this day in 1920. Her funeral service was conducted by Dean Inge of St Paul's Cathedral who considered her to be 'perhaps the greatest Englishwoman of our time'. Ward is buried in the churchyard at Aldbury, not far from her home called Stocks.

Archbishop Edwin Sandys preaches about love

The debt of love is natural and continual. We all owe it, and we owe it unto all. And unto whom we owe it we never pay it, except we acknowledge that we owe it still. In this debt of love we must consider why we must love, whom we must love, and lastly, how we must love. To omit the reasons drawn from nature, this one taken from the God of nature shall suffice. We must love because God hath so commanded, and because it is the fulfilling of all his commandments. 'I give you a new commandment,' saith Christ, 'that ye love one another' (John 13.34). In our new birth or regeneration we are made brethren and fellow-heirs with Christ of God's kingdom. As God therefore for ever loveth us in Christ, so we ought to love our brethren for God, and in Christ, for ever. If ye will be known to be his servants, by this men shall know you. If ye will be counted not hearers only, but also doers of the law, the law is love. He that loveth another fulfilleth the law.

From a sermon *The Debt of Love* edited by J. Ayre

Heavenly Father, kindle in our hearts such love
for you and for our neighbours
that our lives may reflect your very being,
which is love itself;
through Jesus Christ our Lord. Amen.

Nicholas Hawksmoor c.1661–1736

Architect

———

L ITTLE IS KNOWN about Hawksmoor's upbringing in Nottinghamshire other than he was born into a farming family and became fascinated by architecture at an early age. However, we do know that around 1678 he went to London and became a clerk to Christopher Wren. By 1683 he was Wren's Deputy Surveyor at the Royal Hospital in Chelsea and soon after he was working with Wren on Greenwich Hospital, St Paul's Cathedral and Hampton Court Palace. Later on Hawksmoor collaborated with Sir John Vanbrugh on the building of Blenheim Palace and Castle Howard. Hawksmoor never travelled abroad to be influenced by Italianate fashion. Instead, much of his Roman classical style was gained through close study of books. Also, unlike his peers, he made his name with church and university architecture, rather than building houses for the wealthy. Following Wren's death in 1723, Hawksmoor became the surveyor of Westminster Abbey. He died on this day in 1736 and is buried in Shenley.

Origen preaches about being built into a living temple

All of us who believe in Christ Jesus are said to be living stones, according to the words of Scripture: But you are living stones, built as a spiritual house in a holy priesthood, that you may offer spiritual sacrifices acceptable to God through Jesus Christ. When we look at an earthly building, we can see that the larger and stronger stones are the first to be set in place as the foundation, so that the weight of the whole structure may rest on them securely. In the same way understand that some of the living stones become the foundation of the spiritual building. What are these living stones placed in the foundation? They are the apostles and prophets. That is what Paul says when he teaches: We have been built upon the foundation of the apostles and prophets, with our Lord Jesus Christ himself as the cornerstone. You, my hearers, must learn that Christ himself is also the foundation of the building we are now describing, so that you may prepare yourselves more eagerly for the construction of this building and become stones that lie closer to the foundation. As the apostle Paul says: No foundation can be laid other than the one that has been laid already: I mean Christ Jesus. Blessed are those, therefore, who build a religious and holy structure upon such a noble foundation. In this building of the Church, there must also be an altar. I think that if those of you, disposed and eager for prayer, offer petitions and prayers of supplication to God day and night, you will become the living stones for the altar which Jesus is building.

From *A homily on the Book of Joshua*

———

We pray, O God, for the fellowship of the Spirit,
who unites us in the bond of peace as members of the one Body.
Deepen our communion one with another in Christ,
and grant that through your Spirit continually working in us
we may daily increase in the knowledge of your love,
and learn to love our brothers and sisters
with the love you have shown to us in Jesus Christ our Lord. Amen.

Anonymous

Roger Pemberton 1555–1627

Founder of almshouses

———

ROGER PEMBERTON WAS born in 1555 and went up to study at St John's College, Cambridge. Following graduation, he moved to St Albans where he became a prominent burgess. Pemberton had considerable business interests in London and in 1588 he was one of the contributors to the defence against the Spanish Armada. Pemberton was made High Sheriff of Hertfordshire in 1618. He married Elizabeth Moore in 1579 and their six children were all baptised in St Peter's Church, St Albans, where there is still a memorial to the family. Shortly before his death he purchased the manor of Wotton Shelton, in Bedfordshire, and became Lord of the Manor. He also owned extensive lands in the parishes of St Peter and St Stephen in St Albans. In his will, dated 1624, Pemberton left money to build some almshouses on his land in Bowgate in St Peter's Street. This act of charity was reputedly in atonement for an accident when he killed a 'poore widowe' with a bow and arrow. He left an endowment to maintain the almshouses and to provide food and clothing for the widows. These benefits did not come without conditions. If any of the widows caused problems or were difficult, their allowance was withdrawn for a period. They also had to attend worship at St Peter's Church each Sunday.

John Chrysostom offers some thoughts on probity

Let each of us, with an informed conscience, enter into a review of our actions, and bring our whole life before our minds for assessment and try to discern whether we are deserving of correction or punishment. When we are indignant that somebody whom we reckon guilty of various crimes escapes with impunity, let us first reflect upon our own faults, and perhaps our indignation will cease. Crimes appear great because they usually involve great or notorious matters; but once we inquire into our own actions, we will perhaps find numerous other matters for concern. For example, to steal or to defraud a person is the same thing: the gravity of the offence is not lessened by whether it is gold or silver that is at stake. In either case it is the attitude of mind that is the root cause. A person who steals a small object will not baulk at the chance of stealing something bigger. If he does not steal, it is probably because he lacks the opportunity. A poor man who robs a poorer person would not hesitate to rob the rich given half the chance. His forbearance issues simply from weakness, not from choice.

From *Homily 3 on the second Epistle to Timothy*

Generous God, you have placed us in a world of abundance
and provided for all our needs.
Grant us a spirit of thankfulness,
and implant within us the seeds of compassion,
that as we have received from your bounty,
so we may share what we have with others;
for the sake of Jesus Christ our Lord. Amen.

John Dunstaple c.1390–1453

Composer, astronomer and mathematician

———

ALTHOUGH HIS MUSIC is rarely performed today, Dunstaple was one of the most famous composers of his day. His compositions were performed widely across Europe and manuscripts of his music have survived in Italy and Germany. About fifty works are attributed to him, including settings of the mass, motets, hymns and other liturgical texts. It is thought that he composed his motet *Albanus roseo rutilat* for the Duke of Bedford's visit to St Albans Abbey in 1426. In addition to his musical compositions, Dunstaple was also known for his writings on astronomy and mathematics. Details of his life are sketchy. It is clear that he was highly educated although we do not know where he studied. It is thought that he may have been in the service of John of Lancaster and, at a later date, in the service of Humphrey, Duke of Gloucester, who is buried in St Albans Abbey. Taxation records reveal that he owned properties in Hertfordshire, Cambridgeshire, London, Essex and Normandy. He is buried in St Stephen's Church, Walbrook, in London.

Thomas Merton writes about art and worship

If the Church has emphasised the function of art in her public prayer, it has been because she knew that a true and valid aesthetic formation was necessary for the wholeness of Christian living and worship. The liturgy and the chant and Church art are all supposed to form and spiritualise man's consciousness, to give him a tone and a maturity without which his prayer cannot normally be either very deep or very wide or very pure. There is only one reason why this is completely true: art is not an end in itself. It introduces the soul into a higher spiritual order, which it expresses and in some sense explains. Music and art and poetry attune the soul to God because they induce a kind of contact with the Creator and Ruler of the Universe. The genius of the artist finds its way by the affinity of creative sympathy, or con-naturality, into the living law that rules the universe. This law is nothing but the secret gravitation that draws all things to God as to their centre. Since all true art lays bare the action of this same law in the depths of our own nature, it makes us alive to the tremendous mystery of being in which we ourselves, together with all other living and existing things, come forth from the depths of God and return again to him.

From *No Man Is An Island*

———

Holy and eternal God,
whose glory cherubim and seraphim
and all the hosts of heaven proclaim:
sanctify and bless, we beseech thee,
the music of our worship and all who make it;
and grant that the service that we can only offer unworthily here
we may enjoy perfectly in thy heavenly kingdom;
through Jesus Christ our Lord. Amen.

Anonymous

George Gilbert Scott 1811–78

Architect

———

THE CHURCHES OF Christ Church Little Heath, All Saints Leavesden, St John Bourne End, Holy Trinity Frogmore, St Mary Childwick Green and All Saints Ridgmont were all designed by George Gilbert Scott. During his long career he was architect of more than eight hundred buildings and renovated many others, including the churches at Ickleford, Eversholt and Sarratt. He designed the chancel at St Thomas of Canterbury Clapham and drew up the plans for the Orchard Mead Almshouses in Ridge. The Albert Memorial in London stands as one of his most famous landmarks. Scott was also interested in furnishings, and designed the pulpit and communion rails in St James, Thorley. Scott was born in Gawcott in Buckinghamshire in 1811. His grandfather was the biblical commentator Thomas Scott. He trained as an architect under James Edmeston, but soon came under the influence of Pugin which led to his interest in the Gothic Revival Movement. Scott was appointed Professor of Architecture at the Royal Academy and was knighted in 1872. He wrote a number of books including *A Plea for the Faithful Restoration of our Ancient Churches*. In 1838 he married Caroline Oldrid. Two of their sons and one of their grandsons became influential architects. He is buried in Westminster Abbey.

George Herbert stresses the importance of caring for our churches

The Country Parson hath a special care of his church that all things there be decent and befitting his Name by which it is called. Therefore first he takes order that all things be in good repair; as walls plastered, windows glazed, floor paved, seats whole, firm and uniform, especially that the pulpit, and desk, and communion table and font be as they ought, for those great duties that are performed in them. Secondly, that the church be swept and kept clean without dust or cobwebs, and at great festivals strawed and stuck with boughs and perfumed with incense. Thirdly, that there be fit and proper texts of Scripture everywhere painted, and that all the painting be grave and reverend, not with light colours or foolish antics. Fourthly, that all the books appointed by authority be there, and those not torn or fouled, but whole and clean and well bound; and that there be a fitting and sightly communion cloth of fine linen, with an handsome and seemly carpet of good and costly stuff or cloth, and all kept sweet and clean in a strong and decent chest with a chalice and cover, and a stoop or flagon; and a basin for alms and offerings, besides which he hath a poor-man's box conveniently sited to receive the charity of well-minded people, and to lay up treasure for the sick and needy. And all this he doth, not as out of necessity, but as desiring to keep the middle way between superstition and slovenliness.

From *A Country Parson*

———

We thank you for our church buildings,
standing in the heart of our communities,
visual symbols of your presence in our midst.
We thank you for those who designed and built them,
and for those who still care for them.
Grant that our churches may be places of welcome,
where all may experience the good news of your love,
and hear your truth proclaimed;
we ask this in the name of Jesus Christ our Lord. Amen.

Thomas Coram c.1668–1751

Philanthropist

———

THE THOMAS CORAM School in Berkhamsted is named after an important eighteenth-century philanthropist. Captain Thomas Coram is best remembered for founding the Foundling Hospital in Bloomsbury, London, to care for abandoned children. It is thought to be the world's first incorporated charity. Coram was born in Lyme Regis and spent much of his early life at sea. For a period he ran a shipbuilding business in Massachusetts and later became a successful merchant in London. It was here that his philanthropic streak came to the fore, horrified at the number of homeless children living on the city's streets. In 1739 Coram obtained a Royal Charter to establish 'a hospital for the maintenance and education of exposed and deserted young children.' The Foundling Hospital was completed in 1745. William Hogarth, who painted a famous portrait of Coram, was one of the first governors of the hospital and with some fellow artists decorated the Governors' Court Room. As a result, the Foundling Hospital also became the first art gallery open to the public. The composer George Frideric Handel donated the manuscript of his famous Hallelujah Chorus to the hospital. The original hospital building is now the Thomas Coram Foundation for Children.

Geoffrey Studdert Kennedy writes about the nature of God's love

We call it charity when men gave away what they did not want themselves in order to patch up evils and ameliorate bad conditions which their greed, slackness, or stupidity have helped to create. This is not charity, and it is blasphemy to call it by that splendid name. We call it charity when we give a poor devil half a crown to get shut of him and rid ourselves of the sight of his misery, that is blasphemy too. Real charity is not easy, it is always hard, it means that we must be ready to take time, trouble, and infinite pains to create life. The business man who seeks to give good value for money, who prides himself on his fellow workers in the business, and whose aim is to see that by efficiency, and energy, his business produces and sustains fine life, he is the charitable man. Our faith is that God is Charity – that his charity is so great that he spares himself no suffering and no agony in order to create in the world fine life. We are meant to be like him.

From *The New Man in Christ*

We thank you for the gift of children,
for their spontaneous trust and curiosity,
their boundless energy and enthusiasm:
grant that as a society and as a church
we may protect and nurture all young people
that they may grow up
to know and love you, the Living God;
through Jesus Christ our Lord. Amen.

Elizabeth Bowes-Lyon 1900–2002

Queen Elizabeth the Queen Mother

———

ELIZABETH ANGELA MARGUERITE Bowes-Lyon was the ninth of ten children of Lord Glamis and his wife Cecilia. Born at their country house, St Paul's Walden Bury, in Hertfordshire, she was christened in the parish church of All Saints. In 1904 her father inherited the title of 14th Earl of Strathmore and Kinghorne and, as a result, she became Lady Elizabeth Bowes-Lyon. Her childhood was divided between Glamis Castle and Hertfordshire. When she married the second son of King George V and Queen Mary, Albert, Prince of York, she never dreamed that one day she would be Queen herself. As Duchess of York she was known as the 'Smiling Duchess' because of her demeanour. In 1936 following the abdication of Edward VIII and the accession of her husband to the throne as King George VI, she and her family were unexpectedly thrust into the limelight. During the Second World War she was described by Adolf Hitler as 'the most dangerous woman in Europe' as her indomitable spirit provided moral support to the nation. Not long after the end of the war, when Elizabeth was only fifty-one, her husband died. She was to spend more years as a widow than she had as a wife. She oversaw the restoration of the Castle of Mey where she spent August each year. One of her passions was horse racing and she owned many winning horses. She died on this day in 2002 at the age of 101.

From The Admonitions of St Francis of Assisi

'I did not come to be served but to serve' says the Lord. Those who are placed over others should glory in such an office only as much as they would were they assigned the task of washing the feet of the brothers. And the more they are upset about their office being taken from them than they would be over the loss of the office of washing feet, so much the more do they store up treasures to the peril of their souls. Be conscious, O man, of the wondrous state in which the Lord God has placed you, for he created you and formed you to the image of his beloved Son according to the body, and to his likeness according to the spirit. And yet all the creatures under heaven, each according to its nature, serve, know, and obey their creator better than you. And even the demons did not crucify him, but you together with them have crucified him and crucify him even now by delighting in vices and sins.

From *Francis and Clare* edited by Armstrong and Brady

Generous God,
who has taught us through your Son
that from those to whom much has been given,
much will be expected;
and from those to whom much is entrusted, much will be asked:
give grace to all in positions of influence,
to use their gifts and energy for the good of others;
for Jesus Christ's sake. Amen.

John Donne 1572–1631

Poet, politician, lawyer and cleric

———

'FOR WHOM THE bell tolls', 'No man is an island' and 'Death comes equally to us all, and makes us all equal when it comes' are some of the familiar phrases that originate from the pen of John Donne, one of the most important of the Metaphysical Poets. The son of a Catholic, John Donne was born in dangerous times. A number of his relatives were either executed or sent into exile because of their faith. Donne studied at both Oxford and Cambridge Universities, as well as at Lincoln's Inn. Whilst travelling abroad, Donne squandered most of his inheritance and as a consequence spent much of his adult life in poverty, relying on the generosity of wealthy friends. Upon his return to England, he was appointed Chief Secretary to Sir Thomas Egerton, Lord Keeper of the Great Seal, whose niece Donne married in 1601. This led to his dismissal, as the marriage was against her father's wishes. Donne was elected Member of Parliament for Brackley in 1602, and was then ordained in 1615 at King James's behest. In 1621 he was appointed both Rector of Blunham in Bedfordshire and Dean of St Paul's Cathedral in London, positions he held until his death ten years later. He donated a paten and chalice to Blunham church. As well as his poetry, no less than one hundred and sixty of his sermons survive.

Litany to the Father, the Son and the Holy Ghost

Father of Heaven, and Him, by whom
It, and us for it, and all else for us,
Thou madest, and govern'st ever, come
And re-create me, now grown ruinous:
My heart is by dejection, clay, and by self-murder, red.
From this red earth, O Father, purge away
All vicious tinctures, that new-fashioned
I may rise up from death, before I'm dead.

O Son of God, who, seeing two things,
Sin and Death, crept in, which were never made,
By bearing one, tried'st with what stings
The other could Thine heritage invade;
O be Thou nail'd unto my heart, and crucified again;
Part not from it, though it from Thee would part,
But let it be by applying so Thy pain,
Drown'd in Thy blood, and in Thy passion slain.

O Holy Ghost, whose temple I
Am, but of mud walls, and condensèd dust,
And being sacrilegiously
Half wasted with youth's fires, of pride and lust,
Must with new storms be weather-beat, double in my
    heart Thy flame,
Which let devout sad tears intend, and let—
Though this glass lanthorn, flesh, do suffer maim—
Fire, sacrifice, priest, altar be the same.

John Donne

———

Gracious God, who endowed your servant John Donne
with gifts of preaching and poetry
which enrich our worship
and deepen our understanding;
bless all who preach and teach
that their words may draw us into your presence
and strengthen us in your service;
through Jesus Christ our Lord. Amen.

John Saunders Gilliat 1829–1912

Governor of the Bank of England

———

FOR OVER TWO hundred and forty years poor clergy in the Church of England were supported by Queen Anne's Bounty, a fund which had been established in 1704. For many years Gilliat served as one of the trustees of the fund until it was merged with the Ecclesiastical Commissioners in 1947 to form the Church Commissioners. He was a practising Anglican throughout his life and personally paid for the building of the vicarage for Christ Church, Chorleywood. He served as a member of the Bishop of St Albans' Fund and was also on the Church Committee for Church Defence and Church Instruction. Born in Berkshire to John and Mary Gilliat, he was educated at Harrow School and University College, Oxford. His father was a merchant banker and Gilliat followed in his footsteps when he joined the court of the Bank of England, where he was eventually promoted to be Governor. He became Member of Parliament for Clapham in 1886 and represented the constituency of Widnes from 1892 until 1900. He was married to Louisa Babington with whom he had three children.

Archbishop Rowan Williams preaches about finance and the Church

Queen Anne's Bounty was established in order to help the Church of England to be holy. An extravagant statement? No, because it was a move to assist the church to be itself. The situation that prevailed at the beginning of the eighteenth century was more chaotic and unjust than we can easily imagine: a good study for anyone who thinks that our current financial anxieties are uniquely awful. The Church of England had been stripped of its assets by greedy monarchs and gentry ever since the first days of the Reformation. The effects of clerical poverty and the gross inequality of clerical incomes created a situation in which clergy were forced into pluralism or into secular trade to stay afloat, or were at the mercy of unscrupulous patrons. The Church's pastors and teachers were often not free to preach their convictions for fear of losing their position; but the rank injustice of the whole system also, in another and ultimately more serious way, prevented the Church itself proclaiming the truth in which it was created. Queen Anne began to make it possible for the Church to understand itself properly again; to make its own decisions about doctrine and pastoral deployment, to regain self-respect as a supernaturally grounded body, not a badly funded department of state. The Church – for all that the eighteenth century was not one of its great eras – at least was able to shed some of the appalling legacy of unscrupulous depredation by the secular power in the century and a half before. And it very slowly recovered some sense that to put wealth at the service of the most needy was a central aspect of the gospel vision. Without all this, holiness, corporate holiness for the community, could not be realised.

From an unpublished sermon celebrating the anniversary of Queen Anne's Bounty

Heavenly Father
whose Son has taught us that
it is more blessed to give than to receive;
save us from greed and selfishness
and grant to us and to all your people
a spirit of joyful generosity;
we ask this through Jesus Christ our Lord. Amen.

Samuel Vince 1749–1821

Clergyman, mathematician and astronomer

———

IN THE LONG line of distinguished Archdeacons of Bedford stands Samuel Vince. From his humble beginnings as a plasterer's son, Vince went up to study at Caius College and Sidney Sussex College, Cambridge, and in 1779 he was ordained. His academic interests were many and varied. He wrote books on mathematics, physics and a three-volume work on astronomy. His works *Observations on the Theory of the Motion and Resistance of Fluids* and *Experiments upon the Resistance of Bodies Moving in Fluids* were to provide insights into aviation long after his death. He was highly regarded as an academic and in 1780 he was awarded the Copley Medal given by the Royal Society of London for 'outstanding achievements in research in any branch of science'. In 1796 he was appointed the Plumian Professor of Astronomy and Experimental Philosophy in Cambridge and in 1809 he was made Archdeacon of Bedford. Vince held both posts until his death in 1821.

Samuel Vince dedicates his book to the Bishop of Lincoln with these words

When Christianity is attacked by the arguments of the philosopher, and the scoffs and ridicule of the weak, it behoveth us 'to give a reason of the hope that is in us.' A superficial examination of the evidences of Christianity; the vanity of controverting established opinions; or viciousness of life, generally operate as reasons for opposing the truths of the gospel; but whatever be the motive, it is commonly attended with a total indifference to the great end of religion – a due preparation for a future state. Reflection upon the construction of the universe, and the nice laws by which the material world is governed, is the only thing which can bring a man back from atheism to the belief of a supreme being; and when the mind is satisfied of a providence, the evidences of the Christian religion will find an easy admission; the defect not lying in the evidence, but in a previous disposition of the mind to receive it. Little therefore remains, but earnestly to exhort unbelievers to consider the grounds of our belief, with that attention which the importance of the subject demands. These discourses are therefore published, not as an attempt to place the evidences of our religion in a new point of view, but principally to state and consider (what I conceive to be) the only true principle upon which Mr Hume's argument against the credibility of miracles, can be satisfactorily answered. If the reasoning be admitted, the conclusions which are deduced will justify our belief of the Gospel dispensation.

From *The Credibility of Christianity Vindicated*

O gracious and holy Father,
give us wisdom to perceive you,
intelligence to understand you,
diligence to seek you,
patience to wait for you,
eyes to see you,
a heart to meditate on you,
and a life to proclaim you,
through the power of the spirit of Jesus Christ our Lord. Amen.

St Benedict

Henry Graham Greene 1904–91

Author and playwright from Berkhamsted

———

GRAHAM GREENE WAS one of the great English novelists of the twentieth century. He attended Berkhamsted School where his father was the second master and then Headmaster. Greene hated the school, claiming that he was bullied and attempted to commit suicide on several occasions. In desperation he ran away from the school and later underwent psychoanalysis for a period. Greene read history at Balliol College, Oxford, during which time he published his first collection of poetry, *Babbling April*. Whilst at Oxford Greene suffered from depression and later in life he struggled with bipolar disorder. For a period he worked in journalism and it was during this stage of his life that he converted to Roman Catholicism. In 1927 Greene married Vivien Dayrell-Browning but the marriage only lasted until 1948 when they separated. They had two children, Lucy and Francis. After the success of his first novel Greene became a full-time writer. However, some of his early books were not well received and it was not until *Stambour Train*, which was made into the film *Orient Express,* that he became more widely known. Nevertheless it was still necessary for him to earn income by writing reviews and working as the literary editor of *The Spectator*. Throughout his life Greene travelled widely, which enabled him to work undercover for MI6 for a time. Among his most famous books are *Brighton Rock, The Power and the Glory, The Heart of the Matter* and *Our Man in Havana.* He died on this day in 1991 and is buried in a cemetery near Lake Geneva in Switzerland.

Aleksandr Solzhenitsyn gives a speech on literature

Woe betide that nation whose literature is interrupted by the interference of force. This is not simply a violation of the 'freedom of the press': it is the locking-up of the national heart, the carving-up of the national memory. Such a nation does not remember itself, it is deprived of its spiritual unity, and although its population supposedly has a common language, fellow-countrymen suddenly stop understanding each other. Mute generations live out their lives and die without telling their story either to their own or a future generation. If such geniuses as Akhmatova or Zamayatin are walled up alive for the duration of their lives, if they are condemned to create in silence until the grave, without hearing any response to what they have written, then this is not just their own personal misfortune but the deep tragedy of the whole nation – and, too, a threat to the whole nation. And in certain cases it is a danger for the whole of mankind, too: when the whole of history ceases to be understood because of that silence.

From *One Word of Truth*

Heavenly Father
we thank you for the creative gifts of writers,
for their imagination, skill and dedication:
bless those who reflect on our world and on the human condition
that understanding ourselves more fully,
we may follow you more faithfully;
for the glory of your Holy Name. Amen.

Peter Mumford 1922–92

Bishop of Hertford and Truro

———

PETER MUMFORD LOVED the great metaphysical poets of the seventeenth century and named his autobiography *Quick-eyed Love Observed* – a phrase from a poem by George Herbert. Mumford was born in 1922 and educated at Sherborne School. He served in the Royal Artillery for five years and then read theology at University College, Oxford, before training for the ministry at Cuddesdon Theological College. He ministered at several places in the diocese: St Albans Abbey, St Luke's Leagrave and St Andrew's Bedford. In 1969 Mumford was inducted as Rector of St John the Baptist, Crawley, and four years later was made Archdeacon of St Albans. In 1974 he was consecrated Bishop of Hertford where he served for seven years until he was translated to Truro. During his time in Cornwall he became known for his commitment to ecumenism, especially with the Methodists. He retired in 1989. Both Peter and his wife, Jane, were members of the Third Order of the Franciscans. They had two sons and a daughter.

Love bade me welcome; yet my soul drew back,
Guilty of dust and sin.
But quick-eyed Love, observing me grow slack
From my first entrance in,
Drew nearer to me, sweetly questioning
If I lack'd anything.

'A guest,' I answer'd, 'worthy to be here:'
Love said, 'You shall be he.'
'I, the unkind, ungrateful? Ah, my dear,
I cannot look on Thee.'
Love took my hand and smiling did reply,
'Who made the eyes but I?'

'Truth, Lord; but I have marr'd them: let my shame
Go where it doth deserve.'
'And know you not,' says Love, 'Who bore the blame?'
'My dear, then I will serve.'
'You must sit down,' says Love, 'and taste my meat.'
So I did sit and eat.

George Herbert

Gracious God,
you invite us to turn to you in faith and trust:
give us courage to abandon ourselves joyfully to your service,
that you may purify our hearts and minds
and lead us ever deeper into your love;
through Jesus Christ our Lord. Amen.

Edward Young 1681–1765

Priest, playwright and romantic poet

————

NOT MANY CLERICS are remembered for a single poem. Yet Edward Young's *Night Thoughts* (1742) became so famous that it was translated into several languages, including Magyar, and later illustrated by William Blake. It is said that he wrote part of the poem sitting under a yew tree in Datchworth. His plays, which were performed in London, include *Busiris, Revenge* and *The Brothers*. Young's works were praised by Goethe and Samuel Johnson, and were said to have influenced Edmund Burke. Towards the end of his life, Young wrote *Conjectures on Original Composition*, which was translated into German and became hugely influential. Young was educated at Winchester College, and at New College and Corpus Christi College, Oxford. He then became a fellow of All Souls, Oxford. In 1731 he married Lady Elizabeth Lee, daughter of the Earl of Lichfield, but she died nine years later. Young's connection with the diocese began in 1728 when he was appointed Rector of Welwyn, where he was to spend the rest of his life. He died on this day in 1765.

Mark 15.14. And Pilate said unto them 'Why? What evil that he done?' And they cried out more exceedingly 'Crucify Him'

The crucifixion of our blessed Saviour was an event full of terror in its nature, and full of consolation in its consequences, to the whole human race. But neither of these is the proposed subject of the present discourse. I rather choose to contemplate the strong evidences of a divine interposition, which are afforded us in the manner of bringing about this great event: such a manner as was requisite to render it most effectual to the merciful intentions of our great, and most indulgent God in it. I shall observe the most admirable, and adorable wisdom of God through this whole transaction; and make it manifest, that He sees through all the actions, accidents, hearts, and inclinations of men; and conducts them all, however perverse, to the full accomplishment of his own good pleasure. If innocence could ever have been a sufficient fence against injustice, or meekness against calumny, or the most obliging goodness against outrage, our most blessed Lord must have been sufficiently guarded against the prosecution of the Jews. But as human nature stands corrupted, these excellent qualities are no guards at all. They rather expose, and lay us open to malevolent assaults. Innocence itself is often interpreted into a crime, and gives some men as much offence as injury could possibly do. And indeed, as long as envy is mischievous in its attempts, as any other passion; it cannot but happen, that, sometimes, it may be as unsafe (in respect of temporal Interest) to be eminently good, as eminently evil. It was therefore to little purpose that Pilate alleged our blessed Saviour's innocence, in this suggestion, 'Why, what evil hath he done?' He had done none; but that was his offence. Therefore this allegation as it affronted the malice of their proceedings, so it the more inflamed it; making them 'cry out more exceedingly, Crucify Him'.

From a sermon preached by Edward Young before King George II in 1758

Lord Jesus Christ
who prayed for your persecutors, saying,
'Father, forgive them, for they know not what they are doing':
grant us the same spirit of forgiveness
towards all who revile or persecute us;
we ask it for your name's sake. Amen.

Richard Lucy c.1592–1667

Politician

———

RICHARD LUCY WAS born at Charlecote Park in Warwickshire, the son of Thomas Lucy and Constance Kingsmill. He studied at Magdalen College and Exeter College, Oxford, and Lincoln's Inn. In 1617, still in his twenties, Lucy was knighted and a year later created baronet of Broxbourne in Hertfordshire. His was an influential family: one of his brothers was a Member of Parliament and another brother was Bishop of St Davids. Lucy married Elizabeth West, whose father was Sir Henry Cock of Broxbourne. They had two children, but in 1645 Elizabeth died. He married a second time to Rebeccca Chapman of Wormley. He was Member of Parliament for Old Sarum during the Long Parliament of 1647, and continued in the Rump Parliament. He was elected to represent Hertfordshire for both the First and the Second Protectorate Parliaments in 1654 and 1656 respectively. In his will he left a bequest to establish and endow a boys' school in Broxbourne.

Alan Richardson describes the attitudes of the first Christians towards politics

Similarly the Christian churches [in the first three centuries] developed no political programme of their own. This was not merely because they were in no position to do so but rather because the making of political programmes was in itself no part of their concern. They sketched no blueprints for Utopia. An influential strain in Christian thinking was indeed avowedly pessimistic about the prospects for this world; the apocalyptists held that things would get worse before they got better and that it was not until the cup of human wickedness was full to overflowing that the final judgement would begin with the return of Christ in glory. It is hardly surprising that some, like the seer John on Patmos, should read the signs of the times in the light of the gloomier prognostications of the Old Testament scriptures. In general, however, the Christian congregations settled down to the task of making the best of things as they were. They put no trust in political activism and formed no political programme, confident that God was in control of the affairs of the whole world and that in his wisdom he would consummate his age-long purpose of salvation for all mankind…They expressed this conviction by means of the symbol of the 'appearing' or the 'return' of Christ, an image appropriate to ancient cosmography and still capable of being understood in the age of astrophysics. Christians were even now citizens of a heavenly country, whose law was love and whose life was peace; but their present existence was like that of colonists far from their home country, whose duty and privilege it was to transplant the quality of the life of their homeland into the alien environment in which they found themselves. The political attitude of the Gentile churches can be found in a verse from one of Paul's last letters: 'Our citizenship is in heaven, from whence we wait for a Saviour, the Lord Jesus Christ' (Philippians 3.20).

From *The Political Christ*

Lord Jesus Christ, who taught your disciples to pray
'Your kingdom come, your will be done':
strengthen all who work for justice, peace and the common good.
Bring an end to war and strife, and usher in your kingdom;
to the praise and glory of your name. Amen.

William Alabaster 1568–1640

Rector of Therfield

WILLIAM ALABASTER'S ECCLESIASTICAL career was turbulent. His link with Hertfordshire comes from the time when he was Rector of Therfield. Born at Hadleigh in Suffolk and educated at Westminster School, Alabaster was selected as one of the Queen's Scholars and went to Trinity College, Cambridge. Following graduation he was elected to a fellowship in the college and in 1596 appointed the college catechist. Today Alabaster is remembered as a writer on religious subjects, a playwright and a poet, though during his lifetime there was controversy over his tragedy *Roxana* which, it was claimed, he had copied from an Italian play called *La Dalida*. Alabaster wrote a number of books, including *De bestia apocalyptica*, *Ecce sponsus venit* and *Spiraculum tubarum*. Alabaster converted to Roman Catholicism and studied at the English College in Rome. During a spell in Spain he was captured and sent back to England where he was imprisoned in the Tower of London. Pardoned by James I, he travelled to Italy and published a book *Apparatus in revelationem Jesu Christi* which was condemned by the Inquisition. He renounced Catholicism and was made a Prebend of St Paul's Cathedral and instituted into the living at Therfield. Alabaster married Katherine Fludd. He died in 1640 and is buried at St Dunstan-in-the-West, London.

A Divine Sonnet by William Alabaster

Jesu, thy love within me is so main,
And my poor heart so narrow of content,
That with thy love my heart wellnigh is rent,
And yet I love to bear such loving pain.
O take thy Cross and nails and therewith strain
My heart's desire unto his full extent
That thy dear love may not therein be pent,
But thoughts may have free scope thy love to explain.
O now my heart more paineth than before,
Because it can receive and hath no more,
O fill this emptiness or else I die,
Now stretch my heart again and now supply,
Now I want space, now grace. To end this smart,
Since my heart holds not thee, hold thou my heart.

From *The Sonnets of William Alabaster*
edited by G. M. Story and H. Gardner

Lord Jesus Christ,
Living Word of the Father,
bless, we pray, all wordsmiths who use language
to preach, teach, entertain or challenge.
Give them integrity in what they write and say
that they may be grounded in truth and guided by love;
for your name's sake. Amen.

Samuel Trevor Francis 1834–1925

Preacher and hymn writer

———

GENERATIONS OF EVANGELICAL Christians will be familiar with the hymn *O the Deep, Deep Love of Jesus.* It was written by Samuel Francis who was a lay preacher in the Plymouth Brethren. Born in Cheshunt, into a family that loved music, art and poetry, Samuel joined a church choir when he was nine years old. Even as a child he wrote poetry and this gift was to mature as he grew older. The family moved to the north of England, but he was discontented and soon moved back south. Not long afterwards, he had a profound spiritual crisis while walking over one of the bridges across the River Thames. He was contemplating suicide when he had an overwhelming experience of the love of God which led to his conversion to Christianity. During his adult life he worked as a merchant in London, but in his spare time he was a prolific hymn writer. He travelled extensively around the country, teaching and preaching about the Christian faith. Among his better-known hymns are *Now around Thee, Lord, we meet* and *I am waiting for the dawning of the bright and blessèd day.* He died at the age of ninety-two in a nursing home in Worthing.

One of Samuel Francis' most famous hymns

O the deep, deep love of Jesus, vast, unmeasured, boundless, free!
Rolling as a mighty ocean in its fullness over me!
Underneath me, all around me, is the current of Thy love
Leading onward, leading homeward to Thy glorious rest above!

O the deep, deep love of Jesus, spread His praise from shore to shore!
How He loveth, ever loveth, changeth never, nevermore!
How He watches o'er His loved ones, died to call them all His own;
How for them He intercedeth, watcheth o'er them from the throne!

O the deep, deep love of Jesus, love of every love the best!
'Tis an ocean full of blessing, 'tis a haven giving rest!
O the deep, deep love of Jesus, 'tis a heaven of heavens to me;
And it lifts me up to glory, for it lifts me up to Thee!

O God, whom saints and angels delight to worship in heaven:
be ever present with your servants who seek through art and music
to perfect the praises offered by your people on earth;
and grant to them even now glimpses of your beauty,
and make them worthy at length to behold it unveiled for evermore;
through Jesus Christ our Lord. Amen.

From *The Book of Common Prayer* of the Episcopal Church

Francis Bacon 1561–1626

Author, politician, lawyer and scientist

———

IF YOU GO into the church of St Michael in St Albans, where Francis Bacon is buried, you will find a magnificent memorial to him. When translated the inscription reads

Francis Bacon
Baron of Verulam, Viscount St. Albans
or, by more conspicuous titles,
of Science the Light, of Eloquence the Law, sat thus.
Who after all Natural Wisdom and Secrets of Civil Life he had unfolded
Nature's Law fulfilled – Let Compounds be dissolved!

Bacon was born in London and was educated at home, due to poor health. He studied at Cambridge University, where he met Queen Elizabeth I, and then at Gray's Inn and was elected to Parliament in 1584. His father had been Lord Keeper of the Great Seal for the Queen and Bacon held the same post under King James I. He was appointed Lord Chancellor in 1618. Bacon was passionate about science and wrote a seminal book on the scientific method, entitled *Novum Organum*, arguing for the need to observe the natural world. He also wrote about theological and ecclesiastical matters and was sympathetic to the Puritan cause. He was married to Anne Barnham.

Francis Bacon exhorts us to use knowledge for the glory of God

But the greatest error…is the mistaking or misplacing of the last or furthest end of knowledge. For men have entered into a desire of learning and knowledge, sometimes upon a natural curiosity and inquisitive appetite; sometimes to entertain their minds with variety and delight; sometimes for ornament and reputation; and sometimes to enable them to victory of wit and contradiction; and most times for lucre and profession; and seldom sincerely to give a true account of their gift of reason to the benefit and use of men: as if there were sought in knowledge a couch whereupon to rest a searching and restless spirit; or a terrace for a wandering and variable mind to walk up and down with a fair prospect; or a tower of state, for a proud mind to raise itself upon; or a fort or commanding ground, for strife and contention; or a shop, for profit or sale; and not a rich storehouse for the glory of the Creator and the relief of man's estate.

From *The Advancement of Learning* edited by M. Kiernan

———

Thou, O Father! who gavest the visible light as the first-born of thy creatures, and didst pour into man the intellectuall Light as the top and consummation of thy workmanship, be pleased to protect and govern this work, which coming from thy goodness returneth to thy glory. Then, after thou hadst reviewed the works which thy hands had made, beheldest that 'everything was very good'; and thou didst rest with complacency in them. But man reflecting on the works which he had made, saw that 'all was vanity and vexation of Spirit', and could by no means acquiesce in them. Wherefore if we labour in thy works with the sweat of our brows, thou wilt make us partakers of thy vision and thy sabbath. We humbly beg that this mind may be steadfastly in us, and that thou, by our hands and also by the hands of others on whom thou shalt bestow the same spirit, wilt please to convey a largeness of new alms to thy family of mankind. These things we commend to thy everlasting love, by our Jesus, thy Christ, God with us. Amen.

Francis Bacon

Philip Goodwin d.1667

Vicar

———

ANY DIVISIONS IN the Church today are dwarfed by those of the early 1660s when over two thousand clergy were expelled from the Church of England. Among them was Philip Goodwin who had been appointed Vicar of St Mary's, Watford, in 1645, but who was ejected in 1661 because he refused to conform. A few years later, however, he changed his position and was appointed Rector of Liston in Essex. He married Lucy, the daughter of the patron, William Clopton, with whom he had four sons (two of whom were ordained in the Church of England) and a daughter. Goodwin was born in Suffolk and studied at St John's College, Cambridge, graduating in 1627. He was ordained in Peterborough and in 1633 made curate of All Saints', Hertford. Some years later he was appointed to be the market-day lecturer at Hemel Hempstead. He wrote a number of books including *The Evangelicall Communicant in the Eucharisticall Sacrament, The Lord's Day enlivened, Family Religion Revived,* and *The Mystery of Dreames.* He is buried in Watford.

Goodwin exhorts us to focus our thoughts on Christ when taking Holy Communion

To remember Christ his death and sufferings at this Supper, is more then to have some few transient thoughts at that instant of Christ and the things of Christ, and so vanish without any permanent impresse made upon the mindes of men. To remember Christ and his death is to be affected with it, as to draw vertue from it, and feel the effectuall fruit of it. Its more then to look at things in a distance or in a generall notion, its to make all present as if the Sacrament day were Christ suffering day to be at the Lords Table as at mount Calvary, beholding Christ on the crosse bleeding…, to bring all home in a close application to ones own particular interest, and for each ones spiritual advantage. Thus carnall men can never remember Christ, or the sufferings of Christ they are things they do not rightly understand, not highly esteem, and so have no mind to remember, Psalm 106.7 mans memory and Gods mercy hardly hangs together. Two things natarall men are apt to forget: Gods goodnesse and their own sinfulnesse, the goodness of God in Christ is easily forgotten, rarely remembred, alas! sinfull men at the Sacrament, they a little think upon Christ as corporally crucified long since: not as spiritually crucified at present before their eyes, Galatians 3.1. they minde the outward Ordinance but forget Christ, not laying his love, his death, his worth to heart: as a woman whose husband being to travell left her a precious jewel as a token of his love to remember her of him in his absence, she loved oft to look upon her jewell but forgat her husband: her jewell was oft in her hand, but her husband seldome in her heart, far from the desire of her thoughts.

From *The Evangelicall Communicant in the Eucharisticall Sacrament*

———

Lord Jesus Christ, you invite us to supper
to share the sacrament of your body and blood:
forgive us our sins, cleanse us from unrighteousness
and grant that having received you
we may never forget you or fail you;
we ask this for your name's sake. Amen.

Guthlac of Crowland 673–714

Saint and hermit

———

ASTWICK CHURCH IN Bedfordshire is one of a handful of churches in the country dedicated to St Guthlac. He was the son of Penwald and Tette, and was born in the Midlands, then known as the Kingdom of Mercia. It is thought that he belonged to Æthelred's army for a time before becoming a monk in the monastery of the Augustinian Canons at Repton at the age of twenty-four. Two years later Guthlac felt called to a hermit's life and moved to Crowland in Lincolnshire where he lived in a cell next to an oratory. He became famous for his holiness and ascetic way of life, dressing in skins and living almost exclusively on bread and water. Many people visited him there, seeking spiritual guidance. King Æthelbald, in gratitude for Guthlac's kindness in protecting him from his cousin Ceolred, and for Guthlac's prophecy that he would become king, built Crowland Abbey in Guthlac's honour. When Guthlac died, his sister, St Pega, conducted his funeral rites. He is commemorated on this day each year.

Richard Foster argues for the Christian practice of living in simplicity

Asceticism and simplicity are mutually incompatible. Occasional superficial similarities in practice must never obscure the radical difference between the two. Asceticism renounces possessions. Simplicity sets possessions in proper perspective. Asceticism can find no place for a 'land flowing with milk and honey.' Simplicity can rejoice in this gracious provision from the hand of God. Asceticism can find contentment only when it is abased. Simplicity knows contentment in both abasement and abounding (Philippians 4.12). Simplicity is the only thing that can sufficiently reorient our lives so that possessions can be genuinely enjoyed without destroying us. Without simplicity we will either capitulate to the 'mammon' spirit of this present evil age, or we will fall into an un-Christian legalistic asceticism. Both lead to idolatry. Both are spiritually lethal. Scripture abounds in descriptions of the abundant material provision God gives His people…It also abounds in warnings about the danger of provisions that are not kept in proper perspective…The spiritual discipline of simplicity provides the needed perspective. Simplicity sets us free to receive the provision of God as a gift that is not ours to keep, and that can be freely shared with others. Once we recognize that the Bible denounces the materialist and the ascetic with equal vigour, we are prepared to turn our attention to the framing of a Christian understanding of simplicity.

From *Celebration of Discipline*

Grant me, O most sweet and loving Jesus, to rest in thee above every creature,
above all health and beauty, above all glory and honour,
above all power and dignity, above all knowledge and subtlety,
above all riches and arts, above all joy and exultation,
above all fame and praise, above all sweetness and consolation,
above all hope and promise, above all desert and desire,
above all gifts and presents which thou art able to bestow or infuse,
above all joy and gladness which the mind is capable of receiving and feeling;
finally, above angels and archangels, and above all the heavenly host,
above all things visible and invisible, and above all that thou art not, O my God! Amen.

Thomas à Kempis

Lady John Thynne & Daughters

Anna Constantia Thynne 1806–66

Marine zoologist

———

I F YOU GO into the church of St Mary in Haynes, you will see a recumbent effigy of a lady, her hands clasped in prayer. Behind this innocuous-looking memorial is the story of an extraordinary woman, Lady Anna Thynne. Anna was one of a large family, born to an impecunious Irish vicar, the Reverend Charles Cobbe Beresford and his wife Amelia. Anna was adopted by relatives, George and Harriet Byng, who lived at Wrotham Park near Barnet. She married the Reverend Lord John Thynne, who was Sub-Dean and a Canon of Westminster Abbey, and for a time they lived at Haynes Park in Bedfordshire. Anna was fascinated by the natural world and spent much time studying it. Social convention prevented her from publishing her findings, but it is now recognised that she was a distinguished amateur scientist. She was responsible for the birth of the modern aquarium after taking some stone corals from Torquay to her London home in 1846, and the animals – to the horror of her housemaids – then bred. It was the first stable sustained marine aquarium and she maintained the corals and sponges for over three years.

Rebecca Scott describes the debates about evolution during the Victorian era

Alarmed by the spread of materialist ideas, the Earl of Bridgewater, the Right Honourable Reverend Francis, had left £8,000 in his will to the Royal Society to 'appoint persons to write, print and publish one thousand copies of a work on the Power, Wisdom and Goodness of God as manifested in the Creation; illustrating such work by all reasonable arguments'. And in 1830 the search was on for an author of such works. One obvious choice was the charismatic Oxford geologist the Reverend William Buckland who, having accepted the commission, worked for six years to reconcile the apparent conflicts between geology and religion. In 1836 his *Bridgewater Treatise: Geology and Mineralogy Considered with Reference to Natural Theology* was published, and all of the one thousand copies printed were sold out within weeks. The Treatise was a triumph. Everyone in Anna's circle in Clifton, Bristol and London was talking about it. In the book, Buckland turned his mind to a series of paradoxes between the Biblical account of creation and the fossil evidence that seemed to absolutely contradict that account, paradoxes that readers like Anna hoped he could reconcile. He used Paley's language to argue that geology was 'the unfolding records of the operations of the Almighty Author of the Universe, written by the finger of God himself, upon the foundations of the everlasting hills'. The answer, he claimed, to the conflicts between fossil evidence and the Biblical account of Creation was to redefine what was understood by Creation. The Bible's 'beginning', after all, might refer to millions of years of turbulence and creation, not just seven days. And since creation, he claimed, God had been making the world more and more perfect for man.

From *Theatres of Glass*

———

Almighty God, you made the universe with all its order, atoms, worlds, galaxies and the intricate complexities of living creatures. Help scientists and all who study the mysteries of your creation to know you more truly and more surely, to fulfil their role in your eternal purpose, to be true witnesses to your glory, and to be faithful stewards of your gifts. We ask this through Jesus Christ our Lord. Amen.

Based on a prayer from the Society of Ordained Scientists

Edmund Castell 1606–85

Priest and orientalist

———

IT IS ARGUABLE that the Bible has been studied more than any other text in the world. Edmund Castell's extraordinary knowledge of ancient languages enabled him to make a significant contribution to its study. He had been one of the team under the leadership of Brian Walton who produced the *Polyglott Bible*. This gave him the idea for his *magnus opus*, the ambitious *Lexicon Heptaglotton Hebraicum, Chaldaicum, Syriacum, Samaritanum, Aethiopicum, Arabicum, et Persicum*. Castell claimed that he worked on the project between sixteen to eighteen hours each day for eighteen years and had a team of fourteen scholars assisting him. Unfortunately the book did not sell enough copies and Castell lost a great deal of money. However, his work was not wasted. Long after his death both the Syriac and the Hebrew sections of the lexicon were published. Castell was born at Tadlow and studied at Emmanuel College, Cambridge. In 1666 he was appointed Professor of Arabic. Disaster struck in the following year when he was imprisoned for his brother's debts, for which he had stood surety. Castell was later appointed Rector of Higham Gobion in Bedfordshire.

Two reflections from Archbishop Michael Ramsey

If we come closer to the inner heart of Bible reading we are not just stuffing our minds with information; we are letting God feed us through his word, and this means letting the scriptures speak to imagination, conscience, feeling, and will, as well as to the mind. As we read, and read slowly, we pause and let the truth of God come home to us. Our imagination is moved to wonder, our conscience is pricked to penitence, our feelings are moved to love, our will is stirred to resolve, and our mind to whatever understanding we can muster. In that way we quietly let the passage of scripture come home to us, mould us, and be our food and drink.

There is one particular image which I ask you to look at closely. It is the image used by St. John which, more than any other, sums the matter up. St. John writes, 'The Word became flesh and dwelt among us, and we beheld his glory'. *Word*: it is a biblical term denoting one who is living, creative, imperishable, divine. *Flesh*: it is a biblical term denoting what is creaturely, frail, mortal, human. Here then is the paradox. The divine Creator has humbled himself to take on himself the entire experience of existence as man, in all conditions of humanity. Is it credible? It is only just credible. It is credible because there already exists the affinity between God and man, through man being made in God's likeness. This affinity anticipates the closest final fellowship conceivable between God and man. Again, it is credible because of the infinity of God's love, with love's power of entering into the experience of another beyond all the analogies of love's power which we know.

From *Through the Year with Michael Ramsey* edited by Margaret Duggan

———

Blessed Lord, by whose providence all holy scriptures were written and preserved for our instruction, give us grace to study them this and every day with patience and love. Strengthen our souls with the fullness of their divine teaching. Keep from us all pride and irreverence. Guide us in the deep things of thy heavenly wisdom, and of thy great mercy lead us by thy Word unto everlasting life; through Jesus Christ our Lord and Saviour. Amen.

Brooke Foss Westcott

Mary Carbery 1867–1949

Author

———

MARY VANESSA TOULMIN was born and spent her childhood at Childwickbury Manor in Hertfordshire, the daughter of Henry Joseph Toulmin and Emma Louisa Wroughton. Mary was married twice: firstly to Algernon, Baron Carbery of Castle Freke, County Cork, with whom she had a son, then when Algernon died she married Professor Arthur Wellesley Sandford of Frankfield House, County Cork, Ireland. Under the pseudonym Mary Carbery she wrote a number of books, mainly on Irish themes, such as *The Farm by Loch Gur*, *The Germans in Cork* and *West Cork Journal*. However, she also wrote *Hertfordshire Heritage: Ourselves and our Words*. Mary was an inveterate traveller, and spent much of the early part of the last century crossing Europe in *Creeping Jenny*, an ox-drawn caravan. She was also credited with being the first person to install a bath in a mobile home. She died at Eye Manor in Herefordshire.

Mary Carbery describes her longing to travel

I am restless, hearing the call of the road, and the call of mountains with their water courses. I must not listen. I must not leave the children to go away and away. Jesus Christ heard the call of the road and obeyed it. If He had not been able to go here and there, He would have known the pain which comes to those who are thwarted in this respect, again and again, and He would have left some strengthening and encouraging words for those who are prisoners in their home. Just as I am by nature restless, a mover-on, so do I want to grow, and mentally to progress; to have a wider horizon, to cross mountains and seas; glad to be beyond, glad to change; not wishing to return on my tracks; leaving by the wayside the outworn things which have served their purpose; dropping impediments; to go on in the company of those of like mind; to part from those who, like Lot's wife, look back with regret. I want to go from strength to strength, '*im Ganzen, Guten, Wahren, resolut zu leben*' [To live resolutely a whole, good and true life]. I wonder whether either of my sons will inherit my wander-thirst. If they do, I hope they will be able to satisfy it.

From *West Cork Journal*

God of our journeying,
walk with us on life's pilgrimage;
and as your Son drew alongside the disciples on the Road to Emmaus
so open our eyes and ears to recognise your presence with us.
Lead us, together with our fellow pilgrims,
to find our home in heaven with you;
through Jesus Christ our Lord. Amen.

John Tradescant c.1570–1638

Naturalist and gardener

TRADESCANTIA IS A familiar plant in many English gardens, which is named after John Tradescant the Elder (he had a son of the same name). John, the father, was probably born in Suffolk, but first comes to prominence as the head gardener at Hatfield House, the home of Robert Cecil, the Earl of Salisbury. Tradescant also worked for William Cecil, Robert's son, in his gardens at Salisbury House in London. Tradescant's reputation grew rapidly and he designed gardens for Lord Wotton and George Villiers, the 1st Duke of Buckingham, and King James I. He travelled extensively in Europe collecting seeds, bulbs and plants but also went as far as Russia, North America, Algiers and the Eastern Mediterranean. As well as exotic plants, Tradescant collected a wide range of objects and curiosities. He displayed them in a building in Lambeth he named 'The Ark', which was the first public museum in the country, sometimes referred to as the Musaeum Tradescantianum. John Tradescant and his son are buried in the churchyard of St-Mary-at-Lambeth.

Bill Bryson wonders at the amazing diversity of life

Of the organisms that we *do* know about, more than 99 in 100 are only sketchily described – 'a scientific name, a handful of specimens in a museum, and a few scraps of description in scientific journals' is how Wilson describes the state of our knowledge. In *The Diversity of Life*, he estimated the number of known species of all types – plants, insects, microbes, algae, everything – at 1.4 million, but added that that was just a guess. Other authorities have put the number of species slightly higher, at around 1.5 million to 1.8 million, but there is no central registry of these things, so nowhere to check numbers. In short, the remarkable position in which we find ourselves is that we don't actually know what we actually know. In principle you ought to be able to go to experts in each area of specialisation, ask how many species there are in their fields, then add the totals. Many people have in fact done so. The problem is that seldom do any two come up with matching figures. Some sources put the number of known types of fungi at seventy thousand, others at a hundred thousand – nearly half as many again. You can find confident assertions that the number of described earthworm species is four thousand and equally confident assertions that the figure is twelve thousand. For insects, the numbers run from 750000 to 950000 species. These are, you understand, supposedly the known number of species. For plants, the commonly accepted numbers range from 248000 to 265000. That may not seem too vast a discrepancy, but it's more than twenty times the number of flowering plants in the whole of North America.

From *A Short History of Nearly Everything*

We give you praise, Heavenly Father,
for the wonder and glory of this world
with its diversity, its beauty, and its splendour.
Give us grace to live in it with joy
to treat it with reverence
and tend it with care;
for we ask it in the name of Jesus Christ our Lord. Amen.

Frances Milton Trollope 1779–1863

Novelist

———

Affixed to the front of a modest-looking house in Barnet is a plaque to Frances ('Fanny') Trollope. Born in 1863 into a clerical family (her father was Vicar of Heckfield in Hampshire), she was the middle of three children. Fanny's mother died when she was young and her father married Sarah Partington. None of the children had a good relationship with Sarah and they were brought up in London. As a young woman Fanny met Thomas Trollope, a barrister. They married in 1809 and had six children, the most famous of whom, Anthony, followed in Fanny's footsteps by becoming a novelist. Thomas decided to make a living from farming but was so unsuccessful that he was soon in debt. Fanny spent time in America, in an attempt to improve the family's finances, and whilst there became committed to the emancipation of slaves. On her return to England she wrote her first book, *Domestic Manners of the Americans*, in which she attacked what she perceived to be the hypocrisy of the American people. When Thomas died in 1835 Fanny turned to writing again to earn an income and pay off the family debts. She used her novels to explore social issues and dealt with subjects such as slavery, corruption in the Church and the appalling conditions of factory workers in the north of England. Two of her novels, *The Abbess* and *Father Eustace*, expressed strong anti-Catholic views. Trollope travelled extensively and also wrote a number of travel books. She was a prolific author, writing more than one hundred books. She spent the last years of her life living in Florence, where she is buried in the English Cemetery.

Frances Trollope's description of the English countryside

The beauties of an English village have been so often dwelt upon, so often described, that I dare not linger long upon the sketch of Wrexhill, which must of necessity precede my introduction of its vicar. And yet not even England can show many points of greater beauty than this oak-sheltered spot can display. Its peculiar style of scenery, half garden, half forest in aspect, is familiar to all who are acquainted with the New Forest, although it has features entirely its own. One of these is an overshot mill, the sparkling fall of which is accurately and most nobly overarched by a pair of oaks which have long been the glory of the parish. Another is the grey and mellow beauty of its antique church, itself unencumbered by ivy, while the wall and old stone gateway of the churchyard look like a line and knot of sober green, enclosing it with such a rich and unbroken luxuriance of foliage 'never sear', as seems to show that it is held sacred, and that no hand profane ever ventured to rob its venerable mass of a leaf or a berry. Close beside the church, and elevated by a very gentle ascent, stands the pretty Vicarage, as if placed expressly to keep watch and ward over the safety and repose of its sacred neighbour.

The opening paragraph of *The Vicar of Wrexhill*

Grant us the power of your Holy Spirit
that with courage and integrity
we might act justly, love mercy,
and walk humbly with you,
through Jesus Christ our Lord. Amen.

Simon de Beauchamp c.1145–c.1206

Founder of Newnham Priory, Bedford

———

THE ORIGINS OF the Augustinian Priory of Newnham are obscure. What is not in doubt is that the Beauchamp family played a significant role in its foundation. The Anglo-Saxon Chronicles tells us that there were secular canons living around the church of St Paul's in Bedford in 971. By the time of the Conquest in 1066 they had endowments in Biddenham and Bedford and their patron was Hugh de Beauchamp, who held the Barony of Bedford. Hugh was succeeded by his son, Payn de Beauchamp, and it was Payn's son, Simon de Beauchamp, who erected the priory buildings in the middle of the twelfth century during the reign of King Henry II. There were six secular canons, one of whom was Nicholas, the Archdeacon of Bedford. We are told that Simon de Beauchamp, having received advice from King Henry II, Pope Alexander III and Bishop Robert of Lincoln, decided they should become religious canons. The transfer of the endowments was made in front of witnesses in St Paul's Church, Bedford, and the first prior, named William, was appointed in 1166. Simon de Beauchamp's endowment was significant and included the tithes of fourteen churches: St Paul's Bedford, Renhold, Ravensden, Great Barford, Willington, Cardington, Southill, Hatley, Wootton, Stagsden, Lower Gravenhurst, Aspley, Salford and Goldington. In addition the endowment included income from markets, mills, navigation and fishing rights.

St Augustine gives instructions on asking pardon and forgiving offences

You should either avoid quarrels altogether or else put an end to them as quickly as possible; otherwise, anger may grow into hatred, making a plank out of a splinter, and turn the soul into a murderer. For so you read: *Everyone who hates his brother is a murderer* (1 John 3:15). Whoever has injured another by open insult, or by abusive or even incriminating language, must remember to repair the injury as quickly as possible by an apology, and he who suffered the injury must also forgive, without further wrangling. But if they have offended one another, they must forgive one another's trespasses for the sake of your prayers which should be recited with greater sincerity each time you repeat them. Although a brother is often tempted to anger, yet prompt to ask pardon from one he admits to having offended, such a one is better than another who, though less given to anger, finds it too hard to ask forgiveness. But a brother who is never willing to ask pardon, or does not do so from his heart, has no reason to be in the monastery, even if he is not expelled. You must then avoid being too harsh in your words, and should they escape your lips, let those same lips not be ashamed to heal the wounds they have caused.

From *The Rule of St Augustine*

We pray, Heavenly Father,
for the monks, nuns and friars
whom you have called to the religious life:
give them love, grace and patience
that their life together may bear witness
to the coming of your kingdom;
through Jesus Christ our Lord. Amen.

John William Roger Lewis 1924–99

Teacher

———

MILTON ERNEST IS a tiny Bedfordshire village, graced with a medieval church and a Voluntary Controlled Church of England Lower School. Roger Lewis was of a generation of church wardens who had served alongside four vicars and through three interregnums in the parish of All Saints. During the Second World War Roger was a wireless operator in the Royal Navy. When he was demobbed he trained as a teacher and worked at St John's School, Cambridge, for twenty-eight years. Roger returned to Milton Ernest in 1955 to marry a local girl, Betsy Starey. Her family lived in Milton Ernest Hall, the only house designed by the ecclesiastical architect William Butterfield (see the entry for 3 February). They had two children, Sally and Adrian. Roger and Betsy were to return to their roots when they came back to live in the village in 1972 and immersed themselves in the local community and church life. At one stage Roger explored the possibility of being ordained as a priest in the Church of England, but this did not come about. However, his influence as a Christian teacher had a profound impact upon those he taught. Although he was known for being rather disorganised, his patent honesty and goodness shone through. Later in life Roger was licensed as a Reader and exercised a valuable ministry at All Saints Church.

A poem about All Saints Church, Milton Ernest

No great cathedral is this church of ours;
No spire it has that reaches for the sky.
No Betjeman has written of its towers;
No claim it has to fame for those who lie
Within its walls, or in the churchyard nigh.
No word is writ of those who cut the stone;
No knowledge have we of the guiding hand,
The architect, who lived those years far gone,
When Harry III was sat upon the throne.
Small, humble, unpretentious, here it stands,
A witness to long centuries of praise.
That burden falls on ours these present days.
Can we refuse to honour those demands?

Roger Lewis

We thank you for the rural areas in our diocese
and pray for those whose living comes from the land;
Prosper those who care for the countryside
that it may be preserved for future generations.
We ask your blessing upon our hamlets and villages
and for those who sustain our common life:
we thank you for their voluntary service in church and community,
and their hidden acts of kindness and generosity;
we ask this in the name of Jesus Christ our Lord. Amen.

Henry Chauncy 1632–1719

Lawyer and antiquary

———

HENRY CHAUNCY IS celebrated today for writing *The Historical Antiquities of Hertfordshire*, which is the first, and possibly the greatest, history book of the county. It took Chauncy fourteen years to write, assisted by a team of researchers. It was published in a large illustrated volume in 1700 and contained details of the county's terrain, leading families and their properties, clergy, churches and memorials. Chauncy was born at Ardeley, Hertfordshire, and was educated in the school in the local vicarage before going to Stevenage Grammar School and Gonville and Caius College, Cambridge. He was admitted to the Middle Temple, London, in 1650 and called to the Bar in 1656. He held various posts in the Middle Temple over the following years and was also steward of the borough court in Hertford. He played a key role in founding The Blue Coat School in the town. He married three times: firstly to Jane Flyer of Brent Pelham who died in 1672. He then married Elizabeth Wood who also died. Finally he married Elizabeth Thruston. He fathered nine children. There is a memorial to Chauncy in St Lawrence Church, Ardeley.

James Detrich writes about the importance of history

Studying church history is about being with the community of faith. Reading the stories, learning the truths, examining the insights of these faithful men and women down through the centuries gives to us the sense that our faith is not shallow, but as the song used to say, it is 'deep and wide.' Church historian John Hannah claims that studying Christian heritage 'dispels the sense of loneliness and isolation in an era that stresses the peripheral and sensational.' It breaks us away from this modern culture that emphasizes the glitz and the glamour of the here and now, and helps us to establish confidence in the faith by examining the beliefs central to our faith that have been developed over a long period of time. Christian theology does not invent beliefs; it finds beliefs already among Christians and critically examines them. The excavation site for Christian theology is not merely in the pages of Scripture, though that is the starting point, but it expands from there into the many centuries as we find the Holy Spirit leading His church. For us today, it gives us the ability to live each day absolutely sure that what we are believing in actually is true; to know and understand that for over 2000 years men and women have been worshipping, praising, and glorifying the same God that we do today. It's similar to those grand, majestic churches, the cathedrals that overwhelm you with the sense of transcendence. The expansive ceilings, high walls, and stained glass leave the impression that our faith, our Christian heritage, is not small but large. Entering into a contemplation of our faith's history is like going into one of those churches. It takes away the loneliness, the isolation, and reminds us of the greatness of our faith.

From *James Detrich's Blog*

———

Almighty God, you are Ancient of Days
who stands above and beyond our limited understanding of time
and sees all things as in a moment; grant us humility to learn from the past,
that drawing on the experiences of those who have gone before us,
we may have the wisdom and understanding
to live our lives in the light of your eternal changelessness;
for we ask this in the name of Jesus Christ our Lord. Amen.

George Andrew Beck 1904–78

Roman Catholic bishop

———

THE COLLEGE OF St Michael in Hitchin had a strong influence on Roman Catholicism in Britain during the six decades it was in existence. The college was well established when the Assumptionist Fathers came to Hitchin in 1925 to take over its running and also to provide the parish priest. 'Augustinians of the Assumption', as they are properly known, follow the Rule of St Augustine and have a particular interest in education. George Beck had come to the college from Clapham College, London, in 1917 and was so influenced by the order that he decided to become an Assumptionist. He studied at Louvaine before being ordained in 1927 and continued to teach at the college. He was a keen sportsman and played cricket for Hitchin Town Cricket Club. Beck eventually became headmaster of the College of St Michael from 1941 to 1944 before his appointment as headmaster of the Becket School, Nottingham. In 1948 Beck was appointed coadjutor Bishop of Brentwood. Three years later he assumed full responsibility as Bishop of Brentwood and was then Bishop of Salford in 1955–64. His expertise in education was well used during this period and a number of new schools were opened. In 1964–76 he was the Archbishop of Liverpool. Beck was a keen supporter of the Sword of the Spirit Movement, which was introduced into Great Britain by Cardinal Hinsley in 1940. The movement, which had strong ecumenical roots, was committed to working for peace. Today it has evolved into a movement involving more than ten thousand people living in sixty-five communities in twenty-four countries. The Sword of the Spirit Movement seeks to:

- proclaim the good news of Christ through direct evangelisation
- bring together Christians from different traditions and cultures for common mission
- support parents in raising children with character and a clear sense of identity
- envision and train the upcoming generation to take on roles of responsibility
- help bridge the gaps of race, class, and culture
- work in cooperation with the churches to foster Christian renewal and promote unity
- give hope and vision to those seeing their countries destroyed by war and violence

George Beck writes about the role of Christians in rebuilding Europe after the war

The Sword of the Spirit movement has as its purpose the restoration in Europe of a Christian basis for both public and private life by a return to the true principles of international order and Christian freedom. This work, on which the settlement of Europe after the war must be based, can be achieved only by the marshalling of Christian opinion in this country, in Europe, and all over the world in support of a peace and the foundation of a true social order based on Christian principles and infused with a Christian spirit; and it is part of the purpose of this meeting to emphasise the responsibility which is now laid upon Christians of using their influence in national and international life for this purpose, and from the present moment.

From an address given at Rickmansworth on 27 July 1941

Lord of the Universe,
through whom we were created
and by whom we are being redeemed:
forgive our incipient racism,
save us from narrow nationalism,
and grant that we and all peoples
may live together in harmony;
through Jesus Christ our Lord. Amen.

Dorothy Evelyn Sivyer 1901–87

Church warden and organist

———

OUR CHURCHES ARE full of tantalising references to people whose lives are now forgotten, whose stories have never been told and whose Christian faith had never been celebrated. A small plaque on a bookcase in All Saint's Church Sutton to the memory of Dorothy Sivyer records one such person. 'Miss Sivyer', as she preferred to be known, came from humble beginnings as her father was in service as a butler and her mother was a lady's maid, which involved her mother often travelling abroad with the family. Dorothy never married and left no descendants. During her adult life she lived in Biggleswade and worked as clerk to the town council. However, in her spare time Dorothy was deeply involved in the life of Sutton village and church. She cycled from Biggleswade to Sutton every Sunday to play the organ for services. For twenty-five years she served as churchwarden. Throughout the village community she was known for her friendship and for the welcome that she was always ready to give to visitors to the church.

Aelred of Rievaulx reflects on friendship

There are four qualities which must be tested in a friend: loyalty, right intention, discretion and patience, that you may entrust yourself to him securely. The right intention, that he may expect nothing from your friendship except God and its natural good. Discretion, that he may understand what is to be done on behalf of a friend, what is to be sought from a friend, what sufferings are to be endured for his sake, upon what good deeds he is to be congratulated; and, since we think that a friend should sometimes be corrected, he must know for what faults this should be done, as well as the manner, the time and the place. Finally, patience, that he may not grieve when rebuked, or despise or hate the one inflicting the rebuke, and that he may not be unwilling to bear every adversity for the sake of his friend. There is nothing more praiseworthy in friendship than loyalty, which seems to be its nurse and guardian. It proves itself a true companion in all things – adverse and prosperous, joyful and sad, pleasing and bitter – beholding with the same eye the humble and the lofty, the poor and the rich, the strong and the weak, the healthy and the infirm. A truly loyal friend sees nothing in his friend but his heart. Embracing virtue in its proper place, and putting aside all else as if it were outside him, the faithful friend does not value them much if they are present, and does not seek them if they are absent. Moreover, loyalty is hidden in prosperity, but conspicuous in adversity. A friend is tested by necessity. A rich person's friends abound, but whether they are true friends only emerges when adversity proves their worth. Solomon says: 'He that is a friend loves at all times, and a brother is proved in distress.'

From *On Spiritual Friendship*

Heavenly Father,
whose Son Jesus Christ sought us out and called us friends:
we thank you for the gift of companionship
and for the love and support we receive;
may we never take them for granted
but with open hands and open hearts
reciprocate with love and care;
through Jesus Christ our Lord. Amen.

William Dickins 1686–1759

Stonemason

———

THE SMALL VILLAGE of Keysoe lies at the north end of Bedfordshire between Bolnhurst and Pertenhall. The church of St Mary the Virgin has a plaque attached to the outside tower wall which recounts the extraordinary escape of William Dickins. He was pointing the mortar work of the spire when he slipped and fell 132ft, and not only survived but lived for another forty-one years. The plaque commemorates what happened:

In Memory of the Mighty hand of the Great God and Our Saviour Jesus Christ, Who Preserved the Life of Wilm Dickins Aprl 17th 1718 when he was Pointing the Steepel and Fell From the Rige of the Middel Window in the Spiar Over the South West Pinackel he Dropt Upon the Batelment and their Broake his Leg and foot and Drove Down 2 Long Copein Stone and so fell to the Ground with his Neck Upon one Standard of his Chear When the Other End took the Ground Which was the Nearest of Killing him Yet when he See he was Faling Crid Out to his Brother Lord Daniel Wots the Matter Lord Have Mercy Upon Me Christ Have Mercy Upon me Lord Jesus Christ Help me. But Now Almost to the Ground. Died Nov 29, 1759. Aged 73 Years.

Pope John Paul II reflects on work

God's fundamental and original intention with regard to man, whom he created in his image and after his likeness, was not withdrawn or cancelled out even when man, having broken the original covenant with God, heard the words: 'In the sweat of your face you shall eat bread'. These words refer to *the sometimes heavy toil* that from then onwards has accompanied human work; but they do not alter the fact that work is the means whereby man *achieves that 'dominion'* which is proper to him over the visible world, by 'subjecting' the earth. Toil is something that is universally known, for it is universally experienced. It is familiar to those doing physical work under sometimes exceptionally laborious conditions. It is familiar not only to agricultural workers, who spend long days working the land, which sometimes 'bears thorns and thistles', but also to those who work in mines and quarries, to steel-workers at their blast-furnaces, to those who work in builders' yards and in construction work, often in danger of injury or death. It is likewise familiar to those at an intellectual workbench; to scientists; to those who bear the burden of grave responsibility for decisions that will have a vast impact on society. It is familiar to doctors and nurses, who spend days and nights at their patients' bedside. It is familiar to women, who, sometimes without proper recognition on the part of society and even of their own families, bear the daily burden and responsibility for their homes and the upbringing of their children. *It is familiar to all workers* and, since work is a universal calling, it is familiar to everyone.

From *Laborem exercens*

Most merciful Father,
we thank you for miners, fire fighters, and steeplejacks
and for the courage of all whose work
involves risking their lives for others;
give them foresight and concentration,
grant them your protection
and give peace to them and their families;
through Jesus Christ our Lord. Amen.

Elizabeth I 1533–1603

Queen of England

———

LIKE MANY OTHER monarchs Elizabeth often travelled with her court and we know that she stayed in many places in the diocese, including Knebworth House, Old Gorhambury, Woburn Abbey and Toddington Manor. She spent much of her childhood at the Royal Palace of Hatfield, only part of which survives today, and it was there in 1558, allegedly sitting beneath an oak tree in the grounds reading a book, that she was told that she had succeeded to the throne. She held her first Council of State in the Great Hall at Hatfield. Elizabeth's genius was to unite a country which was deeply divided over religious matters and to preside over the 'golden age' of William Shakespeare, Christopher Marlowe and William Byrd.

Queen Elizabeth on religion from a speech at the close of Parliament, 1585

One thing I may not overskip. Religion, the ground on which all other matters ought to take root, and, being corrupted, may mar all the tree. And that there be some fault-finders with the order of the clergy, which so may make a slander to myself, and to the church, whose over-ruler God hath made me, whose negligence cannot be excused, if any schisms or errors heretical were suffered. Thus much I must say, that some faults and negligences must grow and be, as in all other great charges it happeneth; and what vocation without? All which, if you, my lords of the clergy, do not amend, I mean to depose you. Look ye, therefore, well to your charges. This may be amended without needless or open exclamations. I am supposed to have many studies, but most philosophical. I must yield this to be true, that I suppose few (that be no professors) have read more. And I need not tell you, that I am not so simple that I understand not, nor so forgetful that I remember not; and yet, amidst my many volumes, I hope God's book hath not been my seldomest lectures, in which we find that which by reason all ought to believe. I see many overbold with God Almighty, making too many subtle scannings of his blessed will. The presumption is so great that I may not suffer it.

From G. W. Prothero's *Select Statutes and other Constitutional Documents*

———

Stretch forth, O Lord most mighty, Thy right hand over me, and defend me from mine enemies, that they never prevail against me. Give me, O Lord, the assistance of Thy Spirit, and comfort of Thy grace, truly to know Thee, entirely to love Thee, and assuredly to trust in Thee. And that as I do acknowledge to have received the government of this Church and Kingdom at Thy hand, and to hold the same of Thee, so grant me grace, O Lord, that in the end I may render up and present the same again unto Thee, a peaceable, quiet, and well-ordered State and Kingdom, as also a perfect reformed church, to the furtherance of Thy glory. And to my subjects, O Lord God, grant, I beseech Thee, faithful and obedient hearts, willingly to submit themselves to the obedience of Thy word and commandments, that we altogether being thankful unto Thee for Thy benefits received, may laud and magnify Thy Holy Name world without end. Grant this, O merciful Father, for Jesus Christ's sake, our only Mediator and Advocate. Amen.

Queen Elizabeth I

Joseph Arthur Rank 1888–1972

Miller and film maker

————

ARTHUR RANK WAS possibly the most successful film maker in the United Kingdom. In 1946 his companies owned five studios (one of which was at Elstree in this diocese) and 650 cinemas. Throughout his life Rank was a practising Methodist. He established the Religious Films Society in 1933 to promote films with a religious and moral message. On one occasion he declared, 'I am in films because of the Holy Spirit' and never made decisions unless he had prayed about them. Rank was born in Drypool. He did not excel at boarding school in Cambridge and started work with his father's milling business, spending a year as an apprentice in Luton. The business grew quickly under his leadership and he became extremely wealthy. In 1917 he married Laura Ellen Marshall with whom he had three children. As well as its core business of making films, the Rank Organisation diversified into the manufacture of radios, televisions and Rank Xerox photocopiers and also became one of the wealthiest charities in Britain.

Bernard Brandon Scott writes about the power of story

A movie may be popular, and reach a mass audience for a variety of complex reasons. Certainly the media moguls cannot force us to view what we do not want to watch. Nor is a movie's popularity a matter of a good advertising campaign, although that is important. Many movies have failed at the box office even though they had strong campaigns, and others have succeeded without massive advertising. Sometimes the studios are surprised. If the moguls could decree our likes, then movie-making would not be such a risky business. One reason a movie does well is that it intersects with basic struggles, conflicts, or tensions within a society in such a way that it provides a temporarily masked resolution to that conflict. Frequently, people complain that serious movies should be entertaining and make us feel good. In other words, the movies should live up to their mythical dimension. Because the ancients propagated their myths in stories of the gods, we think that myth belongs to the past and has been superseded by Christianity and modern science. But that misunderstanding only allows myth to remain hidden. Basically, myth is a narrative that mediates fundamental conflicts by indirection so that we are not even aware that it is happening. We have seen all these characteristics in the popular movies we have just reviewed. We propagate our myths in films and TV programs. We sit before their flickering light and listen to this new shaman sing our songs. Yet just as these media can be used to propagate myth, they also can be turned against myth when they refuse to mediate the conflict, thereby making us aware of what is really happening. When Job refuses to buy his friends' explanation of why misfortune has befallen him – when he refuses to blame himself – he upsets the order of the universe and exposes for all time the basically unsolved problem of good and evil: how can a good God be implicated in an evil world? Likewise, when Martin Scorsese in *Goodfellas* refuses to ennoble the violence of the mobsters as other gangster movies such as *The Godfather* have, we are forced to come to terms with our own violence. The mask is removed.

From *Hollywood Dreams and Biblical Stories*

Lord Jesus Christ,
who taught your followers through story and parable:
bless writers, actors and film makers with skill, imagination and creativity;
may they practise their art with joy and integrity;
and inspire us to courage and compassion;
through Jesus Christ our Lord. Amen.

William Cowper 1731–1800

Poet, hymn writer and translator

———

TODAY WE REMEMBER Cowper as the hymn writer who wrote *God moves in a mysterious way, Hark my soul it is the Lord, Jesus where'er thy people meet* and *Oh for a closer walk with God*. However, during his life he was celebrated as a translator of classical texts and as one of the outstanding poets of his generation. Wordsworth praised his poetry and Coleridge described him as 'the best modern poet'. His work was deeply influenced by his evangelical faith and also by his love of nature. Cowper's father, who was Rector of St Peter's, Berkhamsted, sent him to Dr Pitman's School in Markyate, before going on to Westminster School. While he was training as a lawyer he had a mental breakdown and attempted suicide on at least three occasions. To recuperate he was sent to St Albans where he was treated in the asylum run by Dr Nathaniel Cotton. When he had recovered Cowper went to Huntingdon to stay with the Reverend Morley Unwin and his wife Mary. When Unwin died two years later, Cowper and Mary moved to Olney and it was there that he and John Newton, the converted slave trader, became friends. Newton included some of Cowper's hymns in his hymnal which became known as the *Olney Hymns*. We know that Cowper was a Deputy Lieutenant of Hertfordshire for a time, as in 1761 he signed an order for one William Dowsing of Ayot St Peter. In 1773 Cowper's mental health again deteriorated and it was largely due to the support of Mary Unwin, who encouraged him to compose more poetry, that he recovered and went on to write *The Task* and *The Diverting History of John Gilpin*. During the last twelve years of his life he translated a number of Greek works into English including Homer's *Iliad* and *Odyssey*. He died on this day in 1800 and is buried at East Dereham in Norfolk, where he and Mary had moved to five years previously.

God moves in a mysterious way
His wonders to perform;
He plants His footsteps in the sea
And rides upon the storm.

Deep in unfathomable mines
Of never failing skill
He treasures up His bright designs
And works His sov'reign will.

Ye fearful saints, fresh courage take;
The clouds ye so much dread
Are big with mercy and shall break
In blessings on your head.

Judge not the Lord by feeble sense,
But trust Him for His grace;
Behind a frowning providence
He hides a smiling face.

His purposes will ripen fast,
Unfolding every hour;
The bud may have a bitter taste,
But sweet will be the flow'r.

Blind unbelief is sure to err
And scan His work in vain;
God is His own interpreter,
And He will make it plain.

Lord Jesus Christ, who for love of our souls
entered the deep darkness of the cross:
we pray that your love may surround all
who are in the darkness of great mental distress
and who find it difficult to pray for themselves.
May they know that darkness
and light are both alike to you
and that you have promised
never to fail them or forsake them.
We ask it for your name's sake. Amen.

Llewellyn Cummings

Guinevere Mary Ashwell 1934–2011

Foster mother and teacher

MANY PARENTS FIND child rearing challenging, but during her lifetime Guinevere Ashwell and her husband Eric fostered more than seventy children. Guinevere Edwards was born in Oswestry and after leaving school she trained as a domestic science teacher at Abergavenny. She worked as a supply teacher for many years and when she moved to Cambridge in 1971 she taught in a number of schools in Bedfordshire. She met Eric Ashwell, whilst working in a Mental Health Unit in Cambridge, and they married in 1963. Their daughter, Helen, was born in 1966. Five years later, the family left Cambridge and moved to Sandy. Eric worked as a civil engineer at Cardington, and they worshipped at St Swithun's Church in Sandy. Guinevere ran the Sunday School for more than nine years, producing an annual Nativity play each Epiphany, and also founded the 'Skyjack' group for teenagers, which met at her house on Sunday afternoons. She also instigated an annual Youth Weekend at Chellington. However, one of her greatest achievements was her commitment to fostering. Some of the children stayed a few days, others for longer periods. Rachel and her sister Natasha were two such – Rachel lived with Guinevere and Eric for eighteen months, and they adopted Natasha when she was twelve; she lived with them for sixteen years.

Mary Sumner, founder of the Mothers' Union, sets out some of the principles of their work

That the prosperity of a nation springs from the family life of the homes. That family life is the greatest institution in the world for the formation of the character of children. That the tone of family life depends in great measure upon the married life of the parents – their mutual love, loyalty and faithfulness the one to the other. That religion is the indispensable foundation of family life, and that the truths of the Christian faith should be taught definitely at home as well as at school. That parents are themselves responsible for the religious teaching of their children. That character is formed during the first ten years of life by the example and habits of home. That example is stronger than precept, and parents therefore must be themselves what they wish their children to be. That the history of the world proves the divine power given by God to parents, and to mothers especially, because children are placed in their arms from infancy, in a more intimate and closer relationship with the mother than with the father, and this moreover, during the time when character is formed. That the training of children is a profession. That it needs faith, love, patience, method, self-control, and some knowledge of the principles of character-training. That it is the duty of every mother with her own lips to teach her child that he is God's child, consecrated body and soul in Holy Baptism to be our Lord Jesus Christ's soldier and servant unto his life's end. That every baptised child should be taught the Creed, the Lord's Prayer and the Ten Commandments and all other things which a Christian ought to know and believe to his soul's health.

From *Mary Sumner: Her Life and Work* by Mary Porter

Gracious God,
whose Son Jesus Christ shared at Nazareth the life of an earthly home:
we pray that parents everywhere may model your unconditional love,
that their children may grow up in an atmosphere of security and trust,
with a sense of right and wrong
and in the confidence that comes from knowing they are loved;
for Christ's sake. Amen.

Angus Campbell MacInnes 1901–77

Bishop of Bedford and Archbishop of Jerusalem

———

BORN INTO A clerical dynasty (his father was Bishop of Jerusalem, and his son and grandson were also ordained) Campbell MacInnes was educated at Harrow and Trinity College, Cambridge. He was ordained and served his curacy at St Mary's Peckham, following which he went on to serve in the Middle East. For a period he was Archdeacon of Palestine, Syria and Trans-Jordan but returned to England in 1950 to become Vicar of St Michael's, St Albans. In 1953 he was consecrated Bishop of Bedford. Four years later he was made Archbishop of Jerusalem and Metropolitan of the Province. He retired in 1969 and died in 1977.

The duties of a bishop according to a Celtic monastic rule of the seventh century

If you are a member of the noble order of bishops, take up your service wholeheartedly, be subject in all honesty to the Lord, and let all be obedient to you. Cure all harmful ailments through the power of the good Lord, establish peace among the people, restrain the noble kings. In your dealings with clergy and laity alike, act as becomes a pastor. Be assiduous in preaching, be gracious, be pleasant. The suppression of the wicked who love to do evil, and the exaltation of the truth, are duties that become you. When accepting holy orders you should be familiar with Scripture, for you will be a stepson of the church if you are unprepared and ignorant. It is true indeed that every ignorant person is uncouth, and someone who does not read the testament of the Lord is not a true successor of his. Truly it belongs to you to condemn all heresy and all evil. Therefore be not yourself guilty of any evil, either in word or in deed. The wicked will not rise at your approach, nor will they obey you. You yourself will be blameworthy if you are gentle with them. It is certain that you will be answerable on the great judgement day for the sins of your subjects, as well as for your own faults.

From *The Rule of Carthage* in R. R. Atwell's *Celebrating the Saints*

———

Grant, O God, we beseech thee, that the same mind may be in all the ministers of thy Church that was in Christ Jesus:
    his self-forgetting humility
    his interest in common things;
    his love for common people;
    his compassion for the fallen;
    his tolerance with the mistaken;
    his patience with the slow;
    and in all their work and converse make them continually sensitive
to thy guidance and ready for thy will; through Jesus Christ our Lord.
Amen.

Methodist Church, Book of Offices

Basil Tudor Guy 1910–75

Bishop of Bedford and Gloucester

———

WHEN BASIL GUY suggested that the Church should use an advertising agency to increase the number of people going to church, he created a stir in the national newspapers and a horrified response in many pews. However, the idea of an advertising campaign was picked up in 1991 when the Diocese of Oxford ran a poster at Christmas 'Wrap up the kids and bring them to church' and in the following year the Churches Advertising Network was established. In 1994 the Church of England report *Paying the Piper* examined the place of advertising and concluded 'We believe that advertising can be a creative, effective, appropriate, even amusing means of communication for the Church.' Clearly Guy was a man ahead of his time. Basil Guy was educated at Forest School, Walthamstow, Keble College, Oxford, and Wells Theological College. He was made a deacon in 1934 and served a seven-year curacy at Wanstead. In 1941 he moved to become Vicar of Bradninch near Cullompton and five years later he was appointed Vicar of Tavistock. Guy was consecrated Bishop of Bedford in 1957 and translated to the See of Gloucester in 1962. He died of cancer whilst still in office in 1975.

Basil Guy writes about the problem of suffering

All suffering and pain are part of the mystery of human life and we shall never understand them fully until 'we know even as we are known' in Heaven. But God has revealed certain great principles which help us to see some way into the mystery even now. 'In the beginning' there was no suffering because everything that God made was 'very good.' And in the end there will 'be no more death, neither sorrow nor crying, neither will there be any more pain' because again everything will be 'very good.' But here and now pain and suffering exist as part of that great disorder that man's sin and foolishness have brought into God's world. We get ill and suffer pain not because we ourselves are especially wicked sinners but because we are men and women and live in a world which sin has spoilt. But God is working in the world. He is using the very disorder which men have made to redeem us and lead us all back again to him. As in the Crucifixion itself, so always God uses evil, to make good if we will co-operate with him. That is the great vocation to which we are called – not to be just 'bearers' suffering dumbly like animals but active partners with God working with him to bring good out of evil.

From *When you are ill*

———

Gracious Lord,
we lift before you those who are ill and the dying:
ease their pains, quell their fears
and grant that they may rest in your perfect love;
give wisdom to the doctors, compassion to the nurses,
patience to their families and to those who are anxious
the gift of your peace which passes human understanding;
for we ask this in the name of Jesus Christ, the suffering servant. Amen.

Richard Field 1561–1616

Theologian

TODAY RICHARD FIELD is mainly remembered for his book *Of the Church*, in which he argued that the Church of England is a natural continuation of the early Church and as such has held true to the apostolic tradition. Field believed that the Church of England should be bound by the decrees of the first seven ecumenical councils. He was an ally of the Anglican theologian Richard Hooker. Field was born in Hemel Hempstead and was educated at Berkhamsted School and Oxford University. He held various posts, including catechism lecturer at Oxford University, divinity reader at Winchester Cathedral, and lecturer in divinity at Lincoln's Inn. He was Rector of Burghclere, Hampshire, Prebend of Windsor, and in 1610 was made Dean of Gloucester. He married twice and had seven children by his first wife. He is buried in St George's Chapel, Windsor Castle.

Richard Field writes about the nature of the Church

There are, and have been always some, who, possessed with a false opinion of absolute sanctity, and spotless righteousness, reject the societies and companies of them in whom any imperfection may be found; which was the furious zeal of the Pelagians in old time, and the Anabaptists in our time. Others there are, which, though they proceed not so far, yet deny those societies of Christians to be the true Churches of God, wherein the severity of discipline is so far neglected, that wicked men are suffered and tolerated without due and condign punishment. These, while they seem to hate the wicked, and fly from their company for fear of contagion, do schismatically rent, and inconsiderately divide themselves from the body of God's Church, and forsake the fellowship of the good, through immoderate hate of the wicked. But these do dangerously and damnably err; the first in that they dream of heavenly perfection to be found amongst men on earth, when as contrariwise the prophet Isaiah pronounceth, that 'all our righteousness is like the polluted and filthy rags...' And David desireth of Almighty God, that he will 'not enter into judgement with him, for that in his sight no flesh shall be justified:' and Augustine denounceth a woe against our greatest perfections, if God do straitly look upon them. The latter, though they do not require absolute and spotless perfection in them that are in and of the Church, yet think it not possible that any wicked ones should be found in so happy and blessed a society: not remembering that the Church of God is compared to 'a net, that gathereth into it all sorts of fishes, great and small, good and bad,' which are not separated one from another, till they be cast out upon the shore; that it is like 'a field sown with good seed wherein the envious man soweth tares'; like 'a floor, wherein wheat and chaff are mingled together;' like the 'ark of Noah, wherein cursed Cham was as well preserved from drowning as blessed Sem.'

From *Of the Church: Five Bookes*

Lord Jesus Christ,
we thank you for your church
which has borne witness to your truth over the centuries:
forgive our sins, heal our divisions
and grant us that unity for which you prayed,
that the world may believe;
for we ask it for your name's sake. Amen.

Edward Miall 1809–81

Journalist and Congregational minister

———

DURING THE SECOND half of the nineteenth century Edward Miall was well known as a passionate campaigner for the disestablishment of the Church of England. To further this cause he founded a newspaper in 1841, *The Nonconformist*, arguing that Nonconformity had to be represented in the House of Commons. By 1852 forty 'dissenters' had been elected to Parliament. Miall himself was elected as Liberal Member of Parliament for Rochdale in 1852 and he represented the constituency of Bradford in 1860–74. He had a close connection with Hertfordshire during the years he served as a Congregational minister at Ware. He died on this day in 1881.

From an article by Edward Miall

We are made 'partakers of the Divine nature,' by possessing ourselves of that which is divine in his acts and truths. He who recognises God's wisdom, has within himself the wisdom of God, to the whole extent of that recognition. He who sympathises with God's purity, has within himself the purity of God, to the whole extent of that sympathy. The life of which we speak is God in the soul up to the measure of the soul's present capacity – and hence our Lord speaks not figuratively but literally when he declares 'And this is life eternal, that they might know thee the only true God, and Jesus Christ, whom thou hast sent.' In the nature of religious life, as thus understood, we shall find, without difficulty, guidance to a vivid apprehension of its growth, to foster which all Christian institutions are maintained. *More of God* made the property of the soul is the radical idea – more of God both as it regards the breadth of our acquaintance with him by increased knowledge, and its intimacy by intenser sympathy. As the bee wings its way from flower to flower, sucks honey from each, and makes its own that subtle element in each which, extracted, constitutes sweetness, so the wakened spirit of man roams over the vast realms of nature, hovers about the proceedings of Providence, or lingers in the richer and more favourite fields of the Gospel, in search of God – and in every object upon which contemplation alights, in every law engraven upon physical being, in every cognisable connection of means with ends, in every principle of moral government, in every historical illustration of its main bent and purpose, and, above all, in the yet more genial, because, so far as our apprehensions are concerned, more hearty exemplifications of the Divine mind and will clustered in the revealed word, whatever of God, whatever of his perfections, his character, his modes of working, his intentions, can be discerned, is appropriated by the soul; – that which, in the truest and highest sense, is the life of all things, is drawn by the renewed spirit into itself, and, made its own by knowledge and sympathy, adds to its amount of life, and constitutes growth.

From *The British Churches in relation to the British People*

———

Grant us, Gracious Lord,
eyes to perceive your hand in all things;
in the beauty and tragedy of nature
in the passion and struggle of human endeavour
in the friends who know us well enough to speak truth to us
and in the strangers who cross our path unexpectedly;
this we ask in the name of Jesus Christ. Amen.

David Livingstone 1813–73

Missionary doctor, abolitionist and explorer

——————

DAVID LIVINGSTONE WAS one of the greatest national heroes of the Victorian era and inspired generations of young men and women to offer themselves for the mission field. He was born into a poor, yet deeply religious, Scottish family. As a boy he and his brother had to work long hours in a cotton mill. Nevertheless, the mill offered a basic education for its workers and in 1836 he was able to go to Anderson's College in Glasgow to study medicine. Believing that God had called him to be a missionary in China, he was accepted for training by the London Missionary Society and completed his studies there. Unable to go to China because of the first Opium War, Livingstone came under the influence of Robert Moffat, who had been working in Africa, and Thomas Buxton (see the entry for 19 February), who was a passionate abolitionist. So in 1841 Livingstone travelled to Kuruman which was to be his base for several years. However, he soon became restless and so began the journeys for which he was to become famous. He was the first European to see Lake Ngami, the Mosi-oa-Tunya waterfall on the Zambesi (which he renamed after Queen Victoria), and Lake Malawi. Livingstone resigned from the London Missionary Society in 1857 and lived for a time in Barnet. He soon continued his explorations, looking amongst other things for the source of the Nile. For a period of six years he lost all contact with the outside world, which prompted an American newspaper to send Henry Stanley to find him. Livingstone died from malaria and dysentery, kneeling in prayer by his bedside. His body, minus his heart, was sent back to England with a message from the local people: 'You can have his body, but his heart belongs in Africa'.

Some famous quotations of David Livingstone

I place no value on anything I have or may possess, except in relation to the kingdom of Christ. If anything will advance the interests of the kingdom, it shall be given away or kept, only as by giving or keeping it I shall promote the glory of Him to whom I owe all my hopes in time and eternity.

I am prepared to go anywhere, provided it be forward.

I never show all my feelings; but I can truly say, my dearest, that I loved you when I married you, and the longer I lived with you, I loved you the better…Let us do our duty to Christ, and He will bring us through the world with honour and usefulness. He is our refuge and high tower; let us trust in Him at all times, and in all circumstances. Love Him more and more, and diffuse His love among the children. Take them all around you, and kiss them for me.

From a letter to his wife

I have nothing better to say to you than to take God for your Father, Jesus for your Saviour, and the Holy Spirit for your sanctifier. Do this and you are safe for ever. No evil can then befall you.

From a letter to one of his children

O Jesus, fill me with thy love now,
and I beseech thee, accept me,
and use me a little for thy glory.
O do, do, I beseech thee, accept me and my service,
and take thou all the glory. Amen.

David Livingstone

George Joye c.1492–1553

Reformer

———

GEORGE JOYE WAS raised in Renhold, Bedfordshire, and went up to Christ's College, Cambridge, in 1509. He was ordained as a subdeacon at Newnham Priory in Bedford in 1515. Two years later he became a Fellow of Peterhouse, Cambridge. In 1527 Joye was found guilty of holding heretical beliefs and was summoned to appear before Cardinal Wolsey in Westminster. He immediately fled to Strasbourg where he published a book defending his views. These were dangerous days as other reformers, such as Thomas Bilney and William Tyndale, were being put to death. On one occasion Joye was nearly captured but he managed to evade his pursuers. During the 1530s Joye spent much of his time on the Continent and published various sections of the Bible translated into English. He returned to live in England for short periods between persecutions. However, in 1546 his books were publicly burnt in London. When Edward VI came to the throne Joye again returned. In 1549 he became Rector of Blunham in Bedfordshire and in the following year he was appointed Rector of Ashwell in Hertfordshire. Joye was married and had eight children.

Myles Coverdale writes about loving others

This excellent learning then of Christ must be established in us, that we think us not to be born unto ourselves, but to the honour of God and wealth of all men: so that, loving him again which bestowed himself on us altogether for our redemption, we also for his sake love other men, and abhor their vices; having not only respect to their need, and what we are able to do for them, but also remembering the manifold causes, that by reason should move us to love them, to tender them, to be at one with them, and not to account them as strangers, or to hate them for any alteration of vesture, or of any such trifle; yea, in no wise to despise them, but esteeming their hurt our own; to consider that, whatsoever we have received, it is given us to bestow upon them, and to increase in edifying of them in charity. This learning will induce men to desire no vengeance, but to be the sons of their Father in heaven, to overcome evil with good, to suffer hurt rather than to do it, to forgive other men's offences, to be gentle in manners; if they be cunning, to forbear and amend the ignorance of the unlearned; if they be rich, to be circumspect in distributing the goods that God hath given them; in poverty, to be as well content as other men; in office, to be more careful and diligent in considering their charge, in noting the manners of evil persons, yet not to despise the profession of virtue.

From *Writings and Translations of Myles Coverdale* edited by G. Pearson

———

O Lord Jesus Christ, draw thou our hearts unto thee;
join them together in inseparable love, that we may abide in thee, and thou in us,
and that the everlasting covenant between us may stand sure forever.
O wound our hearts with the fiery darts of thy piercing love.
Let them pierce through all our slothful members and inward powers,
that we, being happily wounded, may so become whole and sound.
Let us have no lover but thyself alone;
let us seek no joy nor comfort except in thee. Amen.

Myles Coverdale

John Mattock 17th century

Benefactor

LITTLE IS KNOWN about John Mattock, although it is likely that he came from Coventry. The trust document setting up Hitchin Grammar School stated that 'the ancestors of the said John Mattock have for many ages and yeares last past been and continued inhabitants within the Towne of Hitchin of principall Ranke qualitie and degree, and have duringe the tyme of their aboade there been helpfull and beneficiall to the inhabitants there, and from whom the dwellers have had countenance, comfort and reliefe.' It appears that Mattock owned significant tracts of land around the town and a home in Bancroft Street. In 1639 he set up a charity to endow the school, giving it six acres of pasture in an area called Conygree, and three acres of meadow called Cow Close. The trustees had to ensure that the rent from the land should be used 'to the maintenance of an able and learned schoolmaster for instructing the children of the inhabitants of Hitchin in good literature and virtuous education for the avoiding of idleness, the mother of all vice and wickedness.' Thus Hitchin Grammar School, today known as Hitchin Boys' School, was founded. Its first Headmaster was Thomas Heyndy and he was given responsibility to run the school at which the pupils had to learn 'The Eight parts of Speech, the Three Concords of Grammar, the Right Ordering of Sentences, Repetitions, Translations, Declamations, Faire-Wrighting, Cipherage and Castinge of Accompts.'

Jeremy Taylor reflects on the dangers of idleness

God hath given every man work enough to do, that there shall be no room for idlenesse, and yet hath so ordered the world, that there shall be space for devotion. He that hath the fewest businesses of the world, is called upon to spend more time in the dressing of his soul, and he that hath the most affairs, may so order them, that they shall be a service of God; whilst at certain periods they are blessed with prayers and actions of religion, and all day long are hallowed by a holy intention. However, so long as idlenesse is quite shut out from our lives, all the sins of wantonnesse, softenesse and effeminacy are prevented, and there is but little room left for temptation: and therefore to a busie man temptation is fain to climbe up together with his businesses, and sins creep upon him only by accidents and occasions; whereas to an idle person they come in a full body, and with open violence, and the impudence of a restlesse importunity. Idlenesse is called *the sin of Sodom and her daughters*, and indeed is *the burial of a living man*, an idle person being so uselesse to any purposes of God and man, that he is like one that is dead, unconcerned in the changes and necessities of the world.

From *The Whole Works of the Right Reverend Jeremy Taylor*

O Lord and Master of my life,
a spirit of idleness, despondency, ambition, and idle talking give me not.
But rather a spirit of chastity, humble-mindedness, patience,
and love bestow upon me Thy servant.
Yea, O Lord King, grant me to see my failings and not condemn my brother;
for blessed art Thou unto the ages of ages. Amen.

The Prayer of St Ephraim the Syrian

Mary Field d.1792

Housekeeper and grandmother

IN THE CHURCHYARD in Widford we find the grave of Mary Field, known today because of her famous grandson, the poet Charles Lamb. Lamb and his sister spent much of their childhood at Blakesware, a house near Widford, where their grandmother was housekeeper to the Plumer family. Lamb recalled his visits there in his essays *Blakesmoor in H----shire* and *Dream Children* and he held a great affection for the village and the surrounding area. The original of Lamb's 'Rosamund Gray' is said to have been a native of Widford. Lamb's poem *The Grandame* says of his grandmother

> She served her heavenly master. I have seen
> That reverend form bent down with age and pain,
> And ranking malady. Yet not for this
> Ceased she to praise her Maker, or withdraw
> Her trust in Him, her faith, and humble hope;
> So meekly had she learned to bear her cross –
> For she had studied patience in the school
> Of Christ; much comfort she had thence derived,
> And was a follower of the Nazarene.

Mary Field represents all those parents and relatives who will never know the influence their life and example has had on the young people who knew them.

Charles Lamb describes his grandmother

Then I went on to say, how religious and how good their great-grandmother Field was, how beloved and respected by every body, though she was not indeed the mistress of this great house, but had only the charge of it (and yet in some respects she might be said to be the mistress of it too) committed to her by the owner, who preferred living in a newer and more fashionable mansion which he had purchased somewhere in the adjoining county; but still she lived in it in a manner as if it had been her own, and kept up the dignity of the great house in a sort while she lived, which afterwards came to decay, and was nearly pulled down…And then I told how, when she came to die, her funeral was attended by a concourse of all the poor, and some of the gentry too, of the neighbourhood for many miles round, to show their respect for her memory, because she had been such a good and religious woman; so good indeed that she knew all the Psaltery by heart, ay, and a great part of the Testament besides. Here little Alice spread her hands. Then I told what a tall, upright, graceful person their great-grandmother Field once was; and how in her youth she was esteemed the best dancer – here Alice's little right foot played an involuntary movement, till, upon my looking grave, it desisted – the best dancer, I was saying, in the county.

From *Dream Children*

> *Almighty Father*
> *we thank you for grandparents;*
> *for the wealth of their wisdom,*
> *the richness of their experience,*
> *and their gift of perspective.*
> *Strengthen the bonds within the families of our nation*
> *and especially those between grandparents and grandchildren,*
> *for we ask it in the name of Jesus Christ our Lord. Amen.*

St Fremund 9th century

Hermit and martyr

———

MUCH OF FREMUND'S life is shrouded in history but it is likely that he was the son of King Offa of Mercia. When Offa converted to Christianity, Fremund followed his example. Called to a life of prayer, he went to Lundy Island to live as a hermit. When the Vikings invaded and were threatening the kingdom, Fremund was summoned to fight in the battle which took place near Offchurch. The Vikings were defeated and in thanksgiving Fremund knelt to pray. A soldier, jealous of Fremund's prowess, attacked and killed him. His corpse was taken to the church of Cropredy near Banbury, where it was reported that miracles took place. As a result Fremund was made a saint. Around the year 1122 the Prior of Dunstable obtained Fremund's bones and commissioned a casket in which to keep them. It is thought that the Prior wanted to have a shrine similar to the shrine in St Albans. For centuries Dunstable held an annual fair on St Fremund's Day. In 1968 the Bishop of St Albans consecrated a new church dedicated to St Fremund the Martyr which today serves the northern part of Dunstable.

Richard Foster writes about Christian simplicity

Asceticism and simplicity are mutually incompatible. Occasional superficial similarities in practice must never obscure the radical difference between the two. Asceticism renounces possessions. Simplicity sets possessions in proper perspective. Asceticism can find no place for a 'land flowing with milk and honey.' Simplicity can rejoice in this gracious provision from the hand of God. Asceticism can find contentment only when it is abased. Simplicity knows contentment in both abasement and abounding (Philippians 4.12). Simplicity is the only thing that can sufficiently reorient our lives so that possessions can be genuinely enjoyed without destroying us. Without simplicity we will either capitulate to the 'mammon' spirit of this present evil age, or we will fall into an un-Christian legalistic asceticism. Both lead to idolatry. Both are spiritually lethal. Scripture abounds in descriptions of the abundant material provision God gives His people. 'For the Lord your God is bringing you into a good land…a land…in which you will lack nothing' (Deuteronomy 8.7–9). It also abounds in warnings about the danger of provisions that are not kept in proper perspective. 'Beware lest you say in your heart, "My power and the might of my hand have gotten me this wealth"' (Deuteronomy 8.17). The spiritual Discipline of simplicity provides the needed perspective. Simplicity sets us free to receive the provision of God as a gift that is not ours to keep, and that can be freely shared with others. Once we recognize that the Bible denounces the materialist and the ascetic with equal vigour, we are prepared to turn our attention to the framing of a Christian understanding of simplicity.

From *Celebration of Discipline*

———

Almighty God, we thank you for the life of St Fremund
who, following the example of your Son Jesus Christ,
left the comfort of his home to seek you in a life of solitude.
Amidst the frantic busyness of our life,
help us to find oases of silence and contemplation
that we may encounter you in your love and grace
and then be sent out as your witnesses.
We ask this in the name of Jesus Christ our Lord. Amen.

Joseph Finch Fenn 1820–84

Vicar of Stotfold

———

THE BEAUTIFUL MEDIEVAL church of St Mary sits in the middle of the small town of Stotfold, just to the north of Letchworth. One of its most famous vicars was Joseph Fenn, who served there between 1847 and 1860. Fenn had been born in Travancore in India but was educated in England at Blackheath Proprietary School. He studied at Trinity College, Cambridge, and was ordained in 1845. He was elected to a fellowship of Trinity which he held for three years. Following his time as Vicar of Stotfold, he became the perpetual curate of Christ Church, Cheltenham, in 1860. As the population grew he was instrumental in the building of the new church of St Stephen, Tivoli, in the parish. He was appointed as chaplain to the Bishop of Gloucester in 1877 and became an honorary canon two years later. He is buried in a family vault in Leckhampton.

Joseph Fenn preaches on 1 Corinthians 13.1–3

Though I speak with the tongues of men and of angels, and have not charity, I am become as sounding brass, or a tinkling cymbal. And though I have the gift of prophecy, and understand all mysteries and all knowledge; and though I have all faith so that I could remove mountains, and have not charity, I am nothing. And though I bestow all my goods to feed the poor and though I give my body to be burned, and have not charity, it profiteth me nothing. St Paul's most beautiful description of true human love in this chapter ought to be well and often considered by us all. There is a remarkable contrast between his method here and that which he adopts in all other cases, and which is adopted also by St Peter and St John. Here, you will remember, he makes no direct allusion to the example of our Blessed Lord. In other cases he and his fellow apostles base their descriptions of Christian love, and their exhortations to it, on the love of Christ as the example and the motive and the power which are to produce true love in us. Of course everyone who reads the Gospels, and who knows our Lord Jesus Christ in any degree as described in the Gospels, must and will observe that every feature of the portrait of Love here drawn has its true exemplification in the Jesus of the Gospels, in the human character of our Lord. And as certainly every true student of the New Testament will see that in that Character, the true Character of Eternal God, the Father, the Son, and the Holy Spirit, is set forth directly. And all this is most important to observe. The Name is not mentioned. The reality is there. We read, between the lines, St John's principle: 'Herein is love, not that we loved God, but that He loved us and sent His Son to be the propitiation for our sins. Hereby perceive we love because He laid down His life for us.' We seem to hear our Saviour saying to us – 'This is my love. Continue ye in my love.'

From *Lenten Teachings*

Heavenly Father,
who has revealed in the life and teaching of your Son Jesus Christ
the true nature of divine love: teach us to follow his example,
that in loving the unlovely and loving our enemies
we may discover that we too are loved unconditionally;
for we ask it for your Son's sake. Amen.

Georgiana Arabella Caldecott Gall 1825–46

Mother

———

SOME FAMILIES EXPERIENCE terrible suffering. Such was the case with Georgiana Gall's family. She was the daughter of John Thomas James who had been appointed Bishop of Calcutta in 1827 when she was just two years old. Having been consecrated in England he set off to Calcutta with his wife and baby, leaving his two other children (one of whom was Georgiana) behind in East Sheen. The following year he died on a sea journey between Calcutta and Penang. We know little about Georgiana's life, except what is recorded on her memorial in St Mary's Church, Baldock.

> *Behold God is my salvation: I will trust and not be afraid:*
> *For the Lord Jehovah is my strength and my song;*
> *He also is become my salvation*
> *Georgiana Arabella Caldecott*
> *only daughter of John Thomas James, Bishop of Calcutta*
> *wife of George Lawrence Herbert Gall of the Elms in this parish Esq*
> *Captain in the Madras Cavalry*
> *She died at Torquay after giving birth to a daughter which lived*
> *only to be baptised on the 20th of April 1846 aged 21 years.*

The monument shows Georgiana lying on a couch. A young woman is kneeling at her feet. Behind her an angel is bearing her soul up into heaven. Not far away we find another memorial in the church. This is for her husband, whose life also ended tragically when he was killed at Bareilly in India.

Francis de Sales reflects on how a Christian should face suffering

Do not put a limit on your patience in the face of various kinds of injury or affliction, but rather embrace every trial that God permits to come upon you. Be patient, not only in the case of great trials which may befall you, but also in the face of petty things and accidents. Many people do not mind encountering difficulties, provided they are not put out by them. 'I don't mind being poor,' says one person, 'were it not for the fact that it means that I cannot entertain my friends'...'It would not concern me,' says another, 'If I were poor, provided people did not think it was through my fault'...Others are willing to suffer a little, but not too much: they do not mind being ill as long as they have the money to pay for a cure. To all such I say that we must be patient, not only with the fact of illness, but with the particular circumstances in which we suffer. When you become ill, apply the remedies that are in your power, and trust to the will of God. To act otherwise is to tempt divine providence. Having done so, wait with openness to the result that God should be pleased to send. If the remedy overcomes the illness, thank God with humility; if, on the contrary, the sickness does not respond to the medication, then bless God with all patience.

From *Introduction to the Devout Life*

———

> *Holy Father, look with mercy on all who are ill or who suffer:*
> *may they know your everlasting arms holding them*
> *and your indwelling presence sustaining them.*
> *Bless those who care for the sick and suffering*
> *and give them your patience and compassion;*
> *through Jesus Christ our Lord. Amen.*

Joshua Gosselin 1739–1813

Artist

———

GOSSELIN WAS THE eldest child of Joshua and Anne Gosselin. In 1761 he married Martha le Marchant and they had six sons and eight daughters. It was a well-to-do and well-connected family and in 1768 Gosselin took over the post which his father had held as Greffier or Clerk of the Royal Court. He held the post until 1792. He was also Colonel of the North Regiment of the Militia on the island of Guernsey. Among his many and varied interests, Gosselin was a keen botanist, building up a large herbarium, and was the first to list all the plants which were to be found on the island. He was also interested in archaeology. However, it is as a landscape artist that Gosselin is chiefly remembered today. As well as painting many scenes on Guernsey, he also painted several of the churches on the island. For a time he lived at Bengeo Hall in Hertfordshire where he died. His second son married Sarah, daughter of Jeremiah Rament Hadsley of Ware Priory. Gosselin is buried in the vault of the Byde family of Ware Park.

Evelyn Underhill writes about seeing reality

What we have to find is a metaphysical landscape, a way of seeing the world, which shall justify the saint, the artist and the scientist, and give each his full rights. Not a doctrine of watertight compartments, an opposition of 'appearance' to 'reality'. Rather, a doctrine of the indwelling of this visible world by an invisible, yet truly existent, world of spirit which, while infinitely transcending, yet everywhere supports and permeates the natural scene. Even to say this, is to blur the true issue by resort to the deceptive spatial language which colours and controls our thoughts, and translate the dynamic and spiritual into static and intellectual terms. The first demand we must make of such a diagram is, that it shall at least safeguard, though it can never represent, all the best that man has learned to apprehend of the distinct and rich reality of God…For that which above all a genuine theism requires of our human ways of thinking, is the acknowledgement of two sorts or stages of reality, which can never be washed down into one: of a two-foldness that goes right through man's experience, and cannot without impoverishment be resolved. We may call these two sorts of reality, this two-foldness, by various names – Supernature and Nature, Eternity and Time, God and the World, Infinite and Finite, Creator and Creature. These terms do but emphasis one or another aspect of a total fact too great for us to grasp, without infringing the central truth of its mysterious duality: for 'God', as Plotinus says, 'never was the All. That would make Him dependent on His universe'.

From *Man and the Supernatural*

———

Heavenly Father,
whose Son Jesus Christ gave sight to the blind:
open our eyes to appreciate your world as it truly is.
May its beauty nourish our souls
and may its suffering provoke us to compassion;
we ask these things for his name's sake. Amen.

Henry Fanshawe 1569–1616

Member of Parliament

———

BOTH FANSHAWE AND his father before him held the post of the King's Remembrancer. The Remembrancer of the Exchequer is the oldest judicial position in continual existence in our country, created by King Henry II in 1154. Its purpose was 'to put the Lord Treasurer and the Barons of Court in remembrance of such things as were to be called upon and dealt with for the benefit of the Crown.' In practice this meant that the officer holder had to keep a close eye on the collection of taxes. Fanshawe's family home was at Ware Park in Hertfordshire. Henry was a keen gardener and Ware Park became famous for its gardens and particularly for its peaches – so much so that King James I had grapes and peaches sent to him twice weekly. As a young man Fanshawe studied at the Inner Temple and then went into politics. For a time he was Member of Parliament for Westbury in Wiltshire and later for Boroughbridge, Yorkshire. In 1603 he was knighted. Among his many other interests he was a keen breeder of horses and also had a special interest in Italy. He was married to Elizabeth and they had six sons. Fanshawe and his wife are buried in a vault in St Mary's Church, Ware.

D. L. Munby ponders about attitudes to wealth

Can a rich man be saved? Can a rich society be saved? We must first notice that the Christian gospel has never said that material abundance was in itself evil. The Old Testament constantly reiterated that abundance was the fruit that came of following the ways of the Lord; the Son of Man ate and drank with sinners and publicans, though he had nowhere to lay his head, and the Church has constantly prayed for abundance and prosperity for its members and their societies. The evils of riches, to the Christian, are the evils of distraction (the distraction that keeps men from thinking about God), the evils of a false dependence on the created order, and a would-be security that fails to take account of the inevitable fragility of human destiny on this earth. They are spiritual evils, not material evils, and it may be that they lead men to inadequate, not excessive, appreciation and enjoyment of the glories of the material universe; we tend to use, and abuse, material things, rather than to enjoy them.

From *God and the Rich Society*

O Lord Jesus Christ,
by your incarnation you sanctified material things
to be the means of your grace:
grant us a right attitude to money,
and a generous heart in the use of the wealth committed to us,
that by our stewardship we may glorify you,
with the Father and the Holy Spirit,
one God, now and for ever. Amen.

The Central Board of Finance of the Church of England

Charles Fraser-Smith 1904–92

Inventor, missionary and author

———

FRASER-SMITH IS BELIEVED to be the inspiration for 'Q' in the James Bond novels by Ian Fleming. During the Second World War, he worked in the Ministry of Supply and was responsible for providing the Special Operations Executive agents with what they required. Brought up in Hertfordshire, Fraser-Smith was adopted when he was seven. He was a pupil at Brighton College and then worked in a variety of roles including in an aircraft factory. Influenced by the faith of his adoptive family (they had been Christian missionaries) he went to work in Morocco as a missionary. Whilst on furlough and preaching in a church in Leeds, he described the challenges of finding supplies from every possible source. A member of the Ministry of Supply was in the congregation and before long he was offered a job with MI6, developing gadgets for agents who were working undercover in occupied Europe. Soon he was designing cameras hidden in cigarette lighters, pens which doubled as compasses and steel shoelaces that could be used as saws. He called his inventions 'Q gadgets'. Fraser-Smith played a key role in 'Operation Mincemeat' which was later made into a film, *The Man Who Never Was*. After the war, he bought a dairy farm in Devon and wrote several books about his experiences in the war. He married twice and had two children.

Dietrich Bonhoeffer reflects on how Christians should respond to evil

Jesus, however, tells us that it is just because we live in the world, and just because the world is evil, that the precept of non-resistance must be put into practice. Surely we do not wish to accuse Jesus of ignoring the reality and power of evil! Why, the whole of his life was one long conflict with the devil. He calls evil evil, and that is the very reason why he speaks to his followers in this way. How is that possible?

If we took the precept of non-resistance as an ethical blueprint for general application, we should indeed be indulging in idealistic dreams: we should be dreaming of a utopia with laws which the world would never obey. To make non-resistance a principle for secular life is to deny God, by undermining God's gracious ordinance for the preservation of the world. But Jesus is no draftsman of political blueprints; he is the one who vanquished evil through suffering. It looked as though evil had triumphed on the cross, but the real victory belonged to Jesus. And the cross is the only justification for the precept of non-violence, for it alone can kindle a faith in the victory over evil which will enable people to obey that precept. And only such obedience is blessed with the promise that we shall be partakers of Christ's victory as well as of his sufferings.

From *The Cost of Discipleship*

———

We pray to you, O God, the lover of all,
for those whom we have named our enemies.
Deliver us from the hardness of heart that keeps us locked in confrontation.
Deliver us from the hatred that binds us in old ways.
Grant unto all people the blessing of your love.
And grant unto us such transformation of our lives
that we may make peace with our enemies,
and that together we might make this world a safer place for all. Amen.

Vienna Cobb Anderson

Hugh de Beauchamp 12th–13th century

Founder of the Augustinian Priory at Bushmead

———

RECORDS SHOW THAT the Priory of Bushmead, situated between the villages of Little Staughton and Colmworth, was founded around 1195 and that Hugh de Beauchamp of Easton Socon endowed it with twenty-eight acres of land. Within a few years, under the leadership of Joseph of Coppingford, the community adopted the Augustinian Rule, allowing a small group of priests to share in monastic life together. It appears that throughout its existence it was always a tiny community comprising a handful of priest brothers. The Priory was dissolved under Henry VIII and the lands passed into the hands of William Gascoigne of Cardington, who was Controller of the Household to Cardinal Wolsey. The refectory and sections of the kitchen are the only remains of the Priory Church of St Mary.

In his Rule, written for communities such as the one at Bushmead, St Augustine describes how the brothers should order their common life

The main purpose for you having come together is to live harmoniously in your house, intent upon God in oneness of mind and heart. Call nothing your own, but let everything be yours in common. Food and clothing shall be distributed to each of you by your superior, not equally to all, for all do not enjoy equal health, but rather according to each one's need. For so you read in the Acts of the Apostles that 'they had all things in common and distribution was made to each one according to each one's need.' Those who owned something in the world should be careful in wanting to share it in common once they have entered the monastery. But they who owned nothing should not look for those things in the monastery that they were unable to have in the world. Nevertheless, they are to be given all that their health requires even if, during their time in the world, poverty made it impossible for them to find the very necessities of life. And those should not consider themselves fortunate because they have found the kind of food and clothing which they were unable to find in the world. And let them not hold their heads high, because they associate with people whom they did not dare to approach in the world, but let them rather lift up their hearts and not seek after what is vain and earthly. Otherwise, monasteries will come to serve a useful purpose for the rich and not the poor, if the rich are made humble there and the poor are puffed up with pride. The rich, for their part, who seemed important in the world, must not look down upon their brothers who have come into this holy brotherhood from a condition of poverty. They should seek to glory in the fellowship of poor brothers rather than in the reputation of rich relatives…Let all of you then live together in oneness of mind and heart, mutually honouring God in yourselves, whose temples you have become.

From *The Rule of St Augustine*

Lord God, the light of the minds that know you,
the life of the souls that love you,
and the strength of the hearts that serve you:
help us, following the example of your servant Augustine of Hippo,
so to know you that we may truly love you,
and so to love you that we may fully serve you,
and whom to serve is perfect freedom;
through Jesus Christ our Lord. Amen.

The Collect for St Augustine of Hippo

George Chapman c.1559–1634

Poet, translator and dramatist

———

GEORGE CHAPMAN WAS one of the greatest English classicists of his age and produced what became the most popular translations into English of Homer's *Iliad* and *Odyssey*. Born in Hitchin to Thomas Chapman and Joan Nodes, he studied at Oxford but did not graduate. For a period in the 1580s he worked for Sir Ralph Sadler, who had property in Hertfordshire at Standon and Preston. Chapman fought in the Low Countries in the 1590s under Captain Robert Sidney and spent a period in Middelburg Hospital in the Netherlands, presumably recovering from a wound. In 1595 he became part of Philip Henslowe's group of actors, The Admiral's Men. From 1600 until 1609 he belonged to another group of actors, The Children of the Chapel, who were based at Blackfriars Theatre. Like many other poets and playwrights, Chapman was often short of money. Throughout his life he courted, usually unsuccessfully, various patrons, such as Robert Devereux, Earl of Essex; Henry, Prince of Wales; and Robert Carr, Earl of Somerset. Chapman was a prolific and successful writer, producing a large body of poetry during his life, as well as a considerable number of comedies and tragedies, the most famous of which was *Bussy D'Ambois* published in 1607. He also wrote *The Memorable Masque* for the marriage of Princess Elizabeth and Frederick V in 1613. Anthony Wood said that Chapman was a person of 'most reverend aspect, religious and temperate, qualities rarely meeting in a poet'. He died in May 1634 and is buried in the churchyard of St Giles in the Fields, London.

Courage

Give me a spirit that on this life's rough sea
Loves to have his sails filled with a lusty wind
Even till his sailyards tremble, his masts crack,
And his rapt ship runs on her side so low

That she drinks water, and her keel ploughs air;
There is no danger to a man that knows
What life and death is, – there is no law
Exceeds his knowledge: neither is it lawful
That he should stoop to any other law.

George Chapman

———

O God, who hast hitherto supported me,
enable me to proceed in this labour,
and in the whole task of my present state;
that when I shall render up, at the last day,
an account of the talent committed to me,
I may receive pardon, for the sake of Jesus Christ. Amen.

Samuel Johnson

Ronald John Stephens 1913–2009

Vicar

———

IT IS CLAIMED that Stephens was the first British clergyman to appear in a television commercial. In 1970 he was approached to see if he would commend Blue Band Margarine in an advert. He agreed to do so as long as he could write the script which included a mention of God. 'I decided to compare the need of the body for this product to the need of the soul for God. Of course, I would not have agreed to the commercial if I did not believe completely in the product.' Stephens had the support of Bishop John Trillo who was reported to have said 'I am in favour of real people commending real products. Mr Stephens is a man of integrity and I see no reason why a sincere comment on margarine should not be coupled with a sincere word about God'. The advertisement, which was filmed in his study, showed Stephens saying 'Margarine has goodness in it and the body needs the fats in margarine as the soul needs God.' Stephens trained for the ministry at Sarum Theological College. He was made a deacon in Salisbury Cathedral in 1957 and priested a year later. He served his title at Calne and in 1961 was inducted as Vicar of Stanstead Abbotts. In 1981 he retired to Norfolk where he was granted Permission to Officiate. He was married with five children. He died on this day in 2009.

A reflection on the power of personal influence

In an early sermon of 1832, 'Personal Influence, the Means of Propagating the Truth', Newman asks how Christianity has made its way and held its ground in the world. He answers that its chief strength has not been in rational arguments, but rather it has 'been upheld in the world not as a system, not by books, not by arguments, nor by temporal power, but by the personal influence…' It is impossible to understand Newman without grasping the depth of his commitment to the principle of 'personal influence' which pervades all his writings. Personal influence, for Newman, was more important than organisation and books, as he said: 'The heart is commonly reached, not through reason, but through the imagination, by means of direct impressions, by the testimony of facts and events, by history, by description. Persons influence us, voices melt us, looks subdue us, deeds inflame us'.

From *Leadership in Christian Higher Education*

Lord God, whose Son Jesus Christ set before us
an example of a life lived for your glory
and for the good of others;
save us from the hypocrisy of double standards
and give us your grace
that our lives may display the fruits of the Holy Spirit
of love, joy, peace, patience, kindness,
of generosity, faithfulness, gentleness, and self-control;
we ask this for his name's sake. Amen.

William Wright 1752–1807

Teacher

———

WILLIAM WRIGHT WAS, perhaps, the most famous of the headmasters of Aspley Guise Classical Academy. The school had been founded in the early years of the eighteenth century by Thomas Gressam, with the support of the How family (see the entry for 29 May) who lived at the Old House in the village. The Academy educated boys from the higher echelons of society for careers in the services, Church and commerce, and it was during Wright's time as headmaster that the school reached the pinnacle of its success. Wright came from Kempston and was made headmaster in 1778. He married into the Sawell family from Aspley Guise. However, his wife Margaret died in 1792 and soon after he remarried. Wright died in 1807 and is buried in the churchyard of St Botolph, Aspley Guise – the church where eight years previously he had provided a gallery at the west end for his family and the school.

Pope Paul VI's call for the right of a Christian education

Since all Christians have become by rebirth of water and the Holy Spirit a new creature so that they should be called and should be children of God, they have a right to a Christian education. A Christian education does not merely strive for the maturing of a human person as just now described, but has as its principal purpose this goal: that the baptised, while they are gradually introduced to the knowledge of the mystery of salvation, become ever more aware of the gift of Faith they have received, and that they learn in addition how to worship God the Father in spirit and truth (cf. John 4.23) especially in liturgical action, and be conformed in their personal lives according to the new man created in justice and holiness of truth (Ephesians 4.22–24); also that they develop into perfect manhood, to the mature measure of the fullness of Christ (cf. Ephesians 4.13) and strive for the growth of the Mystical Body; moreover, that aware of their calling, they learn not only how to bear witness to the hope that is in them (cf. Peter 3.15) but also how to help in the Christian formation of the world that takes place when natural powers viewed in the full consideration of man redeemed by Christ contribute to the good of the whole society. Wherefore this sacred synod recalls to pastors of souls their most serious obligation to see to it that all the faithful, but especially the youth who are the hope of the Church, enjoy this Christian education.

From *Declaration on Christian Education (Gravissimum Educationis)*

———

God of wisdom and compassion, we pray for all those around the world who want to learn but are denied their right to education. We pray too for those who teach, especially those who work with few resources and little support. We give thanks for the knowledge, skills and understanding we have and we ask your help to remember how much we have still to learn. Teach us to respect wisdom wherever we find it. As you walked with the disciples on the road to Emmaus walk with us as we try to understand. Open our hearts and minds to new learning even when it challenges us to change. Give us the courage to tackle injustice and guide us towards a new, shared future where everyone has the chance to learn and all may grow in wisdom and understanding. Amen.

A Prayer for Education Sunday

Joy Batchelor 1914–91

Film maker

————

MANY OLDER READERS will remember with affection the cartoon *The Candlemaker*. It tells the story of Tom, who makes candles for the altar of his church at Christmas. *The Candlemaker* was just one of the many *Halas and Batchelor Cartoon Films* which a whole generation of young people were brought up with in the middle of the twentieth century. Joy Batchelor was born in 1914 in Watford. She began to work for John Halas in 1938 as an animator, which proved to be the beginning of a long partnership. Not only did they make many films together but they also married in 1940. During the Second World War they made more than seventy propaganda films. As well as writing scripts and directing films, Joy also worked in advertising and produced graphics for books and magazines. She was a governor of the London International Film School, where she also taught for a time.

Don Schwager describes the way that Jesus used stories to teach

Like the rabbis of his time, Jesus used simple word-pictures, called parables, to help people understand who God is and what his kingdom or reign is like. Jesus used images and characters taken from everyday life to create a miniature play or drama to illustrate his message. This was Jesus' most common way of teaching. His stories appealed to the young and old, poor and rich, and to the learned and unlearned as well. Over a third of the Gospels by Matthew, Mark and Luke contain parables told by Jesus. Jesus loved to use illustrations to reach the heart of his listeners through their imagination. These word-pictures challenged the mind to discover anew what God is like and moved the heart to make a response to God's love and truth. Like a skilful artist, Jesus painted lively pictures with short and simple words. A good picture can speak more loudly and clearly than many words. Jesus used the ordinary everyday to point to another order of reality – hidden, yet visible to those who had 'eyes to see' and 'ears to hear'. Jesus communicated with pictures and stories, vivid illustrations which captured the imagination of his audience more powerfully than an abstract presentation could. His parables are like buried treasure waiting to be discovered (Matthew 13.44).

From *The Parables of Jesus*

God who spoke the world into being and communicates with us still today; we give you thanks for writers, producers, broadcasters and journalists, and all who work in the media. We thank you for their creative skills and technical abilities, and their persistence in seeking after truth. We ask that they may have wisdom, integrity, insight and judgement in their work. May they be a voice for the powerless, a challenge to the powerful; bringers of knowledge and clarity to an uncertain and confused world. Help them to reach for the highest professional standards, especially when budgets are stretched, time is tight, and competition increasing. May they resist the temptation to follow the consensus, jump to easy conclusions, pander to prejudice or cut corners. Help us, who read, watch, listen and contribute to the media, to play our part by being wise and discerning, so that truth and beauty will be the hallmarks of our media. We offer these prayers in the Name of the One who brought the Good News, declared himself as the Truth, and gave Himself for a world in need. Amen.

Adapted from a prayer by Peter Crumpler

Edward Henry Bickersteth 1825–1906

Bishop and poet

———

BORN IN WATTON-AT-STONE in Hertfordshire, the son of a clergyman, Edward Bickersteth studied at Trinity College, Cambridge. His considerable poetic gifts won him the Chancellor's Gold Medal for poetry on three occasions. He was ordained in the Diocese of Norwich and served his title at Banningham in Norfolk before moving to Christ Church, Tunbridge Wells. His first living was at Hinton Martell, from where he moved to be Vicar of Christ Church, Hampstead. After three years he was appointed Dean of Gloucester and before the end of the same year he became Bishop of Exeter. During his ministry he wrote many poems, some of which are still sung as hymns today. Among the numerous books he wrote are *The Blessed Dead, The Second Death, After the Mission, The Good News in Africa* and *From Year to Year: Poems and Hymns for all the Sundays and Holy Days of the Church.*

O Christ, Thou hast ascended triumphantly on high,
By cherub guards attended and armies of the sky:
Let earth tell forth the story, our very flesh and bone,
Emmanuel, in glory, ascends His Father's throne.

Heaven's gates unfold above Thee: but canst Thou, Lord, forget
The little band who love Thee and gaze from Olivet?
Nay, on Thy breast engraven Thou bearest every name,
Our Priest in earth and heaven eternally the same.

There, there Thou standest pleading the virtue of Thy blood,
For sinners interceding, our Advocate with God;
And every changeful fashion of our brief joys and cares
Finds thought in Thy compassion and echo in Thy prayers.

Oh, for the priceless merit of thy redeeming cross
Vouchsafe Thy sevenfold Spirit and turn to gain our loss;
Till we by strong endeavour in heart and mind ascend
And dwell with Thee for ever in raptures without end.

E. H. Bickersteth

Gracious God,
your holy word encourages us to worship
with psalms and hymns and spiritual songs,
and to sing and make melody to you with all our hearts:
we thank you for poets and musicians
whose words and tunes capture our imaginations,
enrich our worship and inspire our devotion;
through Jesus Christ our Lord. Amen.

Jennifer Worth 1935–2011

Nurse, writer and musician

———

'MIDWIFERY IS THE very stuff of drama. Every child is conceived either in love or lust, is born in pain, followed by joy or sometimes remorse,' wrote Jennifer Worth. Her experiences were recounted in the three best-selling books entitled *Call the Midwife*, *Shadows of the Workhouse* and *Farewell to the East End*. These were dramatised on television in *Call the Midwife*, a series which described her years as a midwife in the East End of London in the 1950s, working in partnership with the Anglican sisterhood, the Community of St John the Divine. The series was a huge hit both in Britain and in America. Following her death in 2011, her husband said, 'Jennifer didn't know she was going into a convent; she thought she was just going into a small midwifery practice. She was not a religious person at that stage in her life, and I think she contemplated running a mile. Eventually, she came to really admire the nuns; their work and their faith. I'm sure working with sisters shaped the person she became. In later life she was very devout. She never talked about it to anybody – it was something she recognised she couldn't impose on other people – but I think that sense of faith pervades the book.' Jennifer Lee was brought up in Buckinghamshire and worked as a school secretary. While she was training as a nurse, she lived with the sisters in the East End. She then went on to work as a midwife in a number of London hospitals. In 1963 Jennifer married Philip Worth and moved to Hemel Hempstead, where they had two daughters. In 1973 she retired from nursing in order to teach piano and singing as well as performing as a soloist.

Jennifer Worth writes about her early life

Someone once said that youth is wasted on the young. Not a bit of it. Only the young have the impulsive energy to tackle the impossible and enjoy it; the courage to follow their instincts and brave the new; the stamina to work all day, all night, and all the next day without tiring. For the young everything is possible…In the heady days of my early twenties I went to work in the East End of bomb-damaged London as a district midwife. I did it out of a yearning for adventure, not from a sense of vocation. I wanted to experience something different from my middle-class background, something tough and challenging that would stretch me. I wanted a new slant on life. I went to a place called Nonnatus House, which I thought was a small private hospital, but which turned out to be a convent run by the Sisters of St Raymund Nonnatus. When I discovered my mistake I nearly ran away without unpacking my bags. Nuns were not my style. I couldn't be doing with that sort of thing, I thought. I wanted adventure, not religion. I did not know it at the time, but my soul was yearning for both.

From *Farewell to the East End*

———

Lord Jesus Christ, giver of life and health:
we thank you for the skill and compassion of midwives
and all who dedicate their lives to the care of women in labour:
give them patience, wisdom and tenderness in their work
that mothers may have a safe delivery of their children;
we ask this for your name's sake. Amen.

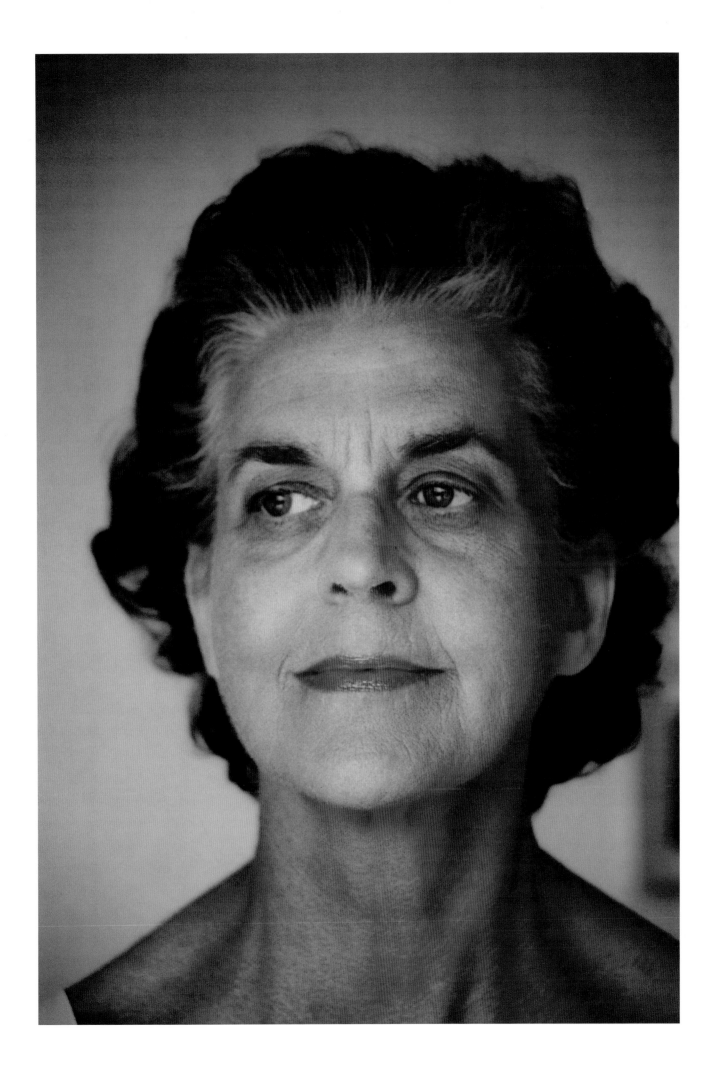

Richard Alliott 1839–99

Free Church headmaster

———

IN 1868 THE Reverend Richard Alliott, a twenty-nine-year-old Cambridge graduate in classics and former Congregational minister from Cheshire, with no teaching experience, was appointed headmaster of the collegiate school in Bishop's Stortford. He took up his position on 1 September and on 23 September the school was formally inaugurated under the name of the Nonconformist Grammar School. The school opened with just forty boys but within ten years numbers had increased to over one hundred and thirty. Alliott led the school for thirty-one years. He also founded the Bishop's Stortford Working Men's Club, which began after he convened a public meeting at the Corn Exchange in December 1873. Supported by two members from the Club and the Institution Union, by the end of the meeting ninety men had joined up. Most Working Men's clubs, even though they were teetotal, started in public houses. But it was soon conceded, even by the Church, that a pint of beer would not hinder the men's mental and moral stimulation for which the clubs were intended. Bishop's Stortford's club was not established in any of the town's many public houses, but in a small private property behind the Corn Exchange that had previously been used as a wine shop.

David Edwards writes about social life in the Victorian era

Victorian Nonconformity eventually came to believe that the first step in its approach to the urban working class was to offer some of these pleasures which the middle classes were now taking for granted. The most sustained effort in this direction, the Pleasant Sunday Afternoon, was invented in West Bromwich in 1875. Its motto was 'Brief, Bright and Brotherly'. This meant a meeting with short addresses (not all of them religious), broken up by non-dogmatic hymns and solos; a hymnal, *Worship Song*, was edited for this purpose in 1907. The PSA was organised with a definite membership by an elected committee and took pride in being non-sectarian. The motive of many of its backers was the hope that working people would return to the normal evening services, and the PSA did produce many thousands of new faces on church premises, particularly in the Midlands; but that hope was not fulfilled on any larger scale, and one disadvantage to the long-term prospects of Nonconformity was that almost all the ministers failed to attach enough importance to the meeting of working people in the trade unions now becoming a major force in non-ecclesiastical surroundings.

From *Christian England*

———

Father, your Son Jesus Christ rooted in earthly living,
the toil of creativity, the energy of interaction.
the hand of movement, the eyes of seeing,
the ears of discerning, the mind of resolving,
the labours of the day, the rest in the night
offered to your praise and glory. Amen.

John Pattison

James Gilmour 1843–91

Missionary

———

JAMES GILMOUR SPENT twenty-one years as a Free Church missionary to the nomadic tribes of Mongolia and died there at the age of forty-seven. Born in Cathkin in Scotland, he studied nearby at Glasgow University. It was during his time there that he became a Christian, and in 1867 he travelled south to study at Cheshunt College in Hertfordshire. In 1870 he was sent as a missionary to China. He made Peking (present-day Beijing) his base, travelling into the interior of China and Mongolia to further his language studies. In the years that followed, Gilmour made several missionary journeys to various parts of Mongolia, returning each time to Peking for the winter to escape the severe weather. In 1874 Gilmour married Emily Prankard. She accompanied him on his travels, preaching the gospel and distributing medicines. They started a family in 1878 and had two sons. Within two years Emily's health had deteriorated, but it was not until 1882 that they were able to return home. As soon as they arrived, Gilmour began a preaching and lecturing tour, and in the following year published his book, *Among the Mongols*. At the end of 1883 Gilmour and his family returned to Mongolia, and in the following year witnessed the conversion of Boyinto, his only convert from the nomadic Mongols. Their third son, Alick, was born in 1884 but their joy was to be short-lived. The following year Emily died, and two years later Alick also died. Gilmour sent the two eldest boys back to Britain to be educated, and joined them in 1889. He returned to Mongolia the following March, but within a year he had died of typhus fever at Tientsin, China.

James Gilmour writes about the Christian understanding of salvation by grace

It frequently appears to a Mongol that salvation, according to Christianity, is altogether too easy. He is surprised to find that a Christian, a teacher of Christianity even, may kill vermin, eat flesh, nay even marry a wife, without infringing any of the doctrines of his religion; his surprise is much increased when he learns that Christianity is free from the almost endless prohibitions, restrictions, vows, and rites with which Buddhism abounds; and when the freedom of Christianity dawns upon him he sometimes expresses himself in terms which are an unconscious echo of the words of Christ, 'My yoke is easy and My burden is light.' A little more knowledge, however, is sufficient to change his opinion. When he learns that salvation, according to the Christian idea, is not merely the cancelling of a long score of old sins, and of the current sins of the present, but purification from sin itself, and the renewal of the heart, he thinks the aim an impossibility, and regards the purification as a process which he is not willing to be put through. To enter upon a contest with evil, and strive to eradicate it from the heart, this is a task from which he shrinks. He is discouraged by the thought on the one hand, that as far as he succeeds, he can claim no merit; and on the other hand, by supposing that he has to maintain the unequal strife in his own strength, an error into which it is quite natural for him to fall, seeing that in working out his own salvation, according to the Buddhistic method, he is not accustomed to rely on any power higher than his own.

From *Among the Mongols*

———

Everliving God,
you have taught us that the law was given by Moses,
but that grace and truth came through your Son, Jesus Christ:
send the Holy Spirit upon us
that we may live in the glorious liberty
which you desire for all your children,
through Jesus Christ our Lord. Amen.

Culling Eardley Eardley 1805–63

Founder of the Bible Lands Charity and the Evangelical Alliance

———

MANY PEOPLE ARE familiar with the Bible Lands Charity (recently renamed *Embrace*) because of their Bethlehem carol sheets that are widely used by churches at Christmas. But they are unlikely to know that the origin of the charity lies in the Turkish Missions Aid Society which Culling Eardley helped found in 1854 and which he chaired. At that time Palestine was part of the Ottoman Empire. Eardley went to Eton and Oriel College, Oxford. He inherited the family estate at Bedwell Park, Essendon, and succeeded to the baronetcy when his father died in 1829. A passionate evangelical, he campaigned on many issues: for the reform of the poor laws, for religious freedom and, although he was a lifelong Anglican, for the disestablishment of the Church of England. He helped found the Evangelical Alliance in 1846. He was Member of Parliament for Pontefract for a short time and although Eardley stood in several other general elections he was never returned to Westminster again. He was married to Isabella Carr and they had three children. He spent most of his life at Bedwell, where he died in 1863.

Eardley's interest in the Holy Land brings to mind Psalm 122. In this passage John Eaton writes about the psalm and about Jerusalem

From the inexhaustible meaning of the holy city, our psalm draws several great themes. It is the place of the fellowship, the loving unity of the Lord's worshippers. It is the place of the name of the Lord, his presence, his self-giving, where his people find their life renewed as they worship and sing praise. And it is the centre and source of justice, the good order sent by God through his anointed ones bringing his law to bear on every aspect of life, rescuing, healing, and guiding. In her deepest meaning, Jerusalem is secure and eternally filled with God's peace upon her walls, gates and stones, and all the servants of the Lord that serve her also. For at the edges of this Jerusalem there is a vulnerability, a divine poverty and exposure, and those who love her must pray for her in her weakness, seeking good for her from God, calling down his peace upon her. And in this work of love, they themselves will find blessing.

From *The Psalms*

I was glad when they said unto me, Let us go into the house of the Lord.
Our feet shall stand within thy gates, O Jerusalem.
Jerusalem is builded as a city that is compact together:
Whither the tribes go up, the tribes of the Lord, unto the testimony of Israel,
to give thanks unto the name of the Lord.
For there are set thrones of judgment, the thrones of the house of David.
Pray for the peace of Jerusalem: they shall prosper that love thee.
Peace be within thy walls, and prosperity within thy palaces.
For my brethren and companions' sakes, I will now say, Peace be within thee.
Because of the house of the Lord our God I will seek thy good.

Psalm 122 from the *King James Version of the Bible*

Helena d.330

Empress and Protector of the Holy Places

———

WHEATHAMPSTEAD AND ELSTOW, two of the ancient churches in the diocese, are dedicated to St Helen (also known as Helena). At Elstow, once a great Benedictine abbey, Helena shares the dedication with Mary, but it is possible that the Marian dedication was a later addition. In Empress Helena we touch the origins of Christianity in our two counties. Helena rose to prominence as the mother of Constantine, the first Christian emperor, who was proclaimed emperor in York in 306 upon the death of Constantius. Helena had been divorced and abandoned by her husband some fifteen years previously, but now gained power, lending support to the new imperial policy of toleration. The persecution of Christians ceased. Already very elderly, in 326 Helena made a pilgrimage to the Holy Land. There she provided funds for the building of two great basilicas: one on the Mount of Olives, and the other at Bethlehem on the reputed site of the nativity. According to fourth-century historians, it was Helena who discovered remains of the cross on which Jesus had been crucified, and arranged for them to be transported back to Rome. Constantine ordered a basilica to be built over the place where his mother had discovered the relic, now known as the Church of the Holy Sepulchre. Helena died some four years later at the great age of eighty.

Socrates Scholasticus writes about Helena's search for the cross

Helena, the mother of the emperor Constantine, being divinely directed by dreams, went to Jerusalem. She sought carefully the sepulchre of Christ, from which he arose after his burial; and after much difficulty, by God's help she discovered it. What the cause of the difficulty was I will explain in a few words. Those who embraced the Christian faith, after the period of his passion, greatly venerated this tomb; but those who hated Christianity, having covered the spot with a mound of earth, erected on it a temple to Venus, and set up her image there, not caring for the memory of the place. This succeeded for a long time; and it became known to Helena. Accordingly, having caused the statue to be thrown down, the earth to be removed, and the ground entirely cleared, she found three crosses in the sepulchre: one of these was that blessed cross on which Christ had hung, the other two were those on which the two thieves that were crucified with him had died. With these was also found the tablet of Pilate, on which he had inscribed in various characters, that the Christ who was crucified was King of the Jews. Since, however, it was doubtful which cross they were in search of, the emperor's mother was not a little distressed; but from this trouble the bishop of Jerusalem, Macarius, shortly relieved her. And he solved the doubt by faith, for he sought a sign from God and obtained it.

From *Ecclesiastical History*

Almighty God,
who in the passion of your blessed Son
made an instrument of painful death
to be for us the means of life and peace:
grant us so to glory in the cross of Christ
that we may gladly suffer for his sake;
who is alive and reigns with you, in the unity of the Holy Spirit,
one God, now and for ever. Amen.

Collect for Holy Cross from *Common Worship*

William Blyth Gerish 1864–1921

Antiquarian

TRADITIONALLY, THE CHURCH of England has had responsibility for burying the dead, with the result that across the land its churchyards are full of interesting memorials. The amateur antiquarian William Gerish surveyed no less than 131 burial grounds in Hertfordshire, and painstakingly recorded the names found on more than 70,000 graves. Today his thirteen volumes of records are kept in the British Library in London. Born in Islington in 1864, Gerish spent much of his childhood in East Anglia. By 1885 he was living in Wormley, but subsequently moved first to Hoddesdon and then to Bishop's Stortford. In 1895 he married Maude Pipe. For most of his life Gerish worked as a bank clerk, writing and researching in his spare time. He was fascinated by local history. He became a member of the East Herts Archaeological Society and wrote a regular column in the *Hertfordshire Mercury* called 'Notes and Queries'. In 1910 the *West Herts and Watford Observer* started to publish a similar column which Gerish helped write. He published lists of monumental inscriptions found in the county, wrote nineteen pamphlets on Hertfordshire folklore, together with a number of short biographies of Hertfordshire people, including Henry Chauncy (see the entry for 19 April). His books, pamphlets and papers are held in St Albans Library and in the Hertfordshire Archives and Local Studies. Eventually he retired to Caister in Norfolk where he died in 1921.

A well-known hymn which is often sung at funerals

Abide with me; fast falls the eventide;
The darkness deepens; Lord with me abide.
When other helpers fail and comforts flee,
Help of the helpless, O abide with me.

Swift to its close ebbs out life's little day;
Earth's joys grow dim; its glories pass away;
Change and decay in all around I see;
O Thou who changest not, abide with me.

I fear no foe, with Thee at hand to bless;
Ills have no weight, and tears no bitterness.
Where is death's sting? Where, grave, thy victory?
I triumph still, if Thou abide with me.

Hold Thou Thy cross before my closing eyes;
Shine through the gloom and point me to the skies.
Heaven's morning breaks, and earth's vain shadows flee;
In life, in death, O Lord, abide with me.

Henry F. Lyte

Gracious Father,
we thank you for those who tend and maintain our churchyards.
May they be places of tranquillity and peace,
where the visitor can be still and reflect,
the bereaved grieve and pray,
and all find hope and consolation
through the power of the resurrection of our Lord Jesus Christ. Amen.

Edward Lowry Henderson 1873–1947

Dean of St Albans

EDWARD HENDERSON WAS educated at Radley College near Abingdon and then went up to Oriel College, Oxford. He was ordained in the Diocese of London and served his title at St Anne's, Limehouse. From there he was appointed to be Rector of Lowestoft. He was made a Residentiary Canon of Gloucester Cathedral before being appointed as Provost of St Mary's Cathedral in Edinburgh in 1919. Henderson's experience stood him in good stead when he became Dean of St Albans in 1925. He stayed there for ten years before being appointed as Dean of Salisbury Cathedral. Henderson retired in 1943.

Richard Baxter exhorts the clergy to practise what they preach

See that the work of saving grace be thoroughly wrought in your own souls. Take heed to yourselves, lest you be void of that saving grace of God which you offer to others, and be strangers to the effectual working of that gospel which you preach; and lest, while you proclaim to the world the necessity of a Saviour, your own hearts should neglect him, and you should miss of an interest in him and his saving benefits. Take heed to yourselves, lest you perish, while you call upon others to take heed of perishing; and lest you famish yourselves while you prepare food for them. Though there is a promise of shining as the stars, to those 'who turn many to righteousness,' that is but on supposition that they are first turned to it themselves. Their own sincerity in the faith is the condition of their glory, simply considered, though their great ministerial labours may be a condition of the promise of their greater glory. Many have warned others that they come not to that place of torment, while yet they hastened to it themselves: many a preacher is now in hell, who hath a hundred times called upon his hearers to use the utmost care and diligence to escape it. Can any reasonable man imagine that God should save men for offering salvation to others, while they refuse it themselves; and for telling others those truths which they themselves neglect and abuse? Many a tailor goes in rags, that maketh costly clothes for others; and many a cook scarcely licks his fingers, when he hath dressed for others the most costly dishes. Believe it, brethren, God never saved any man for being a preacher, nor because he was an able preacher; but because he was a justified, sanctified man, and consequently faithful in his Master's work. Take heed, therefore, to ourselves first, that you be that which you persuade your hearers to be, and believe that which you persuade them to believe, and heartily entertain that Saviour whom you offer to them. He that bade you love your neighbours as yourselves, did imply that you should love yourselves, and not hate and destroy yourselves and them.

From *The Reformed Pastor*

O Thou who in almighty power wast weak,
and in perfect excellency wast lowly,
grant unto us the same mind.
All that we have which is our own is naught;
if we have any good in us it is wholly thy gift.
O Saviour, since thou, the Lord of heaven and earth,
didst humble thyself, grant unto us true humility,
and make us like thyself; and then, of thine infinite goodness,
raise us in thine everlasting glory. Amen.

Thomas Cranmer

John Wesley 1703–91

Priest and evangelist

———

'I LOOK UPON all the world as my parish,' wrote John Wesley, and judging by all the places he visited in this diocese he worked hard to fulfill his ambition. Travelling on horseback, and often preaching several times each day, among the many places he visited in the diocese were Lidlington, Barkway, Hinxworth, Slip End, Cople, Barnet, Stevenage, Wrestlingworth, Cranfield and Wootton Pillinge. Although Wesley was born and died an Anglican, he is chiefly remembered as the founder of Methodism. The great turning point in his life took place on 24 May 1738, at a meeting in Aldersgate Street, London, when hearing part of Martin Luther's preface to the Epistle to the Romans, his heart was 'strangely warmed'. Wesley's mixture of fervent pietism and social action had a profound effect on England. Forming his followers into small groups for prayer and study, Methodists became known for their practical care and service, as well as for campaigning on issues such as the abolition of slavery, prison reform and temperance.

This entry from Wesley's diary describes his spiritual awakening

In the evening I went very unwillingly to a society in Aldersgate Street, where one was reading Luther's preface to the Epistle to the Romans. About a quarter before nine, while he was describing the change which God works in the heart through faith in Christ, I felt my heart strangely warmed. I felt I did trust in Christ, Christ alone, for salvation; and an assurance was given me that He had taken away my sins, even mine, and saved me from the law of sin and death. I began to pray with all my might for those who had in a more especial manner despitefully used me and persecuted me. I then testified openly to all there what I now first felt in my heart. But it was not long before the enemy suggested, 'This cannot be faith; for where is thy joy?' Then was I taught that peace and victory over sin are essential to faith in the Captain of our salvation; but that, as to the transports of joy that usually attend the beginning of it, especially in those who have mourned deeply, God sometimes giveth, sometimes withholdeth, them according to the counsels of His own will. After my return home, I was much buffeted with temptations, but I cried out, and they fled away. They returned again and again. I as often lifted up my eyes, and He 'sent me help from his holy place.' And herein I found the difference between this and my former state chiefly consisted. I was striving, yea, fighting with all my might under the law, as well as under grace. But then I was sometimes, if not often, conquered; now, I was always conqueror.

From *The Journal of John Wesley*

Fix thou our steps, O Lord,
that we stagger not at the uneven motions of the world,
but steadily go on to our glorious home;
neither censuring our journey by the weather we meet with,
nor turning out of the way for anything that befalls us.
The winds are often rough, and our own weight presses us downwards.
Reach forth, O Lord, thy hand, thy saving hand, and speedily deliver us.
Teach us, O Lord, to use this transitory life
as pilgrims returning to their beloved home;
that we may take what our journey requires,
and not think of settling in a foreign country. Amen.

John Wesley

Augustus Shears 1827–1911

Missionary

———

WHEN AUGUSTUS SHEARS was sent by the United Society for the Propagation of the Gospel to Burma (now known as Myanmar) in 1859, he was only the second Anglican missionary to work in that country. In the mid-nineteenth century the Anglican Church in the region came directly under the authority of the Archbishop of Canterbury. Eventually it was incorporated into the Church of India, Pakistan, Burma and Ceylon. Little did Shears and his colleagues realise that they were laying the foundations for what is now known as the Province of Myanmar, which today comprises six dioceses with more than 62,000 worshippers, 125 priests and 330 congregations. Shears had been brought up in Wimbledon and was educated at Rugby School and St John's College, Cambridge. Following his ordination in 1851, he served a curacy at Lutterworth in Leicestershire, and subsequently ministered in the parishes of Escrick, Yorkshire, and in Abbots Langley. It was from Hertfordshire that in 1859 he went to Moulmein, Burma, where he spent the next three years as a missionary. He was instrumental in founding a school there and also translated the *Book of Common Prayer* into Burmese. Augustus married Annie Williams, who had been born into a missionary family, and they had three children. Following a period of debilitating illness, however, he was forced to return to England and served in various parishes until his death on this day in 1911.

Stephen Neill writes about the dynamic witness of the Church in the early centuries

What is clear is that every Christian was a witness. Where there were Christians, there would be a living, burning faith, and before long an expanding Christian community. In later times great Churches were much set on claiming apostolic origin – to have an apostle as founder was a recognised certificate of respectability. But in point of fact few, if any, of the great Churches were really founded by apostles. Nothing is more notable than the anonymity of these early missionaries. In the second century there were three outstanding centres of Christian life in the Mediterranean – Antioch, Rome, and Alexandria. Of the foundation of the Church of Antioch we have just recorded all that is known; Luke does not turn aside to mention the name of a single one of those pioneers who laid the foundation. Peter and Paul may have organised the Church in Rome. They certainly did not found it. And of the foundation of the Church of Alexandria we know nothing for certain – neither when nor whence nor by whom. That was the greatest glory of the Church of those days. The Church was the body of Christ, indwelt by his Spirit; and what Christ had begun to do, that the Church would continue to do, through all the days and unto the uttermost parts of the earth until his unpredictable but certain coming again.

From *A History of Christian Missions*

Everlasting God,
you call us to declare the good news of your Son Jesus Christ
and to be your witnesses to the ends of the earth:
rouse us from apathy, disturb our complacency,
rekindle in us a love for all people
and send us to proclaim the gospel in word and deed,
for the sake of your Son, Jesus Christ our Lord. Amen.

George Newman 1870–1948

Quaker and doctor

———

BORN INTO A Quaker missionary family, George Newman was educated at Sidcot School, Somerset, and Bootham School, York. As a young man, Newman had wanted to be a missionary, but in the end resolved to train as a doctor. He studied medicine at the universities of Edinburgh and London, in the course of which he developed a special interest in bacteriology and the causes of infectious diseases. At the comparatively young age of thirty, he was appointed Medical Officer of Bedfordshire, and immediately began to research the causes of infant mortality in the county, which at that time was a serious problem. In 1906 he published *Infant Mortality: A Social Problem*. This was to be the first of a number of influential studies and books that he published on public health. The following year Newman was appointed Chief Medical Officer to the Board of Education. He was knighted in 1911, and in 1919 appointed Chief Medical Officer at the Ministry of Health. Newman was a committed Christian and Quaker throughout his life, and this shaped both his outlook and his passionate concern to raise the standard of public health in England. For forty years he edited the *Friends' Quarterly Examiner* and also wrote a number of books on Christianity including *George Fox: the Founder of Quakerism*, *Lord Shaftesbury's Legacy to the Children of England*, and *Quaker Profiles*. He was married to an artist, Adelaide Constance Thorp. He died on this day in 1948 in York.

In this passage we read about George Fox, the founder of the Quakers

He was a man that God endued with a clear and wonderful depth, a discerner of others' spirits and very much a master of his own. And though the side of his understanding which lay next to the world, and especially the expression of it might sound uncouth and unfashionable to nice ears, his matter was nevertheless very profound, and would not only bear to be often considered but the more it was so, the more weighty and instructing it appeared…No arts or parts had any share in his matter or manner and nothing of man's wit or wisdom to recommend them. So that as to man, he was an original and no man's copy. Above all he excelled in prayer. The most awful living reverent frame I ever felt or beheld I must say was his in prayer. He was of an innocent life, no busy-body, nor self-seeker, neither touchy nor critical. So meek, contented, modest, easy, steady, tender, it was a pleasure to be in his company. As he was unwearied, so he was undaunted in his services for God and his people; he was no more to be moved to fear then to wrath…His very presence expressed a religious majesty, yet he never abused it. I write my knowledge and not report, and my witness is true, having been with him for weeks and months together on divers occasions, and those of the nearest and most exercising nature, and that by night and by day, by sea and by land, in this and in foreign countries, and I can say I never saw him out of his place, or not a match for every service or occasion. For in all things he acquitted himself like a man, yea, a strong man, a new and heavenly-minded man, a divine and naturalist, and all of God Almighty's making…

From *George Fox, The Founder of Quakerism* by George Newman

———

O God, our strength and our salvation,
bless all engaged in medical research and public health:
give them skill and insight in their work,
that they may bring healing and health within the reach of all;
for Jesus Christ's sake. Amen.

Peter Roddis 1922–88
and Les Waghorn 1912–95
Churchwardens

———

FOR SOME YEARS St Peter's Church Pertenhall in Bedfordshire was served by two outstanding churchwardens who formed a partnership. Their friendship and co-operation was a living example of Christian discipleship. Peter Roddis was born in Pertenhall to a family which had long links with the village; one of his relatives had already been churchwarden. Roddis was educated at the village school and married the churchwarden's daughter, Mary. He and his brother Bob lived in the village all their lives and both of them worked for local farmers. Roddis took over as churchwarden from his father-in-law in 1970 and was also elected secretary to the parochial church council. He fulfilled both roles until his death in 1988.

Les Waghorn came to the village after serving in the Second World War and ran a nursery with his friend and business partner, Jack Packer. The nursery sold its produce at the markets in St Neots and Bedford. After they retired, Les and Jack continued to grow plants and vegetables, often selling them in aid of church funds. Waghorn also ran the plant stall at the annual church fete. He was churchwarden and parochial church council treasurer for over twenty-five years until his death in 1995. Both Peter Roddis and Les Waghorn were deeply involved in village life, each serving on the village hall committee for many years. They also demonstrated true Christian leadership when *The Stodden Benefice* was established in 1980.

Thomas Merton describes the nature of Christian love

The union that binds the members of Christ together is not the union of proud confidence in the power of an organisation. The Church is united by the humility as well as by the charity of her members. Hers is the union that comes from the consciousness of individual fallibility and poverty, from the humility which recognises its own limitations and accepts them, the meekness that cannot take upon itself to condemn, but can only forgive because it is conscious that it has itself been forgiven by Christ. The union of Christians is a union of friendship and mercy, a bearing of one another's burdens in the sharing of divine forgiveness. Christian forgiveness is not confined merely to those who are members of the Church. To be a Christian one must love all people, including not only one's own enemies but even those who claim to be the 'enemies of God'. 'Whosoever is angry with his brother or sister shall be in danger of the judgement. Love your enemies, do good to them that hate you, pray for them that persecute and speak calumny of you, that you may be the children of your Father who is in heaven.' The solidarity of the Christian community is not based on the awareness that the Church has authority to cast out and to anathematise, but on the realisation that Christ has given her the power to forgive sin in his name and to welcome the sinner to the banquet of his love in the holy Eucharist.

From *The Power and Meaning of Love*

———

Gracious God, the source of life and love:
break down our barriers of pride and envy
and give us grace to be loved and to love,
that in giving ourselves to you and to others,
we may discover that life which is your gift and your promise;
through Jesus Christ our Lord, Amen.

Lanfranc c.1005–89

Archbishop of Canterbury

———

I**T IS THOUGHT** that King Offa may have founded the Benedictine Community at St Albans in 793. There had been various plans to rebuild the original abbey, which was situated just to the south of the present building, but these had come to nothing. A few years after Lanfranc became Archbishop of Canterbury he appointed his nephew, Paul of Caen, as abbot and ordered him to build a new abbey. Born in Pavia in Italy, Lanfranc had become a monk in the newly-founded Benedictine Community at Bec in Normandy in 1042. Abbot Herluin recognised Lanfranc's gifts and appointed him as a teacher. It was there that Lanfranc taught Anselm, who was later to succeed him as Archbishop of Canterbury. Lanfranc's reputation spread so widely that the Duke of Normandy made him one of his special advisors. In 1066 he became the abbot of St Stephen's, Caen, and four years later the Pope made him Archbishop of Canterbury. Among his many acts of charity, Lanfranc founded a hospital for lepers on the edge of the city. Lanfranc set about reforming the Church and brought in a number of his fellow countrymen to support his changes. In particular he insisted on clerical celibacy. He had a formidable intellect and played a significant role in the Councils which took place at Vercelli, Tours and Rome. He wrote *De corpore et sanguine Domini*. He died on this day and is buried in Canterbury Cathedral.

H. E. L. Cowdrey describes an incident in Lanfranc's time at Bec

Lanfranc quickly became somewhat disenchanted with monastic life at Bec. He found that there were few literate monks; too many in the community were lax in their personal lives and monastic observance; some feared Lanfranc as a future office-holder who would seek to correct their ways. Bec, as Lanfranc first experienced its life, had not as yet found a sure direction. Upon the evidence of its profession, it was already too large and diluted by monks with a low view of their vocation to facilitate the contemplative life to which Lanfranc currently aspired. Yet, despite Abbot Herluin's personal sanctity and practical acumen, it had not settled down to the ordered and confident observance of a mature cenobitic house. Its unformed state was well illustrated when Lanfranc resolved to escape to the life of a solitary…Lanfranc's intention to escape was frustrated at the last minute when Herluin experienced a vision: his recently deceased nephew Hugh, an exemplary monk who was the son of his brother Baldric of Servaville, informed him of Lanfranc's intention and also of the need for swift remedial action at Bec. When Herluin next day challenged Lanfranc about his intention, Lanfranc admitted it and, having accepted penance, was absolved; he promised never to desert Herluin and to obey his commands absolutely. Herluin speedily appointed Lanfranc to be prior, committing to his oversight both the internal and external affairs of Bec.

From *Lanfranc: Scholar, Monk and Archbishop*

———

Almighty God, the light of the faithful and shepherd of souls,
who set your servant Lanfranc to be a bishop in the Church,
to feed your sheep by the word of Christ and to guide them by good example:
give us grace to keep the faith of the Church and to follow in the footsteps
of Jesus Christ your Son our Lord. Amen.

Collect for a Bishop from *Common Worship*

Richard How 1727–1801

A Quaker from Aspley Guise

————

THE HOW FAMILY lived in a timber-framed Elizabethan house in the little village of Aspley Guise, between Woburn Sands and Husborne Crawley, known for its strong Quaker presence. The house, known as The Old House, belonged to the How family for almost two centuries. Richard How (the younger) was a friend and supporter of the prison reformer John Howard (see the entry for 20 January) and of the abolitionist Thomas Clarkson. How was a Quaker who was passionate in his support for the abolition of slavery. Throughout his life he amassed a library of over five thousand books and manuscripts. During the 1770s he edited and published the letters of Lady Rachel Russell. In 1782 he wrote about Aspley Guise itself, describing his home, family and friends.

George Fox, the founder of the Quakers, writes about pacifism

Our principle is, and our practices have always been to seek peace and ensue it; to follow after righteousness and the knowledge of God; seeking the good and welfare, and doing that which tends to the peace of all. We know that wars and fightings proceed from the lusts of men, (James 4.1–3), out of which lusts the Lord has redeemed us, and so out of the occasion of war. The occasion of war and war itself, arises from the lust, (wherein envious men, who are lovers of themselves more than lovers of God, lust, kill, and desire to have men's lives or estates). All bloody principles and practices we, as to our own basics, do utterly deny, with all outward wars, strife, and fighting with outward weapons for any end, or under any pretence whatsoever: this is our testimony to the whole world. And whereas if someone should object and say: 'But although you now say, that you cannot fight nor take up arms at all; yet if the spirit move you, then you will change your principle, you will sell your coat and buy a sword, and fight for the kingdom of Christ.' To this we answer, Christ said to Peter, 'Put up your sword in its place;' though he had said before, he that had no sword might sell his coat and buy one, (to the fulfilling of the law and the scripture), yet after, when he had bid him put it up, he said, 'He that takes the sword shall perish with the sword.' And Christ said to Pilate, 'Do you not know that I can now pray to my Father, and he shall presently give me more than twelve legions of angels?' And this might satisfy Peter, after he had put up his sword, when he said to him, 'He that took it, should perish by it,' which satisfies us (Matthew 26.52–53).

From A *Declaration from the Harmless and Innocent People of God*

God of grace,
we give you thanks that, being justified by faith,
we have peace with you through our Lord Jesus Christ:
pour your love into our hearts,
that purged of all hatred and enmity,
we may be peacemakers in your world
in the name of the Prince of Peace,
your Son, Jesus Christ. Amen.

Edward Garrard Marsh 1783–1862

Priest and poet

———

EDWARD MARSH CAME from an artistic family. His father, John Marsh, was a prolific composer and the family were friends with writers such as William Hayley and William Blake. Marsh was educated at Wadham College in Oxford and after graduation he was elected a Fellow of Oriel College. He was ordained in the Diocese of Oxford and served as a curate at Nuneham Courtenay. Marsh was made a residentiary canon of Southwell Minster, and it was during his time there that he married Lydia Williams. Their second daughter, Elizabeth Lydia, married the British Royal Navy officer and missionary to Patagonia, Allen Francis Gardiner. Marsh spent a period as Vicar of Sandon in Hertfordshire before moving to Aylesford, Kent. He gave the Bampton Lectures in the University of Oxford in 1848 under the title *The Christian Doctrine of Sanctification*.

Edward Marsh explains that we cannot be saved by obeying the law but only by God's grace

You see, then, my brethren, now, what is the morality of the ten commandments, and how truly it has been summed up by our divine master in those two comprehensive precepts – 'Thou shalt love the Lord, thy God, with all thy heart, with all thy soul, with all thy mind, and with all thy strength, and thy neighbour as thyself.' Yet, if this be our code of duty, what in few words, what in a summary view of it does it imply? Nothing less than this, that we are to love God so entirely, that it would be clearly impossible with our present faculties to love him better, that we are to extend to our neighbour, to every human being, to our personal enemy, if we have one, to every individual, who has in any way deserved ill of us, as well as to those who have deserved well, a degree of love and affection, not second, but equal to that, which we entertain for ourselves, that we are to seek his welfare, as our own, and be willing to deny ourselves, where there is occasion, for his benefit. This is a high standard: and who can reach it? We cannot indeed look at it steadfastly without being at once convinced by it of sin, without perceiving, that we have never come near to the rule, which marks the line of our duty, without acknowledging, that undoubtedly righteousness cannot come by the law.

From *Seven Sermons on the Ten Commandments*

———

Gracious God,
in ancient times you revealed your purposes to the people of Israel
by giving them the ten commandments;
but now, in the fullness of time, your Son Jesus Christ
has revealed your grace and truth;
in response to your love, may we offer ourselves as living sacrifices,
dedicating ourselves to live with integrity and truth;
we ask it for his name's sake. Amen.

Based on John 1.17

Ethel May Baker 1892–1982

Enrolling member of Wigginton Mothers' Union

———

ETHEL BAKER WAS a member of the Figg family who became the licensees of The Fox, the village pub in Wigginton, Hertfordshire, when she was eight years old. All life passed through the pub, and it gave Ethel a unique insight into the families and inhabitants of her beloved village. Throughout her life she immersed herself in village life and in the worship of its parish church of St Bartholomew. As a young woman Ethel taught in local schools. Following her marriage, she had several different roles, including superintendent of the Sunday School and enrolling member of the Mothers' Union. For seventeen years she served as secretary to the Women's Institute, as well as being secretary of the Nursing Association and the Women's Voluntary Society. During the war Ethel served in the Air Raid Wardens' Service and was a member both of her Parish Council and of Berkhamsted Rural District Council. For Ethel, service to God and service to the local community went hand-in-hand.

Bishop Jeremy Taylor reflects upon the joys of motherhood

When the Almighty God meant to stoop so low as to be fixed in our centre, he chose for his mother a holy person and a maid. She received the angel's message with such sublimity of faith that her faith was turned to vision, her hopes into actual possession, and her grace into glory. She who was full of God, bearing God in her virgin womb and the Holy Spirit in her heart, arose with haste and gladness to communicate that joy which was designed for all the world. Let us notice how light and airy was the coming of the Virgin, as she made haste over the mountains; her very little burden which she bear hindered her not but that she might make haste enough; her spirit was cheerful, and her body full of life. And there is this excellency in religion, that when we carry Christ within us, his presence is not so peevish as to disturb our health, nor so sad as to discompose our cheerfulness, but he re-creates our body by charity and fills us with serenity. For as the virgin climbed mountains easily, so there is no difficulty in our life so great but it may be managed by those assistances we receive from the holiest Jesus, when we carry him about us. Mary found no one so fit as her cousin Elizabeth to share the first emanations of her overjoyed heart, for she was to be the mother of the Baptist, who was sent as forerunner to prepare the way of the Lord her son. It is not easy to imagine what collision of joys was at this blessed meeting; two mothers of two great princes, the one the greatest that was born of woman, and the other his Lord. When these who were made mothers by two miracles came together, they met with joy and mysteriousness. The mother of our Lord went to visit the mother of his servant, and the Holy Ghost made the meeting festival. Never, but in heaven, was there more joy and ecstasy. For these women were hallowed and made big with religion and they met to unite their joy and their eucharist.

From *The Life of our Blessed Lord and Saviour Jesus Christ*

Gracious God, who in your providence chose a peasant girl
to be the mother of your only Son, Jesus Christ:
we thank you for love of our mothers,
for the pain they bear in childbirth,
for the care they lavish in childhood,
and for the cost of letting their children go as they grow into adulthood.
May your love affirm them in this holy calling,
for we ask it in the name of Jesus Christ. Amen.

Juliana Berners b. c.1388

Prioress

———

IT IS LIKELY that Juliana Berners cut a Chaucerian figure in the life of medieval St Albans. Her fame is less to do with her life as a cloistered nun, and more to do with her authorship of a book on hunting and fishing. *The Boke of St Albans* was printed on a press brought to St Albans by Abbot Wallingford. At the back of the book we read, 'Explicit Dam Julyans Barnes in her boke of hunting'. It was one of eight books printed at the Abbey in 1486. Little is known about Juliana's life, although it is thought she was Prioress of St Mary at Sopwell sometime between 1430 and 1480. The Priory was a cell of St Albans Abbey, and had been founded by Geoffrey de Gorham. It is probable that she was raised at court and that this was the origin of her passion for hunting and fishing. Some claim that she is the earliest woman author in the English language.

Ruth Tucker reflects on the role of women in society and in the Church

Martyrs, mystics, mothers, scholars, visionaries, missionaries, reformers, rebels – any attempt to categorise and summarise women and their activities, involvement and roles in Christian faith and ministry over eighteen centuries is daunting. But there is good news. No longer are scholars lamenting the paucity of sources. Primary and secondary works abound, and women's names are finding their way into general texts and monographs as never before. No more do Patricia Hill's words (written in 1985) ring true: 'As so frequently happens in the writing of history, the women have simply disappeared'. Yet the story of women – whether incorporated into a broader historical narrative or confined to gender-specific accounts – is difficult to encapsulate. The temptation has been to focus on extraordinary women whose lives exemplified what would have been deemed notable if achieved by their male counterparts. Women have thus been judged by the male standard – assumed to be the only standard by which to reckon success. But by this standard women never fully made the mark. The consequence has often led to a distorted picture. On the one hand, women's contributions have been magnified beyond their actual significance; and on the other hand, the story of women has become the story of male discrimination and dominance. If told from the 'underside', the pages of women's history would reveal tender scenes of nursing the sick, feeding the hungry, tending graves, mending clothes, planting flowers, singing psalms and leading bedtime prayers. But the impartial reporter's eye would also peer behind closed doors to expose infanticide, idleness, cursing, gossip, child abuse and thievery. That women professed faith in Christ did not make them immune from evildoing. And the celebrated 'saints' were as susceptible to sin as were the nameless lowly ones whose voices have long been stilled in the grave.

From *The Changing Roles of Women in Ministry – The Early Church through the 18th Century*

———

Almighty God, in whom there is neither male nor female,
but all are one in Christ Jesus:
by the power of your Holy Spirit release the gifts of men and women
for the mission and ministry of your Church,
that, rejoicing in our differences and celebrating our complementary strengths,
we may work together for the coming of your kingdom;
through Jesus Christ our Lord. Amen.

Cuthbert Carroll Thicknesse 1887–1971

Dean of St Albans

―――

CUTHBERT THICKNESSE WAS Dean of St Albans from 1936 for nineteen years before he retired in 1955. He was ordained in 1913 after receiving his education at Marlborough College, Keble College, Oxford, King's College, London, and Bishop's College Cheshunt. Thicknesse was ordained deacon in the Diocese of London in 1913 and served his title at St John-at-Hackney. He became a military chaplain and was wounded in action at Ypres. Thicknesse was appointed Rector of Badsworth in 1917. Five years later he moved to become Rector of Wigan and an Honorary Chaplain to the king. Thicknesse disagreed with the use of nuclear weapons and created a stir when, in August 1945 at the end of the war with Japan, he would not allow St Albans Abbey to be used for a service of celebration. He was married to Rhoda Oonah Marjorie Madan Pratt. Thicknesse died on this day in 1971.

Antonios Kireopoulos argues that Christians must work for arms reduction

The theological principles upon which the Christian Churches over the years have worked to reduce and eliminate weapons are principles quite fundamental to the Christian faith itself. These theological principles demand that adherents of the faith live their lives through actions reflective of these principles. The belief in God demands that believers turn away from the idolatry of militarism, and not engage in pursuits that support it. The belief in the sovereignty of God requires believers to find their security in God, and not in armaments. The belief in the abundant love of God calls upon believers to love their neighbours, not actively seek *or even passively allow* things that would harm their neighbours. The belief in the dignity of the human person requires that believers seek equity for all, not the advantage of one over another. The belief in God's overriding justice demands that believers seek justice, reconciliation, and peace among nations, and not conflict or policies that breed conflict. In current discussions, these theological principles and behavioural imperatives find their voice in the general appeal to the *moral* and *ethical* leadership that religious communities can offer. It is up to the Churches to articulate as effectively as possible the morals and ethics involved in the disarmament debate. For example, the Churches could better help draw the distinction between legitimate defence needs and superfluous stockpiling of weapons. The Churches could better help point out when the sensible appeal to defence is manipulated, especially through fear, in order to justify unbridled military expenditure. The Churches could better help demonstrate the dangers of the porous boundary between the licit and illicit arms trade. The Churches could better help raise a red flag when weapons are being sold to regimes that imperil human rights through the oppression of their peoples. The Churches could better help expose the irrationality of policies such as 'useable' nuclear weapons. And, as in the case of landmines, the Churches could better help call attention to the senseless destructiveness of certain types of weaponry.

From *Toward a Theology of Non-Proliferation*

Save us, Good Lord, from the sins that lead to conflict and war:
from arrogance and pride, from greed and envy
and from a false nationalism that masks racism.
In your mercy inspire us to work for a peace based on truth and justice,
where all are given equal opportunities;
that your kingdom may come and your will be done,
here as it is in heaven. Amen.

Augustus Orlebar 1824–1912

A cricketing parson

———

AUGUSTUS ORLEBAR COULD hardly have imagined that when he was instituted as Vicar of Willington in 1858 that he would die in office in the same parish fifty-four years later.

Part of a well-known Bedfordshire family (one of Augustus' relatives, Charles Orlebar, was Rector of Whipsnade), he was born at Aspley Guise and confirmed in St Peter's, Sharnbrook. He studied at Rugby School where he became captain of the First XI cricket team. One of his contemporaries at Rugby, Thomas Hughes, was the author of the best selling *Tom Brown's School Days*. In the book, the fight between Tom Brown and Slogger Williams was based on a real fight that took place between Orlebar and a boy called Bulkeley Jones. During his time at Wadham College, Oxford, Orlebar played cricket for the university. He was ordained in 1847 and served curacies in Southover, Lewes, and Hagley Hall. In 1852 he became Vicar of Farndish (now linked with the parish of Podington) and during the next few years played cricket for Bedfordshire and Northamptonshire. In 1858 he became Vicar of Willington and in the same year married Caroline Yarde Scobell. They had six children. Orlebar was instrumental in the restoration of Willington Church, working with the architect Henry Clutton (who also designed the churches at Souldrop, Woburn, Woburn Sands and Steppingley, and restored the churches at Stevington and Houghton Regis). Orlebar also helped establish the church school in Willington. He is buried in the churchyard next to his wife.

Peter van der Veer reflects on Christianity and sport in the Victorian era

Thomas Arnold became Head Master of Rugby in 1827. He was a Christian moralist who insisted that education was essential to the physical and moral improvement of the British nation. By combining the function of head master and pastor, he could deliver a sermon every Sunday in the Rugby chapel. In these sermons he stressed the connections between morality, physicality, and intellectual growth in education. Arnold's influence on the emergence of the English school system can not be overestimated. He organised the public school as a total pedagogic institution of discipline and surveillance, as if it were a monastery…Thomas Hughes popularised Arnold's ideas about Christian righteousness and self-reliant masculinity in his novel. It describes the life of Tom Brown from birth through graduation from Rugby. Pluck and moral strength carry the day, both in sports and life in general. Tom Brown is rescued from moral laxity and religious indifference by the wonderful combination of cricket and Christianity…Cricket, right along with Christianity, carried the imperial mission. Cricket became a political metaphor: 'The greatest game in the world is played wherever the Union Jack is unfurled, and it has no small place in cementing the ties that bond together every part of the Empire… on the cricket grounds of the Empire is fostered the spirit of never knowing when you were beaten, of playing for your side and not for yourself, and of never giving up a game as lost. This is as invaluable in Imperial matters as cricket.'

From *Imperial Encounters: Religion and Modernity in India and Britain*

Give us, O God, the confidence to compete to the best of our ability,
the grace to celebrate when an opponent does well,
the gift of good humour when we lose, and the gift of humility when we win,
that we may rejoice in your gift of life; for Christ's sake. Amen.

John de Cobham d.1355

Benefactor

———

JOHN DE COBHAM was the eldest son of the first Baron Cobham. In 1320 he took over from his father as Warden of the Cinque Ports and Constable of Dover Castle. In 1334 he also became Constable of Rochester Castle and in 1335 was appointed Admiral of the region west of the Thames. In the last years of his life he was Member of Parliament for Kent. He married twice, firstly to Joan of Beauchamp, and then to Agnes Stone of Dartford. Cobham was a benefactor of the Carmelite Priory of St Mary in Hitchin (not to be confused with the Benedictine community at the present-day parish church of St Mary in Hitchin). The Carmelites were an order of hermits founded in the twelfth century in Palestine. They dwelt on Mount Carmel and took their inspiration from the Prophet Elijah who had lived on the mountain. Edward II founded the priory in 1317. In 1351 Cobham gave it an endowment of various properties and six acres of land. The priory was dissolved in 1538.

Carmelites live according to The Rule of Saint Albert

Since man's life on earth is a time of trial, and all who would live devotedly in Christ must undergo persecution, and the devil your foe is on the prowl like a roaring lion looking for prey to devour, you must use every care to clothe yourselves in God's armour so that you may be ready to withstand the enemy's ambush. Your loins are to be girt with chastity, your breast fortified by holy meditations, for as Scripture has it, holy meditation will save you. Put on holiness as your breastplate, and it will enable you to love the Lord your God with all your heart and soul and strength, and your neighbour as yourself. Faith must be your shield on all occasions, and with it you will be able to quench all the flaming missiles of the wicked one: there can be no pleasing God without faith; and the victory lies in this – your faith. On your head set the helmet of salvation, and so be sure of deliverance by our only Saviour, who sets his own free from their sins. The sword of the spirit, the word of God, must abound in your mouths and hearts. Let all you do have the Lord's word for accompaniment.

From *The Rule of Saint Albert* by Bede Edwards

———

Fire is a powerful image in Carmelite spirituality, drawing on the story of Elijah calling down fire from heaven.

Flame, alive, compelling,
yet tender past all telling,
reaching the secret centre of my soul!
Since now evasion's over,
finish your work, my Lover,
break the last thread,
wound me and make me whole!

Burn that is for my healing!
Wound of delight past feeling!
Ah, gentle hand whose touch is a caress,
foretaste of heaven conveying
and every debt repaying:
slaying, you give me life for death's distress.

O lamps of fire bright-burning
with splendid brilliance, turning
deep caverns of my soul to pools of light!
Once shadowed, dim, unknowing,
now their strange new-found glowing
gives warmth and radiance for my Love's delight.

Ah, gentle and so loving
you wake within me, proving
that you are there in secret, all alone;
your fragrant breathing stills me
your grace, your glory fills me
so tenderly your love becomes my own.

A poem by the Carmelite friar St John of the Cross
in *Celebrating the Seasons* by Robert Atwell

Cicely Mary Strode Saunders 1918–2005

Founder of the hospice movement

———

CICELY SAUNDERS SUMMED up her philosophy succinctly 'You matter because you are you and you matter to the last moment of your life. We will do all we can to help you, not only to die peacefully but to live until you die.' As a pioneer in the development of palliative care, Cicely Saunders is rightly hailed as the founder of the modern hospice movement. Born into a prosperous family in Barnet, she was educated at St Anne's College, Oxford. With the outbreak of war, she trained first as a nurse at St Thomas' Hospital in London, and then as an almoner. It was while working in Archway Hospital in north London that she fell in love with David Tasma, a young Jewish refugee from Poland who was dying from inoperable cancer. It was an experience that changed her life. Following his death, she trained and qualified as a doctor in order to devote herself to the care of the dying. She wanted a new approach to terminal care and, in the teeth of considerable opposition and suspicion from the medical establishment, planned to build a hospice. After years of hard work, persuasion and fundraising St Christopher's Hospice was finally opened in south London in 1967. She served as its medical director until 1985. A deeply committed Christian, Cicely Saunders was strongly opposed to euthanasia, but believed that each person had the right to 'die well'. She believed that it is essential that patients receive holistic care which responds not just to their physical needs, but to their social, psychological and spiritual needs as well. She wrote extensively, including *Management of Terminal Malignant Disease* and *Living with Dying*. She died peacefully at St Christopher's in 2005 at the age of eighty-seven.

Cardinal Basil Hume reflects on the approach of death

The Christian faces death realistically, but also knows that death is a gateway, a new beginning, a fulfilment of human life. I fail to understand how anybody can go through life and think there is nothing after death. That is a totally inhuman thought. Now life for the majority is not easy. There are periods of joy and happiness of course; there are times when things go smoothly and happily; yet there are a great number of times when it is a burden. Life is punctuated now with joys, now with sorrows. Within us is the desire to live; we want to go on. There is an urge to go on living fully and totally. We long to enjoy deep down the peace, the joy and happiness which constantly elude us. We cannot grasp them now nor keep them. It is for that deep joy and happiness that we were made. One day it will be ours. If it were not going to be ours our lives would certainly end in frustration and be unfulfilled. That is not only a terrible thing to contemplate, but it is to my way of thinking unreasonable. We are men and women moving through life like pilgrims heading towards our final destination.

From *To be a Pilgrim*

God of our pilgrimage, bless those who accompany us on our final journey,
that in death, as well as in life, we may know your presence
and the assurance of your love; through him who died and rose for us,
your Son, our Saviour, Jesus Christ. Amen.

Charles Boutell 1812–77

Priest and antiquarian

————

CHARLES BOUTELL WAS a priest with extraordinarily wide interests. He carried out extensive archaeological excavations and wrote an important book on heraldry, which remained in print for many years. He wrote other books on monumental brasses, armaments, domestic and ecclesiastical architecture and a guide book to St Albans Abbey. He was also an illustrator, a gift which he used to great effect in some of the books he wrote. Born in Pulham, Norfolk, Boutell was educated at St John's College, Cambridge, before being ordained in Ely Cathedral to a curacy at Hemsby on the Norfolk coast. He then spent nine years as a curate in Sandridge, Hertfordshire, during which time he was one of the founder members of the St Albans Architectural Society. In 1846 Boutell was appointed to the living of Downham Market and Wiggenhall in Norfolk. He belonged to a number of historical, archaeological and architectural societies and regularly gave lectures. In 1838 he married Mary Chevallier with whom he had five children, three of whom predeceased him.

Boutell's career was marred by arguments and disputes which led to his resignation from Downham Market. Towards the end of his life he was Assistant Minister at St Stephen's, Portland Town, London, and Honorary Chaplain to the Royal Naval Artillery Volunteers.

Reflecting on St Antonin, Thomas Merton's French home town during his formative youth, he observes

Here, everywhere I went, I was forced, by the disposition of everything around me, to be always at least virtually conscious of the church. Every street pointed more or less inward to the centre of the town, to the church. Every view of town from the exterior hills, centred upon the long grey building with its high spire. The church had been fitted into the landscape in such a way as to become the keystone of its intelligibility. Its presence imparted a special form, a particular significance to everything else that the eye beheld, to the hills, the forests, the fields, the white cliff of the Rocher d'Anglars and to the red bastion of the Roc Rouge, to the winding river, and the green valley of the Bonnette, the town and the bridge, and even to the white stucco villas of the modern bourgeois that dotted the fields and orchards outside the precinct of the vanished ramparts: and the significance that was imparted was a supernatural one. The whole landscape, unified by the church and its heavenward spire, seemed to say: this is the meaning of all created things: we have been made for no other purpose than that men may use us in raising themselves to God, and in proclaiming the glory of God. We have been fashioned, in all our perfection, each according to his own nature, and all our natures ordered and harmonised together, that man's reason and his love might fit in this one last element, this God-given key to the meaning of the whole. Oh, what a thing it is, to live in a place that is so constructed that you are forced, in spite of yourself, to be at least a virtual contemplative!

From *The Seven Storey Mountain* by Thomas Merton

————

Almighty God,
we thank you for the heritage of our nation,
with its glorious buildings and rich history.
Inspire us by the example of what has gone before
to look with confidence to the future
that we may work for the coming of your kingdom;
through Jesus Christ our Lord. Amen.

Charles Walter Stansby Williams 1886–1945

Poet and novelist

———

CHARLES WILLIAMS WAS one of the most influential writers of his generation. He was friends with Evelyn Underhill, T. S. Eliot and W. H. Auden, and part of the literary circle called 'The Inklings' which included C. S. Lewis and J. R. R. Tolkien. Williams was a committed Anglican and, like a number of literary figures of his day, was interested in theology. He published a history of the Christian Church, called *Descent of the Dove,* and a seminal study on Dante, entitled *The Figure of Beatrice.* Williams was an alumnus of St Albans School. Unable to complete his studies at University College London, for financial reasons, he became a proof reader for Oxford University Press in 1908. He lived in Victoria Street, St Albans, from 1894 until his marriage to Florence Conway in 1917. Williams spent his entire working life with the Press, occupying various roles until he was appointed Editor. He published his first book of poetry, *The Silver Stair,* when he was twenty-eight years old, and this was followed by several other volumes of poetry, most notably *Taliessin through Logres* and *The Region of the Summer Stars.* He was a literary critic, biographer and playwright, though it is his novels that are best known today, such as *War in Heaven* and *All Hallows' Eve.*

In this passage Williams describes the coming of Jesus Christ

There had appeared in Palestine, during the government of the Princeps Augustus and his successor Tiberius, a certain being. This being was in the form of a man, a peripatetic teacher, a thaumaturgical orator. There were plenty of the sort about, springing up in the newly-established peace of the empire, but this particular one had a higher potential of power, and a much more distracting method. It had a very effective verbal style, notably in imprecation, together with a recurrent ambiguity of statement. It continually scored debating-points over its interlocutors. It agreed with everything on the one hand, and denounced everything on the other. For example, it said nothing against the Roman occupation: it urged obedience to the Jewish hierarchy; it proclaimed holiness to the Lord. But it was present at doubtfully holy feasts; it associated with rich men and loose women; it commented acerbically on the habits of the hierarchy; and while encouraging everyone to pay their debts, it radiated a general disapproval, or at least doubt, of every kind of property. It talked of love in terms of hell, and of hell in terms of perfection. And finally it talked at the top of its piercing voice about itself and its own unequalled importance. It said that it was the best and worst thing that ever had happened or ever could happen to man. It said it could control anything and yet had to submit to everything. It said its Father in Heaven would do anything it wished, but that for itself it would do nothing but what its Father in Heaven wished. And it promised that when it had disappeared, it would cause some other Power to illumine, confirm, and direct that small group of stupefied and helpless followers whom it deigned, with the sound of the rush of a sublime tenderness, to call its friends.

From *The Descent of the Dove*

Everliving God,
who in creation, spoke the Word to bring all things into being:
we thank you for the power of word and narrative, image and metaphor;
bless and prosper those who write,
and grant that they may use their skill
to bring insight and understanding;
we ask this through Jesus Christ, the Word made flesh. Amen.

Zacharey Grey 1688–1766

Priest, controversialist and Shakespearean scholar

———

GREY WAS ONE of the more colourful priests who have served in the living of Houghton Conquest. He was a prolific author and his passion for Shakespeare was matched only by his hatred for Puritans. He was educated at Trinity College, Cambridge, and ordained in 1711. Grey held the livings of All Saints, Houghton Conquest, and St Giles and St Peter, Cambridge. His normal practice was to live in Cambridge in the winter months and at Ampthill, not far from Houghton Conquest, during the summer. As a passionate royalist, Grey wrote articles and pamphlets countering the views of the leading republicans. He used his literary skills to defend the Church of England and to argue against the Puritans. Among his published writings are *A Vindication of the Church of England*, *Presbyterian Prejudice Display'd* and *The Spirit of Infidelity Detected*. Grey also engaged in a prolonged dispute with Daniel Neal, criticising each of the four volumes of *The History of the Puritans* as they were published between 1723 and 1739. Among the several books that Grey wrote on William Shakespeare the most significant is his *Critical, Historical, and Explanatory Notes on Shakespeare*, published in 1754. Grey married twice. His second marriage, to Susanna Hatton, produced two daughters, both of whom married clergy. He died at Ampthill in 1766 and is buried at All Saints, Houghton Conquest.

Grey's praise of King Charles I

I shall take the liberty of summing up the character of the royal martyr, in the words of a pious and learned prelate, who lived in those times. 'The heroic virtues, (says he), the flaming charity, the admirable patience, the rare humility, the exemplary charity, the constant and frequent devotions, and the invincible courage of that happy prince, not daunted with the ugly face of a most horrid death hath rendered him the glory of his country, the honour of that church whereof he was the chiefest member, the admiration of Christendom, and a pattern for all princes of what communion soever, to imitate unto the end of the world. His sufferings were psalms, his prison a paradise, and his death-day the birth-day of his happiness; whom his enemies advantaged more by their cruelty, that they could have done by their curtesies. They deprived him of a corruptible crown, and invested him with a crown of glory. They snatched him from the society of his dearest spouse, and from his most hopeful olive branches, to place him in the bosom of his holy angels. This alone is ground enough for his sufferings, to manifest to the world those transcendent graces with which God had enriched him, to which his sufferings gave the greatest lustre, as the stars shine brightest in a dark night'.

A Review of Mr Daniel Neal's History of the Puritans by Zacharey Grey

———

Gracious God,
from whom comes all authority and to whom all must give account,
we give you thanks for our Queen and Government:
may our politicians and leaders rise above personal need and ambition
to work for the good of the whole nation,
pursuing peace, prosperity and justice for all;
this we ask in the name of Jesus Christ our Lord. Amen.

William Ellis 1794–1872

Author and missionary to Madagascar

———

Born into a working-class family, William Ellis worked as a gardener in Stoke Newington. He felt called to missionary service and studied at Homerton College, Hampstead, before being ordained in 1815. The same year Ellis married Mary Moor and within a few weeks they sailed to Eimeo, one of the South Sea Islands. He travelled extensively in the area before settling in Hawaii. However, his wife's health deteriorated and he had to return to England, where he published a book about his travels. In 1830 he took up the post of Assistant Foreign Secretary of the London Missionary Society. Mary died in 1835 leaving Ellis with four children. Two years later he married Sarah Stickney (see her entry for 16 June). The London Missionary Society commissioned Ellis to write a book about Madagascar which was published in two volumes in 1838. Ellis' health broke down, so he and Sarah moved to Hoddesdon where in 1848 he was appointed as the pastor of the Congregational Church. As his health improved, Ellis' thoughts turned again to Madagascar and in 1853 he set sail once again. He wrote about his experiences in *Three Visits to Madagascar*, *Madagascar Revisited* and *Martyr Church of Madagascar*. The toils of his missionary endeavours bore fruit when, in 1868, the new queen who came to the throne was a Christian. Ellis and his wife died within a few days of each other in 1872. He was buried in Abney Park Cemetery in London.

John Patten and Edward Shillito describe the persecutions in Madagascar

The Martyr Church was well named, for many of the faithful suffered death rather than deny the name of Christ. When the hour of trial came these heroic souls met death calmly and with words of triumph upon their lips. The story of the persecution can be told in four chapters. Four times did the fires blaze fiercely. It was in August, 1837, that Rasalama, the first Malagasy martyr, was put to death. Rafaralahy, a young Christian man, seeing her speared, said: 'If I might die so tranquil and happy a death, I would willingly die for the Saviour too.' This was his fate not long afterwards. At this time two hundred Christians were sold into slavery. A second time, in the years 1840–1842, flames were again kindled sevenfold. Sixteen Christians were arrested as they were making their escape to the coast. Paul, a Malagasy and his wife, Joshua and his wife, and Flora, were among the nine who were speared to death. In the year 1849 once more Christians were called to accuse themselves. During this outbreak of persecution eighteen men and women were led forth to die. 'Each Christian man and woman was fastened with cords to two poles, their bodies wrapped in torn and soiled pieces of matting in token of their degradation, their mouths filled with rag to prevent their speaking of the Saviour,' says a trustworthy narrator.

From *The Martyr Church and Its Book*

———

Almighty God,
who called your Church to bear witness
that you were in Christ reconciling the world to yourself:
help us to proclaim the good news of your love,
that all who hear it may be drawn to you;
through him who was lifted up on the cross,
and reigns with you in the unity of the Holy Spirit,
one God, now and for ever, Amen.

Collect for the Thirteenth Sunday after Trinity
from *Common Worship*

Peggy Irene Leech 1929–2012

Church Army Sister

———

THE CHURCH ARMY was founded in 1882 by Wilson Carlile to provide Church of England evangelists to minister in some of the poorest urban areas of the United Kingdom. Today it works in fifteen different countries. Peggy Leech was commissioned in the Church Army in 1956 and, based in the Moral Welfare Department, ministered to women who were working in the sex trade. In 1985 she became a deaconess in the Diocese of St Albans and began working in All Saints, South Oxhey, where she was to stay for the next twenty-four years. In 1987 she was ordained deacon and then in 1994, when she was sixty-five years old, she was among the first women in the diocese to be ordained priest. Peggy Leech was well known in South Oxhey, due to her pastoral ministry of visiting and caring. This was rooted in her life of daily prayer, reflection and Bible reading. For much of her life she suffered from ill health but this did not prevent her from exercising a ministry of healing around the parish. She retired at the age of eighty-one and returned to her home county of Sussex, where she died in 2012.

Wilson Carlile addresses a group of bishops attending the Lambeth Conference of 1930

The Church Army regards our bishops, not only as our dear Fathers in God, but as generals of divisions for their dioceses, whilst the vicars are the colonels of the local regiment. *We* are the captains operating under our colonels to enlist and train companies for our holy war. Church Army evangelists have but little to do with doctrines and ceremonies, theology and philosophy; our first duty is to get each private to fire on the enemy with the love-shots of living witness. We believe that for conversion purposes, a few true testimonies from keen, consistent-living folk are worth hundreds of theological discourses. As evangelists (men and women) we must be able to speak acceptably ourselves, but our chief business is to call forth sincere persons to confess with their mouth as well as with their life. This they promised to do in their baptism. We press for attendance at the holy feast for strength to go forth to bring in the 'bad and the good'; note, the *bad* first. We have so to live and labour that when we fall in the fight, platoon leaders are ready to rally round the colonel to carry on the battle. We want to do the work of an Evangelist and get consecrated communicants enthused with the idea of the early catholic and apostolic days. All must be propagandists or atrophy.

From *Celebrating the Seasons* by Robert Atwell

———

Almighty God,
by whose power and in whose mercy we are shielded from danger
and pardoned when we have done wrong:
Help us to dedicate our lives that we may live for others rather than ourselves,
and grant that through the power of the Holy Spirit we may be steadfast in duty,
patient in hardship and bold at all times to declare the truth
in the name of him who loves us and died for us, Jesus Christ our Lord. Amen.

Adapted from the Collect of the King's Royal Hussars

Samuel Whitbread 1720–96

Brewer and politician

———

SAMUEL WHITBREAD WAS the founder of a dynasty which has made a huge contribution to Bedfordshire for the past 300 years. He was born at Cardington, the seventh of eight children. In his early teenage years Whitbread was apprenticed to a London brewer, John Whiteman. In 1742 Whitbread invested in Thomas Shewell's two breweries. The business prospered and soon became one of the largest breweries in London. Whitbread bought out Shewell in 1765. He was a shrewd entrepreneur and was quick to embrace new methods, including the use of a steam engine in 1786. In 1799 the brewery was renamed Whitbread and Co Ltd. Whitbread married Harriet Hayton, from Ivinghoe, Buckinghamshire, and they had a son, also named Samuel, and two daughters. Harriet died in 1764 and he married Mary Cornwallis. Whitbread was the Member of Parliament for Bedford in 1768–90, after which his son was elected in his place. Whitbread supported the abolition of slavery. Among his philanthropic works were almshouses he built in Cardington. He endowed them with rent from a farm and set up trustees to oversee them. The occupants had to be of 'sober, decent life and conversation' and had to attend public worship regularly. He died on this day in 1796 and is buried in Cardington church in the Whitbread Chapel.

Gregory of Nazianzus preaches about generosity

'Blessed are the merciful, for they shall obtain mercy,' says the Scripture. Mercy is least in importance among the beatitudes. Again it is written: 'Blessed are they who are considerate to the needy and the poor.' And yet again: 'It goes well with those who act generously and lend.' My brothers and sisters, let us lay hold of this blessing, let us earn the name of being considerate, let us be generous. Not even the night should interrupt you in your duty of mercy. Do not ever say: 'Go away and come back later and I will give you something tomorrow.' There should be no delay between your intention and carrying out your good deed. Generosity is the one thing that cannot admit of delay. 'Share your bread with the hungry, and bring the needy and the homeless into your home,' with a joyful and eager heart. 'Whoever does acts of mercy should do so with cheerfulness.' The grace of a good deed is doubled when it is done with promptness and speed. What is given with bad grace or against one's will is distasteful and far from praiseworthy. When we perform an act of kindness we should rejoice and not be glum about it. 'If you undo the shackles and the irons of injustice,' says the prophet Isaiah, that is, if you do away with meanness and counting the cost, with prevarication and grumbling, what will be the result? Something great and wonderful! What a marvellous reward there will be: 'Your light will break forth like the dawn, and your healing will rise up quickly.' Who would not aspire to light and healing?

From *Celebrating the Seasons* by Robert Atwell

Gracious God, give us grace and a spirit of generosity
that in all things we may give rather than take,
share rather than grasp, and contribute rather than consume;
may we use our gifts, our possessions and our time
for the good of others and the glory of your holy name;
through Jesus Christ our Lord. Amen.

Harold Maurice Abrahams 1899–1978

Olympic athlete

———

MANY PEOPLE WILL only know of Harold Abrahams' life through the 1981 film *Chariots of Fire*. Born into an immigrant family, Abrahams' father had come to Bedford from Poland and married a Welsh woman. Harold, the youngest of the four brothers, was a pupil at Bedford School and also Repton School. He joined the army for a time before going to Gonville and Caius College, Cambridge. He was actively involved in many aspects of university life, being a member of the Pitt Club, the Athletics Club, the Liberal Club and the Gilbert and Sullivan Society. His athletic prowess led to his inclusion in the British Olympic Team of 1920 where he competed in the sprinting and the long jump. However, it was in 1924 that he reached the peak of his sporting success, setting the English record for the long jump and, shortly after, winning a gold medal for the 100 metres and a silver medal as part of the relay team. Although he stopped competing in the following year, he was deeply involved in sport for many years, as captain of the 1928 British Olympic Team and as a sports reporter until his retirement. In 1934 Abrahams became a Roman Catholic. Two years later he married an opera singer, Sybil Evers, with whom he adopted two children. He was chairman of the British Amateur Athletic Board in 1948–75. Abrahams worked in the Ministry of Economic Warfare and after the war joined the Ministry of Town and Country Planning until 1963. He was also secretary of the National Parks Commission in 1950–63. Among the books Abrahams wrote are *The Olympic Games* and *The Rome Olympiad*. He is buried in the churchyard of St John the Baptist in Great Amwell in Hertfordshire.

'And if anyone engages in an athletic contest, he does not win the crown unless he observes the rules of the game' (2 Timothy 2.5)

Paul says that the athlete does not win the crown of victory unless he observes the rules of the contest. There is a very interesting point in the Greek here which is difficult to bring out in translation. The Authorised Version speaks of striving lawfully. The Greek is *athlein nomimōs*. In fact that is the Greek phrase which was used by the later writers to describe a professional as opposed to an amateur athlete. The man who strove *nomimōs* was the man who concentrated everything on his struggle. His struggle was not just a spare-time thing, as it might be for an amateur; it was a whole-time dedication of his life to excellence in the contest which he had chosen. Here then we have the same idea as in Paul's picture of the Christian as a soldier. A Christian's life must be concentrated upon his Christianity just as a professional athlete's life is concentrated upon his chosen contest. The spare-time Christian is a contradiction in terms; a man's whole life should be an endeavour to live out his Christianity.

From *The Letters to Timothy, Titus and Philemon* by William Barclay

Almighty and everlasting God,
increase in us your gift of faith
that, forsaking what lies behind
and reaching out to that which is before,
we may run the way of your commandments
and win the crown of everlasting joy;
through Jesus Christ your Son our Lord. Amen.

Collect for the Eighteenth Sunday after Trinity
from *Common Worship*

Thomas Parmiter d.1681

Merchant and benefactor

———

ALTHOUGH THE PRESENT-DAY Parmiter's School is in Garston, in the parish of Leavesden, as far as we know Thomas Parmiter himself never lived in Hertfordshire. He was a successful London silk merchant, married to Elizabeth, who died in 1702. Apart from these facts we know little else about him. As in many medieval wills, Parmiter speaks of his personal faith: *'In the Name of God Amen. I Thomas Parmiter…bequeathe my soule into the hand of God that gave it steadfastly looking and believing through the merritts and mediation of Jesus Christ my Saviour to obtain pardon and forgivenesse of all my sins.'* Parmiter left two farms in Suffolk, the rents from which were to be used to provide £100 per annum for a free school in Bethnal Green to educate ten pupils. A further £30 per annum was bequeathed to pay for six almshouses. Other donors gave land and additional funds, and the school and almshouses were opened in 1722 in St John's Street. As the number of pupils increased the original buildings became too small, so it moved to new premises in 1838 and again in 1887. In 1913 the school and the almshouses became separate charities. In 1945 the almshouses were bombed. Within a few years the trustees decided to sell the land and use the proceeds to provide pensions and annuities. In 1977 the school moved out of London to a new site in Garston. The school was officially opened by the Queen in 1981. Today it is a voluntary aided school with over one thousand students.

Hugh Latimer preaches about the importance of charity

Now to make an end: we are monished here of charity, and taught that God is not only a private Father, but a common Father unto the whole world, unto all faithful; be they never so poor and miserable in this world, yet he is their Father. Where we may learn humility and lowliness: specially great and rich men shall learn here not to be lofty or to despise the poor. For when ye despise the poor miserable man, whom despise ye? Ye despise him which calleth God his Father as well as you; and peradventure more acceptable and more regarded in his sight than you be. Those proud persons may learn here to leave their stubbornness and loftiness. But there be a great many which little regard this: they think themselves better than other men be, and so despise and contemn the poor; insomuch that they will not hear poor men's causes, nor defend them from wrong and oppression of the rich and mighty. Such proud men despise the Lord's prayer: they should be as careful for their brethren as for themselves. And such humility, such love and carefulness towards our neighbours, we learn by this word 'Our'.

From *Love's Redeeming Work* by G. Rowell, K. Stevenson and R. Williams

Father of all,
we live in a world of plenty,
yet many of your children live in poverty and famine:
teach us to be good stewards
and to share what we have,
that we may express our unity with all people
as part of your worldwide family;
we ask this in the name of Jesus Christ our Lord. Amen.

John Eliot c.1604–90

'Apostle to the Indians'

———

THE EAST WINDOW of the parish church of St John the Baptist, Widford, is dedicated to the memory of John Eliot, one of the more unusual sons of the village, who spent most of his adult life as a missionary in North America. Eliot studied at Jesus College, Cambridge, and initially taught in a private school at Little Baddow in Essex. In 1633, however, he sailed to America, landing at Boston in Massachusetts. Eliot was employed to minister at the First Church in Roxbury where in 1645 he set up a school, the Roxbury Latin School. In order to evangelise the Native Americans he learned the language of the Algonquin people, and in 1663 published the Bible in Algonquin, and three years later *The Indian Grammar Begun*. Dismayed at the political and religious divisions tearing England apart, Eliot set his mind as to how best to order society and wrote *The Christian Commonwealth*, a tract in which he argued for an elected theocracy. He was sufficiently committed to new forms of civic life that he set up fourteen towns for Native Americans who had become Christians. In 1689 he donated land and money to found a school to educate children of all races, side by side. It is known today as The Eliot School of Fine and Applied Arts. He married Hanna Mumford and they had six children, though only two survived him. He died on this day in 1690.

A letter from Mr John Eliot directed unto Mr Richard Floyd, Treasurer of the Corporation for New England

To his much respected and Christian friend Mr Floyd, Treasurer of the Corporation for Promoting Religion among the Indians in New England. Christian Friend and Beloved in the Lord.

After salutations in the Lord Jesus. I shall not trouble you with any thing at present save this one businesse of moment, touching the printing of the Bible in the *Indian* language, touching which businesse sundry of the elders did petition unto the Commissioners, moving them to further it, as a principall means of promoting religion among them. And God so guided (without mans contrivance) that I was there when it came in. They moved this doubt whether the translation I had made was generally understood? to which I answered, that upon my knowledge it was understood as farre as *Conecticot* [*Conecticot* is about 100 miles up in the Country.]: for there I did read some part of my translation before many hundred English witnesses, and the *Indians* manifested that they did understand what I read, perfectly, in respect of the language, they further questioned whether I had expressed the translation in true language? I answered that I feared after times will find many infirmities in it, all humane works are subject to infirmity, yet those pieces that were printed, *viz. Genesis* and *Matthew*, I had sent to such as I thought had best skill in the language, and intreated their animadversions, but I heard not of any faults they found.

From *The Eliot Tracts* edited by Michael Clark

———

God of the nations,
we thank you for the gifts of speech and language
enabling us to learn, understand and grow in wisdom:
bless and prosper those who teach languages,
that people of different nations and tongues
may learn to recognise one another as your children;
through your Living Word, Jesus Christ. Amen.

Richard Fletcher c.1544–96

Bishop of London

———

ONE OF THE best-known stories about Richard Fletcher was the unusual manner of his death. On 13 June 1596 he had returned to his home in Chelsea, having assisted at the consecration of the Bishop of Worcester. At 6 o'clock in the evening he lit up his pipe, turned to his servant and said 'Boy, I die' and promptly dropped dead. Born in Watford, Fletcher moved to Bishop's Stortford when his father was made vicar of Holy Trinity Church. Fletcher went up to Trinity College, Cambridge, where he graduated in 1566. He was ordained deacon and priest in 1569 and granted a fellowship at Corpus Christi College. In 1572 he was made a prebendary of St Paul's Cathedral. Fletcher married Elizabeth Holland in 1573, at which point he was forced to vacate his fellowship. He was appointed the town preacher of Rye in Sussex. In 1575 Fletcher was introduced to the court and came to the attention of Queen Elizabeth, not least for his excellent preaching. In 1583 he was appointed Dean of Peterborough, where he played a significant role in the trial of Mary, Queen of Scots, at Fotheringhay. Fletcher's rise through the episcopate was rapid. He was made Bishop of Bristol in 1589, Bishop of Worcester in 1593 and Bishop of London in 1595. Following his first wife's death, Fletcher married Mary Baker in 1595, thereby incurring the displeasure of Queen Elizabeth, at which point she suspended him for five months. He was buried in St Paul's Cathedral.

Gregory the Great reflects on the qualities that are needed in leaders

Christian leaders are enemies to our Redeemer if on the strength of the good works they perform, they desire to be loved by the Church more than by Christ; indeed, such servants are guilty of adulterous thinking. Although in truth it is the bridegroom who sends gifts through his servants to his bride the Church, the servants are busy trying to secure the eyes of the bride for themselves. When such self-love captures the mind, it propels a person either into inordinate laxity or into brutal irascibility. From love of self, the leader's mind becomes lax. He sees people sinning, but dares not correct them because he is frightened their love for him will be weakened; or even worse, rather than reprove them, he will actually go so far as to gloss over their faults with adulation. Leaders tend to display such an attitude to those of whom they are frightened, those whom they think can wreck their pursuit of temporal glory. By contrast, folk who (in their estimation) cannot harm them, they constantly hound with bitter and harsh words. Incapable of admonishing such people gently, they abandon any pretence of pastoral sensitivity, and terrify them into submission by insisting on their right to govern. The divine word rebukes such leaders when the prophet says: 'You ruled over people with force and with a high hand.' Such leaders love themselves more than their Creator, and brag of the qualities of their leadership.

From the treatise *Pastoral Care* by Gregory the Great

God of love and mercy,
you anoint your shepherds with the Holy Spirit
that they might lead and care for your flock:
make them wise, compassionate and courageous.
Give them hearts of love to seek after the lost,
call back the wanderers and protect the weak;
for we ask this in the name of the Good Shepherd
Jesus Christ our Lord. Amen.

Sarah Stickney Ellis 1799–1872

Congregationalist author

———

DURING HER LIFETIME Sarah Ellis was well known as an author, publishing on a wide variety of subjects including art, household management, cookery, travel and missionary work, as well as writing poetry. However, today she is best remembered for her books on moral education and the role of women in society. She was also an accomplished artist and illustrator. Born Sarah Stickney into a Quaker family who farmed in Richmond, Yorkshire, she was the youngest of the five children. Much of her education took place at home, although for three years she attended a Quaker school at Ackworth. In 1837 she married a widower, the Reverend William Ellis, who was also a writer. He was deeply involved in the London Mission Society. Ellis became a Congregationalist and Sarah supported him both in his missionary work and also in the temperance movement. In 1841 they moved to Hoddesdon and it was here that she set up a non-denominational school for young ladies at Rawdon House, aided by a friend, Isabella Hurry. Among the many books she wrote are *Pictures of Private Life*; *The Negro Slave: a Tale Addressed to the Women of Great Britain*; *The Women of England, their Social Duties and Domestic Habit*; and *The Mothers of England, their Influence and Responsibility*. She was not without her critics, some of whom disliked the moralising tone of her writings and suggested that, rather than influencing husbands, she was actually advocating manipulating them. She died on this day in 1872, within a week of her husband's death, and is buried in the Quaker burial ground in Hoddesdon.

David Edwards describes some of the Christian social work in the nineteenth century

When we seek to understand the strength of the Victorian Evangelicals, we ought to see Shaftesbury finding a ragged boy asleep in the roller used in Regent's Park. We ought to think of Elizabeth Gilbert, the blind daughter of a bishop, opening the first workshop for blind men in her home in 1853. We ought to remember the missions to workers in jobs which most of the country was happy to ignore. Evangelicals noticed the navvies who built the Crystal Palace which was the marvel of London; and Catherine Marsh made them seem marvellous in the book she wrote about her work among them, *English Hearts and English Hands*. They cared for the deep sea fishermen who found cheap alcohol the best way of forgetting the cruel conditions on their little boats in the North Sea. The Victorian Evangelicals did not merely condemn. Nor did they live only among the respectable. They followed their Master in seeking out the lost. And without intending to do this, they laid the foundations of the twentieth-century Welfare State by putting into practice their acknowledgement of a duty to interfere in the results of the working of the laws of capitalist economics.

From *Christian England*

Heavenly Father, giver of all good gifts:
open our eyes to see the world in all its suffering,
open our minds to understand how we can make a difference
and open our hands that we might reach out to those in need
in practical caring and generous love.
Give us faith, courage and boldness as we work for the coming of your kingdom;
through Jesus Christ our Lord. Amen.

St Botolph d.c.680

Patron saint of farming and travellers

———

WHAT DO THE village churches at Aspley Guise in Bedfordshire and Eastwick in Hertfordshire have in common? Both are dedicated to an English abbot who lived in the seventh century and who is remembered today as the patron saint of farmers and travellers. *The Anglo-Saxon Chronicle* tells us that Botolph built a church at Ikanho, which is probably in the present-day parish of Iken in Suffolk. In *The Life of St Ceolfrith* there is a reference to an abbot called Botolphus who was 'a man of remarkable life and learning, full of the grace of the Holy Spirit'. It is thought that he was buried at Ikanho and that his body was taken first to Burgh and then to the great Benedictine Abbey of Bury St Edmunds. Four London churches, each near different city gates, were dedicated to St Botolph, presumably because travellers arriving and leaving London could pray to him in thanksgiving and for his protection. The towns of Boston in Lincolnshire and Massachusetts are named after Botolph, being a contraction of St Botolph's town. His feast day is 17 June.

Thoughts for pilgrims and travellers as they prepare for a journey

Just as a true pilgrim, going towards *Jerusalem*, leaveth behind him house and land, wife and children, and maketh himself poor and bare from all things that he hath, that he may go lightly without letting. Right so, if thou wilt be a spiritual pilgrim, thou shalt strip thyself naked of all that thou hast, that are either good deeds or bad, and cast them all behind thee, that thou be so poor in thy own feeling that there be nothing of thy own working that thou wilt restingly lean on; but ever desiring more grace and love, and ever seeking the spiritual presence of Jesus. And if thou dost thus, then shalt thou resolve in thy heart fully and wholly that thou wilt be at *Jerusalem*, and at no other place but there; that is, thou shalt purpose in thy heart wholly and fully that thou wilt nothing have but the love of Jesus and the spiritual sight of Him in such manner as He shall please to show Himself; for to that end only art thou made and redeemed, and He it is that is thy beginning and thy end, thy joy and thy bliss. And therefore whatsoever thou hast, be thou never so rich in other deeds spiritual or corporal (unless thou have this love that I speak of, and know and feel that thou hast it) hold and esteem that thou hast right nothing. Imprint this well in the desire of thy soul, and cleave fast thereto, and it shall save thee from all perils in thy going, that thou shalt never perish, and it shall save thee from the thieves and robbers which call unclean spirits, that though they spoil thee and beat thee by divers temptations, thy life shall ever be safe; and in brief, if thou keep it, as I have said, thou shalt escape all perils and mischiefs, and come to the city of *Jerusalem* in a short time.

From *The Ladder of Perfection* by Walter Hilton

———

O God,
by whose grace the blessed Abbot Botolph,
enkindled with the fire of your love,
became a burning and a shining light in your church;
grant that we may be inflamed with the same spirit of discipline and love,
and ever walk before you as children of the light,
through Jesus Christ our Lord. Amen.

Collect for St Botolph, author unknown

Selina Hastings 1707–91

Benefactress

FROM 1792 UNTIL 1906 Cheshunt was the home of an influential college, founded by Selina Hastings, Countess of Huntingdon. She had set up the college in Brecon in 1768 when six Methodist students were expelled from St Edmund Hall, Oxford, so that they could be trained for the Christian ministry. The college moved to Cambridge in 1906, and in 1967 it merged with Westminster College where it has continued to train ministers for the United Reformed Church and the Presbyterian Church. Selina Hastings was born near Ashby-de-la-Zouch in Leicestershire. In 1728 she married Theophilus Hastings, the ninth Earl of Huntingdon, with whom she had six children. She was drawn into the Methodist revival and following the death of her husband in 1746 she made George Whitfield her personal chaplain. Using her wealth and influence, Selina founded a denomination, known as the Countess of Huntingdon's Connexion, for which she built sixty-four chapels. They had to subscribe to the doctrines of the Church of England and use the *Book of Common Prayer*. Following her death some of the churches became part of the Congregational Church and in 1863 many of the churches joined the Free Church of England. Today the Connexion still has twenty-three churches in England and others in Sierra Leone. Among the English churches are two in the diocese: Wormley Free Church and Rosedale Community Church, Cheshunt.

Alan Harding writes about Selina's work to spread the Christian gospel

Lady Huntington was also involved, in the years immediately following her conversion, in more direct and practical forms of Christian service. She had various plans for schools, including one which the master would combine with selling Wesley's publications. The distribution of religious literature was in fact an important part of her ministry. In 1746 she arranged for some of William Law's works to be printed – probably for free distribution, like the Wesley works that she appears previously to have had reprinted. She took an interest in how the Revival was spreading across the country: when Charles Wesley was in Cornwall in 1743, for example, she sent him a gift for the Methodists in St Ives. She prayed and read with her own servants (not necessarily with their agreement!) and she asked John Wesley if it would be in order for her to expound the Scriptures to them. She used her family chaplain to run 'a little meeting' in her house, and there were schemes to address the physical and spiritual needs of the poor of the neighbourhood. Her ministry was direct and personal:

God show forth his love & power every moment among us and we find many added to the believers. My poor old woman is quite recovered… (and) very faithful to that which is committed to her…I have laboured much among the unawakened. I let none pass by of any rank…God blesses my labours for their bodily health so much that they come many miles to me on that account and many God sends home a seeking…I am brought by reading, singing and talking to them almost past opening my mouth.

From *Selina, Countess of Huntingdon*

Holy Spirit, sent by the Father,
ignite in us your holy fire;
strengthen your children with the gift of faith,
revive your Church with the breath of love,
and renew the face of the earth,
through Jesus Christ our Lord. Amen.

The Collect for Pentecost from *Common Worship*

Michael Bolton Furse 1870–1955

Bishop of St Albans

———

MICHAEL FURSE SERVED as Bishop of St Albans for twenty-four years – longer than any of his predecessors or successors. However, his connection with the patron saint of the diocese goes back even further, as he had been Bishop of Pretoria for eleven years from 1909 to 1920 and his cathedral there was also dedicated to St Alban. Furse had had a privileged education, studying at Eton and Trinity College, Oxford. He trained for the ministry at Cuddesdon College, Oxford, was made deacon in 1896 and then priested the following year. For eight years he was Fellow and Dean of Trinity College before being appointed as Archdeacon of Johannesburg at the age of thirty-three. Furse married Frances Redfield in 1903 and one of the great sadnesses during his time as Bishop of Pretoria was the death of their daughter in 1918 due to scarlet fever. In her memory the Jane Furse Hospital was built. Two years later Furse was translated to St Albans. During his episcopate seventeen new churches were built in the diocese. He was made a Knight Commander of the Most Distinguished Order of Saint Michael and Saint George in 1947. His autobiography is called *Stand Therefore: a bishop's testimony of Faith in the Church of England*. He is buried in the churchyard at Cuddesdon with his wife.

Michael Furse reflects on the incarnation

There are many things in the Christian Faith which baffle our understanding; but one thing is as clear as daylight, and that is the object for which the Son of God became Incarnate. He came, as he said himself, 'that men might have life, and have it more abundantly.' He came to satisfy the deepest and most fundamental instinct in every normal human being, that is to *live*, and live fully, in body, mind, and spirit. In order that His message might be understood by all men, of whatever race or language, he gave that message to the world in the one language which is common to the whole human race – the language of a human life. He has demonstrated in a truly human life, the 'Way' all men should live: by doing so He reveals, to those who will take the trouble to study that life and the principles on which it was based, the truth about God and man and their relation to each other. But he did not merely set before men an ideal; He claimed, as he still claims, to give them the power to live out that ideal in everyday life; for Christianity is not only a code of ethics, but a dynamic force for living life according to God's plan.

From *A School of Prayer*

———

Heavenly Father,
send down the Holy Spirit on all bishops and priests
that they may be faithful shepherds of the flock entrusted to their care:
may they grow daily in love and holiness,
may they guard the faith and proclaim the gospel,
that all people may hear the good news of your salvation;
for we ask this in the name of Jesus Christ our Lord. Amen.

John Evans 1823–1908

Manufacturer, archaeologist and geologist

———

JOHN EVANS WAS one of a number of Victorian industrialists who were able to pursue their academic interests alongside their work. For a significant part of his working life Evans was the manager of the John Dickinson's paper manufacture plant at Nash Mills in Hemel Hempstead. His expertise in the industry led to him becoming the President of the Society of Chemical Industry (1891–3) and the British Association for the Advancement of Science (1897–8). In his spare time Evans became a distinguished antiquary and numismatist. He wrote a number of works including *The Coins of the Ancient Britons* (1864) and *The Ancient Stone Implements, Weapons and Ornaments of Great Britain* (1872). At various times he was President of the Society of Antiquaries, the Numismatic Society, the Geological Society of London and the Anthropological Institute of Great Britain and Ireland. He was elected a Fellow of the Royal Society in 1864 and in 1881 he was High Sheriff of Hertfordshire. Evans was also a trustee of the British Museum and was knighted in 1892. He married three times and had six children. His eldest son, Sir Arthur Evans, excavated King Minos' Palace at Knossos on Crete. Evans died at Berkhamsted and is buried at St Lawrence Church, Abbots Langley.

In this passage the priest and biochemist Professor Arthur Peacocke reflects on the relation between science and religion

Briefly, I think that both science and theology aim to depict reality; that they both do so in metaphorical language with the use of models; and that their metaphors and models are revisable within the context of the continuous communities which have generated them. This philosophy of science ('critical realism') has the virtue of being the implicit, though often not articulated, working philosophy of practising scientists who aim to depict reality but know only too well their fallibility in doing so. A formidable case for such a critical scientific realism has been mounted based on the histories of, for example, geology, cell biology and chemistry, which during the last two centuries have progressively and continuously discovered hidden structures in the entities of the natural world that account causally for observed phenomena. Models and metaphors are in fact widely used in science but this does not detract from the aim of such language to refer to realities while it does entail that the models and metaphors are always in principle revisable. *Theology*, the intellectual formulation of religious experience and beliefs, also employs models which may be similarly described. I urge that a critical realism is also the most appropriate and adequate philosophy concerning religious language and should be regarded as partial, inadequate, and revisable but necessary and, indeed, the only ways of referring to the reality that is named as 'God' and to God's relation with humanity. Models and metaphor obviously play an even wider role in religious language than in science. In theology, we also have to attempt *to infer to the best explanation* by application of the normal criteria of reasonableness: fit with the data, internal coherence, comprehensiveness, fruitfulness and general cogency.

From *God and Science*

God of truth,
you created us with the desire for knowledge and understanding
and implanted in us an insatiable curiosity;
bless the endeavours of all who study and research:
may they use their gifts and abilities to work for the common good
that all mankind may prosper and flourish,
for the sake of Jesus Christ our Lord. Amen.

Nathaniel Vincent c.1639–97

Nonconformist minister

———

NATHANIEL VINCENT WAS among the two thousand clergy who left the Church of England in 1662 in what is known as 'The Great Ejection'. Following King Charles II's return to England in 1660 and the Savoy Conference in the following year, Parliament passed the Act of Uniformity in 1662. Any minister who refused to conform to *The Book of Common Prayer* had to leave their living. Vincent had studied at Oxford University and ministered as chaplain of Corpus Christi College. He was ordained and instituted to the parish of Langley Marish. Refusing to conform, Vincent left the parish and spent three years as chaplain to Sir Henry and Lady Blount at their home at Tyttenhanger House near St Albans (an estate which had belonged to St Albans Abbey before the Reformation). Within a few years Vincent had moved to the meeting-house in Farthing Alley in Southwark where he preached, sometimes in the face of great opposition. Over the next few years Vincent was arrested at least three times and he used his spells in prison to write a large number of books. Among his publications are collections of sermons and *The Conversion of a Sinner Explained and Applied, The Principles of the Doctrine of Christ: a Catechism* and *The Spirit of Prayer*. He was married to Anna with whom he had six children.

Vincent reflects on the nature of prayer

In prayer there must *be thanksgiving for what has been already received*. Praise is the *sublimest* part of prayer: praise is a debt; and how vast is the debt, if we consider the multitude, greatness, freeness and continuance of mercies? Praise sweetens prayer, nothing more pleasing to God; nothing more pleasant to ourselves. And to give thanks for benefits received, is as effectual a way to prevail for more mercy, as the most vehement and strongest cries. Oh therefore, that all who pray, would also *praise the Lord for his goodness, and for his wonderful works to the children of men*? (Psalm 107.8). To pray always, implies, *being always in a disposition and frame to pray when God requires it*. The heart must be reconciled to this duty, and fall in love with it, and to go to the throne of grace with alacrity; much may be gotten at the mercy-seat, and the unsearchable riches of Christ are unlocked, and we may take as much as the hand of faith can grasp, without being checked or upbraided. The God whom we have to do with, *gives liberally and like himself* (James 1.5). The heart should be forward to pray, and be weary of, and through grace subdue more and more that evil, which alas is *present when good is about to be performed* (Romans 7.21). To pray always implies, *laying hold of all opportunities to pray* that are graciously vouchsafed to us. Whenever there is a meet season and emotion to pray, we should catch such an occasion by the forelock, for when it is past, it is past recalling.

From a sermon entitled 'Pray Always' in *The Spirit of Prayer*

———

Save us, Gracious God,
from a spirit of complaining
and grant us instead
a spirit of thankfulness and praise;
grant us the faith to receive all that comes our way with acceptance
and to offer it back to you with gratitude,
that you may take it and redeem it for your praise and glory;
through Jesus Christ our Lord. Amen.

Alban d. c.209

Saint and martyr

———

ALBAN IS THE first recorded Christian martyr in Britain. He was a Roman soldier who lived in Verulamium, present-day St Albans. Alban met a Christian priest who was being persecuted and hid him in his house. He was so impressed by the priest's prayerfulness that he was converted to Christianity. Before long the priest was discovered. Instead of handing him over, Alban put on the priest's cloak and was arrested in his place. Despite being tortured by the Romans, he refused to recant his new-found faith. He was taken out of the town to the top of a nearby hill and beheaded, probably around the year AD 209. The place of his execution became a site for pilgrims. It is now the site of the Cathedral and Abbey Church of St Albans. In this diocese the church at Warners End, Hemel Hempstead, and the chapel at Brickendon in the parish of Bayford, are also dedicated to St Alban, as are many churches around the world.

The Venerable Bede describes Alban's martyrdom

When the judge saw Alban, being much enraged that he should thus, of his own accord, put himself into the hands of the soldiers, and incur such danger on behalf of his guest, he commanded him to be dragged up to the images of the devils, before which he stood, saying, 'Because you have chosen to conceal a rebellious and sacrilegious person, rather than to deliver him up to the soldiers, that his contempt of the gods might meet with the penalty due to such blasphemy, you shall undergo all the punishment that was due to him, if, you abandon the worship of our religion.' But St Alban, who had voluntarily declared himself a Christian to the persecutors of the faith, was not at all daunted at the prince's threats, but putting on the armour of spiritual warfare, publicly declared that he would not obey the command. Then said the judge, 'Of what family or race are you?' 'What does it concern you,' answered Alban, 'of what stock I am? If you desire to hear the truth of my religion be it known to you, that I am now a Christian, and bound by Christian duties.' 'I ask your name,' said the judge; 'tell me it immediately.' 'I am called Alban by my parents,' replied he; 'and I worship and adore the true and living God, who created all things.' Then the judge, inflamed with anger, said, 'If you will enjoy the happiness of eternal life, do not delay to offer sacrifice to the great gods.' Alban rejoined, 'These sacrifices, which by you are offered to devils, neither can avail the subjects, nor answer the wishes or desires of those that offer up their supplications to them. On the contrary, whosoever shall offer sacrifice to these images shall receive the everlasting pains of hell for his reward.' The blessed Alban suffered death on the twenty-second day of June, near the city of Verulam, where afterwards, when peaceable Christian times were restored, a church of wonderful workmanship, and suitable to his martyrdom, was erected.

From *A History of the English Church and People*

———

Eternal Father, when the gospel of Christ first came to our land
you gloriously confirmed the faith of Alban
by making him the first to win a martyr's crown:
grant that, following his example, in the fellowship of the saints
we may worship you, the living God,
and give true witness to Jesus Christ your Son our Lord. Amen.

From *Exciting Holiness* by Brother Tristam

Etheldreda c.636–79

Queen, virgin and saint

———

PEOPLE INTERESTED IN etymology may like to know that the word *tawdry* comes from a shortened version of St Etheldreda's name, St Awdrey. The lace that was sold at the annual fair in Ely was considered to be cheap and of poor quality, thus St Awdrey's lace became known as tawdry. The parish church in Bishop's Hatfield is dedicated to this former Abbess of Ely, Etheldreda. It is thought she was a daughter of Anna (or Onna), King of East Anglia. Records reveal that Etheldreda made a vow of perpetual virginity, so that when in 652 she was married to Tondberct, chief of the South Gyrvians, she asked him not to force her to break her promise. He died three years later at which point she went to live on the Isle of Ely which he had given her. In 660 Etheldreda married the King of Northumbria, Ecgfrith. He came to the throne around 670 at which point Etheldreda became a nun. Desiring to consummate the marriage, Ecgfrith tried to kidnap her but Etheldreda escaped accompanied by two nuns. The Anglo-Saxon Chronicle tells us that she founded her monastery at Ely in 673.

From a sermon preached by Martin Luther

And there was one Anna, a prophetess, the daughter of Phanuel of the tribe of Asher (she was of a great age, having lived with a husband seven years from her virginity, and she had been a widow even unto fourscore and four years), who departed not from the temple, worshipping with fastings and supplications night and day. Here some might say: From the example of Anna you see that good works are exalted, as for instance fasting and praying and going to church, therefore they must not be condemned. But who has ever condemned good works? We only reject hypocritical and spurious good works. Fasting, praying, going to church are good works, if they are done in the right spirit. But the trouble is that these blockheads explain the Scriptures so awkwardly, noticing only the works and examples of the saints and thinking that now they are able to learn from them and imitate them. Thus they become nothing but apes and hypocrites, for they do not perceive that the Scriptures speak more of the heart than of the deeds of men. The sacrifice and works of Abel are praised in Scripture, but he himself a great deal more. They however disregard the person and observe only the example, take notice of the works and pay no heed to faith, eat the bran and throw away the flour, as we read in Hosea 3.1: 'They turn unto other gods, and love cakes of raisins.' If you desire to fast and pray like Anna, well and good. But take good care that first of all you imitate her character, and then her works. Be first of all like Anna. But let us see what Luke says of her works and her character, so that her example may be correctly understood.

From *Of Simeon and Anna*

———

We thank you
for the lives and examples of godly women
who have borne witness to their faith
in singleness of purpose and purity of heart:
bless all women who seek your face,
give them faith, hope and love,
that their lives may reveal your grace and truth;
we ask this in the name of Jesus Christ our Lord. Amen.

Rupert Ernest William Gascoyne-Cecil 1863–1936

Rector of Hatfield and Bishop of Exeter

———

MOST OF US would like to be remembered for some act of compassion or heroism in a time of crisis. William Cecil is usually remembered for neither of these things, but rather for his eccentricity. On one occasion he was travelling by train to conduct a confirmation. When the ticket collector came along the carriage, Cecil could not find his ticket. 'Don't worry, my Lord,' said the collector 'everyone knows who you are.' 'That's all very well,' replied Cecil, 'but without the ticket how do I know where I am going?' On another occasion a guest was astonished to see Cecil feeding crumpets to two rats which emerged from a hole in the floorboards. The second son of Lord Salisbury, the Prime Minister, Cecil was born at Hatfield House and educated at Eton College and University College, Oxford. He was ordained in 1887 and served his title in Great Yarmouth. A year later he became Rector of Hatfield and remained so for the next twenty-eight years. In 1916 he was appointed Bishop of Exeter, a post which he held until his death in 1936. In the year of his ordination he married Florence Bootle-Wilbraham. They had four sons and three daughters. Three of their sons were killed during the First World War. It may have been this tragic loss which caused him to write so movingly about the need for clergy to exercise good pastoral care. Cecil died on this day in 1936.

In this passage Cecil reflects on the importance of pastoral care

There is no duty upon which our Ordinal puts greater emphasis that the duty of taking care of the sick and needy. The Deacon is to search for them, the Priest is to care for them spiritually, and the Bishop is to show himself merciful and gentle towards them.

Therefore, I make no apology for recommending this duty as one of the greatest importance to the clergy. Thirty years' experience in parish work has indeed made me confident that this is one of the most essential duties of the parish priest's life. There are many things that we ought to do; we ought to attend committee meetings, we ought to be careful to read and keep up our studies, we ought to organise clubs and games; but of this I am certain, that if we want to win the hearts of our parishioners we can do it in no other way than by being scrupulously careful to perform this most beautiful act of service to Our Lord. Our Lord in His first sermon said He came to bind up the broken hearts, and we must work, as it were, after Him if we would show ourselves true ministers of Christ and His worthy followers.

From the Primary Visitation Charge given by William Cecil to the Diocese of Exeter

———

God of Compassion
whose Son Jesus Christ brought healing to the sick,
calm to the troubled and peace to the disturbed:
fill us afresh with the power of your Holy Spirit,
that we may bring healing to all
who suffer in body, mind or spirit;
for we ask it in his name. Amen.

Eleanor Anne Ormerod 1828–1901

Entomologist

A S THE FIRST woman to be awarded an honorary doctorate by Edinburgh University, Eleanor Ormerod's contribution to science was well summed up in the citation: 'The pre-eminent position which Miss Ormerod holds in the world of science is the reward of patient study and unwearying observation. Her investigations have been chiefly directed towards the discovery of methods for the prevention of the ravages of those insects which are injurious to orchard, field and forest. Her labours have been crowned with such success that she is entitled to be hailed the protectress of agriculture and the fruits of the earth – a beneficent Demeter of the nineteenth century.' Throughout her life, Ormerod was interested in agriculture and insects. She wrote *Notes for Observations on Injurious Insects, The Injurious Insects of South Africa* and *Handbook of Insects injurious to Orchard and Bush Fruits.* She also published an important work on that well-known pest, the turnip-fly. For some years she lectured in entomology at the Royal Agricultural College, Circencester, and was the first woman to become a Fellow of the Royal Meteorological Society. She lived in St Albans in retirement and worshipped at St Michael's Church. A blue plaque on Holywell Hill marks the house where she lived.

Peter Harrison writes about science and Christianity

It is often assumed that the relationship between Christianity and science has been a long and troubled one. Such assumptions draw support from a variety of sources. There are contemporary controversies about evolution and creation, for example, which are thought to typify past relations between science and religion. This view is reinforced by popular accounts of such historical episodes as the Condemnation of Galileo, which saw the Catholic Church censure Galileo for teaching that the earth revolved around the sun. Adding further credence to this view of history are a few recent outspoken critics of religion who vociferously contend that religious faith is incompatible with a scientific outlook, and that this has always been the case. In spite of this widespread view on the historical relations between science and religion, historians of science have long known that religious factors played a significantly positive role in the emergence and persistence of modern science in the West. Not only were many of the key figures in the rise of science individuals with sincere religious commitments, but the new approaches to nature that they pioneered were underpinned in various ways by religious assumptions. The idea, first proposed in the seventeenth century, that nature was governed by mathematical laws, was directly informed by theological considerations. The move towards offering mechanical explanations in physics also owed much to a particular religious perspective. The adoption of more literal approaches to the interpretation of the Bible, usually assumed to have been an impediment to science, also had an important, indirect, role in these developments, promoting a non-symbolic and utilitarian understanding of the natural world which was conducive to the scientific approach.

Christianity and the Rise of Western Science

Lord of creation, we praise you for the intricacy and diversity
of the ecological systems which sustain our life on earth:
for invertebrates, fish, amphibians, reptiles, mammals, plants and birds.
Bless and prosper, we pray, all who study the natural world,
and help us not only to understand but also to respect and honour your creation;
for the sake of Jesus Christ our Lord. Amen.

Thomas Stanley 1625–78

Poet, author and translator

———

A S WELL AS writing poetry, Thomas Stanley was a gifted linguist who could speak French, Spanish and Italian and read Greek and Latin. He translated an important work on spirituality by the French writer Jean-Hugues Quarré, which was published in 1664 under the title *A Spiritual Treasure: Containing our Obligations to God, and the Vertues necessary to a Perfect Christian*. Stanley was born in Clothall and studied at Pembroke Hall, Cambridge, before following a career in law at the Middle Temple. His inherited wealth allowed him time to travel extensively and write poetry. He knew many of the leading people of his day and may well have been quite conceited as he had his portrait painted at least fifteen times, including by such well-known portraitists as Lely and Kneller. Stanley was one of the last metaphysical poets. His *magnus opus* was the three-volume *The History of Philosophy* in which he describes the lives and thoughts of many of the ancient Greek philosophers. He married Dorothy Enyon and was survived by a son and three daughters. He is buried in St Mary the Virgin's Church, Clothall.

The Loss

Yet ere I go,
disdainful beauty thou shalt be
so wretched, as to know
what joys thou fling'st away with me

A faith so bright,
as time or fortune could not rust;
so firm, that lovers might
have read thy story in my dust.

And crown'd thy name
with laurel verdant, as thy youth,
whilst the shrill voice of fame
Spread wide thy beauty and my truth.

This thou hast lost;
for all true lovers, when they find
that my just aims were crosed,
will speak thee lighter than the wind.

And none will lay
any oblation on thy shrine
but such as would betray
thy faith, to faiths as false as thine.

Yet if thou choose
on such thy freedom to bestow
affection may excuse,
for love from sympathy doth flow.

Thomas Stanley

———

Too late have I loved you, O Beauty so ancient,
O Beauty so new. Too late have I loved you!
You were within me but I was outside myself, and there I sought you!
In my weakness I ran after the beauty of the things you have made.
You were with me, and I was not with you.
The things you have made kept me from you –
the things which would have no being unless they existed in you!
You have called, you have cried, and you have pierced my deafness.
You have radiated forth, you have shined out brightly,
and you have dispelled my blindness.
You have sent forth your fragrance, and I have breathed it in, and I long for you.
I have tasted you, and I hunger and thirst for you.
You have touched me, and I ardently desire your peace. Amen.

St Augustine of Hippo

Anthony Burgess d.1664

Nonconformist minister and writer

———

ANTHONY BURGESS WAS born in Watford, the son of a schoolmaster. He studied at St John's College, Cambridge, in 1623 and after graduation became a Fellow of Emmanuel College, Cambridge. In 1635 he was made Rector of Sutton Coldfield. He was on the Parliamentary side during the Civil War and played an important role in the Westminster Assembly. However, he refused to confirm after the Restoration and in 1662 he was ejected from his living. A prolific writer, many of Burgess' sermons were published during his lifetime and he wrote a number of books defending Reformation theology, such as the pithily titled *The True Doctrine of Justification Asserted and Vindicated from the Errors of Papists, Arminians, Socinians, and Antinomians, in thirty lectures at Lawrence Jury*. He also wrote books on original sin and a commentary on Paul's First Letter to the Corinthians.

Anthony Burgess preaches to a congregation after the death of their minister

There are two actions of the body mentioned in prayer, which denote that excellent deportment that should be at that time in the soul; kneeling of the body, that denoteth self-humiliation; lifting up the hands, that implieth faith and confidence: thus *descendendo ascenditur*, how hardly do the people of God keep these two graces co-operating together, but either their humiliation abateth their faith, or their faith hindreth their humiliation; both these together are the *calidum* and the *humidum*, which maintain the life of holy duties; he prayed as well as kneeled, for that is the only key to open heaven, that is David's harp, to allay all those unruly affections that are apt to disturb us…There is some comfort, though there be cause of much sorrow, that though your faithful pastor be dead, yet the chief pastor of your souls is not. He that sendeth pastors and teachers in the church, he that sendeth forth labourers into his harvest, he liveth for ever…Now the will of God is done, concerning our deceased brother, your duty is to be much in prayer to God, that they may be a Joshua after Moses, that God would join your hearts together as one man, to seek out a pastor for you, which shall feed you according to his holy will. The Lord hath made a great breach upon you, be sensible of it, and seriously consider how all your soul comforts and advantages are bound up in this matter. Ministers are compared to the sun, and salt, *nihil sole et sale utilius*. Can you be without the sun in the heaven? Without bread for your body, or neither without this bread of life for your souls, or without this light to guide you in the wilderness of this world, to eternal happiness?

From Thomas Blake's *Vindiciæ foederis*

Bountiful God,
whose Son has taught us that the harvest is plentiful
but the workers are few:
send the Holy Spirit upon your people,
rousing us from our apathy
opening our eyes to a needy world,
and giving us courage to respond to your call,
that we may declare your good news in word and deed;
through Jesus Christ our Lord. Amen.

Thurcytel d.975

Abbot of Crowland and Abbot of Bedford

———

MEDIEVAL SOCIETY WAS divided into three categories: those who fight, those who labour, and those who pray. During his lifetime, Thurcytel participated in all three. As a young man, he served in the royal household of various of the Saxon kings, including Edward the Elder (*c.*874–924) and Æthelstan (*c.*893–939). Under the command of King Æthelstan he fought in the Battle of Brunanburh in 937. What happened next is unclear, but eleven years later Thurcytel received the Benedictine habit and joined the community at Crowland in Lincolnshire. He was subsequently elected Abbot. It is thought that he is the same Thurcytel who was related to Oscytel, Archbishop of York, and who became the Abbot of Bedford. The *Anglo-Saxon Chronicle* records that in 971 Thurcytel buried Archbishop Oscytel in Bedford Abbey. Thurcytel died on this day in 975.

A poem on the vocation to the monastic life

Not that they beggared be in mind, or brutes,
That they have chosen a dwelling-place afar
In lonely places: but their eyes are turned
To the high stars, the very deep of Truth.
Freedom they seek, an emptiness apart
From worthless hopes: din of the market place
And all the noisy crowding up of things,
And whatsoever wars on the Divine,
At Christ's command and for His love, thy hate.
By faith and hope they follow after God,
And know their quest shall not be desperate,
If but the Present conquer not their souls
With hollow things: that which they see they spurn,
That they may come at what they do not see,
Their senses kindled like a torch that may
Blaze through the secrets of eternity.
The transient's open, everlastingness
Denied our sight: yet still by hope we follow
The vision that our eyes have seen, despising
The shows and forms of things, the loveliness
Soliciting for ill our mortal eyes.
The present's nothing: but eternity
Abides for those on whom all truth, all good,
Hath shone in one entire and perfect light.

St Paulinus of Nola

———

Blessed Lord,
whose service is perfect freedom,
give us grace both to hear and obey your call,
that in all the challenges and opportunities that life brings,
we may know your peace and discover your joy;
through Jesus Christ our Lord. Amen.

Margaret Beaufort c.1443–1509

Mother of Henry VII

———

BORN AT BLETSOE Castle in Bedfordshire, Margaret was the daughter of John Beaufort, Duke of Somerset. She inherited his estate when she was a child and a few years later married John de la Pole, the son of her guardian, William de la Pole. The marriage only lasted three years before it was dissolved and she was put into the care of Jasper and Edmund Tudor, the illegitimate half-brothers of the king. Margaret married Edmund but again the marriage only lasted a short time, as he was killed a few months later by the Yorkist army. Margaret was pregnant by Edmund and gave birth to Henry Tudor, her only child, at Pembroke Castle in 1457. He was to become King Henry VII. In 1462 she married her first cousin, Henry Stafford, son of the first Duke of Buckingham. He died nine years later. Margaret's fourth and final husband was Thomas Stanley, the Lord High Constable and King of Mann. Renowned for her piety, Margaret, perhaps exhausted after so many husbands, took a vow of chastity in 1499 and left her husband's home to live at Collyweston. She organised her son's funeral and for a short time acted as Regent for Henry VIII. Margaret was a generous benefactor of education, founding a school in Wimborne. She established the Lady Margaret's Chair of Divinity, Cambridge, and founded Christ's and St John's Colleges in Cambridge. Lady Margaret Hall, Oxford, is named after her, as is Margaret Beaufort Middle School in Riseley, Bedfordshire, close to Bletsoe where she was born. She died on this day in 1509.

Margaret Beaufort's Book of Hours is kept in the Fitzwilliam Museum in Cambridge. In this passage Gordon Mursell writes about the practice of private prayer in the late medieval period

By the late fourteenth century books of hours and primers (lay prayer books), usually rich elaborations of the psalms and other scriptural texts, had become the primary devotional material used by prosperous and literate people in secular life, a process which in turn reflects the growing importance of the family and household as the primary focus of piety. The primers originated in monastic offices, and since their essential core was liturgical they enabled laypeople to share the regular prayer of clergy and religious: one illustration shows a layman with a book, seated in the church near the officiating priest engaged in his devotion. But they also included extra-liturgical devotions, affective and penitential prayers to Jesus, the office of the dead, prayers for different times of day, and familiar scriptural texts such as the prologue to St John's Gospel. Some households also created their own 'common-place book', a pattern of devotion which remained popular from the fifteenth until the eighteenth centuries, and might include poems, songs and sayings considered worth preserving.

From *English Spirituality from Earliest Times to 1700*

God be in my head and in my understanding.
God be in my eyes and in my looking.
God be in my mouth and in my speaking.
God be in my heart and in my thinking.
God be at my end and at my departing. Amen.

From *The Sarum Book of Hours*

Herbert Thorndike 1598–1672

Orientalist and theologian

———

HENRY THORNDIKE LIVED through the turbulent years following the execution of King Charles I, the Commonwealth and the Restoration of the monarchy. Born in Lincolnshire, he went to Trinity College, Cambridge, in 1613, was elected a fellow of the college in 1620, and taught oriental languages there. In 1636 he was made a Prebendary of Lincoln Cathedral, and four years later was appointed to the living of Claybrook while continuing to teach Hebrew at Cambridge. He was Rector of Barley in 1642–44 and 1662–4. An expert linguist, Thorndike played a key role in contributing to the Syriac sections of the London Polyglot Bible. Thorndike's scholarship was far-reaching. He wrote on a range of topics, such as *Of the Government of Churches, Of Religious Assemblies and the Publick Service of God* and *A Discourse of the Right of the Church in a Christian State*. Following the Restoration of the monarchy he was invited to contribute to the revision of the Prayer Book published in 1662. He is buried in the cloister of Westminster Abbey.

Herbert Thorndike emphasises the importance of preaching

There is one thing that hindereth the effect of the excellence Scripture when it is read, that is, because it is not understood. Thereupon cometh the office of preaching in the Church to expound the word of God; and that which is preached hath the force and virtue of the word of God, because the word of God is not the letters and syllables, but the sense and meaning of the Scriptures. But all men are capable more or less of understanding the Scriptures as they are read: and no man understandeth them so well but may improve by hearing them read in the Church. Let those that slight this part of the Church-service take order first, that all congregations shall be perfect in the knowledge of the Scriptures. And yet were that come to pass we must not give way to leave it out: the better they are acquainted with it the more shall they improve in the understanding of it, by hearing it repeated. But so far as it is understood it is a thing strange and admirable, that any man living should imagine that the effect thereof in enlightening the mind, or converting the heart, is less when it is read than when it is expounded out of the pulpit. The one the word of God as the Holy Ghost inspired it, the other no less, so far as it departeth not from that which is written, but always subject, so long as man is subject to error and mistake, to depart from it. Arid when this precious wine is once dashed with the water of human apprehensions it is no offence to me that it is still called the word of God; for so it should be, and so it is presumed to be, till it appear otherwise: but it will concern every man to look about him, that he pin not on God his own infirmities. As for the necessity and excellence of preaching, let all them that are most affected to it examine their reasons, and they shall not ascribe more to it than here shall be done.

From *The Theological Works of Herbert Thorndike*

———

Living God, from whom every good thought comes
and in whom all our longings find their fulfilment:
bless those who study and translate the scriptures,
that they may work with diligence, and teach with integrity;
through Jesus Christ, your Living Word. Amen.

Robert Barclay 1843–1921

Banker

ROBERT BARCLAY WAS a well-known banker in the City of London. He was also a deeply committed Christian who in 1871 bought a new home for himself and his family in Hoddesdon. It had formerly been known as High Wyches, but Barclay renamed it High Leigh. In 1868 he married Elizabeth Ellen Buxton, the daughter of Thomas Buxton (the abolitionist and social reformer, commemorated on 19 February). They had two sons, William and David. Barclay became a director of First Conference Limited, which had been established to provide places where Christians could hold conferences, especially for the support of overseas missionary work. The first conference centre was at The Hayes at Swanwick, Derbyshire, which was purchased in 1910. When Barclay died in 1921 his home, High Leigh, was sold to the company and since then has been a popular Christian conference centre in the South East of England.

John V. Taylor describes the role of the Holy Spirit as the motivating power of mission

The chief actor in the historic mission of the Christian Church is the Holy Spirit. He is the director of the whole enterprise. The mission consists of the things that he is doing in the world. In a special way it consists of the light that he is focussing upon Jesus Christ. This fact, so patent to Christians in the first century, is largely forgotten in our own. So we have lost our nerve and our sense of direction and have turned the divine initiative into a human enterprise. 'It all depends on me' is an attitude that is bedevilling both the practice and the theology of our mission in these days. That is precisely what Jesus forbade at the start of it all. They must not go it alone. They must not think that the mission is their responsibility.

> While he was in their company he told them not to leave Jerusalem. 'You must wait', he said, 'for the promise made by my Father, about which you have heard me speak: John, as you know, baptised with water, but you will be baptised with the Holy Spirit, and within the next few days'. (Acts 1.4–5)

They were not invited to deploy their resources or plan their strategy.

> 'It is not for you to know about dates or times, which the Father has set within his own control. But you will receive power when the Holy Spirit comes upon you; and you will bear witness for me in Jerusalem, and all over Judaea and Samaria, and away to the ends of the earth' (Acts 1.7–8). The very mandate to engage in this world-wide mission could only be given simultaneously with the gift of the Holy Spirit. This is made quite specific in the fourth Gospel. Jesus repeated, 'Peace be with you', and said, 'As the Father sent me, so I send you'. Then he breathed on them, saying, 'Receive the Holy Spirit!' (John 20.21–22).

From *The Go-Between God*

God of love and truth,
who has reconciled us to yourself
and given us a message of reconciliation:
break down the barriers of pride and anger,
demolish the walls of greed and envy
and open our hearts to you and to our neighbours,
that we may discover that in you
we are all children of the same heavenly Father;
we ask this in the name of Jesus the Reconciler. Amen.

Hannah Riddell 1855–1932

Missionary

———

H ANNAH RIDDELL WAS born in Barnet into a military family. As a young woman she worked for a time as a superintendent for the Young Women's Christian Association in Liverpool, before being selected by the Church Missionary Society in 1890 to serve in Japan. She sailed for Japan the following year and was stationed at Kumamoto on the island of Kyushu. Finding so many people suffering from leprosy, Riddell decided to found a hospital. It took four years of organising and fundraising but eventually in 1895 the Kumamoto Hospital of the Resurrection of Hope was opened. Riddell ceased to be supported by the Church Missionary Society but continued her missionary work independently at Kusatsu, and Okinawa (where the Okinawa Airakuen Leprosy Sanatorium was built). Riddell was not only interested in treating patients but also wanted to prevent the disease, so in 1918 she founded the first leprosy research laboratory in Japan. Riddell's ashes are buried in the grounds of Kumamoto Hospital.

Dietrich Bonhoeffer writes about the cost of following Jesus Christ

The cross is laid on every Christian. The first Christ-suffering which every man must experience is the call to abandon the attachments of this world. It is that dying of the old man which is the result of his encounter with Christ. As we embark upon discipleship we surrender ourselves to Christ in union with his death – we give over our lives to death. Thus it begins; the cross is not the terrible end to an otherwise God-fearing and happy life, but it meets us at the beginning of our communion with Christ. When Christ calls a man, he bids him come and die. It may be a death like that of the first disciples who had to leave home and work to follow him, or it may be a death like Luther's, who had to leave the monastery and go out into the world. But it is the same death every time – death in Jesus Christ, the death of the old man at his call. Jesus' summons to the rich young man was calling him to die, because only the man who is dead to his own will can follow Christ. In fact every command of Jesus is a call to die, with all our affections and lusts. But we do not want to die, and therefore Jesus Christ and his call are necessarily our death as well as our life. The call to discipleship, the baptism in the name of Jesus Christ means both death and life. The call of Christ, his baptism, sets the Christian in the middle of the daily arena against sin and the devil. Every day he encounters new temptations, and every day he must suffer anew for Jesus Christ's sake. The wounds and scars he receives in the fray are living tokens of this participation in the cross of his Lord.

From *The Cost of Discipleship*

———

Almighty God,
whose most dear Son went not up to joy but first he suffered pain,
and entered not into glory before he was crucified:
mercifully grant that we, walking in the way of the cross,
may find it none other than the way of life and peace;
through Jesus Christ your Son our Lord. Amen.

The Collect for the Third Sunday of Lent
from *Common Worship*

William George Lovell d.1909
and Mary Howard Lovell d.1902

Benefactors

WHEN WILLIAM AND Mary Lovell's thirteen-year-old son, Sidney, died of peritonitis in 1891 they wanted to establish a memorial in his name. They decided to leave bequests in their wills to build almshouses for elderly and infirm people who were over sixty years of age. The Lovells also left money for a new marble floor in the chancel of St Paul's Church, Bedford, in Sidney's memory. William's family came from Bedford and he made his money from the family business of brewing. Mary was the daughter of Sir Frederick Howard, one of the founders of the Britannia Ironworks in the town. The almshouses were opened in 1925 with an inscription:

THE SIDNEY HOWARD LOVELL ALMSHOUSES
These almshouses are erected to the Glory of God and in memory of Sidney Howard Lovell
by direction of his parents William George Lovell and Mary Howard Lovell
'Do unto others as ye would that others should do unto you.'

The deed specified that the residents 'may be married or single, and in their selection no question of politics is to be considered, but special regard is to be had to industry and good conduct. They may do casual work and may keep poultry or pigs. The Trustees may, if they think fit, appoint a caretaker or a nurse.'

Gregory of Nyssa preaches about generosity

Be generous on behalf of your unfortunate brethren. That which you withhold from your belly, give to the poor. Let a fear of God level out the differences between you and them: with self-control, carefully avoid two contrary evils: your own gorging and the hunger of your brethren. This is how the physician works: he puts some on diets, and gives supplementary food to others, in this way curing sicknesses with one or the other of these methods. So follow this salutary advice. Let good words open the doors of the rich. This counsel might thus encourage the poor to turn themselves and appeal to the wealthy. But words alone cannot enrich the poor. Let the eternal Word of God give also a house and a light and table, by means of the household of the Word. Speak to them with affection and alleviate their miseries with your own substance. But there are still other wretched ones, those who are not only poor but sick. Let us take care of those in the neighbourhood. Don't let a stranger treat those who are in your neighbourhood. Don't let another rob you of the treasure you are depositing. Embrace the wretched as gold: care for their miseries as if treating yourself, as if saving your wife, your children, your domestics and all your house.

From *The Body of the Poor* by Susan Holman

Teach us, Good Lord,
to serve thee as thou deservest;
to give and not to count the cost;
to fight and not to heed the wounds;
to toil and not to seek for rest;
to labour and not to ask for any reward,
save that of knowing that we do thy will;
through Jesus Christ Our Lord. Amen.

Saint Ignatius Loyola

James Robert Talbot 1726–90
Roman Catholic bishop

———

J AMES TALBOT WAS related to the Earls of Shrewsbury, a well-known Recusant family from the Midlands. Born in Isleworth, he was educated at Twyford School in Hampshire and the English College at Douai. Talbot was ordained as a priest when he was twenty-four and nine years later was consecrated Coadjutor Bishop to Richard Challoner. In 1768 Talbot was prosecuted for saying the Mass but was acquitted on a technicality. He was again prosecuted in 1771 but the case was dismissed. In 1781 he was appointed Vicar Apostolic of the London District. During the final years of his life he was instrumental in the buying of Old Hall Green, near Ware, which was later to become the home of St Edmund's College. He spent his final years in a convent in Hammersmith, where he died. He was remembered as a generous benefactor with the nickname 'Good Bishop Talbot'.

William Law reflects on the worth of money

If a man had eyes, hands and feet that he could remove to give to those who wanted them, if he should then lock them up in a chest, or please himself with some needless or ridiculous use of them, instead of giving them to brothers in need, wouldn't we have every justification in calling him an inhuman beast? If he chose rather to amuse himself with furnishing his house than to entitle himself to an eternal reward by giving those in need the eyes and hands they require, would we not justly class him mad? Now money is very much in the same category as eyes and feet. If we lock it up in chests or waste it in needless and ridiculous expenses while the poor and the distressed are in great need of it, or if we consume it on ridiculous ornaments or clothes while others are starving in nakedness, we are not far from the cruelty of the man who chooses wastefully to dispose of his hands and eyes rather than give them to those who need them. If we choose to indulge ourselves in the kind of expensive enjoyments which have no real value, things which aren't really necessary, rather than to gain for ourselves an eternal reward by disposing our money well, we are guilty of the same madness. Once we have satisfied our own reasonable needs, all the rest of our money is like spare eyes or spare hands. It is something that we cannot keep for ourselves, foolishly wasting it, but is something that can only be used well by giving it to those who need it.

From *A Practical Treatise upon Christian Perfection*

———

I am no longer my own but yours. Put me to what you will,
rank me with whom you will; put me to doing, put me to suffering;
let me be employed for you or laid aside for you,
exalted for you or brought low for you.
Let me be full, let me be empty, let me have all things, let me have nothing.
I freely and wholeheartedly yield all things to your pleasure and disposal.
And now, glorious and blessed God, Father, Son and Holy Spirit,
you are mine and I am yours. So be it.
And the covenant made on earth, let it be ratified in heaven. Amen.

The Methodist Covenant Prayer

Douglas Noel Sargent 1907–79

Missionary and bishop

———

DOUGLAS SARGENT WAS educated at Watford Grammar School for Boys from where he went to read mathematics at King's College, Cambridge. He undertook his theological training at the London College of Divinity and was ordained in the Diocese of St Albans in 1932, where he served his title at Willian. From there Sargent made the unusual transition of becoming a missionary in China by taking up a lectureship at the West China Union University in the Szechuan Province. He then moved to become chaplain to Bishop Song, a post which he combined with his work as assistant secretary for the Church Missionary Society in China. Sargent went to New York in 1948 to undertake further study. Following the Chinese Revolution of 1949 it was decided that it was not sensible for him to return to China so he went instead to minister in Hong Kong. He returned to Britain in 1961 and was appointed as the principal of the Church Missionary Society training college at Chislehurst. However, in the following year he was consecrated to be the third Bishop of Selby. Sargent married Imogene Ward in 1942. She was the daughter of American missionaries and had been born in Foochow. He retired in 1972 and lived in York until his death in 1979.

Douglas Sargent writes about self-sacrifice

In words such as these have countless young men and women offered themselves to God. Some have spoken them at a moment of supreme crisis when they have consciously dedicated their all to God. Others have breathed them hesitantly, hardly daring to conceive what the implications of such a tremendously simple prayer might be. Still others have barely put into words at all their steadily growing conviction that life must be lived for God, and that if that is to be so only God Himself can have the directing of it. But no matter how individual circumstances may vary, the words stand for an experience which should be central in the life of every Christian, the unreserved offering of the self to God from a heart overwhelmed with gratitude to the Son of God, 'who loved me and gave Himself for me'. It is indeed, the first word in this brief prayer that is of primary importance, for however much the emphasis may appear to be on the 'I' and the 'me', it is the Lord Himself who really stands in the centre of the picture. It is the vision of Jesus Christ that calls forth the response. Only when we realise the depth of His love, both for us as individuals and for the whole world, shall we be willing to place our lives unreservedly in His hands.

From *The Making of a Missionary*

———

Heavenly Father, as in days of old,
you call men and women to leave home and family
and follow you to the ends of the earth
to declare the good news of your Son:
guard those who have obeyed your call;
protect them when in danger,
encourage them when disheartened
and grant them the gift of your peace
to keep their hearts and minds fixed on you:
for we ask this in the name of Jesus Christ our Lord. Amen.

Thomas More 1478–1535

Statesman and lawyer

———

FOR SEVERAL CENTURIES the More family had a home at North Mymms called More Hall, later renamed Gobions. Thomas More himself was born in London in 1478 and educated at St Anthony's School before entering the service of John Morton, the Archbishop of Canterbury. He went up to Oxford University but two years later he moved to study law, firstly at New Inn and then at Lincoln's Inn. Following his election to Parliament in 1504 he rose rapidly. He was made a Privy Councillor, Speaker of the House of Commons, and then in 1529 he was appointed Lord Chancellor. More was known as someone who could not be bribed. He did, however, oversee the trial and execution of several 'heretics' during his time in office. More married Jane Colt and together they had four children. Unusually for the time, he insisted that his daughters were given the same education as his son. He wrote a number of devotional books, but his most famous work is *Utopia* which described the political system of an idealised island state. More resigned in 1532 when Henry VIII wanted to annul his marriage to Catherine of Aragon. He withdrew from public life to live quietly in his family home. His disagreement with the king was not over the royal succession but whether the English king could usurp papal authority. In 1534 he was arrested and imprisoned in the Tower of London. He was found guilty of high treason and beheaded. He is honoured as one of the 'Reformation martyrs' by Anglicans and Roman Catholics.

Thomas More writes to his daughter Margaret from prison, just before his execution

Although I know well, Margaret, that because of my past wickedness I deserve to be abandoned by God, I cannot but trust in his merciful goodness. His grace has strengthened me until now and made me content to lose goods, land, and life as well, rather than to swear against my conscience. God's grace has given the king a gracious frame of mind toward me, so that as yet he has taken from me nothing but my liberty. In doing this His Majesty has done me such great good with respect to spiritual profit that I trust that among all the great benefits he has heaped so abundantly upon me I count my imprisonment the very greatest. I cannot, therefore, mistrust the grace of God. By the merits of his bitter passion joined to mine and far surpassing in merit for me all that I can suffer myself, his bounteous goodness shall release me from the pains of purgatory and shall increase my reward in heaven besides. I will not mistrust him, Meg, though I shall feel myself weakening and on the verge of being overcome with fear. I shall remember how Saint Peter at a blast of wind began to sink because of his lack of faith, and I shall do as he did: call upon Christ and pray to him for help. And then I trust he shall place his holy hand on me and in the stormy seas hold me up from drowning.

From *The Complete Works of St Thomas More*

Give me, good Lord,
an humble, lowly, quiet, peaceable, patient,
charitable, kind and filial and tender mind,
every shade, in fact, of charity,
with all my words and all my works,
and all my thoughts,
to have a taste of thy holy blessed Spirit. Amen.

Thomas More

Ralph Gubion d.1151

Abbot of St Albans

———

RALPH GUBION WAS an Englishman whose family had come to England at the time of the Norman Conquest. He was both a monk of the Abbey at St Albans and also chaplain to Bishop Alexander of Lincoln. Gubion was elected Abbot of St Albans in 1146 and was known as a robust leader of the community. It is thought that he forced Alcuin, the Prior, out of office and appointed Geoffrey de Gorham in his place. He persuaded Pope Eugenius III to grant privileges to the Abbey and he also strengthened the finances of the community. Gubion was known as a bibliophile. Ill health forced him to stand down in 1150 and he died in the following year.

St Benedict writes about the role of the prior in a community

It often happeneth indeed, that grave scandals arise in monasteries out of the appointment of the Prior; since there are some who, puffed up with the wicked spirit of pride and thinking themselves to be second Abbots, set up a despotic rule, foster scandals, and excite quarrels in the community, and especially in those places where also the Prior is appointed by the same Bishop or the same Abbots who appointeth his Abbot. How foolish this is can easily be seen; because, from the very beginning of his appointment, matter for pride is furnished him, when his thoughts suggest to him that now he is exempt from the authority of the Abbot, because 'thou too hast been appointed by those by whom the Abbot was appointed.' From this source arise envy, discord, slander, quarrels, jealousy, and disorders. While the Abbot and the Prior are thus at variance with each other, it must follow that their souls are endangered by this discord and that those who are under them, as long as they humour the parties, go to ruin. The fault of this evil resteth on the heads of those who were the authors of such disorders. We foresee, therefore, that for the preservation of peace and charity it is best that the government of the monastery should depend on the will of the Abbot; and if it can be done, let the affairs of the monastery (as we have explained before) be attended to by deans, as the Abbot shall dispose; so that, the same office being shared by many, no one may become proud. If, however, the place require it, or the brotherhood reasonably and with humility make the request, and the Abbot shall deem it advisable, let the Abbot himself appoint as Prior whomever, with the advice of God-fearing brethren, he shall select. But let the Prior reverently do what his Abbot hath enjoined on him, doing nothing against the will or the direction of the Abbot; for the higher he is placed above others, the more careful should he be to obey the precepts of the Rule.

From *The Rule of St Benedict*

Lord our God,
you established the Church as a sign of your continuing presence in the world.
We ask you to raise up faithful ministers to your Church
in the priesthood and religious life,
so that the message of faith, justice and love contained in the gospel
may be brought into the hearts of all people.
We ask this through Christ our Lord. Amen.

John R. Quinn

Charles Longman 1809–75

Publisher and benefactor

———

IF YOU CLIMB up the tower of St Mary's Church, Apsley End, and look at the six bells, you will see from the inscription that the tenor (the heaviest) bell was the gift of Charles Longman. He was heir to the publishing company Longman's and was a partner of the well-known paper mill owner in the village, John Dickinson. Another bell was donated by John Dickinson Junior, the only surviving son of the founder of Apsley Mills. Longman was a wealthy man who had bought Shendish Manor and its estate. Following the death of his wife in 1860 he decided to build a church in her memory. Longman paid for the church, which was opened in 1871 and dedicated by the Bishop of Rochester. (This was just six years before Hertfordshire moved from the Diocese of Rochester into the newly formed Diocese of St Albans.) It was a momentous year for Longman as he was also High Sheriff of Hertfordshire. The Longman family continued to contribute to the church for many years, including donating the beautiful reredos, the church's outstanding feature, in 1915.

Thomas Merton reflects on the role of bells

Bells are meant to remind us that God alone is good, that we belong to Him, that we are not living for this world. They break in upon our cares in order to remind us that all things pass away and that our preoccupations are not important. They speak to us of our freedom, which responsibilities and transient cares make us forget. They are the voice of our alliance with the God of heaven. They tell us that we are His true temple. They call us to peace with Him within ourselves. The gospel of Mary and Martha is read at the end of the Blessing of a Church Bell in order to remind us of all these things. The bells say: business does not matter. Rest in God and rejoice, for this world is only the figure and the promise of a world to come, and only those who are detached from transient things can possess the substance of an eternal promise. The bells say: we have spoken for centuries from the towers of great churches. We have spoken to the saints your fathers, in their land. We called them, as we call you, to sanctity. What is the word with which we called them? We did not merely say, 'Be good, come to church.' We did not merely say 'Keep the commandments' but above all, 'Christ is risen, Christ is risen!' And we said: 'Come with us, God is good, salvation is not hard, His love has made it easy!' And this, our message, has always been for everyone, for those who came and for those who did not come, for our song is perfect as the Father in heaven is perfect and we pour our charity out upon all.

From *Thoughts in Solitude*

———

Changeless God
who has created a world of endless variety,
ever new and ever changing:
we thank you for the art of campanology,
for the physicality involved in ringing,
for the skill of good striking,
for method and composition, and the ability to conduct.
May the sound of bells ringing from our towers each week,
be a constant reminder of your call to us to bow down and worship;
through Jesus Christ our Lord. Amen.

Rosamund Essex 1900–85

Editor of the *Church Times*

———

'THE ELEVENTH COMMANDMENT of journalism is "Thou shalt not be dull, and if thou art dull thou shalt be sacked" ' so Rosamund Essex often said and, judging by her autobiography *Woman in a Man's World*, she lived out this principle in every aspect of her life. After reading Classics at Oxford University, Rosamund became a journalist on the *Church Times*, where she worked for thirty years. For the last ten years of her time there she was the newspaper's editor. In 1952, she started the Train a Priest Fund in response to stories of hardship from ordinands unable to support their family on meagre diocesan grants. Over the years the TAP Fund provided grants for more than 4,650 ordinands during their training. Upon retirement in 1960, Rosamund Essex worked for Inter-Church Aid and Refugee Service, now known as Christian Aid, and travelled abroad extensively. She was a staunch Anglo-Catholic who was strongly convinced she had a vocation to the priesthood. This was never to be fulfilled, although in 1969 she became the first woman Reader in the Diocese of St Albans. Rosamund never married but, most unusually for her time, adopted a young boy when she was thirty-nine. In later years, she was a lay reader at St Albans Abbey, a part-time speaker for Christian Aid, and wrote a weekly column in the *Church Times*.

Richard Thomas writes on communication

God wasn't born in a stable in Bethlehem merely to convey information. Our message is not about God: God himself is the message. As John says: 'That which was from the beginning, which we have heard, which we have seen with our eyes, which we have looked at and our hands have touched – this we proclaim concerning the World of life.' Jesus didn't simply convey a message. He transmits life itself, and everyone he touches is transformed, changed, made more fully alive. His stories acted, and still act today, like yeast in a dough. They work in us, expanding our vision, shattering our illusions and bringing us to life. Our communication does not begin with a decision by a committee or a church council to activate a particular message. Our communication begins with the activity of the Holy Spirit driving us forward, 'into all truth', as John puts it. The initiative is God's. As the proverb says: 'Many are the plans in a man's heart, but it is the Lord's purpose that prevails.' That's what makes Christian communication unique. We begin with neither a product, nor with a message – we begin with the God who is alive and present in his people, and who longs to bring others into a living relationship with himself. Or rather, God begins with us!

From *An Introduction to Church Communication*

———

Living Word,
we thank you for journalists, bloggers and authors
and all who work in communication:
May their words be used to seek the truth,
to protect the weak and to build up the common good;
for the sake of Jesus Christ our Lord. Amen.

Mark Frank 1613–64

Rector of Barley and Archdeacon of St Albans

———

MARK FRANK IS one of the lesser-known Caroline Divines, a group of seventeenth-century clergymen, distinguished by their scholarship and spirituality, who made a formative contribution to Anglican theology. Born in Buckinghamshire, Frank went up to Pembroke College, Cambridge, in 1627 and spent much of his life there in various roles. He was elected to a scholarship in 1630 and four years later to a fellowship. In 1641 Frank became the junior treasurer of the college and in the following year senior treasurer. In 1644, however, he was ejected for his refusal to take the Solemn League and Covenant. Frank served as chaplain to two archbishops: William Juxon and Gilbert Sheldon. With the Restoration of the monarchy in 1660, Frank's fortunes revived. Sheldon appointed him Archdeacon of St Albans and Treasurer of St Paul's Cathedral. He was also able to resume his fellowship at Pembroke College. He was awarded the degree of Doctor of Divinity in the following year, and in 1662 elected Master of the College. Shortly before his death, he was also made Rector of St Margaret of Antioch, Barley, in Hertfordshire. He was a distinguished preacher and a collection of his sermons was published posthumously in 1672 under the title, *A Course of Sermons for all the Sundays and Festivals throughout the Year*. He is buried in St Paul's Cathedral.

In this sermon Mark Frank reflects on St Peter's words when the disciples unexpectedly caught a large haul of fish in response to Jesus Christ's command to let down their nets

Luke 5.8: *Depart from me, for I am a sinful man, O Lord.*

A strange speech for him that speaks, to him 'tis spoken, from St Peter to his Saviour…Yet if we consider what St Peter was when he so cried out, or what made him to do it, or how unfit he, being a sinful son of man, thought himself for the company of the Son of God, we shall cease to wonder, and know it is the sinner's case for ever so to do, to be astonished at miracles, not to bear suddenly the presence of our Lord, and when we first apprehend it, to cry out to him, with St Peter here, to withdraw from us for a while, for that we are not able to endure the brightness and terror of his splendour and majesty. It was a miraculous and stupendous draught of fish (after they had given up all hopes of the least) suddenly came to net, which thus amazed St Peter and his fellows. They had drudged and toiled all night, and not a fish appeared: but when Christ came to them, then came whole shoals, and thrust so fast into the net, that they brake it to get in, as if the mute and unreasonable creatures themselves had such a mind to see him, by whose word they were created, that they valued not their lives, so they might see and serve his pleasure.

From *Fifty-One Sermons*

Give us, O Lord,
after the example of your servant Mark Frank,
a mind to explore the wonders of the world
and an eloquence to speak of them,
that our voices may echo the hymn of all creation
and give you praise through your Son, Jesus Christ. Amen.

Benedict of Nursia c.480–c.547

Founder of the Benedictines and patron saint of Europe

———

BENEDICT WAS BORN into a Roman family in Nursia, Italy. He studied in Rome but then left to live the life of a hermit at Enfide, not far from Subiaco. When the abbot of a nearby monastery died, the monks asked Benedict to take his place. However, relationships in the monastery became so strained that the monks tried to poison him. Attracted by his holiness, people gathered around Benedict and communities sprang up. He moved to Monte Cassino where he founded a community which is still there today. *The Rule of St Benedict* has become one of the most important rules in Western Christianity. It comprises seventy-three chapters which detail how the monastery is to be run, the place of worship, study and manual labour, and the responsibilities of the various members of the community. Benedict died on this day in 547. In 1964 he was made the Patron Protector of Europe. The two branches of the Benedictines today are the Benedictine Federation and the Cistercians. There have been many Benedictine communities within the borders of the Diocese of St Albans. In Bedfordshire there were communities at Beadlow Priory, Bedford Abbey, Elstow Abbey and Millbrook Priory. There is still a Roman Catholic Benedictine Community at Turvey Abbey. In Hertfordshire there were communities at St Albans Abbey and priories at Cathale (near Cuffley), Cheshunt, Flamstead, Hertford, Markyate, Redbourn, Rowney (near Sacombe), Sawbridgeworth, Sopwell, Standon and Ware. The church at Bennetts End in Hemel Hempstead is dedicated to St Benedict.

St Benedict writes about the religious life in one of his monasteries

Hearken, my son, to the precepts of thy Master, and incline the ear of thy heart willingly to hear, and effectually to accomplish, the admonition of thy living Father, that by the labour of obedience thou may return to him, from whom thou didst depart by the sloth of disobedience. To thee therefore is my speech now directed, who, renouncing thy own will, dost take upon thee the strong and bright armour of obedience, to fight under the Lord Christ our true King. First of all whatever good work thou dost begin, beg of him with most earnest prayer to perfect; that he who hath now vouchsafed to reckon us in the number of his children, may not be saddened by our evil deeds. For we must at all times so serve him with the goods he hath bestowed upon us, that he may not either as an angry Father disinherit us his children, or as a dread Lord, exasperated by our offences, deliver us up to perpetual punishment as wicked servants, who would not follow him to glory. We are therefore now about to institute a school of the service of God; in which we hope nothing will be ordained rigorous or burdensome. But if in some things we proceed with a little severity, sound reason so advising, for the amendment of vices or preserving of charity; do not straightway for fear thereof, flee from the way of salvation which is always strait and difficult in the beginning.

From *The Prologue of the Rule of St Benedict*

Almighty and Everlasting Father,
who called your servant Benedict
to share a common life with his brothers in Christ:
guide with your Holy Spirit all members of the Order which he founded,
that they may be a blessing to your Church
and a glory to your name; through Jesus Christ our Lord. Amen.

The Collect for St Benedict

Christopher Rahere Webb 1886–1966

Stained glass designer

———

IF YOU GO into the Lady Chapel of St Peter's Church in St Albans, you will see one of the many examples of the striking stained glass designed by Christopher Webb. The window depicts an angel whose arms are outstretched and the verse 'Of His Kingdom there shall be no end' (Luke 1.33). Webb's unusual middle name comes from the twelfth-century Prior of the Augustinian community at St Bartholomew's, Smithfield, called Rahere. Webb's father was the churchwarden at St Bartholomew's and his uncle, Sir Aston Webb, oversaw its restoration. Webb studied at Rugby School and the Slade School of Art before being articled to Sir Ninian Comper. At the start of the Great War in 1914 he signed up in the Artist's Rifles and served in France. After the war he collaborated with the architect William Randoll Blacking, who had also studied under Comper. Webb then began to design stained glass. After his marriage to Mary Curtis in 1926 he moved from East Grinstead to St Albans and had a studio at Orchard House on Holywell Hill. He designed five windows for St Albans Abbey.

Stained glass should be used to communicate the message of the gospel

Many people believe that stained glass reached the height of its achievement in the great Gothic cathedrals of Europe in the twelfth and thirteenth centuries. To appreciate fully the depth and truth of this view, it is necessary to examine stained glass not in terms of subject matter or craft techniques, but in terms of purpose, specifically *service to the Church*. The view that medieval stained glass achieved what it did because it was able to serve as a sort of 'picture Bible' for the illiterate masses is widely held but is largely inaccurate. The people of medieval Europe were mostly illiterate and uneducated, yes, but they were far from stupid. The great windows of Chartres spoke to them not as 'picture paintings' of far-away Bible stories but on a much more immediate and, importantly, personal level. In this regard, medieval stained glass achieved something that is entirely possible with modern stained glass in our highly educated and widely literate Western world: it served then as it can serve now as a vehicle for God's call to conversion and as a lens through which this call can be more fully understood…and answered. For a stained glass installation to fulfil its proper role, it must be no mere bauble but a good and faithful servant of the Church by acting as a lens through which the faithful can more fully understand and come to live the vital elements for growth in holiness as they develop a sound spirituality that will allow them to 'become as saints,' recognizing their individual dependence on God's mercies and allowing them to forgive – and seek forgiveness – as becomes a true disciple of Christ.

From *Sourcebook 2011: Your guide to Stained, Decorative and Architectural Art Glass*

Almighty God,
whose world is filled with the light of your glory:
we thank you for the stained glass which adorns our churches
declaring the truths of the gospel
and recounting the lives of the saints;
as the light of your love shines upon us,
may we reflect your beauty and walk in your light;
through Jesus Christ our Lord. Amen.

Violet Olivia Cressy-Marcks 1895–1970

Explorer and writer

———

S O EXTENSIVE WERE her travels that in just under forty years Violet Cressy-Marcks made eight journeys around the world and visited every country on earth. She was elected to the Royal Geographical Society in 1922 and was soon exploring the remoter parts of the world, writing about the peoples, the archaeology, and the natural world she found. Never shy of a challenge, she travelled by any means possible including horse-riding, sledging and canoeing. She worked as a war correspondent, sometimes taking photos of the fighting for newspapers, and even drove ambulances for the Red Cross during the Second World War. Violet Rutley was born in West Wickham. She married Maurice Cressy-Marcks with whom she had a son. Following their divorce she then married Francis Fisher from Watford and they had two sons. She wrote *Up the Amazon and over the Andes* and *Journey into China*. Cressy-Marcks is buried at St Paul's Church, Langleybury, in Hertfordshire.

Violet Cressy-Marcks meets some Christian missionaries in China

I saw a European man and woman in Chinese clothes, selling medicine in a tiny shop, and they spoke to us. They were German missionaries. He was formerly with the China Inland Mission, and she had taken vows of celibacy. However, in love they fell, and were now working for an American lady who years ago had given her private fortune to missionary work in China. They very kindly asked us to stay the night, and as we had not yet fixed up with the inn, we gratefully accepted. I have a great admiration for missionaries in China. Much has been written against them, but I have never yet found any who were inhospitable, and they are often grossly imposed upon. I have only stayed two or three times with missionaries, but have very often had a meal with them, and have been given of their best. There are men and women, not so good, everywhere. I realise the missionary field is no exception, but an un-Christian man or woman attached to a mission probably does more harm than anywhere else. However, that is rare. Mostly they are selfless and work hard, with little or no encouragement. I do not mention that they are denied comforts and so-called civilisation, because I know there are many people who would much prefer a missionary's life to their own. There is the woefully ignorant missionary whose limitations are not made up by faith. His contact with so much better educated people than himself, who are often leading a life in accordance with an ancient religion which makes them truthful, honest and tolerant, but whom he is trying to convert to Christianity, is a pitiful sight. On the other hand, there are very fine men and women with first-class brains in the missionary field, and most of them have grown fond of China and look upon it as their real home.

From *Journey into China*

———

Lord Jesus Christ,
you called the disciples to forsake the familiar and the secure
and follow you on a journey of faith and discovery:
open our hearts to those we meet on the way,
open our eyes to the wonders of the world around,
and open our hands that we may walk closely with you,
the Son of Man who had nowhere to lay your head;
we ask it for your name's sake. Amen.

Thomas Legh Claughton 1808–92

First Bishop of St Albans

———

On Northern shores the year's untimely close
Has mantled Nature in her garb of snows;
The glorious Sun is sinking into gloom,
As youth before its time into the tomb:
And in the keen clear air, as fade away
The streamy splendours of departing day,
Fantastic shapes of crystal fretwork gleam,
And drink a borrowed lustre from his beam.

SO BEGINS THOMAS Claughton's poem *Voyages of Discovery to the Polar Regions* for which he won the Newdigate prize for English verse at Oxford University. Claughton was such an accomplished poet that he held the post of Professor of Poetry at Oxford University in 1852–7. The son of a Member of Parliament, he was born at Winwick, Lancashire, and studied at Rugby School and Trinity College, Oxford. Claughton was a high churchman, who having been ordained in 1834 was later appointed to be Vicar of Kidderminster, where he was to have an outstanding ministry over the following twenty-six years. Claughton was nominated Bishop of Rochester in 1867 and oversaw the founding of the Diocese of St Albans which took place in 1877. He was appointed the first Bishop of the Diocese of St Albans. Claughton married Julia Susannah Ward and they had nine children. He is buried at St Albans Abbey.

Thomas Claughton addressed the clergy

My Reverend Brethren, the troubles of the Church of England within are such as might be composed tomorrow, if we could be persuaded to cease from vain contention about matters which can never be regarded alike from different stand-points by those who will not agree to place themselves side by side with those from whom they differ, even for the sake of trying to understand their view. I am afraid that the doctrine of the Real Presence of Christ in the Sacrament must be referred to this head. It is common for those who reject this doctrine as it is ordinarily understood, to impute to their opponents (if I must use the word) that which they distinctly repudiate and deny themselves to hold; while some of those who hold it seem to have no care for that wise rule, that no man put a stumbling-block or occasion to fall in his brother's way, but say and do things which are sure to perplex and irritate those who are of the contrary part. These are the wounds of the Church, which can only be healed by mutual forbearance and a fixed resolution on the part of those that are strong to bear the infirmities of the weak, and not to please themselves; and by the banishment of all shyness and reserve, which would be the unfailing accompaniment of such a resolution seriously taken; to be followed, as it eventually might be, by the disbanding of those organisations which, so long as they subsist, render unity impossible and all but hopeless in the future.

From *A Charge delivered to the Clergy and Churchwardens of the Diocese of St Albans*

———

Gracious God, you bring down the powerful from their thrones
and lift up the lowly:
teach us to listen before we speak, reflect before we judge,
and seek to understand before we criticise;
for we ask this in the name of your Son Jesus Christ. Amen.

William Bill c.1505–61

Liturgist and Dean of Westminster Abbey

———

WILLIAM BILL LIVED through the turbulent years of the English Reformation. One of five children, he was born and brought up in the village of Ashwell in north Hertfordshire. It was from here that he went to Cambridge to study at St John's College. Graduating in 1532, he was elected a Fellow in 1535, and in 1547 became its Master. During the years that followed, he held various posts in the university, including two periods as Master of Trinity College and one as Vice-Chancellor of the University. With the accession of Queen Mary, however, Bill's evangelical sympathies resulted in him being removed from office. In 1558, under Queen Elizabeth, he found himself back in favour. He served as Lord High Almoner and was appointed first as Provost of Eton College and then Dean of Westminster Abbey. It was during this period that he was commissioned to revise the second Prayer Book of King Edward VI, which was authorised for use from 1559. He died on this day in 1561 and is buried in St Benedict's Chapel in Westminster Abbey.

William Bill was concerned with the words and prayers that we use in our worship. Here Michael Perham reflects on worship and liturgy

Worship is the offering to God of praise, glory and honour in reverence and in love. It is something that can be done in community or alone, in church or in a thousand other contexts. But what is this strange thing called 'liturgy' that seems to occupy more of the Church's consciousness than used to be the case? Worship and liturgy are not exactly the same thing. Liturgy is that subtle blend of word, song, movement, gesture and silence that enables the people of God to worship together. Liturgy is, at a certain level, always about compromise, for it is about finding the forms that will enable people to experience something satisfying collectively. In that sense perhaps heaven will be a divine compromise, for that too will provide a setting where people with their infinite variety of personality and preference can experience something overwhelmingly wonderful that binds and draws together. You can worship without liturgy on your own. You can worship without church on your own. But the moment you engage in worship with others, there has to be a shared form, and that is where liturgy comes in. For that form is likely to be shaped by words, by music, by movement, by gesture and by silence. That is what liturgy is – the way into the Church's corporate worship of God, the Father of our Lord Jesus Christ.

From *New Handbook of Pastoral Liturgy*

———

Living God,
may our words, music and song
draw us ever deeper in worship and adoration,
that filling our minds with your glory and your truth
we may offer our lives as a living sacrifice
to your praise and honour;
through Jesus Christ our Lord. Amen.

Henry Peacham 1546–1634
and Henry Peacham 1578–c.1644
Authors from North Mymms

———

BOTH FATHER AND son shared the same name: Henry. The father was curate of North Mymms and is remembered today as the author of *The Garden of Eloquence,* published in 1577. Henry, his second son, was educated at schools in both St Albans and London. He went to Trinity College, Cambridge, in 1592. During his time there he made what is thought to be the earliest illustration of a scene from a Shakespearian play. Peacham continued drawing throughout his life and in 1606 he wrote a treatise on drawing and painting called *Art of Drawing.* This was later expanded and republished as *Graphice.* It became the basis of Peacham's most famous book, *The Compleat Gentleman.* In it he described the literature, philosophy, poetry and art that a young man needed to be acquainted with to become a gentleman. The book was reprinted many times in subsequent years. Throughout his life Peacham struggled to make a living. He dedicated many of his books to wealthy patrons in the hope of receiving their support, but much of the time he was forced to teach in order to earn a living. Peacham wrote many other books, most notably emblem books. These books were very popular in the sixteenth and seventeenth centuries. They contained texts – a quotation, aphorism or motto – illustrated with images. Peacham wrote a number of emblem books, most notably *Minerva Britanna.*

Peacham the younger was an Anglican and a Royalist. Here he sets out his views

'Submit yourselves', says the apostle, 'unto all manner of ordinance of man for the Lord's sake, whom we ought to obey for conscience sake'…again by the same apostle, 'The prince is the minister of God for thy wealth, but if thou doest evil fear, for he beareth not the sword in vain' (or for nought) for he is the servant of God, to take vengeance on him that doth evil, and writing unto his disciple Titus, he says, 'Put them in remembrance that they be subject to principalities and powers, and that they obey their governors for we must acknowledge, that there is no power but of God, and he that resisteth this power, resisteth the ordinance of God, and they that resist, shall receive to themselves judgement'. Seeing therefore it hath pleaseth God to establish this order amongst men, that is, to be governed by kings and sovereign magistrates, unto whom he hath given power of ruling and reigns over them, we must readily and willingly yield them all obedience, tendering unto them our service, as well in times of peace as of war, in peace as ornaments, in war as ramparts and bulwarks against a common enemy; besides, we ought to speak of them with all honour and respect, not to traduce them nor their actions in public or private among inferiors.

From *The Duty of All True Subjects to their King*

———

King of the nations,
the source of authority and power:
inspire the leaders of the nations
to exercise compassion
to lead with integrity
and to govern with justice;
through Jesus Christ our Lord. Amen.

James Fleetwood 1603–83

Rector of Anstey and Bishop of Worcester

———

JAMES FLEETWOOD WAS born in Chalfont St Giles, Buckinghamshire, and educated at Eton and King's College, Cambridge. Following ordination he served for a time as chaplain to the Bishop of Lichfield and incumbent of Prees in Shropshire. During the Civil War Fleetwood supported the Royalist cause, serving as a chaplain in the King's Army. King Charles awarded him the degree of Doctor of Divinity in 1642 for his service at the Battle of Edge Hill. He then became Rector of Sutton Coldfield and Chaplain to Charles, Prince of Wales. In 1647 he was ejected from the living and moved to Barnes where he ran a school. After the Restoration Fleetwood was elected to be Provost of King's College, Cambridge, and reinstituted to the living of Prees. In 1662 he was appointed to the living of Anstey, Hertfordshire. In 1675 he became Bishop of Worcester. Fleetwood married Martha Mercer and the couple had two sons and four daughters. He died on this day in 1683 and is buried in Worcester Cathedral.

St Francis of Assisi writes about the Christian virtue of humility

'I did not come to be served but to serve,' says the Lord. Those who are placed over others should glory in such an office only as much as they would were they assigned the task of washing the feet of the brothers, and the more they are upset about their office being taken from them than they would be over the loss of the office of washing feet, so much the more do they store up treasures to the peril of their souls. Be conscious, O man, of the wondrous state in which the Lord God has placed you, for He created you and formed you to the image of His beloved Son according to the body, and to His likeness according to the spirit. And yet all the creatures under heaven, each according to its nature, serve, know, and obey their Creator better than you. And even the demons did not crucify Him, but you together with them have crucified Him and crucify Him even now by delighting in vices and sins. In what then can you glory? For if you were so subtle and wise that you had all knowledge and knew how to interpret all tongues and minutely investigate the course of the heavenly bodies, in all these things you could not glory for one demon knew more about the things of earth than all men together, even if there may have been someone who received from the Lord a special knowledge of the highest wisdom. Likewise, even if you were more handsome and richer than everyone else and even if you performed wonders such as driving out demons, all these things would be an obstacle to you and none of them would belong to you nor could you glory in any of these things. But in this we can glory: in our infirmities and bearing daily the holy cross of our Lord Jesus Christ.

From *Francis and Clare: the complete works* by R. Armstrong and I. Brady

———

Almighty God,
you have made us for yourself,
and our hearts are restless
till they find their rest in you:
teach us to offer ourselves to your service,
that here we may have your peace,
and in the world to come may see you face to face;
through Jesus Christ our Lord. Amen.

Collect for the Seventeenth Sunday
after Trinity from *Common Worship*

Maurice Berkeley Peel 1874–1917

Priest and army chaplain

———

MAURICE BERKELEY PEEL was an army chaplain who quite literally 'went over the top' with the men in the Welsh battalion to which he was attached in the First World War, and with whom he lost his life in the Pas de Calais in northern France. Peel was the younger son of the First Viscount Peel, for many years the Speaker of the House of Commons. He was educated at Winchester and New College, Oxford, where he read history. He worked for some years at Oxford House in Bethnal Green, where he founded a very successful branch of the Church Lads' Brigade, with some two hundred boys enlisted in three battalions. In 1899 he was ordained and his first parish was in Bethnal Green, where he soon realised his mission would be a prolonged struggle against heavy odds. However, he lived and worked amongst the people of the parish and inspired them with his enthusiasm. By the time he moved to Bedfordshire in 1906 to be Rector of Wrestlingworth and Eyeworth, the church and Sunday School in Bethnal Green were both full and the Church Lads' Brigade had waiting lists of those who wanted to join. Peel founded another branch of the brigade whilst in Eyeworth and arranged holidays for children from the East End with local cottagers. After three years in Bedfordshire, Peel moved to Beckenham in Kent, where he met and married Emily Alington, with whom he had two children. When war was declared, Peel volunteered to be a chaplain with the forces and was sent to France. Early in 1915, he was awarded the Military Cross 'for conspicuous gallantry and devotion to duty'. He was killed by a sniper in 1917 whilst rescuing a wounded man.

Maurice Berkeley Peel preaching about those who died in the war

Well may we believe as we meditate upon the events of this War, that He and His Angels are with us, and that our beloved have not laid down their lives in vain at the feet of the Crucified. Ah, how deep must be their peace and gladness as they wake up from the shock of death into the great calm of God, and enter through the Gate of Sacrifice into the clearer dawn and the wider prospects, and the deeper unions of the promised land. If only the bereaved will set their minds on life instead of death, they will receive the conviction which experience will strengthen that, though the grave of the dust of the dear son or husband may be far away and lost in the shattered trenches, or the devouring waves, the brave, true bright spirit is very near indeed, looking with a purer love, guiding with a steadier hand, comforting with a new joyous confidence. I write this because I want to help those who mourn. I am confident that the human spirit belongs to the Eternal God, and is immortal because of that belonging. I am confident that the essence of life is *Love*, and that those who return to God receive new capacities to love, and to be a blessing to those who love them, and are loved by them.

From *A Hero Saint* by G. V. Sampson

———

God of Peace, the creator of all nations and peoples:
give us grace to banish from our hearts and minds
the greed and ambition which cause enmity and strife;
help us to use our creativity and energy
to work for that peace which is your desire for all people;
for we ask it in the name of Jesus Christ, the Prince of Peace. Amen.

Thomas Quinton Stow 1801–62

Congregational minister

———

A SUFFOLK MAN, THOMAS Stow began preaching the Christian gospel during his teens. He attended a missionary training college in Gosport to train for ministry in the Congregational Church and was appointed the minister at Framlingham in Suffolk. It was there that he married Elizabeth Eppes with whom he was to have four children, one of whom became a judge, one a politician, and another an explorer and writer. Stow spent a period as a Congregational Minister in Buntingford, Hertfordshire, before moving to Halsted in Essex. In 1836 he sailed to Australia under the auspices of the Colonial Missionary Society. He began his work in Adelaide, holding meetings in an old army tent. It was here in 1837 that a church of eleven members was established. Before long they had moved into a log church, with a schoolroom on one end, which Stow had personally constructed. Meanwhile, the Stow family had to live in the tent for another year until a house could be built for them. In November 1840 Freeman Street Chapel was opened and it was here that Stow was to minister for many years. In 1856 Stow's health deteriorated so he resigned but carried on preaching and teaching whenever he was fit enough. In 1862 he travelled to Sydney to help at Pitt Street Congregational Church but he became ill and died there on this day in 1862. He is buried in West Terrace Cemetery in Adelaide. He wrote *Memoirs of R. Taylor* and *The Scope of Piety*.

In this passage Thomas Stow writes about gratitude

Another mode of glorifying God is by acts of devout and grateful attribution. When we ascribe to men the estimable qualities and worthy deeds which belong to them, we honour them; and this ascription may be made as well by our actions as our views, feelings and expressions. Thus we honour God not only by deeply tracing all good to him, as the fountain of living waters – as the Infinite and Everlasting Excellency; by profoundly adoring him, as the 'Father of lights, from whom cometh every good and every perfect gift,' by sincere and solemn avowal of our own entire obligation to his goodness, by our thrill of gratitude, our song of praise, our loud hosanna; but by joyful submission to the bond of cordial, grateful service – by our thankful conduct – by laying our whole being under contribution to the law of gratitude – by making our actions praise God, and our whole life one grand doxology. We cannot in judgment, in disposition, in sincere expression, in unfeigned celebration, ascribe all good to God, and our actions not receive direction, character, impulse, and control from sentiments so pure and powerful. We shall *do* as well as *say* all things to the glory of God. 'All things are for our sakes, that the abundant grace might through the thanksgiving of many redound to the glory of God.' And *thanks*, such as glorify God, may be *given*, by the language and harmony of holy actions, as well as by 'psalms and hymns and spiritual songs.'

From a sermon 'All things to the glory of God' in *The Scope of Piety*

God of all creation,
in work and leisure,
in joy and sorrow,
in sickness and health
in my life and my death,
may I live with thanksgiving,
and glorify your holy name;
through Jesus Christ our Lord. Amen.

St Margaret d.304

Virgin and martyr

———

THE MEMORY OF St Margaret is commemorated in several places in the diocese. The churches at Higham Gobion, Streatley and Ridge are all dedicated to St Margaret and those at Barley and Bygrave are dedicated to St Margaret of Antioch. The name of the parish Stanstead St Margaret's probably arises from the dedication of the medieval chantry chapel, now demolished, which was built on to the Church of the Blessed Virgin Mary. Margaret of Antioch, who is also known as Marina, was thought to be the daughter of Aedesius, a pagan priest. She lived in present-day Turkey. Refusing to renounce her Christian faith in order to marry Olybrius, she was tortured and put to death in the year 304. St Margaret is a popular saint in England and more than two hundred and fifty churches are dedicated to her memory. She is commemorated in the Anglican and Roman Catholic Churches on 20 July and by the Eastern Church on 17 July. She is honoured as the patron saint of pregnant women.

Alan Smith writes about the witness of Christians down through the ages

'God has so arranged the body, giving the greater honour to the inferior member, that there may be no dissension within the body, but the members may have the same care for one another. If one member suffers, all suffer together with it; if one member is honoured, all rejoice together with it' (1 Corinthians 12.24–27). St Paul tells us that the church – God's community past and present – is made up of people with a variety of gifts. Some are called to be apostles, others prophets, teachers or leaders, whilst others are administrators or healers (1 Corinthians 12.27–31). The lives of many such Christians have been recorded by history. They are our role models. However, for every St Peter or St Francis, there have been tens of millions of ordinary Christians who have lived out their faith quietly in their day-to-day lives. No one has written about them in chronicles or history books; today no one even remembers their names or their untold acts of kindness. The glory of Christianity is to be found in these long-forgotten saints who have borne witness to the truth of Christianity. It is these unnamed Christians who make up the bulk of the martyrs; these uncelebrated missionaries who planted most of the churches; these anonymous believers who have kept the light of Christ shining down through the ages in towns and villages across the world through their faith and generosity. We need not be beguiled by the present-day thirst for fame and celebrity as God does not need to look in the newspaper to know of the faithfulness of the great company of Christians who have passed on the baton of faith.

From an unpublished sermon

Faithful God,
we thank you for the holy martyrs
who in every age have borne costly witness
by suffering and dying for their faith:
give us grace and courage that, following their example,
we too may bear witness with humility and generosity,
through Jesus Christ our Lord. Amen.

Richard de Argentein 13th century

Founder of Little Wymondley Priory and the Hospital of St John and St James in Royston

———

TODAY WE FEEL ashamed about the Crusades and view them as some of the saddest episodes in the history of the Christian Church. Like most important men of his time, Richard de Argentein was a soldier and was involved in fighting throughout his life. However, he was a generous benefactor as well as being a Crusader. He went on his first Crusade in 1218 and in the following year was involved in the capture of Damietta in Egypt. He wrote a letter to the Abbot of Bury St Edmunds in which he told how he founded a church dedicated to St Edmund and appointed three chaplains to serve there. Richard went on his second Crusade in 1240. There is an account in the Dunstable Chronicle which records that de Argentein and twenty knights could not hold the Tower of David in Jerusalem and had to call a truce in order to leave the city. Despite being a man of war, de Argentein founded and endowed the Augustinian Priory of Little Wymondley, which was dedicated to St Mary. He also established the Hospital of St John and St James in Baldock Street, Royston, and built a chapel at his manor house at Melbourn. De Argentein married three times. His first wife was Emma de Broy of Bletsoe, whom he married sometime before 1200, although it appears that she had died by 1203, leaving him to bring up their infant daughter, Margaret. He then married Cassandra de Insula, followed by Joan de Lenham. He held many public offices such as Sheriff of Hertfordshire and Constable of Hertford Castle. In 1246 the chronicler Matthew Paris listed de Argentein's death as one of the 'nobles in England' and wrote that he was 'an energetic knight who in the Holy Land had fought faithfully for God for a long time.'

Dietrich Bonhoeffer reflects on Christ's command to love our enemies

To the natural man, the very notion of loving his enemies is an intolerable offence, and quite beyond his capacity: it cuts right across his ideas of good and evil. More important still, to man under the law, the idea of loving his enemies is clean contrary to the law of God, which requires men to sever all connection with their enemies and to pass judgement on them. Jesus however takes the law of God in his own hands and expounds its true meaning. The will of God, to which the law gives expression, is that men should defeat their enemies by loving them. In the New Testament our enemies are those who harbour hostility against us, not those against whom we cherish hostility, for Jesus refuses to reckon with such a possibility. The Christian must treat his enemy as a brother, and requite his hostility with love. His behaviour must be determined not by the way others treat him, but by the treatment he himself receives from Jesus; it has only one source, and that is the will of Jesus.

From *The Cost of Discipleship*

———

Living God,
whose Son Jesus Christ taught that we should neither hate nor kill,
but rather should love our enemies:
we acknowledge that Christians have sometimes committed atrocities in your name.
Help us to make restitution for the harm our forebears caused
and grant that we may always act with love and justice,
for the sake of Jesus who is the Prince of Peace. Amen.

Joyce Crossland 1919–2009

Associate Sister of the Community of St Andrew

———

A S A YOUNG girl Joyce Crossland won a scholarship to Manchester Grammar School but she did not take up the place as the family could not afford to support her. Instead she worked as a cashier in the Co-op. Joyce went on to study at St Brigid's, a college for young women wanting to go to the mission field. She then trained as a nurse at Manchester Royal Hospital and studied to become a deaconess at Gilmore House, Clapham Common. Joyce worked in a Manchester parish for two years but heard a call to the religious life and applied to join the Community of St Andrew. During her novitiate she worked in the community convalescent home in Westgate-on-Sea and then at St Stephen's, Rochester Row, London. In 1954 she was professed as a Sister and sent to Bedford to run the St Albans Diocesan Children's Home in Bromham Road. She became an outstanding leader of the Home, renovating the buildings, admitting boys for the first time and recruiting a large team of volunteers. She wanted it to be a place where young teenagers could cross the bridge to independence. In 1984 the Sisters moved into a house in Conduit Road, Bedford, which was a focus for continuing family life and prayer, and from where they offered meals to the homeless. For many years Joyce had a particular interest in the church in Ghana. In 1984–96 she visited the country annually, working alongside Father Ralph SSM, the Principal of St Nicholas Theological College, Cape Coast. In 1992 she and another Sister moved to Paddock House in Willen, built for them by the Society of the Sacred Mission.

Archbishop Michael Ramsey meditates on Christian service

Think of your ministry as a series of comings of Christ, and the more you learn not to be taken unawares the more you can 'love his appearing.' How does he come? In times of your grief and disappointment he comes; and just when you begin to be oppressed you find that your nearness to *his* grief is the supreme fact: you are near his Cross again, and you are taken out of yourself. In times of joy in your ministry he comes; and just when you are tempted to be pleased with your own success you find that *his* joy is the supreme fact, and it makes an enormous difference. And in times of your complacency of unfaithfulness he comes; and in your sudden painful awareness that it is not well with you he is near in judgement and forgiveness. Watch and be ready. It happens as unexpectedly as the burglar breaking in. But when the master of the house comes, what does he do? We would expect him to sit down and refresh himself, and tell the servants to wait on him. But no. The Lord waits on them. So the Lord always comes to us in order to serve us; and it is for us to let him.

From *The Christian Priest Today*

———

Lord Jesus Christ,
who came not to be served but to serve
and to give your life as a ransom for many:
teach us the same humility
that we may neither consider ourselves too important to serve others,
nor be so arrogant that we do not allow others to serve us;
we ask this for your name's sake. Amen.

John de Warefeld 12th–13th century

Prior of Kings Langley

———

THE DOMINICAN PRIORY at Langley was founded by Edward II in 1308 in response to a vow that he made to God when in a difficult situation. He donated land and money to provide for a priory for fifteen friars and appointed John de Warefeld, a member of his household, to be the first Prior. The conventual church was built in 1312 and it was in the cemetery that Piers Gaveston, the first Earl of Cornwall and favourite of Edward II, was buried two years later. We know that in 1315, when de Warefeld ceased to be Prior, he became Edward's confessor. The priory continued to be an influential place as Richard II was buried there for a while and it was also the resting place of Edmund of Langley, Duke of York, and his wife, Isabella. Little more is known about de Warefeld's life after this period although he appears to have lived in London. His will is extant and probate shows that he died in 1349. In it he is described as a 'citizen and corndealer of London'. He left money to the church of St Mary atte Helle, and after various bequests to members of his family stipulated that the remainder of his goods were to be sold, with half of the proceeds to be given to the poor and the other half divided between his sons.

Thomas Aquinas, one of the great Dominicans, speaks of Christian leadership

Since it is the duty of a teacher of catholic truth not only to build up those who are mature in their faith, but also to shape those who are just beginning…so the declared purpose of this work is to convey things that pertain to the Christian religion in a way that is readily accessible to beginners. We have noticed that newcomers are invariably put off reflecting more deeply upon their faith by various writings, intimidated partly by the swarm of pointless questions, articles, and arguments, but also because essential information is being communicated under the constraints of textual commentary or academic debate, rather than sound educational methods, and because repetition breeds boredom and muddled thinking. Eager, therefore, to avoid these and similar pitfalls, and trusting in the help of God, we shall try in this work to examine the claims of Christian teaching, and to be precise and clear in our language as far as the matter under discussion allows. It is clear that Christian teaching employs human reason, not so as to prove anything because that would undermine the merit of believing, but rather in order to elucidate the implications of its thought. We should note that just as grace never scraps our human nature, but instead brings it to perfection, so in the same way our natural ability to reason should assist faith as the natural loving inclination of our will yields to charity.

From *Introduction to the Summa Theologiae of Thomas Aquinas* by R. McInemy

O Lord my God,
help me to be obedient without reserve,
poor without servility, chaste without compromise,
humble without pretence, joyful without depravity,
serious without affectation, active without frivolity,
submissive without bitterness, truthful without duplicity,
fruitful in good works without presumption,
quick to revive my neighbour without haughtiness,
and quick to edify others by word and example without simulation. Amen.

Thomas Aquinas

Edward Stallybrass 1794–1884

Missionary and Bible translator

———

DOUBTLESS FEW PEOPLE from Royston are fluent in Russian and Mongolian. However, Edward Stallybrass used his gift for languages to translate the Bible into Mongolian. He came from modest beginnings, one of nine children born to William and Susannah Stallybrass. As a young man Stallybrass trained for the Congregational ministry at Homerton College in London before being ordained in 1816. He and his wife Sarah were sent by the London Missionary Society to St Petersburg, where he studied Russian. By 1819 Stallybrass had established a mission station at Selenginsk in Transbaikalia to work among the Buryat Mongols. Three years later he moved to Khodon. Stallybrass collaborated with William Swan and Robert Yuille and eventually they published a version of the New Testament in Mongolian. In 1840 missionary work was banned by the Orthodox Church so in the following year Stallybrass returned to England. He was appointed as minister of Hampden Chapel and headmaster of a school in Walthamstow. In 1858 he moved to take up a post at Burnham in Norfolk. Stallybrass married and was widowed four times. His first wife was Sarah Robinson whom he married in 1817 and they had six children. She died in 1833 and two years later he married Charlotte Ellah who only lived for another six years. In 1844 he married Sarah Bass (who died in 1855) and finally in 1861 he married Mary Ann Oughton, who died in 1874. He died in Kent in 1884 and is buried in Stoke Newington.

Edward Stallybrass reflects on the challenges faced by missionaries

In religious, as well as in secular affairs, men are often mistaken in their estimate of success. They are apt to overlook the difficulties which lie in the way of any great achievements, and to imagine that delay is defeat. Unwarrantable analogies are formed; precedents are found in miraculous and supernatural occurrences; and conclusions are drawn from comparisons, that are sometime invidious, and always fallacious. This is especially the case in reference to missionary labours. Nothing of the *underground* processes is seen by superficial observers. The slow acquisition of oral language, and sometimes the actual formation of a written language, which had never been before reduced to a definite character, or a regular system; the difficult initiation into those habits and manners which it seems requisite in some cases to adopt, in order to any successful intercourse; the still greater difficulty of making either the written or the spoken language of a people the medium of conveying accurate ideas respecting subjects of mysterious import, and which, therefore, sometimes require a *notation*, so to speak, altogether new, either in its symbols, or in the application of them: these, and numberless other circumstances, must inevitably render laborious and persevering exertion necessary, and cause success to be a matter rather of hope than of attainment.

From *Memoir of Mrs Stallybrass*

———

Eternal God, giver of love and power,
your Son Jesus Christ has sent us into all the world
to preach the gospel of his kingdom:
confirm us in this mission,
and help us to live the good news we proclaim;
through Jesus Christ our Lord. Amen.

The Post Communion Prayer for the Seventh Sunday
after Easter from *Common Worship*

Edmund Staunton 1600–71

Clergyman

———

BORN IN WOBURN, Staunton studied at Wadham and Corpus Christi Colleges in Oxford. As a young man he had two profound experiences of his mortality – a serious illness and then an accident, when he nearly drowned. He wrote that these events gave him 'many sad and serious thoughts concerning my spiritual and eternal state'. Staunton was ordained and ministered in Witney, in Oxfordshire. After a short while he moved to Bushey and then to Kingston-upon-Thames where he became known as an energetic visitor and preacher. He was awarded the degree of Doctor of Divinity from Oxford University in 1634 and was also made one of the six preachers at Westminster Abbey. In 1649 he became the president of Corpus Christi College. However, he was ejected from the post in 1660 and retired to Rickmansworth. He continued to preach and teach at Salters Hall in London. He wrote two books, *A Dialogue between a Minister and a Stranger about Soul Affairs* and *A Treatise of Christian Conference*. He spent his final years in Bovingdon.

In this passage Staunton exhorts his readers to be serious in their discipleship

Let me advise you, and the Lord persuade your heart,

1. To make conscience of secret prayer, begging of God for Christ his sake, that he would make you sensible of the ignorance, of the blindness of the mind, of the hardness and impenitency of the heart, of the carelessness and mindlessness of the spirit, in the great things of grace and salvation, be earnest with God to give you knowledge, and consider that the soul be without knowledge is not good.

2. As also, for repentance from dead works, and a true saving faith in Jesus Christ. Beg of God an heart, to seek first the Kingdom of God, and his righteousness, and that you may be of those who strive to enter in at the strait gate, and of those violent ones who take the Kingdom of Heaven by force.

3. Be careful to hear good ministers preach, remembering what concerneth you in what you hear.

4. Be much in searching the Scriptures, and reading of good books, catechisms, and such like.

5. Make choice of good company, of such as fear God, and walk precisely, holily, righteously, and soberly in this present evil world, and improve such acquaintance by good conference with them, putting such questions to them as may make for your edification, and they, let me tell you, will be as glad of your society, as you of theirs.

6. Be sure, if you have a family, to set up the worship of God in your family, reading the Scriptures, and praying morning and evening with the household, catechising, and instructing your children and servants if you have any.

7. And lastly, be strict in sanctifying the Sabbath, spend that day well.

From *A Dialogue: or a Discourse between a Minister and a Stranger*

Lord Jesus Christ,
you invited your followers to lose their lives
for your sake and for the sake of the gospel,
that they might discover the life abundant
that you alone can give:
grant us grace to seek you in all things
and to work for the coming of your kingdom
when we shall see you face to face;
we ask this for your name's sake. Amen.

John of Wallingford d.1214

Abbot of St Albans

———

AN EARLY TRADITION claims that John (also sometimes known as John de Cella) came from the Hyde family of Denchworth. He is sometimes confused with a monk of the same name, the Infirmarius of the Abbey, and also a chronicler who lived slightly later. The details of John's early life are sketchy, although we know that he studied in Paris and was for a time Prior of Holy Trinity Priory in Wallingford, which was a cell of the monastery at St Albans. He was a man of wide interests and among his many achievements was the ability to predict the high water mark of the River Thames. He wrote a history book, the *Chronica Joannis Wallingford*, which dealt with the period from the fifth to the eleventh century. He became Abbot of St Albans Abbey in 1195 and remained in post until his death in 1214. He was buried at the Abbey where there is a memorial stone to him set into the floor of the Presbytery.

St Benedict writes about the qualities that are required in an abbot

Let him make no distinction of persons in the monastery. Let him not love one more than another, unless it be one whom he findeth more exemplary in good works and obedience. Let not a free-born be preferred to a freedman, unless there be some other reasonable cause. But if from a just reason the Abbot deemeth it proper to make such a distinction, he may do so in regard to the rank of anyone whomsoever; otherwise let everyone keep his own place; for whether bond or free, we are all one in Christ, and we all bear an equal burden of servitude under one Lord, 'for there is no respect of persons with God'. We are distinguished with Him in this respect alone, if we are found to excel others in good works and in humility. Therefore, let him have equal charity for all, and impose a uniform discipline for all according to merit. For in his teaching the Abbot should always observe that principle of the Apostle in which he saith: 'Reprove, entreat, rebuke', that is, mingling gentleness with severity, as the occasion may call for, let him show the severity of the master and the loving affection of a father. He must sternly rebuke the undisciplined and restless; but he must exhort the obedient, meek, and patient to advance in virtue. But we charge him to rebuke and punish the negligent and haughty. Let him not shut his eyes to the sins of evil-doers; but on their first appearance let him do his utmost to cut them out from the root at once, mindful of the fate of Heli, the priest of Silo.

From *The Rule of St Benedict*

———

Loving Lord,
we pray for those called to be shepherds in your Church:
give them hearts which yearn for you and the good of your people,
minds which always seek your truth and love to teach it,
hands ever ready to help and bless the poor and the needy,
feet poised to meet those who are seeking after you,
and tongues to speak of your grace and your glory;
through Jesus Christ our Lord. Amen.

Henry Allon 1818–92

Nonconformist minister

———

A YORKSHIREMAN BY BIRTH, Henry Allon (not to be confused with his son, a composer, of the same name) became a prominent minister in the Congregationalist Church. He trained at Cheshunt College in Hertfordshire and then spent most of his life as the minister of the Union Chapel in Islington. For many years he was editor of the *British Quarterly Review*. He wrote many books including *The Psalmody of the Reformation, The Indwelling Christ and Other Sermons, The Congregational Psalmist, the Worship of the Church, The Literary Genius of John Bunyan, The Life Eternal, The Sympathy of Jesus* and biographies of James Sherman and William Ellis. He died whilst still in office in 1892 and is buried in Abney Park Cemetery in London.

Henry Allon preaches on the transfiguration

This was the transfiguration of Moses. We are told also of a transfiguration of Stephen; and of the transfiguration of Christ. And it would be a study both interesting and profitable to trace the resemblances and differences of these three glorifications of great servants of God. Moses saw the glory of Jehovah; Stephen saw Jesus standing on the right hand of God; Christ held converse with glorified saints. Moses was transfigured when the idolatry of the people drove him almost to despair; and the transfiguration strengthened and encouraged him, while it filled the people with penitence and awe. Christ was transfigured when about to accomplish His decease at Jerusalem; and the transfiguration filled Him with calm strength and purpose, while it excited the disciples to rapture and worship. Stephen was transfigured when about to die beneath the murderous stones of a lawless mob; and the transfiguration filled him with martyr faith and Christ-like magnanimity, while it exasperated the Sanhedrin and the people to a more murderous rage. There are supreme moments in the lives of great servants of God, when only Divine visions can sustain them; and there are visions of God adequate to sustain men in straits and agonies that are worse than death.

From *A Sermon* on Exodus 34

———

Low in Thine agony,
Bearing Thy cross for me,
Saviour divine!
In the dark tempter's hour,
Quailing beneath his power,
Sorrowing yet more and more,
Thou dost incline.

In deep and trembling fears,
With crying strong and tears,
Now Thou dost pray.
If it be possible
This cup so terrible,
Father most merciful,
Take it away.

Yet, Lord, Thy will be done;
Lo, I, Thine only Son,
This cup will drink.
O wondrous love of Thine,
Unspeakable, divine;
To save this soul of mine
Thou wilt not shrink.

Thy soul its travail saw,
And in its heavy woe
Was satisfied.
So let Thy sorrow, Lord,
Fullness of joy afford,
To life and God restored,
Through Him who died.

Henry Allon

Francis Russell c.1527–85

Politician and benefactor

———

THE BEDFORD ALMSHOUSES, which are some of the oldest surviving buildings in Watford, sit next to St Mary's Church. Built at the end of the sixteenth century by Francis Russell, they were designed to house 'eight poor women'. He also bequeathed £120 in his will to support poor people in four parishes. Russell studied at King's Hall, Cambridge. He entered politics representing Buckinghamshire and was also High Sheriff of Bedfordshire and Buckinghamshire in 1547. In 1550 he was styled Lord Russell, and on his father's death in 1555 he became the second Earl of Bedford. Living in a period of religious turmoil, Russell was firmly on the side of the reformers. He was one of the signatories of the document which supported Lady Jane Grey as the next monarch, so when Queen Mary I came to the throne he was imprisoned for a time before being pardoned. He then spent time travelling on the Continent, studying Italian and meeting some of the leading reformers of the day. Russell was a soldier and helped put down the Prayer Book Rebellion of 1549 which broke out in Devon and Cornwall. Some years later in 1557 he fought at the Battle of Saint-Quentin in Picardy. When Queen Elizabeth I came to the throne she appointed Russell as one of her privy councillors and he was involved in diplomatic negotiations with France and Scotland. In September 1563 Russell was nominated by the crown to be governor of Berwick and warden of the east marches towards Scotland. He married Margaret, the daughter of Sir John of Bletso in Bedfordshire, and they had eight children. When Margaret died in 1562, he married Bridget Hussey. He died on this day in 1585 in London and is buried in the chapel at Chenies Manor House.

Reinhold Niebuhr writes about politics and faith

The field of politics is not helpfully tilled by pure moralists; and the realm of international politics is particularly filled with complexities which do not yield to the approach of a too simple idealism. On the other hand the moral cynicism and defeatism which easily results from a clear-eyed view of the realities of international politics is even more harmful. The world community must be built by men and nations sufficiently mature and robust to understand that political justice is achieved, not merely by destroying, but also by deflecting, beguiling and harnessing residual self-interest and by finding the greatest possible concurrence between self-interest and the general welfare. They must also be humble enough to understand that the forces of self-interest to be deflected are not always those of the opponent or competitor. They are frequently those of the self, individual or collective, including the interests of the idealist who erroneously imagines himself above the battle. Since all political and moral striving results in frustration as well as fulfilment, the task of building a world community requires a faith which is not too easily destroyed by frustration.

From *The Children of Light and the Children of Darkness*

———

Grant, Lord, to all politicians
a realistic understanding of the world and its ways,
a concern for justice and peace,
a desire to protect the weak and the vulnerable,
a willingness to admit when they get things wrong,
and a passion to work for the good of all;
we ask this in the name of Jesus Christ our Lord. Amen.

Robert Alexander Kennedy Runcie 1921–2000

Bishop of St Albans and Archbishop of Canterbury

———

BORN INTO AN agnostic family in Merseyside, Robert Runcie gained scholarships to Merchant Taylors' School in Crosby and Brasenose College, Oxford, where he read Greats. During the Second World War he was a tank commander in the Scots Guards and was awarded the Military Cross for his bravery at Winnekendonk. After the war he trained for the ministry at Westcott House, Cambridge, and served his curacy in Newcastle-upon-Tyne before returning to Westcott House as chaplain. Later, he was appointed to be the Vice-Principal of the college. In 1956 Runcie was elected Fellow and Dean of Trinity Hall. Four years later he was appointed Principal of Cuddesdon, the theological college near Oxford. In 1970 he was consecrated Bishop of St Albans. He often said that his time at St Albans was one of the happiest periods of his life. As well as his diocesan responsibilities across Bedfordshire and Hertfordshire, he was chairman of the Central Religious Advisory Committee on Broadcasting and joint chairman of the Anglican-Orthodox Commission. After ten years the call came to move to Canterbury where he became the 104th Archbishop. His archepiscopacy is remembered for events such as officiating at the marriage of Prince Charles and Lady Diana Spencer in 1981, and praying with Pope John Paul II at Canterbury Cathedral a year later. It was Runcie who set up a commission on urban priority areas, which resulted in the *Faith in the City* report in 1985. The contents of the report were leaked and there was a concerted effort by the government to rubbish its findings. However, the report led to the setting up of the Church Urban Fund, which raised more than £55 million and made a major contribution to regeneration in urban areas across Britain. Runcie also made news when his sermon at the end of the Falklands War provoked an angry response from the government. He retired in 1991 and was created a life peer, taking the title Baron Runcie of Cuddesdon. He married Rosalind, a professional pianist, in 1957. They had two children, James and Rebecca. He is buried to the north of St Albans Abbey, with his wife who died in 2012 (see entry for 19 December).

Robert Runcie writes about the resurrection of Jesus Christ

The only thing at the first Easter which transformed the disillusioned friends and disciples of Jesus into a world-converting power was the reality of the resurrection. Here is no mere dramatic symbol of an eternal pattern of death and rebirth which can be discerned in nature. The Christian community was formed in the beginning by those who believed that God had acted to open the door through which man could pass to share in the divine life which not even death and time can quench. We believe that the world was charged with new possibilities at the first Easter.

From *Windows onto God*

Come, Lord,
in the fullness of your risen presence,
and make yourself known to your people again
through the breaking of the bread,
and the sharing of the cup. Amen.

Robert Runcie

William Penn 1644–1718

Founder of the Province of Pennsylvania

———

ANYONE WANDERING AROUND Rickmansworth cannot fail to realise that the town has a connection with William Penn: there is a public house called the Pennsylvanian and also a school and leisure centre named after him. The son of an admiral, Penn was born in London and educated at Chigwell School and at Christ Church, Oxford. He did not graduate because he was a Quaker. He lived for a period in Rickmansworth, although his first marriage took place at King John's Farm in Chorleywood. When Penn received a grant of land in America from Charles II in payment of a debt owed to his father, he used it to establish a colony – Pennsylvania – as a refuge for religious dissenters. He was himself a pacifist Quaker. The Penn family owned the colony until the American Revolution. Penn married twice and had fifteen children. He died at Ruscombe in Berkshire. Among his most famous works are *The Great Case of Liberty of Conscience* (1670) and *Christian Quaker and His Divine Testimony* (1673).

William Penn writes about the founder of the Quakers, George Fox

The world began with innocency: all was then good that the good God had made: and as he blessed the works of his hands, so their natures and harmony magnified him their Creator. Then the morning stars sang together for joy, and all parts of his works said Amen to his law…O holy Sabbath, O holy day to the Lord! But this happy state lasted not long: for man, the crown and glory of the whole, being tempted to aspire above his place, unhappily yielded against command and duty, as well as interest and felicity; and so fell below it, lost the divine image, the wisdom, power, and purity he was made in. By which, being no longer fit for paradise, he was expelled from that garden of God, his proper dwelling and residence and was driven out, as a poor vagabond, from the presence of the Lord, to wander in the earth, the habitation of beasts. Yet God, that made him, had pity on him; for he seeing he was deceived, and that it was not of malice, or an original presumption in him, but through the subtlety of the serpent (that had first fallen from his own state, and by the mediation of the woman, man's own nature and companion, whom the serpent had first deluded) in his infinite goodness and wisdom found out a way to repair the breach, recover the loss, and restore fallen man again by a nobler and more excellent Adam.

From *A Journal of Historical Account of the Life … of George Fox*

We give back to you, O God, those whom you gave to us.
You did not lose them when you gave them to us,
and we do not lose them by their return to you.
Your Son has taught us that life is eternal and love cannot die.
So death is only a horizon, and a horizon is only the limit of our sight.
Open our eyes to see more clearly, and draw us closer to you,
so that we may know we are nearer to our loved ones, who are with you.
You have told us that you are preparing a place for us:
prepare us, that where you are we may be always,
O dear Lord of life and death. Amen.

William Penn

Christina of Markyate c.1100-55

Nun and mystic

———

BAPTISED THEODORA, IT was only later in life that she adopted the name by which we know her today: Christina. Tradition has it that while praying at the shrine of St Albans she felt called to become a nun and took a vow of chastity. Against her will, however, she was betrothed by her parents to a nobleman called Berthred. She refused to consummate the marriage and fled from her home in Huntingdon. For two years she took refuge with an anchoress called Alfwen, before moving to Markyate in Hertfordshire, where she sought the protection of a monk called Roger the Hermit. It was whilst in hiding that she received visions of Jesus Christ and of the Blessed Virgin Mary. Eventually Berthred released Christina from her marriage vows. When Roger died around the year 1121, he bequeathed his hermitage to Christina. Her reputation for holiness grew and a number of women came to live alongside her. The Abbot of St Albans, Geoffrey de Gorham, supported her and in 1131 received her vows as a nun. He helped her establish a monastic community and in 1145 the canons of St Paul's Cathedral, who owned the land, allowed her to rent it. A house was built which became known as Markyate Priory. The Priory was dissolved during the reign of Henry VIII. In 1959 a manuscript about Christina was discovered in the British Library. Dated to the 1150s, it was probably written by someone closely associated with the Priory. There are also several references to Christina in the records of St Albans Abbey. The important St Albans Psalter, now in Hildesheim in Germany and a facsimile of which is on display in St Albans Abbey, probably belonged to Christina.

In this passage Thomas Merton, a Trappist monk, reflects on the solitary life

We do not go into the desert to escape people but to learn how to find them; we do not leave them in order to have nothing more to do with them, but to find out the way to do them the most good. But this is only a secondary end. The one end that includes all others is the love of God. The truest solitude is not something outside you, not an absence of people or of sound around you; it is an abyss opening up in the centre of your own soul. And this abyss of interior solitude is a hunger that will never be satisfied with any created thing. The only way to find solitude is by hunger and thirst and sorrow and poverty and desire, and the one who has found solitude is empty, as if he had been emptied by death. He has advanced beyond all horizons. There are no directions left in which he can travel. This is a country whose centre is everywhere and whose circumference is nowhere. You do not find it by travelling but by standing still. Yet it is in this loneliness that the deepest activities begin. It is here that you discover act without motion, labour that is profound repose, vision in obscurity, and beyond all desire, a fulfilment whose limits extend to infinity.

From *New Seeds of Contemplation*

God of eternity,
who at the dawn of time
spoke and brought all things into being:
amongst the noise and busyness of life,
give us grace to be still and enter into that silence
where we may hear your voice of calm;
through Jesus Christ our Lord. Amen.

George Tankerfield d.1555

Protestant martyr

———

SET INTO THE wall surrounding Romeland Garden, opposite the west end of St Albans Abbey, is a slate plaque. It marks the site of the execution of a man from Barnet, George Tankerfield, who was burnt at the stake when he was in his late twenties. During the reign of Mary I (sometimes known as 'Bloody Mary') a number of people were executed as heretics for their refusal to convert from Protestantism to Roman Catholicism. In Hertfordshire, along with Tankerfield, William Hale was burnt at Barnet and Thomas Fust at Ware. We know little about Tankerfield apart from some details in *Foxe's Book of Martyrs*. It is likely that he was born in York and worked in London as a baker. He was arrested and taken to Newgate Prison before being examined by Bishop Bonner. Tankerfield was brought to St Albans by the High Sheriff of Hertfordshire, Edward Brocket, where he was burned to death on 26 August.

A vision of heaven, as described by the lovable Dame Alice at the end of a medieval mystery play

There will be such a kissing and welcoming as never was and a hurrying and hooraying and introducing and forgiving and such a partying, it will be like Christmas and Easter rolled into one. There will be such a telling of stories and retelling of stories and the good Lord will smile and chide us that we did not trust him and we shall see the joke, all of us, and we shall laugh and laugh and there will be such a partying as never was, my loves. And Mary his mother will look to her Son and say it is time for rest and there will be such a sleeping till the morning. And the morning will come and the sun will be bright and the sky will be blue and the meadows will beckon and there will be such an adventuring and exploring. And those who could not walk will run again and those who could not see will see colours such as never were, and those who could not hear will hear music beyond their believing and there will be such an exploring and adventuring and telling of adventures. But the good Lord will say 'Enough. I have work for you and we shall remember those still on earth and will have charge of you to pray for and to weep for and to long for'. But in our weeping there will be laughter, for one day they will be with us and there will be such a partying as never was my love. Easter and Christmas all rolled into one.

From *A Christmas Cracker*

In you, Father Almighty, we have our preservation and our bliss.
In you, Christ, we have our restoring and our saving.
You are our mother, brother, and saviour.
In you, our Lord the Holy Spirit, is marvellous and plenteous grace.
You are our clothing; for love you wrap us and embrace us.
You are our maker, our lover, our keeper.
Teach us to believe that by your grace all shall be well,
and all shall be well, and all manner of things shall be well. Amen.

A prayer of Julian of Norwich

Nathaniel Cotton 1707–88

Doctor and poet

———

NATHANIEL COTTON WAS born in London in 1707. He trained as a doctor in Leiden before moving to a practice in Dunstable, where he developed a particular interest in mental health. Around 1740 he set up an asylum called the Collegium Insanorum in Dagnall Street, St Albans. Perhaps the most famous of his patients were the poets Edward Young and William Cowper. He married Anne Pembroke, who bore him seven children, then after her death he married Hannah Everett, with whom he had another three children. Cotton was famous as a poet. His first collection of poems was called *Visions in Verse for the Entertainment and Instruction of Younger Minds* and was reprinted many times over several subsequent decades. Cotton also wrote *Observations on a particular kind of scarlet fever, that lately prevailed in and about St. Alban's*. He died on this day in 1788 and is buried in St Peter's Churchyard in St Albans.

A poem by Nathaniel Cotton

The subject of my song is health,
A good superior far to wealth,
Can the young mind distrust its worth?
Consult the monarchs of the earth;
Imperial czars and sultans own
No gem so bright, that decks their throne;
Each for this pearl his crown would quit,
And turn a rustic, or a cit.
Mark, though the blessing's lost with ease,
'Tis not recover'd when you please,
Say not that gruels shall avail,
For salutary gruels fail.
Say not, Apollo's sons succeed,
Apollo's son is Egypt's reed.
How fruitless the physician's skill,
How vain the penitential pill,
The marble monuments proclaim,
The humbler turf confirms the same!

Prevention is a better cure,
So says the proverb, and 'tis sure.
Would you extend your narrow span,
And make the most of life you can;
Would you, when med'cines cannot save,
Descend with ease into the grave;
Calmly retire, like evening light,
And cheerful bid the world good-night?
Let temperance constantly preside,
Our best physician, friend and guide!
Would you to wisdom make pretence,
Proud to be thought a man of sense?
Let temperance (always friend to fame)
With steady hand direct your aim;
Or, like an archer in the dark,
Your random shaft will miss the mark;
For they who slight her golden rules,
In wisdom's volume stand for fools.

From *Health*

O God of Wisdom,
in whom we live and move and have our being:
we thank you for our minds;
for memory by which we learn and gain perspective,
for intellect to reflect on our lives and the world
for imagination to glimpse future possibilities
and for understanding of how they may be realised,
for our good and for the good of all people;
we ask this in the name of Jesus Christ our Lord. Amen.

Albert John Trillo 1915–92

Bishop of Bedford and later Bishop of Hertford

———

NOT MANY BISHOPS have begun their working life in the film industry, delivering film-cans around Soho for British Lion. John Trillo's natural gifts and determination enabled him to study at night school and to receive a first class degree from King's College, London. Ordained in 1938 he served his title at Christ Church, Fulham, and was then appointed as Priest in Charge of St Michael's, Cricklewood. Trillo was particularly interested in young people as evidenced by his involvement in theological education and his time as secretary to the Student Christian Movement. For three years he was also chairman of the Church of England Youth Council. Trillo occupied several posts in the Diocese of St Albans, including eight years as the principal of Bishops College in Cheshunt. He was consecrated Bishop of Bedford in 1963 and for the first two years of his episcopate he was also a Residentiary Canon of St Albans Abbey. His final post in the diocese was as Bishop of Hertford from 1968 until 1971, before he was translated to the See of Chelmsford. He retired in 1985. In 1942 he married Patricia Williams and they had two sons and a daughter.

Archbishop Michael Ramsey writes about humility

'Everyone who exalts himself will be abased, and he who humbles himself will be exalted' (Luke 18.14). In these words our Lord sums up his parable of the complacent Pharisee and the penitent Publican. The contrast has run on from the Jewish Church of our Lord's time into the Christian Church in every period; and it recurs today in every parish and in every congregation. You will find in your ministry what a drag the one kind of character is upon the life of the Church and what a source of strength is the other. Indeed to lead men and women from the one state to the other will be one of the chief aims of your pastoral work. The words, however, which occur in a number of contexts in the Gospel tradition, have far wider reference. They concern the predicament of the human race and the answer of the Gospel to that predicament. Here is Man satisfied with himself and with his immense powers and using his powers to aggrandise himself in ways which make the world divided and miserable. And here on the other side is the answer of the gospel, that if Man has lost the power to humble himself before his Creator, the Creator will humble himself towards his creatures. So the divine humility breaks upon the scene of human pride. Bethlehem, Calvary, the feet-washing at the Last Supper, all say, 'he who humbles himself will be exalted'. The saying of Jesus is echoed in the hymn which St Paul cites in Philippians 2, telling of how one who was in the form of God humbled himself and God highly exalted him. Divine humility is the power which comes to make the human race different.

From *The Christian Priest Today*

———

Lord Jesus Christ,
you demonstrated the way of humility
by reaching out to the poor and vulnerable
and by washing the feet of the disciples:
teach us to offer ourselves in humble service,
that counting others better than ourselves,
we may reflect the divine love in our words and deeds:
we ask this in the name of the Suffering Servant,
Jesus Christ our Lord. Amen.

Edgar Jacob 1844–1920

Third Bishop of St Albans

———

EDGAR JACOB WAS born into a clerical family. His father was the Archdeacon of Winchester and Rector of Crawley in Hampshire, while his mother's father had been Vicar of Romney. He studied at Winchester College and went up to New College, Oxford, where he was awarded a first class degree. Ordained in the Diocese of Oxford, Jacob served his title at Witney and a second curacy in Bermondsey. In 1871 he was appointed Domestic Chaplain to the Bishop of Calcutta. After five years he returned to England but continued as Commissary of Calcutta. In 1878 he was appointed Vicar of Portsea and in 1887 he also became an honorary chaplain to Queen Victoria. From 1876 until 1896 he was examining chaplain to the Bishop of Winchester. Jacob was consecrated to the See of Newcastle in 1896 and seven years later he was translated to the See of St Albans. He retired in 1919 and died shortly afterwards.

Edgar Jacob exhorts the clergy

What conception has the average parishioner of his responsibility; *(a)* to his parish, *(b)* to his diocese, *(c)* to the Church of which he is a member, *(d)* to the British Empire, *(e)* to the world? Does every incumbent, every churchwarden, realise that the parish cannot regard its own needs only? Our reformed system of church finance is happily doing much to draw us together, and enables us to realise that we are members of a Body and all concerned with the Body to which we belong; but I want to get beyond the parish and beyond the diocese, and to insist that the stage of missionary zeal cannot be satisfied with a cared-for parish and a well-equipped diocese, but thirsts for the winning of souls to Christ throughout the world. The cheerful willingness of men and women to give themselves up for the Master's service at home and abroad, the earnest intercession of those who cannot give themselves thus wholly up, the sacrifice of time and money by all for the spreading of the life – must be the natural outcome of a realisation of the truth that I am trying to enforce. Is there not need of real repentance, and can we clergy say honestly that no repentance is needed on our part, and that if there is apathy and indifference it is due to laity not heeding the teaching we have tried to give and the example we have tried to set? We have an opportunity during this National Mission showing whether we are afire or not. If we are afire we shall help our Church workers and our communicants to be afire.

From *Addresses to the Clergy of the Diocese of St Albans in Preparation
for the National Mission of Repentance and Hope on March 1916*

———

*Heavenly Father, by the power of the Holy Spirit
kindle a flame of love in our hearts
for you and for your world:
inspire us to witness in word and deed,
that all people may turn to you in hope and trust
and your kingdom may come and your will be done;
for we ask this in the name of Jesus Christ our Lord. Amen.*

Edward Wilkes d.1646

Founder of almshouses

————

EDWARD WILKES IS one of the countless number of Christians who has left a lasting mark on our diocese. The Wilkes family had arrived in Leighton Buzzard around 1575. In 1630 Edward Wilkes established ten almshouses for 'poor widows'. He instructed that they should 'constantly repair to the Church on Sundays, and also on the days when sermons are preached', otherwise they might be removed from the almshouses. He also specified that on Rogation Day each year, the trustees of the charity, the town crier and ten boys from each church choir in the parish must make a tour of the properties of the charity. Upon arrival at the almshouses, one of the choirboys had to be stood on his head while details of Wilkes' bequest were read out aloud to the assembled crowd. This custom is still observed annually. Wilkes left money, specifying that a sermon should be preached on the anniversary of his death, 24 March, for which the preacher was to be paid ten shillings. Wilkes died in 1646 and is buried in All Saints Church, Leighton Buzzard, with his wife. In 1692 one of his descendants, Matthew, added to the endowment with land and property, including a public house, The Three Horseshoes. The almshouses were rebuilt in 1857 and extended in 1873.

Basil the Great preaches about love

Are you poor? There is someone much poorer than you are. You have enough bread for ten days; another has enough for one. As a good and kind hearted person, make your surplus equal by distributing it to the needy. Do not shrink from giving of the little you have; do not treat your own calamity as if it is worse than the common suffering. Even if you possess only one loaf of bread, and the beggar stands at the door, bring one loaf out of the storeroom and, presenting it to the hands lifted up towards heaven, offer this merciful and considered prayer:

> *One loaf of which you see, O Lord, and the problem is evident, but as for me, I prefer your commandment to myself and I give of the little I have to the starving brother; for you also give to your servant in trouble. I know your great goodness and I also confidently believe in your power, for you do not defer your grace for another time, but dispense your gifts when you wish.*

And if you speak and act in this way, the bread that you should give out of your scarcity would become seed for planting, would bear rich fruit, a pledge of sustenance, a patron of mercy. Say to your self what the widow of Sidon said in a similar situation – remember well the story – 'As the Lord lives, I have only this in my house to feed my children and myself.' And if you should give out of your state of deprivation you too would have the vessel of oil abounding with grace, the unemptying pot of flour. For God's lavish grace on the faithful is exactly like that of the always emptying, never-exhausting, double-giving vessels of oil.

From *The Body of the Poor* by Susan Holman

————

Generous God, whose Son Jesus Christ
taught that it is more blessed to give than to receive:
forgive our greed and acquisitiveness
and teach us the way of hospitality and generosity,
that following the example of your Son,
we may share freely with others
the good things we have received from your hand;
We ask this for his name's sake. Amen.

William Cecil 1521–98

Secretary of State and Lord High Treasurer

——

FROM MODEST ROOTS, William Cecil became one of the most important men of his day. He was educated at the King's School in Grantham, Stamford School and St John's College, Cambridge. For a time he was in the service of Edward Seymour, Duke of Somerset, and then in 1547 entered Parliament, representing Stamford. When Seymour was ousted from his post as Lord Protector, Cecil was imprisoned in the Tower of London. However, he was released within a few weeks and shortly after became Secretary of State to Edward VI. During the short reign of Mary I Cecil's fortunes waned for a time. When Elizabeth came to the throne Cecil was made Secretary of State and took control of the finances and the Privy Council. He was convinced that Mary Queen of Scots had to be executed if she was not to be the focus of Catholic plots against the Crown. He played an important part in the Religious Settlement of 1559. In 1572 Cecil was also appointed as Lord High Treasurer, which gave him even more influence over the queen. Cecil lived at Theobalds in Hertfordshire. He married Mary Cheke who only lived a year after the birth of their child, Thomas. In 1546 he married Mildred Cooke.

The relation between politics and the Church has always been complex. Here, David McIlroy describes what he believes to be the role of the Church

The church, at its best, performs four useful tasks for politicians. First, it expresses what it understands the content of God's just requirements for human society to be. Yet in enunciating a Christian morality it should do so in a way that reckons – as do Scripture and tradition – with the complexities and contingencies of the societies within which Christian politicians reach their judgements. Second, it may indicate what approaches it believes would be unprincipled accommodations and which would be unprincipled. For example, the Christian politician Ann Widdecombe voted in favour of amendments to the 1967 Abortion Act that reduced the normal time limit for abortion but allowed late abortions of handicapped babies. She did so because she believed that, on balance, the amendments would lead to fewer babies being aborted even though the change in the law meant that some handicapped babies were now at greater risk of abortion. In deciding how to vote on this issue of conscience, she was guided by the Catholic Church's teaching regarding the lesser of evils. The church's teaching gave her guidance on how to act in accordance with her Christian principles in a political context in which compromise is unavoidable. The political discernment of the right (just) thing to do in all the circumstances, which I have called 'shallow justice' and which the Bible calls 'just judgement', is a demanding task to which the church ought to offer its very best reflection. Third, the church may, where the need demands it, offer sharp critique of government. Archbishop Desmond Tutu's stance against apartheid was both peaceable and yet uncompromising. Fourth, and by no means least, the church prays for politicians.

From *The Role of Government in Classical Christian Political Thought*

Heavenly Father,
we pray for the leaders of nations:
give them wisdom that they may govern for the good of all people
compassion to seek the welfare of the poor and vulnerable
and a determination to work for peace and justice;
through Jesus Christ our Lord. Amen.

Rohese de Vere c.1110–67

Founder of the Gilbertine Priory at Chicksands

———

Rohese de Vere was born in Hedingham and baptised at Waldon in Essex. Her father was Aubrey de Vere II and her mother was Alice of Clare. Rohese married Geoffrey de Mandeville, the Earl of Essex, and we know they had at least three sons: Geoffrey, William and Robert. Records reveal that in 1143 Rohese's husband took up arms against King Stephen. He died the following year and Rohese married Payn de Beauchamp, Baron of Bedford. They founded a priory at Chicksands, near Shefford, for canons and nuns which was a part of the Gilbertine Order, a religious order founded by Gilbert of Sempringham (c. 1083–1190). There were only eight other religious houses in England for men and women. Their living quarters were separate and they sat on different sides of a screen in church. Rohese was also involved in the move of the secular canons from St Paul's, Bedford, to Newnham in Bedfordshire. She was buried at Chicksands Priory. All that survives of the priory today is a cloister.

Just before his death Gilbert writes a letter of encouragement

Gilbert of Sempringham, by God's mercy whatever he is, or rather was, to his dear sons the canons and brethren of Malton, everlasting salvation in the Lord together with God's blessing and his own. While it was allowed and while in his mercy God furnished me with the ability, I used occasionally to pay personal visits to you as to my dearest sons; and with such teaching as matched my knowledge and my powers, I would summon and draw you towards the love of God. Oh that success had crowned my efforts! But now I am entirely bereft of bodily strength, so that by passing beyond the veil of flesh I must depart from this life which has been bitter and wearisome to me for a long while. And because from now on I shall not be able to speak with you face to face, I do not hesitate in this written form to urge you as strongly as I can: for God's sake and for the salvation of your souls pay more careful attention to divine love than you have up until now, but repressing vice, exalting truth and justice, and keeping the rules and traditions of your Order. And you can do this the more carefully and strictly because you are free from the concerns which occupy others in the Order, and because you have the opportunity to exercise discipline within the Order in such a way that the unruliness of others may be prevented. For this is why I have particularly brought you together, that our Order may be protected and exalted through the strictness of your religious observance.

A reading from a letter of Gilbert of Sempringham to his canons at Malton

---

O God, by whose grace your servant Gilbert,
kindled with the flame of your love,
became a burning and a shining light in your Church:
Grant that we also may be aflame with the spirit of love and discipline,
and walk before you as children of light;
through Jesus Christ our Lord, who lives and reigns with you,
in the unity of the Holy Spirit, one God, now and for ever. Amen.

From *The Book of Common Prayer*
of the Episcopal Church of the USA

Henry Atkins 1558–1635

Physician

———

H ENRY ATKINS' FAMILY came from Great Berkhamsted in Hertfordshire. He studied at Trinity College, Oxford, and the University of Nantes. Atkins' outstanding abilities were recognised when he became a fellow, and later president, of the College of Physicians and was subsequently re-elected president on six occasions. He is remembered as a generous benefactor of the college. The Earl of Essex appointed Atkins as his doctor, so that he could accompany him on the Spanish Expedition. However, Atkins was such a poor sailor that he had to resign his post. He was then employed by James I to accompany the king's son from Scotland to England and also to give medical care to Henry, Prince of Wales, in his final illness. Atkins was married to Mary Pigot and they had one son, also called Henry. The family lived in Warwick Court in London, where Atkins died. He is buried in St Mary's, Cheshunt. The inscription on his monument begins:

> Henry Atkins, D^r in Physique, Physician in Ordinary for the space of 32 years to king James and king Charles; was the son of Richard Atkins of Great Barkhamstead in this co. of Hertford Gent. and dyed anno 1635, aged 77, and lyeth here interred in this vault, which hee caused to bee made anno 1623, for himselfe and his only wife Mary

Stephen Parsons writes about health

A Christian will never regard healing or wholeness as simply adequate physical functioning. Wholeness or 'Shalom' is the experience, as the hymn puts it, of being 'ransomed, healed, restored, forgiven'. It is a state of being right with God, one's self, one's neighbours and the whole created world. To be whole is to be as God meant us to become and to partake of the 'Kingdom' that Christ came to share. None of us achieve that state of wholeness but everything we do as Christians, our prayer, worship, self-examination and care for one another, helps us to move towards that target. The Christian ministry of healing must be seen in the context of this complete process. When a Christian prays with another Christian for healing, there is the implicit prayer that not only will the 'sick' individual find relief from their physical ailment, but that they will also move further into the wholeness that God wills for them. That wholeness will include forgiveness of their sin, a new beginning in their relationships with God and their fellows and a deeper grasp of the journey through life that God has prepared for them. From this perspective of the meaning of wholeness, the offerings of alternative medicine and spirituality look a little thin. Likewise when Christian healing is divorced from the whole Christian notion of wholeness, it too seems rather shallow. If we do start from a 'high' notion of Christian wholeness, then our critique of other healing systems is that they are, whether or not contaminated by power issues, incomplete and less than totally adequate.

From The Guild of St Raphael

> We humbly beseech thee, of thy goodness, O Lord,
> to comfort and succour all them who in this transitory life
> are in trouble, sorrow, need, sickness, or any other adversity:
> help us to minister to them thy strength and consolation,
> and so endow us with the grace of sympathy and compassion
> that we may bring to them both help and healing;
> through Jesus Christ our Lord. Amen.

From The Book of Common Prayer

St Walthen c.1095–1159

Monk of Warden and Abbot of Melrose

———

WALTHEN WAS BORN into a wealthy and privileged family. His father was Simon, Earl of Huntingdon, and his mother, Maud, was the grand-niece of William the Conqueror. After Walthen's father died, Maud married King David of Scotland. Although he lived in the Scottish Court, Walthen wanted to enter the religious life. He joined the Austin Canons at the monastery at Nostell in Yorkshire. His godliness was recognised and before long he was made Prior of the Monastery of Kirkham. Walthen, however, felt called to become a Cistercian monk and moved to Warden in Bedfordshire to join the community. He was sent to Rievaulx in Yorkshire where the famous abbot, St Aelred, allowed him to make his profession as a monk. Towards the end of his life he was elected Abbot of Melrose in Scotland, where he is buried.

John Cassian writes about the monastic vocation

The whole purpose of the monk, and indeed the perfection of his heart, amount to this – total and uninterrupted dedication to prayer. He strives for unstirring calm of mind and for never-ending purity, and he does so to the extent that this is possible for human frailty. This is the reason for our tireless and unshakeable practice of both physical work and contrition of heart. Indeed, there is a mutual and undivided link between these. For just as the edifice of all the virtues strives upward toward perfect prayer so will all these virtues be neither sturdy nor enduring unless they are drawn firmly together by the crown of prayer. This endless, unstirring calm of prayer that I have mentioned can neither be achieved nor consummated without these virtues. And likewise virtues are the prerequisite foundation of prayer and cannot be effected without it. It is pointless for me simply to talk about prayer, simply to direct attention to its ultimate reality, with its presupposition of the practice of all the virtues. The first task is to look at the succession of obstacles to be overcome and then to examine the necessary preliminaries to success. With the gospel parable for a guide, one must carefully calculate and gather together everything required for the construction of this most sublime tower of the spirit. And preliminary work will be necessary if the assembled materials are to be of any use, for they will not be able to support the sublime reality of perfection unless we unload all our vices and rid our souls of the wreck and rubble of passion. Then simplicity and humility must be laid as sure foundations on, as they say, the living solid earth of our hearts, on that rock of which Scripture speaks.

From *Conferences*

Lord, I seek you with all my heart, with all the strength you have given me.
I long to understand that which I believe.
You are my only hope; please listen to me.
Do not let my weariness lessen my desire to find you, to see your face.
You created me in order to find you; you gave me strength to seek you.
My strength and my weakness are in your hands:
preserve my strength, and help my weakness.
Where you have already opened the door, let me come in;
where it is shut, open at my knocking.
Let me always remember you, love you, meditate upon you,
and pray to you, until you restore me to your perfect pattern. Amen.

Augustine of Hippo

Lawrence 3rd century

Deacon and martyr

SEVEN CHURCHES IN the Diocese of St Albans are dedicated to the memory of St Lawrence of Rome: Abbots Langley, Ardeley, Bovingdon, Nettleden, Steppingley, Willington and Wymington. Lawrence was one of seven deacons who served under Pope Sixtus II. They were all martyred during the persecution in the reign of Emperor Valerian the Elder. The Prefect of Rome was eager to get hold of the treasures belonging to the Church and so commanded Lawrence to assemble them in one place. Lawrence requested that he be granted three days to gather them. When the time came for him to meet with his persecutors, Lawrence arrived with a group of crippled and blind people, saying, 'These poor are the treasures of the church.' Tradition recounts that Lawrence was martyred at the site of the church of San Lorenzo in Panisperna, by being burned to death on a gridiron, which explains, rather bizarrely, why he is the patron saint of chefs. Today is his feast day.

Leo the Great preaches about St Lawrence

How gloriously powerful is the blessed martyr Lawrence whose sufferings we commemorate today. Even his persecutors felt the power of his teaching when they were confronted by his courage, a courage born of love for Christ, which not only refused to yield to them, but actually gave strength to those around him. When the fury of the pagans was raging against Christ's most chosen members and attacking those especially who were ordained, the wicked persecutor's wrath was vented on Lawrence the deacon, who was outstanding not only in the performance of the liturgy, but also in the management of the Church's property. The persecutor promised himself a double spoil from this man's capture, reasoning that if once he could force Lawrence to surrender the Church's treasures, his action would also discredit him irredeemably. Greedy for money and an enemy to the truth, the persecutor armed himself with a double weapon: with avarice to plunder the gold, and with impiety to carry off Christ. And so it was that he demanded that the Church's wealth, on which his greedy mind was set, should be brought out to him. The holy deacon then showed him where he had it stored. He pointed to a crowd of holy poor people, in the feeding and clothing of whom, he said, was to be found a treasury of riches which could never be lost, and which was entirely secure because the money had been spent on so holy a cause. At first the plunderer was completely baffled, but then his anger blazed out into hatred for a religion which should put its wealth to such a use. Determined to pillage the Church's treasury, and finding no hoard of money, he resolved then to carry off a still greater prize by carrying off that sacred deposit of faith with which the Church was enriched. He ordered Lawrence to renounce Christ, and prepared to test the deacon's stout courage with terrifying tortures.

From *The Nicene and Post-Nicene Library of the Fathers* by P. Schaff and H. Wace

---

God of the Poor,
who inspired Lawrence the Deacon
to a life of loving service:
give us grace to follow his example,
that defending the weak and supporting the needy,
we may bear witness to your love for all people;
this we ask in the name of Jesus Christ our Lord. Amen.

Herbert Whitton Sumsion 1899–1995

Composer and musician

———

HERBERT SUMSION WAS one of the greatest English composers of church music of the twentieth century. He was also known for his teaching, conducting and performing. As well as composing for choirs and the organ, Sumsion wrote chamber and orchestral works. His connection with the Diocese of St Albans dates from the time when he was Director of Music at Bishop's Stortford College. Following the sudden death of Herbert Brewer in 1928, Sumsion was appointed organist of Gloucester Cathedral, a post he held for almost forty years. With little time for preparation he had to conduct several major works at the Three Choirs Festival which was taking place at Gloucester that year. This prompted Elgar to joke 'What at the beginning of the week was assumption has now become a certainty'. Sumsion's connection with the Festival was to continue until his retirement in 1967. He died on this day in 1995.

Some reflections on the role of music in worship

I, Doctor Martin Luther, wish all lovers of the unshackled art of music grace and peace from God the Father and from our Lord Jesus Christ! I truly desire that all Christians would love and regard as worthy the lovely gift of music, which is a precious, worthy, and costly treasure given to mankind by God. The riches of music are so excellent and so precious that words fail me whenever I attempt to discuss and describe them…In summa, next to the Word of God, the noble art of music is the greatest treasure in the world. It controls our thoughts, minds, hearts, and spirits…Our dear fathers and prophets did not desire without reason that music be always used in the churches. Hence, we have so many songs and psalms. This precious gift has been given to man alone that he might thereby remind himself that God has created man for the express purpose of praising and extolling God. However, when man's natural musical ability is whetted and polished to the extent that it becomes an art, then do we note with great surprise the great and perfect wisdom of God in music, which is, after all, His product and His gift; we marvel when we hear music in which one voice sings a simple melody, while three, four, or five other voices play and trip lustily around the voice that sings its simple melody and adorn this simple melody wonderfully with artistic musical effects, thus reminding us of a heavenly dance, where all meet in a spirit of friendliness, caress and embrace. A person who gives this some thought and yet does not regard music as a marvellous creation of God, must be a clodhopper indeed and does not deserve to be called a human being; he should be permitted to hear nothing but the braying of asses and the grunting of hogs.

From the foreword to Georg Rhau's *Symphoniae iucundae*

God of Eternity,
to whom the angels in heaven sing their everlasting song,
declaring you worthy to receive glory and honour and power:
inspire composers with melody and harmony
opening our hearts and minds in wonder and awe
and leading us ever deeper in worship and praise;
through Jesus Christ our Lord. Amen.

Walter John Lawrance 1840–1914

First Dean of St Albans

———

WALTER JOHN LAWRANCE was educated at St Paul's School, London, from where he went to Trinity College, Cambridge. He had intended to follow his father in a career as a lawyer, but instead was ordained deacon in 1863 by the Bishop of Rochester. He served two curacies and then in 1868 was appointed as the Rector of St Albans Abbey. The building was in such a terrible state that in 1870 worship had to be moved into the nave as the tower was unstable. For many years Lawrance had a turbulent relationship with the architect Lord Grimthorpe, who was willing to pay for the repairs on the Abbey but in return insisted that they should be done in the way he specified. In 1877 the Diocese of St Albans was founded and the Abbey became the Cathedral of the new diocese. In 1884 Lawrance, in addition to being the Rector, was appointed Archdeacon of St Albans (a post he held for twenty-five years) and in 1900 he became the first Dean of the Cathedral. Under his leadership the number of services and the size of the congregations grew greatly. Lawrance had boundless energy. He chaired the St Albans School of Music, the Governors at the Grammar School and the Committee of Management of the St Albans and Mid Herts Hospital and Dispensary. He was chaplain to the mayor for forty-six years. In 1871 Lawrance married Caroline Grant and they had five children. He died on this day in 1914.

Lawrance preaches about the Christian hope

We are accustomed to consider all that is best in human life to be a kind of type, at least a foreshadowing, of the life to come. Our moments of highest and truest pleasure, our times of most elevated thought, do not end with themselves. They carry our spirits on further. They make us feel that there is something else beyond in store for us; that we were not meant to perish, but are created to be immortal. And doubtless the feeling, like all that is deepest in our nature, is a true one. Very poor in comparison with heaven are the best things of earth; very fleeting are its most enduring joys. And if we form our fancies of heaven merely from what we know of the delights of earth, they will of course be most inadequate. What eye hath not seen, nor ear heard, neither hath entered into the heart of man to conceive, it is clear we cannot judge from our seeing, or from hearing, or from imagination. But for all this, as I have said, the instinct is a true one, which makes us see a likeness to things above in the noblest and best of things below.

A sermon preached in the Abbey Church of St Albans on Septuagesima Sunday 1871
being the Sunday after the Funeral of Mrs Lipscomb

———

Gracious Father,
you have created a world of beauty and delight;
grant that at the time of my death
I may enter into your presence
and see you, the source of all beauty, face to face,
when all that I am and all that I shall be,
will be enveloped in your burning love,
through Jesus Christ our Lord. Amen.

Hippolytus 170–235

Theologian, martyr and patron saint of horses

——

ONE OF THE strangest place names in Hertfordshire is St Ippolyts, a village just outside Hitchin. Equally strange is the ancient tradition that during the Middle Ages sick horses used to be brought to the church to be blessed by the parish priest. This is because the name of the village is a corruption of Hippolytus, who is the patron saint of horses. The name of the village comes from an important Roman theologian of the third century, St Hippolytus. He studied under Irenaeus and was renowned for his intellect and his eloquence. Hippolytus was a hard liner and opposed a number of the popes, including Pope Callixtus I who he thought was too lenient in offering absolution to Christians who had fallen into grave sin. When persecution broke out in 235 during the reign of the Emperor Maximinus Thrax, Hippolytus was sent into exile. However, it seems that he soon returned to Rome as he was buried there in 236. Within a few years Hippolytus was being commemorated as a martyr. Hippolytus wrote on a variety of subjects, including liturgy and ecclesiastical law, his most important book being the *Refutation of all Heresies*. He also wrote *On Christ and the Antichrist, The Twelve Apostles of Christ, On the Seventy Apostles of Christ*, and commentaries on the books of Daniel and the Song of Songs. Hippolytus is commemorated on 13 August in both the Eastern and Western churches.

Hippolytus explores the human and the divine natures of Jesus

When He came into the world, He was manifested as God and man. And it is easy to perceive the man in Him, when He hungers and shows exhaustion, and is weary and athirst, and withdraws in fear, and is in prayer and in grief, and sleeps on a boat's pillow, and entreats the removal of the cup of suffering, and sweats in an agony, and is strengthened by an angel, and betrayed by a Judas, and mocked by Caiaphas, and set at nought by Herod, scourged by Pilate, and derided by the soldiers, and nailed to the tree by the Jews, and with a cry commits His spirit to His father, and drops His head and gives up the ghost, and has His side pierced with a spear, and is wrapped in linen and laid in a tomb, and is raised by the Father on the third day. And the divine in Him, on the other hand, is equally manifest, when He is worshipped by angels, and seen by shepherds, and waited for by Simeon, and testified of by Anna, and inquired after by wise men, and pointed out by a star, and at a marriage makes wine of water, and chides the sea when tossed by the violence of winds, and walks upon the deep, and makes one see who was blind from birth, and raises Lazarus when dead for four days, and works many wonders, and forgives sins, and grants power to his disciples.

From *The Refutation of all Heresies* by Hippolytus by J. H. MacMahan

———

Christ is risen: the world below lies desolate.
Christ is risen: the spirits of evil are fallen.
Christ is risen: the angels of God are rejoicing.
Christ is risen: the tombs of the dead are empty.
Christ is risen indeed from the dead, the first of the sleepers.
Glory and power are his forever and ever. Amen.

Hippolytus of Rome

Marianne Margaret Alford 1817–88

Artist and benefactor

———

LADY MARIAN ALFORD (the name by which she is usually remembered) lived at a time when most ordinary children would have only received the most elementary education. Following the death of her husband in 1849 she became a generous benefactor of what is now known as Little Gaddesden Church of England Primary School. Born in Rome, Marian was the daughter of the second Marquis of Northampton. Much of her childhood was spent in Italy and she was to return there regularly throughout her life. Following the death of her mother, she came to live in England when she was thirteen. She married John Hume Oust, the Viscount Alford, who was heir to the Egerton estate. After he inherited the title they moved to Ashridge Park in Hertfordshire and he changed his surname to Egerton. They had two sons. Marian was interested in every aspect of art. She was an excellent painter, but also created the designs for Alford House, her London home. She was one of a group of women who founded the Royal School of Needlework and later in life she wrote *Needlework as Art*. It is said that she died with her brother, the Bishop of Ely, at her side reading prayers as she made the responses.

Some thoughts on beauty in the writings of Dean Inge

The Beauty of the world, as many have felt, is the strongest evidence we have of the goodness and benevolence of the Creator. Not, of course, that the world was made beautiful for our sakes. It is beautiful because its Author is beautiful, and we should remember that when the old writers spoke of God as the Author of nature, they used the word in much the same sense as if we said that a man was the author of his own photograph. But we are allowed to see and enjoy beauty, although the gift cannot be proved to promote our own survival. It looks like a free gift of God. Beauty is a general quality of nature, and not only of organic nature; crystals are very beautiful; the perceiving mind must also be beautiful and healthy. The vile or vulgar mind not only cannot discern beauty; it is a great destroyer of beauty everywhere. The love of beauty is super-personal and disinterested, like all spiritual values; it promotes common enjoyment and social sympathy. Unquestionably it is one of the three ultimate values, ranking with Goodness and Truth.

From *Outspoken Essays*

———

God of Glory,
whose beauty is revealed in creation,
in mountain and valley, in plant and flower;
grant that artists may also reflect your beauty
in their works of art and compositions of music.
But above all, may we show forth your beauty
in human kindness and acts of compassion;
through Jesus Christ our Lord. Amen.

The Blessed Virgin Mary 1st century

Mother of Jesus

———

BY FAR THE saint with the greatest number of churches in the diocese dedicated in their honour is Mary, the Mother of the Lord. In churches from the south of the diocese, such as East Barnet and Potters Bar, to Salford and Yelden in the north, from Puttenham and Studham in the west to Gilston and Braughing in the east, we find her name honoured. Nothing for sure is known of her parentage or the place of her birth. Only her name is known for certain: Mary or Miriam (in Hebrew), and that she had an aged relative called Elizabeth. According to the Gospel of Luke, Mary was a young Jewish girl living in Nazareth, engaged to a man called Joseph, when a messenger from the Lord announced that she was to be the bearer of the Son of God to the world. Her response, 'Let it be to me according to your word', and her life of obedience and faithfulness have been upheld ever since as a model for all who hear and obey God's word. For this reason, in Christian tradition Mary is often described as 'the second Eve', the one who unlocks Eve's disobedience, and we find this theme recurring in many carols and hymns. We know that Mary was present at the crucifixion of Jesus, standing at the foot of the cross, and was with the apostles and others on the Day of Pentecost. According to the Gospel of John, as Jesus was dying, he commended the care of his mother to the beloved disciple.

Julian of Norwich writes about the Blessed Virgin Mary

With the same cheerful joy our good Lord looked down to his right and thereby brought to mind the place where our Lady was standing during his passion. 'Do you want to see her?' he said, saying in effect, 'I know quite well you want to see my blessed Mother, for, after myself, she is the greatest joy I can show you, and most like me and worthy of me. Of all my creation, she is the most desirable sight.' And because of his great, wonderful, unique love for this sweet maiden, his blessed Mother our Lady St Mary, he showed her to be rejoicing greatly. This is the meaning of the sweet words. It was as if he were saying, 'Do you want to see how I love her, so that you can rejoice with me in my love for her, and hers for me?' Here to understand this word further our Lord God is speaking to all who are going to be saved, as it were to all humankind in the person of one individual. He is saying, 'Can you see in her how greatly you are loved? For love of you made her so exalted, so noble, so worthy. This pleases me, and I want it to please you too.' For after himself, Mary is the most blessed of all sights.

From *Revelations of Divine Love*

Heavenly Father,
who chose Mary to bear your Son:
we thank you for her ready obedience,
for her mother's tender and watchful care,
and for her waiting and watching at the foot of the cross;
give us grace to follow her example
by offering ourselves to your service and the service of others;
through Jesus Christ our Lord. Amen.

The Annunciation of the Blessed Virgin Mary
see entry for 15 August

Anne Jane Charles Williamson d.1927

Benefactress

THE WILLIAMSONS ARE a long-established Bedfordshire family, indeed Williamson Road in Kempston was named after Anne's grandfather, the Reverend Edmund Williamson who bought Kempston Manor in the early nineteenth century. He was Rector of Campton from 1791 until 1839 and was well-known as a hunting and fishing parson of the old school. He was succeeded in the post by Anne's father, the Reverend Edmund Ryland Williamson, who was rector from 1839 until 1864. In 1878 Anne married the Reverend George Charles. They changed their surname by royal licence to Charles Williamson. Sadly George died within a few years without them having any children. Anne then devoted her time and energy to the Church and to charitable work in and around Kempston. She built St John's Almshouses, Bedford Road, in her husband's memory to provide accommodation for members of the Church of England. Before long she had moved from the manor into the central first floor flat of the almshouses and lived there until she died. In her will Anne left £8000 to build the Church of the Transfiguration in Kempston, which was consecrated in 1939.

St Augustine exhorts us to be generous

My brothers and sisters, I beg you above all else to show charity not only towards one another, but also to those who are outside our communion whether they be pagans who do not yet know Christ, Christians separated from us, those who profess their faith in the head Jesus Christ while separated from the body. Let us grieve for them, my friends, as though they were our own brothers and sisters. For that is what they are, whether they like it or not. They will only cease to be our brothers and sisters when they cease to say 'Our Father'. They claim no longer to be in fellowship with us and want to rebaptise us, saying that we do not possess what only they can truly confer. They ridicule our baptism and reject us as their brothers and sisters. But why did the prophet in Scripture tell us: 'Say to them: you are our brothers,' if not because we recognise in them what we ourselves refuse to repeat. They, by not repeating theirs, and acknowledging it as valid as our own, are saying to them: 'You are our sisters and brothers.' They may say to us: 'Why do you seek us out? Why do you want us?' And we will answer: 'Because you are our brothers and sisters.' They may say: 'Go away! We have nothing in common with you.' But we shall reply that we absolutely do have something in common: we profess one Christ; thus we ought to be united in one body under one head.

From *A Commentary on the Psalms* by Augustine

Heavenly Father,
whose Son Jesus Christ taught that it is more blessed to give than to receive:
set us free from greed and covetousness,
teach us the joy of giving and sharing
and grant that our lives may reflect your grace and generosity;
through Jesus Christ our Lord. Amen.

Henry Joseph Wood 1869–1944

Conductor and composer

———

THE PROMS (OR to give them their full title The Henry Wood Promenade Concerts) are an English institution known the world over. Their fame is due largely to Henry Wood who conducted the annual series of concerts for more than fifty years. Wood's bust is still placed centre stage at the Royal Albert Hall throughout the season of concerts. Henry Wood was born into a musical family in Barnet. He had organ lessons during his childhood and before long he was playing for church services and giving organ recitals. He studied composition, organ and piano at the Royal Academy of Music, and then took up conducting and giving singing lessons. In the mid-1890s he was employed to conduct a series of classical and light music concerts in the Queen's Hall. Tickets were offered at affordable prices and concert-goers were allowed to promenade, smoke and even eat during the concerts. In 1941, the Queen's Hall was destroyed by German bombers and the Proms were temporarily transferred to the Bedford Corn Exchange. Since then they have been held annually in the Royal Albert Hall. As a composer Wood is best known for his *Fantasia on British Sea Songs*, *Fantasia on Welsh Melodies* and *Fantasia on Scottish Melodies*. He also wrote choral works such as *St. Dorothea*, *Daisy* and *Returning the Compliment*. His dedication to music in this country was such that he turned down two posts as chief conductor to major symphony orchestras in America. Wood married Olga Michailoff in 1898. She died in 1909 and two years later Wood married his secretary, Muriel Ellen Greatrex, with whom he had two daughters. He died in Hitchin Hospital and his funeral was held in St Mary's Church in the town.

Easter by George Herbert

Rise, heart, thy lord is risen. Sing his praise
Without delays,
Who takes thee by the hand, that thou likewise
With him may'st rise:
That, as his death calcinèd thee to dust,
His life may make thee gold, and, much more, just.

Awake, my lute, and struggle for thy part
With all thy art,
The cross taught all wood to resound his name
Who bore the same.
His stretchèd sinews taught all strings what key
Is best to celebrate this most high day.

Consort, both heart and lute, and twist a song
Pleasant and long;
Or, since all music is but three parts vied
And multiplied
O let thy blessèd Spirit bear a part,
And make up our defects with his sweet art.

From *The Temple*

———

O Divine Composer,
whose praises are sung by sun, moon and stars:
may our lives as well as our voices echo their song,
give us grace to live in harmony with you and with our neighbour,
working for that day when creation will reach its fulfilment
in a perfect cadence of your loving purposes;
through Jesus Christ our Lord. Amen.

John Incent c.1480–1545

Dean of St Paul's Cathedral and founder of Berkhamsted School

———

STANDING ON THE High Street in Berkhamsted, opposite St Peter's Church, is a half timbered house, built in the year 1500, with a blue plaque mounted on the wall. This was the home of John Incent's family, and still today it is known locally as 'Dean Incent's House'. John's father, Robert, was Secretary to the Duchess of York who lived at Berkhamsted Castle; and there is a memorial brass to Robert and his wife, Katherine, in St Peter's Church. John Incent studied at both the University of Cambridge and the University of Oxford. At the age of twenty-nine he was appointed to the Chancellor's Court as an ecclesiastical lawyer. In 1512 he was ordained and some time afterwards became Master of the Hospital of St Cross in Winchester. Incent was appointed chaplain to King Henry VIII and, as a faithful servant to the Crown, he became one of Thomas Cromwell's agents, supervising the sequestration of monastic properties following the Dissolution of the Monasteries. In 1540 he was appointed Dean of St Paul's Cathedral, a position he held for five years until his death in 1545. His lasting memorial is Berkhamsted School, which he founded using money obtained from selling the lands of the Brotherhood of St John the Baptist. It received its Royal Charter in 1541 and the building was completed three years later.

Archbishop Michael Ramsey writes about forgiveness

The priest is the minister of reconciliation; and by this office he links the common life of the Church to the gospel of divine forgiveness upon which its common life depends. Now the priest today is only one among many skills and agencies designed to help people in their troubles. The psychiatrist, the doctor, the welfare officer, the marriage guidance counsellor, and many kinds of social worker bring relief to the problems with which people get entangled. The parson's monopoly has long ceased, the confessional no longer stands pre-eminent as the seat of counsel and direction. Yet amidst all the various activities for the putting right of human ills there is so often a whole dimension missing, the dimension of sin and forgiveness. It not seldom happens that psychiatry, instead of liberating the patient into the realm of moral responsibility and the issues of conscious sin and forgiveness, can substitute medicine for moral responsibility. It is this dimension of sin and forgiveness which the priest keeps alive by an office which represents the forgiving Church and the forgiving Lord Jesus. He will do this by his ministry in Confession and Absolution and by his preaching of the gospel of God's reconciliation. He will bear witness to the cost of forgiveness to the divine holiness, and he will remember that the familiar phrase in 2 Corinthians 5:20 which we translate 'the ministry of reconciliation' means 'the ministry of *the reconciliation*', the reconciliation once for all wrought on the hill of Calvary and subsequently to be applied through the centuries to every penitent heart. 'Whose sins thou dost forgive they are forgiven.'

From *The Christian Priest Today*

———

Merciful God,
who has promised forgiveness of sins
to all those who turn in penitence and faith:
in the power of the Holy Spirit
enable us to examine our lives
that we may offer to you all that is good
and repent of all that is selfish or evil:
for we ask this in the name of Jesus Christ our Lord. Amen.

Robert Bloomfield 1766–1823

Poet

——

I N A CORNER of the churchyard in the small Bedfordshire village of Campton stands the headstone of the poet Robert Bloomfield. His most famous poem, *The Farmer's Boy,* was published in 1800 thanks to the patronage of a Suffolk squire, Capel Lofft. Not only did it sell 26,000 copies within three years, but it was translated into French, Italian and Latin. The painter John Constable even quoted Bloomfield's poem as the source of inspiration for two of the paintings he exhibited in London. Bloomfield was born in Suffolk and was educated by his mother. Showing little propensity for agricultural work, he was apprenticed as a shoemaker to his brother who was working in London. One of his duties was to read aloud the newspapers in the workshop and it was this which introduced him to the poetry in *The London Magazine.* With his interest kindled, he began writing poems and, shortly after, *The Village Girl* was published. Bloomfield was fortunate to be taken under the patronage of Augustus Henry FitzRoy, the third Duke of Grafton, who granted him an annuity and found him employment. He continued to write and publish poetry and one of his poems was turned into the libretto for the opera *The Miller's Maid.* When his publisher went bankrupt Bloomfield was forced to move to Shefford, where he made a meagre living selling books. Following the death of his wife, he started to lose his eyesight and, despite the friendship and personal support of the rector, Mr Williamson, he died on this day in 1823.

O Thou, who bidst the vernal juices rise!
Thou, on whose blasts autumnal foliage flies!
Let Peace ne'er leave me, nor my heart grow cold,
Whilst life and sanity are mine to hold.
Shorn of their flow'rs that shed th' untreasur'd seed,
The withering pasture, and the fading mead,
Less tempting grown, diminish more and more,
The dairy's pride; sweet Summer's flowing store.
New cares succeed, and gentle duties press,
Where the fire-side, a school of tenderness,
Revives the languid chirp, and warms the blood
Of cold-nipt weaklings of the latter brood,
That from the shell just bursting into day,
Through yard or pond pursue their vent'rous way.

From *The Farmer's Boy* by Robert Bloomfield

Almighty God, Lord of heaven and earth,
in whom we live and move and have our being;
who doest good unto all men,
making thy sun to rise on the evil and on the good,
and sending rain on the just and on the unjust:
favourably behold us thy servants, who call upon thy name,
and send us thy blessing from heaven, in giving us fruitful seasons,
and satisfying us with food and gladness;
that both our hearts and mouths shall be continually filled with thy praise,
giving thanks to thee in thy holy church;
through Jesus Christ our Lord. Amen.

John Cosin

William Booth 1829–1912

Founder of the Salvation Army

———

WILLIAM BOOTH WAS pretty clear about a Christian's duty. It was, he said, about 'loosing the chains of injustice, freeing the captive and oppressed, sharing food and home, clothing the naked, and carrying out family responsibilities.' He practised what he preached and in 1865 he and his wife set up the Whitechapel Christian Mission in London's East End, where they provided shelter and food for the poor. Determined that it should be run as efficiently as possible, they organised themselves along military lines and soon all the workers were given uniforms and ranks. Not surprisingly, Booth became the first general. Born in Nottingham, Booth was converted in 1844 and immediately felt called to be a Methodist lay preacher. He moved to London, where he worked in a pawnbroker's shop, but in 1853 he gave up his job to devote himself full-time to his calling. When the Methodist Conference refused to give him permission to work as a full-time evangelist, he resigned and worked independently. His book *In Darkest England* was a best-seller. In it he set out his blueprint for abolishing poverty and providing employment. The Salvation Army expanded rapidly and by the time Booth died it had personnel in fifty-eight countries. Today there are Salvation Army Corps in many different places in the Diocese of St Albans including Bedford, Dunstable, Eaton Bray, Hemel Hempstead, Luton, Leighton Buzzard, Potton and Watford. For much of his life Booth was the object of criticism, for his opposition to alcohol, for using women to preach ('My best men are women') and for the exuberant worship which was characteristic of the Salvation Army. He was 'promoted to glory' on this day in 1912.

William Booth writing to his wife

I enjoyed a special season in prayer the other night. Never since I knew you have I so completely given you up to God, to do with you as he will. I felt for a few minutes an agonising desire for the will of God to be done, even though it should be crucifixion to mine. I pleaded in such a way and impelled by such motives and feelings as I know were acceptable to God. I felt myself to be the vilest thing in creation, and entreated Him with all the earnestness of my being that if he saw your union with me would injure your usefulness, or endanger your salvation, or endanger both our souls, or otherwise diminish his glory in its remotest consequences, that he would, even at any cost, avert it. I believe I was heard. It was the greatest sacrifice; the most precious, the most tender I could make. But praise the Lord I rose from my knees and have felt several times since a sweet assurance that the sacrifice, though offered and bound to the altar, need not be slain, that God's glory may be best promoted by giving my Isaac back into my bosom.

From *The Letters of William and Catherine Booth*

God of compassion, whose Son Jesus Christ was anointed
to bring good news to the poor, release to the captives,
sight to the blind, freedom for the oppressed
and to proclaim the year of the Lord's favour:
rouse your Church in the power of the Holy Spirit,
that we may share in his ministry in the world;
for we ask this for his name's sake. Amen.

John Sayer d.1682

Cook and benefactor

———

I F YOU GO into the Lady Chapel of St Peter's Church in Berkhamsted you will see an elaborate marble tomb which commemorates the life of John Sayer. His home was Berkhamsted Place, a large country house near the town. When the monarchy was restored in 1660, King Charles II appointed Sayer as his chief cook. He was a friend of the diarist Samuel Pepys, who wrote about him, 'I went with Captain Morrice at his desire into the King's Privy Kitchen to Mr. Sayres, the Master Cook, and there we had a good slice of beef or two to our breakfast, and from thence he took us into the wine cellar where, by my troth, we were very merry, and I drank too much wine, and all along had great and particular kindness from Mr. Sayres, but I drank so much wine that I was not fit for business.' Sayer died in 1682 and in his will he left £1000 to build almshouses in the High Street. The twelve rooms were to house six poor widows. They were to be given two shillings each week and fuel to keep warm. The almshouses can still be seen today and record his generosity with the words 'A gift of John Sayer, 1684.'

A meditation on the centrality of mercy for the Christian life

'Blessed are the merciful for they shall obtain mercy'. Sweet is the name of mercy, dear friends; and if the name is sweet, how much more so the reality! Yet though everyone wants to receive it, sadly not everyone lives in such a way as to merit it. Everyone wants to receive mercy: few are ready to show it to others. What incredible effrontery to want to receive something one constantly refuses to give! You must show mercy in this life if you hope to receive it in the next. And so, dear friends, since we all wish for mercy, let us make her our patroness in this age that she may free us in the life to come. There is mercy in heaven, but we attain it through the exercise of mercy on earth. This is what Scripture says: 'O Lord, your mercy is in heaven.' There are two kinds of mercy then, mercy on earth and mercy in heaven, one human, the other divine. What is human mercy like? It makes you concerned for the misery in which the poor live. What is divine mercy like? It forgives sinners. Whatever generosity human mercy shows during our life on earth divine mercy replays when we reach our heavenly country. In this world God is cold and hungry in the person of the poor, as he himself said: 'As you did it to one of the least of these my brothers and sisters, you did it to me.' God who is pleased to give from heaven, desires to receive on earth. What sort of people are we if we want to take what God gives, but refuse to give when he asks? When a poor person is hungry, Christ is in need, as he said himself: 'I was hungry and you gave me no food'.

———

From a sermon of Caesarius of Arles
Almighty God, whose Son Jesus Christ had nowhere to lay his head:
be with those who are homeless this day,
especially the poor, the elderly and the asylum seeker.
Forgive our apathy and rouse us to support all your children
that they may have security and shelter;
We ask this through Jesus Christ our Lord. Amen.

Peter Bulkeley 1583–1659

Puritan minister

———

PETER BULKELEY MUST be the only Anglican clergyman from Bedfordshire who is the ancestor of a President of the United States of America. His famous descendant is former president George Bush. Bulkeley's father, Edward, was Rector of All Saints Odell, Bedfordshire. After studying at St John's College, Cambridge, Peter succeeded his father in 1610, and spent the next twenty-four years in Odell as the parish priest. In 1613 he married Jane Allen at Goldington and they had nine children. Jane died in 1626 and in 1635 he married Grace Chetwode with whom he had another four children. In the early years of the seventeenth century there were passionate disputes between Puritans like Bulkeley and the 'Caroline Divines', such as the Archbishop, William Laud. When in 1634 the Archbishop made a visitation Bulkeley refused to wear a surplice or make the sign of the cross and Laud suspended him. Consequently Bulkeley decided to emigrate to Massachusetts. In 1635, Bulkeley and Simon Willard bought land from a tribe of native Indians and founded a town which they named Concord. He was to become the first Christian minister of the small community. He died there in 1659. Bulkeley's most famous book was the *Gospel Covenant* which was published in London in 1646.

Evelyn Underhill, the writer and spiritual director, writes about the Church

The old Flemish painters loved to represent the Church as a vast cathedral, with many side chapels opening from one great nave. In the centre of that stood the Crucifix. In the surrounding chapels those Sacraments were dispensed through which the Incarnate Charity pours itself out to purify, feed, restore, and at last transform the feeble lives of men; dependent on that ceaseless self-giving, as branches upon the Vine. That was a wonderful image of what Christianity really is; the manifestation in and through men of the self-spending Charity of God, and the binding together in one Divine Society of all who have been touched by that supernatural generosity and depend on its life-giving life. Thinking of this, we are no longer surprised that the Creed which once ended by stating its belief in the Spirit, should go on to insist on belief in the Body, the Temple, that Spirit indwells; asserting the social and organic character of real spirituality, endorsing its authority and repudiating the claims of the religious individualist. 'I believe One Catholic and Apostolic Church.' We must believe someone. We believe, then, the united voice of Christendom; its statements about Reality, as given in its Scriptures, its Liturgy, its Sacraments, and by its Saints. We make its Creeds, its solemn pronouncements regarding the essentials of Faith, our standard, trust them, take them seriously: not as a particular way of dealing with life – something that happens to appeal to us – but as *the* way of dealing with life. Though the architecture be old-fashioned and the lighting defective, here God in His humility tabernacles among men.

From *The School of Charity*

Heavenly Father,
we thank you for adopting us as your children
and making us part of your family, the Church:
give us humility to honour one another,
patience towards those we find difficult
and love for those with whom we disagree;
through Jesus Christ our Lord. Amen.

Jane Cart 17th–18th century

Benefactress

———

JANE CART WAS the youngest of eight children born to Thomas Chew, a haberdasher from London, and Elizabeth Marche from Dunstable. In 1684 she married James Cart who was a distiller and merchant. They had nine children, all of whom died before Jane, and then in 1706 her husband died. Six years later Jane's brother, William, died and he left his estate to Cart, her sister Frances and her nephew Thomas Aynscombe. Together they decided to build Chew's School, providing free education for poor children from Church of England families in Dunstable. During her lifetime, Cart inherited a great deal of money and property from members of her family, including two public houses. She used it for charitable purposes, setting up a trust for the poor and funding apprenticeships for pupils of Chew's School. She also paid for the construction of the Cart Almshouses. Built in 1723, the almshouses comprised six brick-built houses. They were to be allocated to poor women of Dunstable who were members of the Church of England. Cart is buried, as she requested in her will, in the Priory Church, next to William Chew, her brother. The Jane Cart Trust still makes charitable grants today.

Jean-Pierre Camus records a dialogue about loving God

Once I asked Blessed François how one may best become perfect. 'You must love God with your whole heart,' he answered, 'and your neighbour as yourself.' 'I did not ask in what perfection consists,' I replied, 'but how to attain it?' 'Charity,' he repeated, 'is both the means and the end, the one and only way by which we can attain that perfection which in truth is charity itself. It was St Paul who said: "I will show you a more excellent way"; and then he elaborates more fully upon charity. It is the one way to God, the only truth, the only life of the soul, for it carries us out of the death of sin into the life of grace. It nourishes faith and hope. And just as the soul is the life of the body, so charity is the life of the soul.' 'I am aware of that,' I said, 'But I want to know *how* one is to love God with one's whole heart and one's neighbour as oneself?' Again he answered the same: 'We must love God with our whole heart and our neighbour as ourselves.' 'I am still just where I was,' I rejoined. 'Tell me how I may acquire such love.' 'The best way, the shortest and easiest way of loving God with one's whole heart – is simply to love Him wholly and heartily!' This is the only answer he would give.

From *The Spirit of St Francis de Sales*

Dear Jesus, help us to spread your fragrance everywhere we go.
Flood our souls with your Spirit and life.
Penetrate and possess our whole being so utterly
that our lives may only be a radiance of yours.
Shine through us and be so in us that every soul
we come in contact with may feel your presence in our soul.
Let them look up and see no longer us but only Jesus.
Stay with us and then we shall begin to shine as you shine,
so to shine as to be light to others.
The light, O Jesus, will be all from you. Amen.

From a prayer by Mother Teresa

Owen d.684

Bishop and saint

———

WHAT IS THE connection between the Normandy city of Rouen in France and the small Bedfordshire village of Bromham? The answer is St Owen, to whom the fine church in Bromham is dedicated. In past centuries there were a number of churches dedicated to Owen but it is thought that this is now the only church in England to be named in his honour. Owen (sometimes spelt Ouen) was born in Sancy, in what is now the Province of Picardy in northern France. He was sent to the courts of the Frankish kings Chlotar II and Dagobert I and eventually was appointed Chancellor. He founded the abbey at Rebais, was ordained, and around the year 640 he was made Bishop of Rouen. He was renowned as a zealous bishop, who cared for the poor and was committed to reforming the Church. At the same time he was known to be a wise counsellor to the Merovingian rulers. He wrote a biography of St Eligius. He died on this day in 684 and is buried in Rouen.

Olegario González de Cardedal asks 'What does a bishop do?'

What Christ is in his divinity for all men, that should the bishop be to all his diocese, both believers and unbelievers. Three avenues are open to the bishop if he is to succeed in his immense task. These are: teaching and prophecy in proclaiming the word of the gospel; priestly action in celebrating the sacrament of the faith; pastoral work by giving his life for the service of others. The best definition of a bishop is therefore the etymological one. A bishop is one who, representing Christ, 'watches over' and 'cares for' the gospel and the Church. Furthermore, he cares for all those who have not heard the gospel nor been welcomed as part of it, as well as for those who have already received the gospel and live in communion with the Church. The figure of Jesus as 'pastor and bishop of souls,' will be the only rule of life for the bishop in his ministry to sinner and saint; in the celebration of the holy mysteries; in the conduct of daily life. He can be described as witness, vicar and ambassador of Christ, bearer of the gospel, overseer of the Church of God, doctor, judge, interpreter of the Holy Scripture, pastor and father. At the same time he is called to be the actual and authorised representative of the one gospel and of the one Christ in one place, and therefore the basis of unity, the head and pastor of his local church. He could not take up nor bear such a task alone. It must be borne in union with all those who belong to the Church and above all in co-operation with all those who are joined together in it and in the 'ecclesial ministry' of priest and deacon.

From *Bishops But What Kind?* edited by Peter Moore

———

Almighty and everlasting God,
the only worker of great marvels,
send down upon our bishops and other pastors
and all congregations committed to their care
the spirit of your saving grace;
and that they may truly please you,
pour upon them the continual dew of your blessing.
Grant this, O Lord,
for the honour of our advocate and mediator, Jesus Christ. Amen.

A prayer for bishops and other pastors from *Common Worship*

Ronald Arbuthnott Knox 1888–1957

Priest, novelist and broadcaster

————

A LTHOUGH RONALD KNOX is chiefly remembered as a writer, he also holds an unusual place in the history of broadcasting. In 1926 he presented a radio programme called *Broadcasting from the Barricades*. This dramatic presentation contained live reports of a revolution taking place in London, during which listeners heard that the Houses of Parliament had been destroyed. Broadcast on a weekend when snow prevented the delivery of newspapers, it caused widespread consternation in listeners who thought it was reporting actual events. It is likely that this programme was the inspiration for Orson Welles' 1938 broadcast *War of the Worlds*. The son of a Bishop of Manchester, Ronald Knox was educated at Eton and Balliol College, Oxford. He was such an outstanding classicist that after he graduated he was elected to a fellowship at Trinity College, Oxford. Ordained as an Anglican in 1912, Knox was appointed the college chaplain. However, in 1917 he converted to Roman Catholicism and a year later was ordained as a Roman Catholic priest. He recounts his spiritual journey in two books, *Apologia* and *A Spiritual Aeneid*. For seven years he taught at St Edmund's College, Ware – a seminary in Hertfordshire – before returning to Oxford as the Roman Catholic chaplain. Knox was a prolific writer. The bulk of his writing was on religious themes, in books such as *The Belief of Catholics* and *The Gospel in Slow Motion*. However, he also wrote satirical essays and detective novels. He used his language skills in his translations of the Vulgate Bible, *The Imitation of Christ*, and the autobiography of Thérèse of Lisieux into English.

Ronald Knox writes about the nature of faith

Faith comes in to encourage us, when we are hesitating to make an affirmation; and that is why we can say that faith is a gift – there is a bestowal of grace which confirms our wills, and makes it possible for us to assert, and to go on asserting, truths of religion over which, if we were left to our indolent and cowardly selves, we might be tempted to suspend judgment. That is why faith can be exercised in equal measure, and is needed in equal measure, by a trained theologian and by a simple peasant. If faith were a mere affair of the intellect, then the theologian would need a greater measure of faith, or at least a different kind of faith, as compared with the peasant. But it is not so; either needs the same gift, either has the same moral responsibility – that of asserting positively what he sees to be true, and identifying himself whole-heartedly with the assertion. The theologian understands the doctrine with all its niceties and interpretations, as far as it is possible for the human mind to understand such things; the peasant understands it in terms of his own thought, using crude analogies and words inadequate to the situation. But either needs, and either might lose, the gift of faith which transforms, for him, a mere intellectual conclusion into a conviction which is really part of himself.

From a sermon 'Faith Lost and Found' in *In Soft Garments*

————

Gracious God, teach us to trust
when life is good and we forget you,
when the going is rough and we doubt you,
when the busyness of life absorbs us
and when ambition and pride obsess us;
that whatever comes our way, we may walk in simple trust;
through Jesus Christ our Lord. Amen.

William Barringer 16th–17th century

Benefactor

———

WE KNOW LITTLE about William Barringer's life, but we do know a great deal about the good he did by bequeathing land and almshouses, which for nearly three hundred years have helped the people of the Bedfordshire village of Stevington. The son of Thomas Barringer, William held land in Stevington called Fishpond Close, forty-two acres of meadow and a cottage. We do not know the date of Barringer's death but his will is dated 1632. In it he is described as 'William Barringer of St Faith's London, stationer.' He left the residue of his estate for 'the building and making of…almshouses of poor men'. The almshouses were built in 1634. However, it seems that not all of Barringer's wishes were carried out, for in 1639 George Daniel, the Vicar of Stevington, and his churchwardens brought an action against the executors of his will, claiming that they had 'combined together to make the intention of so pious and charitable a work to come to none effect'. The result was that the executors had to pay over £400 which was to be used to purchase land to endow the almshouses and support the residents. Records reveal that in 1651 the charity also owned land in Pavenham. The five almshouses were rebuilt in 1841 and they are still run by the Barringer Charity.

Octavia Hill, famous for her charitable work in providing housing for the poor, writes about her work

The subject of dwellings for the poor is attracting so much attention, that an account of a small attempt to improve them may be interesting to many readers, especially as the plan adopted is one which has answered pecuniarily, and which, while it might be undertaken by private individuals without much risk, would bring them into close and healthy communication with their hard-working neighbours. Two years ago I first had an opportunity of carrying out the plan I had long contemplated, that of obtaining possession of houses to be let in weekly tenements to the poor. That the spiritual elevation of a large class depended to a considerable extent on sanitary reform was, I considered, proved; but I was equally certain that sanitary improvement itself depended upon educational work among grown-up people. I purchased three houses in my own immediate neighbourhood…It should be observed that well-built houses were chosen, but they were in a dreadful state of dirt and neglect. The repairs required were mainly of a superficial and slight character: slight in regard to expense – vital as to health and comfort. The place swarmed with vermin; the papers, black with dirt, hung in long strips from the walls; the drains were stopped, the water supply out of order. All these things were put in order, but no new appliances of any kind were added, as we had determined that our tenants should wait for these until they had proved themselves capable of taking care of them.

From *Homes of the London Poor*

———

Lord Jesus Christ, who had nowhere to lay your head,
we pray for the homeless and destitute:
protect those who are living on the streets,
bless those providing food and shelter for them
and help us as a society to provide housing for those in need;
for we ask it in the name of Jesus Christ. Amen.

Ellen Mansfield 1908–98

Church member

———

ELLEN MANSFIELD WAS a baby when the new church of St Cuthbert's in Rye Park was consecrated in 1908. She was not baptised until she was three and in that year the congregation was thriving, with ninety-one communicants on Easter Day, a choir of thirty-eight men, and seventeen Sunday School teachers with responsibility for more than two hundred children. The church had a Mothers' Union, a Scripture Union and ran Bible classes, a football team, a dispensary for health care and a 'coal club', helping people save for their winter fuel. In 1927 Ellen was confirmed and joined the Girls' Friendly Society, which in those days had branches in most Anglican parishes. However, Ellen's involvement with others was not limited to the Church. In her thirties, with another war looming, Ellen became a parish councillor, and during the war was an Air Raid Precautions (ARP) warden, spotting enemy bombers from the tower of St Cuthbert's. Her air raid shelter at home was an iron bathtub in the back garden. Like many of her generation, when so many of the young men had been killed in the Great War, Ellen never married. For many years she was a member of the church choir and taught in the Sunday School, so when St Cuthbert's ran its first crèche in 1967 she was put in charge. Ellen died in 1998, having devoted much of her life to St Cuthbert's. She, and many others like her, represent those Christians whose stories are seldom told but who are the backbone of the mission and ministry of the Church.

Evelyn Underhill writes about the nature of prayer

The first thing this vast sense of God does for us, is to deliver us from the imbecilities of religious self-love and self-assurance; and sink our little souls in the great life of the race, in and upon which this One God in His mysterious independence is always working, whether we notice it or not. When that sense of His unique reality gets dim and stodgy, we must go back and begin there once more; saying with the Psalmist, 'All my fresh springs are in thee.' Man, said Christ, is nourished by every word that proceeds out of the mouth of God. Not the words we expect, or persuade ourselves that we have heard; but those unexpected words He really utters, sometimes by the mouths of the most unsuitable people, sometimes through apparently unspiritual events, sometimes secretly within the soul. Therefore seeking God, and listening to God, is an important part of the business of human life: and this is the essence of prayer. We do something immense, almost unbelievable, when we enter that world of prayer, for then we deliberately move out towards that transcendent Being whom Christianity declares to be the one Reality: a Reality revealed to us in three ways as a Creative Love, a Rescuing Love, and an Indwelling, all-pervading Love, and in each of those three ways claiming and responding to our absolute trust. Prayer is the give and take between the little souls of men and that three-fold Reality.

From *The School of Charity*

———

Heavenly Father,
we thank you for the witness of those Christian men and women
whose stories will never be written in a book or portrayed in a film:
we bless you for the example of their lives,
for their acts of kindness and charity
and for their words of encouragement and hope;
strengthen us by your Holy Spirit and through the grace of the sacraments
may we follow their example in holy living and compassionate caring;
for we ask this in the name of Jesus Christ our Lord. Amen.

John Browne d. c.1736

Rector of Wallington

———

W E KNOW LITTLE about of the life and ministry of the Reverend John Browne who was Rector of Wallington in Hertfordshire for over twenty years from around 1714 until 1736. However, Browne is typical of many clergy in the eighteenth century in his concern for the provision of education for children in his parish. In his will, dated 6 July 1736, he left £100 in trust, specifying that the rectors and churchwardens of the parish should use 'the interest thereof to be paid by them to a mistress or dame for teaching the children of all the day labourers of Wallington and instructing them in church catechism, without fee or reward'. He also left £20 so that the interest could be used to help poor people each Easter Monday. The moneys were invested and in 1868 some of the capital was used to buy a cottage to house the teacher. In 1904 the charities became known as 'Browne's Educational Foundation' and 'Browne's Charity for the Poor'. The school closed in 1939.

Carlo Caretto explores the connection between faith and action

We say we want faith, but we don't want to open our purses to the poor. We claim we are looking for Christ, but we make no effort to change our lives, even though we can see how mistaken they are. I feel we must give the lie to the man who says, 'I'm looking for God, but I can't find him!' Let him try to do everything in the truth, free from the demon of pride and the suffocating density of egoism. Let every trace of racism be rooted out, let every man be welcomed as a brother, and…you will see, you will see! Live *love*. Act *truth*. Honour *life*. And it will be God within you whom you live, act, and honour. God will not come to you because you have been 'good'. He was already there. He has always been coming and always is coming. But now you can see Him because you have purified your eyes, softened your heart, and stooped down. Remember! He was already there, He was already there, He was already there. The only difficulty was that you were unable to see him.

From *The God Who Comes*

O Lord,
who though thou wast rich
yet for our sakes didst become poor,
and has promised in thy holy gospel
that whatsoever is done to the least of thy brethren
thou wilt receive as done to thee:
give us grace, we humbly beseech thee,
to be ever willing and ready to minister,
as thou enablest us, to the needs of others,
and to extend the blessings of thy kingdom
over all the world to thy praise and glory,
who art God over all, blessed for ever. Amen.

St Augustine

Minnie Kingsley c.1841–1929
and Constance Demain Saunders 1871–1955

Mother and daughter: gardeners and benefactresses

———

THE DEMAIN SAUNDERS family has played a significant role in the life of the small Hertfordshire village of Brickendon. Henry Wilson Demain Saunders came to the village in 1874 when he leased Brickendon Grange. Over the next few years he bought up much of the property in the village and in 1883 built Fanshaws, a large country house. In 1871 Henry married his second wife, Minnie Edenborough, at Waltham Cross and ten months later they had their first and only child, Constance. After Henry's death Minnie and Constance alternated between living in Fanshaws and Bourne Orchard, until in 1892 Minnie married Arthur Kingsley. The family were generous benefactors. They gave land and money to build the village chapel in 1932. In 1944 Constance gave the village hall and recreation grounds to the local community. She was also a magistrate, school governor, chairman of the parish council and published several articles on genealogy. Minnie and Constance were passionate gardeners and made detailed records in a diary called *Our Garden Book*. Poignantly, among the descriptions of the garden, Constance records her mother's death: *Minnie Kingsley my dear mother who made this garden and who stands in the midst of it here, died on Wednesday morning the twenty eighth of August 1929. She walked in this garden in the late evening of August the twenty sixth, and saw the white roses there.*

Bishop Lancelot Andrewes preaches about Jesus the gardener

The risen Christ comes unknown, stands by Mary Magdalene, and she little thought it had been he. Not only not knew him, but misknew him, took him for the gardener. Tears will dim the sight, and it was not yet scarce day, and she seeing one, and not knowing what any one should make in the ground so early but he that dressed it, she might well mistake. But it was more than so; her eyes were not holden only that she did not know him, but over and beside he did appear in some such shape as might resemble the gardener whom she took him for. Proper enough it was, it fitted well the time and place, this person. The time, it was the spring; the place, it was the garden: that place is most in request at that time, for that place and time a gardener doth well. Yet Mary did not mistake in taking him for a gardener; though she might seem to err in some sense, yet in some other she was in the right. For in a sense, and a good sense, Christ may well be said to be a gardener, and indeed is one. A gardener he is. The first, the fairest garden that ever was, paradise, he was the gardener, for it was of his planting. And ever since it is he as God makes all our gardens green, sends us yearly the spring, and all the herbs and flowers we then gather; and neither Paul with his planting, nor Apollos with his watering, could do any good without him. So he is a gardener in that sense.

From a sermon preached before King James I at Whitehall on Easter Day 1620

God of the Universe, who created our planet and saw that it was very good:
awaken in us a sense of wonder, and renew our delight in its beauty;
give us respect for all you have created
that we may hand it onto our children for the good of all;
through Jesus Christ our Lord. Amen.

Henry Aylmer Skelton 1884–1959

Rector, archdeacon and bishop

———

HENRY SKELTON WAS educated at Felsted School in Essex and graduated from Keble College, Oxford, in 1908. He spent a year at the newly-opened Bishop's College, Cheshunt, in Hertfordshire before being ordained to a title at Chertsey in 1910. Following a second curacy at St Barnabas, Epsom, Skelton was appointed as Vicar of Mentmore and chaplain to the Earl of Rosebery. In 1922 he took up a post as curate of St Mary's Cathedral, Auckland, New Zealand and a year later moved to become Rector of North Yorke Peninsula Mission. Skelton returned to England in 1924 and ministered as Rector of St George's, Toddington. Within three years he moved to be Sub-Dean of the Cathedral and Abbey Church of St Alban. From there he became Archdeacon of St Albans and in 1939 he was consecrated Bishop of Bedford in Westminster Abbey. In 1942 he was translated to be Bishop of Lincoln at which point he was also made a Doctor of Divinity. He retired in 1946 and died on this day in 1959.

How bishops are to defend and pass on the faith

Bishops are also to be upholders of the faith. Sometimes this is interpreted in a negative way, as guardian of the faith in some medieval manner – a bishop with a pike and a halberd in his hand rather than a crozier and a blessing. The faith, however, is something which needs to be defended as well as proclaimed. There is such a thing as orthodoxy, right teaching, just as there is such a thing as wrong teaching, heresy. Heresies abound as much today as they did in the times of the apostles. The proclamation of the faith is one of the basic ministries of the bishop – the true faith of Jesus Christ as handed down by his family, the Church. From this there are deviations, there are misinterpretations – 'Councils have been known to err.' But it would also seem that in all minds of leadership a measure of discipline is required. Leadership in whatever sphere it is exercised requires a surrender of personal liberty. It may mean, perhaps it does, that if a bishop is to exercise his ministry as an upholder of the faith, he may be required to suspend his academic ventures as a speculative theologian. For a bishop is to edify, to build up; and there are too many theological demolition contractors in the world today.

From *Bishops But What Kind?* edited by Peter Moore

Gracious Father,
we humbly beseech thee for thy universal church.
Fill it with all truth, in all truth with all peace.
Where it is corrupt, purge it;
and where it is in error, direct it;
where it is superstitious, rectify it;
where anything is amiss, reform it;
where it is right, strengthen and confirm it;
where it is in want, furnish it;
where it is divided and rent asunder,
make up the breaches therefore,
O thou holy one of Israel.

William Laud

John Bunyan 1628–88

Writer and preacher

———

THE BUNYAN FAMILY originally came from Pulloxhill, although John Bunyan was born near Elstow, in a place now called Bunyan's End. As a young man he worked as a tinker, one of the lowliest of occupations. In 1644 he enlisted in the New Model Army and served at the garrison in Newport Pagnell. In his autobiographical book *Grace Abounding* Bunyan claims that as a young man he led a sinful life of swearing, dancing and bell-ringing. He came under the influence of John Gifford, the minister of St John's Church in Bedford, and was baptised. Shortly afterwards he began public preaching. He was arrested for preaching on several occasions, most notably at Eaton Socon and Harlington, and was famously imprisoned in Bedford Gaol. In 1672 Bunyan became pastor of St John's Church, Bedford. He also established a church in Mill Street, Bedford, which is now a Baptist church known as Bunyan Meeting. Bunyan wrote his most famous book, *The Pilgrim's Progress*, during his periods of imprisonment. He was a prolific writer, producing about sixty books and tracts. Bunyan married twice. He and his first wife had four children and he also had two children by his second wife, Elizabeth. He died on this day in 1688 in Holborn and is buried in the cemetery at Bunhill Fields in London.

Christian's pilgrimage described

I see myself now at the end of my journey, my toilsome days are ended. I am going now to see that head that was crowned with thorns, and that face that was spit upon for me. I have formally lived by hearsay and faith; but now I go where I shall live by sight, and shall be with him in whose company I delight myself. I have loved to hear my Lord spoken of; and wherever I have seen the print of his shoe in the earth, there I have coveted to set my foot too. His name has been to me as a civet-box; yea, sweeter than all perfumes. His voice to me has been most sweet, and his countenance I have more desired than they have most desired the light of the sun. His word I did use to gather for my food, and for antidotes against my faintings. 'He has held me, and hath kept me from mine iniquities; yea, my steps hath he strengthened in his way.' Now, while he was thus in discourse, his countenance changed, his strong man bowed under him; and after he had said, Take me, for I come unto thee, he ceased to be seen of them. But glorious it was to see how the open region was filled with horses and chariots, with trumpeters and pipers, with singers and players on stringed instruments, to welcome the pilgrims as they went up, and followed one another in at the beautiful gate of the city.

From *The Pilgrim's Progress* by John Bunyan

———

Who would true valour see
let him come hither;
one here will constant be,
come wind, come weather.
There's no discouragement,
shall make him once relent,
his first avow'd intent,
To be a pilgrim. Amen.

John Bunyan

Giles 8th century

Hermit

————

LITTLE IS KNOWN of St Giles beyond the fact that he was a hermit of outstanding holiness who died around the year AD 710 in Provence. Like many of the early Christian monastics, he lived a life of solitude given to prayer. Later in life, he founded a monastery under the Benedictine Rule in a wooded valley now called, in his honour, Saint-Gilles-du-Gard. The monastery's proximity to Arles, one of the most important towns in medieval Gaul, resulted in it becoming a famous resting-place on the pilgrimage routes both to Santiago de Compostela (the Way of St James) and to the Holy Land. Returning pilgrims and Crusaders brought back stories of the saint, including his care for the wounded and those crippled by disease, as a result of which Giles became the patron saint of disabled people, and particularly of those suffering from leprosy. In medieval Europe, those who suffered from leprosy were forbidden to enter towns and cities, and often congregated in settlements on the edge of major populations, or close to trading routes. The churches built to meet their needs were regularly dedicated to St Giles, the most famous of which is St Giles-without-Cripplegate in London. In the Diocese of St Albans no less than four medieval churches are dedicated in his honour: Totternhoe, South Mymms, Wyddial and Codicote. Behind their dedication may be glimpsed the world of our forebears, because it is possible that these churches were originally built to care for settlements of handicapped and disabled people, or perhaps even a colony of those suffering from leprosy.

Roy McCloughry and Wayne Morris discuss the dignity that God gives to all people

At many times in the history of the world, disabled people have had their humanity called into question. Sometimes this has been done explicitly such as through support of eugenics. At other times it has been more subtle with disabled people being treated as second-class citizens and being marginalised from the community. Yet the creation narrative states that we are all without exception made in the image of God. If this means anything it must mean that each person is worthy of respect and dignity because each person has been made by God to convey something unique about God to the world. It says something about the high degree of worth that God attaches to each human being regardless of race, religion, orientation or ability. The idea that we are all made in the image of God is also an invitation. It invites us to discover that image in each other. It poses us a challenge to treat people as if they are made in the image of God rather than anything less. There are many contexts in which this is forgotten, whether it be in the treatment of prisoners of war, the treatment of 'bogus' asylum seekers or even those with severe learning disabilities. It is easy to neglect the invitation to explore the ways in which the other person is made in God's image. This statement and this invitation are essential insights in a world that is made for relationship.

From *Making a World of Difference*

————

Everlasting God
whose servant Giles ministered to the sick and disabled
with gentleness and compassion:
give us grace to perceive your image in all people,
treating them with dignity and respect,
for the honour of him who died and rose for us,
your Son, our Saviour, Jesus Christ. Amen.

Henry Spencer Moore 1898–1986

Sculptor and artist

———

H ENRY MOORE'S FATHER was an engineer who worked in the Yorkshire pits. Not wanting his sons to follow him down the mines, he determined that they should receive a good education. Moore's artistic ability was evident at an early age and when he was just eleven he resolved to become a sculptor, against the advice of his parents. He won scholarships to Castleford Secondary School, to Leeds School of Art (where he first met Barbara Hepworth) and, in 1921, to the Royal College of Art in London. He was later to spend seven years teaching at the college before moving to a post at the Chelsea School of Art where he was Head of the Department of Sculpture. He married the artist Irina Radetsky and they had a daughter, Mary. Moore was a modernist sculptor who preferred to work in bronze and marble. His works were abstract and many of them were based on the human form. His first large public bronze, *Family Group*, was produced in 1950 and is sited in Stevenage. Today, his sculptures are found in many different parts of Europe and America. Some of these are in churches and cathedrals including the *Circular Altar* at St Stephen's Walbrook in London, and *Mother and Child* in St Paul's Cathedral. Moore used his wealth to endow the Henry Moore Foundation which is based at Perry Green, near Much Hadham in Hertfordshire, where he lived and worked from 1940 until his death.

Henry Moore describes one of his sculptures

I began thinking of the Madonna and Child for St. Matthew's by considering in what ways a Madonna and Child differs from a carving of just a 'Mother and Child' – that is, by considering how in my opinion, religious art differs from secular art…It's not easy to describe in words what this difference is, except by saying in general terms that the Madonna and Child should have an austerity and a nobility, and some touch of grandeur (even hieratic aloofness) which is missing in the everyday 'Mother and Child' idea. Of the sketches and models I have done, the one chosen has, I think, a quiet dignity and gentleness. I have tried to give a sense of complete easiness and repose, as though the Madonna could stay in that position for ever (as, being in stone, she will have to do). The Madonna is seated on a low bench, so that the angle formed between her nearly upright body and her legs is somewhat less than a right angle, and in this angle of her lap, safe and protected, sits the Infant…The Madonna's head is turned to face the direction from which the statue is first seen, in walking down the aisle, whereas one gets the front view of the Infant's head when standing directly in front of the statue…In sculpture, which is related to architecture, actual life-size is always confusing, and as St Matthew's is a large church, spacious and big in scale too, the Madonna and Child is slightly over life-size.

From *Church of St Matthew, Northampton, 1893–1943*

———

Gracious God,
who have revealed yourself to us in human form:
we thank you for the inspiration and gifts of sculptors;
may their art broaden our horizons, stimulate our imaginations
and draw us more deeply to praise and worship;
through Jesus Christ our Lord. Amen.

Mother Jane 1927–95

Mother General of the Community of the Sisters of the Love of God

———

FOR SOME YEARS, Jane was Sister-in-Charge of one of the daughter houses of the Community of the Sisters of the Love of God at Boxmoor, Hemel Hempstead. This Anglican community of nuns, rooted in the Carmelite tradition of contemplative prayer, had been founded in 1906. Originally based in a small house in East Oxford, the community moved to a new site in Fairacres Road in Oxford in 1911. As the number of Sisters grew so new buildings were commissioned, including a large chapel. Daughter houses were opened, including one at Boxmoor in 1928, known as the Convent of St Mary and the Angels. The house closed in 2005. The community also had daughter houses at Burwash in Sussex, and Bede House at Staplehurst in Kent, together with a number of hermit Sisters, including one on Bardsey Island. Before she entered the religious life, Jane worked as a librarian in the Bank of England. She joined the community in 1956 at the age of twenty-nine. In 1973 she was elected Mother General, a position she held for fifteen years until 1988. Jane was a generous person of wide sympathies. Self-effacing, wise, approachable, down-to-earth, Jane brought the holy within the reach of the ordinary. Archbishop Robert Runcie said of her, 'There is a streak of natural scepticism in her character which makes her words of faith and fortitude still accessible to those who find it hard to believe'. She died in 1995 on the Feast of St Patrick.

Sister Jane writes about the Christian journey

First and foremost, we are a pilgrim people…We cannot settle down to the comfortable; we must always be moving on, and always exposed: at the mercy of God, and in that mercy finding all we need. This involves being in close touch with our contemporary world at a level below conscious knowledge of events – though I believe that such knowledge is in fact something required of the majority of us: receiving information can be costly, and if we accept this it will not distract our Godward attention. But much more important is a right understanding of Father Gilbert Shaw's maxim: 'We are a microcosm of the macrocosm.' Our community mirrors the world in miniature. We contain within and among ourselves all the potential forces for good and evil that are in humanity, and it is for us to be open to the Spirit so that He can work through us to draw humankind to the full measure of the image and likeness of God. Our experience of the sorrows and happiness of the human condition is underpinned by 'perpetual gladness', because, if our only hope is in God, it cannot be shaken by what seems to us tragedy and disaster for others and for ourselves.

From *Loving God Whatever*

———

Teach us, good Lord, to view our life as a pilgrimage of grace,
that we may seek you in every face, and listen for you in every voice.
Teach us to be attentive to your will, open and expectant, receptive and obedient.
Teach us to be still, and to move into that deeper communion
which is your gift and your will for us;
through Jesus Christ our Lord. Amen.

Walter de Standon 13th century

Prior of Beadlow

———

IN 1233 WALTER became the conventual prior of Beadlow Priory situated just outside Clophill, a few miles south of Bedford. It had been founded as a Benedictine Community in the middle of the twelfth century by Robert D'Albini. It is likely that a number of monks came from Millbrook Priory, which had been dissolved in 1143, to establish the new priory in Beadlow. It was a daughter house of the Abbey at St Albans. Over the next few decades a number of the priors were local men, such as John of Stopsley (elected 1285), John of Stagsden (transferred 1296), Gregory of Saint Albans (elected 1302) and Richard of Hertford (elected 1312). Throughout most of its history the priory was financially weak and it eventually closed in 1428, when the remaining monks joined the community at St Albans. Today there are no monastic buildings to be seen, although the site was excavated in the 1960s when the foundations of the priory were exposed.

Columbanus extols the virtue of humility

Monks must everywhere beware of a proud independence and learn true humility as they obey without murmur or hesitation, by which, according to the word of the Lord, the yoke of Christ may be sweet to them and his burden light. Otherwise while they are learning the humility of Christ, they will not feel the sweetness of his yoke or the lightness of his burden. For humility is the response of the soul when wearied with vices and effort, its only refuge from so many evils, and insofar as it is drawn to consideration of this from so many errant and empty things without, to that extent it enjoys repose and recuperation within, so that even bitter things are sweet to it and things which it previously found difficult and demanding it now feels to be plain and easy. Mortification too, which is intolerable to the proud and hard-hearted, becomes the comfort of those who take pleasure only in what is humble and gentle. But we should realise that no one can perfectly enjoy either this joy of martyrdom or any other benefit that follows unless he has paid particular attention to not being found unready. For if, along with this aim, he has wishes to pursue or to nourish any of his desires, both entirely preoccupied and thrown into confusion by these intrusions, he will not always be able to follow thankfully where the commandment leads, nor can someone who is stirred up and lacking in gratitude act as he should. Thus there are three ways of mortification: not to argue back in mind, not to speak with an unbridled tongue, not to go wherever we wish. It demands that we should always say to a senior monk, however unwelcome his instructions, 'Not as I will, but as you will.'

From a Rule for Monks in *Celtic Spirituality* by O. Davies

———

Lord, you have undertaken to repay many times over your servants
who give up brothers or sisters, father, mother or children,
land or houses, for the sake of your name.
We praise you for all who have sought God,
following the way of St Benedict
in lives of obedience, stability and conversion of life.
Bless their communities, their worship and their service;
increase the number of those who heed your call to join them;
granting them in this life the fulfilling of your promises,
and in the world to come life everlasting. Amen.

Based on a prayer by John Poulton

Henry Frank Johnston 1834–1908

Vicar of High Wych

———

EDUCATED AT ETON and Trinity College, Cambridge, Henry Frank Johnston initially entered the army in 1856 following his graduation. For two years he served as a junior officer in the Royal Dragoon Guards, before resigning his commission to study for the ministry. Following his ordination, he served a curacy in Richmond, Surrey, before moving to Hertfordshire as Vicar of St James, High Wych, Sawbridgeworth. This was followed by a period as Rector of Chelmsford, an important living in the fast-growing county town of Essex. It was the parish church of St Mary the Virgin over which Johnston presided that would subsequently be chosen to become the Cathedral of the new Diocese of Chelmsford when it was created in 1914. Johnston was an able priest, and his success in Chelmsford led to his appointment first as Archdeacon of Essex, and then as Suffragan Bishop of Colchester in 1895, a position he held until his death in 1908.

A reflection on the origins of the Church

The society of this new and blessed people began in the apostles, whom Christ the anointed Saviour of the world did choose to be his followers, and to be witnesses of all the things he did and suffered among sinful men. To these our Saviour Christ after his resurrection gave most ample commission to teach the nations and people of the world, and to preach repentance and remission of sins in his name, opening their understanding that they might understand the Scriptures, that so it behoved him to suffer, and to rise again the third day, whereof they were witnesses. Yet commanded he them to tarry in Jerusalem, till they were endued with power from above, which was performed unto them in the feast of Pentecost, when all they that looked for the redemption of Israel by this anointed Saviour, and had been his followers, after his departure from them and returning from the heavens, were assembled into one place, and suddenly heard as it were the noise of a mighty and rushing wind, and there appeared unto them cloven tongues like fire, and sat upon every one of them, and they were all filled with the Holy Ghost, and began to speak with other tongues, as the spirit gave them utterance; so that though there were dwelling at Jerusalem, men that feared God of every nation under heaven, yet they all heard them speak in their own tongues the wonderful works of God. Here was the beginning of that blessed company, which for distinction's sake we call the Christian Church, as consisting of them that believe in Christ now already come in the flesh.

From *Of the Church* by R. Field

———

Give to your Church, O God, the grace to follow in the steps of Jesus Christ,
who came not to be served, but to serve, and to give his life as a ransom for many.
Anoint us afresh with your Spirit, and fill us with power from on high.
May we be ready to spend and be spent in your service, that the hungry may be fed,
the homeless clothed, and the sick and destitute cared for.
So may we work with you for the dignity and freedom of all.
Grant this, heavenly Father, for your world's sake. Amen.

Joan Wilkins 1918–2001

Churchwarden

———

MRS JOAN WILKINS, known to one and all as 'Dorkie', was born in a workhouse. At an early age she was farmed out to various relatives who sadly, or so it would appear, abused her and treated her as an unpaid servant. Not surprisingly, at the first opportunity she obtained a job as scullery maid and escaped. She was a hard worker and later managed to procure a job as live-in housekeeper in the tiny village of Shelton. A devout and faithful Christian, she became churchwarden at St Mary's Church, a role she held for forty years. As churchwarden, Dorkie undertook all the practical tasks involved in keeping a village church alive, including looking after the building, churchyard maintenance, cleaning, flower arranging, verging and preparing for worship. She had a great capacity for friendship and providing pastoral care and support to everyone in the village. The Church was the centre of her life and, thanks to her, thrived in a village with barely fifty residents.

A well-known hymn about Christian service

Teach me, my God and King,
in all things thee to see,
and what I do in anything
to do it as for thee.

A man that looks on glass,
on it may stay his eye;
or if he pleaseth, through it pass,
and then the heaven espy.

All may of thee partake;
nothing can be so mean,
which with this tincture, 'for thy sake,'
will not grow bright and clean.

A servant with this clause
makes drudgery divine:
who sweeps a room, as for thy laws,
makes that and the action fine.

This is the famous stone
that turneth all to gold;
for that which God doth touch and own
cannot for less be told.

From *The Elixir* by George Herbert

———

Teach us, O God, to see you in all things:
grant that whatever we do, in word or deed,
may be for the strengthening of the Church and the coming of the kingdom,
and may it be offered in your name and for your glory;
for Jesus' sake. Amen.

Nathanael Ball 1623–81

Rector and linguist

———

A POLYGLOT BIBLE SETS out the text of the Christian scriptures in the original languages side by side. It is used by scholars to study the meaning of the text and how it has been translated. Nathanael Ball is remembered for his role in helping compile the *London Polyglot,* published in six volumes in 1657, which was considered to be one of the best polyglots ever produced. It included texts in Latin, Hebrew, Greek, Syriac, Ethiopic, Arabic and Persian. Ball was born in Somerset and studied at King's College and Pembroke College, Cambridge, where he was known as a gifted linguist. In 1650 the Westminster Assembly approved him as a minister and he was made Vicar of Furneux Pelham and, two years later, Rector of Barley. However, in the late 1650s his predecessor, Herbert Thorndike, was allowed to return to the benefice from which he had been deprived and it was Ball's turn to be ejected. For a time Ball lived and ministered in Royston, probably employed as a curate. Following the Act of Uniformity of 1662 he became a Nonconformist. Ball worked as an evangelist in various places such as Little Chishill, Bayford, Epping and Cambridge, and it appears that he was a teacher to a conventicle in Thaxted in 1669. He wrote *Spiritual Bondage and Freedom* and *Christ the Hope of Glory*, both of which were published after his death. He married Mary Parr and they had thirteen children. He died of consumption, probably in Epping.

Gordon Mursell writes about the role of the Bible following the Reformation

The influence of the Bible on English spirituality of the sixteenth and seventeenth centuries can hardly be overestimated. We have already noted the part it played in the spiritual life of the Lollards; but the invention and development of printing rendered it more accessible still, especially since this coincided with a concern to make the scriptures available in the vernacular. This concern was rooted in two things: the humanist commitment to returning *ad fonts*, to the pristine purity of early Christianity; and the concern of both Catholics and Protestants to foster lay education and piety. Hence it is not surprising to find both Protestants and Catholics seeking to make the Bible available in the vernacular. In England it was Thomas Cromwell, in 1536, who arranged for an English Bible to be made available in every parish church for the laity to hear and read; during Mary's reign, Cardinal Pole sought to make use of the vernacular Bible in his plans for the education of the clergy; and exiled Jesuits took advantage of its availability for their own work of catechesis and spiritual formation: indeed in 1582 the first Catholic English version of the New Testament appeared at Reims. By the early seventeenth century, cheap Bibles, Psalters, catechisms and Prayer Books were all widely available.

From English Spirituality from the Earliest Times to 1700

Heavenly Father,
who on the day of Pentecost sent the Holy Spirit on the disciples
causing them to speak in many tongues:
bless those with gifts of language and translation
that our knowledge and understanding may be deepened,
and we may share the good news of our Lord Jesus Christ
with confidence and joy. Amen.

Alexander of Neckam 1157–1217

Augustinian canon and scholar

———

SAILORS THE WORLD over owe a debt of gratitude to Alexander of Neckam for his books, *De utensilibus* and *De naturis rerum*. In them he described how ships can be navigated when the sky was cloudy by using a needle suspended over a magnet. Although the compass was well known in other parts of the world, Neckam was the first Westerner to write about the way that sailors could utilise the compass to help them navigate. He also wrote on many other subjects including natural history, medical science, grammar and the Bible. Neckam translated various texts, including Aesop's Fables. He composed poetry and wrote a major theological tome entitled *Speculum Speculationum*. Although Neckam was born in St Albans and taught at Dunstable, he also studied and lectured in the University of Paris. An Augustinian monk, he was to become the Abbot of Cirencester Abbey in 1213. He died at Kemsey and is buried at Worcester.

Pilgrims have often used the sea as a metaphor for God

Celtic monasticism is coloured by the peregrinations of the Celtic Saints and, consequently, is of a very different character than western European monasticism. While the Rule of Benedict emphasized stability, the Celtic saints were travellers who journeyed far and wide, leaping into their tiny coracles and setting sail on the sea, often without oars or sails, and often without a specific destination, content to let God take them where God would. The peregrinations of the saints is aptly illustrated by the story of the three Irishmen who drifted over the sea for seven days w/o oars, were found, and brought to the court of King Alfred. When asked where they were heading, they responded that they 'stole away because they wanted for the love of God to be on pilgrimage, we cared not where.' Their love of travel was motivated by their love of God; their journey was undertaken in order to come closer to God. Theirs was a journey in which oars or sails were not necessary, for that for which they were searching was to be found not without, but within: It has been said that, 'The longest journey is the journey inward' (Dag Hammarskjold). The peregrinations of the Celtic saints were ways of expressing outwardly a journey which they wanted to undertake inwardly. Columbanus was quick to remind his companions to, 'Let us not love the roadway rather than the homeland lest we lose our eternal home…Therefore, let this principle abide with us, that on the road we live as travellers, as pilgrims, as guests of the world…'

Deborah Vess

———

Steer the ship of my life, good Lord, to your quiet harbour,
where I can be safe from the storms of sin and conflict.
Show me the course I should take.
Renew in me the gift of discernment,
so that I can always see the right direction in which I should go.
And give me the strength and the courage to choose the right course,
even when the sea is rough and the waves are high,
knowing that through enduring hardship and danger
in your name we shall find comfort and peace, Amen.

Basil of Caesarea

John Allen Manton 1809–64

Methodist minister

———

JOHN MANTON WAS one of a generation of young Methodist ministers who were sent to Australia as missionaries. He was born in Biggleswade and at the age of sixteen was admitted into the Methodist Society. He became a local preacher and was ordained when he was twenty-two. Within a few months he sailed to New South Wales and served at Parramatta, Van Diemen's Land and Port Arthur. Manton was particularly involved in educating adult and adolescent convicts. He then served in various places including Launceston and as the superintendent minister in Hobart. He married Anne Green in 1833 with whom he had several children. In 1855 Manton became the first principal of Horton College in Tasmania. He left two years later and moved to New South Wales. Manton set up another school there, Newington House, in 1863, but died the following year.

Michael Green writes

There are three definitions of evangelism which I have found helpful. The first is one word: 'overflow'. It gives the right nuance, of someone who is so full of joy about Jesus Christ that it overflows as surely as a bath that is filled to overflowing with water. It is a natural thing. It is a very obvious thing. Accordingly, it has that quality which so much evangelism lacks, spontaneity. The second definition is a phrase attributed to C. H. Spurgeon, the famous nineteenth-century British preacher and evangelist. Evangelism, he maintained, 'is one beggar telling another beggar where to get bread'. I like that definition. It draws attention both to the needs of the recipient and to the generosity of the giver: God will not give us a stone when we ask him for bread. I like the equality it underscores. There is no way that an evangelist is any better or on any higher ground than the person to whom he is talking. The ground is level round the cross of Christ. The only difference between the two hungry beggars is that one has been fed and knows where food is always available. There is no great mystique about it. Evangelism is simply telling a fellow searcher where he can get bread. But there is another touch which is important in this definition. It reminds us that we cannot bring this good news to others unless we personally have come to 'taste and see that the Lord is good' (Psalms 34.8). But perhaps the most all-embracing definition of evangelism, and one which has won the most wide-reaching acceptance, belongs to the English Archbishop William Temple: 'To evangelise is so to present Jesus Christ in the power of the Holy Spirit, that men shall come to put their trust in God through him, to accept him as their Saviour, and serve him as their King in the fellowship of his church.'

From *Evangelism through the Local Church*

Most gracious God,
who has called us to make disciples of all the nations:
give us confidence and courage
to proclaim your good news in word and deed;
for the building up of your Church
and for the sake of your son Jesus Christ. Amen.

Gerrard Winstanley 1609–76

Quaker and leveller

———

GERRARD WINSTANLEY WAS the leader of the group who called themselves 'The True Levellers'. They practised a form of Christian Communism, renouncing private property, demanding the redistribution of land, and campaigning against the hereditary rights of the aristocracy. As Winstanley put it in his pamphlet entitled *The New Law of Righteousness*, 'In the beginning of time, God made the earth. Not one word was spoken at the beginning that one branch of mankind should rule over another, but selfish imaginations did set up one man to teach and rule over another.' As a young man, Winstanley had been an apprentice in London and became a freeman of the Guild of Merchant Taylors. In 1643 he was declared bankrupt and was forced to work as a cowherd. It was this experience that transformed his attitude to property and radicalised him. Some six years later, in around 1649, Winstanley and his fellow Levellers began cultivating common land in various parts of the south-east of England (hence their nickname 'Diggers') and giving away the produce. Opposition was fierce and the experiment had to be abandoned. This led Winstanley to move to Pirton in Hertfordshire for a short period, where he managed the estates of Lady Eleanor Davies. In 1657 Winstanley was given some property in Cobham by his father-in-law and he set up business as a corn chandler. Following the death of his first wife, Susan, he married Elizabeth Stanley. He died on this day in 1676.

Gerrard Winstanley pleads for the rights of poor people

We whose names are subscribed, do in the name of all the poor oppressed people in *England*, declare unto you, that call your selves lords of Manors, and Lords of the Land, That in regard the King of Righteousness, our Maker, hath inlightened our hearts so far, as to see, That the earth was not made purposely for you, to be Lords of it, and we to be your Slaves, Servants, and Beggers; but it was made to be a common Livelihood to all, without respect of persons: And that your buying and selling of Land, and the Fruits of it, one to another, is *The cursed thing*, and was brought in by War; which hath, and still does establish murder, and theft, In the hands of some branches of Mankinde over others, which is the greatest outward burden, and unrighteous power, that the Creation groans under: For the power of inclosing Land, and owning Propriety, was brought into the Creation by your Ancestors by the Sword; which first did murther their fellow Creatures, Men, and after plunder or steal away their Land, and left this Land successively to you, their Children. And therefore, though you did not kill or theeve, yet you hold that cursed thing in your hand, by the power of the Sword; and so you justifie the wicked deeds of your Fathers; and that sin of your Fathers, shall be visited upon the Head of you, and your Children, to the third and fourth Generation, and longer too, till your bloody and theeving power be rooted out of the Land.

From *A Declaration from the Poor Oppressed People of England*

———

God of justice and compassion,
whose Son Jesus Christ gave freely to all whom he met
and taught us to follow his example:
imbue your Church with a spirit of reckless generosity,
that we may give with joy and work for a world in which
all have shelter, food and clothing; for we ask this in his name. Amen.

Ellen Holesgrove 1820–1904

Clergy wife and philanthropist

——————

ELLEN HOLESGROVE REPRESENTS the many clergy spouses who have worked quietly behind the scenes in a supportive role. Ellen Mary Shurlock was married to the Reverend William Holesgrove, who was the Vicar of Henlow from 1875 to 1892. William died in 1892 and his name is inscribed on the tenor bell in the tower of St Mary's Church, Henlow. In his memory Ellen erected the Vicar's Club Room. It was built on glebe land in the High Street and opened in December 1893. This facility, which was to be a resource for the whole community, still bears the inscription 'Vicar's Club Room' above the front entrance. It was designed so that one end was a reading room and the other was used for meetings and social events. When she died, Ellen Holesgrove left £1,000 in her will to '…secure the use of accommodation for religious or other charitable purposes of the Church of England approved by the Vicar of Henlow, any clear income being applied for religious or other charitable work of the Church of England in Henlow.'

Michael Ramsey, a former Archbishop of Canterbury, writes about rest

In his work *The City of God* St Augustine told of heaven thus. 'We shall rest and we shall see, we shall see and we shall love, we shall love and we shall praise, in the end which is no end.' Rest: we shall be freed from the busy and fussy activity in which we get in our own light and expose ourselves to our self-centredness. Resting, we shall find that we see in a new way, without the old hindrances. We shall see our neighbours as what they really are, creatures and children of God in whom is the divine image, and that image will become newly visible to us. We shall see ourselves too as God's infinitesimally small creatures: and we shall begin to see God himself in his beauty. Seeing, we shall love, for how shall we not love God in his beauty and how shall we not love all our neighbours in whom the image of God is now visible to us? Praise will be the last word, for all is of God and none is of our own achievement, and we shall know the depth of gratitude and adoration. St Augustine adds 'in the end which is no end'. It will be the end, for here is perfection and nothing can be more final. It will be no end, for within the resting, seeing, loving and praising there is an inexhaustible adventure of new and ceaseless discovery. Such is the heaven for which we were created. Resting, seeing, loving and praising: these words describe not only the goal of heaven but the message of Christianity in the world.

From *Be Still and Know: A Study in the Life of Prayer*

God of eternity
who calls us to a pattern of work and rest, a balance of labour and recreation:
save us from the drivenness of our unresolved needs,
teach us to find a rhythm of activity and stillness,
and give us a trusting faith that commits all things into your hands,
knowing that you are working your purposes out as year succeeds to year;
for we ask these things for the sake of Jesus Christ our Lord. Amen.

Henry Hucks Gibbs 1819–1907

Governor of the Bank of England and politician

———

HENRY GIBBS WAS a high-churchman and a generous benefactor. He worked actively towards the setting up of the new Diocese of St Albans and supported the appeals for the restoration of St Albans Abbey and St John the Baptist Church, Aldenham. He was a prominent lay Anglican who served on the Council of Keble College, Oxford. Gibbs was president of the English Church Union, served on the house of laymen for the Province of Canterbury, and was treasurer of Church House. The eldest of fourteen children, Gibbs went to Redland School and Exeter College, Oxford, then worked for the family firm of Anthony Gibbs and Sons, who were merchants and merchant bankers. In 1853 Gibbs became a director of the Bank of England and was on the court until 1901. He was Governor of the Bank of England from 1875 to 1877 and was also a member of the royal commission on the stock exchange between 1877 and 1878. He was a Justice of the Peace and for a short time he was the Member of Parliament for the City of London. In 1884 Gibbs was High Sheriff of Hertfordshire. He was elevated to the peerage in 1896 and took the title Baron Aldenham, of Aldenham in the County of Hertford. Gibbs was a bibliophile with a large library. He was fascinated with words and was a member of the Philological Society. He was also a benefactor of the *Oxford English Dictionary*. Gibbs married Louisa Anne Adams in 1845 and had seven children. Their fifth son, Kenneth Francis Gibbs, became Archdeacon of St Albans. Gibbs is buried in the churchyard in Aldenham.

Richard Foster reflects on the Christian understanding of money

Martin Luther astutely observed, 'There are three conversions necessary: the conversion of the heart, mind, and the purse.' Of these three, it may well be that we moderns find the conversion of the purse the most difficult. It is hard for us even to talk about money…And yet Jesus spoke about money more frequently than any other subject except the kingdom of God. He gave an unusual amount of time and energy to the money question. In the moving story about the 'widow's mite,' we are told that Jesus intentionally sat in front of the treasury and watched people putting in their offerings (Mark 12.41). By design, he saw what they gave and discerned the spirit in which they gave. For Jesus, giving was not a private matter. He did not – as we so often do today – glance away embarrassed at prying into someone's personal business. No, Jesus considered it public business and used the occasion to teach about sacrificial giving. Jesus' careful attention to the money question is one of the truly amazing things about the Gospel narratives. The range of his concern is startling: from the parable of the sower to the parable of the rich farmer, from the encounter with the rich young ruler to the encounter with Zacchaeus, from teachings on trust in Matthew 6 to teachings on the dangers of wealth in Luke 6.

From *Money, Sex and Power*

Generous God,
the source of all good things:
save us from avarice and greed;
teach us to be faithful stewards of that which has been entrusted to us
and open our hearts so that we may share with those in need;
for the sake of your Son Jesus Christ. Amen.

Philip Stubbs 1665–1738

Archdeacon of St Albans

———

MANY PEOPLE HAVE been profoundly influenced by some event that made its mark on them. This was the experience of Stubbs, who was born during the Great Plague of London. Thousands of people were dying each week from the bubonic plague and life felt very precarious. It is thought that over one hundred thousand people may have died of the plague in London in 1665. Perhaps it was this formative memory which inspired Stubbs' commitment to founding schools for poor children, both when he was Rector of St Alphage, London Wall, and later when he was Rector of Launton, near Bicester. Stubbs himself had benefited from a good education at Merchant Taylors' School and at Wadham College, Oxford, from where he graduated in 1686. He was ordained to serve his title at St Benet, Gracechurch, and St Leonard, Eastcheap, in London. After chaplaincies with the Bishop of Chichester and with the Earl of Huntingdon, he became Rector of Woolwich and Chaplain to Greenwich Hospital. In 1715 Stubbs also became Archdeacon of St Albans, a post he held in plurality with his chaplaincy at Greenwich Hospital and the living at Launton. A priest with wide interests, he was elected a Fellow of the Royal Society in 1703 and wrote several books of sermons. One of his sermons, 'God's Dominion over the Seas and the Seaman's Duty', was reprinted several times and was even translated into French. He was an active supporter of the Society for the Propagation of the Gospel in Foreign Parts and the Society for Promoting Christian Knowledge. In 1696, he married Mary Willis and they had three children. He died on this day in 1738 at Greenwich Hospital and was buried in the hospital's old cemetery. His tombstone survives there in the mausoleum.

In this diary entry Stubbs laments the suffering caused by the plague

1665 Oct 2. I was born, within the Parish of St Andrew Undershaft, London, in which parish 14 died of the Plague that week; in the City 68,596 that year; Lord! what respect hadst thou to me and my Father's House? That many should fall in that great sickness on the right hand and on the left, but no evil happen'd unto me, nor did the Plague approach o'r dwelling. Let me thro' ye whole course of my Life make Thee my refuge even the most High, my Habitation.

From the diary of Philip Stubbs in *Archdeacon Philip Stubbs* by William Scott

———

Grant, merciful Lord,
your help and comfort to all those who suffer
through tragedy, sickness or bereavement;
strengthen those who are working to bring relief and aid
and bless those who are seeking cures for plagues and diseases;
through Jesus Christ our Lord. Amen.

Ernest Urban Trevor Huddleston 1915–98

Monk and anti-apartheid activist

———

'Father Huddleston walked alone at all hours of the night where few of us were prepared to go. His fearlessness won him the support of everyone. No-one, not the gangster, tsotsi, or pickpocket, would touch him.' *Nelson Mandela*

TREVOR HUDDLESTON IS remembered for his tireless campaign against apartheid. This costly prophetic ministry in South Africa was a long way from his birth in Bedford and education at Lancing College and Christ Church, Oxford. After ordination, Huddleston became a member of the Community of the Resurrection, an Anglican religious order based in Mirfield. He was sent to live in Rosettenville, Sophiatown, a suburb of Johannesburg, and it was there that his courageous witness earned him the nickname *Makhalipile* (meaning 'the one who is fearless'). Huddleston returned to England in 1956 to serve as the novice master of the community. Four years later he was consecrated Bishop of Masasi in Tanzania before coming back to England to serve as Bishop of Stepney. His final appointment was as Bishop of Mauritius, during which time he was also the Archbishop of the Province of the Indian Ocean. During his retirement he continued his anti-apartheid work for which he was honoured by the Tanzanian and Indian governments. He was made a Knight Commander of the Order of St Michael and St George in 1998. He died in the same year at Mirfield and his ashes are interred in the garden of Christ the King Church in Sophiatown, where he had served for 13 years.

Trevor Huddleston draws out the meaning of a familiar parable

There is nothing in the parable of the Good Samaritan which is even a hint that the racial arrogance of the Jew is to be excused or palliated because of his background or his history. There is nothing in it either to indicate that Christ accepted the 'official' excuse of the hierarchy for its attitude toward that intolerable division. The priest and the Levite in the parable who 'passed by on the other side' are the representatives, for all time, of those for whom fear is a more powerful motive than love. They are respectable citizens who like to observe the conventions: but they are more – for they are the leaders of religion whose very office redoubles their responsibility, and who fail in their task. The whole point and purpose of the parable is to show that charity, if it is real, must be prepared to break through convention, to shatter preconceptions, to take by force the citadels of prejudice: and that if in doing so it hurts people's feelings and outrages their sense of what is decent, what matter? Nothing could be further from the sentimental sob-stuff that we so often call 'love', than the exposition of that virtue in the parable of the Good Samaritan.

From *Naught for your Comfort*

———

God bless Africa;
guard her children;
guide her leaders
and give her peace,
for Jesus Christ's sake. Amen.

Trevor Huddleston

Richard Hale d.1620

Founder of Hertford Grammar School

———

THE ELDEST SON of Thomas Hale of Codicote, Richard went to London where he made his fortune as a merchant. We know that in 1595 he purchased the manor of Kings Walden Bury, which was to remain in the family until 1884. Hale was granted Letters Patent by King James I in 1616 to establish a school in Hertford. In the following year he gave a benefaction of £800 to 'erect a grammar school for the instruction of children in the Latin tongue and other literature in the town of Hertford'. The original building, which was close to All Saints Church, was in use until the school moved to new premises in 1930. It was known as Hertford Grammar School until the mid-1970s, when it became a comprehensive and was renamed Richard Hale School.

Richard Livingstone explores the role of education

What is a complete human being? Again I shall take the Greek answer to this question. Human beings have bodies, minds and characters. Each of these is capable of what the Greeks called 'virtue' (*arete*) or what we might call 'excellence'. The virtue or excellence of the body is health and fitness and strength, the firm and sensitive hand, the clear eye; the excellence of the mind is to know and to understand and to think, to have some idea of what the world is and of what man has done and has been and can be; the excellence of the character lies in the great virtues. This trinity of body, mind and character is man: Man's aim, besides earning his living, is to make the most of all three, to have as good a mind, body and character as possible; and a liberal education, a free man's education, is to help him to this; not because a sound body, mind and character help to success, or even because they help to happiness, but because they are good things in themselves, and because what is good is worth while, simply because it is good. So we get that clear and important distinction between technical education which aims at earning a living or making money or at some narrowly practical skill, and the free man's education which aims at producing as perfect and complete a human being as may be. This is not to despise technical education which is essential; everyone has to learn to make a living and to do his job, and he cannot do it without training: Technical or vocational education is as much wanted as liberal education. But they are not to be confused. They are both important, both necessary, but they are different. And yet to some extent they overlap.

From *On Education*

———

Almighty God,
who promises the gift of the Holy Spirit to lead us into truth:
enlighten with your Spirit places of education and learning,
and in particular all schools, colleges and universities,
that those who teach and those who study
may grow in knowledge and holiness,
for the good of all people and the flourish of society;
through Jesus Christ our Lord. Amen.

Amphibalus c.3rd century

Priest and martyr

————

HIDDEN AWAY IN a corner of St Albans Abbey are the remains of the medieval shrine of St Amphibalus. For most of the period of the Roman occupation of Britain, Christians were persecuted. Legend records that a Christian priest called Amphibalus was fleeing for his life and was given shelter by Alban, a Roman soldier in Verulamium, present-day St Albans. Alban was so impressed with the priest's faith that he was converted to Christianity. When the pursuing Roman soldiers arrived to arrest Amphibalus, Alban swopped cloaks with him so that the priest could escape. Alban was executed in his place, becoming the first Christian martyr in Britain. We are not sure that Amphibalus was the priest's real name. One tradition says that he was arrested by the Romans and was executed in St Albans. In 1178 the grave of Amphibalus was discovered at Redbourn and his remains were taken to St Albans Abbey.

George Herbert writes about the importance of hospitality

The Country Parson owing a debt of charity to the poor, and of courtesy to his other parishioners, he so distinguisheth, that he keeps his money for the poor, and his table for those that are above alms. Not but that the poor are welcome also to his table, whom he sometimes purposely takes home with him, setting them close by him, and carving for them, both for his own humility, and their comfort, who are much cheered with such friendliness. But since both is to be done, the better sort invited, and meaner relieved, he chooseth rather to give the poor money, which they can better employ to their own advantage, and suitably to their needs, than so much given in meat at dinner. Having then invited some of his parish, he taketh his times to do the like to the rest; so that in the compass of the year, he hath them all with him, because country people are very observant of such things, and will not be persuaded, but being not invited, they are hated. Which persuasion the parson by all means avoids, knowing that where there are such conceits, there is no room for his doctrine to enter. Yet doth he oftenest invite those, whom he sees take best courses, that so both they may be encouraged to persevere, and other spurred to do well, that they may enjoy the like courtesy. For though he desire that all should live well and virtuously, not for any reward of his, but for virtue's sake; yet that will not be so: and therefore as God, although we should love him only for his own sake, yet out of his infinite pity hath set forth heaven for a reward to draw men to piety, and is content, if at least so, they will become good: so the country parson, who is a diligent observer, and tracker of God's ways, sets up as many encouragements to goodness as he can, both in honour and profit and fame; that he may, if not the best way, yet any way, make his parish good.

From *The Country Parson*

———————

Almighty and everlasting God, who alone workest great marvels:
send down upon our bishops, and clergy,
and all congregations committed to their charge,
the healthful spirit of thy grace:
and that they may truly please thee, pour upon them the continual dew of thy blessing.
Grant this, O Lord, for the honour of our advocate and mediator, Jesus Christ. Amen.

From *The Book of Common Prayer*

Germanus c.378–c.448

Bishop

———

IT IS EASY to assume that we are much better travelled than our forebears. Yet in past centuries many people made long and arduous journeys, without any of the comforts we take for granted today. One such person was Germanus, whose life was recorded by Constantius of Lyon at the end of the fifth century. Germanus was a lawyer who became the provincial governor of Autissiodorum, known today as Auxerre, in the Bourgogne region of France. His holiness of life was widely recognised and he was consecrated Bishop of Auxerre. Among some of the British bishops there was concern at the rapidly growing influence of a heresy, Pelaginianism, which was being propounded by Agricola, the son of Bishop Severianus. They appealed to the Bishops of Gaul for help, who sent Germanus of Auxerre and Lupus of Troyes to dispute with the heretics. Bede describes how they sailed to Britain and through their oratory and argument persuaded the believers to hold to orthodox Christian doctrine. Following the meeting Germanus visited the shrine of St Albans. It appears that Germanus made such an impact that he found himself at the head of an army fighting against the Picts and the Saxons at Mold in North Wales. In preparation for the battle he baptised his troops. We are told that the sound of the soldiers shouting 'Alleluia' was so loud that the other army fled into the hills in fear. Germanus died in Ravenna and is buried in the Abbey of Saint-Germain d'Auxerre.

St Augustine reflects on martyrdom

The Lord Jesus Christ not only instructed his martyrs through his teaching, he strengthened them through his own example. In order that those who would suffer for him might have an example to follow, he first suffered for them. He showed the way and became it. When we talk of death, we speak in terms of the body and the soul. In one sense, the soul cannot die, but in another it can. It cannot die inasmuch as the awareness of itself endures; yet it can die if it loses God. For just as the soul is the life of the body, so God is the life of the soul. The body perishes when the soul that is its life departs: the soul perishes when God casts it away. So lest God cast our souls away, let us always live in faith. Only so will we not fear to die for God, and not die abandoned by God. The death of the body will always remain a fear. And yet Christ the Lord has made his martyrs a counter-balance to our fear. Why worry about the safety of limbs when we have been reassured that the hairs on our head are secure? Does not Scripture say that 'the very hairs on your head are numbered'? Why should our human frailty cause us to be so frightened when the truth has spoken thus?

From *A sermon of St Augustine* in *Patrologiae cursus completus* by J. Migne

---

We thank you for your holy martyrs
who held steadfast in the face of opposition:
grant to us the gifts of faith and courage
that we may witness to your truth in word and action,
proclaiming your good news with an irrepressible joy,
in the sure and certain knowledge that our lives are held in your loving arms;
through Jesus Christ our Lord. Amen.

John Briant 1748–1829

Bell founder and clock maker

———

JOHN BRIANT WAS a bell founder who came to Hertford because of the patronage of the Sixth Earl of Salisbury. His foundry was in Parliament Square. It is thought that he cast 422 bells, most of which are still being rung regularly today. His bells can be found in churches in many places in the diocese, including Stanbridge, Houghton Regis, Brent Pelham, North Mymms, Rushden, Stevenage and Tewin. As well as casting bells, Briant was a clockmaker and was famous for his grandfather (or long case) clocks. He married Mary Hanley in St Andrew's, Hertford, in 1786 and they had two children. Mary died in 1793 and in 1802 he married a second time, to Ann Fyson, and they also had two children. As an accomplisher bell ringer, Briant was elected a member of the Ancient Society of College Youths in 1782. Competition between bell founders was fierce and Briant eventually had to sell his business to Thomas Mears of London. He died in poverty, living in the Marlborough Almshouses in St Albans, and is buried in All Saints, Hertford. In 1929 a tablet to John Briant, cast in bell metal, was unveiled in All Saints Church. It reads:

I'm satisfied with the station of life that God has placed me in. I've enjoyed more real pleasure in my favourite pursuits than the wealth of India could afford – John Briant.

Lift it gently to the steeple,
Let our bell be set on high;
There fulfil its daily mission,
Midway 'twixt the earth and sky.

As the birds sing early matins
To the God of nature's praise,
This its nobler daily music
To the God of grace shall raise.

And when evening shadows soften
Chancel-cross, and tower, and aisle,
It shall blend its vesper summons
With the day's departing smile.

Year by year the steeple-music
O'er the tended graves shall pour
Where the dust of saints is garner'd,
Till the Master comes once more.

From *Original Sequences*
by J. M. Neale

We pray, Heavenly Father, for bell ringers
who summon us to worship week by week:
May their ringing stir our hearts
and their tolling rouse our consciences,
may it chime with our hopes and our longings
and draw us afresh to you, the living God;
for we ask this in the name of Jesus Christ. Amen.

Theodore of Tarsus 602–90

Archbishop of Canterbury

———

THE MEDIEVAL CHURCH was a truly international body. Several of the Archbishops of Canterbury came from France and Italy. Theodore, however, was a Greek, born in Tarsus and educated at Antioch and Constantinople. When Pope Vitalian had to appoint a new Archbishop of Canterbury, Hadrian recommended Theodore, who was a monk living in Rome. Although he was only a subdeacon the Pope consecrated him Archbishop of Canterbury at a service in Rome in 668. He arrived in Britain in the following year and immediately began a visitation of the whole country. It was Theodore who was responsible for convening the Synod of Hertford in 673. The Synod agreed on many things: that bishops should not interfere in each other's dioceses; that monks should live in their monastery and be obedient to the Abbot; and how Easter should be celebrated. He also decided that the northern dioceses should be divided, a decision which caused much disagreement amongst the other bishops. Theodore wrote biblical commentaries and taught sacred music and liturgy. At a national level Theodore proved to be a peace maker, brokering a truce between Northumbria and Mercia. He died on this day in 690.

The Venerable Bede writes about the new archbishop

Theodore arrived at his church the second year after his consecration, on Sunday, the 27th of May, and held the same twenty-one years, three months, and twenty-six days. Soon after, he visited all the islands, wherever the tribes of the Angles inhabited, for he was willingly entertained and heard by all persons; and everywhere attended and assisted by Hadrian, he taught the right rule of life, and the canonical custom of celebrating Easter. It was the first archbishop whom all the English church obeyed. And forasmuch as both of them were, as has been said before, well read both in sacred and in secular literature, they gathered a crowd of disciples, and there daily flowed from them rivers of knowledge to water the hearts of their hearers; and, together with the books of holy writ, they also taught them the arts of ecclesiastical poetry, astronomy, and arithmetic. A testimony of which is, that there are still living at this day some of their scholars, who are as well versed in the Greek and Latin tongues as in their own, in which they were born. Nor were there ever happier times since the English came into Britain; for their kings, being brave men and good Christians, they were a terror to all barbarous nations, and the minds of all men were bent upon the joys of the heavenly kingdom of which they had just heard; and all who desired to be instructed in sacred reading had masters at hand to teach them.

From *A History of the English Church and People*

Almighty God,
you called your servant Theodore of Tarsus
from Rome to the See of Canterbury,
and gave him gifts of grace and wisdom
to establish unity where there had been division,
and order where there had been chaos.
Create in your Church, by the operation of the Holy Spirit,
such godly union and concord that it may proclaim,
both by word and example,
the gospel of the Prince of Peace. Amen.

Penny Nash

Barclay Fowell Buxton 1860–1946

Missionary to Japan

———

BARCLAY BUXTON'S NAME connects him with two family dynasties which have played an important part in the history of this area. His Christian name comes from the family who founded Barclays Bank (see the entry for 1 July) and his surname from the Buxton family of Easneye, Ware (see the entry for 20 March). Following a privileged education at Harrow and Trinity College, Cambridge, Barclay Buxton was ordained in 1884 and served curacies at Onslow Square, London, and Stanwix in Cumberland. He heard a call to the mission field and in 1890 sailed to Japan, when he worked as a missionary with the Church Missionary Society. He founded several churches around Matsuye and Yonago. In 1897 Barclay invited Alpheus Paget Wilkes to help him with the mission. In 1903 they were back in Britain for the launch of the Japan Evangelistic Band (called *Kyodan Nihon Dendo Tai* in Japanese) which took place during the Keswick Convention that year. They returned to Japan and worked there together for a number of years. Barclay came back to live in England in 1917 and was appointed Vicar of Tunbridge Wells in 1921. He continued to visit Japan and to chair the Japan Evangelistic Band until his death. Buxton married Margaret Railton in 1886 and they had four sons. One of them, Godfrey Buxton, wrote his father's biography, ran a missionary training college and continued to chair the Japan Evangelistic Band after his father's death.

A letter written by Barclay Buxton

I pray indeed that you may have clear light from God, and that you may faithfully live out all that the Lord teaches you. I pray that you may increase more and more in deep personal knowledge of God and of love to Him. I pray that you may indeed be fruitful Christians and that others may always perceive in you the sweet gospel fruits of love, joy, and peace. And therefore I beg you be diligent in seeking God. Especially let the Word of God be your delight. Feed upon it in your hearts day by day. Seek to be all that God wants you to be. Seek to receive all the grace He will give. Be much in prayer, both for yourselves and also for the work of God amongst all the Japanese. Be diligent to seek an outpouring of the Holy Spirit in revival blessing. Diligently attend the meetings. There are many blessings which are missed by those who do not join with others in prayer and the study of God's Word. Be diligent in testifying to what the Lord is to you, and in seeking to bring others to Christ. I pray God that such a revival may be given to you, that multitudes of Japanese may be saved, and the fire spread from you to Japan. May God march on to victory there, and bring in His kingdom of righteousness and peace and joy in the Holy Ghost. I shall always have happy and grateful recollections of all your kindness to me and Brother Sasao.

From *The Reward of Faith in the Life of Barclay Fowell Buxton* by Godfrey Buxton

---

God of Glory, shine in the darkness of this world
that all people may see your salvation:
may your radiance banish the shadows of sin
and draw us to worship and bow down
and kneel before you our Maker;
we ask this in the name of him who is the Light of the World,
Jesus Christ our Lord. Amen.

Frederick George Field 1917–89

Churchwarden

———

WITHOUT THE SKILL and determination of George Field, St Peter's Church in Thurleigh in Bedfordshire might be a ruin. During the 1940s the church had fallen into disrepair and had to be closed. The roof was leaking, the roof timbers were rotten and it was estimated that the five hundred parishioners would need to raise £20,000 for the repairs. At one stage it was suggested that the nave should be preserved as a shell and that the chancel alone should be used for worship. Field, who was born and farmed in Stevington, moved to Thurleigh in 1951 and was among the band of parishioners who were determined that the entire church should be repaired and re-opened. Alongside the builders, Field and a team of volunteers spent many hours restoring and repairing pews, windows and cleaning the walls. After years of hard work the church was rededicated in 1971. The Parish Notes of 1971 records 'Everyone recognises that Mr George Field has done an incredible amount of work himself and has been the driving force behind it all. To him we owe a very great debt of gratitude. He, himself, does not want our thanks; what he has done he has done for God.' Field served for many years as churchwarden and undertook many of the maintenance jobs that needed doing. He was married to Kath.

Richard Kieckhefer muses on the significance of church buildings

Entering a church is a metaphor for entering into the presence of the holy. A church is sometimes called a house of God, or *domus Dei*. This is not to suppose God is limited to a particular place, as if a church could place objective boundaries on the divine. Rather, to speak of a house of God is to recognise community and its culture as a means of allurement toward God – to recognise that the house made by the community is an apt setting for the people to assemble in the alluring presence of the divine. In the prophet's formulation, God says of Israel, 'Behold, I will allure her, and will lead her into the wilderness, and speak tenderly to her' (Hosea 2.14). The image of encounter with God in a starkly natural setting, a world untouched by human culture, finds its complement in the theme of being allured by God also within a kind of house, a work of people formed by a particular culture and linked in common effort, and thus within a community and its works. Cultural creations and activities that might distract from the life of the spirit are here specifically designed for recalling attention to that life. Entering into a church is a metaphor for recognising that prayer – being allured by God – is possible not only in solitude and in nature but also in community and in culture. And essential to that allurement are a church's aesthetic qualities.

From *Theology in Stone*

We thank you, O God,
for the silent witness of our church buildings,
standing in the midst of our communities:
grant that in the power of the Holy Spirit,
we the people of the living Church,
may also bear witness through our words and deeds;
through Jesus Christ our Lord. Amen.

Henry Cockayne Cust 1780–1861

Rector and Lord of the Manor

———

W HEN HENRY COCKAYNE Cust succeeded to the Cockayne Hatley estate, he not only became Lord of the Manor, but also Rector of the Church of St John the Baptist, as he had taken Holy Orders. Cust arrived in Cockayne Hatley in 1806, a year before his father's death, and lived in the rectory in the village. However, he eventually moved into the mansion after it had been refurbished, and appointed a curate, who lived in the rectory in his place. Around 1850, he demolished the rectory and built a new one, which survives today as a private residence. Cust was keen on building improvements, and these can best be seen in the church itself. When he first arrived, the church was in a poor state of repair – it was reported that snow had fallen on the altar on Christmas Day. Cust re-roofed the church, and furnished it with both medieval and new stained glass. He purchased magnificent carved woodwork from Flanders, and even a pulpit from Antwerp Cathedral (which was eventually sold to Carlisle Cathedral). Cust was married to Anna Maria, and they had five children. He died in 1861, having spent his last years in Windsor, where he had been appointed a canon. He and his wife, and two of their children, are buried in the family vault in the churchyard at Cockayne Hatley.

Lancelot Andrewes reflects on the responsibility of the minister

Let the preacher labour to be heard intelligently, willingly, obediently. And let him not doubt that he will accomplish this rather by the piety of his prayers than by the eloquence of his speech. By praying for himself, and those whom he is to address, let him be their beadsman before he becomes their teacher; and approaching God with devotion let him first raise to Him a thirsting heart before he speaks of Him with his tongue; that he may speak what he hath been taught and pour out what hath been poured in. I cease not therefore to ask from our Lord and Master, that He may, either by the utterances of His scriptures or the conversations of my brethren, or the internal and sweeter doctrine of His own inspiration, deign to teach me things so to be set forth and asserted, that in what is set forth and asserted I may ever hold me fast to the Truth; from this very Truth I desire to be taught the many things I know not, by Him from whom I have received the few I know.

From *The Private Prayers of Lancelot Andrewes*

We pray for those entrusted with the responsibility
of teaching and preaching the Christian faith:
grant them diligence in their preparation,
creativity in their choice of illustration
and clarity in their presentation;
but above all give them the gift of your Holy Spirit
that the words that they speak with their lips
may be lived out in their lives,
to the glory of your holy name;
through Jesus Christ our Lord. Amen.

Muriel Arthington 1924–2009

Sister of the Community of St Andrew

———

MURIEL ARTHINGTON WAS born and raised in Manchester. She won a scholarship to Levenshulme High School and then went to work for Imperial Chemical Industries (ICI) and for the aircraft manufacturing company AVRO. Following the death of her mother, Muriel pursued her vocation with the Community of St Andrew. In 1964 she was sent to work with the Sisters in Bedford, who were running the St Albans Diocesan Children's Home. She was soon deeply involved in the life of the Home, helping at Bedford prison and running family groups. She was professed in 1966. When the Community of St Andrew decided to withdraw from the orphanage in 1967, Muriel was one of the three Sisters who decided to stay on in Bedford and continue caring for the children. She trained in childcare for a year at Sidcup and when the house for teenagers was built, she moved there and had responsibility for their welfare. In 1992 Sister Muriel moved into the Christie Almshouses, where she continued her work with the prison. She was also deputy warden of the Almshouses for a while. She was closely involved in St Paul's Church, Bedford. In 2002, she moved back to live with the Sisters in Willen and died in Easter week 2009.

Evelyn Underhill writes about love and prayer

If we ask of the saints how they achieve spiritual effectiveness, they are only able to reply that, in so far as they did it themselves, they did it by love and prayer. A love that is very humble and homely; a prayer that is full of adoration and of confidence. Love and prayer, on their lips, are not mere nice words; they are the names of tremendous powers, able to transform in a literal sense human personality and make it more and more that which it is meant to be – the agent of the Holy Spirit in the world. Plainly then, it is essential to give time or to get time somehow for self-training in this love and this prayer. It is true that in their essence they are 'given', but the gift is only fully made our own by a patient and generous effort of the soul. Spiritual achievement costs much, though never as much as it is worth. It means at the very least the painful development and persevering, steady exercise of a faculty that most of us have allowed to get slack. It means an inward if not an outward asceticism: a virtual if not an actual mysticism. People talk about mysticism as if it were something quite separate from practical religion; whereas, as a matter of fact, it is the intense heart of all practical religion, and no-one without some touch of it is contagious and able to win souls. What is mysticism? It is in its widest sense the reaching out of the soul to contact with those eternal realities which are the subject matter of religion. And the mystical life is the complete life of love and prayer which transmutes those objects of belief into living realities.

From *Concerning the Inner Life*

Teach us, Good Lord, the way of love and prayer:
love for the loveless, the troubled and the doubting,
love for the lonely, the sick and the dying;
we commit them into your hands and ask that we may be given grace
to support them in practical acts of care and compassion;
for the sake of Jesus Christ our Lord. Amen.

George Wilfrid Blenkin 1861–1924

Dean of St Albans

———

'As to character,' said Tom Staple, 'I don't think much of that. They rather like loose parsons for deans; a little fast living, or a dash of infidelity, is no bad recommendation to a cathedral close' (Anthony Trollope in *Barchester Towers*).

MANY PEOPLE OUTSIDE the Church have little idea of what qualities of character are required to be the dean of a cathedral. However, George Blenkin could not be described as 'loose' and we have no reason to believe that he liked fast living. Blenkin was born into a clerical family and had a privileged education. After school at Harrow and Trinity College, Cambridge, he was ordained in 1886. He remained at Cambridge as Chaplain of Emmanuel College and later at Trinity College. Blenkin was appointed Vicar of Brading on the Isle of Wight in 1906. The First World War broke out on 28 July 1914 by which time Blenkin's appointment to be the new Dean of St Albans had already been announced. He took up his new office in November that year and remained in post, dying on this day in 1924. He was a scholarly dean, a Doctor of Divinity, who specialised in teaching the New Testament.

George Blenkin writes about St Peter

But with all his faults St Peter was specially dear to his Master, as may be seen from the prayer that his faith might not fail and the charge to strengthen his brethren (Luke 12.32), the pitying glance in the hour of his shame (Luke 12.61), the special message about Resurrection (Mark 16.7). He was the first of the Twelve to see the Risen Lord (Luke 24.34; 1 Corinthians 15.5), and finally on the lake side St Peter, greatly forgiven, proved how greatly he loved, and was entrusted with a share in the Good Shepherd's own work and learned that he should glorify God by sharing his Master's fate in death (John 21.15 ff.). In the Acts of the Apostles St Peter seems at once to take the lead among his brethren. He proposes the election of a new Apostle (1.15 ff.) and was the spokesman on the Day of Pentecost. In the successive stages of the development of the Church traced by St Luke, (a) Jerusalem, (b) Judaea, (c) Samaria, (d) 'unto the uttermost part of the earth' (1.8), St Peter takes the initiative. He, with St John, performs the first miracle (3.1–8) and acts as spokesman when they are tried by the Sanhedrin (2.11 ff.). He asserts his primacy in the first visitation of judgment (v.1–11). Although all the Apostles are described as working 'signs and wonders', St Peter's personality seems to have created the greatest impression, so that his very shadow was thought to bring healing (v.15). When the Apostles were imprisoned and miraculously released, St Peter again acted as spokesman before the Sanhedrin (5.29 ff.).

From *The First Epistle of Peter*

Give us grace, Good Lord,
to follow the example of your apostle Peter:
may we be eager to offer ourselves in your service,
quick to repent when we fall,
ready to take responsibility when it is given,
and willing to tend your sheep;
through Jesus Christ our Lord. Amen.

Thomas Clarkson 1760–1846

Abolitionist

———

A SMALL MONUMENT ON the side of the old A10 at Wadesmill, just between Thundridge and High Cross, marks the place where Thomas Clarkson decided to devote his life to the abolition of slavery. In 1785 he was riding his horse on a journey from Cambridge, where he had just won a prize for his Latin essay on slavery. He was tired and sat by the side of the road where he had a 'spiritual revelation from God'. He recorded the event: 'A thought came into my mind that if the contents of the essay were true, it was time some person should see these calamities to their end'. Clarkson translated his essay into English and published it. It made a great impact and as a result the *Committee for the Abolition of the Slave Trade* was formed. The fight for abolition was long and difficult. It has been estimated that Clarkson rode over 35,000 miles around the country in his campaigning. The law banning the slave trade was eventually passed in 1807 although it was not until 1833 that slavery itself was prohibited in the British Empire.

The poet William Wordsworth wrote Sonnet, To Thomas Clarkson, On the final passing of the Bill for the Abolition of the Slave Trade, March, 1807

Clarkson! it was an obstinate Hill to climb:
How toilsome, nay how dire it was, by Thee
Is known,—by none, perhaps, so feelingly;
But Thou, who, starting in thy fervent prime,
Didst first lead forth this pilgrimage sublime,
Hast heard the constant Voice its charge repeat,
Which, out of thy young heart's oracular seat,
First roused thee.—O true yoke-fellow of Time
With unabating effort, see, the palm
Is won, and by all Nations shall be worn!
The bloody Writing is for ever torn,
And Thou henceforth wilt have a good Man's calm,
A great Man's happiness; thy zeal shall find
Repose at length, firm Friend of human kind!

From *Wordsworth and his Circle* by David Rannie

O God, our Leader and our Master and our Friend,
forgive our imperfections and our little motives,
take us and make us one with thy great purpose,
use us and do not reject us, make us all servants of thy kingdom,
weave our lives into thy struggle to conquer
and to bring peace and union to the world.
We are small and feeble creatures,
we are feeble in speech, feebler still in action,
nevertheless let but thy light shine upon us,
and there is not one of us who cannot be lit by thy fire
and who cannot lose himself in thy salvation.
Take us into thy purposes, O God,
let thy kingdom come into our hearts and into this world. Amen.

H. G. Wells

Richard of Wallingford 1292–1336

Mathematician and Abbot of St Albans

———

RICHARD WAS A person of huge intellect and enormous energy. Born in Wallingford to Isabella and William Smith, the village blacksmith, Richard's path to greatness was meteoric by anyone's standards. Following the death of his father, he was taken to the Priory of the Holy Trinity in his village to be cared for and placed under the protection of the Prior, William de Kirkeby. From there Richard was sent to study at Oxford, probably at Merton College. In 1315 he became a monk of St Albans, though he continued to reside in Oxford, studying theology and philosophy. He acquired a reputation as a distinguished mathematician and has been called the 'Father of Trigonometry'. He designed a clock called 'Albion' which displayed the time, date and seasons as well as the courses of the planets and the sun. In 1327, at the age of thirty-five, Richard was elected Abbot of St Albans and gave himself to renewing the life of the monastery. He repaired the roof of the Abbey Church, built the cloisters and an almonry to support the poor and destitute. Richard suffered from leprosy. By 1333 he had become so ill that he agreed to the appointment of a coadjutor-abbot but died three years later. Throughout his life Richard was respected for his holiness and erudition. Leland says that Richard was 'circumspect and timid in prosperity, in adversity patient and magnanimous; in all things and towards all men, both in word and by example, thoughtful and kindly.'

When suffering is offered to God, it can become the means of spiritual growth

Recall just a few ways in which this Gospel of transfiguration is for us a great reality. Suffering is transfigured. That is something that every priest has the joy of seeing, again and again, in the lives of people he meets. People who suffer greatly, and yet through their nearness to Christ, something different happens. They suffer still, but yet there is a sympathy, a gentleness, a sweetness, a power of love, a power of prayer that makes all the difference to them and to those who know them. Suffering transfigured. Situations transfigured. We find ourselves up against something that completely baffles us in any kind of rational terms. We are completely perplexed, and we cannot, as it were, get through the situation, or get round the situation, or retreat from the situation. But see it in the larger context of Jesus crucified and risen, and while it goes on being the painful situation that it was before, somehow it is in a different light, and a different light comes to us, and it was wrong for us to be making hasty judgements about it before we took it into the context of Jesus crucified and risen. The human lives are transfigured. That is what we have all seen happening in human lives, where by God's grace the mingled experiences of sorrow and joy bring about a transforming, the growth in grace, the growth in Christlikeness in reality.

From a retreat address given by Archbishop Michael Ramsey

Father of all mercies and giver of all comfort,
we lift into your presence all who are crushed by suffering:
in your tenderness sustain and strengthen them with your presence,
and grant them healing in body, mind and spirit, according to your will,
and for the sake of Jesus Christ our Lord. Amen.

Benjamin Rogers 1686–1771

Clergyman

———

BENJAMIN ROGERS WAS born in 1686 into a middle-class Bedfordshire family. The names of several generations of his family are to be found in the parish registers of St Paul's, Bedford, and in the burgess-rolls of the borough. His father, Thomas Rogers, was a vintner in the town. Rogers was educated at Mr Wentworth's School at Houghton Conquest and then in 1693 he transferred to the Free School at Bedford. He went up to Sidney Sussex College, Cambridge, in 1702 at the age of sixteen. It appears that he did not complete his degree and was appointed usher, or second master, of his old school, a post he held from 1707 until 1726. In 1712 he was ordained both deacon and priest and became Vicar of Stagsden. He moved to be Rector of Carlton in 1720. He married Jane Hothersall at Podington in 1728. They had twelve children, although only eight of them survived until adulthood. Jane died in 1742. Rogers remained as Rector of Carlton until his death in September 1771. We still have his diary which gives us a rich description of the daily life of a country parson in eighteenth-century Bedfordshire.

We get a glimpse of Benjamin Rogers' life from his diary in 1729

November the 6th. I finished Mr. Rudd's will, which he signed and sealed in the evening. Harry Fenn, John Clason and myself were witnesses.

The 7th. Went to Goldington to see Mr. Favel (where I had been the 4th), Mr. Collins, Mr. Tipping, Mr. Goodhall and his father in law Mr. Richards being there also. I promised to meet the company there on Tuesday night at Mr. Goodhall's, being November the 19th.

The 1st. My cousin Ridge's house was burnt; the fire was occasioned by his sister's looking under a bed with a candle for an halfpenny that one of the children had lost there, as was said. Some of the children narrowly escaped.

March the 16th. I gave the Sacrament to Mr. Carter Senior of Turvey, he being very weak.

The 17th. I went to Bedford where Mr. Collins, Mr. Alderman Battison, Mr. Haslewood, and myself had a discharge in full from Mrs. Priscilla Whalley, sole administratrix to Mr. Aspinall's effects.

The 18th. Mr. Carter Dyed. **The 22nd.** He was buried.

The 25th. I prayed by Henry Fenn. **The 31st.** I went to see Mrs. Carter.

April the 1st. Sow'd Abbot's pieze with Barley; about 4 bushel per acre. Ordered William Allen of Brigend to be blooded for the pleurisie.

2nd. Order'd him to be blouded again. The first time about 11 ounces was taken away; the 2nd about 9. He grew better after the 1st blouding; his blood was worse at the 2nd blooding than at the 1st.

4th. He dyed.

From *The Diary of Benjamin Rogers, Rector of Carlton, 1720–1771*

Gracious Father, we thank you for the faithful mission and ministry
of countless men and women of earlier generations;
although so much of their lives is unknown to us,
you do not forget their acts of love and kindness
which witnessed to you and to the coming of your kingdom.
Give us grace that we may be faithful in our generation
as we pass on the good news in word and deed;
to the glory of your name. Amen.

Lady Mabel de Pattishall 13th century

Founder of the Greyfriars in Bedford

———

THE WRITER OF the book of Hebrews encourages us to 'run with perseverance the race that is set before us,' reminding us that 'we are surrounded by so great a cloud of witnesses' (Hebrews 12.1). The names of most of those witnesses are lost. They are not recorded in any books nor does anyone living remember them; they are known to God alone. However, every so often someone's name is recorded. One such person was Lady Mabel de Pattishall or Mabilea de Plateshull. According to one ancient record, she founded a house in Bedford for Franciscan Friars. Commonly known as the Greyfriars because of the colour of their habit, the brothers worked among the poorest of the poor. Some early records credit the foundation to John St John, so it is possible that there might have been a group of benefactors or a lay fraternity who funded the house and supported the work of the brothers in Bedford. The Franciscan church was dedicated on 3 November 1295. The house was closed during the Dissolution of the Monasteries and the church demolished.

Gordon Mursell describes the world in which Lady Mabel lived and prayed

For much of the Middle Ages, lay piety remained firmly dominated by those who had embraced the religious life. Thus those of aristocratic status (many of whom would have either endowed, or at least generally contributed to, monastic houses) were sustained spiritually by private prayers written or collected together by monks: those of Anselm, which we shall explore later, exerted a particularly important influence on this pattern of spirituality. Many monasteries had confraternities, comprising lay supporters and benefactors, most of whom would have been wealthy, and who would have been rewarded for their gifts by having prayers offered for them: indeed, until the late twelfth century such people might even receive the monastic habit on their deathbed in order to ensure salvation. Others, known as 'corrodians', received either an income from, or actual residence in, a monastery, normally in return for some kind of endowment or grant of land. These relationships between laypeople and monasteries fitted well into a feudal world, for it was based on the familiar feudal practice of 'gift-exchange', i.e. gifts made in expectation of a return; and the return came gradually to be more clearly specified: lay benefactors might expect anything from the saying of some prayers for a departed relative to the recitation of masses for the dead in perpetuity. But they would certainly also expect the monks they were endowing to live lives appropriate to their vocation, not least for fear that otherwise their prayers might not prove efficacious.

From *English Spirituality: From Earliest Times to 1700*

———

Gracious God,
we thank you for our religious communities
and especially for those who are Franciscan tertiaries:
grant that after the example of Francis, the poor man of Assisi,
we may live in simplicity and joy
to the glory of your name;
through Jesus Christ our Lord. Amen.

Gerard Heath Lander 1861–1934

Bishop

———

WHEN GERARD LANDER arrived in Hong Kong in 1907, as the fifth Bishop of Victoria, it was a very different place from today. There were no skyscrapers nor international banks: Hong Kong was a port and a military base, with a population of under a quarter of a million people and a small English ex-patriot community. Christian missionaries had already opened a number of schools and a medical college and St Andrew's Church in Kowloon had been consecrated in the previous year. Lander was educated at Trinity College, Cambridge, and was ordained to a curacy at St Bride's, Liverpool, in 1885. He remained in the Diocese of Liverpool for over twenty years, serving successively as incumbent of St Benedict Everton, St Philip Litherland and St Cyprian Durning Road. From there he was consecrated Bishop of Victoria, Hong Kong, where he served for thirteen years. He returned to England to become Vicar of Holy Trinity, New Barnet, and assistant bishop in the Diocese of St Albans. In 1933 he was made Archdeacon of Bedford but died the following year.

Richard Baxter gives a warning to Christian ministers

Take heed to yourselves, because there are many eyes upon you, and there will be many observers of your falls. You cannot miscarry but the world will ring of it. The eclipses of the sun by day time are seldom without witnesses. As you take yourselves for the lights of the churches, you may expect that men's eyes should be upon you. If other men may sin without observation, so cannot you. God forbid that we should prove so impudent as to do evil in the public view of all, and to sin wilfully while the world is gazing on us. Take heed therefore to yourselves and do your works as those that remember that the world looks on them, and that with the quicksighted eye of malice, ready to make the worst of all, and to find the smallest faults where it is, and aggravate it where they find it, and divulge it and make it advantageous to their designs, and to make faults where they cannot find them. That man, therefore, that is not himself taken up with the predominant love of God, and is not himself devoted to Him and doth not devote to Him all that he hath and can do; that man that is not addicted to the pleasing of God and maketh Him not the centre of all his actions, and liveth not to him as his God and happiness; that is, that man that is not a sincere Christian himself, is utterly unfit to be a pastor of a church. No man is fit to be a minister of Christ that is not of a public spirit as to the Church and delighteth not in its beauty and longeth not for its felicity. As the good of the Commonwealth must be the end of the magistrate (his nearer end) so must the felicity of the Church be the end of the pastor of it.

From *The Reformed Pastor*

———

We thank you, Gracious God, for those who hear your call to service,
leave the security of home and family and venture to serve you overseas;
bless all missionaries who offer themselves in costly service,
sustain them in times of loneliness, protect them in times of danger
and encourage them in times of conflict;
for we ask this in the name of Jesus Christ our Lord. Amen.

Thomas Snagge 1536–93

Speaker of the House of Commons

———

THE BEAUTIFUL FOURTEENTH-CENTURY church of St Mary's, Marston Moretaine, is home to the elaborate alabaster effigies of Thomas Snagge and his wife, Elizabeth. Snagge was an influential lawyer and politician during the second half of the sixteenth century. Born in Letchworth, his father was lord of the manor of Marston Moretaine. Snagge studied law at Gray's Inn and was called to the bar in 1554. He retained his property at Howell Bury and in 1569 purchased the barony and castle of Bedford and the manor of Kempston Daubeney. Snagge also acquired the large estates of the Reynes family in Bedfordshire by marrying Elizabeth Thomas Dikons. They had two sons, Thomas and Robert. As well as practising as a lawyer, Snagge was elected Member of Parliament for Bedfordshire in 1571. Queen Elizabeth I appointed him Attorney General for Ireland, a post which he held in 1577–80. He represented the constituency of Bedfordshire again in 1586 and in the same year was involved in the trial of Mary, Queen of Scots. Two years later he was elected Speaker of the House of Commons. He was returned as Member of Parliament for the Borough of Bedford in the following year. Throughout his parliamentary career Snagge was deeply involved in matters concerning the Church, such as preventing patrons from making corrupt presentations and attendance at worship (this was the period when you could be fined if you missed church).

Austin Farrer reflects on human and divine governance

The plans of government are concerned with statistical charts, with something highly general and impersonal, with persuading the curve on the economic graph to sweep handsomely upwards and, in short, with giving contemporary history a streamlined look. But God's plan is not concerned with streamlining, let us say, the ecclesiastical system, it is concerned with the living body of mankind in all its warmth and variety; not from the point of view of its rationalisation, but from that of its eternal salvation. New every morning is the love, and new every hour the loving foresight, which sees the openings for our happiness, and sets the opportunities of good ready to our hand. Reach out and take them, for now is the appointed time. God's plan is not a five years plan, but a five minutes plan; or, again, from another point of view, neither a five years plan nor a five thousand years plan, but a plan for our eternity, starting here.

From Said or Sung

We pray, good Lord, for all who hold public office
and especially for our politicians and civil servants:
inspire them with a vision of the common good,
that the weak and vulnerable may be protected,
that the powerful may be held to account,
and that together we build a society
where all may thrive and flourish;
for the sake of Jesus Christ our Lord. Amen.

Richard de Morins c.1161–1242

Lawyer and prior

———

I T IS THOUGHT that Morins was born in Lincolnshire and studied in Paris. It was there that he wrote his *Summa Questionium*. He went on to teach canon law in Bologna where he wrote a number of other works. Morins returned to England and became prior of the Augustinian canons at Merton, before being elected prior of Dunstable Priory in 1202. It was only at this point that he was ordained a priest, having been in deacon's orders up to that time. Henry I had founded the Augustinian priory in Dunstable around 1132, and endowed it with the lordship of the manor. In 1203 King John sent Morins as an ambassador to Pope Innocent III. On his return to England he travelled with Giovanni da Crema, the papal legate. In 1206 the legate appointed Morins as the visitor of all the religious houses in the Diocese of Lincoln (which at that time included most of Bedfordshire and Hertfordshire). We know that in 1212 he travelled around both counties preaching the Crusades. In 1215 he attended the Fourth Lateran Council in Rome. There are many records of Morins appearing in ecclesiastical courts on behalf of the papacy and acting as an arbitrator in disputes. In 1235 he assisted the monks of St Albans as they elected a new abbot. Despite Morins' considerable gifts, relations between the prior and the town of Dunstable were often difficult. From 1210 until his death Morins oversaw the compilation of the Annals of Dunstable.

St Augustine lays down how the Christian community should be governed

1. The superior should be obeyed as a father with the respect due him so as not to offend God in his person, and, even more so, the priest who bears responsibility for you all.

2. But it shall pertain chiefly to the superior to see that these precepts are all observed and, if any point has been neglected, to take care that the transgression is not carelessly overlooked but is punished and corrected. In doing so, he must refer whatever exceeds the limit and power of his office, to the priest who enjoys greater authority among you.

3. The superior, for his part, must not think himself fortunate in his exercise of authority but in his role as one serving you in love. In your eyes he shall hold the first place among you by the dignity of his office, but in fear before God he shall be as the least among you. He must show himself as an example of good works toward all. Let him admonish the unruly, cheer the fainthearted, support the weak, and be patient toward all. Let him uphold discipline while instilling fear. And though both are necessary, he should strive to be loved by you rather than feared, ever mindful that he must give an account of you to God.

From *The Rule of St Augustine*

———

Breathe in me, O Holy Spirit, that my thoughts may all be holy.
Act in me, O Holy Spirit, that my work, too, may be holy.
Draw my heart, O Holy Spirit, that I love but what is holy.
Strengthen me, O Holy Spirit, to defend all that is holy.
Guard me, then, O Holy Spirit, that I always may be holy. Amen.

St Augustine

Deborah Louise Ellson 1961–2005

Wood carver and priest

———

DEBORAH ELLSON'S FIRST career was as a physical education teacher. However, she heard a call to the religious life and became a nun of the Community of All Hallows, Ditchingham, in Norfolk, where she remained for seventeen years. Deborah was a spiritual director to a number of people and led many retreats and quiet days. During her time in the Community she discerned a vocation to the priesthood and trained for the ministry on the East Anglian Ministerial Training Course. She was made deacon in the Diocese of Norwich in 2000 and priested in the following year. Deborah served her title at St Margaret's, Lowestoft, from 2000 until 2004. She is remembered there particularly for her pastoral care and her gift for working with children. She was then appointed as Priest-in-Charge of Langleybury, Watford. As well as her parochial duties, she took groups on pilgrimages to Iona and Lindisfarne. Deborah was a gifted wood carver and used her skill to produce many items, including Stations of the Cross, and a processional cross which is still in use at St Margaret's Lowestoft.

A reflection on how we can become more like Christ

The block of marble that became Michelangelo's larger-than-life sculpture of David lay almost untouched in the cathedral storehouse in Florence for decades. Two other sculptors had attempted to make something of it before it was offered to Michelangelo. One started working with it, but soon quit because his talents lay in more delicate work. The great Leonardo da Vinci turned down an opportunity to transform it, preferring to pursue another project more suited to his taste. When offered the opportunity, Michelangelo agreed to do what others could not. He built a shed around the block of marble, which he kept locked at all times. For three years he laboured to transform it from its natural state to an eternal work of art. At first Michelangelo examined the marble minutely to see what poses it would accommodate. He made sketches and models of various possible creations and then tested his ultimate image in a small-scale wax version of his final result. Finally he picked up his mallet and chisel and began to work. When Michelangelo looked at that block of marble, he did not see what it couldn't be; he saw what it could be. He didn't reject it because it was flawed. He saw a way to work around the flaws, even to incorporate them into his design. What he did was so great, even evident flaws could not scar its beauty. There are drill marks in David's thick curled hair, some of the original quarry marks are on the very top of the head, and one can see traces of the cuttings made by an earlier sculptor who, forty years before, failed to do what Michelangelo did: create one of the greatest masterpieces of all time. Michelangelo, the sculptor of David, is a picture of what pastors do as sculptors of the soul if we can but see what so many others have missed.

Bill Lawrence

———

Gracious God,
as a sculptor sees the potential of a rough hewn stone,
so you too see what we can become:
through the sacraments of your Church
and in the power of the Holy Spirit
chip away all that is destructive and sinful
and sculpt us into the people you would have us be;
through Jesus Christ our Lord. Amen.

John Schorne 13th century

Priest

———

PROBABLY THE MOST famous resident of the village of Steppingley was one of the early rectors, John Schorne, who took up office in 1273. He became well known as a healer and was credited with having imprisoned the devil, or demon of pain, in an old boot. It is thought that the French Horn pub in the village is named after him. He moved to North Marston Church in 1283 where, during a drought, he discovered a well, the waters of which were reputed to have miraculous properties. When he died North Marston became a place of pilgrimage. Small models of Schorne holding a boot with the devil's head poking out were sold as pilgrim tokens and this is believed to have been the inspiration for the Jack-in-the-Box, which was so popular in Victorian times. John Schorne's remains lie in St George's Chapel, Windsor.

The Passionate Man's Pilgrimage

Give me my scallop-shell of quiet,
 My staff of faith to walk upon,
My scrip of joy, immortal diet,
 My bottle of salvation,
My gown of glory, hope's true gage;
 And thus I'll take my pilgrimage.

Sir Walter Raleigh

My Lord God,
I have no idea where I am going.
I do not see the road ahead of me.
I cannot know for certain where it will end…
Nor do I really know myself,
and the fact that I think I am following your will
does not mean that I am actually doing so.
But I believe that the desire to please you,
does in fact please you.
And I hope I have that desire in all that I am doing.
I hope that I will never do anything apart from that desire.
And I know that if I do this,
You will lead me by the right road, though
I may know nothing about it.
Therefore will I trust you always though
I may seem lost in the shadow of death.
I will not fear, for you are ever with me,
and you will never leave me to face my perils alone. Amen.

A Pilgrim's Prayer by Thomas Merton

Samuel Horsley 1733–1806

Rector and bishop

————

I F YOU GO to visit the church of St James the Great, Thorley, you will find that members of the Horsley family are buried on the north side of the chancel. Horsley had been the rector of the church from 1779 to 1782. He was an intelligent man who wrote a number of books on a wide variety of subjects, including mathematics and theology, and he translated several books from Greek and Latin into English. Horsley was educated at Trinity Hall, Cambridge, where he read law. For a period he was private tutor to the son of the Earl of Aylesford before being made Archdeacon of St Albans in 1781. He was elected a fellow of the Royal Society in 1767 and was made secretary to the Society in 1773. He was bishop in three different dioceses: firstly, St Davids (1788), then Rochester (1793) and finally St Asaph (1802). Horsley was a passionate apologist for the Christian faith and is remembered for his lengthy debate with Joseph Priestley about the Trinity.

Samuel Horsley preaches on the resurrection

The prop and pillar of the Christian's hope, (which being once removed the entire building would give way), is the great event which we at this season commemorate, the resurrection of our Lord; insomuch that the evidence of that fact may properly be considered as the seal of his pretensions, and of the expectation of his followers. If, notwithstanding the pure and holy life which Jesus led, the sublimity of the doctrine which he taught, and the natural excellence of the duties which he enjoined; if after all the miracles which he performed, he was at last forsaken of the God to whose service his life had been devoted, if his soul at last was left in hell, and the Holy One of God was suffered like a common man, to become the prey of works and putrefaction, then truly is our preaching in vain, and your faith in vain…If Christ be not risen from the dead, the consequence must either be, that he was an imposter, and that his whole doctrine was a fraud; or if the purity of his life might still screen him from so foul an imputation and the truth of his pretensions be supposed consistent with a failure of his predictions in the most important article, you would only have in him a discouraging example of how little estimation in the sight of God is the utmost height of virtue to which human nature can attain…His *resurrection* was the accomplishment both of the ancient prophecies and of his own prediction; a declaration on the part of God that the great atonement was accepted; an attestation of the truth of our Saviour's doctrine and of his high pretensions; a confirmation of the hope of his followers, which renders it no less unreasonable, as the case stands, to doubt of the ultimate completion of his largest promises, than it would have been to hope, had his promises been actually found to fail in so principal an instance.

From *Four Discourses*

————

God of Resurrection,
you raised your Son Jesus Christ from the grave,
and named him the first-born from the dead:
we thank you that in baptism we have passed through the waters of death;
give us grace to walk each day in newness of life
and seek the things that are above, where Christ is sat at your right hand;
to him be the glory, now and for ever. Amen.

Alpheus Paget Wilkes 1871–1934

Missionary

———

BORN INTO A clerical dynasty, Alpheus Paget Wilkes was born at Titchwell in Norfolk. For the first few years of his life he was educated at home but, following the death of his mother, he was sent to Bedford School and then to Lincoln College, Oxford. It was while he was at university that he made a Christian commitment and offered himself for overseas missionary service. In 1898 Paget Wilkes joined a Hertfordshire man, Barclay Fowell Buxton (see the entry for 20 September), who had gone to Japan nine years earlier. Paget Wilkes went to Matsue and Osaka and worked there for the next fourteen years. In 1903 the two men founded the Japan Evangelistic Band during the Keswick Convention. The Band was responsible for establishing around one hundred and fifty churches in Japan, as well as a Bible College in Kobe. Paget Wilkes visited Japan on many occasions over the following years. He wrote poetry and a large number of books including *Missionary Joys in Japan*, *Modern Thought* and *The Dynamic of Life*. He was married to Gertrude Hamilton Barthorp. He died on this day in 1934.

Alpheus Paget Wilkes writes about humility

Many a professor, teacher, minister, or Christian worker, convicted of inward sin and the need of inward holiness, will not, alas, take the position of a humble seeker for purity of heart. They declare that they would lose the confidence of their flock if they publicly owned their need in other than vague and general terms. They seek not the honour that cometh from God, but desire to stand well in the eyes of men! There is not a real and complete surrender to the Lord Jesus. There may not appear to be much connection between faith and this humble and sincere attitude of soul. But there is; and faith is utterly unable to stretch forth her hands, either to lay hold of the promise and receive the blessing, until the soul is determined at all costs to be wholly the Lord's; but as soon as the surrender is complete it can fully and easily believe!

From *The Dynamic of Faith*

Almighty and everlasting God,
in whom we live and move and have our being,
who hast created us for thyself,
so that our hearts are restless until they find rest in thee:
Grant unto us such purity of heart and strength of purpose,
that no selfish passion may hinder us from knowing thy will,
and no weakness from doing it.
In thy light may we see life clearly,
and in thy service find perfect freedom;
through Jesus Christ our Lord. Amen.

From *The Methodist Book of Worship for Church and Home*

St Faith d. c.303

Martyr

THE WITNESS OF St Faith is still honoured in three Hertfordshire churches, each built in different periods. There is the thirteenth-century church in Hexton near Barton-le-Clay, the fifteenth-century church at Kelshall and the Victorian church in Hitchin built in 1894. What is it about St Faith which has caught the imagination of those building churches at such different times? Perhaps it was the idea of a young, innocent girl choosing a painful death rather than compromise her Christian beliefs. Not a great deal is known about St Faith. It is thought she was a young girl from Agen in Aquitaine, who was arrested during the persecutions in the time of Diocletian. She was obliged to make sacrifices to pagan gods but refused, even though she was threatened with torture. St Faith was killed by being burned to death.

Diarmaid MacCulloch writes about martyrdom in the early Church

The Christian sense of certainty in belief was especially concentrated in their celebration of constancy in suffering, even to death. From time to time, they faced mob harassment and official persecution, which in the worst cases ended in public executions preceded by prolonged torture and ritual humiliation, the victims stripped naked in front of a gleeful crowd in sporting arenas. Among the early victims were such Christian leaders as Peter, Paul, Ignatius of Antioch and Polycarp of Smyrna, a very old man when he died around 155 and the first Christian to be recorded as having being burnt alive. That grisly fate Christians later visited on each other a good deal once they gained access to power, yet alongside a continuing Christian inclination to persecute other Christians, there has survived an intense celebration of martyrdom. The first people whom Christians recognised as saints (that is, people with a sure prospect of Heaven) were victims of persecution who died in agony rather than deny their Saviour, who had died for them in agony on the Cross. Such a death, if suffered in the right spirit (not an easy matter to judge) guarantees entry into Heaven…The attractive feature of a martyr's death was that it was open to anyone, regardless of social status or talent. Women were martyred alongside men, slaves alongside free persons. The necessary ability was to die bravely and with dignity, turning the agony and humiliation into shame and instruction for the spectators. Martyrs' bones were treasured and their burial places became the first Christian shrines. From the end of the third century onwards, even while martyrdoms were still being suffered, there is evidence of Christians wanting to be buried near such tombs.

From *A History of Christianity*

We pray for those Christians who this day
will be threatened by violence because of their beliefs,
and those who face injury or death for standing up for the truth;
give them courage and perseverance,
that they may hold firm as they bear witness to the good news;
may their example inspire us in our discipleship
and strengthen us in our faith;
through Jesus Christ our Lord. Amen.

Tom Harris 1917–2010

Churchwarden, bell ringer and fundraiser

———

Tom harris was involved in nearly every area of life at St James' Church in Silsoe, Bedfordshire: bell ringer, organist, choir member and churchwarden. However, he was also a dedicated supporter of Christian Aid and over the years he raised more than £70,000 for the charity. Tom was a founding member of the local Christian Aid Committee in the 1960s and was also Chairman for more than twenty-five years, only giving up due to ill-health. In 1996, in recognition of his years of dedication, he was awarded an MBE for his 'services to the community and to Christian Aid'. Tom was born in Silsoe, the youngest son of a local farmer. He left school at fourteen to work on the family farm and knew just how hard farming could be in the days when there was no electricity or mains water. In 1948 he married Phyllis Smith and they had two sons and three daughters. They were married for sixty-one years. A bell ringer from 1939 to 2003, Tom was also Ringing Master for over fifty years. He sang in the choir, was a Sunday School teacher in his teens, and church organist for fourteen years after the early death of his mother (who herself had been the organist).

St Augustine preaches about practical love

So then, begin by loving your neighbour: 'Share your bread with the hungry, and bring the homeless poor into your own house; when you see the naked, cover them, and do not hide yourself from your own kin.' In doing this what will happen? 'Then shall your light break forth like the dawn.' Your light is your God; to you he is 'morning light', because after the night of this present world he will come to you: God, who neither rises nor sets; God, who always abides. Remember too what is said by the apostle Paul: 'Bear one another's burdens, and in this way you will fulfil the law of Christ.' The law of Christ is charity; and charity is not fulfilled unless we bear one another's burdens. When you were weak, your neighbour carried you. Now you are strong, carry your neighbour. In so doing, my brothers and sisters, you will make up what is lacking in you. By loving your neighbour and being concerned about your neighbour you make progress on your journey. And where is that journey bound if not to the Lord God, the God whom it is our duty to love with all our heart, with all our soul, and with all our mind? We may not yet have reached the Lord, but we do have our neighbour with us. So then, support your fellow traveller that you may come to the One with whom you long to dwell.

From the *Commentary on St John's Gospel*

Lord Jesus Christ, who taught your followers,
by word and example, the lesson of self-less service:
root out of our hearts all greed and envy
and grant us that love which is the fruit of your Holy Spirit
that we may give ourselves freely in service to you and to one another;
we ask this for your name's sake. Amen.

Basil Henry William Carr 1924–2011

Reader

———

BILL CARR CAME to faith through a slightly unusual route as he was curious to know why his wife was always attending the parish church and he was not happy at being known as 'Pat Carr's husband'. Pat was much involved with the church and the Mothers' Union at St Thomas' Church in Wilbury. Bill himself was drawn into church activities, appointed churchwarden, and later he and Pat began a charismatic prayer group in their home. Eventually, Bill was encouraged by the incumbent, the Reverend Donald Dowling, to explore a vocation to Readership which, despite initial misgivings about his lack of further education, he undertook and was licensed in 1988 at Elstow. One of Bill's many talents was his capacity for articulating the faith in a way which ordinary folk could understand. In his preaching, he drew on his own life experiences with both insight and humour, and he had a capacity to empathise with those who were experiencing problems in their personal lives. He and Pat were much in demand for their 'Bible Road Show' where they acted out Bible stories. During his working life Bill had served as a sergeant pilot in the Royal Air Force in East Africa and also worked for ICL in Stevenage.

Henri Nouwen reflects on the healing power of community

Perhaps the main task of the minister is to prevent people from suffering for the wrong reasons. Many people suffer because of the false supposition on which they have based their lives. That supposition is that there should be no fear or loneliness, no confusion or doubt. But these sufferings can only be dealt with creatively when they are understood as wounds integral to our human condition. Therefore ministry is a very confronting service. It does not allow people to live with illusions or immortality and wholeness. It keeps reminding others that they are mortal and broken, but also that with the recognition of this condition, liberation starts. A Christian community is therefore a healing community not because wounds are cured and pains are alleviated, but because wounds and pains become openings and occasions for a new vision. Mutual confession then becomes a mutual deepening of hope, and sharing weakness becomes a reminder to one and all of the coming strength.

From *The Wounded Healer*

———

Almighty and tender Lord Jesus Christ,
Just as I have asked you to love my friends so I ask the same for my enemies.
You alone, Lord, are mighty, you alone are merciful.
Whatever you make me desire for my enemies,
give it to them and give the same back to me.
If I ever ask for them anything which is outside your perfect rule of love,
whether through weakness, ignorance or malice,
Good Lord, do not give it to them and do not give it back to me.
You who are the true light, lighten their darkness.
You who are the whole truth, correct their errors.
You who are the incarnate word, give life to their souls.
Tender Lord Jesus, let me not be a stumbling block to them nor a rock of offence.
My sin is sufficient to me, without harming others.
I, a slave to sin, beg your mercy on my fellow slaves.
Let them be reconciled with you, and through you reconciled to me. Amen.

Anselm of Canterbury

Robert Grosseteste c.1170–1253

Theologian, scientist and bishop

———

IT WOULD BE considered impolite today to name someone on the basis of their anatomy. Yet Grosseteste simply means 'big head' in Norman French. He was born in Suffolk and went to school in Lincoln, before studying in Cambridge and Paris. Robert became part of the household of William de Vere, the Bishop of Hereford, and stayed in the diocese for the next twenty-five years, involved in administrative work and writing a number of scientific works including *On the Calendar*, *On the Movements of the Planets* and *On the Origin of Sounds*. He also wrote the first commentary on Aristotle's *Posterior Analytics*. From 1225 until 1231 he taught in the University of Oxford, following which he became lector to the Franciscans, who lived just outside the city walls. He continued his scientific studies, publishing a book, *On Light*, as well as theological works, *On the ten commandments*, *On the end of the Old Testament law* and *On the six days of creation*. In 1235 he was elected Bishop of Lincoln, the largest diocese in the country with nearly two thousand parishes, which covered most of the present-day Diocese of St Albans. He began a visitation of the diocese and soon became known as a reformer, meeting with much opposition, not least from the dean and chapter in Lincoln. He travelled extensively, attending the Council of Lyons and visiting Rome. He died on this day in 1253 and is commemorated in the Church of England on 9 October.

Robert Grosseteste preaches before Pope Innocent IV at Lyons

But what is the cause of this hopeless fall of the church? Unquestionably, the diminution in the number of good shepherds of souls, the increase of wicked shepherds, and the circumscription of the pastoral authority and power. Bad pastors are everywhere: the cause of unbelief, division, heresy, and vice. It is they who scatter the flock of Christ, who lay waste the vineyard of the Lord, and desecrate the earth. No wonder, for they preach not the Gospel of Christ with that living word which comes forth from living zeal for the salvation of souls, and is confirmed by an example worthy of Jesus Christ: and to this they add every possible form of transgression – their pride is ever on the increase, and so are their avarice, luxury, and extravagance; and because the life of the shepherds is a lesson to the laity, they became thus the teachers of all error and all evil. Instead of being a light of the world, they spread around, by their godless example, the thickest darkness and the icy coldness of death.

From *John Wycliffe and his English Precursors* by G. V. Lechner

———

Heavenly Father,
you call bishops to be shepherds of Christ's flock,
to guard the faith of the apostles,
to proclaim the gospel of the kingdom
and to lead your people in mission:
fill all bishops with your Holy Spirit
that they may live holy lives
and be faithful in their calling
through Jesus Christ our Lord. Amen.

Thomas Ravenscroft c.1582–1635
James and Mary Ravenscroft 17th century
Musicologist and benefactors

———

THOMAS RAVENSCROFT WAS a musicologist and composer who collected popular songs and folk music, which he had heard being sung in the streets and markets of London. He published three collections called *Pammelia*, *Deuteromelia* and *Melismata*. The second volume contains the earliest record of 'Three Blind Mice'. Ravenscroft also produced a metrical psalter called *The Whole Booke of Psalmes* and wrote anthems and motets. His son, James, and daughter in law, Mary, founded the Jesus Hospital Charity in Chipping Barnet in 1670. Its purpose was to provide almshouses for 'poor and ancient women'. These six 'sisters' had to be 'of holy report and innocent conversation'. The trustees were not allowed to admit anyone 'suspected of Sorcery or Witchcraft or Charming. Or if Common Drunkard, Common Scold or Backbiter. Nor idiot or lunatic or infected with any foul or loathsome disease.' There is a chapel dedicated to the Ravenscrofts in St John the Baptist, Chipping Barnet, with a fine alabaster effigy of Thomas, dated 1630, and marble busts of James and Mary. There is also a park, public gardens and a school in the town named after them.

Leo, a fifth-century Pope, exhorts us to be generous

If God is love, charity should know no limit, for God cannot be confined…Let us now extend to the poor and those afflicted in different ways a more open-handed generosity, so that God may be thanked through many voices and the relief of the needy supported by our fasting. No act of devotion on the part of the faithful gives God more pleasure than that which is lavished on his poor. Where he finds charity with its loving concern, there he recognizes the reflection of his own fatherly care…In these acts of giving do not fear a lack of means. A generous spirit is itself great wealth. There can be no shortage of material for generosity where it is Christ who feeds and Christ who is fed. In all this activity there is present the hand of him who multiplies the bread by breaking it, and increases it by giving it away…The giver of alms should be free from anxiety and full of joy. His gain will be greatest when he keeps back least for himself. The holy apostle Paul tells us 'He who provides seed for the sower will also provide bread for eating; he will provide you with more seed, and will increase the amount of your goodness.'

From a sermon of Leo the Great

Gracious God,
whose Son Jesus Christ poured out his life
for the salvation of the world:
put into our hearts the same spirit of reckless generosity,
that, walking in the way of the cross,
we may give our lives for you
and for the good of the world:
we ask this for his name's sake. Amen.

Hildred Carlile 1852–1942

Businessman and politician

————

LIFE IS SOMETIMES stranger than fiction. Two elderly brothers, living miles apart, fall ill and die within three hours of each other. So it was in 1942 with Hildred Carlile and his brother, Wilson Carlile, founder of the Church Army. Hildred Carlile was born in Surrey and educated at St Albans School. He worked in business before being elected as the Conservative Member of Parliament for St Albans in 1906. He remained in politics until 1919 when he resigned due to ill health. He served as a Justice of the Peace for Hertfordshire, an Honorary Colonel of a Battalion of the King's Own Yorkshire Light Infantry Regiment, a Deputy Lieutenant, and in 1922 he was High Sheriff of Hertfordshire. He was also a Vice President of the Church Army. Carlile was a generous benefactor and donated one hundred thousand guineas to endow a number of academic chairs in Botany, English, Latin and Physics at Bedford College, University of London. He was knighted in 1911. Six years later he was created a baronet for his public service and took the name Baron Carlile of Ponsbourne Park. He was also made a CBE.

Herbert Hensley Henson reflects on Christianity and politics

We are rightly suspicious of appeals to conscience in the region of public policy, on this very account. Whatever may be the value of intuitions to those who receive them, they are clearly of no more value to others than their own judgment allows. Political wisdom is not learned in the sanctuary or in the assemblies of the saints, but in the patient study of the past and in the school of actual experience. Hardly any lesson is more consistently taught by the chequered and various history of mankind than this: that high character is no security against political folly, and noble intentions no effectual barrier against unworthy methods. We are not, therefore, to suppose that, as Christians, we possess some distinctive insight into public affairs which others do not possess, that we can take a short cut to our political decisions, and that those decisions are morally binding on the acceptance of others. To think in that way is to think fanatically, and thinking fanatically is the condition of intemperate speech and, when opportunity comes, of intolerant action. Christianity no more commits us to a specific political doctrine, or party, or programme, than to a specific nationality or government.

From 'Christianity and Politics' in *Christ and the Nation*

Lord of the Nations,
we pray for our Members of Parliament:
may their ambition be to work for the good of all,
may their determination drive them to fight for truth and justice
and may they lead by personal example,
protecting the weak and shielding the vulnerable;
through Jesus Christ our Lord. Amen.

William Jones 1755–1821

Clergyman

———

NOT MANY CLERGY minister in the same parish for forty years, yet this was precisely what William Jones did in his parish in Hertfordshire between 1781 and 1801. Jones was born in Abergavenny and studied at Jesus College, Oxford. He spent a short spell as a private tutor in Jamaica before being ordained. He was first curate and then Vicar of Broxbourne and Hoddesdon until his death on this day in 1812. Jones kept a diary which gives us a graphic account of the struggles in his life and ministry. His wife was called Theodosia and they argued constantly. He wrote that she was 'a lawyer's daughter and possessed such a wonderful volubility of speech, such a miraculous power of twirling and twisting every argument to her own interest that I am no match for her High Mightiness'. Jones also had a long running disagreement with a local farmer, who insisted on putting his cattle on Jones' glebe and who wrote to the bishop 'a letter full of calumnies and misrepresentations' to block his appointment as vicar. The famer did not succeed in his campaign and in frustration he cut off some of the bell ropes. In revenge the vicar's friends got their own back 'that night and many succeeding days and nights, not only by the ringing, but by hisses, hootings, and various insults of the populace'. Jones is also remembered for having purchased a coffin for himself which he used as a bookshelf. Ironically, when he died he was too big to fit into it.

Harry Williams reflects on suffering

In page after page of the New Testament we are told that in so far as we share in Christ's sufferings we are made partakers here and now of His resurrection. This is the great and glorious paradox of Christian experience: that it is by dying that we live, that it is by sharing with Jesus the horror of His agony that we live with Him reigning indestructibly in peace. Once we are willing to see and feel the desert in which we live, the desert becomes fertile, bringing forth every tree whose fruit shall be for meat, and the leaf thereof for healing. Once we know that we are poor, the Kingdom of Heaven is ours. So when our lot is cast with somebody who is finding his cross, his desert, his poverty overwhelming, we are on holy ground. For it is precisely here that God is present to save, to save us as well as them. So our identification with the other person brings to our lives and to theirs the power, the joy, the victory which is already ours and all mankind's in Christ Jesus our Lord. That, I believe, is the message which our age is waiting to hear – a realistic recognition of suffering and evil in the universe, not trying apologetically to pretend that things are better than they are, together with the first-hand affirmation of this suffering and evil as the place where the Son of Man is glorified and with Him we and all mankind.

From *The True Wilderness*

———

O God, give us strength to change those things that we can change,
the patience to accept those that we cannot change,
and the wisdom to know the difference, always;
through Jesus Christ's sake. Amen.

Reinhold Niebuhr

Edward Aveling Green 1842–1930

Sculptor

———

IN THE EARLY years of the twentieth century the Rector of Eversholt gave the artist Edward Green permission to decorate the nave and chancel arch of the parish church. The painting over the nave depicts Christ surrounded with angels, all of whom appear to have the same face. Green only used one person as his model, Mary Taylor, a young girl from the village who worked for his family. In 1908 he donated the reredos, with its carving of the Last Supper, and also designed a stained glass window for the church. The bronze cast of St Michael in the war memorial in the village is also by Green.

Edward Green was born in Woburn in 1842. As a young man he studied engineering but became increasingly frustrated as he was so passionate about art. He enrolled at the Royal Academy Schools and travelled extensively around Europe, visiting the great galleries. He spent part of the year in London, painting in his studio in Haverstock Hill, London, and the rest of his time at his sister's home, Berrystead in Eversholt, where he also had a studio in a former tithe barn. Towards the end of his life he settled at Berrystead permanently and died there in 1930.

Ray Hutchinson writes about art

He pressed a switch, and in a corner of the small, shabby room the light from hidden globes broke evenly on an unframed canvas, some eighteen inches square, which showed a Virgin of unconventional youthfulness in a robe and fillet of Aegean blue…

'You may get my meaning,' he said, 'when I tell you that picture does more to me than twenty sermons. For one thing it tells me what religious faith can do with ordinary things. You look at that face – you know that girl's had some experience no other woman had before or since. But the model's nothing unusual – you'll see girls like that today, any time you like to walk around the fields in Tuscany. Look at her skin – look at the freckles. That's not the daughter of a rich storekeeper even. That's a peasant girl.'

From *A Child Possessed*

Robert Henri describes the power of the artist

When the artist is alive in any person, whatever his kind of work may be, he becomes an inventive, searching, daring, self-expressing creature. He becomes interesting to other people. He disturbs, upsets, enlightens, and he opens ways for a better understanding. Where those who are not artists are trying to close the book, he opens it, and shows there are still more pages possible.

From *The Art Spirit*

———

God of beauty,
we thank you for the gift of creativity
enabling us to see the world afresh:
open our eyes this day
that we may truly see the beauty around us
and then direct our gaze to you,
the source of all beauty;
for we ask this in the name of Jesus Christ our Lord. Amen.

Henry John Temple 1784–1865

Prime Minister

———

BROCKET HALL IN Lemsford has been the setting for many significant events, not least the death of Lord Palmerston while he was still Prime Minister. Christened Henry John Temple, Palmerston was educated at Harrow and the Universities of Edinburgh and Cambridge. He was elected as the Tory Member of Parliament for Newport in 1807 and rapidly rose to high office. He was Secretary of War in 1809–28, Foreign Secretary for most of the time in 1830–51, Home Secretary in 1852–5 and Prime Minister for the Whigs in 1855–8 and of the newly-formed Liberal Party from 1859 until his death. Palmerston argued for penal reform, the abolition of slavery, Catholic emancipation, and he also supported the Factory Act of 1853, which outlawed young people from working between 6pm and 6am. He was known for his patriotism and oratory. Not a lot is known about Palmerston's faith, although he supported the establishment of the Church of England and was keen to maintain a balance of churchmanship among the bishops. On his death bed his doctor asked if he believed in the regeneration of the world through Jesus Christ, to which Palmerston replied: 'Oh, surely'. He was married to Emily, Lady Cowper.

Here the Dutch priest and humanist Erasmus writes about the responsibility of rulers

The first requisite of a king is to judge rightly about each matter, because opinions are like sources from which all the actions of life flow, and when they are infected everything must needs be mismanaged. The next essential is to recoil from evil and to be led towards good. For true wisdom consists not only in the knowledge of truth, but in the love and eager striving for what is good…And for first of all the mind of the prince must be freed from all false ideas, so that he can see what is truly good, truly glorious, truly splendid. The next thing is to instil the hatred of what is base, the love of what is good, so that he can see clearly what is becoming to a prince, and wish for nothing but what is worthy of a good and beneficent ruler. Let him recognise the good where it may be found, and always measure everything by it, never varying from this aim. This is what is meant by wisdom, and it is in this that the prince must so far excel other mortals, as he excels them in dignity, in wealth, in splendour, and in power.

From *The 'Adages' of Erasmus* translated by Margaret Mann Phillips

O God, Almighty Father,
King of kings and Lord of all our rulers,
grant that the hearts and minds of all who go out as leaders before us,
the statesmen, the judges, the men of learning, and the men of wealth,
may be so filled with the love of thy laws,
and of that which is righteous and life-giving,
that they may serve as a wholesome salt unto the earth,
and be worthy stewards of thy good and perfect gifts;
through Jesus Christ our Lord. Amen.

Prayer of the Order of the Garter

POPE ADRIANIV

Nicholas Breakspear c. 1100–59

Pope

———

POPE ADRIAN IV was baptised Nicholas Breakspear. He is the only Englishman ever to have been elected Pope. It is thought that he was born at Breakspear Farm in Bedmond, Hertfordshire, and was educated at St Albans School. Breakspear had wanted to be a monk in the Benedictine Community at St Albans but he was told to wait. In his frustration, he went to France, where he became a canon regular of the monastery of St Rufus at Arles and eventually its Abbot. Breakspear imposed such strict discipline on the community that some of the monks made a formal complaint to the Pope. However, Pope Eugene III was so impressed with him that, rather than rebuke him, he made him Bishop of Albano in 1149. Within a few years he was sent by the Pope to Norway where he formed the Diocese of Hamar and founded a number of schools. Soon after his return to Rome in 1154, Pope Anastasius IV died and Breakspear was elected Pope. During his papacy he made an alliance with the Byzantine Emperor in a war against the Sicilians. Not only did the Byzantines lose the war but the hope of healing the schism between the Church in the East and the West, which had started in 1054, was not realised either. Breakspear died at Anagni, according to one tradition, after choking on a fly.

Dietrich Bonhoeffer, who was martyred for his faith, writes about following Christ

Cheap grace is the preaching of forgiveness without requiring repentance, baptism without church discipline, Communion without confession, absolution without personal confession. Cheap grace is grace without discipleship, grace without the cross, grace without Jesus Christ, living and incarnate. Costly grace is the treasure hidden in the field; for the sake of it a man will gladly go and sell all that he has. It is the pearl of great price to buy which the merchant will sell all his goods. It is the kingly rule of Christ, for whose sake a man will pluck out the eye which causes him to stumble, it is the call of Jesus Christ at which the disciple leaves his nets and follows him. Costly grace is the gospel which must be *sought* again and again, the gift which must be *asked* for, the door at which a man must *knock*. Such grace is *costly* because it calls us to follow, and it is *grace* because it calls us to follow *Jesus Christ*. It is costly because it costs a man his life, and it is grace because it gives a man the only true life. It is costly because it condemns sin, and grace because it justifies the sinner. Above all, it is *costly* because it cost God the life of his son: 'ye were bought at a price,' and what has cost God much cannot be cheap for us. Above all, it is *grace* because God did not reckon his Son too dear a price to pay for our life, but delivered him up for us. Costly grace is the Incarnation of God.

From *The Cost of Discipleship*

———

Lord Jesus Christ
you took on the form of a servant and humbled yourself,
becoming obedient even unto death:
grant us grace to embrace the cross and follow you,
that in dying to self, we may discover your gift of true life,
life in all its fullness;
we ask this for your name's sake. Amen.

Nicholas Ridley c.1500–55

Bishop and martyr

———

RIDLEY CAME FROM Northumberland and was educated at the Royal Grammar School in Newcastle. He studied at Pembroke College, Cambridge, and after ordination attended the Sorbonne in Paris and Louvain University. When he returned to Cambridge he was involved in the debates about the Pope's supremacy. Around 1540 he was made Master of Pembroke College. Ridley was already supporting the Reformation and was accused of heresy. However, in 1547 he was appointed as the Bishop of Rochester. Ridley collaborated with Cranmer in producing the 1549 *Book of Common Prayer*. In 1550 he was translated to the See of London. During this period he lived in Palace House, Much Hadham, and it was from there in 1552 that he travelled to visit the king's half sister, the Catholic Mary, at Hunsdon. He was known for his passionate support for the poor and it was mainly due to him that King Edward VI founded St Thomas's Hospital and Christ's Hospital. Ridley supported Lady Jane Grey's claim to the throne, so at Mary's accession he had to resign his Bishopric. During the Marian persecutions, he was taken to Oxford to be examined and tried. Ridley was condemned to death and he was burned at the stake on this day in 1555.

Nicholas Ridley writes about his forthcoming death

Let us not then fear death, which can do us no harm, otherwise than for a moment to make the flesh to smart; for that our faith, which is surely fastened and fixed unto the word of God, telleth us that we shall be anon after death in peace; in the hands of God, in joy, in solace, and that from death we shall go straight unto life. For St John saith, 'He that liveth and believeth in me, shall never die.' And in another place, 'He shall depart from death unto life.' And therefore this death of the Christian is not to be called death, but rather a gate or entrance into everlasting life. Therefore Paul calleth it but a dissolution and resolution: and both Peter and Paul, a putting off of this tabernacle or dwell-house, meaning thereby the mortal body, as wherein the soul or spirit doth dwell here in this world for a small time. Yea, this death may be called, to the Christian, an end of all miseries. For so long as we live here, 'we must pass through many tribulations, before we can enter into the kingdom of heaven.' And now, after that death hath shot his bolt, all the Christian man's enemies have done what they can, and after that they have no more to do. What could hurt or harm poor 'Lazarus, that lay at the rich man's gate'? His former penury and poverty, his miserable beggary, and horrible sores and sickness? For so soon as death had stricken him with his dart, so soon came the angels, and carried him straight up into Abraham's bosom.

From *Foxe's Book of Martyrs*

———

O Heavenly Father,
the author and fountain of all truth,
the bottomless sea of all understanding,
send, we beseech thee, thy Holy Spirit into our hearts,
and lighten our understandings
with the beams of thy heavenly grace.
We ask this, O merciful Father, for thy dear Son,
our Saviour, Jesus Christ's sake. Amen.

Nicholas Ridley

William Warham c.1480–1557

Rector and archdeacon

———

NOT TO BE confused with his uncle of the same name (who was Archbishop of Canterbury), it is thought that Warham was educated at Winchester College and New College, Oxford. From his library, we know that he studied canon law. As he was a layman he had to be given a dispensation by the Pope to be appointed Archdeacon of Canterbury around 1505. As well as being Rector of Barley in Bedfordshire, he held many other offices including the livings of Orpington, Hayes, Shoreham, Wrotham and Harrow-on-the-Hill. He was also a Prebendary of St Paul's Cathedral and a Canon of Exeter Cathedral for many years. In his role as archdeacon for the Archbishop of Canterbury he was involved in a number of diplomatic missions for Henry VIII. Towards the end of his life he lived near St George's Chapel, Windsor.

Basil Hume writes about the priesthood of every Christian

The whole Church at different levels is concerned with fulfilling its priestly mission. This is not the place to explore the full extent of this priestly role. Fundamental is the offering by the people of the sacrifice of their own lives. This is expressed in the communal celebration of the Eucharist, the representing to God of Christ's sacrifice, which reconciles man to God. That adoration, thanksgiving and intercession offered by the whole people of God is, when properly understood, of the most profound importance to the human family. It creates and expresses community. It bridges the abyss between God and man. It reconciles man to man in a communal meal which is both a sacrifice and a healing. The priesthood of the baptised goes further. It finds expression also in the signs and symbols of the sacraments which sanctify the major moments and experiences of life. In this way, the Christian explores and intensifies the deeper experience of what it means to be human. Again, there is the daily personal relationship with God which exists through prayer and is nourished by it. Here once more the baptised, as priests, represent the whole of mankind when they pray; through Christ, with Christ and in Christ they offer prayer, praise and constant intercession for the needs of themselves and their neighbours. Perhaps unfashionably, in an age of social concern and action, I would claim that the priestly role of the Christian and of the whole people of God is the most essential for the coherence of our society, for its wellbeing and for its spiritual and psychic health. Uprooted and superficial as we have become individually, we have lost, too, our sense of identity with each other in community. The priesthood of each Christian, consciously embraced, can serve to restore awareness of the transcendent and a sense of true community, and can help society to rebuild its hierarchy of human values and priorities. But awareness of the transcendent is the essential starting-point.

From *To be a Pilgrim*

Heavenly Father,
in baptism you have adopted us as your children
and in confirmation commissioned us in your service:
fill us, your people, with the fullness of the Holy Spirit
and give us grace to live lives worthy of our calling;
through Jesus Christ our Lord. Amen.

Sarah Churchill 1660–1744

Duchess of Marlborough

———

SARAH JENNINGS WAS born in Holywell House in St Albans. Her father was the Member of Parliament for the borough. When her brother died in 1677 Sarah inherited land in Hertfordshire and Kent, and the following year she married a young soldier, John Churchill, with whom she had five children. Sarah's only son died in 1703 but her four daughters all married aristocrats. Sarah had a long and deep friendship with Princess Anne and they corresponded over many years using the pseudonyms of 'Mrs Freeman' and 'Mrs Morley.' When Anne came to the throne in 1702 she gave John Churchill a dukedom and an annuity and appointed Sarah as Mistress of the Robes and Keeper of the Privy Purse. However, Sarah was both strong willed and opinionated and before long the two friends fell out. Her strong Whig views and her determination to get her own way were regarded as a threat by the Queen. In 1712 Sarah and her husband, who by now was the Duke of Marlborough, travelled abroad and did not return to England until the day Queen Anne died. In 1736 Sarah left a lasting legacy by erecting the Marlborough Almshouses in St Albans. She died on this day in 1744.

Griffith Jones writes about the importance of charity

An uncharitable Christian is a downright contradiction. Of all the enjoyments of this world, of all endowments of the human mind, and of all the heaven-born graces which adorn a pious soul, the most amiable and excellent charity is the greatest. It is charity that crowns and consummates the Christian character; which every genuine Christian aspires after, and can never be a Christian indeed without it. In brief, it is the substance of every virtue, of every duty, and of all obedience: without it, faith itself can avail no more to salvation, than infidelity. It unites the spirits of all good men in the bond of peace, and smothers all contention; softens all severe censure, and covereth a multitude of sins. It is indeed the sum of present and future bliss; and its nature, reward and joy never fail, but remains for ever, durable as eternity! In a word, it is the divine nature, and the offspring of God; and, if I may presume to advance one step farther, charity is so essential to goodness, perfection and felicity, that the want of it, if that was possible, (with awful reverence I write it) would divest the great Jehovah of his divinity; for God is love. And can we then be Christian, good or happy, without it?

From *Selections from the Welsh Piety*

O God, the father of the forsaken,
the help of the weak, the supplier of the needy;
you teach us that love towards the human race
is the bond of perfectness and the imitation of your blessed self.
Open and touch our hearts that we may see and do,
both for this world and that which is to come,
the things that belong to our peace.
Strengthen us in the work which we have undertaken;
give us wisdom, perseverance, faith and zeal,
and in your own time and according to your pleasure prosper the issue;
for the love of your Son, Christ Jesus. Amen.

Lord Shaftesbury

Daniel Axtell 1622–60

Soldier and Baptist

———

DANIEL AXTELL'S LIFE illustrates the conflicts and contradictions that Christians face when they take up arms. Axtell was the son of William Axtell, the chief burgess of Berkhamsted. He was a Puritan and a Baptist who was keen to propagate the Baptist faith. Although he was not ordained he preached regularly, forcing other ministers to allow him into the pulpit. He fought at York and Marston Moor and also commanded the soldiers during the trial of Charles I in 1649. Later that year Axtell sailed to Ireland as part of Cromwell's army, where he was involved in battles in Drogheda, Kilkenny and Meelick. He was arrested and court marshalled because some of the Irish prisoners were executed. He returned to Ireland in 1684 but objected to Henry Cromwell's policy of compromise and decided to resign, complaining that 'the Godly were discouraged and wicked men countenanced.' Axtell was married to Elizabeth with whom he had two sons, William and Daniel. Following the Restoration of the monarchy he was arrested for regicide. He prayed publicly for the conversion of King Charles II and stated defiantly 'If I had a thousand lives I could lay them all down for the cause'. He was hung, drawn and quartered for treason at Tyburn on this day in 1660 and his head was displayed in Westminster Hall.

Michael Ramsey, a former Archbishop of Canterbury, writes about pacifism

Through the centuries probably only a minority of considering Christians have held that Christ's teaching demands the totally pacifist position. I would hold myself that the injunction to turn the other cheek and to offer no resistance to evil, like many other of Christ's injunctions, concerns motive. Faced with a violent attack the follower of Christ must have total selflessness in motive; so far as his own pride or comfort or security is concerned he must be ready to accept death and have no self-concern. But given that selflessness in motive which Christ demands, he may strike, or risk killing, or even kill if his concern is to protect others, whether family, friends, neighbours, enemies, or the community itself. It has been found possible, however hazardous, to strike in defence of others without hatred, anger, or self-concern; and conversely it is possible to be physically passive while bearing anger and hatred. It is such considerations which cause many conscientious Christians not to endorse total pacifism.

From *Canterbury Pilgrim*

Blessed God,
you call us to be bridge builders and peace makers:
dispel from our minds all pride and anger,
banish from our hearts all selfish ambition and enmity,
and grant us that peace which comes from the knowledge
that all that we are and all that we shall be
is held secure in your love;
we ask this in the name of Jesus Christ, the Prince of Peace. Amen.

Ursula Taylor 17th–18th century

Benefactress

———

THE TAYLOR FAMILY owned Clapham Manor in Bedfordshire for several generations until it passed into the hands of the Ashburnham family through marriage. Dame Ursula was the wife of Sir Thomas Taylor. The church of St Thomas à Becket in Clapham still owns a paten and chalice that was given by the Taylor family, dated 1687. She is remembered today for the school which bears her name: Ursula Taylor Voluntary Controlled Lower School in Clapham. There is also an Ursula Taylor Charity which was founded in 1724. The charity owned a field, the rent from which was used to support poor children to get an apprenticeship. The charity still makes grants to young people between the ages of thirteen and twenty-five who live in the parish, to support them in training or education.

Evelyn Underhill, a well-known spiritual director, reflects on love

The Creed, our list of the spiritual truths to which our inner life must be conformed, is all about a God who *is* Charity, a Charity that *is* God. It tells us that what we call creation is the never-ceasing action of a self-spending personal love; and all the experiences and acts of religion are simply our small experience of, and response to, the pressure and the call of that same creative Love which rules the stars. 'Behold, Lord, from whence such love proceedeth!' exclaims Thomas a Kempis. It proceeds from the very heart of the universe. For Christians this is the ultimate fact, which must govern the whole conduct of life. We are each created, sought, possessed and maintained by a living Reality that is Charity; truly known by us in and through His free, generous self-giving, and in no other way. The life which we are called upon to manifest in space and time is a living spark of this generous Love. That means that the true demand of religion will never be a demand for correct behaviour or correct belief; but for generosity, as the controlling factor in every relation between man and God and man and man. To look at ourselves and our lives after looking at this great truth is surely enough to bring self-satisfied piety down with a run. When we look out towards this Love that moves the stars and stirs in the child's heart, and claims our total allegiance and remember that this alone is Reality and we are only real so far as we conform to its demands, we see our human situation from a fresh angle; and perceive that it is both more humble and dependent, and more splendid, than we had dreamed. We are surrounded and penetrated by great spiritual forces, of which we hardly know anything. Yet the outward events of our life cannot be understood, except in their relation to that unseen and intensely living world, the Infinite Charity which penetrates and supports us, the God whom we resist and yet for whom we thirst; who is ever at work, transforming the self-centred desire of the natural creature into the wide-spreading, outpouring love of the citizen of Heaven.

From *The School of Charity*

———

Bountiful God,
whose servant St Paul taught that
whoever sows sparingly will also reap sparingly,
and whoever sows generously will also reap generously:
send the Holy Spirit on your church
and open our hearts
that we may live joyfully,
give generously and share freely;
through Jesus Christ our Lord. Amen.

George Frederick Bodley 1827–1907

Architect

———

GEORGE BODLEY WAS one of the foremost architects of his day. His impact on the Diocese of St Albans can be seen today in the repairs, restoration and re-ordering of three churches: All Saints St Paul's Walden, St Mary's Cheshunt and St Paul's Bedford. He was also the architect of the new chapel at Bedford School. The son of a doctor, Bodley was born in Hull. Under the influence of Sir George Gilbert Scott, he became known as one of the leading proponents of the English Gothic Revival and was responsible for the building and re-ordering of many churches. He designed buildings at Magdalen College, Oxford, and the Anglican Cathedral in Washington D.C. He also worked closely with William Morris and Charles Kempe. Bodley was awarded the Royal Institute of British Architects' gold medal in 1899 and was elected as a Royal Academician in 1902. As well as his buildings, he is also remembered for his wallpaper designs and a book of poetry, which was published in 1899. In 1872 Bodley married Minna Reavely and they had one son. He died on this day in 1907 near Oxford and is buried at Kinnersley in Herefordshire.

Saint Augustine preaches about the living Church

Christ the Lord wants to come in to us and dwell in us. Like a good builder he says: A new commandment I give you: love one another. He says: I give you a commandment. He means: Before, you were not engaged in building a house for me, but you lay in ruins. Therefore, to be raised up from your former state of ruin you must love one another. Dear brethren, remember that this house is still in process of being built in the whole world: this is the promise of prophecy. When God's house was being built after the Exile, it was prophesied, in the words of a psalm: Sing a new song to the Lord; sing to the Lord, all the earth. For a new song our Lord speaks of a new commandment. A new song implies a new inspiration of love. To sing is a sign of love. The singer of this new song is full of the warmth of God's love. The work we see complete in this building is physical; it should find its spiritual counterpart in your hearts. We see here the finished product of stone and wood; so too your lives should reveal the handiwork of God's grace. Let us then offer our thanksgiving above all to the Lord our God, from whom every best and perfect gift comes. Let us praise his goodness with our whole hearts.

From *Prayers for Dedication of a Church* by David Philippart

---

We give you thanks for the church buildings of our diocese,
for the generations of people who gathered
at significant points in their lives
for baptisms, weddings and funerals,
and for those who have assembled week by week
for prayer and worship;
may our churches continue to be places where people
hear your word proclaimed,
receive you in the sacraments
and encounter you in spirit and in truth,
through Jesus Christ our Lord. Amen.

Michael Clement Otway Mayne 1929–2006

Dean of Westminster

———

BORN INTO A clerical family in Harlestone, Michael Mayne was educated at the King's School, Canterbury, and Corpus Christi College, Cambridge. After graduation he training for the ministry at Cuddesdon Theological College, Oxford, and was ordained in the Diocese of St Albans to serve his title at St John's, Harpenden. At the end of his curacy he became chaplain to Mervyn Stockwood, the Bishop of Southwark. In 1965 he became Vicar of Norton in Letchworth Garden City and seven years later was appointed Head of Religious Programmes for BBC Radio. From 1979 until 1986 Mayne was Vicar of Great St Mary's, Cambridge, during which time he published *Prayers for Pastoral Occasions*. The Queen appointed him Dean of Westminster Abbey in 1986. During his time at Westminster he suffered from chronic fatigue syndrome (ME) for several years and wrote about his experience of the condition in *A Year Lost and Found*. He worked for many years with Dame Cicely Saunders (see entry for 5 June) in the hospice movement and also for the Medical Foundation for the Victims of Torture. A year before he died he was diagnosed with cancer and wrote about his illness and imminent death in *The Enduring Melody*. He married Alison McKie in 1965 and they had a son and a daughter. He died on this day in 2006.

Michael Mayne reflects on suffering

Each of us learns – or fails to learn – from illness in our own way. What I have learned is that, while God may often seem remote and your faith less resistant than you would wish, yet that Kingdom-melody which has been fashioned in me over a lifetime has survived and has proved a strength. I have sought to keep faith with the Psalmist: *My heart is firmly fixed, O God, my heart is fixed; I will sing, and make melody.* The melody that endures. I have learned that in a crisis God's grace works through the kindness and thoughtfulness of the countless people whose lives we have touched, hopefully (and often unawares) for the good. I have learned a little more of what the cost of marriage may be for my wife and loved ones, as together we explore the demands of 'in sickness and in health'. I have grown in admiration for the skill and dedication of the best in the medical profession. I have learned how scary it can be when drugs stifle your reason and leave you confused and drowning in a world adrift somewhere between logic and nonsense. These ten months have been unlike any others I have known. Many people have helped redeem them, and not least the discipline (and therapy) of writing, the pleasure of reading, and the observing of the changing seasons. Which is to say: the communication of what it feels like to be part and parcel of this messy, unpredictable, often distressing but always beautiful world.

From *The Enduring Melody*

———

Come, O Spirit of God,
and make within us your dwelling place and home.
May our darkness be dispelled by your light,
and our troubles calmed by your peace;
may all evil be redeemed by your love,
all pain transformed through the suffering of Christ,
and all dying glorified by his risen life. Amen.

A collect from the service of Compline

Geoffrey Chaucer c.1343–1400

Author and diplomat

———

KNOWN AS 'THE Father of English Literature', Geoffrey Chaucer was born in London around 1343. His father was a vintner. It is thought that he studied law at the Inner Temple in London. Chaucer became a member of the Royal Court of Edward III and we know that he travelled extensively around Europe, both as a soldier and as a diplomat, on behalf of Richard II. In 1367 he was appointed Clerk of the King's Works and as such had responsibility for the upkeep and repairs of Berkhamsted Castle. Chaucer is best known today as the author of *The Canterbury Tales*, but he also wrote many other books, including *The Book of the Duchess*, and *Troilus and Criseyde*. As well as being a poet Chaucer was also famous as an alchemist, philosopher and astronomer. He married Phillipa de Roet, a lady-in-waiting to the Queen, around 1366 and they had three or four children. He died, probably on this day, in the year 1400 and was the first poet to be buried in Poet's Corner in Westminster Abbey.

Geoffrey Chaucer writing about a priest

A good man of religion was with us
A parish priest, and impecunious,
But he was rich in faith and charity,
And a great scholar of theology.
When preaching, the truth of Christ's gospel would tell.
He taught his whole flock most devoutly and well.
Benign and conscientious as can be
He was all patience in adversity,
As was all too often proved in his life.

His parish was wide with houses far spread
Yet though it rained and thundered round his head
He would still visit the sick, sad and sore,
However far and whether rich or poor,
Walking the whole way, his staff in his hand.
He was an example to every man
For he did a thing first and then preached it.

And though he was holy and virtuous,
He would never despise the unrighteous
Nor was he arrogant or cruel in speech
But kind and careful when he had to teach.
To draw folk to heaven by his fairness,
By good example, this was his business.

From 'The Parson' in *The Canterbury Tales*

———

O God,
who chose the written word to speak an eternal gospel to every age,
give to those who handle words as writers, speakers, journalists and broadcasters
a constant loyalty to truth and a heart concerned with wisdom.
May they raise, and not lower, our moral standards;
may they increase, not diminish, the true welfare of mankind;
for the sake of Jesus Christ our Lord. Amen.

Timothy Dudley-Smith

Robert Fayrfax 1464–1521

Composer and organist

———

AMONG THE MANY distinguished musicians who have worked in the diocese, one of the most famous is Robert Fayrfax. He served in the courts of both Henry VII and Henry VIII, and was one of the singing men at the Field of the Cloth of Gold in France in 1520. He was considered to be the most important composer of his generation and had a considerable influence on both John Taverner and Thomas Tallis. Fayrfax was born in Deeping Gate, Lincolnshire. In his early twenties he became a Gentleman of the Chapel Royal and from 1498 until 1502 was organist at St Albans Abbey. He was awarded a degree in music from Cambridge University and was made a Doctor of Music in 1504. Seven years later he was also made a Doctor of Music of Oxford University. Henry VIII became a generous patron and made him a Poor Knight of Windsor, which provided him with money to help supplement his income from teaching and composing. Six of Fayrfax's settings of the mass survive, as well as motets, songs and instrumental music. He died on this day in 1521 and is buried in St Albans Abbey. There is a brass memorial plaque to him set into the floor of the presbytery.

God as composer and improviser

God sings the blues with us, humming along with our words of pain and despair. But God's voice doesn't end there. If we listen we can hear God's Spirit transposing our notes of despair into a new key of hope. We live each day, each moment, as an improvisational prayer on God's theme of grace. With God's grace we learn to 'perform under pressure'; we learn along the way. The blues reflect the way in which we turn the messiness of our lives into a fine art, improvising what seems like total chaos into a beautiful order. From moment to moment, in the daily hours of our lives, we learn: note by note, step by step, beat by beat. In the words of Jean-Pierre de Caussade, a seventeenth-century Jesuit: 'We learn from experience for which Jesus came on earth to teach us…And so we listen each moment to God in order to become learned in that divine theology which is founded on practice and experience.' We practise our faith. We listen again and again to the movements and moments of God's grace, learning how to perform with grace under pressure, to create art from the mundane. We learn by how we live, working out our salvation with fear and trembling, each day from beginning to end.

From *The Music of Creation* by Arthur Peacocke and Ann Pederson

———

Eternal Lord God, source of all beauty and harmony,
we praise you for the gift of music:
    for the inspiration given to those who compose it,
    for the skill and devotion of those who perform it,
    for the faculties and powers which enable us to enjoy it;
    and we pray that as by this gift our lives are enriched and renewed,
so we may glorify you in a fuller dedication of ourselves,
giving thanks always for all things in the name of our Lord Jesus Christ. Amen.

Frank Colquhoun

John Tyrrell Holmes Hare 1912–76

Bishop of Bedford

———

EDUCATED AT BRIGHTON College and Corpus Christi College, Oxford, John Hare trained for the priesthood at Cuddesdon Theological College. He was ordained in the Diocese of Lichfield and served his title at St Francis of Assisi in West Bromwich. From there he moved to be Vicar of St Matthias, Colindale, in the Diocese of London. In 1951 he was appointed Archdeacon of Bedford, a post which he held until he was made Bishop of Bedford in 1968. He died on this day in 1976 whilst still in office. St John's Hospice in Moggerhanger was founded by local people in his memory in 1980 and is now part of the Sue Ryder organisation (see entry for 16 February).

Archbishop Michael Ramsey writes about the qualities of a priest

The priest, in the Church and for the Church, is the *man of prayer*. Do not all Christians pray? They do indeed, and from many of them we priests can learn to pray and to pray better. Yet 'man of prayer' is in a special way the role of the priest, and because it is so the Church's prayer will be the stronger. As the teacher of theology, the priest must pray, as theology which is alive includes not only bookwork but the authentic knowledge of God which comes through prayer alone. So too as the minister of reconciliation the priest will pray, for he is one with those who are sinful in the bitter estrangement of their sin and in the hopeful grief of their penitence; and at the same time he is one with Christ in his sorrow for sinners and his joy at sin's conquest. As absolver and pastor, no less than as theologian and teacher, the priest has a prayer which focuses the Church's prayer. In him the Church's prayer is expressed in strength, and it thereby becomes the stronger. The priest is the *man of the Eucharist*. The liturgy indeed belongs to all the people. We being many are the one bread, one body. We take, we break, we offer, we receive; and the more vivid realisation of this has been one of the exciting marks of liturgical renewal in our time. Where then, and why then, the priests? As celebrant he is more than the people's representative. In taking, breaking, and consecrating he acts in Christ's name and in the name not only of the particular congregation but of the Holy Catholic Church down the ages. By his office as celebrant he symbolises the focusing of the Eucharist in the givenness of the historic gospel and in the continuing life of the Church as rooted in that gospel. He finds that at the altar he is drawn terribly and wonderfully near not only to the benefits of Christ's redemption but to the redemptive act itself.

From *The Christian Priest Today*

———

Lord Jesus Christ,
who in your grace called the disciples
to leave their nets and follow you:
summon, we pray, men and women
into the sacred ministry of your Church,
endow them with the gifts of the Holy Spirit
for the tasks entrusted to them,
and bless them in their mission and ministry,
that together we may work for the coming of your kingdom;
we ask this for your name's sake. Amen.

Alfred the Great c.849–99

King of Wessex

————

ALFRED WAS THE son of Aethelwulf, King of the West Saxons. He married Ealhswith of Mercia, with whom he had five children. Alfred was crowned king in 871 and fought the Danes on numerous occasions. However, he was unable to rout them and eventually had to make peace. Following the Battle of Ethandun in 878, he struck an agreement with King Guthrum the Old to divide the territories. The land to the east was under Danelaw, while Alfred had control of what is now Hertfordshire and the west of Bedfordshire. It is thought that it was Alfred who ordered the building of weirs on the River Lea at Hertford and Ware. He reorganised the military fortifications of the country, building a number of garrison towns. He also reformed the monetary and fiscal systems and adopted a new legal code. To protect the country from further invasions, Alfred ordered the building of a small fleet of ships. He was concerned that standards of education had declined due to the Danish invasions and so started a school in his court, recruiting scholars from the Continent and decreeing that primary education should be in English. As there were few books in English, Alfred ordered that some of the more significant texts should be translated. A scholar in his own right, Alfred himself translated several works from Latin into English, most famously Gregory the Great's *Pastoral Care*. Alfred founded monasteries at Athelney and Shaftesbury. He died on this day in 899 and is buried in Winchester.

Alfred's love of learning

He learned by heart the 'daily round', that is, the services of the hours, and then certain psalms and prayers; these he collected in a single book, which he kept by him day and night, as I have seen for myself; amid all the affairs of the present life he took it around with him everywhere for the sake of prayers, and was inseparable from it. But alas, he could not satisfy his craving for what he desired the most, namely the liberal arts; for, as he used to say, there were no good scholars in the entire kingdom of the West Saxons at that time. He used to affirm with repeated complaints and sighing from the depths of his heart, that among all the difficulties and burdens of his present life this had become the greatest: namely, that at the time when he was of the right age and had the leisure and the capacity for learning, he did not have the teachers. For when he was older, and more incessantly preoccupied day and night – or rather harassed – by all kinds of illnesses unknown to the physicians of this island, as well as by the cures (both domestic and foreign) of the royal office, and also by the incursions of the Vikings by the land and sea, he had the teachers and scribes to some extent, but he was unable to study.

From *Asser's Life of King Alfred* by L. C. Jane

————

O Sovereign Lord,
who brought your servant Alfred to a troubled throne
that he might establish peace in a ravaged land
and revive learning and the arts among the people:
Awake in us also a keen desire to increase our understanding
while we are in this world,
and an eager longing to reach that endless life
where all will be made clear;
through Jesus Christ our Lord. Amen.

A Collect for Alfred the Great

Margaret Rogers 1923–2009

Diocesan Adviser in Children's Work

———

MARGARET ROGERS, WHO was both the daughter and granddaughter of Bedfordshire incumbents, gave a long life of distinguished service to the Diocese of St Albans.

She was Head Girl at Bedford High School, after which she trained as a church worker at St Christopher's College, Blackheath. Her father's sudden death prevented her completing the Lambeth Diploma at Oxford, and her mother, as a clergy widow, was given just six weeks to vacate the rectory. Margaret, as an only child, became responsible for her mother's support for many years. In 1945 she was appointed Sunday School Adviser in the Diocese of Lincoln, the youngest person to hold such a post at that time. She came to the St Albans Diocese in 1951 as Diocesan Sunday School Adviser, and in 1966 she became part-time Children's Work Adviser in Stevenage and played a significant part in the changing style of church work with children. In 1974, Margaret was appointed to the new post of Diocesan Adviser in Children's Work and Secretary to the Committee for Women's Ministry. This meant she was, in effect, the lay equivalent of the Diocesan Director of Ordinands for women and laity. She saw the diaconate opened up to women, and rejoiced as sixty-two women were ordained to the priesthood in St Albans Abbey in 1994, though she chose not to be ordained herself. For many years she was a member of the congregation of St Augustine's, Limbury in Luton. She was made a Lay Canon of St Albans in recognition of her services to the Church and the diocese.

The rights of children

By the present Declaration of the Rights of the Child, commonly known as the 'Declaration of Geneva,' men and women of all nations, recognising that mankind owes to the child the best that it has to give, declare and accept it as their duty that, beyond and above all considerations of race, nationality or creed:

1. The child must be given the means requisite for its normal development, both materially and spiritually;
2. The child that is hungry must be fed; the child that is sick must be nursed; the child that is backward must be helped; the delinquent child must be reclaimed; and the orphan and the waif must be sheltered and succoured;
3. The child must be the first to receive relief in times of distress;
4. The child must be put in a position to earn a livelihood, and must be protected against every form of exploitation;
5. The child must be brought up in the consciousness that its talents must be devoted to the service of fellow men.

The Geneva Declaration of the Rights of the Child based on work by Eglantyne Jebb and others

———

Bless our children with healthful bodies,
with good understandings,
with the graces and gifts of thy Spirit,
with sweet dispositions and holy habits;
and sanctify them throughout their bodies, souls and spirits,
and keep them unblamable to the coming of our Lord Jesus Christ. Amen.

Jeremy Taylor

John Ball c.1665–1745

Minister and scholar

————

JOHN BALL, ONE of thirteen children, was raised in Barley, Hertfordshire, where his father, Nathanael Ball, was the rector (see entry for 7 September). A Puritan, he studied under the Reverend John Short of Lyme Regis and also at the university in Utrecht. Ball was ordained in 1695, and became minister of a church in Honiton, Devon, where he remained for forty years. He was famous as a biblical scholar who preached from the Hebrew text, which may have proved rather challenging to the good people of the town, not least when he was expounding the text of Leviticus. He also taught theology at a Nonconformist seminary attended by the sons of local Anglican gentry.

Oscar Wilde reads the Bible in Reading Gaol

At Christmas I managed to get hold of a Greek Testament, and every morning, after I had cleaned my cell and polished my tins, I read a little of the Gospels, a dozen verses taken by chance anywhere. It is a delightful way of opening the day. Everyone, even in a turbulent, ill-disciplined life, should do the same. Endless repetition, in and out of season, has spoiled for us the freshness, the naïveté, the simple romantic charm of the Gospels. We hear them read far too often and far too badly, and all repetition is anti-spiritual. When one returns to the Greek; it is like going into a garden of lilies out of some narrow and dark house. And to me, the pleasure is doubled by the reflection that it is extremely probable that we have the actual terms, the *ipsissima verba*, used by Christ. It was always supposed that Christ talked in Aramaic. But now we know that the Galilean peasants, like the Irish peasants of our own day, were bilingual, and that Greek was the ordinary language of intercourse all over Palestine, as indeed all over the Eastern world. I never liked the idea that we knew of Christ's own words only through a translation of a translation. Christ, like all fascinating personalities, had the power of not merely saying beautiful things himself, but of making other people say beautiful things to him; and I love the story St. Mark tells us about the Greek woman, who, when as a trial of her faith he said to her that he could not give her the bread of the children of Israel, answered him that the little dogs who are under the table eat of the crumbs that the children let fall. Most people live for love and admiration. But it is by love and admiration that we should live. If any love is shown us we should recognise that we are quite unworthy of it. Nobody is worthy to be loved. The fact that God loves man shows us that in the divine order of ideal things it is written that eternal love is to be given to what is eternally unworthy.

From *De Profundis*

————

Heavenly Father,
plant deep within us the desire to read and study holy scripture:
may it be to us the word of life and truth,
may it mould us, form us and train us in righteousness and godly living;
that at the final day we may enter into your presence
to stand before him who is the Living Word,
your Son Jesus Christ. Amen.

Samuel Medley 1738–99

Baptist minister

———

SAMUEL MEDLEY'S FATHER had been Attorney-General to the Island of St Vincent in the Caribbean and also tutor to the Duke of Montague. Medley was educated by his grandfather, William Tonge, and then apprenticed to an oilman in London. In 1755 he joined the navy but was discharged four years later, when he was seriously wounded in a battle near Cape Lagos whilst serving under Admiral Boscawen. Recovering from his injuries, he asked God for healing and later claimed that he had been miraculously cured. Medley was converted in 1760 having heard a sermon by Isaac Watts being read. He was baptised and became a member of Eagle Street Church, Holborn. For a time he ran a school in King Street, Soho. In 1767 he was ordained and served at a Baptist Church in Watford, whilst also running a school. During his lifetime Medley was known as an outstanding preacher and prolific hymn writer. We still have around twenty of his hymns, the most famous of which is *I know my redeemer lives*. He married Mary Gill in 1762 and their son, also called Samuel, became a famous portrait painter. Medley died in 1799 and is buried in Liverpool.

I know that my Redeemer lives;
What comfort this sweet sentence gives!
He lives, He lives, who once was dead;
He lives, my ever living Head.

He lives to bless me with His love,
He lives to plead for me above.
He lives my hungry soul to feed,
He lives to help in time of need.

He lives triumphant from the grave,
He lives eternally to save,
He lives all glorious in the sky,
He lives exalted there on high.

He lives to silence all my fears,
He lives to wipe away my tears
He lives to calm my troubled heart,
He lives all blessings to impart.

He lives and grants me daily breath;
He lives, and I shall conquer death:
He lives my mansion to prepare;
He lives to bring me safely there.

He lives, all glory to His Name!
He lives, my Jesus, still the same.
Oh, the sweet joy this sentence gives,
I know that my Redeemer lives!

Samuel Medley

Living Word, we thank you for the poets
who stimulate our imaginations,
evoke our emotions
and stir our wills:
may they enrich our worship
and inspire us to serve you and your people;
through Jesus Christ our Lord. Amen.

Robert Smirke 1780–1867

Architect

———

MEMORIALS TO THE Victorian architect Robert Smirke are to be found in every corner of England, in the buildings that he designed. Among these the best known are the British Museum, the Royal Opera House in Covent Garden, and the great house of Luton Hoo in Bedfordshire. Smirke was one of twelve children born to the Bedfordshire artist of the same name. He went to school in Aspley Guise and then studied at the Royal Academy. Like many of his contemporaries, Smirke went on a grand tour around Europe for four years. He worked on many prestigious projects including the Royal Mint. He was elected a Royal Academician in 1811. Smirke designed and renovated a large number of churches and wrote *Specimens of Continental Architecture*. In 1819 he married Laura Freston, with whom he had a daughter, also called Laura.

Bishop John V. Taylor writes about sculpture

Walking down the long gallery of the Academy of Fine Arts in Florence one meets three of Michelangelo's supreme statements in marble which seem to present a progression of insight. First comes the group of four slaves, unfinished giants struggling to emerge from the raw stone that still imprisons them. Next one's attention is caught and held by the gigantic David which, as one studies the face from different angles, presents all the conflicting emotions of a moment of decision, doubt, resolution and terror. And the third, also unfinished, is the Palestrina Pietà, which some find theatrical; but the monumental grief of the Virgin and the peace of total abandonment in the dead Christ combine to speak the ultimate word about sacrifice. These are the three aspects of the creative activity of the Holy Spirit, the Lord, the Giver of Life. From within the depths of its being he urges every creature again and again to take one more tiny step in the direction of higher consciousness and personhood; again and again he creates for every creature the occasion for spontaneity and the necessity for choice, and at every turn he opposes self-interest with a contrary principle of sacrifice, of existence for the other. And, in the fullness of time, all of this was perfectly disclosed in Jesus Christ, who was conceived by the Holy Spirit and to whom the Holy Spirit has been directing men's attention ever since. It is not difficult to see how this must affect our understanding of that mission which is the continuing Christ-centred activity of that same Holy Spirit.

From *The Go-Between God*

———

Creator God,
who has made us in your image and planted within us the seeds of creativity:
we thank you for artists, sculptors and architects
who stimulate us to see the world in new ways;
open our eyes and broaden our imaginations
that we may share in your creative work in the world;
through Jesus Christ our Lord. Amen.

Fanny Elizabeth Eagles 1836–1907

Deaconess and nun

I F YOU GO into St Paul's Church in Bedford you will find that the stained glass window in the north wall of the sanctuary is dedicated to the memory of Sister Fanny. Who was she and why is she commemorated in such a prominent place? Fanny was the daughter of Ezra Eagles, a solicitor, clerk of the peace and coroner for the Borough of Bedford. From the day of her confirmation at the age of sixteen, she knew that she wanted to dedicate her life to God. Fanny trained as a nurse at King's College Hospital and then spent some time at an Anglican sisterhood in Brompton Square. She was admitted Deaconess in Ely Cathedral in 1869 and was later asked to run the Ely Diocesan Deaconess Institution to train deaconesses for parish work. Before long other deaconesses joined her and they lived together under a common rule. The Sisters ran Sunday Schools, evening classes and visited the poor and sick in their homes. During the smallpox epidemic of 1871–2, Fanny worked tirelessly visiting the sick, washing and caring for them, and even arranging the funerals. On one occasion Fanny was persuaded to look after an orphan and before long the Sisters were caring for more than twenty children. The orphanage became the St Albans Diocesan Children's Home and the community was known as St Etheldreda's. Sister Fanny died in 1907 and is buried in Ampthill. In 1933 the orphanage was taken over by the Community of St Andrew.

Carlo Carretto writes about the prayer which is at the heart of the religious life

If the prophets did so, and if Jesus did so, we too must go out into the desert from time to time. It is not a question of transporting oneself there physically. For many of us that could be a luxury. Rather, it implies creating a desert space in one's own life. And to create a desert means to seek solitude, to withdraw from men and things, one of the undisputed principles of mental health. To create a desert means learning to be self-sufficient, learning to remain undisturbed with one's own thoughts, one's own prayer, one's own destiny. It means shutting oneself up in one's room, remaining alone in an empty church, setting up a small oratory for oneself in an attic or at the end of a passage in which to localise one's personal contact with God, to draw breath, to recover one's inner peace. It means occasionally devoting a whole day to prayer, it means going off into the loneliness of the mountains, or getting up alone in the night to pray. When all is said and done, creating a desert means nothing more than obeying God. Because there is a commandment – arguably the most forgotten of all, especially by the 'committed', by militants, by priests, and even bishops – which requires us to interrupt our work, to put aside our daily tasks and seek the refreshing stillness of contemplation.

From *In Search of the Beyond*

Father of the Fatherless:
we thank you for those who have given up their lives to follow you
and especially for the Sisters of St Etheldreda:
give us grace to follow their example
that we too may root our lives in prayer and service,
caring for the weak and vulnerable and especially for children and orphans;
for we ask this in the name of Jesus Christ our Lord. Amen.

Robert Brett 1808–74

Surgeon

———

ROBERT BRETT STANDS in the long tradition of doctors who have viewed their medical work as a Christian vocation. One of the fruits of this was the Guild of St Luke, which Brett founded and which provided a forum where doctors and clergy could work together. Born in 1808 near Luton, Brett studied at St George's Hospital in London. He had hoped to be ordained and work as a missionary but was persuaded to remain in medicine. Following his wife's death, he moved to Stoke Newington where he married the sister of Samuel Reynolds, a surgeon with whom he was working. He remained there until his death. Brett was an ardent supporter of the Tractarian Movement within the Church of England and he used much of his time, energy and money to further the cause. He was one of the prime movers in the building of St Matthias, Stoke Newington, and was a Vice-President of the English Church Union. Brett wrote several Christian books, mainly about faith in the face of sickness, including *Devotions for the Sick Room*, *Devout Prayers on the Life and Passion of the Lord Jesus* and *The Duty and Blessedness of Intercessory Prayer*.

Robert Brett writes about sickness and healing

No amount of sorrow, no bitterness of anguish, no number of failings, no enormity of sins, should drive you to despair or too great fear. However much you have sinned, the mercy of God infinitely exceeds your sins: however weak and infirm you may be, His goodness is ever ready to help you. God is as willing as He is able to heal and deliver, if you will truly turn to Him, humbly and devoutly call upon Him, and trust Him. Although we are great sinners, and most imperfect men, why should we not turn in firm and humble faith to God, who is an abyss of inexhaustible pity, whose nature is goodness, and whose property it is always to have mercy and to spare. It is very right that we should love Him in our inmost souls, who is so gracious towards sinners, that although we daily offend Him in our thoughts, words and deeds, He receives us with joy, and freely forgives us if we turn to Him, and hope and trust in Him. O how excellent is that gift of God, a firm, humble, loving faith! He who has this, must live in holiness, and die in peace. Whoever, relinquishing hope of pardon, plunges himself into the gulf of despair, not only believes not God omnipotent, thinking there are certain sins which He cannot forgive, but also makes Him a liar, since He has promised by His Prophet, 'If the wicked will turn from all his sins that he hath committed, and keep all My statutes, and do that which is lawful and right, he shall surely live, he shall not die.'

From *Thoughts during Sickness* by Robert Brett

———

O holy, merciful, loving Redeemer,
my health and salvation, my strength and my God!
Have mercy, have mercy upon me, for I am poor and destitute.
Help me, infirm and sick.
Be propitious to a vile sinner, plead for me,
and by Thy merits satisfy for me, for I have none of my own;
heal, teach and direct me in all things; confirm me to Thy will,
and make me what Thou wouldst have me to be. Amen.

From *Thoughts during Sickness* by Robert Brett

Nicholas Stratford 1633–1707

Bishop

———

BORN IN HEMEL Hempstead, Nicholas Stratford studied at Trinity College, Oxford. He graduated in 1654 and was made a Fellow of the College in 1657. Ten years later he became warden of the Collegiate and Parish Church of Manchester. He was a strong Royalist, who supported the divine right of kings, and reinstated the Anglican traditions that had been abandoned during the Commonwealth. Stratford maintained good relationships with Dissenters but was worried at the growing influence of Roman Catholics at court. He became Dean of St Asaph in 1673 and Vicar of St Mary Aldermanbury in London in 1683. His opposition to King James II's Roman Catholic sympathies, and his support for William and Mary, led to his appointment as Bishop of Chester in 1689. He is remembered as a pastoral bishop who was deeply involved in the life of the diocese. Stratford wrote *Dissuasive from Revenge* and some of his Latin poetry is to be found in *Britannia Rediviva*. He married and had two sons and two daughters. He died in post in 1707 and money from his estate contributed to the founding of the Blue Coat School in Chester.

John Locke writes about toleration

Since you are pleased to inquire what are my thoughts about the mutual toleration of Christians in their different professions of religion, I must needs answer you freely that I esteem that toleration to be the chief characteristic mark of the true Church. For whatsoever some people boast of the antiquity of places and names, or of the pomp of their outward worship; others, of the reformation of their discipline; all, of the orthodoxy of their faith – for everyone is orthodox to himself – these things, and all others of this nature, are much rather marks of men striving for power and empire over one another than of the Church of Christ. Let anyone have never so true a claim to all these things, yet if he be destitute of charity, meekness, and good-will in general towards all mankind, even to those that are not Christians, he is certainly yet short of being a true Christian himself. 'The kings of the Gentiles exercise leadership over them,' said our Saviour to his disciples, 'but ye shall not be so.' The business of true religion is quite another thing. It is not instituted in order to the erecting of an external pomp, nor to the obtaining of ecclesiastical dominion, nor to the exercising of compulsive force, but to the regulating of men's lives, according to the rules of virtue and piety. Whosoever will list himself under the banner of Christ, must, in the first place and above all things, make war upon his own lusts and vices. It is in vain for any man to usurp the name of Christ, without holiness of life, purity of manners, benignity and meekness of spirit. 'Let everyone that nameth the name of Christ, depart from iniquity.' 'Thou, when thou art converted, strengthen thy brethren,' said our Lord to Peter. It would, indeed, be very hard for one that appears careless about his own salvation to persuade me that he were extremely concerned for mine.

From *A Letter Concerning Toleration*

———

*Merciful Lord, you have taught us through your Son
that love is the fulfilling of the law.
Grant that we may love you with our whole heart
and our neighbours as ourselves;
through Jesus Christ our Lord. Amen.*

The Collect for the Sixteenth Sunday
after Trinity in *Common Worship*

Mary I 1516–58

Queen

———

QUEEN MARY'S INCLUSION in this book may raise some eyebrows: her nickname was 'Bloody Mary' (see the entry for 1 August). Yet, during this period of religious conflict, many Catholics and Protestants truly believed that they were doing God's will. Mary, and those who opposed her, are a powerful reminder that, however strong our convictions may be, we need the humility to see that we might not have the whole truth on our side. Mary was the daughter of Henry VIII and Catherine of Aragon. A staunch Roman Catholic throughout her life, she was removed from the line of succession when the king married Anne Boleyn. During this period Mary lived for a time at Hunsdon in Hertfordshire. It was here that Bishop Nicholas Ridley tried to persuade her to become a Protestant, to which Mary replied 'The doore of the parish church adioyning shalbe open for you if you come, and ye may preach if you list, but neither I, nor none of myne shall heare you'. Mary came to the throne after the death of Edward VI and the abortive attempt by the Duke of Northumberland to crown Lady Jane Grey. Mary was not popular and in 1554 had to put down a rebellion led by Sir Thomas Wyatt. Determined to re-establish the Catholic faith, Mary had many Protestants burned at the stake. She died of influenza and is buried in Westminster Abbey.

Pope Paul VI writes about the need to respect those with whom we disagree

Respect and love ought to be extended also to those who think or act differently than we do in social, political and even religious matters. In fact, the more deeply we come to understand their ways of thinking through such courtesy and love, the more easily will we be able to enter into dialogue with them. This love and good will, to be sure, must in no way render us indifferent to truth and goodness. Indeed love itself impels the disciples of Christ to speak the saving truth to all men. But it is necessary to distinguish between error, which always merits repudiation, and the person in error, who never loses the dignity of being a person even when he is flawed by false or inadequate religious notions. God alone is the judge and searcher of hearts, for that reason He forbids us to make judgments about the internal guilt of anyone. The teaching of Christ even requires that we forgive injuries, and extends the law of love to include every enemy, according to the command of the New Law: 'You have heard that it was said: Thou shalt love thy neighbour and hate thy enemy. But I say to you: love your enemies, do good to those who hate you, and pray for those who persecute and calumniate you' (Matthew 5.43–44).

From *Gaudium et Spes*

———

Gracious God,
who sent your Son, Jesus Christ,
to reveal the way of love:
teach us to follow his example
by loving our enemies
as well as our neighbours,
that at the last we may enter into your presence
you who are the source and fountain of all love;
we ask this in the name of Jesus Christ our Lord. Amen.

Edward Bickersteth 1786–1850

Rector

───────

EDWARD BICKERSTETH WAS part of a large clerical family. His son was Edward Henry Bickersteth, Bishop of Exeter (see entry for 16 May). One of his nephews, Robert, became Bishop of Ripon and another, Edward, was Dean of Lichfield. His eponymous grandson was the Bishop of South Tokyo. Born in Kirby Lonsdale in the Lake District, Bickersteth practised as a solicitor for three years in Norwich. He was ordained in 1816 and worked for the Church Missionary Society. He was made Rector of Watton-at-Stone in Hertfordshire in 1830 but continued his interest in overseas missions, preaching on behalf of the Society for the Conversion of the Jews and supporting the Foreign Aid Society and the Irish Church Missions. He was involved in the Evangelical Alliance. He wrote many hymns and also *A Scripture Help* and *Christian Psalmody*. His brother was Baron Langdale, Master of the Rolls.

In this passage Bickersteth stresses the importance of studying the scriptures

The possession of a Bible, if it be rightly used, is one of the greatest privileges you can enjoy. But it would have been better for you never to have had a Bible, than to have one and neglect to use it; because the Bible is a talent entrusted to your charge, for the improvement or neglect of which you must account – besides, to disregard it, as if it were of no value, is a high affront to that great God who gave it. Suppose a parent wrote a letter to a child at a distance, full of affectionate admonitions and kind promises, and the child never opened it, or only read a line now and then; what an unworthy part such a child would act; – just so are we acting if we neglect that book which our heavenly Father has sent to us, his children. I propose to shew the importance of frequently, patiently, and thoroughly studying the Bible; from the command of Christ – the character and conduct of pious men – the knowledge, practical benefits, and real happiness gained by it – and then to answer some objections, and point out the danger of neglecting it. I know indeed there are persons, such as servants and others, who have not the command of their own time, and from whom so much cannot be expected as from those who have more leisure; but even these may still do something, and I would seriously ask them, 'Cannot *you* often find time for folly, or perhaps for sinful books and company?' Let no excuse then satisfy you for a slight performance of the great duty of studying your Bible, but such as you are convinced will stand good in the solemn day of account.

From *A Help to the Study of the Scriptures*

───────────────────────────────

O Gracious God and most Merciful Father,
who has vouchsafed us the rich
and precious jewel of thy holy Word:
Assist us with thy Spirit that it may be written in our hearts
to our everlasting comfort, to reform us,
to renew us according to thine own image,
to build us up into the perfect building of thy Christ,
and to increase us in all heavenly virtues.
Grant this, O heavenly Father,
for the same Jesus Christ's sake. Amen.

The Geneva Bible

Hubert von Herkomer 1849–1914

Artist

———

HUBERT VON HERKOMER'S *Judas and the Thirty Pieces of Silver for Betraying Christ* portrays a seated group of hard-faced priests refusing to take back the pieces of silver. The look of anxiety and pain on Judas' face expresses his inner turmoil as he realises the full implications of his treachery. Herkomer is chiefly remembered as a portraitist (including a famous portrait of Archbishop Benson), but as well as religious themes, he also painted some gritty scenes depicting the reality of suffering and poverty (most famously *Hard Times*). Born in Germany, Herkomer's family came to Britain in 1857. He studied at the Southampton School of Art, the Munich Academy and the South Kensington Art School and worked as a freelance illustrator. He moved to Bushey and it was there that he married Anna Weise in 1874. Herkomer's reputation grew steadily and he became an Associate of the Royal Academy in 1879. Herkomer founded his own school of art at Bushey in 1883. He was appointed Slade Professor of Art at Oxford in 1885 and five years later he became an Academician. As well as painting, he also composed music and directed a number of films. Herkomer, who was knighted in 1907, died in 1914 and is buried in St James, Bushey.

John Ruskin, the Victorian artist and critic, writes of God's self-revelation

It is clearly necessary, from the beginning to the end of time, that God's way of revealing Himself to His creatures should be a simple way, which all those creatures may understand. Whether taught or untaught, whether of mean capacity or enlarged, it is necessary that communion with their Creator should be possible to all; and the admission to such communion must be rested, not on their having a knowledge of astronomy, but on their having a human soul. In order to render this communion possible, the Deity has stooped from His Throne, and has not only, in the person of His Son, taken upon Him the veil of our human flesh, but, in the person of the Father, taken upon Him the veil of our human thoughts, and permitted us, by His own spoken authority, to conceive Him simply and clearly as a loving Father and Friend; a being to be walked with and reasoned with; to be moved by our entreaties, angered by our rebellion, alienated by our coldness, pleased by our love, and glorified by our labour; and finally, to be beheld in immediate and active presence in all the powers and changes of creation. This conception of God, which is the child's, is evidently the only one which can be universal, and therefore the only one which for us can be true.

From *Modern Painters*

Lord Jesus Christ,
image of the invisible God,
firstborn over all creation:
give us grace to embody your love
with humility and compassion,
that our acts of compassion and kindness
may reveal your presence in the world;
for we ask this for your name's sake. Amen.

Agnes d.1245

Prioress

————

FOR JUST UNDER four hundred years there was a priory of nuns in the small Bedfordshire village of Harrold. The Augustinian community was established in 1138 by Sampson le Fort and dedicated to the Blessed Virgin Mary and St Peter. It is likely that it was built on land that had been granted to Abbot Gervase of Arrouaise so that he could establish a religious community there. For a time a prior and canons were appointed to look after the Sisters, an arrangement which ceased with the appointment of the first Prioress, Agnes. We know little about her except that she was the Prioress from 1227 until her death in 1245. The seal of the Priory depicted St Peter dressed in a mitre and chasuble. He is holding two keys in his right hand and a crosier in his left. The Priory surrendered to the Crown in 1536 as part of the Dissolution of the Monasteries under Henry VIII. Its lands continued as a supposed manor in secular hands and the buildings were eventually replaced by Harrold Hall, built between 1608 and 1610.

Dietrich Bonhoeffer writes about the nature of Christian communities

Innumerable times a whole Christian community has broken down because it had sprung from a wish dream. The serious Christian, set down for the first time in a Christian community, is likely to bring with him a very definite idea of what Christian life together should be and try to realise it. But God's grace speedily shatters such dreams. Just as surely God desires to lead us to a knowledge of genuine Christian fellowship, so surely must we be overwhelmed by a great general disillusionment with others, with Christians in general, and, if we are fortunate, with ourselves. By sheer grace God will not permit us to live even for a brief period in a dream world. He does not abandon us to those rapturous experiences and lofty moods that come over us like a dream. God is not a God of the emotions but the God of truth. Only that fellowship which faces such disillusionment, with all its unhappy and ugly aspects, begins to be what it should be in God's sight, begins to grasp in faith the promise that is given to it. The sooner this shock of disillusionment comes to an individual and to a community the better for both. A community which cannot bear and cannot survive such a crisis, which insists upon keeping its illusion when it should be shattered, permanently loses in that moment the promise of Christian community. Sooner or later it will collapse. Every human wish dream that is injected into the Christian community is a hindrance to genuine community and must be banished if genuine community is to survive.

From *Life Together*

————

Lord Jesus Christ,
in your great love you draw all people to yourself,
and in your wisdom you call us to your service.
We pray at this time you will kindle in the hearts of men and women
the desire to follow you in the Religious Life.
Give to those whom you call,
grace to accept their vocation readily and thankfully,
to make the whole-hearted surrender which you ask of them,
and for love of you, to persevere to the end;
this we ask in your name. Amen.

From *The Anglican Religious Communities Yearbook*

Elizabeth Harvey 1820–76

Founder of almshouses

———

ELIZABETH HARVEY WAS the eldest of the three children of the Reverend James Harvey and his wife Catherine, of Caldecote near Biggleswade. The Harvey family came from nearby Ickwell Bury, which is between Northill and Old Warden. Elizabeth's younger sister, Susan, and younger brother, Edmund, both died before her, so in their memory she had five almshouses built in 1876 in Upper Caldecote. Each one had a hall, living room and pantry with one bedroom above. An earth closet and common washhouse stood outside. On the front of the Elizabeth Harvey Almshouses there is a plaque which reads:

Erected by Elizabeth Harvey AD 1876
In memory of Edmund Harvey who died AD 1870
And of Susan Harvey who died AD 1866

Octavia Hill reflects on Christian charity

I dealt last year with that portion of our Donation Fund which had been devoted to the sick, the old, the dying, or the helpless; not that spent in putting men or women into self-supporting positions, or in training the young for the battle of life, but that spent on the alleviation of pain, the comfort of those who will never work again. I said, and I feel it always, that this kind of help should have the very first place of honour in any scheme of Christian Charity. It is greatly to be impressed on almsgivers that the best way of helping the destitute is to find, if possible, some radical remedy for their destitution, such as training a widow's children: but that does not alter the great law that it is the helpless who are to be aided. Let us be clear therefore a certain portion of what we give should be just spent on the aged, the dying, and the disabled, not as if it were invested in preparation for life, but spent as in merciful help. But, oh! my friends, do not let us deceive ourselves. We may not enter into the blessing of thus sharing with the stricken-down people what God has given us of money, by subscribing to any huge, general, far-away scheme; we cannot delegate the duty, nor depute the responsibility on a large scale and without thought. If we are not prepared to give ourselves, at least to some extent, at least to the extent of choosing thoughtfully, watchfully, whom we will depute; and if those, who have not much time, but whose wealth claims from them large gifts, are not ready to choose large objects, so that the thought demanded may be possible to them; if they will not give in individual charity regularly and quietly, undertaking definite duty to groups of pensioners among the aged, or incurable, or to costly cases of training; and if they will not see that the personal care they cannot give is at least rendered by those whom they know and trust; then, believe me, their gifts are in terrible danger of doing harm.

From *Letter to My Fellow-Workers: Work Among the Poor During 1886*

———

Make us worthy, Lord,
to serve our fellow human beings throughout the world
who live and die in poverty and hunger.
Give them, through our hands, this day their daily bread,
and by our understanding love, give peace and joy. Amen.

Mother Teresa of Calcutta

Theophilus Dillingham 1613–78

Archdeacon of Bedford

———

THEOPHILUS DILLINGHAM WAS born at Over Dean in the parish of Northill, Bedfordshire, where his father was the rector. He studied at Emmanuel College, Cambridge, and after graduation he was elected a fellow of Sidney Sussex College and took the degree of Doctor of Divinity. He became the Master of Clare Hall in 1654. However, at the Restoration he was ejected and replaced by his predecessor Thomas Paske. Dillingham then went on to marry Paske's daughter, Elizabeth, with whom he had six children. In 1661 Paske resigned and Dillingham was re-elected to the mastership. He also became a Prebendary of York Minster and Rector of Offord Cluny in Huntingdonshire. In September 1667 he was installed as Archdeacon of Bedford. Dillingham also served as Vice-Chancellor of Cambridge University on three occasions. He died in 1678 and was buried at St Edward's Church in Cambridge.

William Law meditates on the Christian life

Devotion is neither private nor public prayer; but prayers, whether private or public, are particular parts or instances of devotion. Devotion signifies a life given, or devoted, to God. He, therefore, is the devout man, who lives no longer to his own will, or the way and spirit of the world, but to the sole will of God, who considers God in everything, who serves God in everything, who makes all the parts of his common life parts of piety, by doing everything in the Name of God, and under such rules as are conformable to His glory. We readily acknowledge, that God alone is to be the rule and measure of our prayers; that in them we are to look wholly unto Him, and act wholly for Him; that we are only to pray in such a manner, for such things, and such ends, as are suitable to His glory. Now let any one but find out the reason why he is to be thus strictly pious in his prayers, and he will find the same as strong a reason to be as strictly pious in all the other parts of his life. For there is not the least shadow of a reason why we should make God the rule and measure of our prayers; why we should then look wholly unto Him, and pray according to His will; but what equally proves it necessary for us to look wholly unto God, and make Him the rule and measure of all the other actions of our life. For any ways of life, any employment of our talents, whether of our parts, our time, or money, that is not strictly according to the will of God, that is not for such ends as are suitable to His glory, are as great absurdities and failings, as prayers that are not according to the will of God.

From *A Serious Call to a Devout and Holy Life*

———

O God, who madest me for thyself, to show forth thy goodness in me,
manifest, I humbly beseech thee, the life-giving power of thy holy nature within me;
help me to such a true and living faith in thee, such strength of hunger and thirst
after the birth, life, and spirit of thy Holy Jesus in my soul,
that all that is within me, may be turned from every inward thought,
or outward work, that is not thee,
thy holy Jesus, and heavenly working in my soul. Amen.

William Law

Arthur ('Brandy') William Wesley 1908–99

Stockman

————

ARTHUR WESLEY WAS the second generation of his family to be born in Pavenham. He was the eldest of ten children and, as was common in those days, all of them had to do what they could to help provide for the family. By the age of six Arthur was already helping a local farmer and was able to earn a few pennies by collecting eggs and catching rats. He recalled the hard work during the harvest and that when he was just ten years old he slept in a barn with the farm workers until the crops had all been brought in. Arthur spent the whole of his working life on the land. Starting out as a labourer, he eventually became a stockman, caring for the animals. He worked on the same farm for around seventy years and towards the end of his life his achievement was acknowledged when he was given a long service award. During the Second World War Arthur remained at home, as agricultural workers were a reserved occupation. He enlisted in the Home Guard and in addition to his work on the farm he also became the village odd job man, chimney sweep and grave digger. Arthur was passionate about cricket and for some years coached a team formed of the young people of the village. As coach he was delighted when the team won the local league. Throughout his life Arthur worshipped at St Peter's Church, Pavenham, where he often helped with the maintenance of the building. Before the war he married Marjorie. He is buried in Pavenham churchyard.

The psalmist wonders at God the creator

God sendeth the springs into the valleys, which run among the hills.
They give drink to every beast of the field: the wild asses quench their thirst.
By them shall the fowls of the heaven have their habitation, which sing among the branches.
He watereth the hills from his chambers: the earth is satisfied with the fruit of thy works.
He causeth the grass to grow for the cattle, and herb for the service of man:
that he may bring forth food out of the earth;
And wine that maketh glad the heart of man, and oil to make his face to shine,
and bread which strengtheneth man's heart.
The trees of the LORD are full of sap; the cedars of Lebanon, which he hath planted;
Where the birds make their nests: as for the stork, the fir trees are her house.
The high hills are a refuge for the wild goats; and the rocks for the conies.
He appointed the moon for seasons: the sun knoweth his going down.
Thou makest darkness, and it is night: wherein all the beasts of the forest do creep forth.
The young lions roar after their prey, and seek their meat from God.
The sun ariseth, they gather themselves together, and lay them down in their dens.
Man goeth forth unto his work and to his labour until the evening.

From Psalm 104 from the *Authorised Version of the Bible*

————

God of Creation,
we pray for the farmers who grow the grain for our bread,
tend the cattle for our milk and the chickens for our eggs:
may they be good stewards of the land, the livestock and the crops
that they may be conserved for future generations;
for we ask this in the name of Jesus Christ our Lord. Amen.

Stephen Hellard d.1506

Priest and benefactor

———

EVERYONE GETS FRUSTRATED when jobs are left undone. However, Stephen Hellard was not around to complain about his incomplete memorial brass in St Nicholas Church, Stevenage. In his day, it was usual to have your memorial plaque engraved when you made your will. Your executors were then charged with adding the final details after your death. Unfortunately for Hellard his memorial was never completed. It reads

Here lies Master Stephen Hellard of the Diocese of York, Bachelor in degrees, once Rector of his church and also Canon of the Cathedral Church (of St Asaph) who died on the…day of the month of…in the year (of Our Lord) fifteen hundred and …

It is thought he become Rector of Upminster in 1470 before he was appointed as Rector of Stevenage in 1472. A year later he was granted a Papal dispensation so that he could hold two livings at the same time. In 1485 he was also Rector of Ellington, Huntingdonshire. He died in office in 1506. In his will, dated 1501, Hellard instructed that a property in Dead Lane, Stevenage, should be used to provide free accommodation for three people. He also left other land to provide rental income. The almshouses were named 'All Christian Soul House' and the residents were obliged to pray for Hellard's soul each day. The almshouses were rebuilt after a fire in 1807 and they are now known as the Hellard Almshouses.

Cyprian of Carthage reflects after a virulent outbreak of the plague in the city

There are certain people who are disturbed because this disease has attacked equally pagans and Christians. They talk as if being a Christian somehow guaranteed the enjoyment of happiness in this world and immunity from contact with illness, rather than preparing us to endure adversity in the faith that our full happiness is reserved for the future. It disturbs some of our number that death seems to have no favourites. And yet what is there in this world that is not common to us all? As long as we are subject to the same laws of generation we have a common flesh. As long as we are in this world we share an identical physicality with the rest of humankind, even if our spiritual identity singles us out. Until this corruptible form is clothed with incorruptibility, and this mortal frame receives immortality, and the Spirit leads us to God the Father, we share with the rest of humanity the burden of our flesh. When the soil is exhausted and harvest poor, famine makes no distinction of persons. When an army invades and a city is taken, everyone suffers a common desolation. When the skies are cloudless and the rains fail, all alike suffer from the drought. When a ship goes aground on treacherous rocks, the shipwreck affects all who sail in her without exception. Disease of the eye, attacks of fever, weakness in limbs, are all as common to Christians as to anyone else because this is the lot of all who bear human flesh in this world.

From 'On the Mortality Rate' in *Corpus Christianorum: Series Latina*

———

We praise you, Lord Jesus Christ, for your generosity:
you were rich, yet for our sake you became poor,
so that through your poverty we might become rich.
With our praise, O Lord, accept these our gifts,
and use them for the enrichment of others
and for the glory of your names. Amen.

Anon

Isaac Watts 1674–1748

Pastor, hymn writer and scholar

———

ISAAC WATTS WAS born into a Nonconformist family in Southampton and educated at King Edward VI School. As a child he was known to be a gifted linguist and he loved composing verse. As he could not subscribe to the Thirty Nine Articles he was unable to study at university and instead attended a dissenting academy at Stoke Newington. He was appointed pastor of the Independent Chapel at Mark Lane in London. Later he was employed as tutor to the children of the Hartopp family and then to the Abney family who lived at Theobalds, Cheshunt. As well as writing theological books, Watts also wrote *Logic, or The Right Use of Reason in the Enquiry After Truth With a Variety of Rules to Guard Against Error in the Affairs of Religion and Human Life, as well as in the Sciences* which was to go through twenty editions. For many years it was used at the universities of Oxford, Cambridge, Yale and Harvard as a text book for the teaching of logic. Watts wrote over seven hundred and fifty hymns. He is buried at Bunhill Fields in London. There is a memorial to him in Westminster Abbey and statues at Abney Park and in Southampton.

One of Isaac Watts' most famous hymns

O God, our help in ages past,
Our hope for years to come,
Our shelter from the stormy blast,
And our eternal home.

Under the shadow of Thy throne
Still may we dwell secure;
Sufficient is Thine arm alone,
And our defence is sure.

Before the hills in order stood,
Or earth received her frame,
From everlasting Thou art God,
To endless years the same.

A thousand ages in Thy sight
Are like an evening gone;
Short as the watch that ends the night
Before the rising sun.

Time, like an ever rolling stream,
Bears all its sons away;
They fly, forgotten, as a dream
Dies at the opening day.

O God, our help in ages past,
Our hope for years to come,
Be Thou our guard while life shall last,
And our eternal home.

Isaac Watts

Almighty God,
who gave to your servant Isaac Watts
singular gifts of rendering your praises in verse,
that he might write for your Church an abundant supply
of psalms, and hymns, and spiritual songs:
Stir up the hearts of your people,
that they may joyfully sing your praises in this life and the life to come;
through your Son Jesus Christ our Lord. Amen.

A Collect for Isaac Watts

John Jamieson Willis 1872–1954

Bishop of Uganda

———

'THE CHRISTIANISATION OF the densely populated lake region began when Mr J. J. Willis sailed across the Victoria Nyanza from Uganda, and, in default of a church, held the first baptism under a tree at Maseno.' Bishop Stephen Neill's description of John Willis' travels in *A History of Christian Missions* reveals the extraordinarily difficult challenges that he must have faced in his early years as a missionary in Africa. Willis' connection with the Diocese of St Albans dates from his time as a pupil at Haileybury, the school just outside Hertford. From there he went to study at Pembroke College, Cambridge. He was ordained in 1895 and served his title in Great Yarmouth. Willis went as a missionary to Africa under the auspices of the Church Missionary Society. He served there in various capacities before being appointed Archdeacon of Kavirondo. In 1912 he was consecrated Bishop of Uganda. In 1934 he returned to Britain and was Assistant Bishop in the Diocese of Leicester. He died on this day in 1954.

An extract from a charge given by John Willis in 1913 to missionaries in Uganda

For me this past year has been one of extraordinary interest. It has been a privilege such as few men have enjoyed to visit the widely-scattered stations of the Uganda Missions, and to enter as far as might be into the life of the workers, and the infinitely varied details of the work. I come to the close of this year and the eve of another Synod with a deep feeling of appreciation of what I have been privileged to see, and in a sense to share, and with a very real and lasting sense of gratitude for the unnumbered acts of kindness, and the welcomes that have more than made up for sometimes wearying rides. I can only say that I am proud to be at the head of such a mission, even while humiliated by the thought of the overwhelming responsibility. But when I think of all the work done – the pressing needs of education and pastoral supervision, and the unprecedented openings for evangelisation within and around Uganda – there is one need which stands out as supreme. I dwelt upon it in speaking to the native clergy at Budo; I would close with speaking of it to you tonight. It is the need of *shepherding*. 'Feed My lambs…Tend My sheep…Feed My sheep.' I know of no part of our multitudinous work at the present time more vitally and urgently important than this duty and sacred privilege of ministering to these our brethren in Christ. They are passing as a Church and as individuals through supremely difficult times; they need now, if they ever needed, all the help and all the friendship that we can give them. I commend this to you – I lay it upon myself – as the greatest need that lies before us in the coming year.

From *The Church in Uganda*

———

Lord Jesus Christ,
who taught us that the harvest is plentiful but the workers are few:
we thank you that your Holy Spirit is at work in the world;
help us seize the opportunities for witness and service
that you open up before us,
that your kingdom may come and your will may be done;
for we ask this in the name of Jesus Christ our Lord. Amen.

Stephen Gardiner c.1483–1555

Lord Chancellor and bishop

———

IT IS CLAIMED that the final words of Stephen Gardiner were *Erravi cum Petro, sed non flevi cum Petro* (Like Peter, I have erred, unlike Peter, I have not wept). Gardiner was born into a prosperous family in Bury St Edmunds. He studied law and classics at Trinity Hall, Cambridge. Cardinal Wolsey appointed him as his secretary and he accompanied the Cardinal when King Henry VIII and the French Ambassador signed the Treaty of the More at More Park near Rickmansworth in Hertfordshire and was also sent by Wolsey on a number of diplomatic missions. However, even with his consummate skills, Gardiner was unable to persuade the Pope to grant the king a divorce from Catherine of Aragon. Despite this, Henry made Gardiner his secretary and successively Archdeacon of Taunton, Norfolk and Leicester. In 1551 he was made Bishop of Winchester but continued to travel widely on the Continent as an envoy for the king. During the reign of King Edward VI, Gardiner was imprisoned in the Tower of London and deprived of his See, but was released when Mary I came to the throne. Once again in favour, he was given back the bishopric and also made Lord Chancellor. He is buried in Winchester Cathedral.

Howard Snyder, a Methodist theologian from Canada, reflects on the Church and the kingdom of God

The church gets in trouble whenever it thinks it is in the church business rather than the Kingdom business. In the church business, people are concerned with church activities, religious behaviour and spiritual things. In the Kingdom business, people are concerned with Kingdom activities, all human behaviour and everything God has made, visible and invisible. Kingdom people see human affairs as saturated with spiritual meaning and Kingdom significance. Kingdom people seek first the Kingdom of God and its justice; church people often put church work above concerns of justice, mercy and truth. Church people think about how to get people into the church; Kingdom people think about how to get the church into the world. Church people worry that the world might change the church; Kingdom people work to see the church change the world…If the church has one great need, it is this: To be set free for the Kingdom of God, to be liberated from itself as it has become in order to be itself as God intends. The church must be freed to participate fully in the economy of God.

From *Liberating the Church: The Ecology of Church and Kingdom*

Heavenly Father,
whose Son gave his life for the salvation of others:
save us from our petty obsessions and self-absorption,
open our eyes and set us free from our captivity
that we may serve you joyfully and work for the coming of your kingdom;
through Jesus Christ our Lord. Amen.

Agnes Beaumont 1652–1720

Follower of John Bunyan

———

AGNES BEAUMONT WAS born in the Bedfordshire hamlet of Edworth. At the age of twenty she heard John Bunyan preach and was converted to Christianity. However, her life was not without controversy. In *The Narrative of the Persecution of Agnes Beaumont* she tells us how on one occasion she persuaded Bunyan to allow her to ride with him on horseback to a meeting. When her father heard about this he was so enraged that when she returned home he refused to allow her back into the house. Some time later when her father died, the family lawyer (whom she had refused to marry) claimed that she had poisoned him. Agnes was arrested and after a trial was eventually acquitted of the charges. In her will Agnes asked to be buried next to the minister of Tilehouse Street Chapel, John Wilson, who had been a close friend.

John Bunyan writes about the Christian's pilgrimage

Now when Christian got as far as the Spring of Life he drank of it, and then went up the hill. But when the two men saw that it was steep and high, and that there were three ways to choose from, one of them took the path the name of which is Danger, and lost his way in a great wood, and one of them went by the road of Destruction, which led him to a wide field full of dark rocks, where he fell, and rose no more. I then saw Christian go up the hill, where at first I could see him run, then walk, and then go on his hands and knees, so steep was it. Now half way up was a cave made by the Lord of that hill, that those who came by might rest there. So here Christian sat down, and took out the scroll and read it, till at last he fell off in a deep sleep which kept him there till it was dusk; and while he slept his scroll fell from his hand. At length a man came up to him and woke him, and said: 'Go to the ant, thou man of sloth, and learn of her to be wise.' At this Christian gave a start, and sped on his way, and went at a quick pace. When he had got near to the top of the hill, two men ran up to meet him, whose names were Timorous and Mistrust, to whom Christian said, 'Sirs, what ails you? You run the wrong way'. Timorous said that Zion was the hill they meant to climb, but that when they had got half way they found that they met with more and more risk, so that great fear came on them, and all they could do was to turn back…Christian said 'You rouse my fears. Where must I fly to be safe? If I go back to my own town I am sure to lose my life, but if I can get to The Celestial City, there shall I be safe. To turn back is death; to go on is fear of death, but when I come there, a life of bliss that knows no end. I will go on yet'.

From *The Pilgrim's Progress*

God of Grace,
whose perfect love casts out fear:
set us free to serve you with gladness and joy,
as we entrust ourselves into your care,
confident in your steadfastness and faithfulness:
through Jesus Christ our Lord. Amen.

Edmund Beckett 1816–1905

Horologist, lawyer and architect

———

EDMUND BECKETT IS chiefly remembered for two things. Firstly, in 1851 he designed the mechanism for the clock of the Palace of Westminster, which rings the famous chimes. Secondly, he designed and paid for extensive repairs and alterations principally to the west front of St Albans Abbey. These were deemed to be so awful by some critics that a new verb was coined, 'to grimthorpe' (his title was Baron Grimthorpe), which meant 'to restore an ancient building with lavish expenditure rather than skill and taste.' Grimthorpe also undertook major works on St Peter's Church and St Michael's Church in St Albans. As he was extremely wealthy he could afford to pay for the works, but insisted that they were done according to his plans. He is reputed to have said, 'I am the only architect with whom I have never quarrelled.' Born in Nottinghamshire, Beckett went to Eton and Trinity College, Cambridge. He was called to the bar at Lincoln's Inn in 1841 and became a Queen's Counsel in 1854. He was Chancellor and Vicar-General of the province of York from 1877 until 1900. In 1845, he married Fanny Catherine Lonsdale, who was the daughter of the Bishop of Lichfield. Beckett lived at Batchwood in St Albans. He is buried in the grounds of St Albans Cathedral beside his wife.

A reading about time from the Bible

To every thing there is a season,
and a time to every purpose under the heaven:
A time to be born, and a time to die;
A time to plant, and a time to pluck up that which is planted;
A time to kill, and a time to heal;
A time to break down, and a time to build up;
A time to weep, and a time to laugh;
A time to mourn, and a time to dance;
A time to cast away stones, and a time to gather stones together;
A time to embrace, and a time to refrain from embracing;
A time to get, and a time to lose;
A time to keep, and a time to cast away;
A time to rend, and a time to sew;
A time to keep silence, and a time to speak;
A time to love, and a time to hate;
A time of war, and a time of peace.

Ecclesiastes 3.1–8 from the *Authorised Version of the Bible*

God of eternity
for whom a thousand years is but a day:
forgive us when we squander the precious gift of time
and grant us grace to live our lives wisely
that each moment may be filled with thanksgiving and praise
and offered to you and for your service:
for the sake of Jesus Christ our Lord. Amen.

Ælfric of Abingdon d.1005

Abbot of St Albans and Archbishop of Canterbury

———

ÆLFRIC WAS A monk of Abingdon who became Abbot of St Albans around the year 969. When he was elected Bishop of Ramsbury in 992 his brother, Leofric, succeeded him as Abbot of St Albans. Three years later Ælfric was translated to the See of Canterbury. Records show that two members of the cathedral chapter objected to his appointment and travelled to Rome to try to block it. They were unsuccessful and in 997 Ælfric went to Rome to receive his pallium (a small band of material worn only by the Pope and archbishops) from Pope Gregory V. It is highly likely that he conducted the marriage service of King Æthelred the Unready and Emma of Normandy in 1002. He also ordered the composition of the first *Life of Dunstan*. It is probable that Ælfric was born into a wealthy and influential family, possibly in Kent. His will reveals that, at the time of his death, he owned three ships and he bequeathed properties to his family and to the Abbey at St Albans. Ælfric died on this day in 1005 and was buried at Abingdon. Some years later his remains were taken to Canterbury.

Evelyn Underhill meditates on the resurrection of the dead

The Christian account of the nature of Reality ends with a declaration of absolute confidence. 'I look for the resurrection of the dead, and the life of the world to come': or, more literally, 'I expect the life of the age that is drawing near.' I expect Eternity as the very meaning and goal of all full human life, and especially of the Christian art of living. I expect it because I have already experienced it; if not in my own person, then by my share in the experience of the Saints. 'Let us press on to perfection,' says the writer of the Epistle to the Hebrews, 'because we have *tasted* of the heavenly gift and the powers of the world to come.' The closing phrases of the Creed call us to ascend in heart and mind to the world of the Eternal Perfect, the Thought of God, the Country of Everlasting Clearness, and find the meaning of existence there. It is as if the soul said, 'I believe in and utterly trust one living Perfect God, and His creative purpose, His ceaseless action. And because of that – because I have glimpsed the sparkle of His mysterious radiance and heard the whisper of His inexorable demands – I trust and go on trusting, in spite of all disconcerting appearances, my best and deepest longings. I expect the fulfilment of that sacramental promise which is present in all beauty: the perfect life of the age, the world, that keeps on drawing near. I look past process and change, with all their difficulties and obscurities, to that Perfection which haunts me; because I know that God is perfect, and His supernatural purpose must prevail.'

From *The School of Charity*

———

God of Eternity,
the Alpha and Omega
in whom all people and all things
have their beginning and their end:
we thank you for the lives
of the saints who have trodden the path before us;
grant us grace and the gift of your Holy Spirit
that, following their good example,
we may live lives worthy of our calling;
through Jesus Christ our Lord. Amen.

Hugh c.1135–1200

Patron saint of the sick, swans and shoemakers

———

T HUGH'S LIFE is honoured in the three churches in the diocese which are dedicated to him: St Hugh's Lewsey; St Hugh and St John, Chells, in Stevenage; and St Hugh, which is the daughter church of St Francis, Luton. Born in Avalon, Hugh's mother died when he was eight and his father moved to a local priory with his son. His considerable gifts were soon noticed and he was made a deacon when he was just nineteen years old. Within a short time he became Prior of the Augustinian monastery at Saint-Maximin and a year later in 1160 he entered the Grand Chartreuse, which was famous for the rigorous and disciplined life of the monks. Around 1179, at King Henry II's request, he was sent to become Prior of the first English Charterhouse, which was at Witham in Somerset. Hugh's piety became so well known that in 1186 he was appointed to the See of Lincoln, which at that time was the largest diocese in England. It is significant that most of the Diocese of St Albans was part of the Diocese of Lincoln until 1837. Hugh was assiduous in visiting his vast diocese and he repaired and extended the cathedral in Lincoln, which had been damaged by an earthquake. He also improved the education in the cathedral school. Hugh had a particular concern for the vulnerable, protecting Jews from persecution and caring for those with leprosy. He died in London and is buried in Lincoln Cathedral.

A description of Hugh's life

It is impossible to record among the other marks of his devotion Hugh's great compassion and tenderness toward the sick, and even to those afflicted with leprosy. He used to wash and dry their feet and kiss them affectionately, and having refreshed them with food and drink give them alms on a lavish scale. He often did this privately to thirteen patients in his chamber with few people present, when that number could be found in the place where he was. There were hospitals on certain of the episcopal manors, where many men and women afflicted by this disease were maintained. He made a practice of giving gifts of many different kinds to these in addition to the revenue already assigned to them by his predecessors, and frequently visited them himself with a few of his more God-fearing and devout retainers. He would sit in their midst in a small inner room and would comfort their souls by his kindly words, relieving their sorrow by his motherly tenderness, and encouraging those who were so desolate and afflicted in this life to hope for an eternal reward, combining with amazing gentleness words of consolation and exhortations to good conduct.

From the *Great Life of Hugh* by Adam, Monk of Eynsham, in *They Still Speak* by Robert Wright

---

O holy God,
you endowed your servant and bishop Hugh of Lincoln
with wise and cheerful boldness,
and taught him to commend to earthly rulers the discipline of holy life:
give us grace like him to be bold in the service of the Gospel
putting our confidence in Christ alone;
who is alive and reigns with you
in the unity of the Holy Spirit,
one God, now and for ever. Amen.

From *Exciting Holiness* by Brother Tristam

Gore Ouseley 1770–1844

Diplomat, linguist and businessman

———

IF YOU WANDER into St Mary's Church, Hertingfordbury, you will find a memorial to Gore Ouseley. Ouseley lived nearby at Panshanger Park, although he spent much of his working life abroad. As a young man he was posted to Lucknow, where he played such an important role on behalf of the British Government that he was made a baronet at the age of thirty-eight. In 1810 he was appointed ambassador to Persia, where he helped negotiate the Treaty of Gulistan, which established a new border between Persia and Russia. Ouseley was a brilliant linguist and learnt Sanskrit, Arabic and Persian. He became friends with the famous missionary, the Reverend Henry Martyn, who had completed the first translation of the New Testament into Persian. Following Martyn's death, Ouseley proof read the text and had it published. On his return to England he became President of the Society for the Publication of the Oriental Texts. He wrote *Remarks on the Statistics and Political Institutions of the United States* and *Biographical Notices of Persian Poets*. His son was the Reverend Canon Professor Sir Frederick Arthur Gore Ouseley who was a composer and musicologist. Gore Ouseley died on this day in 1844 in Beaconsfield.

A poem by the Christian Persian Jalil Qazzaq

These hands of ours, which spiritual gifts have gained
These bodies, which Thy grace imparted has sustained
O Lord, do not uphold and strengthen day and night,
To offer Thee a loyal service, as is right!

Our tongues, which glorify thine ever worthy name,
And sing Thy praise, and Thy beneficence proclaim
O Lord, restrain from harm of harsh and hurtful word;
May no unkind or thoughtless phrase from us be heard!

Our eyes, which Thy benevolence and love have viewed
Our ears, which Thy commands have heard with certitude
O Lord, make open to the needs of those around;
Where love is giv'n and sought may love from us abound!

Our spirit's lantern from Thyself illuminate,
That it may still more brightly shine and scintillate;
And may our lamp, by fullness of Thy grace secured,
Maintain a constant light and never be obscured!

From *Christ and Christianity in Persian Poetry*
by Bishop Hassan Dehqani-Tafti

———

Faithful God, we pray for the ancient churches of the East
and especially for Armenian, Assyrian and Chaldean Christians in Iran.
We thank you for their faithful witness down through the centuries
and pray that, in partnership with Anglicans in that troubled country,
they may have grace to persevere in the face of intimidation and opposition;
through Jesus Christ our Lord. Amen.

Adam the Cellarer 12th century

Monk

———

WHEN THE NEW Chapter House was being built on the south side of St Albans Cathedral in 1978, archaeologists were surprised to discover the remains of a monk called Adam the Cellarer buried amongst the abbots. His prestigious resting place is eloquent testimony to the honour in which Adam must have been held during his lifetime. St Albans, like the other large medieval monasteries, was extremely expensive to maintain. The community needed someone who knew how to organise its finances, repair its buildings and provide food and clothes for the monks. A good cellarer was invaluable and vital for the survival of the community. We know nothing about Adam. His remains now lie under a slab in the Quire of the Cathedral, which records his name along with abbots from the same period.

St Benedict writes about the role of the cellarer

Let there be chosen out of the Community as Cellarer of the Monastery, a man who is wise, ripe in manners, and sober; not a great eater, not haughty, nor hasty, nor insulting; not slow, nor wasteful, but fearing God, and acting as a father to the whole Brotherhood. Let him have care of all things, and without the command of the Abbot do nothing. Let him take heed of all that is ordered, and not sadden his Brethren. But if any Brother shall perchance ask anything of him that is not reasonable, let him not, by contemptuously spurning, grieve him, but reasonable and with all humility refuse what he asks for amiss. Let him have regard for his own soul, mindful of that rule of the Apostle: 'They that have ministered well, shall purchase for themselves a good degree.' Let him care diligently for the sick, the children, the guests, and the poor; knowing, without doubt, that for all these he shall give an account on the judgment day. Let him look upon all the vessels and goods of the Monastery as if they were the sacred vessels of the Altar. Let him neglect nothing; neither let him be covetous, nor prodigal, not wasteful of the goods of the Monastery, but do all things with moderation, and according to the command of his Abbot. Above all things, let him have humility, and give at least a gentle answer unto him, on whom he hath nothing else to bestow; for it is written: 'A good word is above the best gift.' Let him have under his care all that the Abbot shall appoint, and presume not to meddle with anything from which he shall forbid him.

From *The Rule of St Benedict*

———

God our Father,
make the door of our church wide enough to receive
all who need human love and fellowship and a Father's care,
and narrow enough to shut out all envy, pride and lack of love;
here may the tempted find help, the sorrowing receive comfort,
the careless be awakened to repentance,
and the penitent be assured of your mercy;
and here may all you children renew their strength
and go on their way in hope and joy
through Jesus Christ our Lord. Amen.

Bishop Thomas Ken

James Janeway 1636–74

Puritan author and preacher

———

JAMES JANEWAY WAS one of the most famous children's authors of his day. His best-known book was a collection of children's conversion stories called *A Token for Children*. Many wealthier families in the mid-seventeenth century would have been familiar with the book. Son of William Janeway, the Rector of Kelshall, James was baptised at St Peter's Church, Lilley. He studied at Christ Church, Oxford, and then worked as a private tutor. We know that he was ejected under the Act of Uniformity in 1662, after which he became a Nonconformist minister serving in Rotherhithe. Janeway faced much opposition and unsuccessful attempts were even made to murder him. On one occasion the meeting house was attacked and destroyed but the congregation replaced it with another, even larger, building. Janeway lived through the Great Plague of London in 1665 and the Great Fire of London in the following year. He wrote a number of books including *Heaven Upon Earth* and *The Saints' Encouragement to Diligence in Christ's Service* and several of his sermons were published. He died of tuberculosis (as did his five brothers) at a young age and is buried at Aldermanbury.

A description of James Janeway's last days

His mother and brethren standing by him, he said 'Dear mother, I beseech you earnestly as ever I desired any thing of you in my life, that you cheerfully give me up to Christ. Do not hinder me, now I am going to rest and glory. I am afraid of your prayers, lest they pull one way, and mine another'. And then turning to his brethren, he spake thus to them 'I charge you all, do not pray for my life any more, you do me wrong, if you do. Oh that glory, that unspeakable glory that I behold. My heart is full, my heart is full. Christ smiles, and I cannot choose but smile. Can you find in your heart to stop me, who am going to the complete and eternal enjoyment of Christ? Would you keep me from my crown? The arms of my blessed Saviour are open to embrace me; the angels stand ready to carry my soul into his bosom; Oh, did you but see what I see, you would all cry out with me, how long, dear Lord; come, Lord Jesus, come quickly! Oh why are his chariot-wheels so long a coming?' And all this while he lay, like a triumphing conqueror, smiling and rejoicing in spirit. There was never a day towards his end but (as weak as he was) he did some special piece of service for his great master. Yea, almost every hour did produce fresh wonders.

From *An Extract of the Life and Death of Mr John* [sic] *Janeway* by James Wheatley

———

Living God,
give us health in body and mind
that during our time on earth
we may so live our lives
that when you call us home
we may be ready and waiting,
confident in your mercy and grace;
through our Lord and Saviour Jesus Christ. Amen.

John Tillotson 1630–94

Curate of Cheshunt and Archbishop of Canterbury

———

TILLOTSON WAS A Yorkshireman from Sowerby. A statue of him still stands in the churchyard of St Peter's Church in the town. He studied at Clare Hall, Cambridge, and in 1651 became a fellow of the college. Ordained in 1661 by a Scottish bishop, he was closely aligned to the Presbyterians in the early years of his ministry. However, following the Act of Uniformity of 1662, he became curate of Cheshunt and later Rector of Kedington in Suffolk. In 1664 he married the niece of Oliver Cromwell, Elizabeth French. He moved on to become Dean of Canterbury and later Dean of St Paul's Cathedral. Tillotson was known for his eloquent, and sometimes combative, preaching. As a result a large number of his sermons were published. He edited John Wilkins' *Principles of Natural Religion* and he wrote *Discourse against Transubstantiation.* He became a confidant to King William and Queen Mary and was made Clerk of the Closet. He was Archbishop of Canterbury for just over three years, during which time he worked on a number of reforms, in particular trying to stamp out non-residence of the clergy.

From a sermon by John Tillotson

And what infinite cause have we to bless God for the gift of his Holy Spirit, and to say with St Paul, 'Blessed be God for his unspeakable gift.' That he hath given his Holy Spirit to his church, at first in miraculous powers and gifts for the preaching of the Christian religion in the world, and ever since in such degrees of assistance, as were necessary in the several ages of the church, for the preservation of the Christian religion in the world; that he hath given his Holy Spirit to every particular member of his church, for the sanctifying and renewing of our natures, 'to strengthen us to every good word and work, and to keep us by his mighty power through faith unto salvation?' And this sanctifying virtue of the Holy Ghost, enabling us to do the will of God, is more than any miraculous powers whatsoever. So our Saviour tells us, (Matthew 7.21–23) 'Not every one that saith unto me, Lord, Lord, shall enter into the kingdom of heaven, but he that doth the will of my Father which is in heaven. Many will say to me in that day, Lord, Lord, have we not prophesied in thy name? and in thy name have cast out devils? and in thy name done many wonderful works? and then will I profess unto them, I never knew you: depart from me, ye that work iniquity.' Men may do wonders by the power of the Holy Ghost, and yet be shut out of the kingdom of heaven; only they that are assisted by the Spirit of God to do the will of God shall be admitted into heaven.

From 'The Reasonableness of Fearing God more than Men' in *Sermons*

———

O God, the Holy Spirit,
come to us, and among us:
*   come as the wind, and cleanse us;*
*   come as the fire, and burn;*
*   come as the dew, and refresh:*
convict, convert and consecrate
*   many hearts and lives*
*   to our great good*
*   and thy greater glory*
and this we ask for Jesus Christ's name. Amen.

Eric Milner-White

Saint Cecilia d. c.180

Martyr and patron saint

—————

THE LATE MEDIEVAL church at Little Hadham in Hertfordshire is the only one in the diocese dedicated to St Cecilia. Little is known for sure about her life. In the sixth century the Bishop of Poitiers, Venantius Fortunatus, claimed that she was martyred sometime around AD 180 in Sicily. It is thought that Cecilia's husband and brother were executed first and that her persecutors tried to kill her by smothering. When that failed they attempted to cut off her head on three occasions. However, as they were beheading her, Cecilia continued to sing praises to God, which is why she is known as the patron saint of musicians. She did not die for a further three days. We know that as early as the fifth century there was a church in Rome dedicated to her memory. Cecilia is often portrayed playing a musical instrument. A stained glass window to her can be found in St Mary's Church, Watford. Cecilia's story is told in The Second Nun's Tale in *The Canterbury Tales* by Chaucer. Many poems have been written about her, including those by Dryden, Pope and Auden, and Handel, Britten and Finzi all composed works in her honour.

Geoffrey Chaucer describes the life of St Cecilia

According to her Life, the fair virgin Cecilia was born of a noble Roman family and brought up from her cradle in the faith of Christ, whose gospel was never absent from her thoughts. And I find it written that she never ceased to love and fear God or to pray Him to preserve her maidenhood. Now when she was to be married to a youth named Valerian, and the day came of her wedding, such was the humbleness and piety of her spirit, she wore a haircloth next her skin under the golden robe which so well became her…Night came, when according to custom she must go to bed with her husband; but she spoke privately to him, saying, 'Sweet and dearly beloved husband, there is a secret you may wish to hear, and which I will gladly tell you if you swear not to reveal it.' Valerian bound himself with an oath that he would never betray her under any circumstances, come what may; and then at last she said, 'I have an angel who loves me with a love so great that waking or sleeping he is always at hand to watch over my body. If he perceives you touch me or make carnal love, he will slay you in the act without hesitation, and you will die in the flower of youth. But if you protect me with a pure love, for your purity he will love you as myself and reveal his radiance and his joy.'

From The Second Nun's Tale in *The Canterbury Tales*

—————

Gracious God,
whose servant Cecilia remained steadfast
singing a song of defiance
as she witnessed to your truth and faithfulness:
write a new song in our hearts,
a hymn of humble trust and confident faith
that we may bear witness in our generation
to the good news of the gospel;
we ask this for the sake of Jesus Christ our Lord. Amen.

Joseph Beaumont 1616–99

Priest, poet and scholar

———

JOSEPH BEAUMONT IS remembered today for his great allegorical poem *Psyche* published in 1648, which took him nearly a year to write. It is the account of 'a soul led by Divine Grace and her Guardian Angel through the assaults of lust, pride, heresie, and persecution.' Written in the style of Spenser, even in its abridged version published after his death by his son, it contains thirty thousand lines – not a poem for the faint hearted or anyone in a hurry. Born in Hadleigh, Suffolk, the son of a clothier, Beaumont went up to Peterhouse, Cambridge. He graduated and was elected to a fellowship in the college in 1636. He was appointed Rector of Kelshall, Hertfordshire, in 1643 but was ejected in the following year and returned to his home town of Hadleigh. Over the following years he held various posts and in 1650 became chaplain to Bishop Matthew Wren of Ely. Beaumont married in 1650 and had six children, but his wife died in 1662 leaving him with a young family. In the same year he was made Master of Jesus College and in the following year Master of Peterhouse. He became the Regius Professor of Divinity in 1674. Beaumont wrote *Some Observations upon the Apologie of Dr. Henry More* and after his death his collected poems were published. He died on this day in 1699 and is buried in the college chapel of Peterhouse, Cambridge.

Jesus inter Ubera Mariae

In the coolness of the day,
The old world even, God all undressed went down
Without His robe, without His crown,
Into His private garden, there to lay
On spicy bed His sweeter head.

There He found two beds of spice,
A double mount of lilies in whose top
Two milky fountains bubbled up.
He soon resolved: 'And well I like!' He cries,
'My table spread upon my bed.'

Scarcely had He 'gun to feed
When troops of cherubs hovered round about,
And on their golden wings they brought
All Eden's flowers. But we cried out: 'No need
Of flowers here! Sweet spirits, forbear.'

'True, He needs no sweets,' say they;
'But sweets have need of Him, to keep them so;
Now paradise springs new with you,
Old Eden's beauty all inclined this way;
And we are come to bring them home.

'Paradise spring new with you,
Where 'twixt those beds of lilies you may see
Of life the everlasting Tree.'
'Sweet is your reason,' then said we: 'come strew
Your pious showers of eastern flowers.'

(Chorus) Winds awake! and with soft gale
Awake the odours of our garden too;
By which yourselves perfumed go
Through every quarter of your world, that all
Your sound may hear and breathe your air.

Joseph Beaumont

———

Humble God, who stooped low to enter our world in human form,
becoming human that we might become divine:
open our minds and hearts to the wonder of your grace,
set us free from greed and envy
and give us grace to live with open hands and open hearts;
through Jesus Christ our Lord. Amen.

Edward Willes 1693–1773

Royal decipherer and rector

———

BORN IN WARWICKSHIRE and educated at Oriel College, Oxford, Willes' linguistic skills (he was fluent in Latin, French, Spanish and Swedish) and his ability to decipher messages (something he learnt while he was at Oxford) brought him to the attention of King George I. He was so successful at unlocking the meaning of the ciphers that were passing between those with pro-Jacobite sympathies that in 1718 he was rewarded with the living of Barton-le-Clay. This is not a skill that has been sought when appointing rectors to that benefice in recent years. Willes' work led directly to the conviction of the Bishop of Rochester, Francis Atterbury, who was sent into exile. Over the following years Willes was given a succession of preferments, when he was appointed to a canonry at Westminster, the deanery of Lincoln, and the livings of Bonsall, Derbyshire, and St John's, Westminster. Despite holding several offices at the same time, he appears to have been assiduous in his clerical responsibilities. In 1743 he was elected Bishop of St Davids and in the following year was translated to the See of Bath and Wells. He and his wife Jane had nine children. He died on this day in 1773, and is buried in Westminster Abbey.

Dietrich Bonhoeffer, the Second World War martyr, writes about listening

The first service that one owes to others in the fellowship consists in listening to them. Just as love of God begins with listening to his Word, so the beginning of love for the brethren is learning to listen to them. It is God's love for us that he not only gives us his Word but also lends us his ear. So it is his work that we do for our brother when we learn to listen to him. Christians, especially ministers, so often think they must always contribute something when they are in the company of others, that this is the one service they have to render. They forget that listening can be a greater service than speaking. Many people are looking for an ear that will listen. They do not find it among Christians, because these Christians are talking where they should be listening. But he who can no longer listen to his brother will soon be no longer listening to God either; he will be doing nothing but prattle in the presence of God too. This is the beginning of the death of the spiritual life, and in the end there is nothing left but spiritual chatter and clerical condescension arrayed in pious words. One who cannot listen long and patiently will presently be talking beside the point and be never really speaking to others, albeit he be not conscious of it. Anyone who thinks that his time is too valuable to spend keeping quiet will eventually have no time for God and his brother, but only for himself and for his own follies.

From *Life Together*

———

Give us grace, Good Lord, to honour our brothers and sisters:
save us from treating others as nothing more than an audience for our opinions,
forgive us our self-obsessions and judgmental attitudes
and grant that we may be quick to listen, slow to speak and ready to understand;
through Jesus Christ our Lord. Amen.

Catherine of Alexandria 4th century

Saint and martyr

———

THERE ARE THREE churches in Hertfordshire dedicated to St Catherine (sometimes spelt Katherine) at Sacombe, Hoddesdon and Ickleford. There are several St Catherines in Christian history, but most churches are dedicated to St Catherine of Alexandria. The obvious exception in this diocese is the church in Dunstable which is dedicated to St Katherine of Genoa. Tradition records that Catherine was the daughter of King Costus and Queen Sabinella, who governed Alexandria. At the age of fourteen she converted to Christianity and soon found herself in discussion with fifty philosophers who, it is claimed, were so persuaded by her arguments that they too converted. Refusing to deny her faith, the Emperor had Catherine tortured by having her tied to a wheel (hence the firework known as a Catherine Wheel) and then beheaded. She is honoured as the patron saint of maidens, female students, wheelwrights and mechanics, and her feast day is 25 November.

Father Christopher Bryant preaches about suffering

The Epistle to the Hebrews declares 'Ours is not a high priest unable to sympathise with our weaknesses, but one who, because of his likeness to us, has been tempted every way, only without sin.' Christians while paying lip service to the true humanity of Christ have often failed to think of him as fully human. People have thought of him as physically human but psychologically divine. They have thought that he suffered intensely in body but was sustained by a more than human perception of what he had to do and how things would turn out. It seems to me that if this had been so, he would have been spared one of the sharpest trials a good man has to endure, uncertainty as to what will be the effect of his actions and the nagging fear that he may have made the wrong decision. It seems to me both more compatible with the reality of our Lord's manhood and with such indications that the Gospels give that Christ, though he saw plainly the human probabilities, did not know clearly what was going to happen, that the unborn future was hidden from him. I believe that we grasp better both what actually happened and its meaning for our own lives, if we understand him as suffering not with a clear vision of the good that would flow from his endurance but in human weakness, in uncertainty and in ignorance of the outcome of it all; clinging only to the Father's will, relying solely on the Father's power; trusting the Father, even at that moment near the end when he felt as though forsaken.

From *The Psychology of Prayer*

Almighty and everlasting God,
who strengthened Your blessed martyr Catherine
with the virtue of constancy in faith and truth:
Grant us in like manner for love of You
to despise the prosperity of this world,
and to fear none of its adversities;
through Jesus Christ our Lord. Amen.

From *The Book of Common Prayer* of the
Episcopal Church of the USA

Thomas Wolsey 1473–1530

Statesman and archbishop

———

AMONG HIS MANY properties, Thomas Wolsey owned one of the greatest houses in Hertfordshire: More Park in Rickmansworth. It was an extraordinary achievement to possess such a magnificent home, considering his modest beginnings. The son of an Ipswich butcher, Wolsey studied at Magdalen College, Oxford, and was ordained around 1498. Before long he was chaplain to the Archbishop of Canterbury and later served as chaplain to Henry VII. Wolsey was a brilliant administrator and diplomat and he soon came to the attention of the newly-crowned Henry VIII. The king was only twenty-three and needed a trusted advisor to deal with matters of state on his behalf. Wolsey proved to be such a wise counsellor that the king made him Archbishop of York when he was just forty-one years old. Other influential posts, some of them ecclesiastical and most of them lucrative, quickly followed and in 1515 he was made a cardinal and became the Lord Chancellor. This gave him a powerful position in advising on matters of state and foreign policy. It was Wolsey who organised the famous summit at the Field of the Cloth of Gold, near Calais, when Henry met King Francis I of France. He used his considerable wealth to build Cardinal College (now known as Christ Church) in Oxford and his two main London homes, York Place and Hampton Court Palace. However, Wolsey was unable to persuade the Pope to annul Henry's marriage to Catherine of Aragon which infuriated the king. In 1530 he was arrested and accused of treason. He died in Leicester before he could be put on trial.

Kenneth Kaunda writes about Christianity and politics

Of course Jesus's choice of the image of the Kingdom of Heaven does not mean that he thought of God's will being done on earth exclusively through some sort of political arrangement – turning the Gospel, in fact, into a political manifesto. We must not make the mistake of identifying the Kingdom of Heaven with any ideology or political philosophy. That way lies fascism. Nevertheless, I do not think Jesus was solely concerned with individual morality and holiness. The ultimate state of blessedness on earth is to be able to love God with all our heart and mind and soul and strength and our neighbour as ourselves. Now if such a wonderful state has no effect upon our organised political, social and economic life then I and all those who share my search for the Kingdom of Heaven are wasting our time. I do not believe I am wasting my time. I have great faith in my fellow men and women and believe there can be no higher vocation than that of trying to create the conditions of life which enable them to be fully human. This is not just a political goal, it has profound religious significance. Everything we do which makes it easier for men and women to show love towards one another enables them, however imperfectly, to share the life of God who is Love.

From *Kaunda on Violence*

Almighty God,
grant that those exercising power here on earth
may use it for the common good,
for the establishing of justice
and for the protection of the weak and vulnerable,
ever mindful that one day they will be called to account
before you, the God of righteousness and compassion;
through Jesus Christ our Lord. Amen.

William Hale Hale 1795–1870

Historian and Archdeacon of St Albans

———

WILLIAM HALE HALE was one of those historians who delighted in researching and writing about obscure subjects. His interests ranged from the wills of bishops to the history of medieval hospitals. His book *Pontifical Law on the Subject of the Utensils and Repairs of Churches as set forth by Fabius Alberti* must surely have been the talk of inns and taverns of London when it was published in 1838. The son of John Hale, a surgeon from Lynn in Norfolk, William Hale was orphaned when he was four. His guardian, James Palmer, had him educated at Charterhouse from where he went up to Oriel College, Oxford. He graduated in classics and mathematics. Hale was ordained deacon in 1818 and served his first curacy at St Benet Gracechurch in London and his second curacy at St Botolph, Bishopsgate. His training incumbent, Charles Blomfield, was made Bishop of Chester in 1824 and Hale moved north to become his chaplain, until Blomfield was translated to the See of London four years later. Hale also moved back to London, ministering at Charterhouse and St Paul's Cathedral. He was successively the Archdeacon of St Albans, Middlesex and London. He married Ann Caroline Coles and together they had eight children. William died on this day in 1870 and he is buried, along with Ann, in St Paul's Cathedral.

William Hale Hale preaches at an ordination in Chester Cathedral in 1824

And first, I would recommend the example of the apostle in the text, as a pattern of that humble spirit in which the Christian Minister should strive to give effect to the authority with which he is invested. No one could be more conscious of the rank and dignity of an apostle, than was St Paul, nor more aware of the wonders which his preaching had wrought. The contemplation of the spiritual blessings which through him God had conferred upon the Gentiles, often filled his breast with joy, and caused him to 'glory through Jesus Christ in things pertaining to God.' In many parts of this epistle we discern abundant proof, that he was as alive to the superior nature of his power over the Churches which he had founded, as to the success which had attended his exertions, and to the obligations which his office imposed on him, to devote himself entirely to the work of the gospel. He was one who knew how to govern and how to serve the church; but it was not until his flock became unmindful of his labours for their salvation, that he taught them the full extent of his apostolical commission, reminding them, 'that the Kingdom of God was not only in word but also in power,' and that he had power 'to come to them with the rod,' if they were unwilling to receive him 'in the spirit of meekness and of love.'

From a sermon on the text 'Let a man so account of us, as of the Ministers of Christ, and Stewards of the Mysteries of God'

Eternal God, the Ancient of Days,
who stands above time and sees all things as in a moment:
give us grace to live our lives in the light of your eternity,
trusting our past, our present and our future
into your everlasting arms;
through Jesus Christ our Lord. Amen.

Eleanor of Castile 1241–90

Queen Consort of King Edward I

———

FOR HUNDREDS OF years there were 'Eleanor Crosses' in four different places in the diocese – at Woburn, Dunstable, St Albans and Waltham Cross. These date from the time when Eleanor was travelling with her husband, King Edward, to Lincoln. She fell ill with a fever at Harby and died on this day in 1290. Edward accompanied her body on its journey back to London and at the twelve places where he spent a night he had a cross erected in her memory. The most famous of these is Charing Cross. The only surviving cross in the diocese is the one at Waltham, although this has been restored and is not on its original site. Eleanor was buried in Westminster Abbey. Eleanor was the daughter of Saint Ferdinand, King of Castile and Leon, and his second wife, Joan, Countess of Ponthieu. Eleanor married Edward in a monastery in Burgos in 1254 and they had sixteen children. It appears that Edward and Eleanor were devoted to each other. She was constantly at his side, even when he was at war, and she accompanied him on the Eighth Crusade. It was during this period that his father died and Edward returned to England in 1274 to be crowned, with Eleanor by his side. She was a generous patron of the Dominican Order of Friars and endowed several priories. Eleanor was an educated woman who commissioned and collected books on a wide range of subjects.

The 'Eleanor Crosses' are a powerful reminder of God's self-giving love. In this passage William Inge, a former Dean of St Paul's Cathedral, writes about the cross

The great message of the *Cross* stands or falls with the divinity of Christ. Is it not the truth that all the rivals of Christianity fail just here? All the religious philosophies of antiquity, it seems to me, shrink, in the last resort, from grasping the nettle of suffering quite firmly. They all want to make us invulnerable, somehow. There must always be a back-door of escape if the ills of life become too overpowering. Either defiant resistance, or suicide, or complete detachment, is recommended. By some means or other, the man himself must be rescued from circumstance, he must provide himself with a magic impenetrable armour. And *therefore*, the sting of pain is never drawn. The good news of Christianity is that suffering is itself divine. It is not foreign to the experience of God Himself. 'In all their afflictions He was afflicted.' 'Surely He hath borne our griefs and carried our sorrows.' 'If thou be the Son of God,' said His enemies, 'come down from the Cross.' No; not while any man remains unredeemed. The divine suffering is not an episode, but a revelation. It is the necessary form which divine love takes, when it is brought into contact with evil. To overcome evil with good means to suffer unjustly and willingly.

From *Speculum Animae*

Generous God,
whose Son Jesus Christ emptied himself,
taking the role of a servant,
and gave his life for us and for our salvation:
grant us grace to follow his example and take up the cross daily,
that with open hands and open hearts
we may discover the source of true life;
we ask it for his name's sake. Amen.

Legh Richmond 1772–1827

Rector

———

LEGH RICHMOND IS best remembered as the author of a novel called *The Dairyman's Daughter*. It was one of the most widely-read books of his day, selling more than four million copies, and was translated into many different languages. Less popular was his work, which was published in eight volumes, called *Fathers of the English Church*. An interesting fact about Richmond is that he invented 'hymn boards' into which the numbers of the hymns could be inserted, a practice that is used in churches all over the world. Born in Liverpool, Richmond studied at Trinity College, Cambridge, and after ordination served his title in Brading and Yaverland on the Isle of Wight. He was a keen supporter of a number of Christian charities, including the Church Missionary Society and the British and Foreign Bible Society. He was appointed to the living of Turvey, Bedfordshire, in 1805 and stayed there until he died. There is a memorial to him in the parish church.

Legh Richmond describes the grief of Elizabeth's parents

Elizabeth's [the dairyman's daughter] features were altered, but much of her likeness remained. Her father and mother sat at the head, her brother at the foot of the coffin. The father silently and alternately looked upon his dead child, and then lifted up his eyes to heaven. A struggle for resignation to the will of God was manifest in his countenance; the tears, rolling down his aged cheeks, at the same time declared his grief and affection. The poor mother cried and sobbed aloud, and appeared to be much overcome by the shock of separation from a daughter so justly dear to her. The weakness and infirmity of old age added a character to her sorrow, which called for much tenderness of compassion. A remarkably decent looking woman who had the management of the few simple though solemn ceremonies which the case required, advanced towards me, saying 'Sir, this is rather a sight of joy than of sorrow. Our dear friend Elizabeth finds it to be so, I have no doubt. She is beyond *all* sorrow. Do you not think she is, Sir?' 'After what I have known, and seen, and heard', I replied, 'I feel the fullest assurance, that while her body remains here, her soul is with her Saviour in Paradise. She loved him *here*, and *there* she enjoys the pleasures which are at his right hand for evermore.'

From *The Dairyman's Daughter*

———

Support us, O Lord,
all the day long of this troublous life,
until the shadows lengthen and the evening comes,
the busy world is hushed,
the fever of life is over
and our work is done.
Then, Lord, in your mercy grant us a safe lodging,
a holy rest, and peace at the last;
through Christ our Lord. Amen.

From the funeral service in *Common Worship*

Alice de Claremont 1098–1142

Founder of the Preceptory of Melchbourne

———

'There was at one time in Melchbourne a preceptory of the Knights of Jerusalem. Its site can still be traced to the south of the Cottage, and it is thus described by Leland, writing in the 16th century: "Here is a right fair place of square stone standing much upon pillared vaults of stone, and there be goodly gardens orchards and ponds and a parke thereby." The Knights Hospitallers had the right to hold a weekly market on Friday, and an annual fair on the vigil, feast and morrow of St. Mary Magdalene. The site of the old market cross is at the junction of the lane from the village with the road to Knotting.' (From Volume Three of *Victorian History of the County of Bedford*.)

ALICE DE CLAREMONT was born and died in Hertford. She was the daughter of Ranulf de Briquessart (or Ranulf the Viscount) of Normandy and Lucia Lucy Bolingbroke. It was during the reign of Henry II that Agnes founded Melchbourne Preceptory in Bedfordshire. It was disestablished around 1550 and re-established for a short time in 1557 during the reign of Mary I. When it was founded the Preceptory was granted the manor and church of Melchbourne, the churches of Dean, Riseley, Souldrop, Eaton Socon and also a number of churches in other parts of the country.

John of the Cross writes about the in-dwelling God

God dwells secretly in all souls and is hidden in their substance for, were this not so, they would be unable to exist. But there is a difference between these two manners of dwelling, and a great one. For in some He dwells alone, and in others He dwells not alone; in some He dwells contented and in others He dwells displeased; in some He dwells as in His house, ordering it and ruling everything, while in others He dwells as a stranger in the house of another where He is not allowed to do anything or to give any commands. Where He dwells with the greatest content and most completely alone is in the soul wherein dwell fewest desires and pleasures of its own; here He is in His own house and rules and governs it. And the more completely alone does he dwell in the soul, the more secretly He dwells; and thus in this soul wherein dwells no desire, neither any other image or form or affection of aught that is created, the Beloved dwells most secretly, with more intimate, more interior and closer embrace, according as the soul, as we say, is the more purely and completely withdrawn from all save God.

From *Living Flame of Love* by Allison Peers

———

Lord, since you exist, we exist.
Since you are beautiful, we are beautiful.
Since you are good, we are good.
By our existence we honour you.
By our beauty we glorify you.
By our goodness we love you.
Lord, through your power all things were made.
Through your wisdom all things are governed.
Through your grace all things are sustained.
Give us power to serve you, wisdom to discern your laws,
and grace to obey those at all times. Amen.

Edmund of Abingdon

Thomas Brand 1635–91

Free Church minister

————

S ON OF A Church of England clergyman who served in Great Hormead in Hertfordshire, Thomas Brand was educated at Bishop's Stortford and Merton College, Oxford. He had planned a career in the law and indeed had been admitted to the Middle Bar. However, he came under the influence of Samuel Annesley, and decided to go into the ministry. After leaving university he was appointed tutor to the four children of the Lady Dowager Roberts of Glassenbury, Kent. In this deeply-religious household he preached twice every Sunday. In 1674 Brand was appointed minister of the Presbyterian chapel at Staplehurst where he was ordained. Within a short time he married a widow, by whom he had several children and who tragically all died young. Eventually opposition to Brand's ministry was so strong that he had to leave Staplehurst. He moved to Bethnal Green where he set up an academy for dissenters. He used his wealth to help build meeting houses and to employ ministers. It is thought that he financed the printing of twenty thousand copies of Joseph Alleine's *Treatise on Conversion* so he could give copies away freely. He was passionate about helping the poor, paying personally for a number of children to learn trades and selling Bibles to poor people at a much reduced price on the condition that they did not sell them at a profit. He died on this day in 1691 and is buried in Bunhill Fields.

C. S. Lewis describes his conversion to Christianity

You must picture me alone in that room in Magdalen College, Oxford, night after night, feeling, whenever my mind lifted even for a second from my work, the steady, unrelenting approach of Him whom I so earnestly desired not to meet. That which I greatly feared had at last come upon me. In the Trinity Term of 1929 I gave in, and admitted that God was God, and knelt and prayed: perhaps, that night, the most dejected and reluctant convert in all England. I did not then see what is now the most shining and obvious thing; the Divine humility which will accept a convert even on such terms. The Prodigal Son at least walked home on his own feet. But who can duly adore that Love which will open the high gates to a prodigal who is brought in kicking, struggling, resentful, and darting his eyes in every direction for a chance of escape? The words *compelle intrare*, compel them to come in, have been so abused by wicked men that we shudder at them; but, properly understood, they plumb the depth of the Divine mercy. The hardness of God is kinder than the softness of men, and His compulsion is our liberation.

From *Surprised by Joy*

Lord Jesus Christ,
you summoned the disciples to leave everything,
to take up the cross and follow you:
bless all who seek to proclaim
the good news of your saving love;
grant them generosity and joy,
compassion and courage,
but above all, a winsome vision of your glory;
for your name's sake. Amen.

Bridget Ruth Adams 1952–2012

Priest and business consultant

———

BRIDGET ADAMS CAME late to ordination. She studied at the University of Sussex, graduating in physics, and went on to obtain a doctorate. Bridget worked in the laser industry for almost thirty years, initially as a research scientist at the National Physical Laboratory. After serving as a school governor in Radlett, a Sunday School teacher, and the press officer for her local church, she began to train for the ordained ministry in 2003. The final year of Bridget's ministry course was spent studying for a Master's degree in Business Chaplaincy at the London School of Theology. Her thesis *Christ in the Marketplace: The Unique Role of a Christian Business Chaplaincy* was published in 2008. She worked as a Business Chaplain in Watford from 2004, holding group meetings in such diverse places as Pizza Express, a coffee house and even a pub. Especially gifted at helping people discover the relevance of Christianity in all aspects of life, she felt strongly that 'if Christ can redeem and transform, then the business world should not be beyond the scope of his redemption and transformation. Christian business people working in the global economy are uniquely placed to help transform the circumstances of the world's poor and to help protect the environment.' One of the founders of *The Hub* in Watford, which evolved into the Kingdom Business School, Bridget Adams and two colleagues set up the Lion's Den, the Christian equivalent of the television show *Dragon's Den*. Aspiring entrepreneurs presented their business plans to the panel, who vetted each project and offered advice and free coaching. The aim was to launch new businesses and re-energise existing ones. At the time of her death she was Assistant Curate of St James, St Paul and Holy Trinity, Bushey. She was married with three children.

> *Dorothy Sayers reflects on work*
>
> Perhaps if the Churches had had the courage to lay their emphasis where Christ laid it, we might not have come to this present frame of mind in which it is assumed that the value of all work, and the value of all people, is to be assessed in terms of economics. We might not so readily take for granted that the production of anything (no matter how useless or dangerous) is justified so long as it issues in increased profits and wages; that so long as a man is well paid, it does not matter whether his work is worthwhile in itself or good for his soul; that so long as a business deal keeps on the windy side of the law, we need not bother about its ruinous consequences to society or the individual. Or at any rate, now that we have seen the chaos of bloodshed which follows upon economic chaos, we might at least be able to listen with more confidence to the voice of an untainted and undivided Christendom.
>
> From *Unpopular Opinions*

> *Everlasting God,*
> *give to those who work in commerce and industry*
> *the qualities of integrity and honesty,*
> *and the energy and vision to work for the common good,*
> *that people and communities may flourish,*
> *and every person may have the opportunity to thrive;*
> *to the glory of your name. Amen.*

Robert Hobbes d.1538

Last Abbot of Woburn

———

LIKE MANY MEDIEVAL monks, we know little about Robert Hobbes' personal life. Woburn Abbey was a Cistercian foundation and Hobbes was elected Abbot in 1524. In 1530 he was granted permission to hold two annual fairs in the town. We also know that two years later he was appointed by King Henry VIII to undertake a visitation of the Cistercian Order and that he was involved in the delegation which investigated John Chascombe, the Abbot of Bruern. At the beginning of the Reformation Hobbes and his community supported the king and took the Oath of Supremacy. However, in the wake of the separation from Rome, Hobbes realised that all the monasteries would be suppressed. He was horrified and recanted, declaring in 1538, that 'The Bysshop of Rome's Auctorite is good and lawful within this Realme accordyng to the old trade, and that is the true waye. And the contrary of the kynges parte but usurpacion disceyved by flattery and adulacion'. Hearing of his protest, Thomas Cromwell dispatched John Williams and William Petre to investigate. Hobbes continued to oppose the suppression of the monasteries. He was arrested, tried in Bedford and convicted of treason. He claimed that he had acted 'out of a scrupulous conscience that he then had, considering the long continuance of the Bishop of Rome in that trade being, and the sudden mutation thereof'. Hobbes was executed along with two other monks. Tradition says that they were hanged from an ancient oak in the grounds of Woburn Abbey.

David Knowles concludes his book on the dissolution of the monasteries

At the end of this long review of monastic history, with its splendours and its miseries, and with its rhythm of recurring rise and fall, a monk cannot but ask what message for himself and for his brethren the long story may carry. It is the old and simple one; only in fidelity to the Rule can a monk or a monastery find security…When once a religious house or a religious order ceases to direct its sons to the abandonment of all that is not God, and ceases to show them the rigours of the narrow way that leads to the imitation of Christ in His Love, it sinks to the level of a purely human institution, and whatever its works may be, they are the works of time and not of eternity. The true monk, in whatever century he is found, looks not to the changing ways around him or to his own mean condition, but to the unchanging everlasting God, and his trust is in the everlasting arms that hold him. Christ's words are true: He who doth not renounce all that he possesseth cannot be my disciple. His promise also is true: He that followeth me walketh not in darkness, but shall have the light of life.

From *Bare Ruined Choirs*

Your kingdom, O God, is an everlasting kingdom,
and your dominion endures through all generations;
You are trustworthy in your promises
and faithful in all that you do;
you uphold all who fall
and lift up all who are bowed down;
give us grace to entrust ourselves into your loving arms,
that we may live for your glory and work for the coming of your kingdom:
through Jesus Christ our Lord. Amen.

Based on Psalm 145

Andrew Willet 1562–1621

Rector of St Margaret of Antioch, Barley, and St Mary, Reed

———

WITH OUR STRONG ecumenical links with other Christian denominations today, it is hard to understand the virulence with which some of our forebears were in dispute with one another over religious matters. Following the Reformation, the teachings of John Calvin spread quickly across Europe, and by the early seventeenth century a significant number of Anglican clergy had been influenced by them. Some of these clergy were virulently anti-Roman Catholic, among them Andrew Willet. He was a prolific writer and preacher who used his pen and his tongue to denounce Catholic teaching on the Mass. His most famous polemical book was *Synopsis Papismi*, published in 1594. Born and schooled in Ely, Willet studied first at Peterhouse and then at Christ's College, Cambridge. He was ordained in 1585 and held livings in Huntingdonshire and Cambridgeshire. For the last twenty-two years of his life he was Rector of Barley, and for a period also held the living of Reed in plurality. Willet married Jacobine Goad in 1588 and they had no less than eighteen children. One of his sons, Thomas, later became the first Mayor of New York. Willet was injured after being thrown from his horse when riding through Hoddesdon and died a few days later on this day in 1621. He is buried in the parish church in Barley.

Andrew Willet preaches on living in God's presence

'I rejoiced, when they said unto me, Let us go up into the house of the Lord' (Psalm 122.1). This princely prophet rejoices in the public and peaceable exercise of religion, that the people of God had now free recourse unto the house of God. And indeed, this is a benefit wherein all Christian people are much to joy, that they are not exiled from God's house, but may cheerfully and quietly thither assemble.

1. So says the prophet David 'Blessed are they, that dwell in thy house, they will ever praise thee' (Psalm 84.4). Therefore our Saviour notes this, as a fearful sign of future miseries, 'when they shall see the abomination of desolation standing in the holy place: then let them that be in Judea flee unto the mountains' (Matthew 24.15). When the holy place of God's worship begins to be desolate and forsake, what comfort can elsewhere be expected?

2. Therefore David desires this as first and principal above all other, that he might dwell in God's tabernacle all the days of his life (Psalm 27.4). And he professes, that he had rather be one day in God's courts, than a thousand elsewhere (Psalm 84.10). And he pours out his heart for grief, when he remembered how he had gone up with the people to God's house, as a multitude keeping a feast (Psalm 42.4) but was not tossed from place to place, and banished from that place of joy and comfort.

From *Ecclesia Triumphans on the Coronation of James: An Exposition of Psalm 122*

Heavenly Father,
you desire that your children should be one in heart and mind:
forgive us the divisions which separate us from one another.
Give us imagination and courage to overcome suspicion,
and grant your Church that unity which is your will;
through Jesus Christ our Lord. Amen.

Dame Laetitia Monson 18th century

Benefactress from Broxbourne

———

ALMSHOUSES CAN STILL be found in many towns and villages across Europe. The first almshouses in Britain were built in the tenth century, usually as part of a religious foundation, to house the poor, especially widows. They often incorporated a chapel where the residents were required to pray for the soul of the founder. During the Reformation many almshouses, being attached to religious houses, were dissolved by Act of Parliament in 1547 and their endowments confiscated. In later centuries we see new foundations being made and endowed by wealthy benefactors. Such was the case in Broxbourne. Laetitia Monson was married to William, brother of Sir Henry Monson, who lived at Broxbourne Manor. William died around 1726 and Laetitia three years later in 1729. The year before she died she built almshouses for six poor widows, and in her will provided grants for their fuel and clothing. These almshouses can still be seen today in Broxbourne High Street. The inscription over the main door reads:

> This Building is Erected at the Sole charge of Dame Laetitia Monson
> Relict of Sr William Monson Bart and was Daughter of John Lord Poulett
> of Hinton St George in the County of Somersett, which Gift is for the Relief
> and Benefitt of poore Widows of the Parish of Broxborne in Hartfordshire
> in the year of our Lord 1728.

John Chrysostom preaches on giving

It is not enough to give to the poor: we must give to them with generosity and without grumbling. It is not even enough to give without grumbling: we must give gladly and willingly…When the poor are helped two conditions ought always to be evident: generosity and joy. Why do you moan about having to give something to charity? Why do you display such resentment in giving alms? If you resent almsgiving, you are showing no mercy: you expose merely your callousness and lack of humanity. If you are full of resentment, how exactly are you going to help someone who is in the pit of depression? Afterwards you will be happy when you see that they are neither demeaned nor humiliated because you have helped them joyfully. Nothing causes embarrassment so much as having to be beholden to others. But by showing joy when you give you will enable your brother or sister to overcome their suspicion. They will realise that in your own estimation, you are receiving yourself in the process of giving. On the other hand, if you show resentment, far from raising their spirits, you will succeed only in depressing them still further. That is why Paul says: 'Let he who gives, do so cheerfully.' If you give gladly, even if it be only a small thing, it can be munificent. If you give unwillingly, even if you give substantially, it will turn into a pittance. It is the attitude of the giver that determines the assessment of our deeds.

From *Homily on Romans*

———

> *Bountiful God,*
> *we thank you for those who alleviate the suffering of others:*
> *grant your blessing on those who provide*
> *shelter for the homeless, food for the hungry*
> *comfort for the distressed and companionship for the lonely;*
> *we ask this in the name of Jesus Christ our Lord. Amen.*

St Nicholas 270–343

Patron saint of pawnbrokers, bankers and sailors

———

THE CHURCHES IN Barton-le-Cley, Elstree, Great Hormead, Harpenden, Hinxworth, Hockliffe, Hulcote, Norton, Stevenage, Swineshead, Tingrith and Wilden all share a dedication to St Nicholas. Born on the southern coast of what is now Turkey, Nicholas was the son of wealthy Christians. His parents died when he was still young, and Nicholas used his inheritance to help the poor and the sick. He was ordained and became Bishop of Myra. During the persecution under the Roman Emperor, Diocletian, he was exiled and imprisoned. With the toleration of Christianity under the Emperor Constantine, Nicholas was allowed to return to his see and in 325 attended the Council of Nicea where he defended the divinity of Christ. Several stories connect Nicholas with the sea. It is said that as a young man he was returning from a pilgrimage to the Holy Land when a storm arose and threatened to wreck the ship. Nicholas was found calmly praying, and the sailors were amazed when the storm abated and they were all spared. This story led to Nicholas becoming the patron saint of sailors. On another occasion Nicholas heard about a father who could not afford a dowry for his three daughters. He went to their house at night and threw three bags of gold coins through their open window, saving the honour of the girls. This is reputed to be the origin of the custom of giving bags of gold chocolate coins to children in their Christmas stockings. It is also why Nicholas is known as the patron saint of pawnbrokers and why the traditional sign for a pawnbroker's shop is to hang three gold balls by the door. There is a real person behind the mythical Father Christmas, Santa Claus being a corruption of the Dutch for St Nicholas. He died on this day in AD 343.

St Nicholas is the patron saint of sailors. Samuel Francis' hymn uses the image of the sea as a metaphor of God's love in Jesus Christ

O the deep, deep love of Jesus, vast, unmeasured, boundless, free!
Rolling as a mighty ocean in its fullness over me!
Underneath me, all around me, is the current of Thy love
Leading onward, leading homeward to Thy glorious rest above!

O the deep, deep love of Jesus, spread His praise from shore to shore!
How He loveth, ever loveth, changeth never, nevermore!
How He watches o'er His loved ones, died to call them all His own;
How for them He intercedeth, watcheth o'er them from the throne!

O the deep, deep love of Jesus, love of every love the best!
'Tis an ocean vast of blessing, 'tis a haven sweet of rest!
O the deep, deep love of Jesus, 'tis a heaven of heavens to me;
And it lifts me up to glory, for it lifts me up to Thee!

———

Steer the ship of my life, good Lord, to the quiet harbour,
where I can be safe from the storms of sin and conflict.
Show me the course I should take.
Renew me in the gift of discernment,
so that I can always see the right direction in which I should go;
and give me the strength and courage to choose the right course,
even when the sea is rough and the waves are high,
knowing that through enduring hardship and danger
we shall find comfort and peace. Amen.

St Basil of Caesarea

John Ashwell d. c.1541

Prior of Newnham in Bedfordshire

———

Newnham, a small village between Radwell, Caldecote and Ashwell, is served today by the small fourteenth-century church of St Vincent, but for nearly four hundred years it was home to an Augustinian monastery. Founded in 1166, the monastery was endowed by Simon de Beauchamp with the tithes of fourteen churches: St Paul's Bedford, Renhold, Ravensden, Great Barford, Willington, Cardington, Southill, Hatley, Wootton, Stagsden, Lower Gravenhurst, Aspley, Salford and Goldington. John Ashwell was the penultimate prior before the community was closed. He studied at Cambridge and became first Rector of Mistley, and later Rector of Littlebury and Halstead, Essex. He served as a military chaplain in France in 1515, and in 1521 was made a Prebendary of St Paul's Cathedral. He was appointed Prior of Newnham around 1527. Although Ashwell was an opponent of the Reformation, he took the Oath of Supremacy in 1534 along with sixteen other members of his community. It is thought that he resigned as Prior around the year 1539 and died two years later.

St Augustine set out how the monks should order their life

1. The main purpose for you having come together is to live harmoniously in your house, intent upon God in oneness of mind and heart.

2. Call nothing your own, but let everything be yours in common. Food and clothing shall be distributed to each of you by your superior, not equally to all, for all do not enjoy equal health, but rather according to each one's need.

3. Those who owned something in the world should be careful in wanting to share it in common once they have entered the monastery.

4. But they who owned nothing should not look for those things in the monastery that they were unable to have in the world. Nevertheless, they are to be given all that their health requires even if, during their time in the world, poverty made it impossible for them to find the very necessities of life.

5. And let them not hold their heads high, because they associate with people whom they did not dare to approach in the world, but let them rather lift up their hearts and not seek after what is vain and earthly. Otherwise, monasteries will come to serve a useful purpose for the rich and not the poor, if the rich are made humble there and the poor are puffed up with pride.

6. The rich, for their part, who seemed important in the world, must not look down upon their brothers who have come into this holy brotherhood from a condition of poverty.

7. Let all of you then live together in oneness of mind and heart, mutually honouring God in yourselves, whose temples you have become.

From *The Rule of St Augustine*

———

Breathe in me, Holy Spirit, that my thoughts may reflect you.
Act in me, Holy Spirit, that my life may further God's reign.
Fill my heart, Holy Spirit, that I may love with great kindness.
Strengthen me, Holy Spirit, that I may defend the poor and needy.
Embolden me, Holy Spirit, that my life may be a witness to the Gospel.
Preserve me, Holy Spirit, that I may always remain your dwelling place. Amen.

Based on a prayer by St Augustine of Hippo

Evelyn Christina Busby 1898–1977

Diocesan Secretary for St Albans Diocese

———

EVELYN BUSBY WAS a woman of many parts: formidable but compassionate. For twenty years she was the Diocesan Secretary for the Diocese of St Albans, based at Holywell Lodge. She was renowned for her administrative skills, her financial competence, her foresight, her understanding of the problems of clergy and laity, and for her dedication to the work of the diocese. Not only was she Diocesan Secretary, but she also worked with local authorities, the Church Assembly and the Church Commissioners. Evelyn also acted as Bursar to the Community of the Sisters of the Love of God, an Anglican community of nuns based in Oxford which has a daughter house at Boxmoor, Hemel Hempstead. As one of their Oblate Sisters, she had a close link with the community, living by a Rule which embodied the nuns' commitment to contemplative prayer, but which was adapted to take account of the person's everyday life and career in the wider world. Evelyn was PCC secretary of St John's Harpenden and in the 1960s she was made a lay canon of St Albans Abbey. She served as a JP, was chairman of the St Albans Divisional Bench, and became the first woman chairman of Harpenden Urban District Council. Her other interests were varied, including cooking and embroidery. In 1959 she was appointed OBE and died in 1977, after a long illness through which she was steadfastly nursed by the friend who shared her home.

Never underestimate the value of good administration

People often complain about administration, yet those of us who have been privileged to work with an excellent administrator know just how invaluable they can be. St Paul also understood this. In one of his letters he says that he left Titus behind to 'put in order what remained to be done' (Titus 1.5). Paul knew he needed help and he could not do everything on his own. It is interesting that hidden in the list of spiritual gifts in Paul's Letter to the Corinthians (1 Corinthians 12.28) is *administration* – ranked equally alongside apostles, prophets and teachers, who always seem to get a higher profile. The Greek word that St Paul uses is *kyberneseis* which means 'helmsman'. This person is not necessarily the captain of the boat, nor the one who has to study the stars to chart the boat's course. This is the person who has the responsibility of steering the vessel, who watches out for rocks in the water and lighthouses on the land. The helmsman is only one of a team. He or she cannot do it alone. Helmsmen need others to raise and lower the sails and to help when casting off and docking. Yet without a helmsman the ship is not going to get far. So too with the church. Without those who work behind the scenes, we would rapidly grind to a halt. So let's celebrate and affirm the administrators who set others free to do their jobs, who see that the practical arrangements are made, and who make things run smoothly.

From an unpublished talk by Alan Smith called *Oiling the Wheels*

———

We thank you, Lord, for those who serve your Church in unseen ways:
for organizers and administrators, for those who care for our buildings.
set up our meetings, and oversee our finances.
May they use their gifts for the building up of your Church
and for advancement of your kingdom;
through Jesus Christ our Lord. Amen.

John Lightfoot 1602–75

Priest and scholar

———

MANY SCHOLARS HAVE been interested in the Jewish roots of the Christian faith. Lightfoot's interest in the subject was nurtured during his time as chaplain to Sir Rowland Cotton of Bellaport, who was a skilled Hebraist. Lightfoot wrote many books (his complete works were published in the nineteenth century in thirteen volumes), many of which were on the Old Testament. Among his best-known books are *Erubhin*, or *Miscellanies, Christian and Judaical*, *A Handful of Gleanings out of the Book of Exodus* and *The Polyglot Bible*, which he worked on with Brian Walton. He also wrote a number of books on the New Testament. Born in the Potteries, the son of a clergyman, Lightfoot was educated in Congleton and at Christ's College, Cambridge. Following graduation, he taught at Repton and was ordained to a curacy at Norton-under-Hales in Shropshire. In 1630 he became Rector of Ashley in Staffordshire, a position he held for twelve years before becoming incumbent of St Bartholomew the Great in London until 1644. In that year he was appointed Master of Catharine Hall, Cambridge, and Rector of Great Munden where he remained for thirty-one years until his death. He was a member of the Westminster Assembly. In 1654 Lightfoot became Vice-Chancellor of the University of Cambridge, although he continued to live at Great Munden.

John Lightfoot writes about the creation

Two ways we come to the knowledge of God, by his works and by his word. By his works we come to know there is a God; and by his word, we come to know what God is. His works teach us to spell; his word teaches us to read. The first as it were his back parts, by which we behold him far off; the latter shows him to us face to face. The world is a book consisting of three leaves, and every leaf printed with many letters, and every letter a lecture. The leaves heaven, the air and earth with the water. The letter in heaven, every angel, star, and planet. In the air, every meteor and soul. In the earth and waters, every man, beast, plant, fish and mineral: all these set together, spell to us that there is a God, and the Apostle says no less though in less space, Romans 1.20 'For the invisible things of him, that is, his eternal power and Godhead are seen by the creation of the world, being considered in his works'…If we mark not the works of God, we are like stones that have no eyes, wherewith to behold. If we wonder not at the works of God, when we mark them, we are like beasts that have no hearts wherewith to admire. And if we praise not God for his works, when we admire them, we are like devils that have no tongues wherewith to give thanks.

From *Erubhin*, or *Miscellanies, Christian and Judaical*

Blessed Lord, by whose providence all Holy Scriptures
were written and preserved for our instruction,
give us grace to study them each day with patience and love.
Strengthen our souls with the fullness of their divine teaching.
Keep from us all pride and irreverence.
Guide us in the deep things of Thy heavenly wisdom;
and, of thy great mercy, lead us by thy Word into everlasting life,
through Jesus Christ our Saviour. Amen.

Brooke Foss Westcott

George Stephen 1829–1921

Industrialist and philanthropist

———

FOR RAIL ENTHUSIASTS the Canadian Pacific Railway, with its stunning route through the Rocky Mountains, is legendary. One of the prime movers behind it was a man who had been born in Scotland, George Stephen. In 1850 Stephen was offered a job in Montreal by one of his cousins. Within a few years he became the owner of the firm and also moved into the manufacture of textiles. His hard work and business acumen drew him into banking. In 1873 he became a director of the Bank of Montreal and in 1876 he was elected its president. He was now in charge of Canada's largest banks and unlike many other bankers was willing to take high-risk decisions. His investments in the railways proved to be so lucrative that he and a small group of colleagues built the Canadian Pacific Railway. It was an extremely challenging undertaking and on several occasions nearly went bankrupt. When it was complete Stephen turned his attention to the more profitable St Paul Minnesota and Manitoba Railroad. In 1892 Stephen settled permanently in England, living at Brocket Hall in Hertfordshire. He was made a baron, taking the title Baron Mount Stephen. Stephen used his considerable wealth to support hospitals in London, Montreal and Aberdeen. He also endowed a fund for the Bishop of St Albans to use for the pastoral support of clergy. Stephen married twice, firstly to Charlotte Annie Kane. After her death he married Georgina Mary Tufnell. Stephen is buried at St John the Evangelist's Church, Lemsford.

A Christian reflection on work

Human work is not simply a burden to be endured, as though a punishment for sin, but rather an essential part of human nature, just as the creative power is an essential part of God's nature. God created the universe out of his infinite love; and so too, if a person is to love in God's image, he must work. In Paradise, man did not work out of material need, since his every need was provided. Rather, Adam 'tilled the ground' in union with the creative Love by which he had being. His work was a pure image of the creative Love by which God loved him. Indeed, so close is the power of work to the nature of the human person, and thus so close to the image of God which resides in the person, that human work was one of the primary victims of sin. When Adam fell from grace by choosing himself instead of love, he also abandoned his power of work, because in Paradise (where every material need was fulfilled) love was the only reason for work. Yet creative love is so close to God's nature, and thus so close to God's will for the human person, that it could not be that man would not work: for then man would not love as he was created to love, and he would thus lose an essential part of his nature.

From *Industrial Theology*

———

Protect, Gracious God,
those who risk their lives for others in their daily work:
for miners, deep sea fishermen,
construction workers and those engaged in heavy industry;
keep them alert to the dangers that surround them
and grant them your presence and your protection;
we ask it in the name of Jesus Christ our Lord. Amen.

John Scott 1731–83

Quaker poet and writer

———

HIDDEN AWAY IN the backstreets of Ware is an unusual grotto created by John Scott. It consists of six underground chambers, decorated with flint, shells and glass, and connected by over thirty metres of tunnels. It was built in the 1760s but subsequently fell into such a bad state of repair that it was nearly demolished. It was restored in 1990 and is now a popular tourist attraction. It would be unfair to portray Scott as nothing more than a creator of a folly. As a committed Quaker, Scott was deeply concerned for the poor. He wrote a book about the degradation and evil of poverty called *Observations on the Present State of the Parochial and Vagrant Poor,* and argued against the Poor Laws. Scott also used his poetic gifts to reflect on poverty and war, published as *Poetic Works.* In 1778 he published *Digests of the General Highway and Turnpike Laws,* which must surely have been a best-seller in his day. Scott was a man with a wide circle of acquaintances, among them Samuel Johnson (who began writing Scott's biography but which was never completed), David Barclay (one of the famous family of bankers) and the artist and poet William Blake.

A poem by John Scott

I hate that drum's discordant sound,
Parading round, and round, and round:
To thoughtless youth it pleasure yields,
And lures from cities and from fields,
To sell their liberty for charms
Of tawdry lace, and glittering arms;
And when Ambition's voice commands,
To march, and fight, and fall, in foreign lands.

I hate that drum's discordant sound,
Parading round, and round, and round;
To me it talks of ravag'd plains,
And burning towns, and ruin'd swains,
And mangled limbs, and dying groans,
And widows' tears, and orphans' moans;
And all that Misery's hand bestows,
To fill the catalogue of human woes.

From *The Miseries of War*

Lord of justice, Lord of mercy,
we cry out to you, longing for the day
when warfare and violence will cease,
and poverty and injustice will be no more.
We yearn for the time when people everywhere
will be more concerned about the good of their neighbour,
than protecting their own rights.
We pray for the coming of your kingdom,
in which mercy, justice and peace will reign;
for the sake of Jesus Christ our Lord. Amen.

James Lumsden Barkway 1878–1968

Rector of Little Gaddesden and Bishop of Bedford

———

JAMES BARKWAY WAS educated at University College, Liverpool University, and Fitzwilliam Hall, Cambridge. Initially he trained for the Presbyterian ministry at Westminster College, Cambridge. However, after ten years as a Presbyterian minister he became an Anglican and served successively at Christ Church Luton, St Albans Abbey, and at Little Gaddesden. In 1933 he became the Diocesan Missioner and in 1935 was appointed Bishop of Bedford. Sadly, he only served in Bedford three years before being elected Bishop of St Andrews, Dunkeld and Dunblane in Scotland. For four years, during his time as bishop, he was also the Provost of St Ninian's Cathedral, Perth. He retired in 1949. He wrote *The Creed and its Credentials* and *The Christian Belief about Christ*.

Archbishop Michael Ramsey writes about Christian leadership

'It's a pity that the leaders of the church are so rotten.' Yes, indeed. It is a worse pity that, when leaders are picked, there is only you to pick them from! But what is the leadership which the human race needs? It is the leading of the human race into fellowship with the Creator, so as to reflect him in all human affairs. This leadership is the role of the *whole* Christian Church. 'As the soul is in the body, so are the Christians in the world.' Within the Church, this leadership is shared by different people in different roles. There are the prophets. God raises them up with particular insight into the divine will and purpose in human affairs. The prophet has eyes which see what the rest of us do not see. There are statesmen. These are practical people with the gift of carrying out particular implications of the divine will in this or that situation. There are all the members of the Church. They all share in the task of leading the human race the right way; of healing that derangement of the relation of creatures to their Creator by which humanity is poisoned. Each will look to his or her own share in that derangement. What is it in *me* that must be put right?

From *Through the Year with Michael Ramsey*

Gracious God, grant that all members of your Church
    may be faithful in their ministry and calling:
for bishops that they may be true shepherds of the flock
    and leaders in mission;
for priests that they may conduct worship
    in our parishes, schools and chaplaincies
    with reverence and imagination;
for deacons that they may serve the poor and needy with joy and kindness;
and for Christians everywhere that they may be bold in their witness and
    compassionate in your service;
give us grace that we may all work together
    for your glory and the coming of your kingdom;
through Jesus Christ our Lord. Amen.

Samuel Johnson 1709–84

Poet, essayist, critic, biographer and lexicographer

———

DR SAMUEL JOHNSON had many connections with people who lived in this diocese. Writing of a visit to Bedfordshire in 1781 when he stayed at Luton Hoo, he says, 'This is one of the places I do not regret coming to see…in the house magnificence is not sacrificed to convenience, nor convenience to magnificence'. Johnson was born in Lichfield where his father worked as a bookseller. He was a prodigious child with an outstanding memory. When he could not afford to complete his studies at Oxford University he began to earn his living by writing. His reputation grew quickly and in 1747 he was commissioned to write a *Dictionary of the English Language*. It was a mammoth task which was to last nine years and which required six researchers to help him. It was to become the most important dictionary of the period. He wrote a significant body of poetry, many essays, a number of biographies and an important annotated edition of Shakespeare's plays. Johnson knew many of the most famous people of his day, including Joshua Reynolds, Edmund Burke, Oliver Goldsmith and David Garrick. However, he did not have an easy life. He was in debt on many occasions and had long periods of ill health. As well as suffering bouts of depression it is thought that he had Tourette syndrome. Johnson was a committed Anglican throughout his life. In the first of his essays published under the title *The Rambler* he desired, 'that in this undertaking thy Holy Spirit may not be withheld from me, but that I may promote thy glory, and the salvation of myself and others.' He was married to Elizabeth Porter who predeceased him in 1752. Johnson is buried in Westminster Abbey.

Samuel Johnson prays

Almighty God, by whose will I was created, and by whose providence I have been sustained, by whose mercy I have been called to the knowledge of my Redeemer, and by whose grace whatever I have thought or acted acceptable to Thee has been inspired and directed; grant, O Lord, that in reviewing my past life, I may recollect Thy mercies to my preservation, in whatsoever state Thou preparest for me; that in affliction I may remember how often I have been succoured; and in prosperity may know and confess from whose hand the blessing is received. Let me, O Lord, so remember my sins, that I may abolish them by true repentance, and so improve the year to which Thou hast graciously extended my life, and all the years which Thou shalt yet allow me, that I may hourly become purer in Thy sight; so that I may live in Thy fear, and die in Thy favour, and find mercy at the last day, for the sake of Jesus Christ. Amen.

From *Prayers and Meditations*

———

Almighty God, the Giver of wisdom,
without whose help resolutions are vain,
without whose blessing study is ineffectual;
enable me, if it be thy will, to attain such knowledge
as may qualify me to direct the doubtful,
and instruct the ignorant;
to prevent wrongs and terminate contentions;
and grant that I may use that knowledge which I shall attain,
to thy glory and my own salvation, for Jesus Christ's sake. Amen.

Samuel Johnson

Eleanor Hull c.1394–1460

The earliest-known woman translator from French into English

———

HISTORICAL STUDY IS gradually unearthing a great deal of information about the role of women in the closing decades of the medieval period. It is now clear that there were many educated women among the gentry; women like Eleanor Hull, who could read and write in French, Latin and English. Eleanor's father was Sir John Malet from Somerset, who was in the service of the Duke of Lancaster. She married Sir John Hull and they had a son, Edward. Both her husband and her son predeceased her. By virtue of her husband's position in the House of Lancaster, Eleanor was present at the marriage between King Henry VI and Margaret of Anjou in France in 1444. In 1417 Eleanor was admitted to the Confraternity of the Abbey of St Albans. Over the years that followed, she gave many gifts to the Abbey, including a copy of Nicholas de Lyra's *Postillae*. When she was widowed she stayed at the Benedictine nunnery of Sopwell Priory, a daughter house of St Albans Abbey. It is thought that it was during this period that she made her translations from a French commentary of the penitential psalms and a collection of prayers and meditations. She is buried at the Benedictine Priory Church at Cannington, Somerset.

William Temple, a former Archbishop of Canterbury, meditates on penitence

It is penitence which creates intimacy with Our Lord. No one can know Him intimately who has not realised the sickness of his own soul and obtained healing from the physician of souls. Our virtues do not bring us near to Christ – the gulf between them and His holiness remains unbridgeable. Our science does not bring us near Him, nor our art. Our pain may give us a taste of fellowship with Him, but it is only a taste unless the great creator of intimacy – penitence – is also there. For in my virtue, my art, my knowledge, there is sure to be some pride – probably, indeed, a great deal of pride. But I cannot be proud of sin which is really admitted to be sin. I can be proud of my dare-devilry; oh, yes, and of anything I do to shock respectability. But then I am not admitting to myself that it is sin – only that other people think it so. When I find something in myself of which I really am ashamed, I cannot at the time be proud of that – though, alas I may be proud of my shame at it, and so make this, too, worthless. In straightforward shame at my own meanness there is no pride and no expectation of forgiveness except through trust in the love of Him who forgives. So it is penitence which brings me in all simplicity to appeal to the sheer goodness and love of God. And we can turn our very sins into blessings if we will let them empty us of pride and cast ourselves upon the generosity of God. 'We receive the due reward of our sins: Jesus, remember me.'

From *Palm Sunday to Easter*

Holy God, who desires truth in my inmost being:
purge me that I may be clean,
wash me, that I may be whiter than snow.
Fill me afresh with your Holy Spirit.
Create in me a clean heart,
and restore in me the joy of your salvation;
through Jesus Christ our Lord. Amen.

A prayer based on Psalm 51

Izaak Walton 1593–1683

Writer

———

BORN AND EDUCATED in Stafford, Izaak Walton moved to London as a young man and took up an apprenticeship with his brother-in-law. Within a few years he was running his own draper's business, trading in linen. In 1626 he married Rachel Floud. They had six children, but all died in infancy. After Rachel's death he married Anne Ken, and they had three children. Walton was acquainted with John Donne (who was his local parish priest) and with many other influential men of the period. Most of them were part of the 'Great Tew Circle', a group of intellectuals who met regularly to discuss topical and philosophical subjects at Great Tew in Oxfordshire. Walton became famous for his biographies of Anglican Divines such as Richard Hooker, Henry Wotton and George Herbert, though today he is better remembered for his book *The Compleat Angler*. The Quaker poet John Scott, who lived in Amwell, referred to Izaak Walton, who

Oft our fair haunts explored; upon Lea's shore
Beneath some green tree oft his angle laid,
His sport suspending to admire their charms.

During the English Civil War Walton was a strong Royalist. After the war he became the business agent for George Morley when he was Bishop of Worcester, and later when he became Bishop of Winchester. Walton bequeathed his farm in Staffordshire to support poor people in Stafford and today the cottage houses a small museum about his life. It was written of Walton, 'Of this blest man, let his just praise be given. Heaven was in him, before he was in heaven.' He died on this day in 1683.

The opening paragraph of Izaak Walton's will

The Last Will August the ninth, one thousand six hundred eighty-three. In the name of God, Amen. I Izaak Walton the elder, of Winchester, being this present day, in the ninetyeth year of my age, and in perfect memory, for which praised be God; but considering how suddainly I may be deprived of both, do therefore make this my last will and testament as followeth: And first, I do declare my belief to be, that there is only one God, who hath made the whole world, and me and all mankind; to whom I shall give an account of all my actions, which are not to be justified, but I hope pardoned, for the merits of my Saviour Jesus: And because the profession of Christianity does, at this time, seem to be subdivided into Papist and Protestante, I take it, at least to be convenient, to declare my belief to be, in all points of faith, as the Church of England now professeth: and this I do the rather, because of a very long and very true friendship with some of the Roman Church.

From *Izaak Walton* by E. G. Marriott

God, grant that I may live
to fish until my dying day
and when it comes to my last catch,
I then most humbly pray,
when in the Lord's safe landing net
I'm peacefully asleep,
that in his mercy I be judged
as good enough to keep. Amen.

The Fisherman's Prayer
(Anonymous)

Samuel Lee 1783–1852

Linguist, lexicographer and Rector of Barley

———

WHEN LEE WAS born in the small Shropshire village of Longnor, his parents could not have imagined that he was destined to become a linguist of international repute. His early years did not look very promising. He was educated in a village school and began work as an apprentice to a carpenter. However, in his spare time he began learning languages and was soon giving lessons in Persian and Hindustani. The Church Missionary Society heard about his abilities and paid for him to study at Cambridge University. In 1819 he was appointed Professor of Arabic at the university and twelve years later became Regius Professor of Hebrew. He was involved in producing the first dictionary of Te Reo Māori, the language of the indigenous population of New Zealand. He held various livings including Bilton-with-Harrogate, Yorkshire, and Banwell, Somerset. In 1838 he became Rector of Barley.

Samuel Lee writes about God's grace

Allow me to suggest to you, that there are but two ways in which Religion can be, or ever has been, taught: one, through 'The Commandments of God' the other, by 'The Traditions of men.' Under the first of these, as already shewn, an active faith is, as it necessarily must be, the only means whereby we can so apply these, as to make them available to our salvation, and ourselves acceptable to God. And, as this takes it for granted that we willingly receive all that He has presented to us, both in His Word, and in His dealings with His Church; so it also does, that we thankfully and sedulously apply all the means of grace thus afforded to us. And of these Sacraments of His Church necessarily claim the highest place. But it is the Spirit of man only, as already shewn, that can enter into, appreciate, duly apply, or profit by these, both for its instruction and final salvation: and to this, it is the Spirit of God alone that can supply, and make effectual to salvation, the means so granted. The means themselves must be earthy, and, so long as they are earthy, they can lay claim to no divine energy; but the end sought must be spiritual: nothing short of this can possibly reach the wants of the human soul, and make it at once holy and happy: and this must, as necessarily, consist in the demonstration of a power, exceeding every thing that is earthy, in order to make believers meet to be partakers of the inheritance of the Saints in light, to grow up to the measure of the stature of Christ, and to be filled with the fullness of God.

From *Some Remarks on the Sermon of the Rev. Dr. Pusey*

Almighty God,
by whose grace alone we are accepted
and called to your service:
strengthen us by your Holy Spirit
and make us worthy of our calling;
through Jesus Christ our Lord, Amen.

Collect for the Fifth Sunday before Lent
from *Common Worship*

Ann Thetis Blacker 1927–2006

Artist, singer and embroiderer

———

BORN IN SURREY, Ann Blacker's father was a psychiatrist and her grandfather a friend of Oscar Wilde. As a young woman, she pursued a career in opera, singing in both lead roles and in the chorus at Glyndebourne. However, it was in the field of the visual arts that her gifts blossomed. She studied at the Chelsea School of Art and became a distinguished artist. Her best-known series of paintings was a celebration of Creation. During her stay in the Far East in 1970, she developed a particular skill in batik, becoming one of its most eminent and visionary practitioners. In 1973 she wrote a book about the vivid dreams she experienced, *A Pilgrimage of Dreams*, and was compiling a second volume at the time of her death in 2006. Her artistic ability was also reflected in the large number of banners and altar frontals she designed and made for a variety of churches, including St Albans Abbey, St George's Chapel Windsor, Durham Cathedral and Grey College, Durham. Ann Blacker's inclusion in this book is a tribute to all ecclesiastical embroiderers.

Some thoughts on art and beauty

Let every dawn of morning be to you as the beginning of life, and every setting sun be to you as its close…Then let every one of these short lives leave its sure record of some kindly thing done for others – some goodly strength or knowledge gained for yourselves; so from day to day, and strength to strength, you shall build up indeed, by Art, by Thought and by Just Will, an Ecclesia of England, of which it shall not be said, 'See what manner of stones are here,' but, 'See what manner of men.'

From *Lectures on Art* by John Ruskin

The Beautiful, says Hegel, is the spiritual making itself known sensuously. It represents, then, a direct message to us from the heart of Reality; ministers to us of more abundant life. Therefore the widening of our horizon which takes place when we turn in prayer to a greater world than that which the senses reveal to us, should bring with it a more poignant vision of loveliness, a more eager passion for Beauty as well as for Goodness and Truth. When St. Augustine strove to express the intensity of his regret for wasted years, it was to his neglect of the Beauty of God that he went to show the poignancy of his feelings, the immensity of his loss. 'O Beauty so old and so new! Too late have I loved thee!' It needs a special training, I think – a special and deliberate use of our faculties – if we are to avoid this deprivation; and learn, as an integral part of our communion with Reality, to lay hold of the loveliness of the First and only Fair.

From *The Essentials of Mysticism* by Evelyn Underhill

God of Truth and Beauty,
open our eyes to all that is noble and gracious
that we may see reflections of your glory
in the world about us, in music and art,
in the face of the child and the stranger,
and be drawn to your eternal goodness;
through Jesus Christ our Lord. Amen.

Arthur Kenneth Mathews 1906–92

Naval chaplain and Dean of St Albans

———

IN HIS OBITUARY in *The Independent* Kenneth Mathews was described as 'a sailor's padre to the end'. Early on in his career he had been padre to the tanker fleet of the Anglo-Saxon Petroleum Company. At the start of the Second World War, he enlisted as a chaplain in the Royal Naval Volunteer Reserve and was awarded the Distinguished Service Cross in recognition of 'gallantry during active operations against the enemy at sea'. Mathews was born into a clerical family and went to Monkton Combe School near Bath. He studied at Balliol College, Oxford, and was ordained in 1933 in the Diocese of Wakefield to a curacy at Penistone. He served as Vicar of Forest Row in East Sussex and after the war was appointed Vicar of Rogate and Rural Dean of Midhurst in the Diocese of Chichester. He served as Dean of St Albans for eight years from 1955 until 1963, when he left St Albans to become Rector of Peebles. He retired in 1971 and died on this day in 1992.

E. B. Pusey, one of the leaders of the Oxford Movement, writes about conscience

It is tacitly assumed, that intellect is a safe and unbiased guide; that its determinations, though not infallible, are sure and unblamable; that, if any implicitly follow it, – as a Pagan philosopher might follow it, apart from any grace of God or prayer for His illumining, nay abstracting oneself for the time from the light of the Gospel, – its conclusions, although in different minds naturally contradictory and self-destructive, are necessarily right for each; that in the things of God too, what is newest is right, what is old is superannuated and wrong, forgetting that the truths of God are eternally new as Himself, being a transcript of a portion of His unchangeable wisdom. Anyhow, men will have it, that no responsibility is incurred, be the result of any process of reasoning what it may, any more than in a proposition of mathematics; that there is no right or wrong about it; in a word, that if a person thinks he is pursuing truth, though he be more anxious to have truth on his side, than to be on the side of truth, conscience and Almighty God have no voice in the matter. The thought that each shall have to give account for his 'opinions' (as people call them), or the process by which he arrived at them, seems to them as strange an imagination, as if the subject-matter were some proposition of pure mathematics.

From a sermon called *The Responsibility of Intellect in Matters of Faith*

Almighty God,
who hast sent the Spirit of truth unto us to guide us into all truth:
so rule our lives by thy power that we may be truthful
in thought and word and deed.
May no fear or hope ever make us false in act or speech;
cast out from us whatsoever loveth or maketh a lie,
and bring us all into the perfect freedom of thy truth;
through Jesus Christ our Lord. Amen.

Brooke Foss Westcott

John Gifford d.1655

John Bunyan's pastor in Bedford

———

JOHN GIFFORD CAME from Kent and served as a major in King Charles II's army. In 1648, during the Civil War, he was captured at Rochester, escaping execution only with the assistance of his sister. He made his way to Bedford and there began work as a physician. Despite his self-confessed dissolute lifestyle of drinking and gambling, he joined a group of Puritans and was converted to Christianity. Gifford soon became known as a passionate and persuasive preacher, and his evident gifts of leadership led to him being appointed pastor of the Puritan Church in 1650. Three years later, during the Commonwealth, he became Master of the Hospital and Rector of St John the Baptist, Bedford, even though he had never been ordained. It was to Gifford that John Bunyan turned to find spiritual help and which led to his own conversion. After Gifford's death, Bunyan succeeded him as pastor of the church. Gifford was married to Mary and they had three daughters, Mary, Elizabeth and Martha. He is buried in St John the Baptist Church, Bedford.

John Bunyan writes about God's grace

Wherefore Christian was left to tumble in the Slough of Despond alone…but I beheld in my dream, that a man came to him, whose name was Help, and asked him, What he did there?
Sir, said Christian, I was bid go this way by a man called Evangelist, who directed me also to yonder gate, that I might escape the wrath to come; and as I was going thither I fell in here.
HELP: But why did not you look for the steps?
CHRISTIAN: Fear followed me so hard, that I fled the next way, and fell in.
HELP: Then said he, Give me thy hand: so he gave him his hand, and he drew him out, and set him upon sound ground, and bid him go on his way.
Then I stepped to him that plucked him out, and said, Sir, wherefore, since over this place is the way from the City of Destruction to yonder gate, is it that this plat is not mended, that poor travellers might go thither with more security? And he said unto me, This miry slough is such a place as cannot be mended; it is the descent whither the scum and filth that attends conviction for sin doth continually run, and therefore it is called the Slough of Despond; for still, as the sinner is awakened about his lost condition, there ariseth in his soul many fears, and doubts, and discouraging apprehensions, which all of them get together, and settle in this place. And this is the reason of the badness of this ground.

From *The Pilgrim's Progress*

O God, the strength of all those who put their trust in you,
mercifully accept our prayers and,
because through the weakness of our mortal nature
we can do no good thing without you,
grant us the help of your grace,
that in the keeping of your commandments
we may please you both in will and deed;
through Jesus Christ your Son our Lord. Amen.

The Collect for Trinity 1 from *Common Worship*

Rosalind Runcie 1932–2012

Pianist, teacher and gardener

———

THE DAUGHTER OF an avowed humanist, Rosalind Turner was one of six children. She was educated at the Perse School for Girls in Cambridge, and studied piano at the Guildhall School of Music, London. As an accomplished concert pianist she regularly gave recitals. She was a gifted teacher and continued to give music lessons until a few days before she died. Lindy, as she was known to her friends, used her musical skills to raise over half a million pounds for the Church and for charity. She was a knowledgeable and passionate gardener and redesigned the gardens at Lambeth Palace when her husband was Archbishop of Canterbury. As a consequence the gardens at the Palace were often opened for charity events. Lindy was also actively involved in the campaign to save the Early Diagnostic Unit for breast cancer at The Royal Marsden. She was made Honorary President of the Anglo-Armenian Association in 1988. Throughout her life she was a regular worshipper although she was famous for commenting that 'too much religion makes me go pop'. In 1956 she married Robert Runcie when he was Dean of Trinity Hall. They had two children. Lindy died a few days before her eightieth birthday and is buried with her husband, next to St Albans Abbey.

Rosemary Verey encourages us to look closely at nature

If our gardens are to be more than graves commemorating summer's beauty, we must start by using our eyes. The problem all too often is that, when we look, we do not see. We fail to appreciate to the full the beauty around us. And if we do not look, beauty will be denied to us. 'It is the old story of "eyes and no eyes",' wrote the great Edwardian gardener Vicary Gibbs. 'Given bright sunlight, without which no colours can be fully seen, there they are if we will only observe them, and the more we look the more we see. It is the perfect harmony of Nature's work which hides her brilliant hues from the careless, though to the patient watcher she reveals fresh beauties both of form and colour every day…things which many a countryman has lived and died without noticing.' Today, mid-December, the light in the Cotswolds is electrifying, brilliant. The air is cold and crisp, the sky a reflecting blue, the earth black, the leaves and the sky motionless, the clouds a thin haze on the horizon. The only movement to be seen is the swift flight of the finches, tits, sparrows and the occasional wren as they search for food in bushes and borders. Wherever I look, there is a feeling of repose and happiness among the plants.

From *The Garden in Winter*

———

O Lord Jesus, true gardener,
work in us what you want of us,
for without you we can do nothing.
For you are indeed the true gardener,
at once the maker and tiller
and keeper of your garden,
you who plant with the word,
water with the spirit
and give your increase with your power. Amen.

Guerric of Igny

Judith of Huntingdon c.1054–86

Founder of Elstow Abbey

———

A NIECE OF WILLIAM the Conqueror, Judith was born in Normandy. In the wake of the Conquest, however, she came to England and in 1070 married Waltheof of Huntingdon and Northumbria with whom she had two daughters: Maud of Northumbria (who married David I of Scotland) and Adelise (who married Raoul III de Conches). Waltheof was part of the Revolt of the Earls who rebelled against William I. It must have been an agonising conflict of loyalties for Judith and it is thought that she betrayed her husband Waltheof to her Uncle William, who had him beheaded in 1076. Shortly afterwards Judith founded Elstow Abbey in Bedfordshire as a Benedictine foundation for nuns, dedicated to St Mary and St Helen. She also established churches at St Ippolyts and Kempston, and owned land at a number of places including Potton, Silsoe, Wilshamstead and Maulden. William wanted Judith to re-marry Simon de Senlis, the Earl of Northampton, but she refused. As a consequence she was stripped of her titles and lands, and fled to Normandy. The parish of Sawtry Judith in Huntingdonshire is named after her.

St Benedict highlights the importance of hospitality in a Christian community

Let all guests who arrive be received as Christ, because He will say: 'I was a stranger and you took Me in'. And let due honour be shown to all, especially to those 'of the household of the faith' and to wayfarers. Let the Abbot pour the water on the guest's hands, and let both the Abbot and the whole brotherhood wash the feet of all the guests. When they have been washed, let them say this verse: 'We have received Thy mercy, O God, in the midst of Thy temple.' Let the greatest care be taken, especially in the reception of the poor and travellers, because Christ is received more specially in them; whereas regard for the wealthy itself procureth them respect. Let the kitchen of the Abbot and the guests be apart, that the brethren may not be disturbed by the guests who arrive at uncertain times and who are never wanting in the monastery. Let two brothers who are able to fulfil this office well go into the kitchen for a year. Let help be given them as they need it, that they may serve without murmuring; and when they have not enough to do, let them go out again for work where it is commanded them. Let this course be followed, not only in this office, but in all the offices of the monastery – that whenever the brethren need help, it be given them, and that when they have nothing to do, they again obey orders.

From *The Rule of St Benedict*

Lord Jesus Christ, you shared your table with all who would come;
give us grace to follow your example of hospitality:
to entertain the stranger as if we are entertaining you,
to visit the prisoner as if we are visiting you,
to care for the sick as if we are caring for you,
to sit with the dying as if we are sitting with you;
we ask this for your name's sake. Amen.

John Ninian Comper 1864–1960

Architect

———

THE WORK OF this Scottish architect can be seen in various places in the Diocese of St Albans. Ninian Comper's most famous commission was the chapel at London Colney, which until 1973 was the home of the Community of the All Saints Sisters of the Poor. He designed stained glass windows for St Albans Abbey and St Nicholas' Elstree. Other examples of his work can be seen in St Mary's Westmill and All Saints Long Marston. Another interesting connection with Bedfordshire is that Comper designed the John Bunyan window in Westminster Abbey. Ninian Comper was the son of an Anglican clergyman from Aberdeen, who had been deeply influenced by the Tractarian Movement. In 1874 he was sent to Trinity College, Glenalmond, and then in 1882 he attended the Ruskin School of Art in Oxford. Comper continued his studies at the South Kensington School of Art, financing these studies by working for the famous stained glass artist, C. E. Kempe. The following year he was articled to the ecclesiastical architect G. F. Bodley. Comper was a close friend of John Betjeman. He married Grace Bucknall in 1890 and they lived most of their lives in London. He was knighted by King George VI in 1950. Comper died on this day in 1960 in Clapham and his ashes are interred in Westminster Abbey.

Ninian Comper writes about the meaning and purpose of a church building

A church built with hands, as we are reminded at every Consecration and Dedication Feast, is the outward expression of that spiritual Church built of living stones, the Bride of Christ. *Urbs beata* Jerusalem, which stretches back to the foundation of the world and onwards to all eternity. With her Lord she lays claim to the whole of His Creation and to every philosophy and creed and work of man which His Holy Spirit has inspired. And so the temple here on earth, in different lands and in different shapes, in the East and in the West, has developed or added to itself fresh forms of beauty and, though it has suffered from iconoclasts and destroyers both within and without, and perhaps nowhere more than in this land, it has never broken with the past: it has never renounced its claim to continuity. To enter therefore a Christian church is to enter none other than the House of God and Gate of Heaven. It is to leave all strife, all disputes of the manner of Church government and doctrine outside – 'Thou shalt keep them secretly in Thy tabernacle from the strife of tongues' – and to enter here on earth into the Unity of the Church Triumphant in Heaven. It cannot be otherwise, since He himself, who is the Temple of it, the Lamb slain from the foundation of the world, is there also. Such a conception of a church, however faintly realised, must put to shame the quarrels of Catholic Christians, who profess the same creeds but set up Church against Church.

From *Of the Atmosphere of a Church*

———

Father in heaven, whose Church on earth is a sign of your heavenly peace,
an image of the new and eternal Jerusalem:
grant to us in the days of our pilgrimage that,
fed with the living bread of heaven,
and united in the body of your Son,
we may be the temple of your presence,
the place of your glory on earth,
and a sign of your peace in the world;
through Jesus Christ our Lord. Amen.

Post Communion Prayer for a Dedication Festival from *Common Worship*

Thomas Babington Macaulay 1800–59

Historian and politician

———

THOMAS MACAULAY WAS a prodigiously bright child, who was able to read by the age of three and shortly after was writing poetry. He was deeply religious, influenced by his parents' large circle of evangelical friends, most of whom were involved in the campaign against slavery. However, in later life, his religious views did not prevent him being critical of religious cant. Deeply immersed in the language of the King James Version of the Bible, whenever he learned a new language he found the best way was to buy a Bible in the language, rather than purchase a dictionary. Macaulay went to a school at Little Shelford (which moved to Aspenden Hall in East Hertfordshire) and then up to Trinity College, Cambridge, where he won a number of prizes. He entered the law but continued his interest in politics, and in particular his opposition to slavery. He entered Parliament in 1830 where his sympathies were with the Whigs. In 1834 Macaulay spent four years in India during which time he was a member of the Supreme Council of India. On his return to England he held various posts including Secretary of War and Paymaster-General. He was made Baron Macaulay of Rothley in 1857 and is buried in Westminster Abbey. His most famous work is *History of England from the Accession of James the Second*. It became a best seller and was translated into at least twelve languages.

Dies Irae

On that great, that awful day,
This vain world shall pass away.
Thus the sibyl sang of old,
Thus hath Holy David told.

There shall be a deadly fear
When the Avenger shall appear,
And unveiled before his eye
All the works of man shall lie.

Hark! to the great trumpet's tones
Pealing o'er the place of bones:
Hark! it waketh from their bed
All the nations of the dead,
In a countless throng to meet,
At the eternal judgment seat.

Nature sickens with dismay,
Death may not retain his prey;
And before the Maker stand
All the creatures of his hand.

The great book shall be unfurled,
Whereby God shall judge the world:
What was distant shall be near,
What was hidden shall be clear.

To what shelter shall I fly?
To what guardian shall I cry?
Oh, in that destroying hour,
Source of goodness, Source of power,
Show thou, of thine own free grace,
Help unto a helpless race.

Thomas Babington Macaulay

———

Most Merciful God,
by whose grace we live and move and have our being:
grant that we may abide in your unfailing love
and trust in your unending mercy,
that at the last, we may see you face to face;
through Jesus Christ our Lord. Amen.

Peter Denny 1917–2009

Model railway enthusiast

ANYONE WHO KNOWS the clergy well will be aware of just how many exhibit a passion for railways. Denny was one such enthusiast. In 1947 he attended the Model Railway Club at Waterloo Station, and this started an interest which was to last for more than sixty years, during which time he wrote many articles for *Railway Modeller* and published three books on the subject. Denny was so well known by fellow enthusiasts that he was invited to open the permanent model railway exhibition at the National Railway Museum in York. Denny's father, who was a tailor by trade, had come from Biggleswade but had moved to St Leonards-on-Sea in Sussex before his son was born. Denny was an only child and taught himself to read before he started school. After the death of his father in 1927 his mother moved to Bexhill-on-Sea where she started taking Peter to church regularly. In 1930 he bought a fret machine and considered a career as a woodwork teacher, but two years later felt a call to ordination. Although registered for military service in the Royal Air Force, he was allowed to train for the ministry at Cheshunt Theological College. In 1943 he was ordained in St Albans Abbey and served his title at St Peter's, Bushey Heath. In 1949 he married Sylvia with whom he had two sons. After a period in secular employment, he served a second curacy at Calstock. In 1956 he was made Vicar of St Newlyn East where he remained for the next twenty-seven years and where he created one of the most intricate model railways ever built, painstakingly soldering every inch of track himself and creating authentic-looking buildings from cardboard. He served two terms as Rural Dean of Pydar, finally retiring to Truro in 1983 where he had a room purpose-built to house his railway network, the 'Buckingham Central' system.

Bill Vanstone observes two young boys making a model

As I watched this microcosm of creative activity, and as later I reflected upon it, three things gradually became evident to me. The first was that, in such activity, there was both working and waiting. One could say that the activity of creating included the passivity of waiting – of waiting upon one's workmanship to see what emerged from it, and to see if that which emerged was 'right'. The second, which followed from the first, was that, in such activity, the creator gave to, or built into, his workmanship that which, if it were not his workmanship, it would not possess a power to affect himself, to have value, significance or importance for himself. The third, which followed from the second, was that in such activity disproportion between creator and workmanship, or between creator and material, was overcome by the gift of value. That which in itself was nothing was transformed, in the creative process, into a thing of value: as the work of a creator, it received a new status in relation to the creator. The incongruity between the great and the small was overcome when the creativity of the great was expended in and upon the small.

From *Love's Endeavour, Love's Expense*

Creator God,
who fashioned humankind in your image,
endowing us with gifts of creativity;
stir our imaginations, reawaken our vision
and open our eyes to the beauty of your world;
for we ask this in the name and for the sake of Jesus Christ. Amen.

Hubert Victor Whitsey 1916–87

Bishop of Hertford and Chester

———

WHITSEY, WHO WAS always known by his second name, Victor, spent most of his life and ministry in the north of England. He went to Queen Elizabeth's Grammar School in Blackburn and studied at St Edmund Hall, Oxford. He was ordained in the Diocese of Blackburn and served his title in Chorley. In the following years he served in parishes in Farington, Halliwell, Langley and Downham. He was consecrated Bishop of Hertford in St Albans Abbey in 1971 and held the post for four years until he was translated to Chester. He retired in 1981 and died on this day in 1987.

Austin Farrer preaches on power and vulnerability in the events of the first Christmas

The universal misuse of human power has the sad effect that power, however lovingly used, is hated. To confer benefits is surely more godlike than to ask them; yet our hearts go out more easily to begging children than they do to generous masters. We have so mishandled the sceptre of God which we have usurped, we have played providence so tyrannically to one another, that we are made incapable of loving the government of God himself or feeling the caress of an almighty kindness. Are not his making hands always upon us, do we draw a single breath but by his mercy, has not he given us one another and the world to delight us, and kindled our eyes with a divine intelligence? Yet all his dear and infinite kindness is lost behind the mask of power. Overwhelmed by omnipotence, we miss the heart of love. How can I matter to him? we say. It makes no sense; he has the world, and even that he does not need. It is folly even to imagine him like myself, to credit him with eyes into which I could ever look, a heart that could ever beat for my sorrows or joys, a hand he could hold out to me. For even if the childish picture be allowed, that hand must be cupped to hold the universe, and I am a speck of dust on the star-dust of the world. Yet Mary holds her finger out, and a divine hand closes on it. The maker of the world is born a begging child; he begs for milk, and does not know that it is milk for which he begs. We will not lift our hands to pull the love of God down to us, but he lifts his hands to pull human compassion down upon his cradle. So the weakness of God proves stronger than men, and the folly of God proves wiser than men. Love is the strongest instrument of omnipotence, for accomplishing those tasks he cares most dearly to perform; and this is how be brings his love to bear on human pride; by weakness not by strength, by need and not by bounty.

From *Said or Sung*

Almighty God, you have given us your only-begotten Son
to take our nature upon him and as at this time to be born of a pure virgin:
grant that we, who have been born again
and made your children by adoption and grace,
may daily be renewed by your Holy Spirit;
through Jesus Christ your Son our Lord, who is alive and reigns with you,
in the unity of the Holy Spirit, one God, now and for ever. Amen.

The Collect for Christmas Day from *Common Worship*

Nathaniel Micklem 1888–1976

Congregationalist theologian and politician

———

SON OF A politician, Nathaniel Micklem was brought up in Boxmoor in Hertfordshire. He went to Rugby School, New College, Oxford, and later to Mansfield College, Oxford, where he trained for the Congregationalist ministry. Whilst at Oxford he became President of the Oxford Union. Following his ordination, he served as Minister of Highbury Chapel, during which time he married Agatha Silcock. After a period with the YMCA in Dieppe he returned to become Chaplain of Mansfield College. He went on to teach theology at the Selly Oak Colleges. From Birmingham he moved to Canada, taking up in 1927 a post at the Queen's Theological College in Kingston, Ontario. Five years later he returned to Oxford as Principal of Mansfield College, a post he occupied until his retirement in 1953. In 1944 Micklem was elected Chairman of the Congregational Union, and became deeply involved in ecumenism. He wrote *Christ and Caesar, Prophecy and Eschatology, National Socialism and the Roman Catholic Church, A Book of Personal Religion* and *The Creed of a Christian*. After his retirement from Mansfield College, he became more involved in politics, serving as Chairman of the Liberal Party in 1956–7. He died on this day in 1976.

Kenneth Leech writes about Christian involvement in politics

Prayer and politics, far from being alternative modes of discipleship or even opposites, are necessary to each other. If they are divided, the result is either a superficial 'Christian radicalism' which stresses action and service at the expense of awe and vision, or a pietism which reduces spirituality to the private sector. At the turn of the century Nicolas Berdyaev observes that Christian piety had all too often become a withdrawal from the world and from men, an unwillingness to share human suffering. The world has risen in protest against this form of piety, this indifference to the world's sorrow. Yet against this protest Berdyaev insisted, only a reborn piety can stand. The choice is not between spirituality and action, but between true spirituality and false. Christian prayer is rooted in a revolutionary vision, it is Kingdom-directed prayer. It is therefore marked by a sense of fulfilment, of yearning, of stretching out into the future and tasting the powers of the age to come. It is never the prayer of security, ease, and the smug certainty. It is a crying out for the Kingdom that is coming. Prayer and politics meet at the point at which this vision of the new age comes into collision, as it must, with political structures based upon a different view of man and of human life. At the heart of our Gospel and our prayer there lies an inescapable core of conflict. This core of conflict is central to the Kingdom which must be the motive force and the visionary cumulus for Christian action.

From *The Meaning of Prayer and Politics*

———

God of all power, we pray for the leaders of the nations:
grant them understanding when grappling with complexity,
wisdom when confronted with conflict,
integrity when faced with temptation,
burning justice when faced with wrongdoing,
and compassion to protect the weak and vulnerable;
through Jesus Christ our Lord. Amen.

Arthur Bennett 1915–94

Clergyman

———

ARTHUR BENNETT IS one of the few Hertfordshire clergy to have written a best-selling book. He compiled an anthology of Puritan prayers entitled *The Valley of Vision*, which was first published in 1975 and which is still selling well, especially in America. A Yorkshireman by birth, Arthur was converted at a Salvation Army mission during his teenage years. He joined the Church Army and worked as an evangelist among the homeless. For several decades the Church Army had a number of horse-drawn caravans and Bennett travelled around East Anglia running parish missions. He trained for the ordained ministry at Clifton Theological College in Bristol, and was ordained to a curacy in Huddersfield. Following a second curacy at Chesham, he was made Rector of St Peter's, Gunton, and from there in 1949 to become Vicar of St Paul's, St Albans. In 1964 Bennett was appointed Rector of Sacombe and Little Munden. His ministry was recognised in 1970 when he was made an honorary canon of the cathedral. Beside his anthology of Puritan prayers, he wrote *Rural Evangelism*, *Travels with a Horse-Drawn Caravan* and *Calvary's Hill*. He married Margarette in 1942. They spent their retirement together in Clapham and are buried in the churchyard at Little Munden where the text on their headstone reads 'Let me find thy joy in my valley.'

Richard Baxter's advice to Christian ministers

Our whole work must be carried on in a sense of our insufficiency, and in a pious believing dependence upon Christ. We must go to him for light, and life, and strength, who sends us on the work; and when we feel our own faith weak, and our hearts grown dull and unsuitable to so great a work as we have to do, we must have recourse to the Lord. Prayer must carry on our work as well as preaching. We must also be very studious of union and communion among ourselves, and of the unity and peace of the churches that we oversee. We must be sensible how needful this is to the prosperity of the whole, the strengthening of our common cause, the good of the particular members of our flock, and the further enlargement of the kingdom of Christ.

From *The Reformed Pastor*

———

Giver of all good, streams upon streams of love overflow my path. Thou hast made me out of nothing, hast recalled me from a far country, hast translated me from ignorance to knowledge, from darkness to light, from death to life, from misery to peace, from folly to wisdom, from error to truth, from sin to victory. Thanks be to thee for my high and holy calling. I bless thee for ministering angels, for the comfort of the Word, for the ordinances of thy church, for the teaching of thy Spirit, for thy holy sacraments, for the communion of saints, for Christian fellowship, for the recorded annals of holy lives, for examples sweet to allure, for beacons sad to deter.

Thy will is in all thy provision to enable me to grow in grace, and to be meet for thy eternal presence. My heaven-born faith gives promise of eternal sight, my new birth a pledge of never-ending life. I draw near to thee, knowing thou wilt draw near to me.

I ask of thee, believing thou hast already given. I entrust myself to thee, for thou hast redeemed me. I bless and adore thee, the eternal God, for the comfort of these thoughts, the joy of these hopes. Amen.

From *The Valley of Vision*

Nicholas Bacon 1510–79

Politician and Lord Keeper of the Great Seal

———

NICHOLAS BACON STUDIED law at Corpus Christi College, Cambridge, and from there was called to the Bar. As a committed Protestant, he profited from the dissolution of the monasteries and was granted by Henry VIII the manor of Gorhambury, near St Albans. Bacon had a meteoric rise. From being the Member of Parliament for Dartmouth, he rose to become the Attorney of the Court of Wards and Liveries, and Treasurer of Gray's Inn. Unsurprisingly, his fortunes waned under Catholic Queen Mary, but revived when her sister Elizabeth succeeded her in 1558. The newly-crowned Elizabeth made him Lord Keeper of the Great Seal and, in 1559, Lord Chancellor. Bacon was deeply involved in the life of the Church of England and also became a generous benefactor. He supported St Albans School by persuading Queen Elizabeth to grant it a wine charter to provide it with a regular income. He married Jane Ferneley (with whom he had six children) and after her death in 1552 he married Anne Cooke. One of his sons was Francis Bacon.

A Prayer Of A Penytente

If the iuste mann seaven tymes eache daye
Ohe Lorde dothe fall, what shall I saye?
Of all iniuste moste sinfull manne
My falles my fautes whoe nvmber canne?
And therewith Lorde soe great they be
That to dispayer they woulde force me.

But that of grace thou haste me taughte
Mercye is more then all my naughte,
Aud that thou wilte with readye care
Here aye all suche as in thye feare
Doe call for helpe and mercye crye
With harte contryte repentantelye.

ffaythe geven to this thus taughte by grace
Dothe breede good hope in dispayers place,
Styll sturringe me mercye to crave
Where for thaskeinge I maye it have,
As by thye worde thou doeste me teache
Where aske and have thy Sonne dothe preache.

Agayne ohe Lorde whoe canne compare
Thye free geven giftes and those not rare,
Provokeinge love eache daye and tyme,
With their rewardes of synne and cryme,
But with moyste eye and hevye harte
Muste nedes repente his sinfull parte?

Repentaunce thus grounded of love
And hope of faythe dothe me nowe move
On knees to fall and mercye crye:
Mercye ohe Lorde mercye mercye:
ffrom iustice Lorde I doe appeale
To thye mercye myne onelye weale.

My Lorde my god my Savyour dere,
My hope my truste and all my chere,
fforgett forgive all my offence,
And graunte by grace me assistance
Thye benefittes soe to remember
That love for love I maye thee render.

Nicholas Bacon

———

Lord Jesus Christ,
you humbled yourself and were born in human flesh
for us and for our salvation:
grant us the same humility,
that we may fashion our lives according to your Word,
and walk in the way of your commandments;
for your name's sake. Amen.

Thomas Becket c.1118–70

Rector of Bramfield, Archbishop of Canterbury and martyr

———

FEW BISHOPS HAVE had a play written about their life and death, but Becket has had at least three written about him, the most famous being T. S. Eliot's *Murder in the Cathedral* which is still regularly performed. During his lifetime, Becket had various connections with the diocese. Henry II granted him the honour of Berkhamsted Castle in 1151 and, according to Matthew Paris, Becket was Rector of Bramfield for a period. Three years after his martyrdom, he was canonized by the Pope. Several churches in Hertfordshire and Bedfordshire are dedicated to him, including those at Clapham, Northaw, Knebworth and West Hyde. There are also medieval wall paintings of Becket in the churches in Chalgrave and Abbots Langley. A chapel in Meppershall dedicated to Becket (which is now on private land) became a place of pilgrimage. Born of Norman stock in Cheapside, London, Becket was sent to Merton Priory for his schooling. From there he went to Bologne and Auxerre to study Canon Law. Archbishop Theobald was not slow to recognise Becket's gifts and appointed him to various posts including that of Archdeacon of Canterbury and Provost of Beverley. His outstanding ability and skills also came to the notice of King Henry II, who in 1155 made him Lord Chancellor. Following the death of Theobald in 1162, the king nominated Becket as Archbishop of Canterbury. Nine days later he was ordained priest and the following day he was consecrated bishop. Against the king's wishes he resigned as Lord Chancellor and soon found himself in conflict with Henry as he sought to reassert the rights of the Church against the Crown. Four of Henry's knights killed Becket in Canterbury Cathedral on this day in 1170.

A description of Becket's death

The wicked knight leapt suddenly upon him, cutting off the top of the crown which the unction of sacred chrism had dedicated to God. Next he received a second blow on the head, but still he stood firm and immovable. At the third blow he fell on his knees and elbows, offering himself a living sacrifice, and saying in a low voice, 'For the name of Jesus and the protection of the Church, I am ready to embrace death.' But the third knight inflicted a terrible wound as he lay prostrate. By this stroke, the crown of his head was separated from the head in such a way that the blood white with the brain, and the brain no less red from the blood, dyed the floor of the cathedral. The same clerk who had entered with the knights placed his foot on the neck of the holy priest and precious martyr, and, horrible to relate, scattered the brains and blood about the pavements, crying to the others, 'Let us away, knights; this fellow will arise no more.'

From an eyewitness account by Edward Grim

Lord God, who gave grace to your servant Thomas Becket
to put aside all earthly fear and be faithful even to death:
grant that we, disregarding worldly esteem, may fight all wrong,
uphold your rule, and serve you to our life's end;
through Jesus Christ your Son our Lord. Amen.

From *Exciting Holiness* by Brother Tristam

John Wogan Festing 1837–1902

Second Bishop of St Albans

———

THROUGHOUT HIS LIFE John Wogan Festing was interested in travel, which may partly account for his passionate support for overseas missions. For nearly forty years he was involved in the Universities' Mission to Central Africa which was inaugurated in Cambridge in November 1859. Festing was born in Stourton and educated first at King's School, Bruton, and then at King's College School, London. In 1860 he studied at Trinity College, Cambridge. He spent a year at Wells Theological College and following ordination served as Vicar of Christ Church, Westminster, and then Vicar of St Luke's, Berwick Street. In 1878 he moved to become Vicar of Christ Church, Albany Street, and a few years later was made a Prebendary of St Paul's Cathedral. He was consecrated Bishop of St Albans in 1890. As his predecessor was still living in the See House, Festing chose to reside in London but near to the railway so that he could the more easily travel both to Essex (which at that time was in the Diocese of St Albans) and to Hertfordshire. He died in December 1902 and is buried outside the north side of St Albans Cathedral.

John Festing's final words to the Diocese of St Albans

I see the need for all Christians of that injunction of St Paul's which I have taken as my text, 'Finally, my brethren, be strong in the Lord and in the power of His might.' Strength, that is what we all need, strength of purpose, strength in action; not the exercise only for our natural strength, but strength in the consciousness of union with the Lord Jesus Christ, strength in purposing and doing what He would have purposed and done, strength in the power of that might which is nothing less than His and which He gives to those, who are united to Him and who seek to use it. For if a Christian were strong in the Lord what would follow? He would always do what was right, always keep in God's ways; he would increase in the knowledge of Christ; he would become holier and better continually; grace and peace would be multiplied to him; all good plans would be carried out; there would be no standing still, no falling short, no growing careless about God's worship, or private prayers, or any good habit; no falling before the devil's assaults. Such one would certainly be ready for the coming of the Lord whenever that coming might be, and would then certainly enter into the joy of His Lord…My brethren, you have started in that Christian course. You are Christians. God has made you His children, He has given you His Holy Spirit, for you were made by Him in baptism members of Christ. You are in Christ. It is for you to continue in Him.

From the *Farewell Sermon*

———

Give us, O Lord, a steadfast heart, which no unworthy thought can drag downwards;
an unconquered heart, which no tribulation can wear out;
an upright heart, which no unworthy purpose may tempt aside.
Bestow upon us also, understanding to know thee, diligence to seek thee,
wisdom to find thee, and a faithfulness that may finally embrace thee;
through Jesus Christ our Lord. Amen.

Based on a prayer by *St Thomas Aquinas*

Samuel Fairclough c.1625–91

Rector of Houghton Conquest

————

TODAY THE *Book of Common Prayer* is celebrated as one of the great treasures of the Church of England. However, when it was introduced in 1662 it was accompanied by the Act of Uniformity, the result of which was that over two thousand clergy who were not episcopally ordained were ejected from their parishes. Among the thirteen hundred clergy who chose to become 'nonconforming ministers' was Samuel Fairclough who had been Rector of Houghton Conquest. Born at Barnardiston, Suffolk, Fairclough was the son of the local rector. He studied at Emmanuel College, Cambridge, becoming a Fellow of Gonville and Caius College, before going to Houghton Conquest. Following the Great Ejection he continued to preach in London before taking up a post as a Congregationalist teacher in the village of Chippenham in East Cambridgeshire in 1672. From 1681 he was living in London. Samuel Fairclough died on this day in 1691; and he and his wife, Frances, are buried in a vault in the church at Heveningham, Suffolk.

A well-known hymn, written by a fellow Nonconformist, who was also ejected in 1662

My song is love unknown,
My Saviour's love to me;
Love to the loveless shown,
That they might lovely be.
O who am I, that for my sake
My Lord should take frail flesh and die?

Sometimes they strew His way,
And His sweet praises sing;
Resounding all the day
Hosannas to their King:
Then 'Crucify!' is all their breath,
And for His death they thirst and cry.

They rise and needs will have
My dear Lord made away;
A murderer they save,
The Prince of life they slay,
Yet cheerful He to suffering goes,
That He His foes from thence might free.

Here might I stay and sing,
No story so divine;
Never was love, dear King!
Never was grief like Thine.
This is my Friend, in Whose sweet praise
I all my days could gladly spend.

Samuel Crossman

————

Grant, O Lord, that as the years change,
we may find rest in your unchangeableness.
May we meet this new year bravely,
sure in the faith that while men come and go,
and life changes around us, you are ever the same,
guiding us with your wisdom and protecting us with your love;
through Jesus Christ our Lord. Amen.

After William Temple

Bibliography

Every effort has been made to identify the sources of readings and prayers, and to ensure that authors have been correctly attributed and acknowledged. In some cases this has not been possible and the author would be grateful to be notified of any omissions or mistakes so they can be rectified in subsequent editions.

Allon, H. (1876) 'The Transfigured Power' in *The Vision of God*, London: Hodder and Stoughton.

Allott, S. (1974) *Alcuin of York*, York: Ebor Press.

Andrewes, L. (1841) *The Works of Lancelot Andrewes*, Oxford: J. H. Parker.

—————— (1957) *The Private Prayers of Lancelot Andrewes*, London: SCM.

The Anglican Religious Communities' Yearbook (2008), Norwich: Canterbury Press.

Armstrong, R. J. and Brady, I. C. (eds) (1982) *Francis and Clare: The Complete Works*, New York: Paulist Press.

Atwell, R. (1995) *Spiritual Classics from the Early Church*, London: Church House Publishing.

Augustine's sermon in Migne, J. P. (ed.) *Patrologiae cursus completus: Series* (1953 onwards), vol. 38, Paris.

Augustine's *Commentary on St John's Gospel* in Atwell, R. (1995) *Spiritual Classics from the Early Church*, London: Church House Publishing.

Ayre, J. (ed.) (1981) *The Sermons of Edwin Sandys*, Cambridge: CUP.

Barclay, F. L. (1909) *The Rosary*, London: G. P. Putnam.

Barclay, W. (1975) *The Letters to Timothy, Titus and Philemon*, Edinburgh: The St Andrew Press.

Barratt, W. G. (1855) *Geological Facts*, London: A. Hall and Co.

Bartel, D. (c.1997) *Musica Poetica: musical-rhetorical figures in German Baroque Music*, Lincoln: University of Nebraska Press.

Baxter, R. (1956) *The Reformed Pastor*, London: SCM.

Beaumont, J. (1877) *The Complete Poems of Joseph Beaumont, 1615–1699*, 2 vols, printed for private circulation.

Beck, G. A. (1941) *Christian Responsibility: an address given in Rickmansworth in 1941*, London.

Bede, The Venerable (1955) *A History of the English Church and People*, Harmondsworth: Penguin.

Bennett, A. (1975) *The Valley of Vision*, London: Cox and Wyman.

Bennett, D. M. (ed.) (2003) *The Letters of William and Catherine Booth*, Brisbane: Camp Hill Publications.

Bickersteth, E. (1815) *A Help to the Study of the Scriptures*, Norwich: Bacon, Kinnebrook and Co.

Blake, T. (1658) *Vindiciæ foederis; or, A treatise of the covenant of God entered with mankinde*, London: printed for Abel Roper, Fleet Street.

Blenkin, G. W. (1914) *The First Epistle of Peter*, Cambridge: Cambridge Greek Testament for Schools.

Bloom, A. (1999) *Living Prayer*, London: Darton, Longman and Todd.

Bloomfield, R. (1821) *The Poems of Robert Bloomfield*, London: printed for the author.

Board for Social Responsibility of the Church of England (1999) *Prisons: a study in vulnerability*, London: Church House Publishing.

Bonhoeffer, D. (1954) *Life Together*, London: SCM.

—————— (2001) *The Cost of Discipleship*, London: SCM.

The Book of Common Prayer: The Administration of the Sacrament and other Rites and Ceremonies of the Church, together with the Psalter or Psalms of David according to the use of the Episcopal Church (2009) New York: OUP.

Brett, R. B. (1870) *Thoughts during Sickness*, Oxford: J. Parker and Co.

Brook, P. (1969) *The Empty Space*, London: MacGibbon and Kee.

Bryant, C. (1969) *The Psychology of Prayer*, Guild of Pastoral Psychology.

Bryson, B. (2003) *A Short History of Nearly Everything*, London: Doubleday.

Bulkeley, P. (1651) *The Gospel-Covenant*, London: M. Simmons.

Bulwer-Lytton, C. G. (1914) *Prisons and Prisoners: some personal experiences*, London: William Heinemann.

Bunyan, J. (1874) *The Pilgrim's Progress*, London: John G. Murdoch.

Burgmann, E. (1944) *The Education of an Australian*, London: Angus and Robertson.

Buxton, G. B. (1949) *The Reward of Faith in the Life of Barclay Fowell Buxton, 1860–1946*, London: Lutterworth Press.

Buxton, T. F. (1840) *The African Slave Trade and its Remedy*, London: John Murray.

Caesarius of Arles in *Corpus Christianorum: Series Latina* (1953 onwards), Turnhout, Belgium.

Camus, J.-S. (1910) *The Spirit of St Francis de Sales*, London: Burns and Oates.

Carbery, M. (1998) *West Cork Journal*, ed. by J. Sandford, Dublin: Lilliput Press.

Caretto, C. (1974) *The God who Comes*, London: Darton, Longman and Todd.

_____ (1975) *In Search of the Beyond*, London: Darton, Longman and Todd.

Cassian, J. (1998) *Conferences*, ed. by Colm Luibheid, Mahwah: Paulist Press International.

Cecil, R. W. E. G. (1920) *Difficulties and Duties; being the substance of a charge given on his primary visitation*, London: Nisbet and Co.

Chapman, G. (1904) *The Works of George Chapman*, London: Chatto and Windus.

Chaucer, G. (1964) *The Canterbury Tales*, St Albans: Panther Books.

Church Publishing (Corporate author) (2010) *Holy Women, Holy Men: Celebrating the Saints*, The Episcopal Church.

Chrysostom's Homily on Romans in Atwell, R. (1995) *Spiritual Classics from the Early Church*, London: Church House Publishing.

Chrysostom's Homily 3 on the second Epistle to Timothy in Atwell, R. (1999) *Celebrating the Seasons*, London: Church House Publishing.

Clapsis, E. (n.d.) Wealth and Poverty in Christian Tradition, http://www.myriobiblos.gr/texts/english/clapsis_wealth.html#10_bottom

Clark, M. P. (2003) *The Eliot Tracts*, London: Praeger.

Claughton, T. L. (1829) *Voyages of Discovery to the Polar Regions*, Oxford: J. Vincent.

_____ (1878) *A Charge Delivered to the Clergy and Churchwardens of the Diocese of St. Albans October–November, 1878*, London: Rivington.

Colquhoun, F. (1967) *Parish Prayers*, London: Hodder and Stoughton.

_____ (1975) *Contemporary Parish Prayers*: London: Hodder and Stoughton.

_____ (1982) *New Parish Prayers*, London: Hodder and Stoughton.

Common Worship: Daily Prayer (2005) London: Church House Publishing.

Comper, J. N. (1947) *Of the Atmosphere of a Church*, London: Sheldon Press.

Cotton, N. (1796) *Health: A Poem*, Glasgow: printed for and sold by Brash & Reid.

Cowdrey, H. E. L. (2003) *Lanfranc: Scholar, Monk and Archbishop*, Oxford: OUP.

Cox, J. E. (ed.) (1846), *Miscellaneous Writings and Letters of Thomas Cranmer*, Cambridge: CUP.

Cressy-Marcks, V. (1940) *Journey into China*, London: Hodder and Stoughton.

Cyprian of Carthage in *Corpus Christianorum: Series* (1953 onwards), Turnhout, Belgium.

Davies, O. (ed.) (1999) *Celtic Spirituality*, New York: Paulist Press.

The Declaration of the Rights of the Child (1959) http://www.un.org/cyberschoolbus/humanrights/resources/child.asp

Dehqani Tafti, H. (1990) *Christ and Christianity in Persian Poetry*, Sohrab Books.

Dell, W. (1817) 'Christ's Strength: a Christian's Strength' in *The Works of William Dell*, London: E. Huntington.

Detrich, J. (2011) *Why Study Church History?* http://www.probe.org/site/c.fdKEIMNsEoG/b.7715375/k.6A08/Why_Study_Church_History.htm

Donne, J. (2002) *The Collected Poems of John Donne*, Ware: Wordsworth Editions.

Duggan, M. (1975) *Through the Year with Michael Ramsey*, London: SPCK.

Eaton, J. (2003) *The Psalms*, London: T. and T. Clark.

Edwards, B. (1973) *The Rule of St Albert*, Aylesford and Kensington: Carmelite Press.

Edwards, D. (1989) *Christian England*, London: Fount Paperbacks.

Erasmus, D. in Phillips, M. M. (1964) *The 'Adages' of Erasmus*, Cambridge: CUP.

Farrer, A. M. (1960) *Said or Sung*, London: Faith Press.

_____ (1964) *Saving Belief: a discussion of essentials*, London: Hodder and Stoughton.

Fenn, J. N. (1885) *Lenten Teachings, 1877–1884*, Cheltenham: Geo. Norman.

Field, R. (1606) *Of the Church*, London: H. Lownes for S. Waterson.

Foreville, R. and Keir, G. (1987) *The Book of St Gilbert*, Oxford: Clarendon.

Forster, E. M. (1925) *Anonymity – an Enquiry*, London: The Hogarth Press.

Foster, R. J. (1978) *Celebration of Discipline*, London: Harper and Row.

_____ (1985) *Money, Sex and Power*, London: Hodder and Stoughton.

Foxe, J. (1910) *Foxe's Book of Martyrs*, London.

Francis of Assisi in Armstrong, R. J. and Brady I. C. (1982) *Francis and Clare: the complete works*, New York: Paulist Press.

Frank, M. (1672) *LI sermons preached by the Reverend Dr. Mark Frank*, London: printed by A. Clark for J. Martyn, H. Brome, and R. Chiswell.

Furse, M. (1928) *A School of Prayer*, London: St Christopher Press.

George, M. (1986) *The Autobiography of Henry VII*, London: Macmillan.

Gilmour, J. (1888) *Among the Mongols*, London: Religious Tract Society.

Green M. (1990) *Evangelism through the Local Church*, London: Hodder and Stoughton.

Gregory the Great (1950) *Pastoral Care*, London: Longmans, Green and Co.

Grey, Z. (1744) *A Review of Mr Daniel Neal's History of the Puritans*, Cambridge.

Guy, B. T. (1950) *When you are Ill*, London: SPCK.

Hale, W. H. (1824) *The Apostle Paul: A Pattern for Christian Ministers*, London.

Harding, A. (2007) *Selina, Countess of Huntingdon*, Peterborough: Epworth.

Harrison, P., *Christianity and the Rise of Western Science* in http://www.abc.net.au/religion/articles/2012/05/08/3498202.htm

Headlam, S. D. (1878) *Priestcraft and Progress*, London.

Henri, R. (1960) *The Art Spirit: notes, articles, fragments of letters and talks to students*, Philadelphia: Lippincott and Co.

Hensley Henson, H. (1908) *Christ and the Nation*, London: T. Fisher Unwin.

Herbert, G. (1898) in *George Herbert's Country Parson*, ed. by H. C. Beeching, Oxford: Blackwells.

Herring, T. (1739) *A Sermon preached before the Lord Mayor*, London: J. and J. Pemberton.

_____ (1961) *The Poems of George Herbert*, Oxford: OUP.

Higham, F. (1939) *Faith of our Fathers*, London: SCM.

Hill, O. (1883) *Homes of the London Poor*, London: Macmillan and Co.

Hilton, W. (1957) *The Ladder of Perfection*, London: Penguin.

Holman, S. R. (1998) *The Body of the Poor in Fourth Century Cappadocia*, Brown University.

_____ (2001) *The Hungry are Dying: Beggars and Bishops in Roman Cappadocia*, Oxford: OUP.

Howard, J. (1777) *The State of the Prisons in England and Wales*, Warrington.

Hume, B. (1984) *To be a Pilgrim*, London: St Paul's Publications.

Hutchinson, R. C. (1964) *A Child Possessed*, London: Geoffrey Bles.

Industrial Theology http://www.industrialtheology.com/ (author unknown)

Inge, W. R. (1911) *Speculum Animae: Four Devotional Addresses*, London: Longmans and Co.

_____ (1923) *Outspoken Essays*, London: Longmans and Co.

_____ (1926) *Lay Thoughts of a Dean*, London: G. P. Putnam's Sons.

Jacob, E. (1916) *Five Addresses to the Clergy of the Diocese of St Albans in Preparation for the National Mission of Repentance and Hope*, London: SPCK.

Jane, L. C. (1908) *Asser's Life of King Alfred*, London: Chatto and Windus.

Jane, Sister (2008) *Loving God Whatever: Through the Year with Sister Jane*, Oxford: Fairacres Publications.

Jeanne, D'Arc, Sister (1968) *The Listening Heart: a book on prayer*, London: Geoffrey Chapman.

Jones, G. (2003) *Selections from the Welsh Piety*, quoted in Rowell, G., Stevenson, K. and Williams, R. (2003) *Love's Redeeming Work: The Anglican Quest for Holiness*, Oxford: OUP.

Jonson, B. (2005) *Ben Jonson: poems*, London: Faber.

Julian of Norwich (1973) *Revelations of Divine Love*, Harmondsworth: Penguin.

Kaunda, D. K. (1980) *Kaunda on Violence*, ed. by C. M. Morris, London: Collins.

Kelly, M. (2000) 'John Cassian: The Conferences' in *Mystics Quarterly* 26, 2: The University of Cincinnati.

Kennaby, N. M. (1951) *To Start You Praying*, London: Society for the Propagation of the Gospel in Foreign Parts.

Kieckhefer, R. (2004) *Theology in Stone: Church Architecture from Byzantium to Berkeley*, Oxford: OUP.

Kiernan, M. (ed.) (2000) *The Advancement of Learning*, Oxford: Clarendon.

Kireopoulos, A. (2004) *Toward a Theology of Non-Proliferation* in http://www.ncccusa.org/news/060616TKonproliferation.html

Knowles, D. (1976) *Bare Ruined Choirs*, Cambridge: CUP.

Knox, R. A. (1942) 'Faith Lost and Found', in *In Soft Garment*, London: Burns Oates.

Küng, H. (1977) *On being a Christian*, London: Collins.

Law, W. (1901) *A Practical Treatise upon Christian Perfection*, London, Longmans, Green and Co.

Lawrance, W. J. (1871) *A Sermon preached in the Abbey Church of St Albans on Septuagesima Sunday 1871 being the Sunday after the Funeral of Mrs. Lipscomb*, The archive of St Albans Abbey.

Lawrence, W. http://m.crosswalk.com/church/pastors-or-leadership/sculptors-of-the-soul.html

Lechler, G. V. (1904) *John Wycliffe and his English Precursors*, London: Religious Tract Society.

Lee, S. (1843) *Some Remarks on the Sermon of the Rev. Dr. Pusey lately Preached and Published at Oxford in a letter addressed to that Gentleman*, London.

Leech, K. (1982) 'The Meaning of Prayer and Politics', in *The Times*, 13 February 1982.

Leo the Great, *Sermon* in Atwell, R. (1999) *Celebrating the Saints*, Norwich: Canterbury Press.

Lewis, C. S. (1942) *The Weight of Glory*, London: SPCK.
_____ (1964) *Surprised by Joy*, London: Fontana.

Lightfoot, J. (1629) *Erubhin; or Miscellanies, Christian and Judaicall*, London.

Livingstone, R. W. (1960) *The Future in Education and Education for a World Adrift*, Cambridge: CUP.

Locke, J. (1689) *A Letter concerning Toleration*, London.

Loyd, P. (1952) *The Holy Spirit in the Acts*, London: Mowbray.

Luther, M. (1983) *The Sermons of Martin Luther*, Grand Rapids: Baker Book House.

MacCulloch, D. (2010) *A History of Christianity: The First Three Thousand Years*: London: Penguin.

MacMahan, J. H. (1868) *The Refutation of all Heresies by Hippolytus*, Edinburgh: T and T Clark.

Main, J. (1989) *The Joy of Being*, London: Darton, Longman and Todd.

Manning, H. (1850) *Sermons IV*, in Rowell, G., Stevenson, K. E. and Williams, R. (2003) *Love's Redeeming Work: The Anglican Quest for Holiness*, Oxford: OUP.

McCloughry, R. and Wayne Morris, W. (2002) *Making a World of Difference*, **London: SPCK.**

McIlroy, D. 'The role of government in classical Christian political thought' in Spencer, N. and Chaplin, J. (eds) (2009), *God and Government*, London: SPCK.

McInemy, R. (ed.) (2004) *Introduction to the Summa theologiae of Thomas Aquinas*, Indiana: St Augustine's Press.

March, E. G. (1832) *Seven Sermons on the Ten Commandments*, London: R. B. Seeley and W. Burnside.

Marriott, E. G. (1987) *Izaak Walton: 1593–1683, his life and work, the will, probate details*, Nottingham.

Mayne, M. (2006) *The Enduring* Melody, London: Darton, Longman and Todd.

Merton, T. (1950) *Seeds of Contemplation*, London: Hollis and Carter.
_____ (1955) *No man is an Island*, London: Hollis and Carter.
_____ (1976) *The Power and Meaning of Love*, London: Sheldon Press.
_____ (1997) *Thoughts in Solitude*, Tunbridge Wells: Burns and Oates.

Methodist Church (1965) *The Book of Offices, being the orders of service authorized for us in the Methodist Church*, London: Methodist Publishing House.

Miall, E. (1849) *The British Churches in relation to the British People*, London.

Miller, J. (1996) *New Paintings: Annual Exhibition 1996*, London: Messum.

Moore, H. (1943) quoted in Church of St. Matthew, Northampton, 1893–1943, St Matthew's Church, Northampton.

Moore, P. (1982) *Bishops but what kind?* London: SPCK.

More, T. (1963) *The Complete Works of St Thomas More*, London: Yale University Press.

Mother Mary Clare (1981) *Encountering the Depths: Prayer, Solitude, and Contemplation*, London: Darton, Longman and Todd.

Mumford, P. (1985) *Quick-Eyed Love, Observing – Recollections and Reflections*, Shaftesbury.

Munby, D. L. (1961) *God and the Rich Society*, Oxford: OUP.

Mursell, G. (2001) *English Spirituality from Earliest Times to 1700*, London: SPCK.
_____ (2001) *English Spirituality from 1700 to the Present Day*, London: SPCK.

Neale, J. M. (1866) *Original Sequences, Hymns and other Ecclesiastical Verses*, Hayes.

Neill, S. (1984) *A History of Christian Missions*, London: Penguin.

Newman, G. (1924) *George Fox, the Founder of Quakerism*, London: British Periodicals.

Niebuhr, R. (1945) *The Children of Light and the Children of Darkness*, London: Nisbet and Co.

Norwich, J. J. (1975) *A Christmas Cracker*, Huntingdon: Hambledon Press.

Nouwen, H. (1979) *The Wounded Healer: Ministry in Contemporary Society*, Garden City New York: Doubleday.

Oman, C. (1965) *Ayot Rectory*, London: Hodder and Stoughton.

Origin (1940) 'Homilies on Joshua' in *Sources Crétiennes*, Paris.

Parsons, S. *The Guild of St Raphael Website* http://www.guild-of-st-raphael.org.uk/topics-alternative.htm

Patten, J. A. and Shillito, E. (1935) *The Martyr Church and its Book*, London: London Missionary Society.

Peacham, H. (1639) *The Duty of All True Subjects to their King*, London: H. Seyle.

Peacocke, A. R. (1996) *God and Science: A Quest for Christian Credibility*, London: SCM.

_____ and Pederson, A. (2006) *The Music of Creation*, Edinburgh: Alban.

Pearson, G. (ed.) (1844) 'Opinions meet for a Christian Man' in *The Means to be Used in Christian Warfare* by Myles Coverdale, in *Writings and Translations of Myles Coverdale*, Cambridge: Parker Society.

Peers, A. (ed.) (1972) St John of the Cross, *Living Flame of Love*, Doubleday Company.

Penman, D. (1985) *A Garden of Many Colours: The report of the Archbishop's Commission on multicultural ministry and mission presented to the synod of the Anglican Diocese of Melbourne*, Melbourne: Anglican Diocese of Melbourne, Diocesan Registry.

Penn, W. (1836) *A Journal of Historical Account of the Life of George Fox*, Leeds.

Perham, M. (2000) *New Handbook of Pastoral Liturgy*, London: SPCK.

Petrie, C. (ed.) (1935) *The Letters, Speeches and Proclamations of King Charles I*, London: Cassell and Co.

Philippart, D. (1997) *Prayers for Dedication of a Church*, Chicago: Archdiocese of Chicago.

Phillips. M. M. (1964) *The 'Adages' of Erasmus*, Cambridge: CUP.

Pieper, J. (1999) *Leisure: The Basis of Culture*, Indianapolis: Liberty Fund Inc.

Pope John Paul II (1981) *Laborem Exercens*, London: Catholic Truth Society.

Pope Paul VI (1965) *Declaration on Christian Education (Gravissimum Educationis)*, London: Catholic Truth Society.

Pope Paul VI (1965) *Gaudium et Spes*, London: Catholic Truth Society.

Porter, M. (1921) *Mary Sumner: Her Life and Work*, Winchester: Warren.

Pott, J. H. (1796) *A Charge delivered to the Clergy of the Archdeaconry of St Albans at the Visitation held May 20th 1796*, London.

Prideaux, D. (1944) 'Prayer and Contemplation' in *Laudate* (Quarterly Review), Nashdom Abbey.

Prothero, G. W. (1913) *Select Statutes and other Constitutional Documents*, Oxford: Clarendon.

Pusey, E. B. (1973) *The Responsibility of Intellect in Matter of Faith*, Oxford: James Parker.

Raleigh, W. in Alexander, C. F. (1887) *The Sunday Book of Poetry*, London: Macmillan.

Ramsey, M. (1964) *Canterbury Essays and Addresses*, London: SPCK.

_____ (1972) *Retreat Address*, quoted in Rowell, G., Stevenson, K. and Williams, R. (2003) *Love's Redeeming Work: The Anglican Quest for Holiness*, Oxford: OUP.

_____ (1974) *Canterbury Pilgrim*, London: SPCK.

_____ (1975) *Through the Year with Michael Ramsey*, ed. by Margaret Duggan, London: SPCK.

_____ (1982) *Be Still and Know: A Study in the Life of Prayer*, London: Collins.

_____ (1985) *The Christian Priest Today*, London: SPCK.

Rannie, D. W. (1907) *Wordsworth and his Circle*, London: Methuen and Co.

Reformed Reflections www.reformedreflections.ca/

Rhau, G. (1538) *Symphoniae iucundae* quoted in U. S. Leopold (1965) *Luther's Works*, Philadelphia: Fortress Press.

Richardson, A. (1973) *The Political Christ*, London: SCM.

Richmond, L. (1820) *The Dairyman's Daughter*, London: J. Evans and Sons.

Robertson, W. A. S. (1889) *Archdeacon Philip Stubbs*, London: Mitchell and Hughes.

Rogers, B. (1950) *The Diary of Benjamin Rogers, Rector of Carlton, 1720–1771*, Streatley.

Rose, J. H. (1834) *The Law of Moses viewed in connexion with the history and character of the Jews*, The Hulsean Lectures 1834, Cambridge: The Pitt Press.

Rowell, G., Stevenson, K. and Williams, R. (2003) *Love's Redeeming Work: The Anglican Quest for Holiness*, Oxford: OUP.

The Rule of St Augustine (1984), London: Darton, Longman and Todd.

Runcie, R. (1983) *Windows onto God*, London: SPCK.

Ruskin, J. (1900) *Lectures on Art*, New York: John W. Lovell.

_____ (1910) *Modern Painters* (Volume IV), George Allen and Sons.

Sales, F. de (1953) *Introduction to the Devout Life*, London: Longmans, Green and Co.

Sampson, G. V. (1917) *A Hero Saint: A Memoir of the Rev. the Hon. Maurice Berkeley Peel*: T. W. Thornton.

Sargent, D. N. (1960) *The Making of a Missionary*, London: Hodder and Stoughton.

Sayers, D. L. (1946) *Unpopular Opinions*, London: Victor Gollancz.

Schaff, P. and Wace, H. (eds) (1983 onwards) *The Nicene and Post-Nicene Library of the Fathers*, Michigan: Grand Rapids.

Scholasticus, S. (1891) *The Ecclesiastical History*, London.

Schwager, D. (2008) http://www.rc.net/wcc/parable1.htm

Scott, B. B. (1994) *Hollywood Dreams and Biblical Stories*, Minneapolis: Fortress Press.

Selby, P. (2009) *Grace and Mortgage*, London: Darton, Longman and Todd.

Shepherd, R. (1788), *The Ground and Credibility of the Christian Religion*, Oxford: Lockyer Davis.

Snyder, H. (1983) *Liberating the Church: The Ecology of Church and Kingdom*, Basingstoke: Marshalls.

Solzhenitsyn, A. (1972) *One Word of Truth: the Nobel speech on literature, 1970*, London: Bodley Head.

Sourcebook 2011: Your guide to Stained, Decorative and Architectural Art Glass, http://sgaaonline.com/?page_id=41

The SPCK Book of Christian Prayer (1995), London: SPCK.

Spencer, A. G. (1826) *Sermons on Various Subjects*, London: Rivington.

St Paulinus of Nola in Waddell, H. (1951) *Mediæval Latin Lyrics*, London: Constable.

Stalleybrass, E. (1836) *Memoir of Mrs Stallybrass*, London.

Stanley, T. (1647) *Poems and Translations*, printed for the author and his friends.

Stark, R. (2006) *Cities of God*, New York: HarperCollins.

Staunton, E. (1673) *A Dialogue: or a Discourse between a Minister and a Stranger* in Mayo, R. (1673) in *The life and death of Edmund Staunton D.D.*, London: Printed for T. Parkhurst.

Stewart, D. M. (2002) *The Westminster Collection of Christian Prayers*, John Knox Press.

Story, G. M. and Gardner, H. (eds) (1959) *The Sonnets of William Alabaster*, Oxford: OUP.

Stow, T. Q. (1836) *The Scope of Piety*, London: Halstead.

Studdert Kennedy, G. A. (1932) *The New Man in Christ*, London: Hodder and Stoughton.

Taylor, J. (1758) *The Life of our Blessed Lord and Saviour Jesus Christ*, London.

_____ (1828) *The Whole Works of the Right Rev. Jeremy Taylor*, volume 5, London: Rivington.

Taylor, J. V. (1972) *The Go-Between God*, London: SCM.

Teilhard de Chardin, P. (1965) *Hymn of the Universe*, London: Collins.

Temple, W. (1948) *Palm Sunday to Easter*, London: SCM.

Thomas, R. (1994) *An Introduction to Church Communication*, Oxford: Lynx Communication.

Thorndike, H. (1856) *Theological Works of Herbert Thorndike* in Haddan, W. A. (ed.), *The Library of Anglo-Catholic Theology*, Oxford: J. H. Parker.

Tristam, Brother (1997) *Exciting Holiness*, Norwich: Canterbury Press.

Trollope, F. (1996) *The Vicar of Wrexhill*, Stroud: Alan Sutton.

Tucker, R. A. (2005) 'The Changing Roles of Women in Ministry – The Early Church through the 18th Century' in Pierce, R. W. and Merrill Groothuis, R. (eds) (2005) *Discovering Biblical Equality: Complementarity without Hierarchy*, Leicester: IVP.

Tyndale, W. (2000) *The Obedience of a Christian Man*, London: Penguin.

Underhill, E. (1920) *The Essentials of Mysticism and Other Essays*, London: J. M. Dent and Sons.

_____ (1926) *Concerning the Inner Life*, London: Methuen and Co.

_____ (1927) *Man and the Supernatural*, London: Methuen and Co.

_____ (1934) *The School of Charity: Meditations on the Christian Creed*, London: Longmans, Green and Co.

Unitatis Redintegratio (1982) in Stransky, T. F. and Sheerin, J. (eds) *Doing the Truth in Charity*, Paulist Press International.

Vanstone, W. (1977) *Love's Endeavour, Love's Expense*, London: Darton, Longman and Todd.

Verey, R. (2002) *The Garden in Winter*, London: Frances Lincoln.

van der Veer, P. (2001) *Imperial Encounters: Religion and Modernity in India and Britain*, Oxford: Princeton University Press.

van der Weyer, R. (ed.) (1993) *The Fount Book of Prayer*, London: HarperCollins.

Vanier, J. (1997) *The Scandal of Service: Jesus Washes Our Feet*, London: Darton, Longman and Todd.

Vess, D. http://deborahvess.org/ids/medieval/celtic/celtic.html

Vince, S. (1798) *The Credibility of Christianity Vindicated, In Answer to Mr. Hume's Objections*, Cambridge.

Vincent, N. (1677) *The Spirit of Prayer*, London.

Ward, B. (1975) *The Sayings of the Desert Fathers*, London: Mowbray.

Wesley, J. (1987) *The Journal of John Wesley*, ed. by E. Jay, Oxford: OUP.

Wheatley, J. (1797) *An Extract from the Life and Death of Mr John Janeway*, London: printed for George Whitfield.

White, W. H. (2007) *Mark Rutherford's Deliverance*, edited by his friend Reuben Shapcott, Brighton: Victorian Secrets.

Whitelock, A. (2009) *Mary Tudor: England's First Queen*, London: Bloomsbury.

Wilde, O. (1917) *De Profundis*, London: Methuen and Co.

Willet, A. (1603) *Ecclesia Triumphans…With a brief exposition of 122 Psalme*, Cambridge: John Legat, printer to University of Cambridge.

Williams, C. W. S. (1949) *The Descent of the Dove*, London: Faber and Faber.

Williams, H. A. (1994) *The True Wilderness*, London: Mowbray.

Wilkes, A. N. P. (1916) *The Dynamic of Faith*, London: Oliphants.

Willis, J. J. (1914) *The Church in Uganda*, London: Longmans and Co.

Winkworth, S. (1950) *Theologia Germanica*, London: Victor Gollancz.

Winstanley, G. (1649) *A Declaration from the poor oppressed people of England, directed to all that call themselves Lords of Manors*, London.

Woodforde, J. (1968) *The Diary of a Country Parson*, ed. by J. Beresford, Oxford: OUP.

Index of names

Index of places

Index of themes